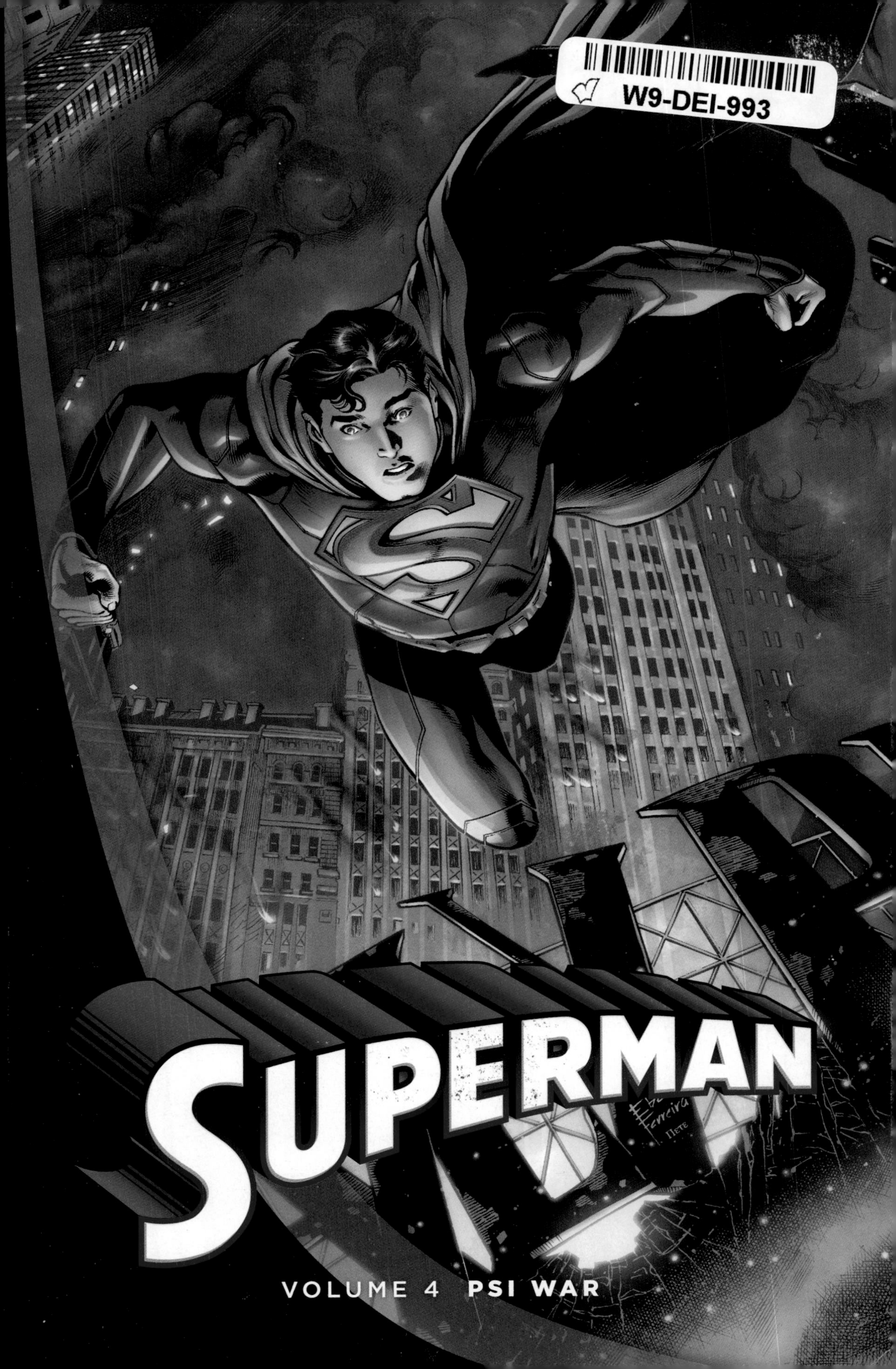
SUPERMAN
VOLUME 4 PSI WAR

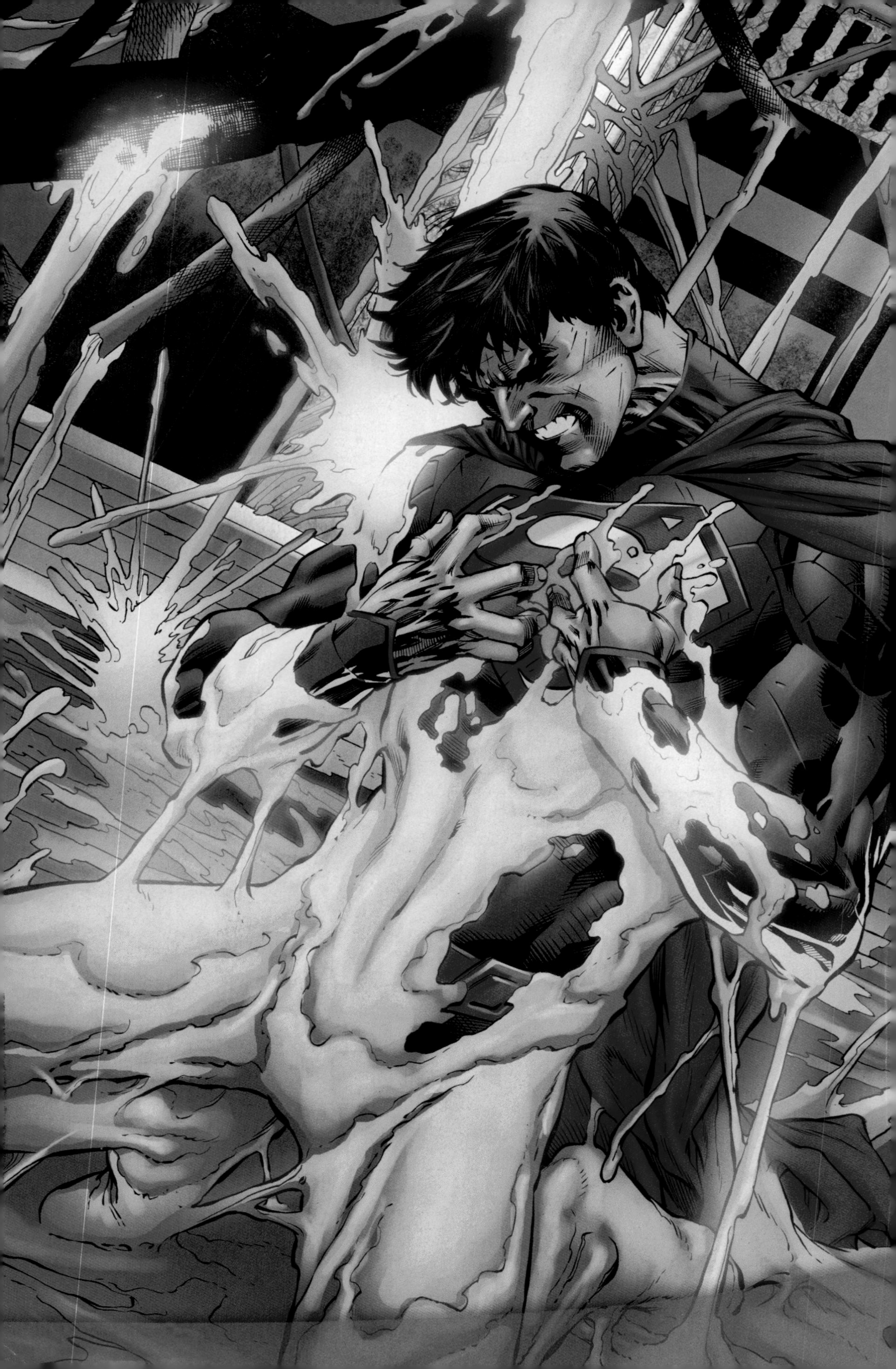

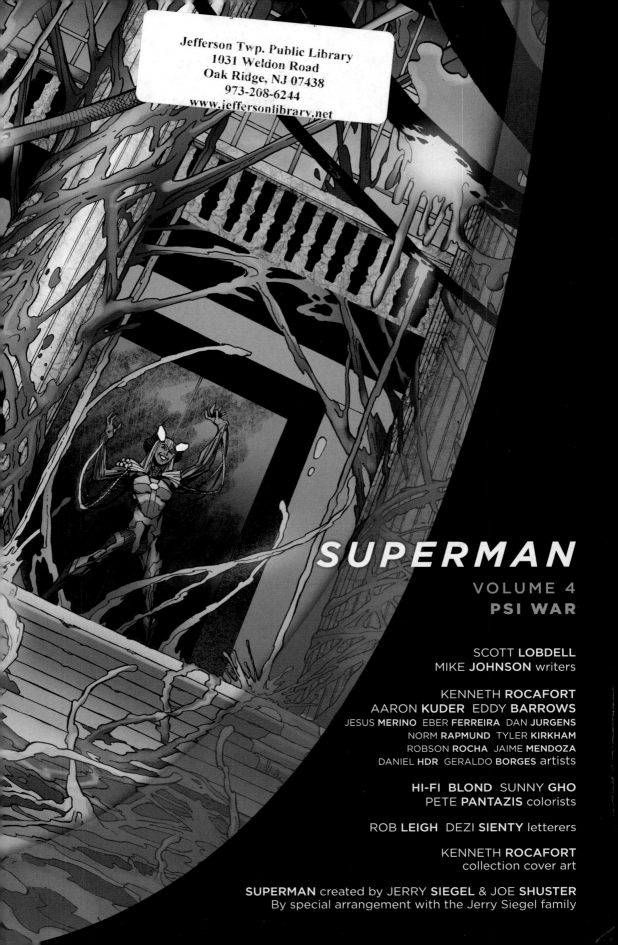

SUPERMAN

VOLUME 4
PSI WAR

SCOTT **LOBDELL**
MIKE **JOHNSON** writers

KENNETH **ROCAFORT**
AARON **KUDER** EDDY **BARROWS**
JESUS **MERINO** EBER **FERREIRA** DAN **JURGENS**
NORM **RAPMUND** TYLER **KIRKHAM**
ROBSON **ROCHA** JAIME **MENDOZA**
DANIEL **HDR** GERALDO **BORGES** artists

HI-FI BLOND SUNNY **GHO**
PETE **PANTAZIS** colorists

ROB **LEIGH** DEZI **SIENTY** letterers

KENNETH **ROCAFORT**
collection cover art

SUPERMAN created by JERRY **SIEGEL** & JOE **SHUSTER**
By special arrangement with the Jerry Siegel family

EDDIE BERGANZA Editor – Original Series ANTHONY MARQUES Assistant Editor – Original Series
ROWENA YOW Editor ROBBIN BROSTERMAN Design Director – Books ROBBIE BIEDERMAN Publication Design

BOB HARRAS Senior VP – Editor-in-Chief, DC Comics

DIANE NELSON President DAN DIDIO and JIM LEE Co-Publishers GEOFF JOHNS Chief Creative Officer
AMIT DESAI Senior VP – Marketing and Franchise Management AMY GENKINS Senior VP – Business and Legal Affairs
NAIRI GARDINER Senior VP – Finance JEFF BOISON VP – Publishing Planning
MARK CHIARELLO VP – Art Direction and Design JOHN CUNNINGHAM VP – Marketing
TERRI CUNNINGHAM VP – Editorial Administration LARRY GANEM VP – Talent Relations and Services
ALISON GILL Senior VP – Manufacturing and Operations HANK KANALZ Senior VP – Vertigo and Integrated Publishing
JAY KOGAN VP – Business and Legal Affairs, Publishing JACK MAHAN VP – Business Affairs, Talent
NICK NAPOLITANO VP – Manufacturing Administration SUE POHJA VP – Book Sales FRED RUIZ VP – Manufacturing Operations
COURTNEY SIMMONS Senior VP – Publicity BOB WAYNE Senior VP – Sales

SUPERMAN VOLUME 4: PSI WAR

DC Comics, 1700 Broadway, New York, NY 10019
A Warner Bros. Entertainment Company.
Printed by RR Donnelley, Owensville, MO, USA. 1/09/15. First Printing.

ISBN: 978-1-4012-5094-2

Library of Congress Cataloging-in-Publication Data

Lobdell, Scott, author.
Superman. Volume 4, Psi War / Scott Lobdell ; illustrated by Kenneth Rocafort and Aaron Kuder.
pages cm. — (The New 52!)
ISBN 978-1-4012-5094-2
1. Graphic novels. I. Rocafort, Kenneth, illustrator. II. Kuder, Aaron, illustrator. III. Title. IV. Title: Psi War.
PN6728.S9L586 2014
741.5'973—dc23
2014011610

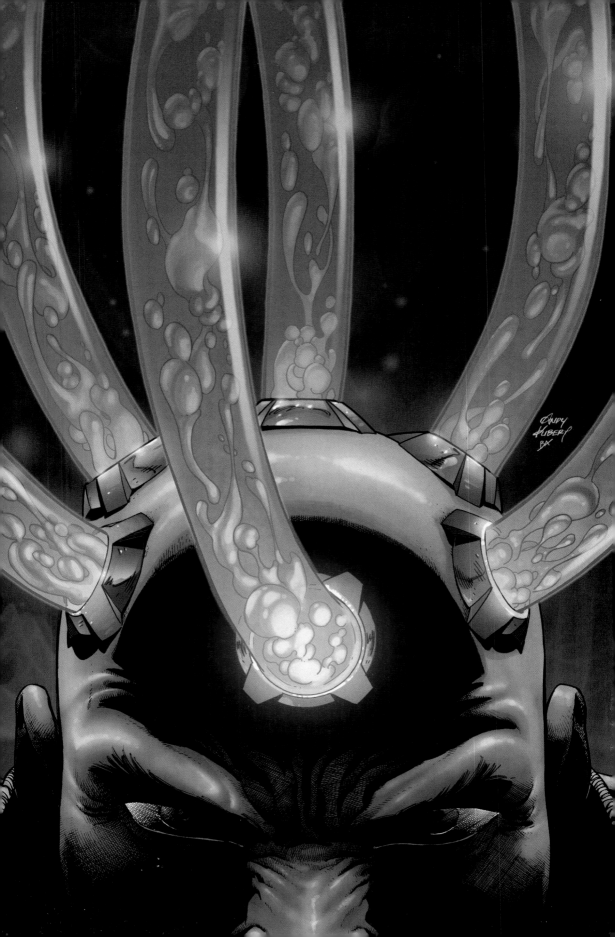

THE LAST BYLINE

SCOTT LOBDELL writer **DAN JURGENS** penciller **NORM RAPMUND** inker *cover art by* **ANDY KUBERT & BRAD ANDERSON**

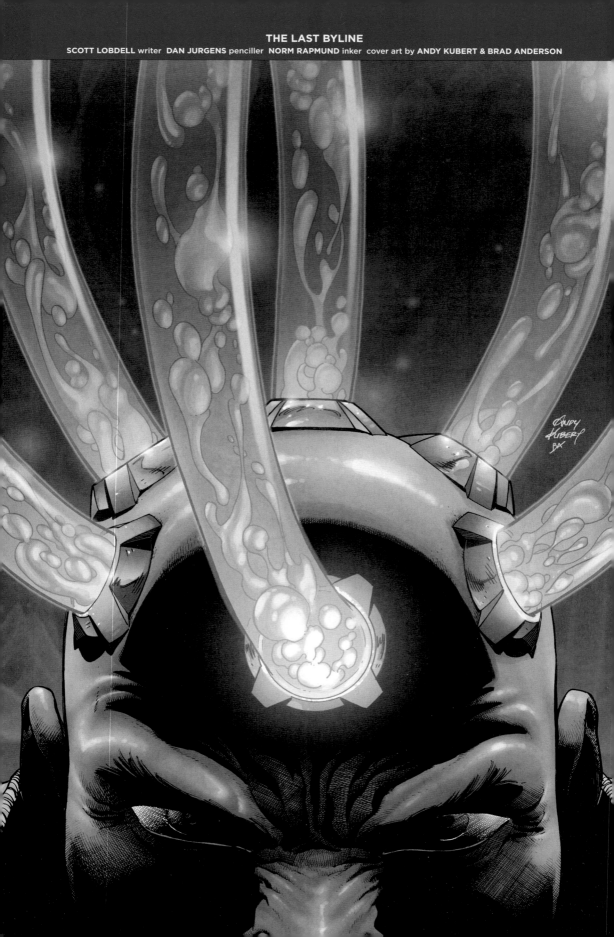

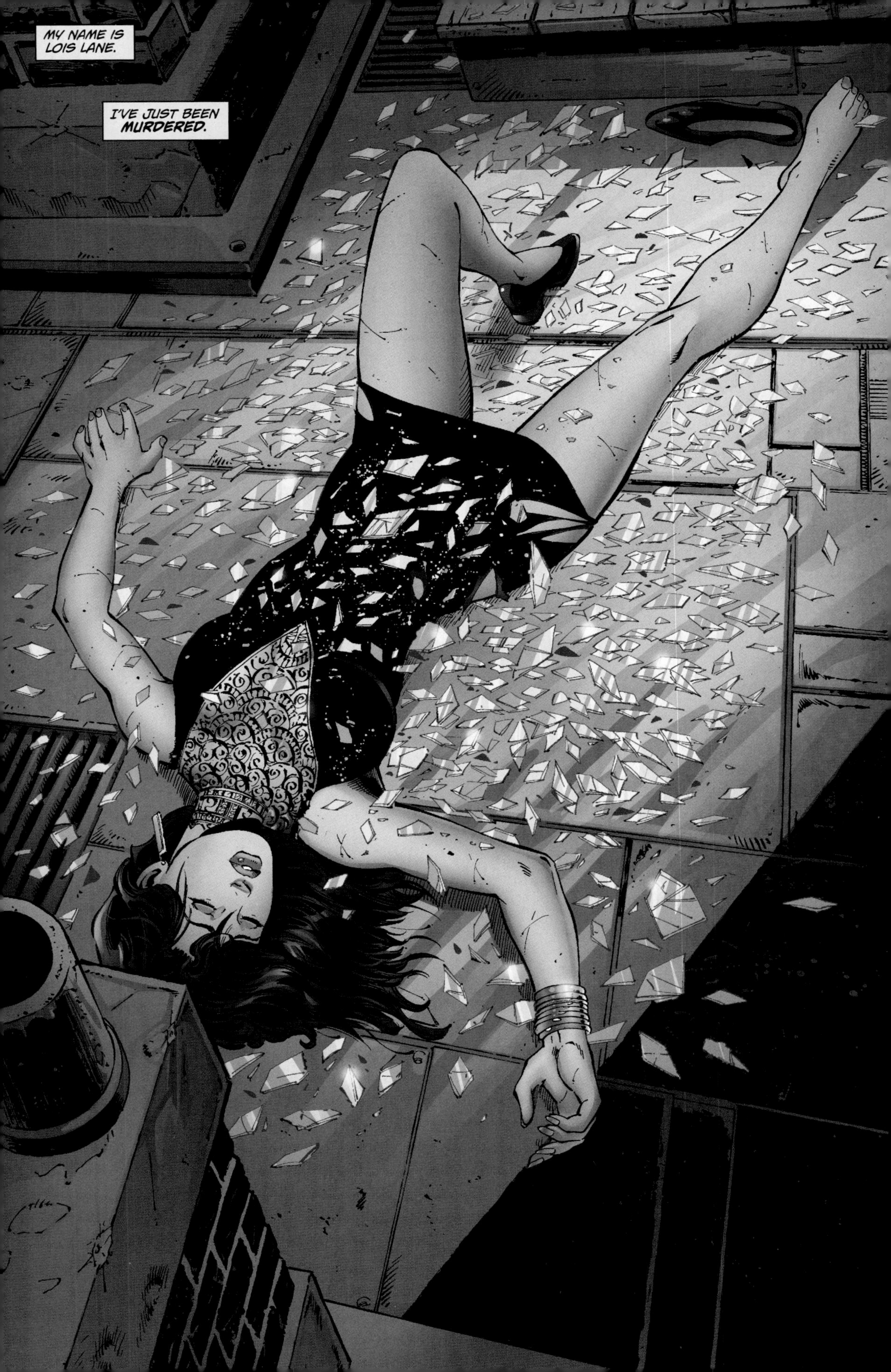
MY NAME IS LOIS LANE.
I'VE JUST BEEN MURDERED.

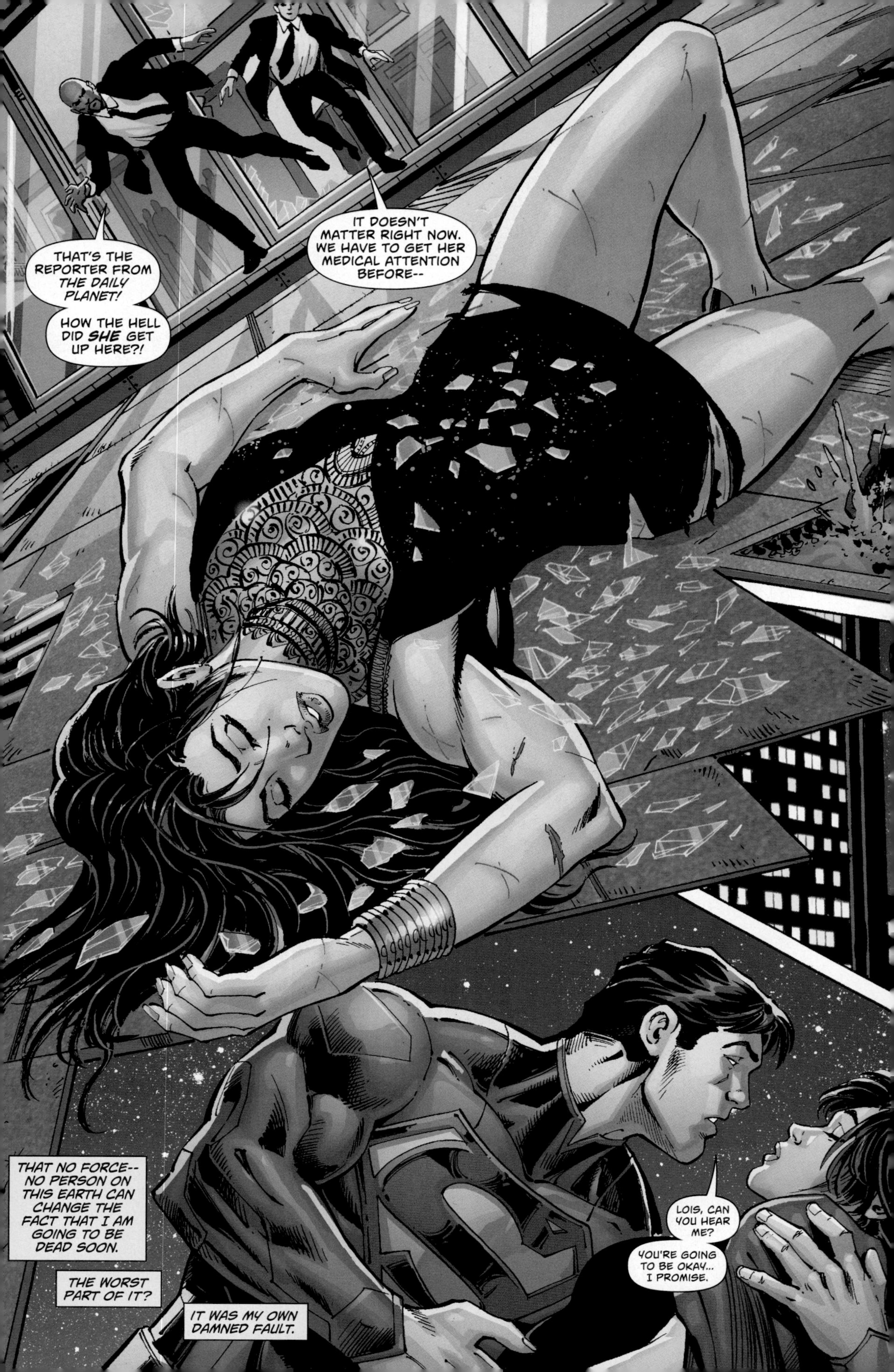
THAT'S THE REPORTER FROM *THE DAILY PLANET!*
HOW THE HELL DID **SHE** GET UP HERE?!
IT DOESN'T MATTER RIGHT NOW. WE HAVE TO GET HER MEDICAL ATTENTION BEFORE--
THAT NO FORCE-- NO PERSON ON THIS EARTH CAN CHANGE THE FACT THAT I AM GOING TO BE DEAD SOON.
THE WORST PART OF IT?
IT WAS MY OWN DAMNED FAULT.
LOIS, CAN YOU HEAR ME?
YOU'RE GOING TO BE OKAY... I PROMISE.

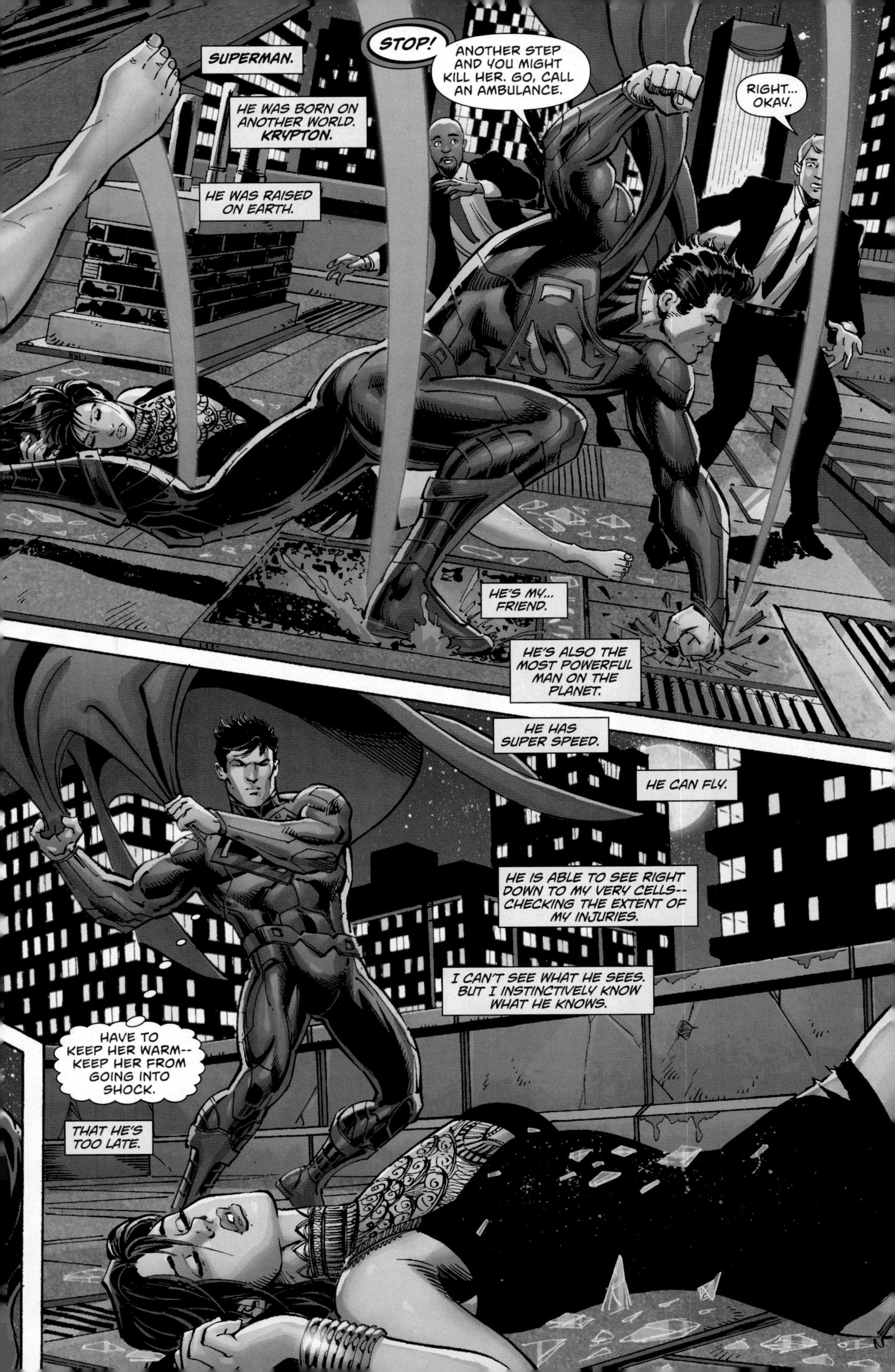
SUPERMAN.
HE WAS BORN ON ANOTHER WORLD. KRYPTON.
HE WAS RAISED ON EARTH.
STOP!
ANOTHER STEP AND YOU MIGHT KILL HER. GO, CALL AN AMBULANCE.
RIGHT... OKAY.
HE'S MY... FRIEND.
HE'S ALSO THE MOST POWERFUL MAN ON THE PLANET.
HE HAS SUPER SPEED.
HE CAN FLY.
HE IS ABLE TO SEE RIGHT DOWN TO MY VERY CELLS-- CHECKING THE EXTENT OF MY INJURIES.
I CAN'T SEE WHAT HE SEES. BUT I INSTINCTIVELY KNOW WHAT HE KNOWS.
HAVE TO KEEP HER WARM-- KEEP HER FROM GOING INTO SHOCK.
THAT HE'S TOO LATE.

Chapter One

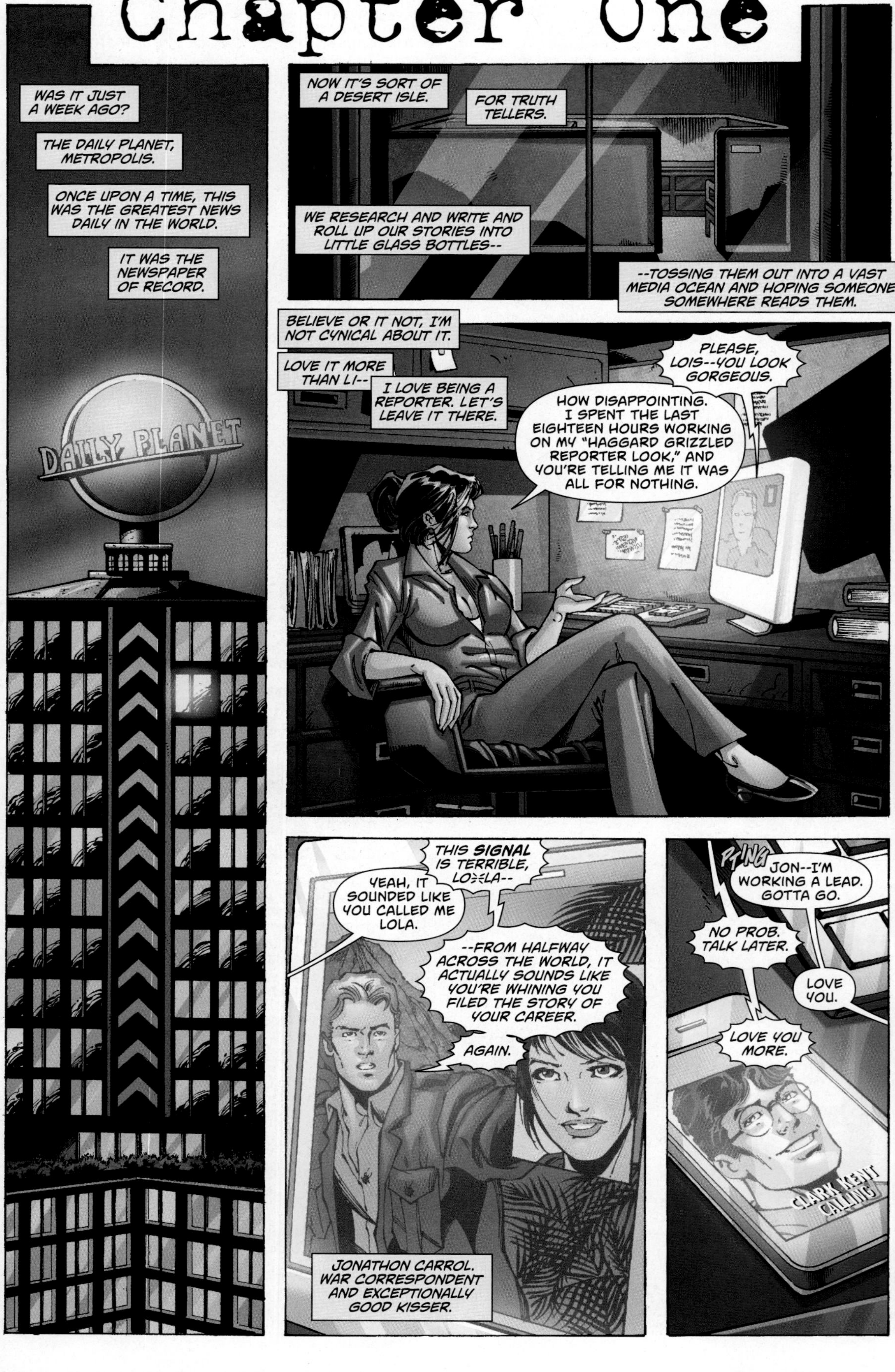
WAS IT JUST A WEEK AGO?
THE DAILY PLANET, METROPOLIS.
ONCE UPON A TIME, THIS WAS THE GREATEST NEWS DAILY IN THE WORLD.
IT WAS THE NEWSPAPER OF RECORD.
DAILY PLANET
NOW IT'S SORT OF A DESERT ISLE.
FOR TRUTH TELLERS.
WE RESEARCH AND WRITE AND ROLL UP OUR STORIES INTO LITTLE GLASS BOTTLES--
--TOSSING THEM OUT INTO A VAST MEDIA OCEAN AND HOPING SOMEONE SOMEWHERE READS THEM.
BELIEVE OR IT NOT, I'M NOT CYNICAL ABOUT IT.
LOVE IT MORE THAN LI--
I LOVE BEING A REPORTER. LET'S LEAVE IT THERE.
PLEASE, LOIS--YOU LOOK GORGEOUS.
HOW DISAPPOINTING. I SPENT THE LAST EIGHTEEN HOURS WORKING ON MY "HAGGARD GRIZZLED REPORTER LOOK," AND YOU'RE TELLING ME IT WAS ALL FOR NOTHING.
THIS SIGNAL IS TERRIBLE, LO-LA--
YEAH, IT SOUNDED LIKE YOU CALLED ME LOLA.
--FROM HALFWAY ACROSS THE WORLD, IT ACTUALLY SOUNDS LIKE YOU'RE WHINING YOU FILED THE STORY OF YOUR CAREER.
AGAIN.
JONATHON CARROL. WAR CORRESPONDENT AND EXCEPTIONALLY GOOD KISSER.
PING
JON--I'M WORKING A LEAD. GOTTA GO.
NO PROB. TALK LATER.
LOVE YOU.
LOVE YOU MORE.
CLARK KENT CALLING

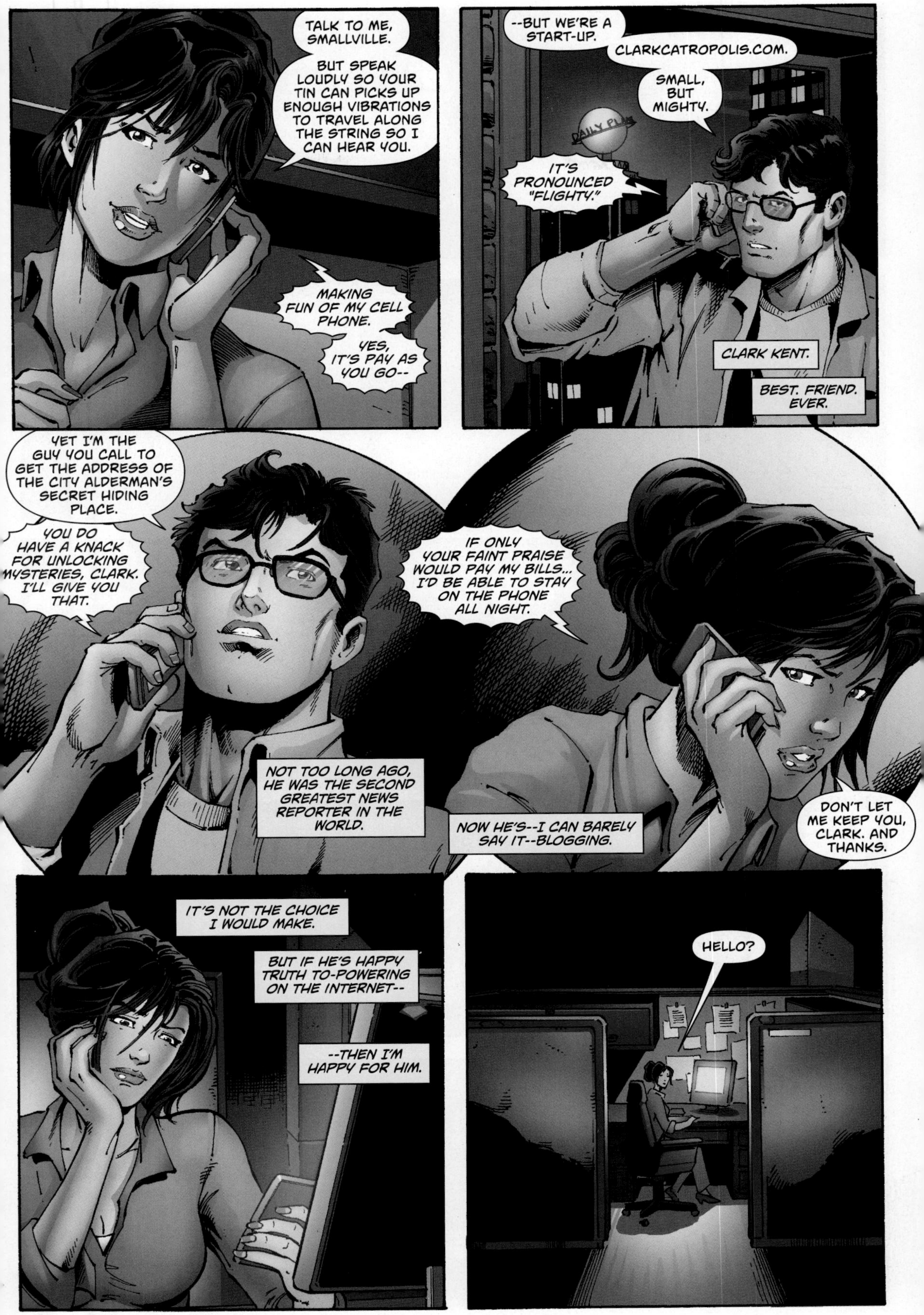
TALK TO ME, SMALLVILLE.
BUT SPEAK LOUDLY SO YOUR TIN CAN PICKS UP ENOUGH VIBRATIONS TO TRAVEL ALONG THE STRING SO I CAN HEAR YOU.
MAKING FUN OF MY CELL PHONE.
YES, IT'S PAY AS YOU GO--
--BUT WE'RE A START-UP.
CLARKCATROPOLIS.COM.
SMALL, BUT MIGHTY.
IT'S PRONOUNCED "FLIGHTY."
CLARK KENT.
BEST. FRIEND. EVER.
YET I'M THE GUY YOU CALL TO GET THE ADDRESS OF THE CITY ALDERMAN'S SECRET HIDING PLACE.
YOU DO HAVE A KNACK FOR UNLOCKING MYSTERIES, CLARK. I'LL GIVE YOU THAT.
IF ONLY YOUR FAINT PRAISE WOULD PAY MY BILLS... I'D BE ABLE TO STAY ON THE PHONE ALL NIGHT.
NOT TOO LONG AGO, HE WAS THE SECOND GREATEST NEWS REPORTER IN THE WORLD.
NOW HE'S--I CAN BARELY SAY IT--BLOGGING.
DON'T LET ME KEEP YOU, CLARK. AND THANKS.
IT'S NOT THE CHOICE I WOULD MAKE.
BUT IF HE'S HAPPY TRUTH TO-POWERING ON THE INTERNET--
--THEN I'M HAPPY FOR HIM.
HELLO?

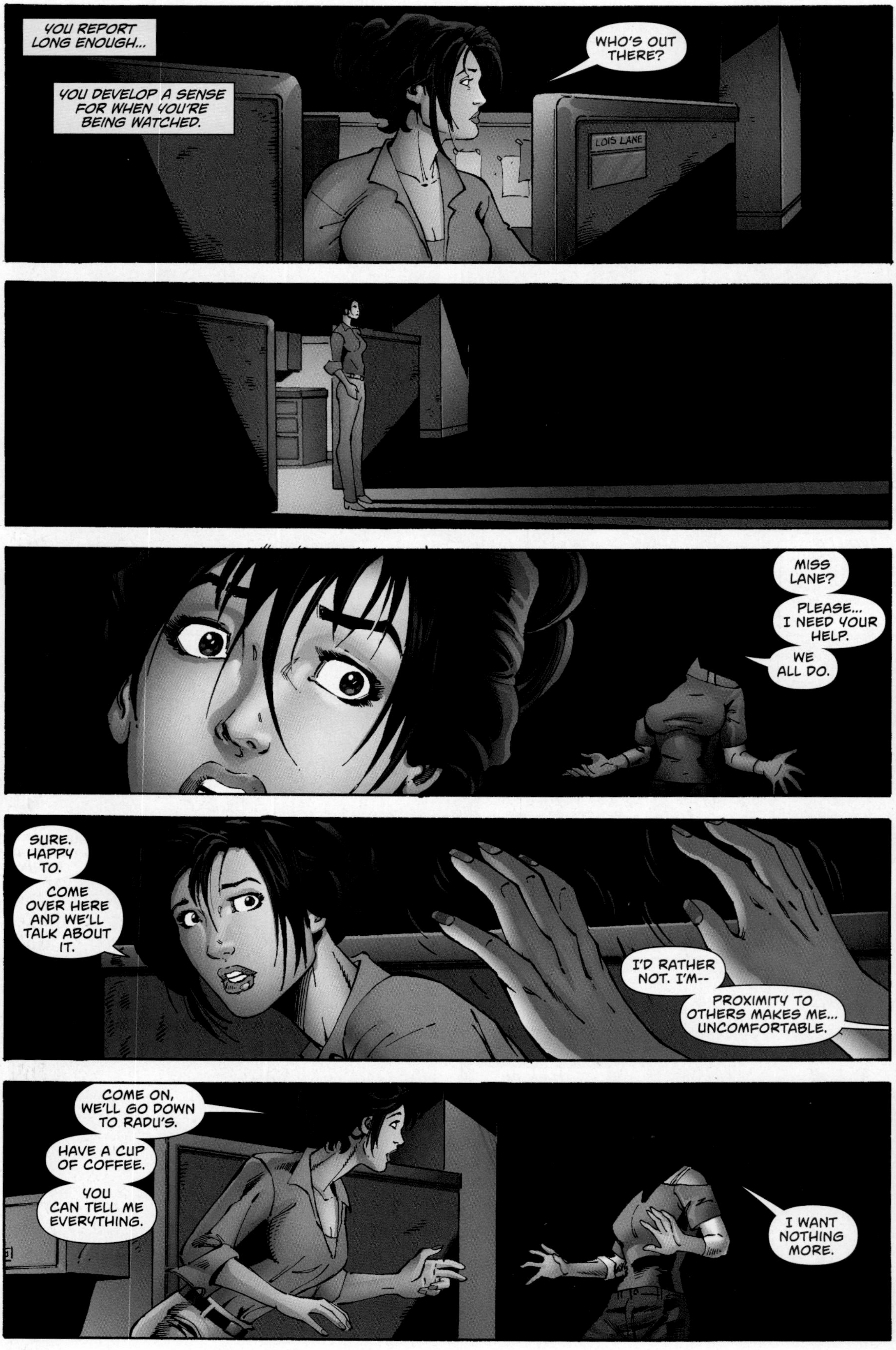
YOU REPORT LONG ENOUGH...
YOU DEVELOP A SENSE FOR WHEN YOU'RE BEING WATCHED.
WHO'S OUT THERE?
LOIS LANE
MISS LANE?
PLEASE... I NEED YOUR HELP.
WE ALL DO.
SURE. HAPPY TO.
COME OVER HERE AND WE'LL TALK ABOUT IT.
I'D RATHER NOT. I'M--
PROXIMITY TO OTHERS MAKES ME... UNCOMFORTABLE.
COME ON, WE'LL GO DOWN TO RADU'S.
HAVE A CUP OF COFFEE.
YOU CAN TELL ME EVERYTHING.
I WANT NOTHING MORE.

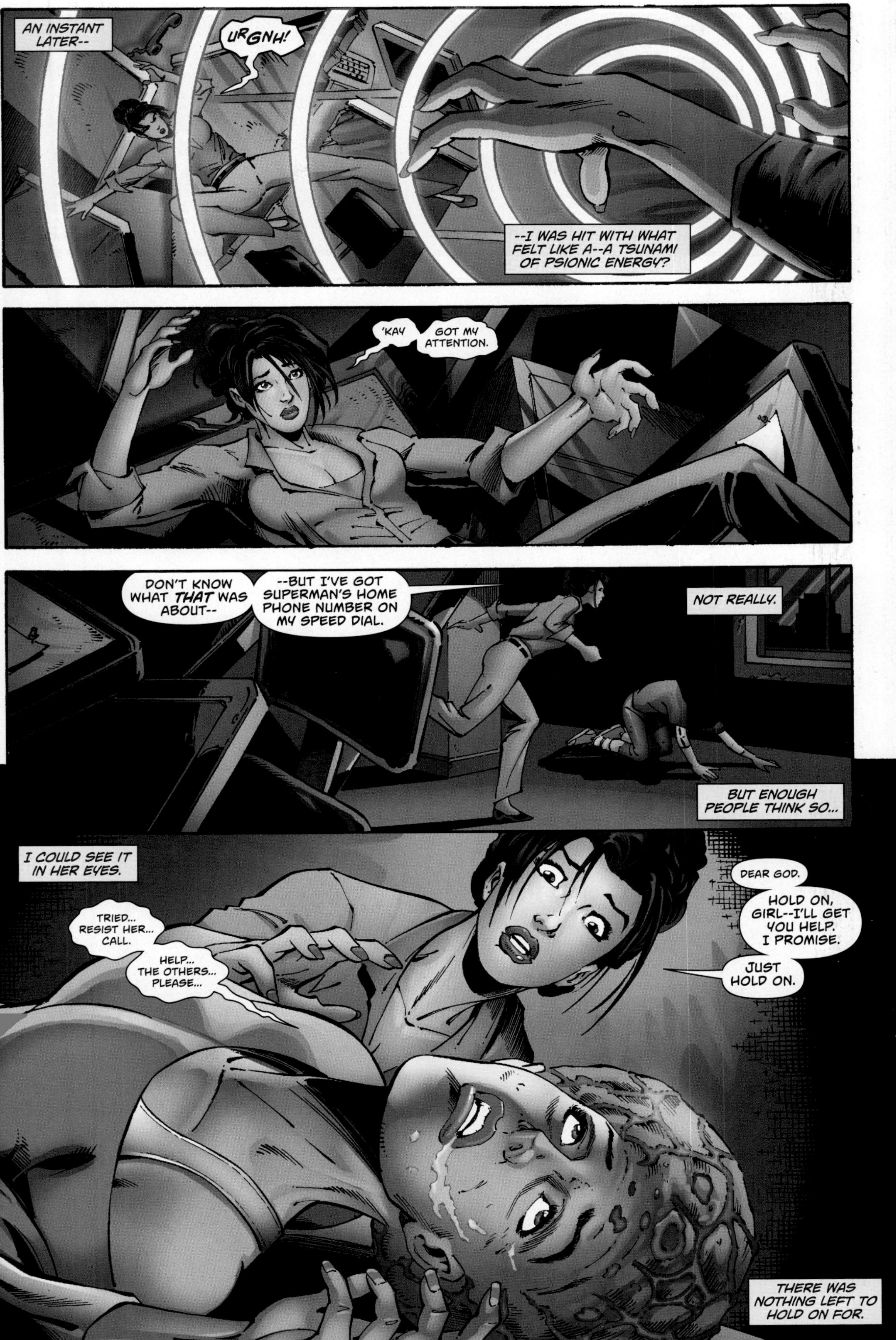
AN INSTANT LATER--
URGNH!
--I WAS HIT WITH WHAT FELT LIKE A--A TSUNAMI OF PSIONIC ENERGY?
'KAY
GOT MY ATTENTION.
DON'T KNOW WHAT THAT WAS ABOUT--
--BUT I'VE GOT SUPERMAN'S HOME PHONE NUMBER ON MY SPEED DIAL.
NOT REALLY.
BUT ENOUGH PEOPLE THINK SO...
I COULD SEE IT IN HER EYES.
TRIED... RESIST HER... CALL.
HELP... THE OTHERS... PLEASE...
DEAR GOD.
HOLD ON, GIRL--I'LL GET YOU HELP. I PROMISE.
JUST HOLD ON.
THERE WAS NOTHING LEFT TO HOLD ON FOR.

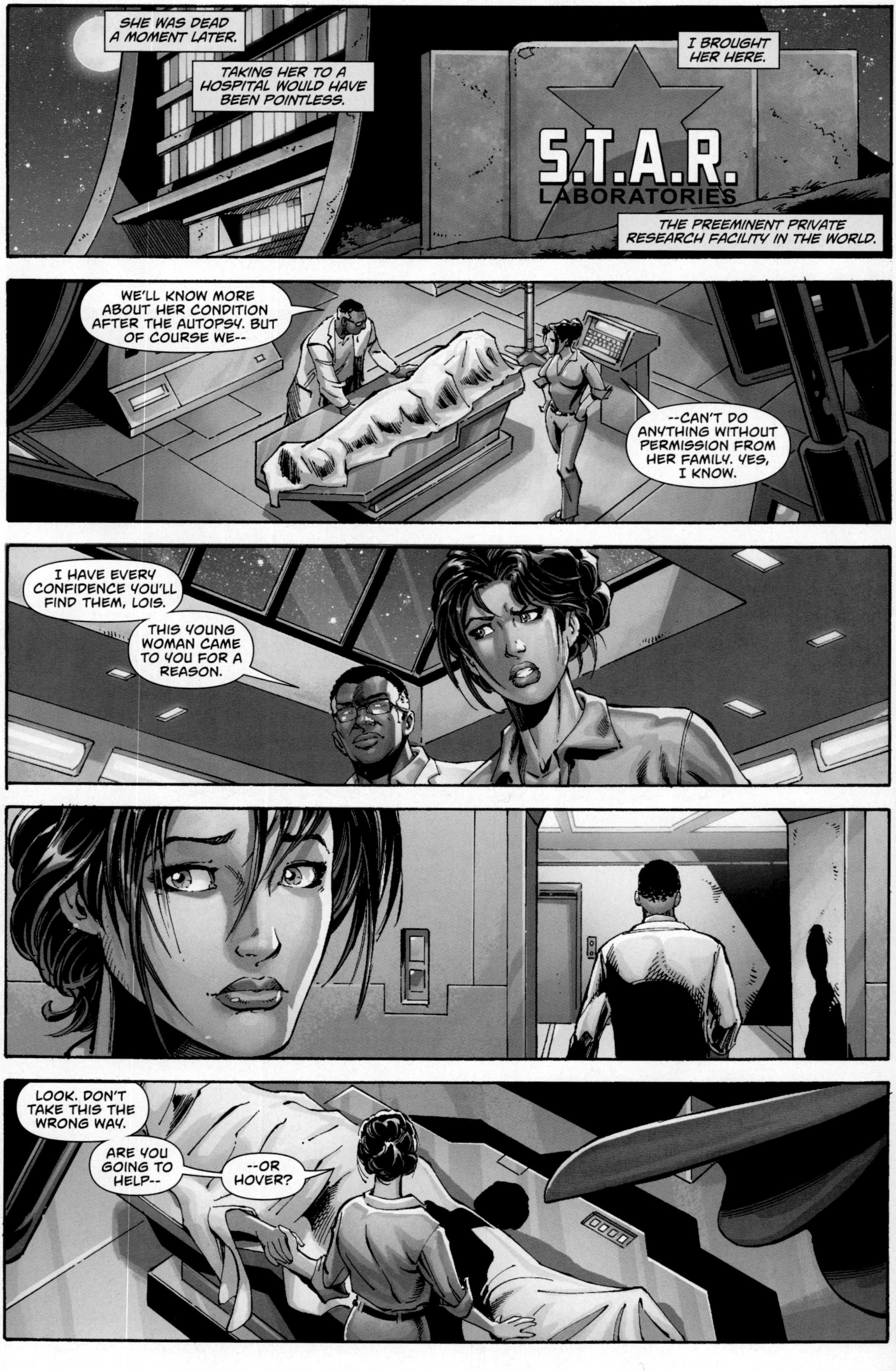
SHE WAS DEAD A MOMENT LATER.
TAKING HER TO A HOSPITAL WOULD HAVE BEEN POINTLESS.
I BROUGHT HER HERE.
S.T.A.R. LABORATORIES
THE PREEMINENT PRIVATE RESEARCH FACILITY IN THE WORLD.
WE'LL KNOW MORE ABOUT HER CONDITION AFTER THE AUTOPSY. BUT OF COURSE WE--
--CAN'T DO ANYTHING WITHOUT PERMISSION FROM HER FAMILY. YES, I KNOW.
I HAVE EVERY CONFIDENCE YOU'LL FIND THEM, LOIS.
THIS YOUNG WOMAN CAME TO YOU FOR A REASON.
LOOK. DON'T TAKE THIS THE WRONG WAY.
ARE YOU GOING TO HELP--
--OR HOVER?

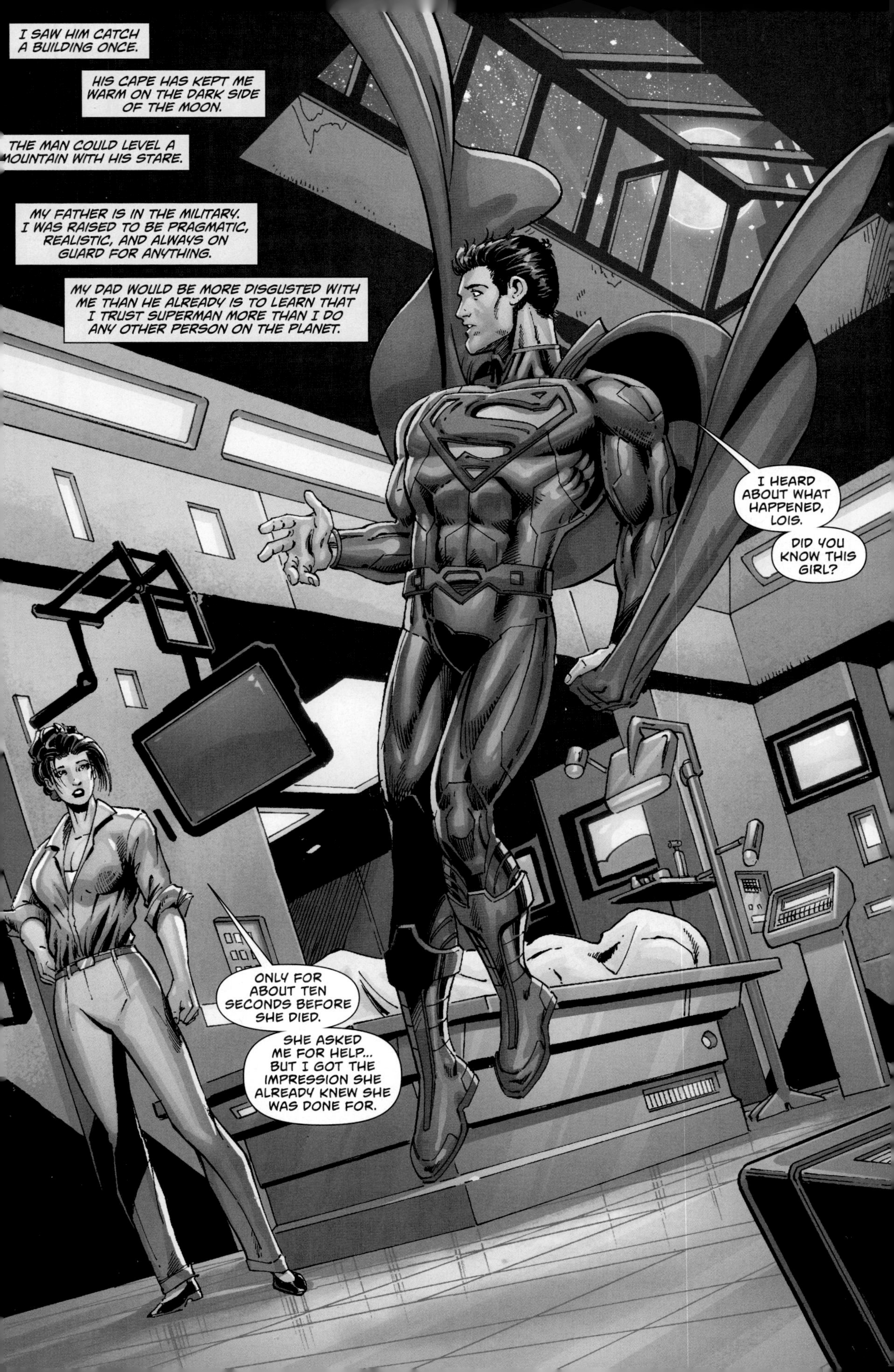
I SAW HIM CATCH A BUILDING ONCE.
HIS CAPE HAS KEPT ME WARM ON THE DARK SIDE OF THE MOON.
THE MAN COULD LEVEL A MOUNTAIN WITH HIS STARE.
MY FATHER IS IN THE MILITARY. I WAS RAISED TO BE PRAGMATIC, REALISTIC, AND ALWAYS ON GUARD FOR ANYTHING.
MY DAD WOULD BE MORE DISGUSTED WITH ME THAN HE ALREADY IS TO LEARN THAT I TRUST SUPERMAN MORE THAN I DO ANY OTHER PERSON ON THE PLANET.
I HEARD ABOUT WHAT HAPPENED, LOIS.
DID YOU KNOW THIS GIRL?
ONLY FOR ABOUT TEN SECONDS BEFORE SHE DIED.
SHE ASKED ME FOR HELP... BUT I GOT THE IMPRESSION SHE ALREADY KNEW SHE WAS DONE FOR.

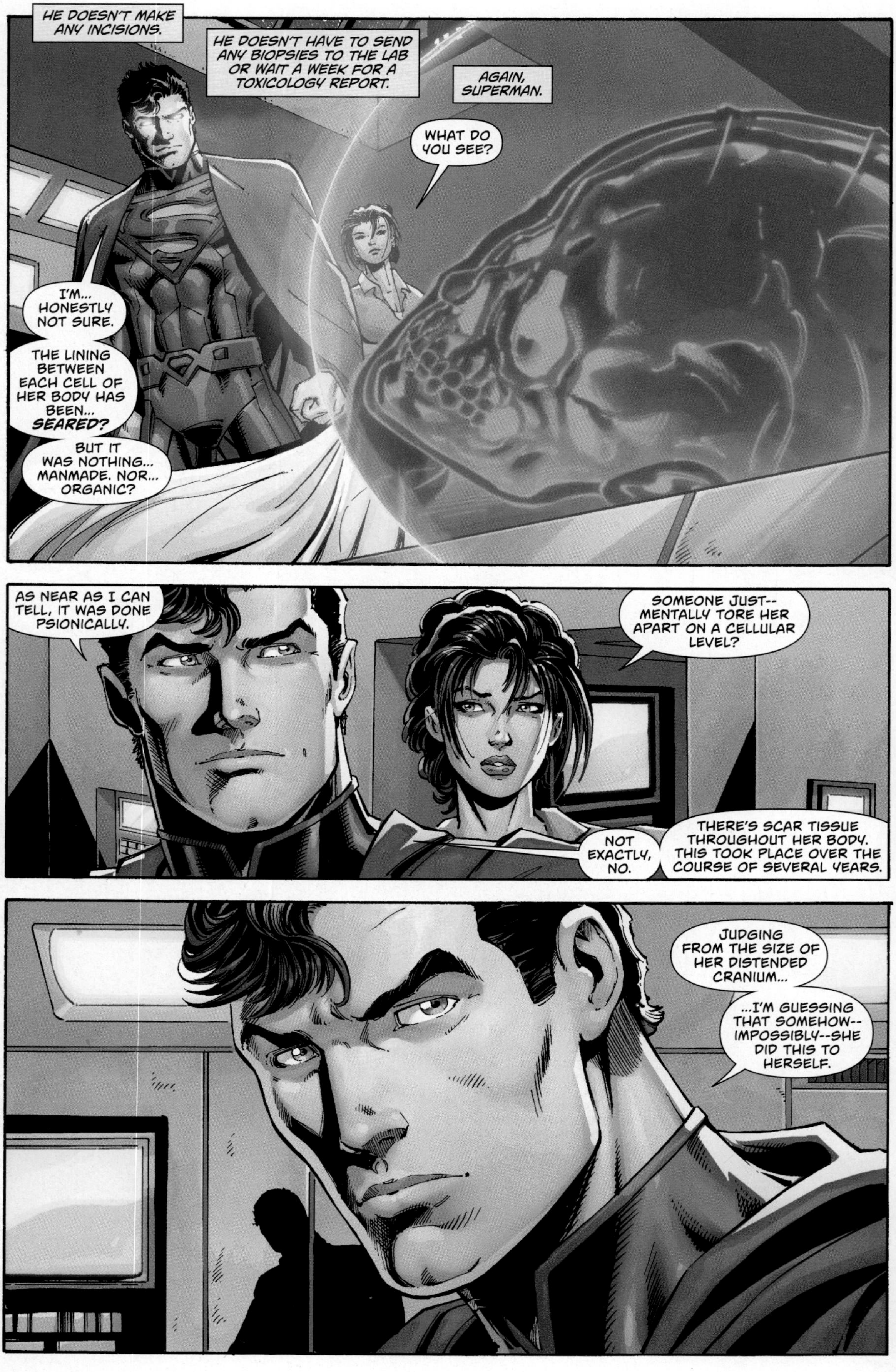
HE DOESN'T MAKE ANY INCISIONS.
HE DOESN'T HAVE TO SEND ANY BIOPSIES TO THE LAB OR WAIT A WEEK FOR A TOXICOLOGY REPORT.
AGAIN, SUPERMAN.
WHAT DO YOU SEE?
I'M... HONESTLY NOT SURE.
THE LINING BETWEEN EACH CELL OF HER BODY HAS BEEN... SEARED?
BUT IT WAS NOTHING... MANMADE. NOR... ORGANIC?
AS NEAR AS I CAN TELL, IT WAS DONE PSIONICALLY.
SOMEONE JUST--MENTALLY TORE HER APART ON A CELLULAR LEVEL?
NOT EXACTLY, NO.
THERE'S SCAR TISSUE THROUGHOUT HER BODY. THIS TOOK PLACE OVER THE COURSE OF SEVERAL YEARS.
JUDGING FROM THE SIZE OF HER DISTENDED CRANIUM...
...I'M GUESSING THAT SOMEHOW--IMPOSSIBLY--SHE DID THIS TO HERSELF.

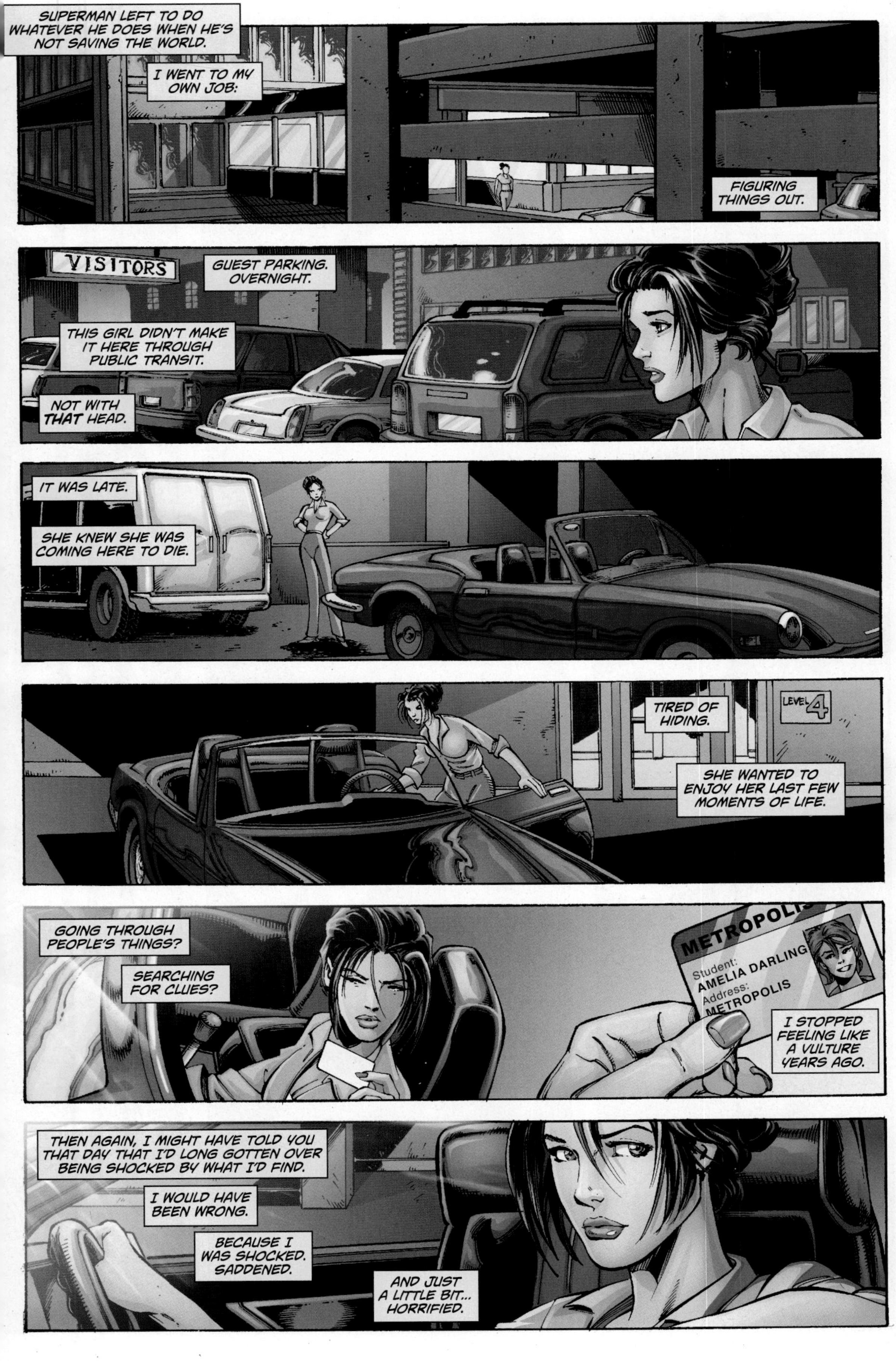
SUPERMAN LEFT TO DO WHATEVER HE DOES WHEN HE'S NOT SAVING THE WORLD.
I WENT TO MY OWN JOB:
FIGURING THINGS OUT.
VISITORS
GUEST PARKING. OVERNIGHT.
THIS GIRL DIDN'T MAKE IT HERE THROUGH PUBLIC TRANSIT.
NOT WITH THAT HEAD.
IT WAS LATE.
SHE KNEW SHE WAS COMING HERE TO DIE.
TIRED OF HIDING.
LEVEL 4
SHE WANTED TO ENJOY HER LAST FEW MOMENTS OF LIFE.
GOING THROUGH PEOPLE'S THINGS?
SEARCHING FOR CLUES?
METROPOLIS
Student: AMELIA DARLING
Address: METROPOLIS
I STOPPED FEELING LIKE A VULTURE YEARS AGO.
THEN AGAIN, I MIGHT HAVE TOLD YOU THAT DAY THAT I'D LONG GOTTEN OVER BEING SHOCKED BY WHAT I'D FIND.
I WOULD HAVE BEEN WRONG.
BECAUSE I WAS SHOCKED. SADDENED.
AND JUST A LITTLE BIT... HORRIFIED.

Chapter Two

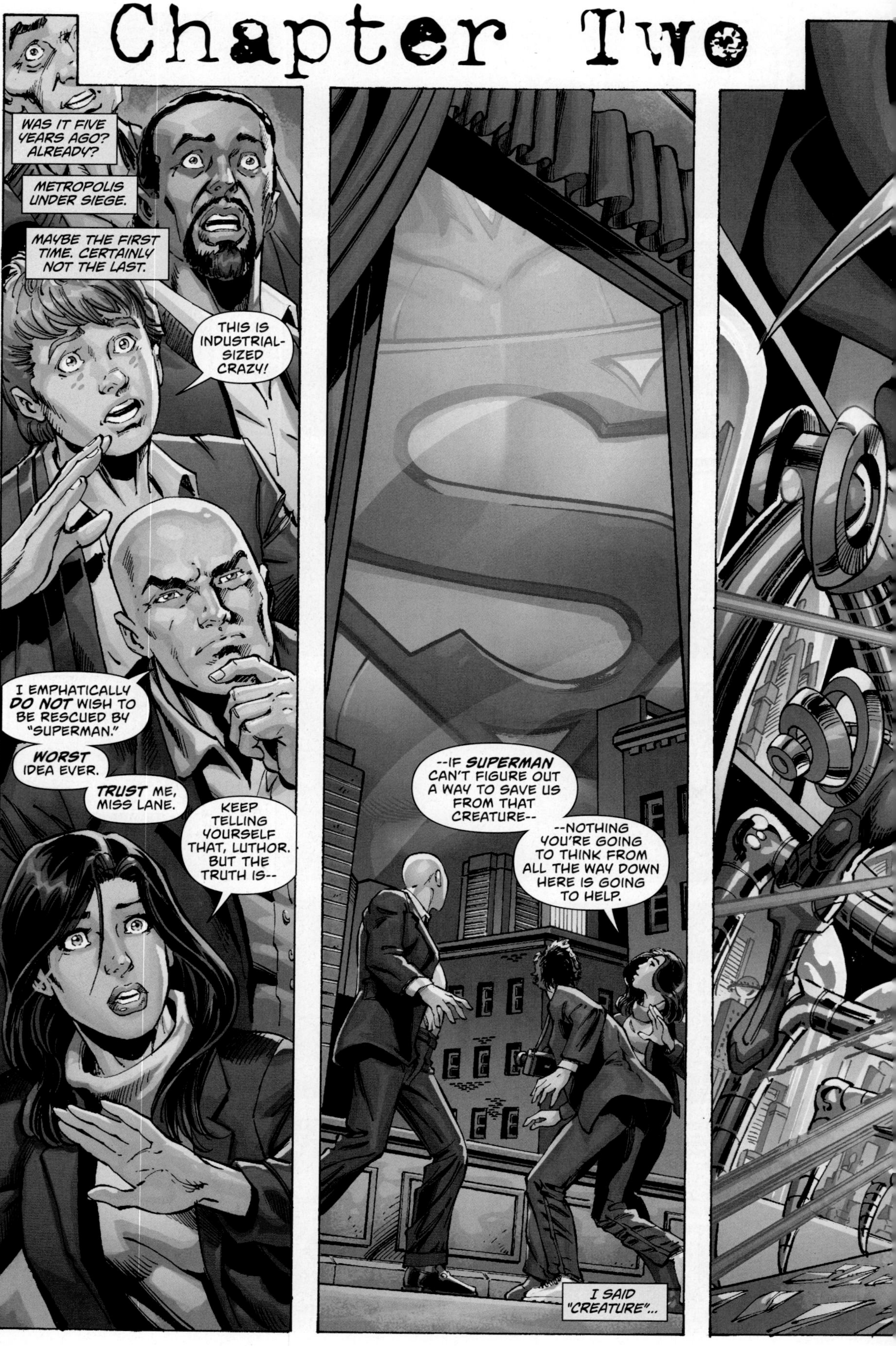
WAS IT FIVE YEARS AGO? ALREADY?
METROPOLIS UNDER SIEGE.
MAYBE THE FIRST TIME. CERTAINLY NOT THE LAST.
THIS IS INDUSTRIAL-SIZED CRAZY!
I EMPHATICALLY DO NOT WISH TO BE RESCUED BY "SUPERMAN."
WORST IDEA EVER.
TRUST ME, MISS LANE.
KEEP TELLING YOURSELF THAT, LUTHOR. BUT THE TRUTH IS--
--IF SUPERMAN CAN'T FIGURE OUT A WAY TO SAVE US FROM THAT CREATURE--
--NOTHING YOU'RE GOING TO THINK FROM ALL THE WAY DOWN HERE IS GOING TO HELP.
I SAID "CREATURE"...

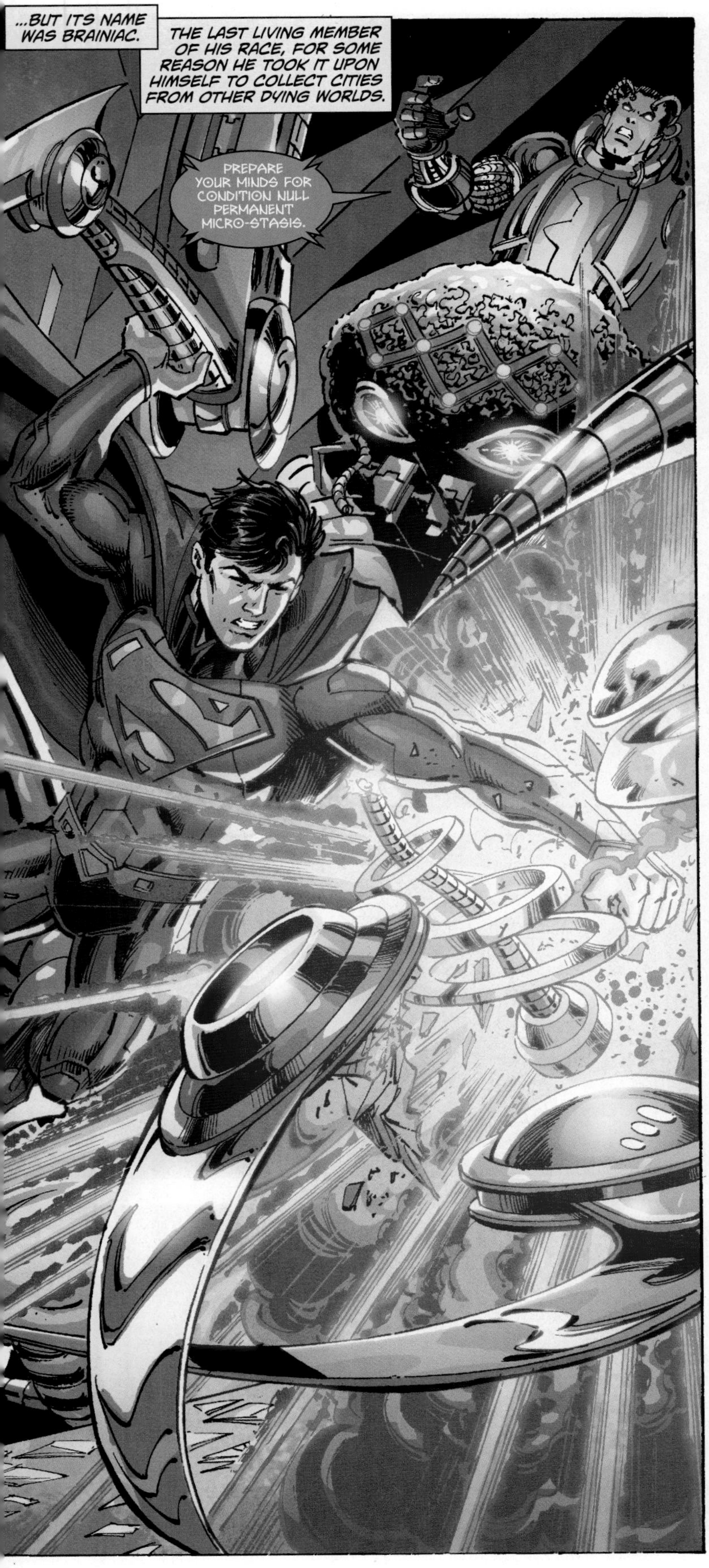
...BUT ITS NAME WAS BRAINIAC.
THE LAST LIVING MEMBER OF HIS RACE, FOR SOME REASON HE TOOK IT UPON HIMSELF TO COLLECT CITIES FROM OTHER DYING WORLDS.
PREPARE YOUR MINDS FOR CONDITION NULL PERMANENT MICRO-STASIS.

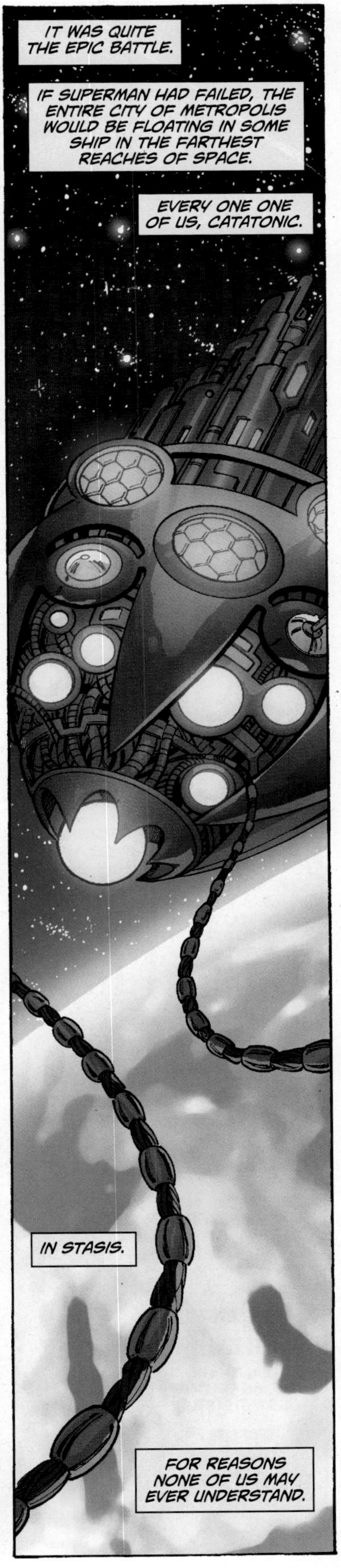
IT WAS QUITE THE EPIC BATTLE.
IF SUPERMAN HAD FAILED, THE ENTIRE CITY OF METROPOLIS WOULD BE FLOATING IN SOME SHIP IN THE FARTHEST REACHES OF SPACE.
EVERY ONE ONE OF US, CATATONIC.
IN STASIS.
FOR REASONS NONE OF US MAY EVER UNDERSTAND.

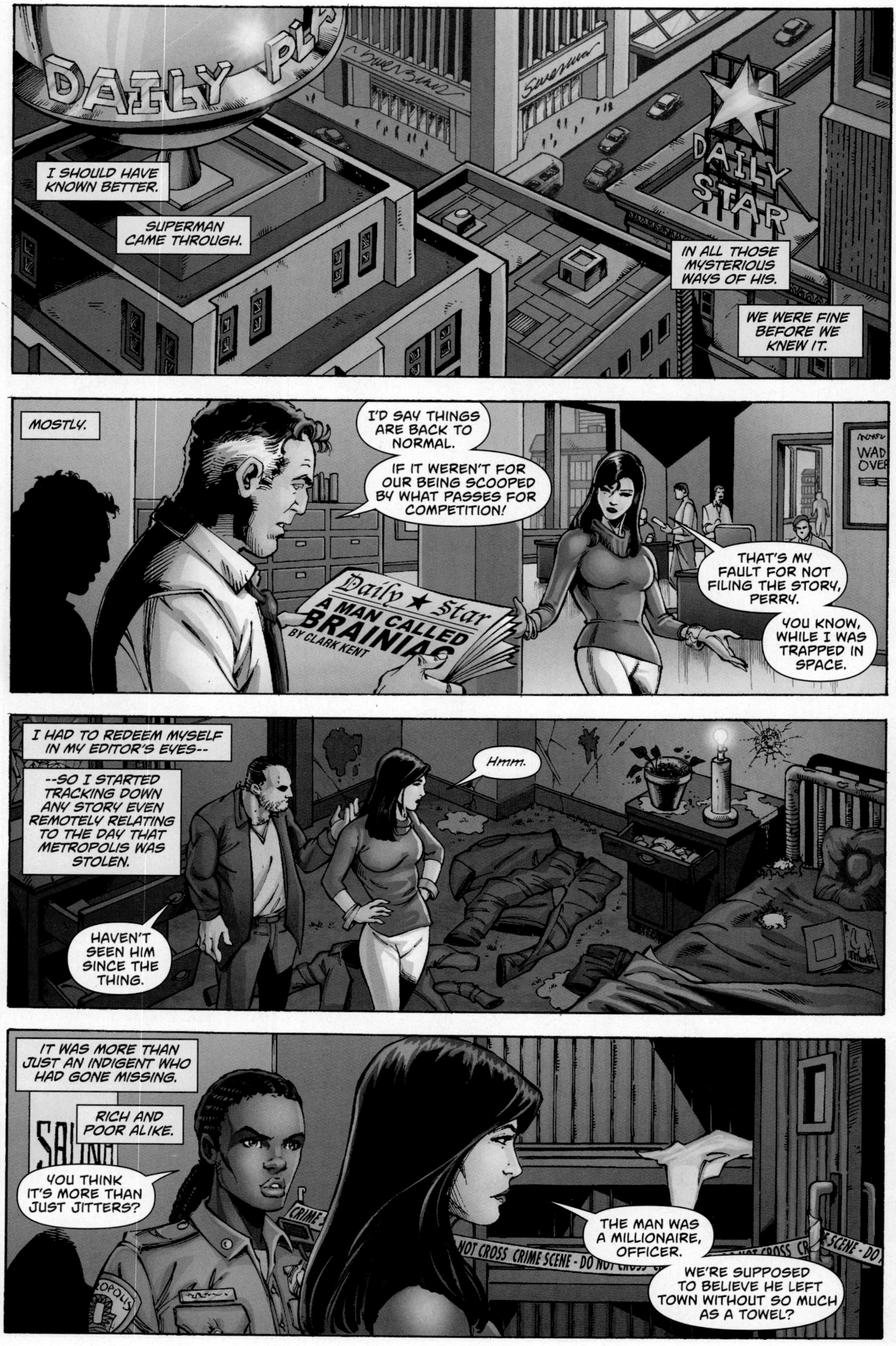
DAILY PL
DAILY STAR
I SHOULD HAVE KNOWN BETTER.
SUPERMAN CAME THROUGH.
IN ALL THOSE MYSTERIOUS WAYS OF HIS.
WE WERE FINE BEFORE WE KNEW IT.
MOSTLY.
I'D SAY THINGS ARE BACK TO NORMAL.
IF IT WEREN'T FOR OUR BEING SCOOPED BY WHAT PASSES FOR COMPETITION!
Daily ★ Star
A MAN CALLED BRAINIAC
BY CLARK KENT
THAT'S MY FAULT FOR NOT FILING THE STORY, PERRY.
YOU KNOW, WHILE I WAS TRAPPED IN SPACE.
I HAD TO REDEEM MYSELF IN MY EDITOR'S EYES--
--SO I STARTED TRACKING DOWN ANY STORY EVEN REMOTELY RELATING TO THE DAY THAT METROPOLIS WAS STOLEN.
Hmm.
HAVEN'T SEEN HIM SINCE THE THING.
IT WAS MORE THAN JUST AN INDIGENT WHO HAD GONE MISSING.
RICH AND POOR ALIKE.
YOU THINK IT'S MORE THAN JUST JITTERS?
THE MAN WAS A MILLIONAIRE, OFFICER.
WE'RE SUPPOSED TO BELIEVE HE LEFT TOWN WITHOUT SO MUCH AS A TOWEL?
NOT CROSS CRIME SCENE - DO NOT CROSS

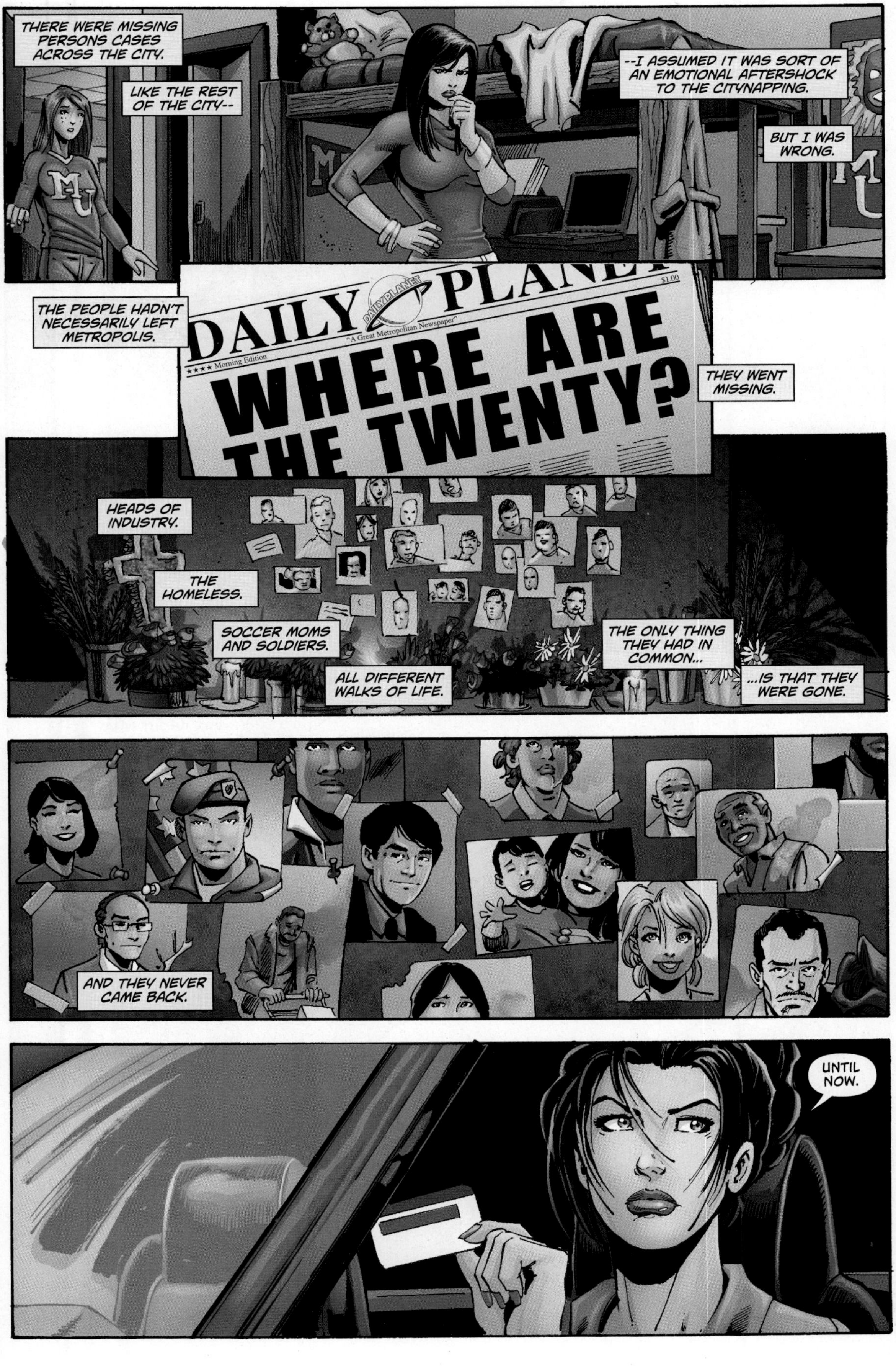
THERE WERE MISSING PERSONS CASES ACROSS THE CITY.
LIKE THE REST OF THE CITY--
--I ASSUMED IT WAS SORT OF AN EMOTIONAL AFTERSHOCK TO THE CITYNAPPING.
BUT I WAS WRONG.
THE PEOPLE HADN'T NECESSARILY LEFT METROPOLIS.
DAILY PLANET
$1.00
"A Great Metropolitan Newspaper"
Morning Edition
WHERE ARE THE TWENTY?
THEY WENT MISSING.
HEADS OF INDUSTRY.
THE HOMELESS.
SOCCER MOMS AND SOLDIERS.
ALL DIFFERENT WALKS OF LIFE.
THE ONLY THING THEY HAD IN COMMON...
...IS THAT THEY WERE GONE.
AND THEY NEVER CAME BACK.
UNTIL NOW.

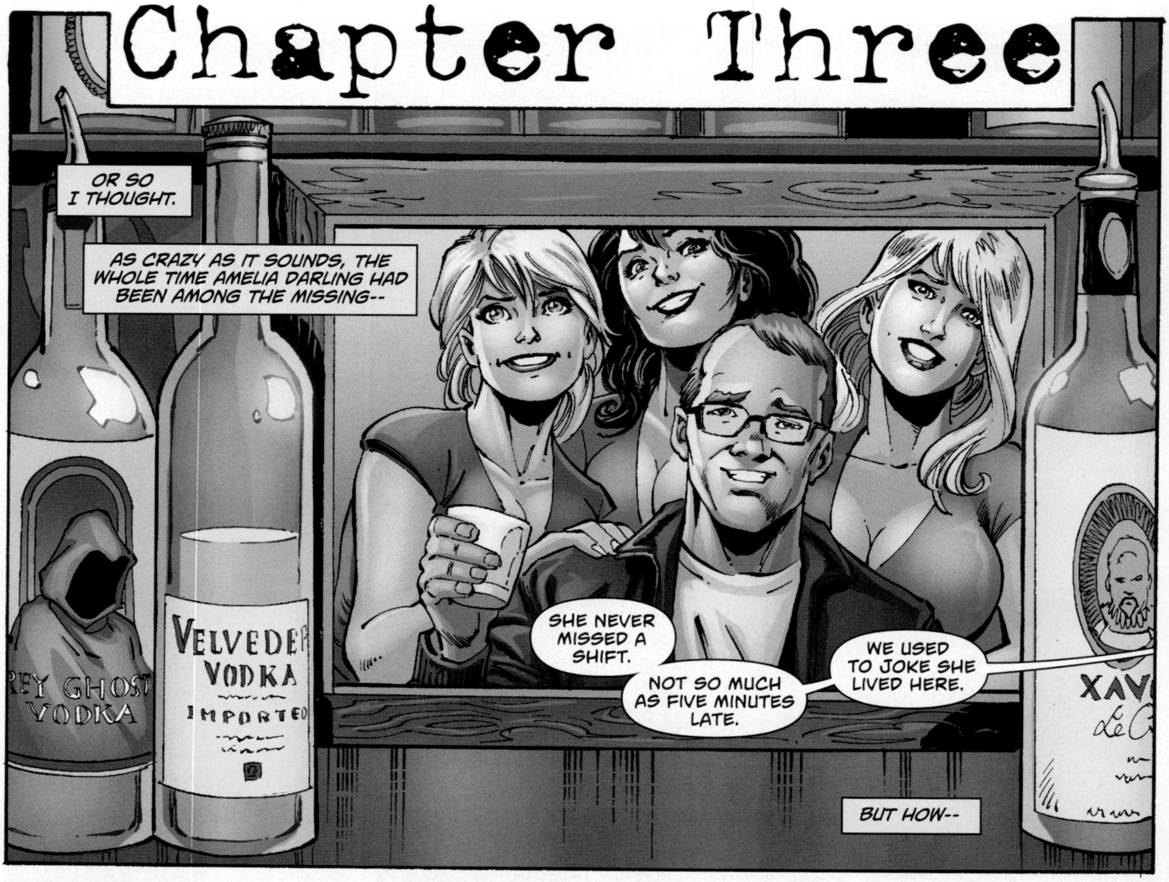
Chapter Three
OR SO I THOUGHT.
AS CRAZY AS IT SOUNDS, THE WHOLE TIME AMELIA DARLING HAD BEEN AMONG THE MISSING--
SHE NEVER MISSED A SHIFT.
NOT SO MUCH AS FIVE MINUTES LATE.
WE USED TO JOKE SHE LIVED HERE.
BUT HOW--

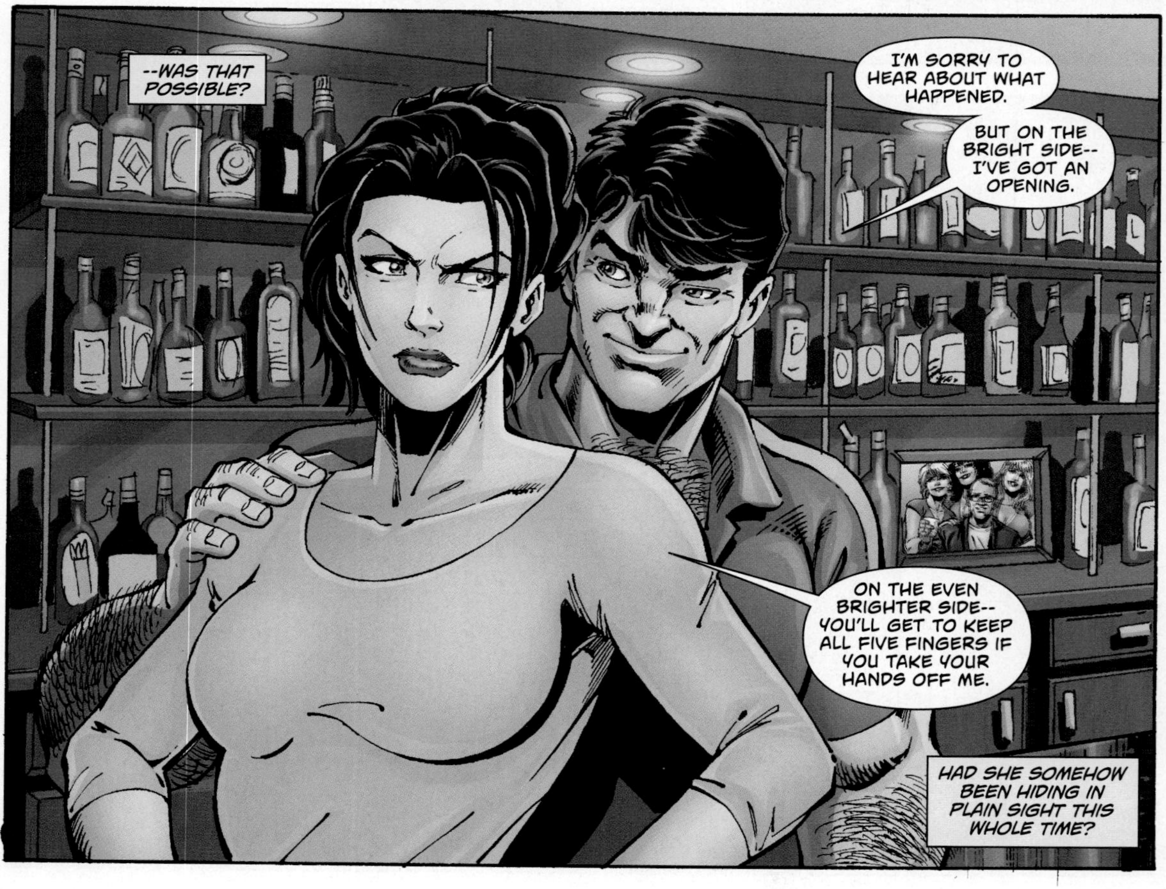
--WAS THAT POSSIBLE?
I'M SORRY TO HEAR ABOUT WHAT HAPPENED.
BUT ON THE BRIGHT SIDE-- I'VE GOT AN OPENING.
ON THE EVEN BRIGHTER SIDE-- YOU'LL GET TO KEEP ALL FIVE FINGERS IF YOU TAKE YOUR HANDS OFF ME.
HAD SHE SOMEHOW BEEN HIDING IN PLAIN SIGHT THIS WHOLE TIME?

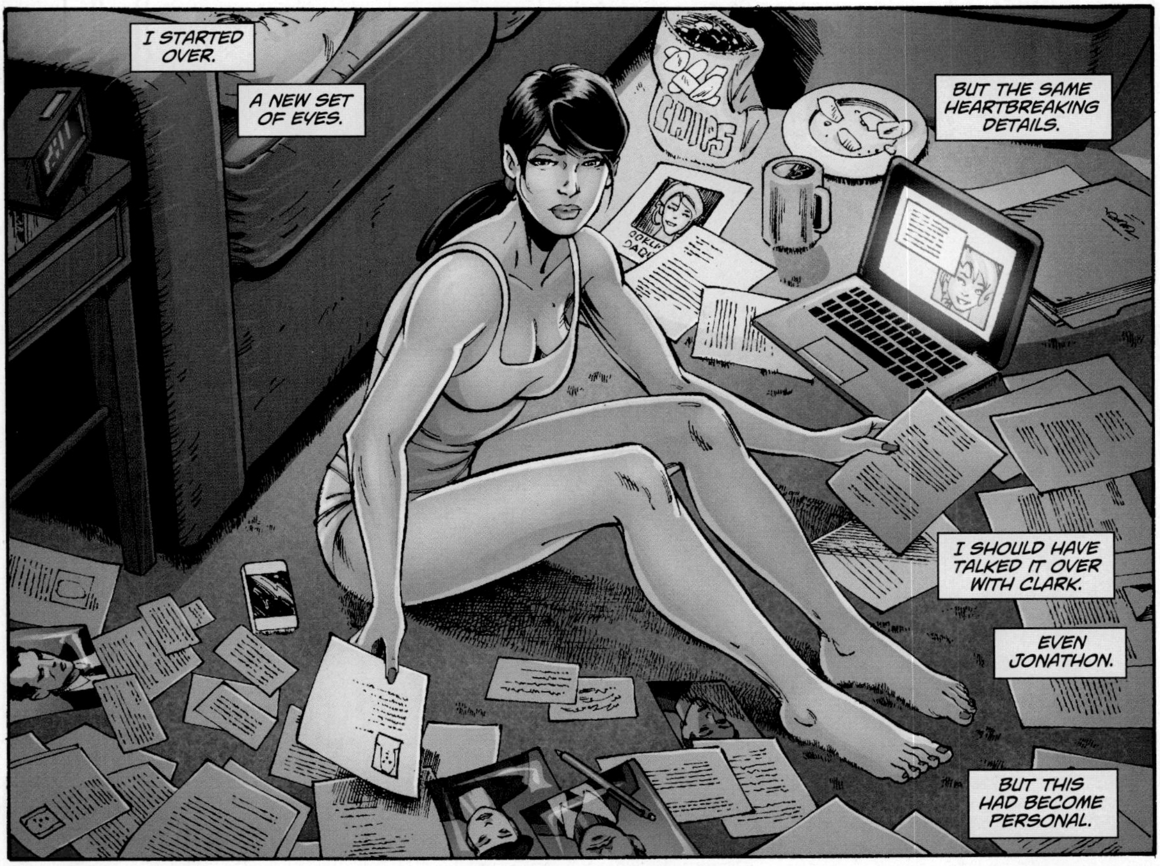
I STARTED OVER.
A NEW SET OF EYES.
BUT THE SAME HEARTBREAKING DETAILS.
I SHOULD HAVE TALKED IT OVER WITH CLARK.
EVEN JONATHON.
BUT THIS HAD BECOME PERSONAL.

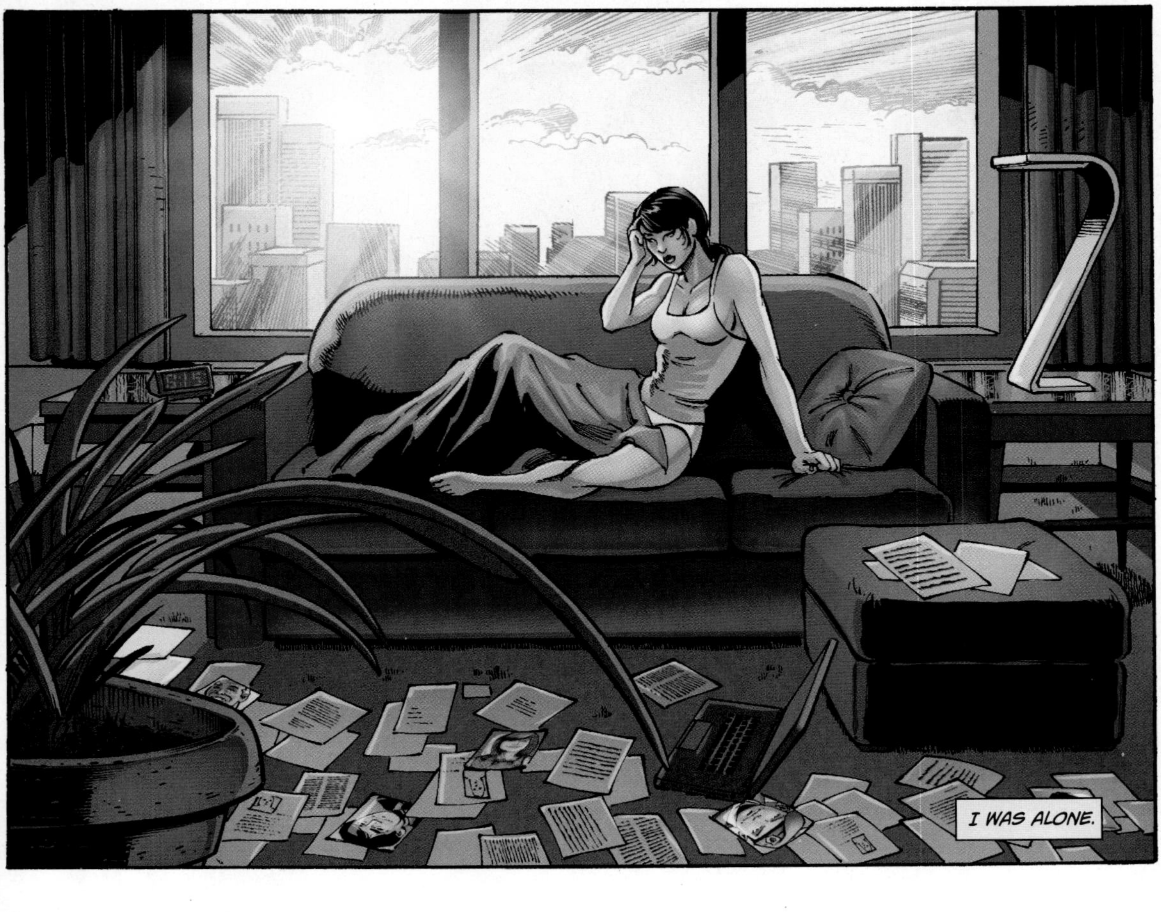
I WAS ALONE.

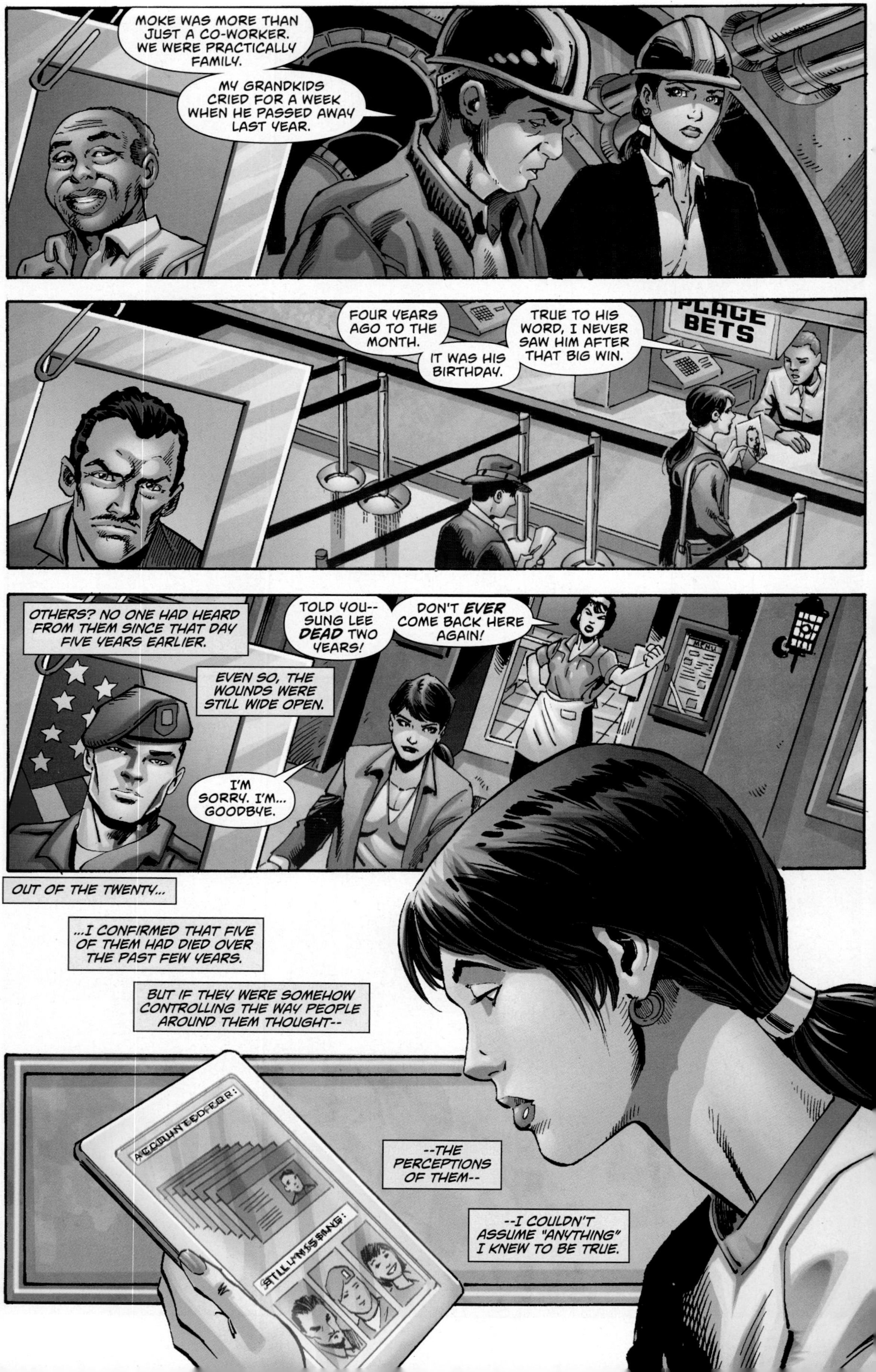
MOKE WAS MORE THAN JUST A CO-WORKER. WE WERE PRACTICALLY FAMILY.
MY GRANDKIDS CRIED FOR A WEEK WHEN HE PASSED AWAY LAST YEAR.
FOUR YEARS AGO TO THE MONTH.
IT WAS HIS BIRTHDAY.
TRUE TO HIS WORD, I NEVER SAW HIM AFTER THAT BIG WIN.
PLACE BETS
OTHERS? NO ONE HAD HEARD FROM THEM SINCE THAT DAY FIVE YEARS EARLIER.
TOLD YOU-- SUNG LEE **DEAD** TWO YEARS!
DON'T **EVER** COME BACK HERE AGAIN!
MENU
EVEN SO, THE WOUNDS WERE STILL WIDE OPEN.
I'M SORRY. I'M... GOODBYE.
OUT OF THE TWENTY...
...I CONFIRMED THAT FIVE OF THEM HAD DIED OVER THE PAST FEW YEARS.
BUT IF THEY WERE SOMEHOW CONTROLLING THE WAY PEOPLE AROUND THEM THOUGHT--
ACCOUNTED FOR:
STILL MISSING:
--THE PERCEPTIONS OF THEM--
--I COULDN'T ASSUME "ANYTHING" I KNEW TO BE TRUE.

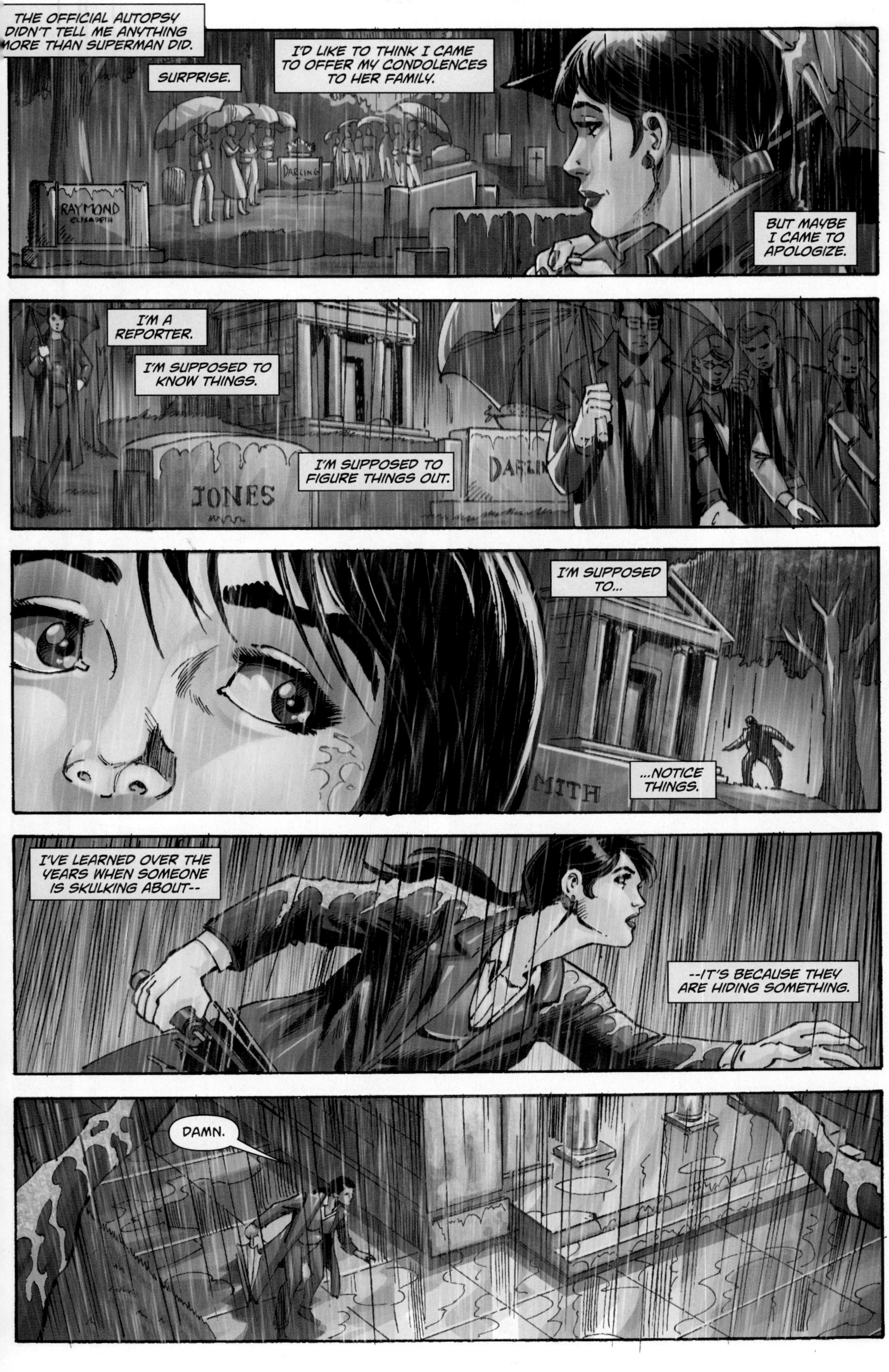
THE OFFICIAL AUTOPSY DIDN'T TELL ME ANYTHING MORE THAN SUPERMAN DID.
SURPRISE.
I'D LIKE TO THINK I CAME TO OFFER MY CONDOLENCES TO HER FAMILY.
BUT MAYBE I CAME TO APOLOGIZE.
RAYMOND
DARLING
I'M A REPORTER.
I'M SUPPOSED TO KNOW THINGS.
I'M SUPPOSED TO FIGURE THINGS OUT.
JONES
I'M SUPPOSED TO...
...NOTICE THINGS.
I'VE LEARNED OVER THE YEARS WHEN SOMEONE IS SKULKING ABOUT--
--IT'S BECAUSE THEY ARE HIDING SOMETHING.
DAMN.

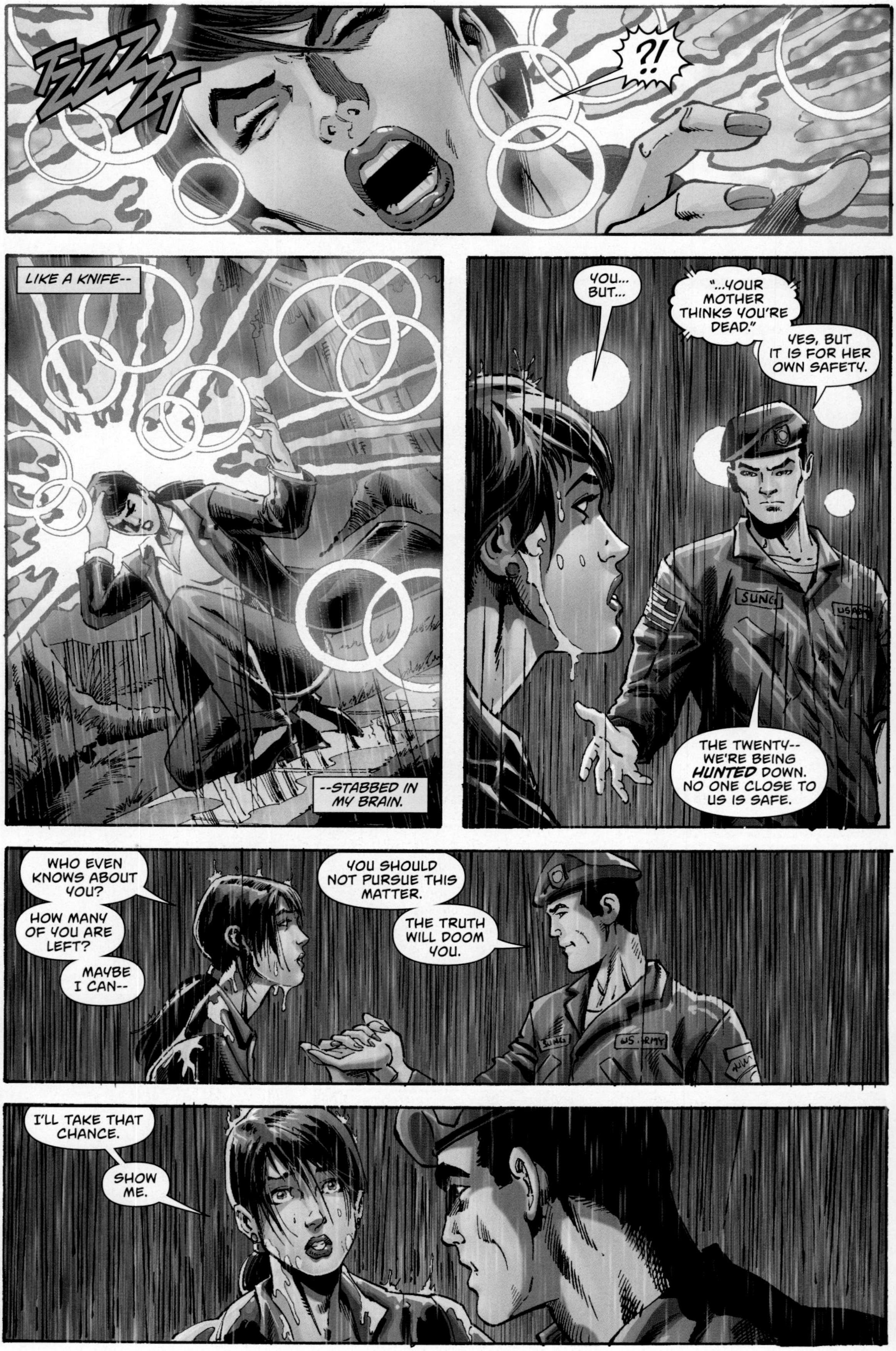
TZZZZT
?!
LIKE A KNIFE--
--STABBED IN MY BRAIN.
YOU... BUT...
"...YOUR MOTHER THINKS YOU'RE DEAD."
YES, BUT IT IS FOR HER OWN SAFETY.
SUNG
THE TWENTY-- WE'RE BEING HUNTED DOWN. NO ONE CLOSE TO US IS SAFE.
WHO EVEN KNOWS ABOUT YOU?
HOW MANY OF YOU ARE LEFT?
MAYBE I CAN--
YOU SHOULD NOT PURSUE THIS MATTER.
THE TRUTH WILL DOOM YOU.
SUNG
US ARMY
I'LL TAKE THAT CHANCE.
SHOW ME.

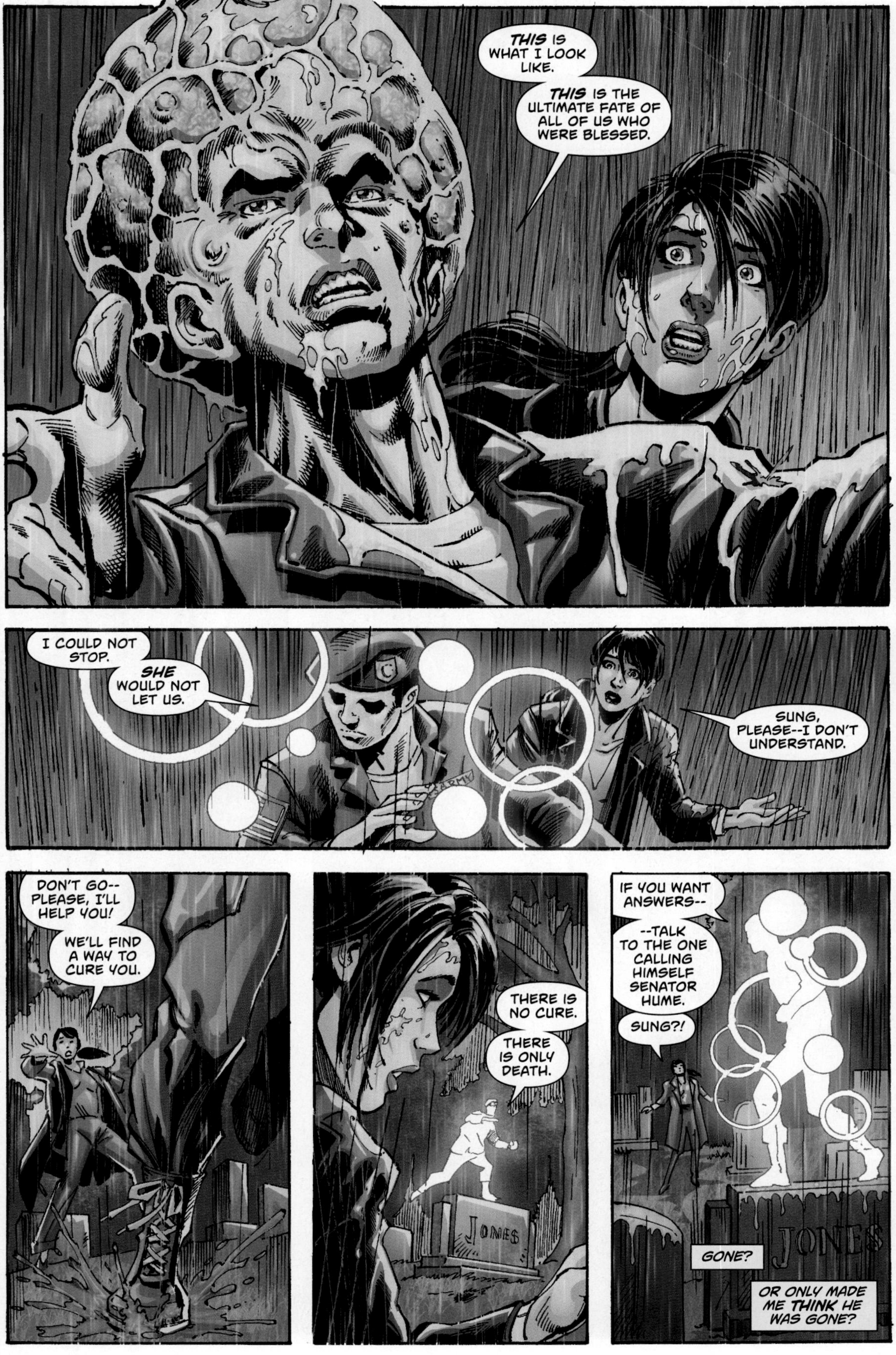
THIS IS WHAT I LOOK LIKE.
THIS IS THE ULTIMATE FATE OF ALL OF US WHO WERE BLESSED.
I COULD NOT STOP.
SHE WOULD NOT LET US.
SUNG, PLEASE--I DON'T UNDERSTAND.
DON'T GO--PLEASE, I'LL HELP YOU!
WE'LL FIND A WAY TO CURE YOU.
THERE IS NO CURE.
THERE IS ONLY DEATH.
JONES
IF YOU WANT ANSWERS--
--TALK TO THE ONE CALLING HIMSELF SENATOR HUME.
SUNG?!
JONES
GONE?
OR ONLY MADE ME THINK HE WAS GONE?

Chapter Four

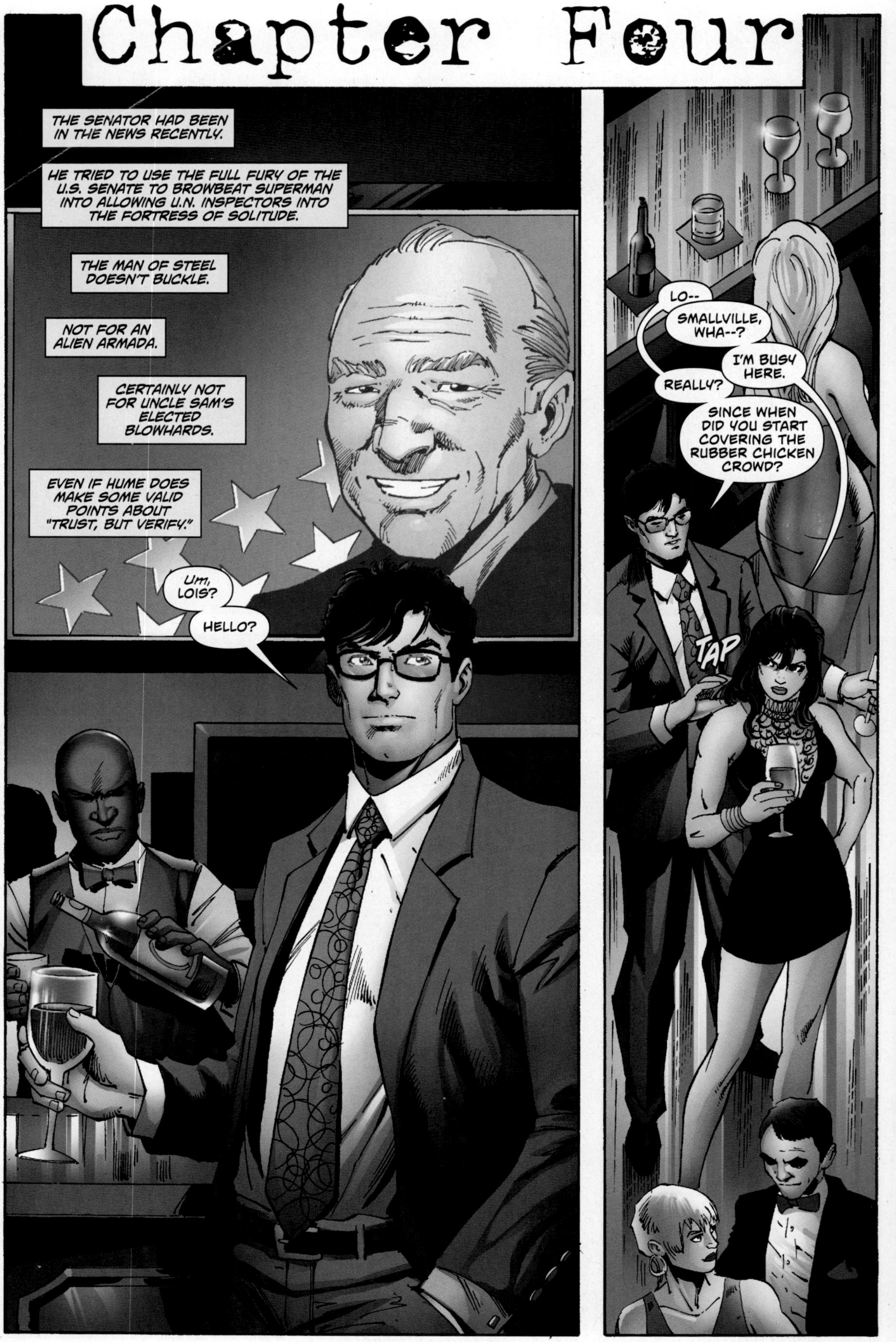

THE SENATOR HAD BEEN IN THE NEWS RECENTLY.
HE TRIED TO USE THE FULL FURY OF THE U.S. SENATE TO BROWBEAT SUPERMAN INTO ALLOWING U.N. INSPECTORS INTO THE FORTRESS OF SOLITUDE.
THE MAN OF STEEL DOESN'T BUCKLE.
NOT FOR AN ALIEN ARMADA.
CERTAINLY NOT FOR UNCLE SAM'S ELECTED BLOWHARDS.
EVEN IF HUME DOES MAKE SOME VALID POINTS ABOUT "TRUST, BUT VERIFY."
UM, LOIS?
HELLO?
LO--
SMALLVILLE, WHA--?
I'M BUSY HERE.
REALLY?
SINCE WHEN DID YOU START COVERING THE RUBBER CHICKEN CROWD?
TAP

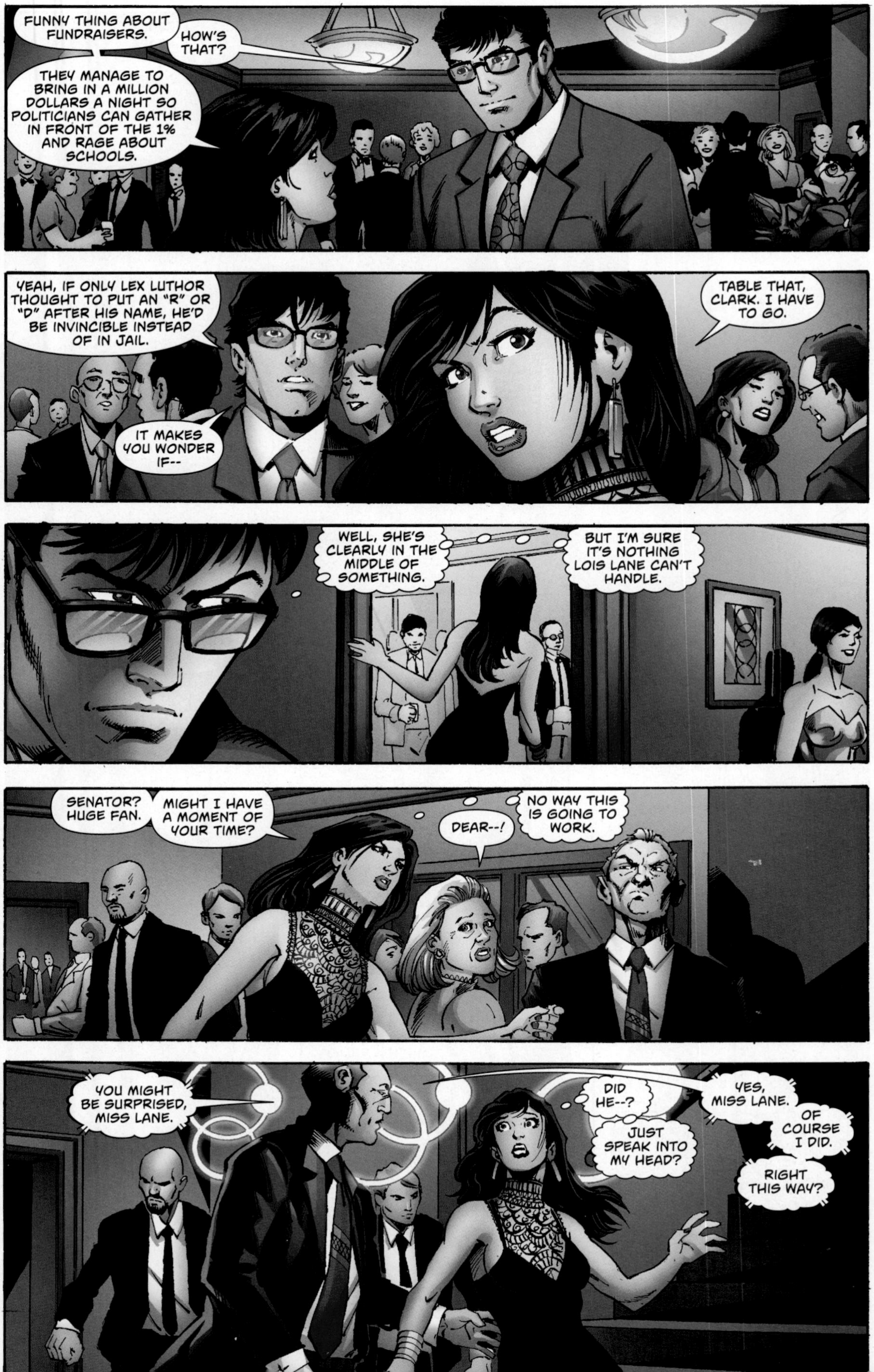
FUNNY THING ABOUT FUNDRAISERS.
HOW'S THAT?
THEY MANAGE TO BRING IN A MILLION DOLLARS A NIGHT SO POLITICIANS CAN GATHER IN FRONT OF THE 1% AND RAGE ABOUT SCHOOLS.
YEAH, IF ONLY LEX LUTHOR THOUGHT TO PUT AN "R" OR "D" AFTER HIS NAME, HE'D BE INVINCIBLE INSTEAD OF IN JAIL.
IT MAKES YOU WONDER IF--
TABLE THAT, CLARK. I HAVE TO GO.
WELL, SHE'S CLEARLY IN THE MIDDLE OF SOMETHING.
BUT I'M SURE IT'S NOTHING LOIS LANE CAN'T HANDLE.
SENATOR? HUGE FAN.
MIGHT I HAVE A MOMENT OF YOUR TIME?
DEAR--!
NO WAY THIS IS GOING TO WORK.
YOU MIGHT BE SURPRISED, MISS LANE.
DID HE--?
JUST SPEAK INTO MY HEAD?
YES, MISS LANE.
OF COURSE I DID.
RIGHT THIS WAY?

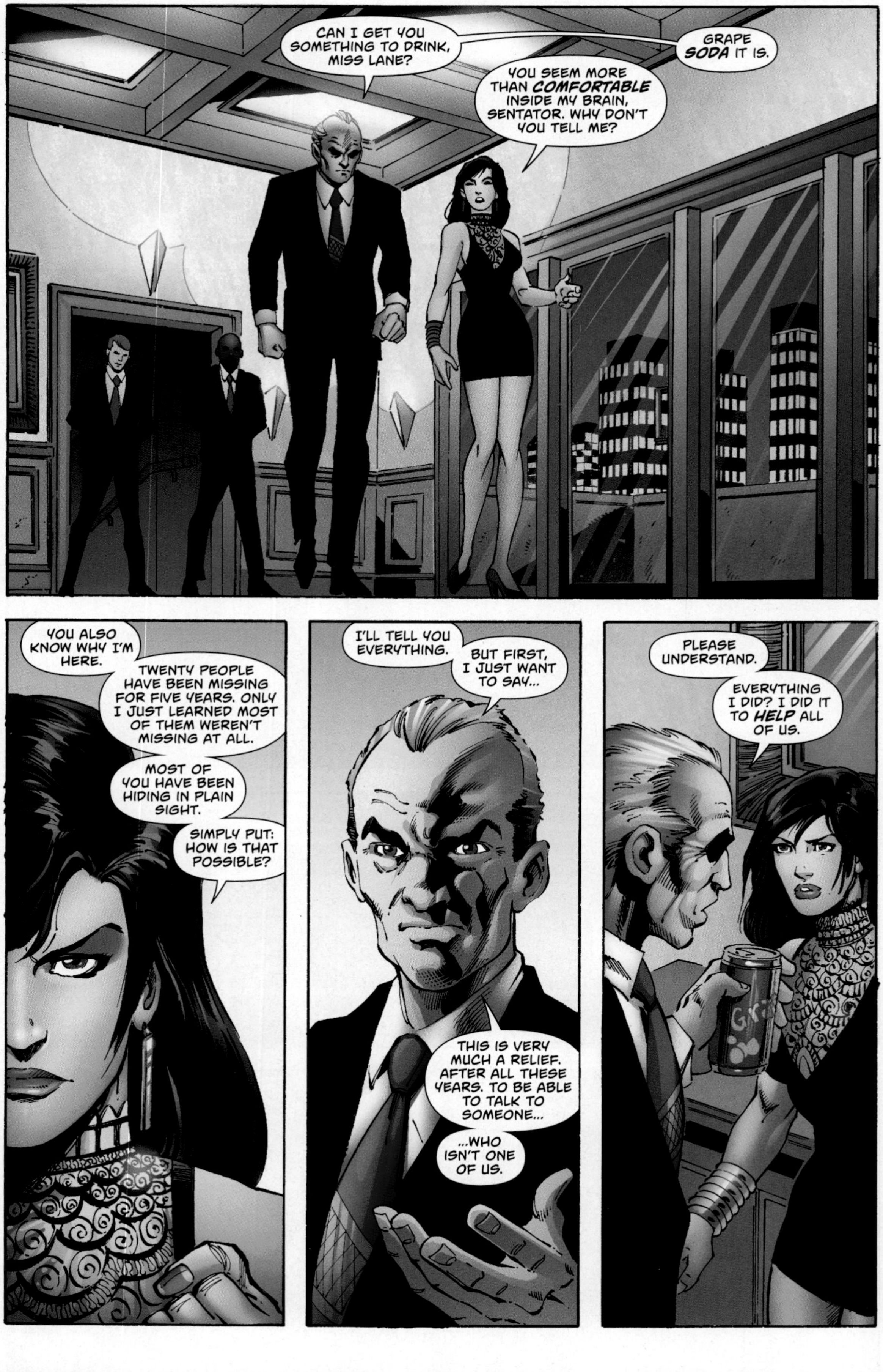
CAN I GET YOU SOMETHING TO DRINK, MISS LANE?
YOU SEEM MORE THAN COMFORTABLE INSIDE MY BRAIN, SENTATOR. WHY DON'T YOU TELL ME?
GRAPE SODA IT IS.
YOU ALSO KNOW WHY I'M HERE.
TWENTY PEOPLE HAVE BEEN MISSING FOR FIVE YEARS. ONLY I JUST LEARNED MOST OF THEM WEREN'T MISSING AT ALL.
MOST OF YOU HAVE BEEN HIDING IN PLAIN SIGHT.
SIMPLY PUT: HOW IS THAT POSSIBLE?
I'LL TELL YOU EVERYTHING.
BUT FIRST, I JUST WANT TO SAY...
THIS IS VERY MUCH A RELIEF. AFTER ALL THESE YEARS. TO BE ABLE TO TALK TO SOMEONE...
...WHO ISN'T ONE OF US.
PLEASE UNDERSTAND.
EVERYTHING I DID? I DID IT TO HELP ALL OF US.

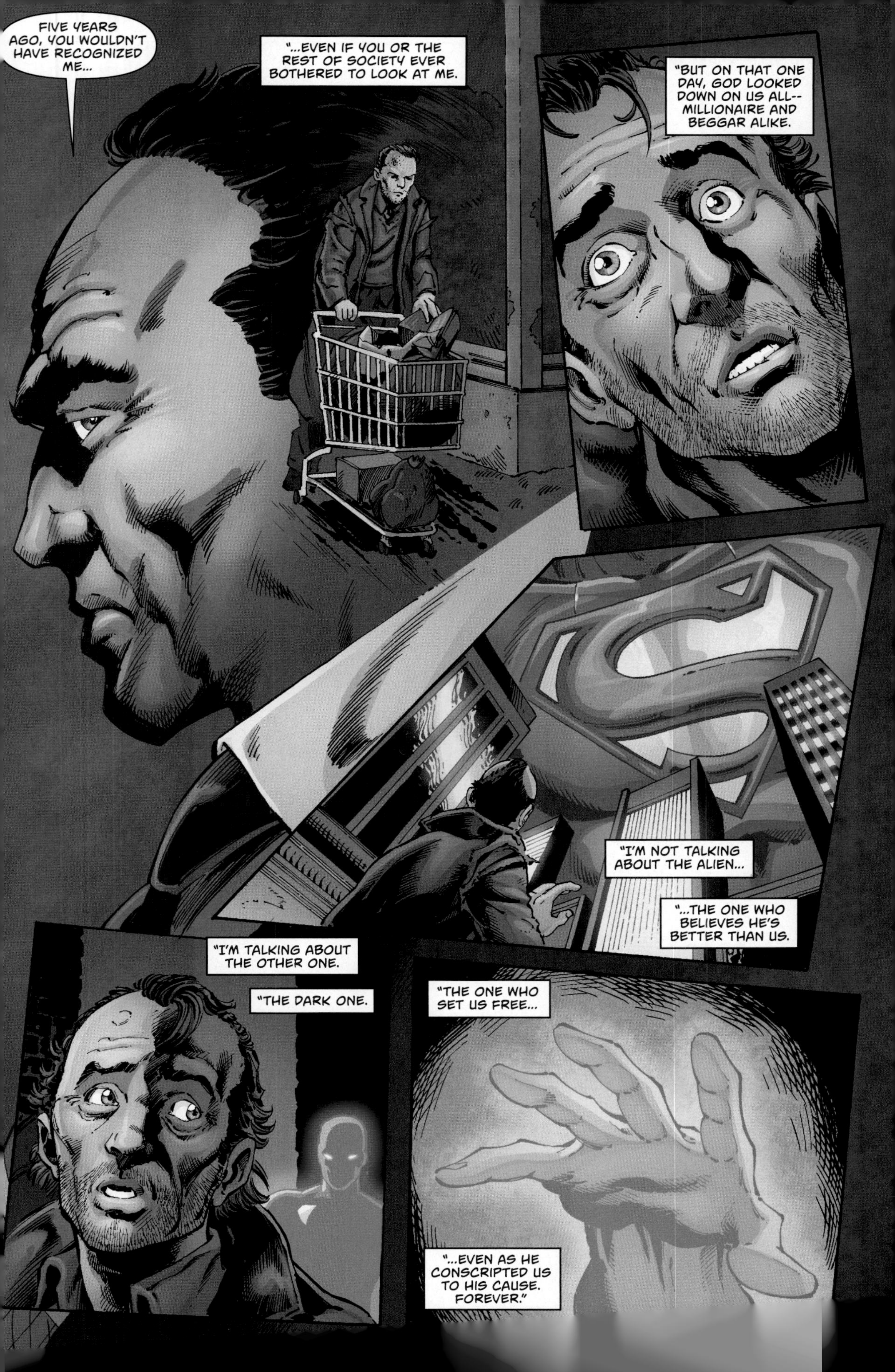
FIVE YEARS AGO, YOU WOULDN'T HAVE RECOGNIZED ME...
"...EVEN IF YOU OR THE REST OF SOCIETY EVER BOTHERED TO LOOK AT ME.
"BUT ON THAT ONE DAY, GOD LOOKED DOWN ON US ALL-- MILLIONAIRE AND BEGGAR ALIKE.
"I'M NOT TALKING ABOUT THE ALIEN...
"...THE ONE WHO BELIEVES HE'S BETTER THAN US.
"I'M TALKING ABOUT THE OTHER ONE.
"THE DARK ONE.
"THE ONE WHO SET US FREE...
"...EVEN AS HE CONSCRIPTED US TO HIS CAUSE. FOREVER."

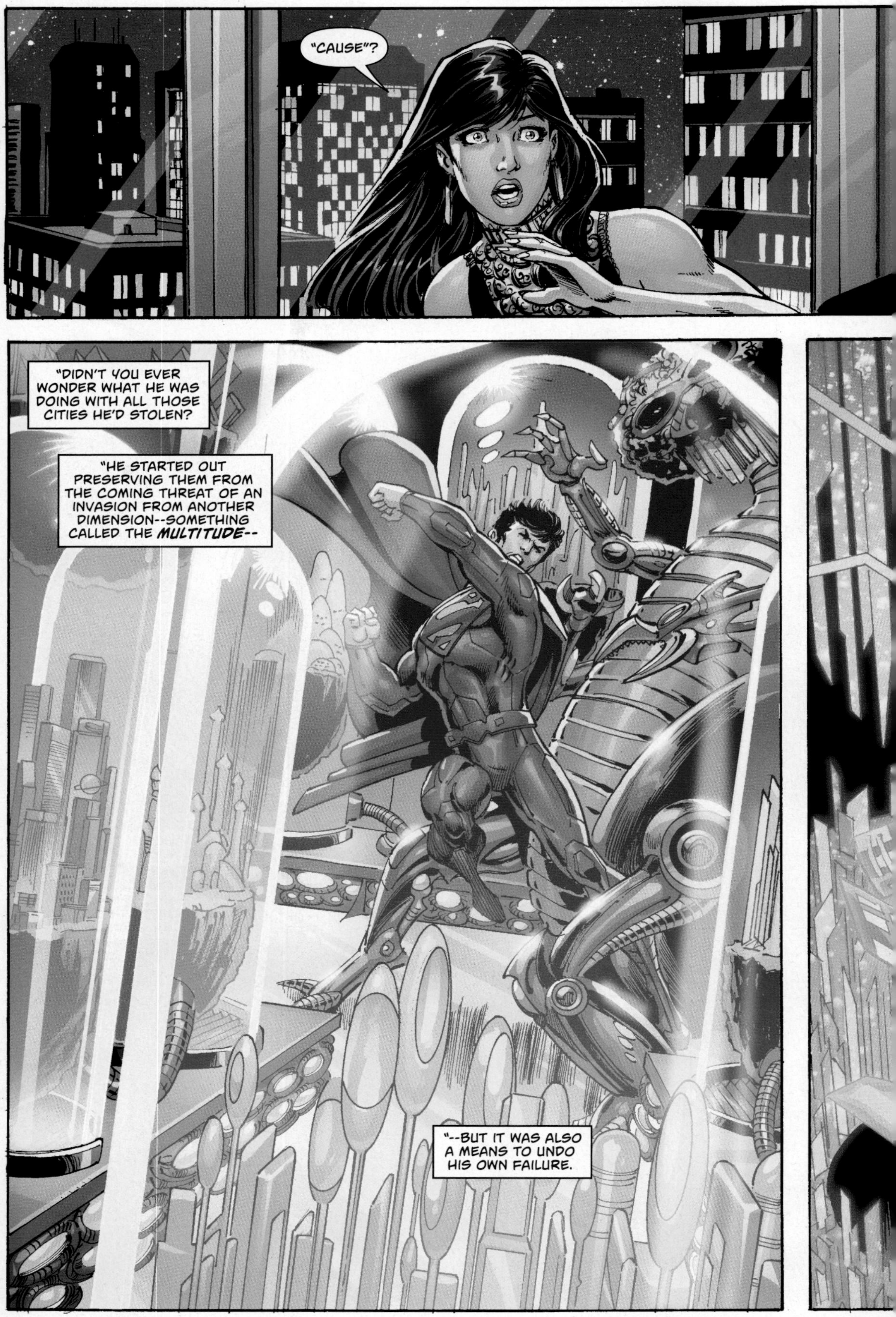
"CAUSE"?
"DIDN'T YOU EVER WONDER WHAT HE WAS DOING WITH ALL THOSE CITIES HE'D STOLEN?
"HE STARTED OUT PRESERVING THEM FROM THE COMING THREAT OF AN INVASION FROM ANOTHER DIMENSION--SOMETHING CALLED THE *MULTITUDE*--
"--BUT IT WAS ALSO A MEANS TO UNDO HIS OWN FAILURE.

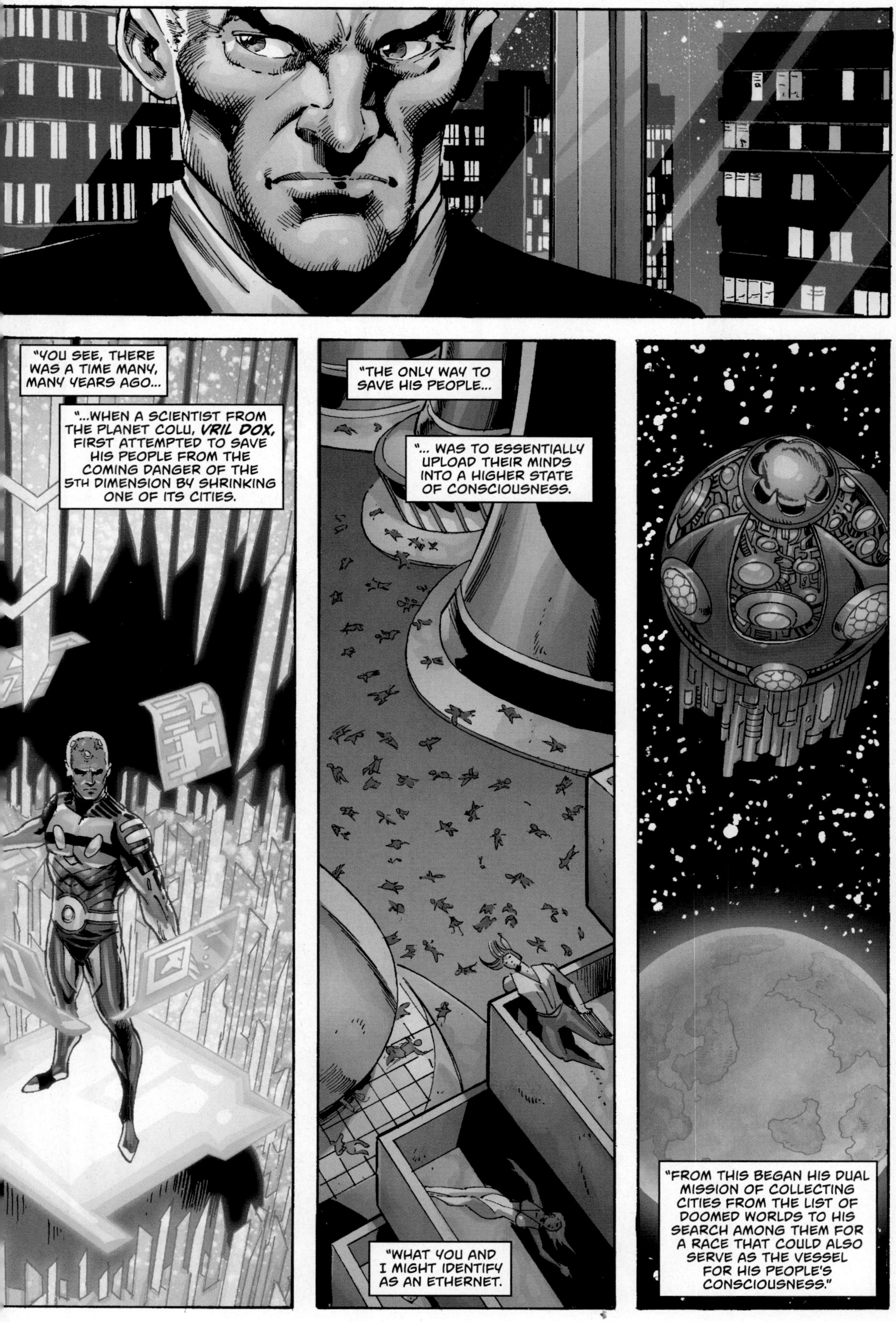
"YOU SEE, THERE WAS A TIME MANY, MANY YEARS AGO...
"...WHEN A SCIENTIST FROM THE PLANET COLU, VRIL DOX, FIRST ATTEMPTED TO SAVE HIS PEOPLE FROM THE COMING DANGER OF THE 5TH DIMENSION BY SHRINKING ONE OF ITS CITIES.
"THE ONLY WAY TO SAVE HIS PEOPLE...
"... WAS TO ESSENTIALLY UPLOAD THEIR MINDS INTO A HIGHER STATE OF CONSCIOUSNESS.
"WHAT YOU AND I MIGHT IDENTIFY AS AN ETHERNET.
"FROM THIS BEGAN HIS DUAL MISSION OF COLLECTING CITIES FROM THE LIST OF DOOMED WORLDS TO HIS SEARCH AMONG THEM FOR A RACE THAT COULD ALSO SERVE AS THE VESSEL FOR HIS PEOPLE'S CONSCIOUSNESS."

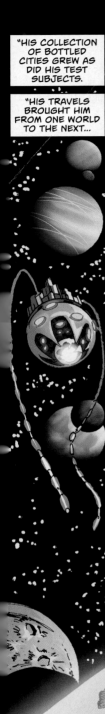

"HIS COLLECTION OF BOTTLED CITIES GREW AS DID HIS TEST SUBJECTS.

"HIS TRAVELS BROUGHT HIM FROM ONE WORLD TO THE NEXT...

"...TAKING 'SAMPLES' IN A WAY THAT ONLY HE COULD.

"IF HE WAS GOING TO USE THESE PEOPLE AFTER ALL AS HOSTS, HE HAD TO MAKE CERTAIN HIS OWN PEOPLE COULD CONTINUE TO EXIST IN THEIR NEW HOMES.

"I UNDERSTAND IT WAS AN ACTION OTHERS MIGHT CALL 'EVIL'...

"...BUT UNDERSTAND, HE WAS TRYING TO SAVE HIS PEOPLE.

"BUT WORLD AFTER WORLD--CITY AFTER CITY-- ALL HIS MACHINATIONS AND MANIPULATIONS

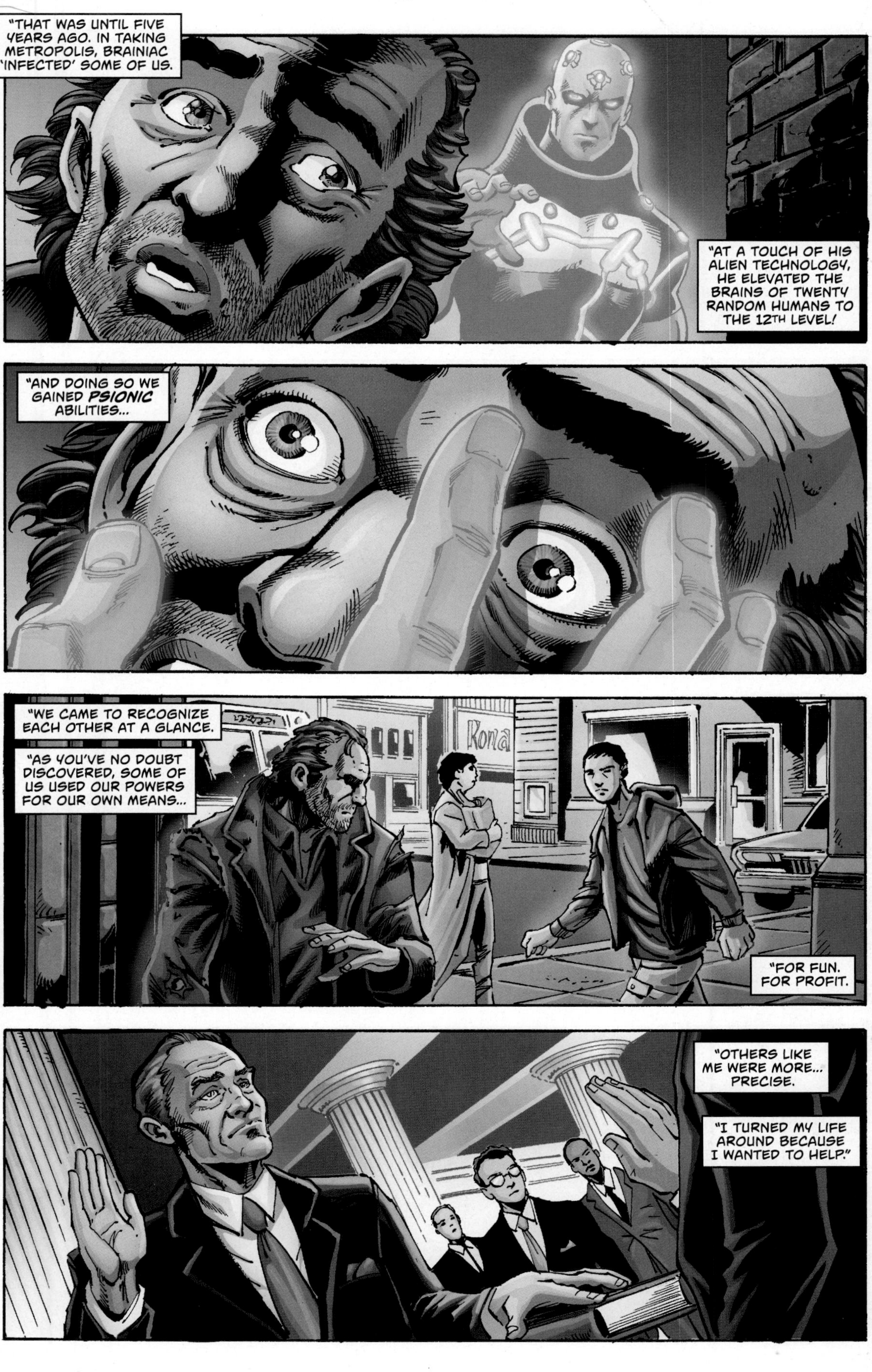
"THAT WAS UNTIL FIVE YEARS AGO. IN TAKING METROPOLIS, BRAINIAC 'INFECTED' SOME OF US.
"AT A TOUCH OF HIS ALIEN TECHNOLOGY, HE ELEVATED THE BRAINS OF TWENTY RANDOM HUMANS TO THE 12TH LEVEL!
"AND DOING SO WE GAINED *PSIONIC* ABILITIES...
"WE CAME TO RECOGNIZE EACH OTHER AT A GLANCE.
"AS YOU'VE NO DOUBT DISCOVERED, SOME OF US USED OUR POWERS FOR OUR OWN MEANS...
Rona
"FOR FUN. FOR PROFIT.
"OTHERS LIKE ME WERE MORE... PRECISE.
"I TURNED MY LIFE AROUND BECAUSE I WANTED TO HELP."

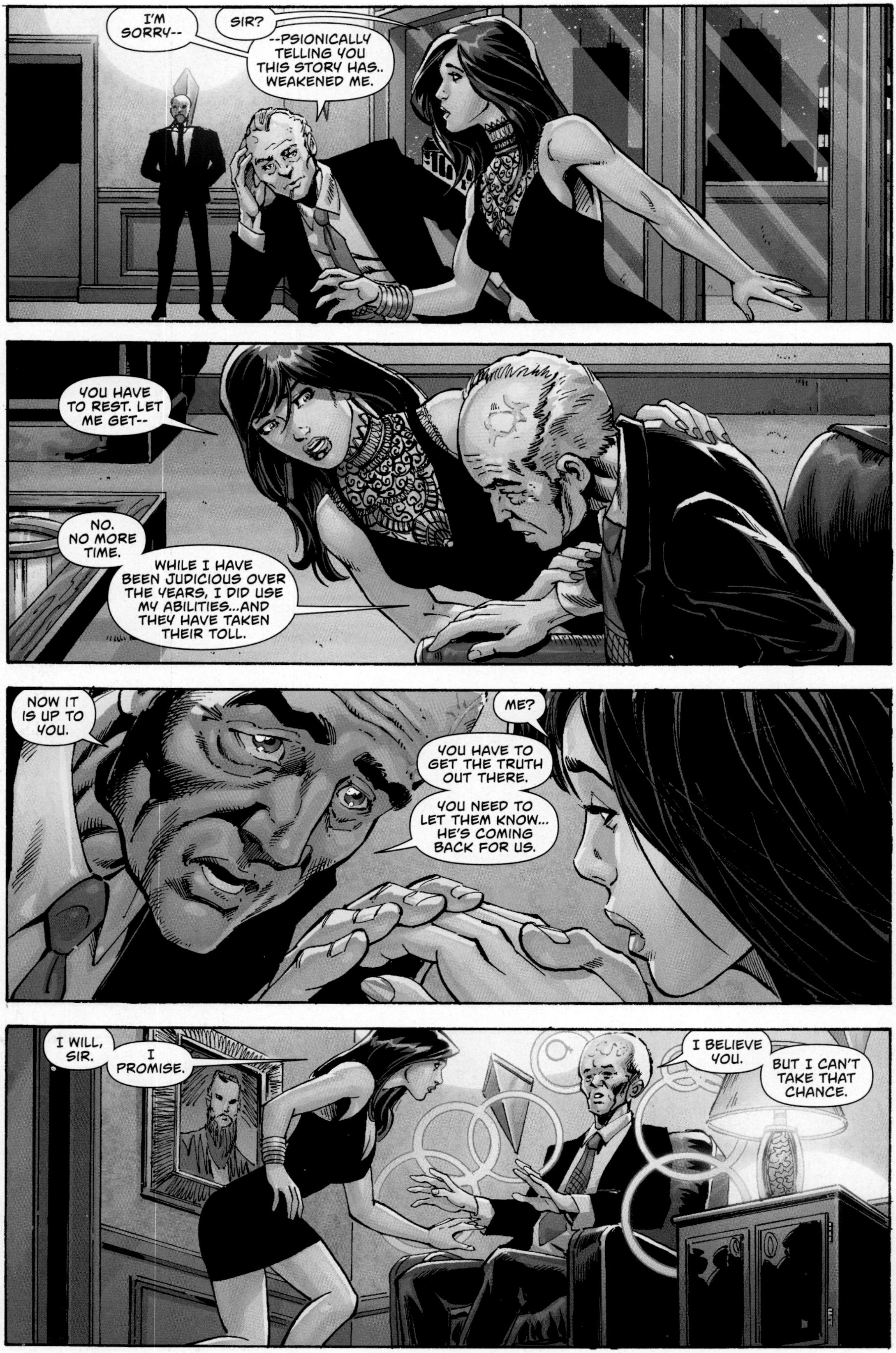
I'M SORRY--
SIR?
--PSIONICALLY TELLING YOU THIS STORY HAS.. WEAKENED ME.
YOU HAVE TO REST. LET ME GET--
NO. NO MORE TIME.
WHILE I HAVE BEEN JUDICIOUS OVER THE YEARS, I DID USE MY ABILITIES...AND THEY HAVE TAKEN THEIR TOLL.
NOW IT IS UP TO YOU.
ME?
YOU HAVE TO GET THE TRUTH OUT THERE.
YOU NEED TO LET THEM KNOW... HE'S COMING BACK FOR US.
I WILL, SIR.
I PROMISE.
I BELIEVE YOU.
BUT I CAN'T TAKE THAT CHANCE.

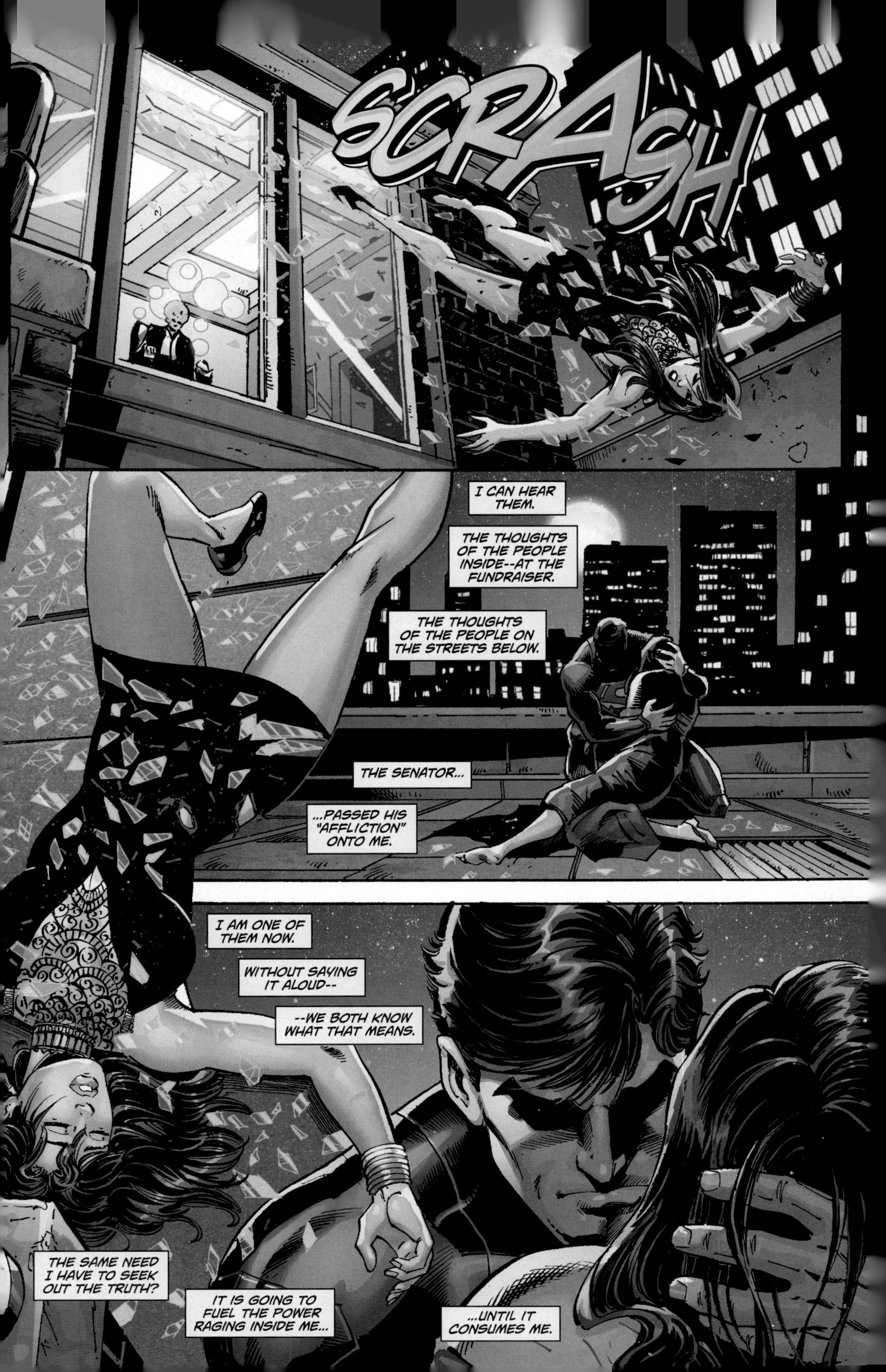
SCRASH
I CAN HEAR THEM.
THE THOUGHTS OF THE PEOPLE INSIDE--AT THE FUNDRAISER.
THE THOUGHTS OF THE PEOPLE ON THE STREETS BELOW.
THE SENATOR...
...PASSED HIS "AFFLICTION" ONTO ME.
I AM ONE OF THEM NOW.
WITHOUT SAYING IT ALOUD--
--WE BOTH KNOW WHAT THAT MEANS.
THE SAME NEED I HAVE TO SEEK OUT THE TRUTH?
IT IS GOING TO FUEL THE POWER RAGING INSIDE ME...
...UNTIL IT CONSUMES ME.

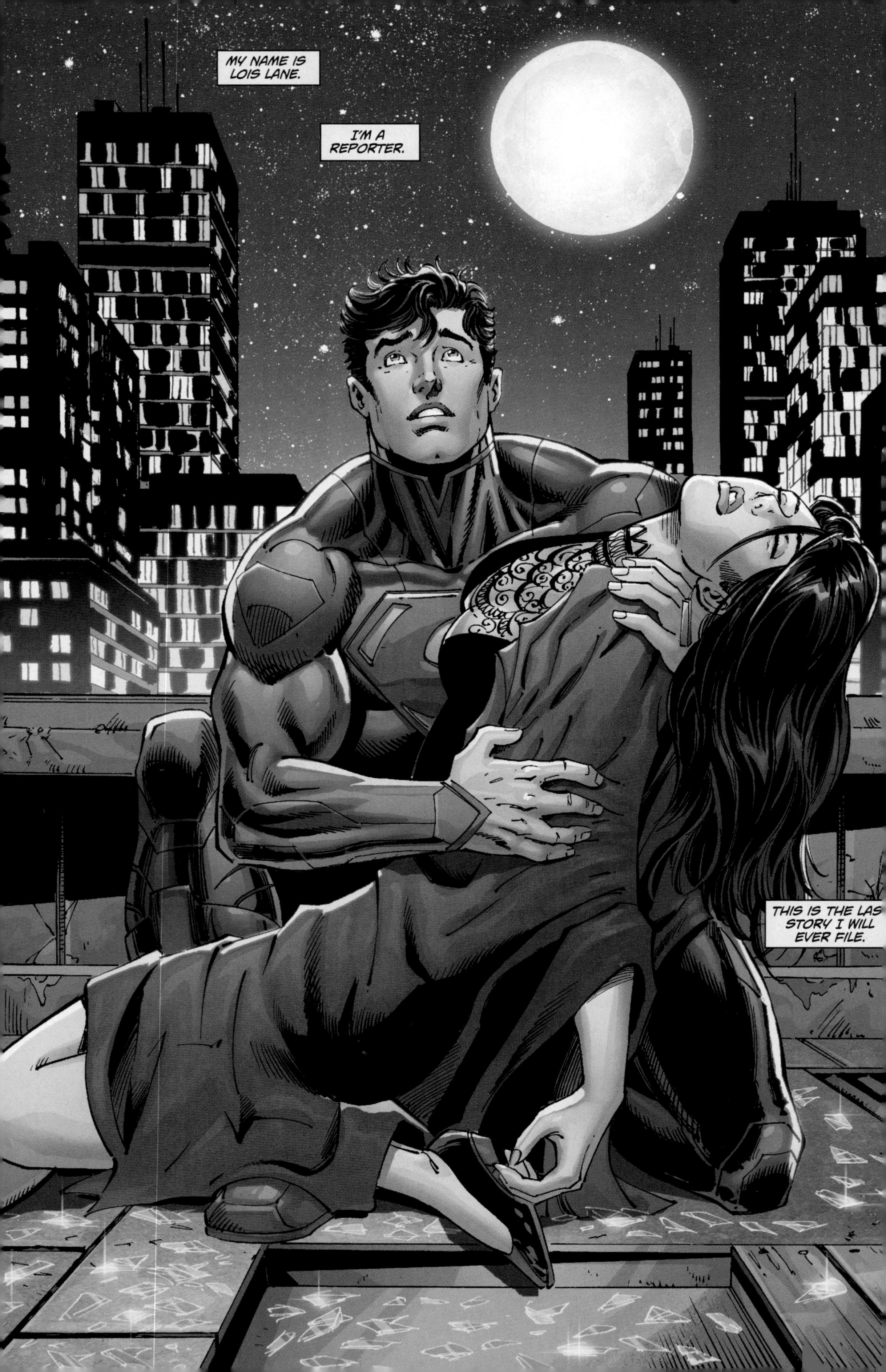
MY NAME IS LOIS LANE.
I'M A REPORTER.
THIS IS THE LAS STORY I WILL EVER FILE.

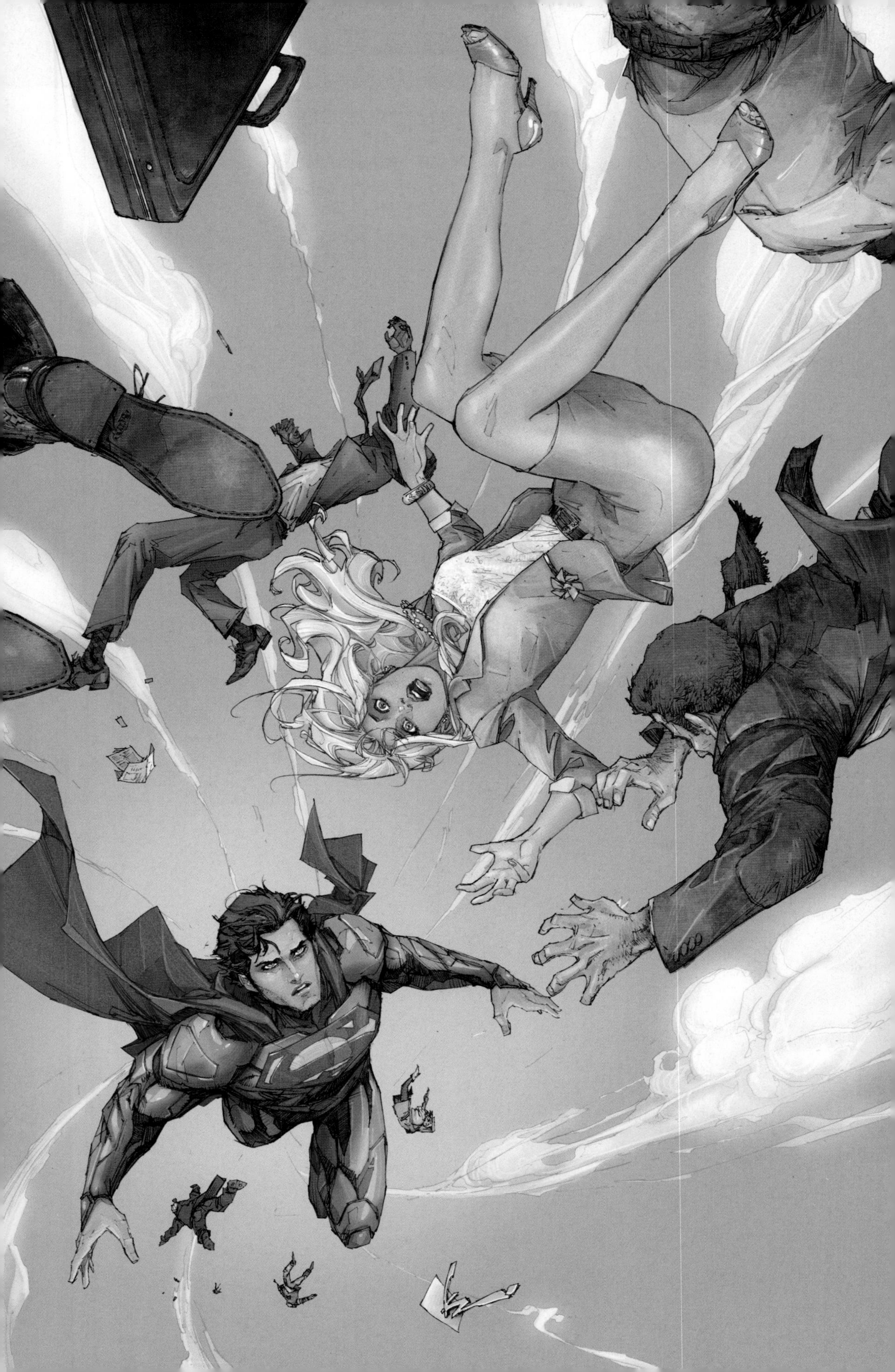

METROPOLITAN NIGHTMARE

SCOTT LOBDELL writer **AARON KUDER** – PGS 1-4 & 17-20 **TYLER KIRKHAM** – PGS 5-9 **ROBSON ROCHA** – PGS 10-16 pencillers
AARON KUDER – PGS 1-4 & 17-20 **JAIME MENDOZA** – PGS 10-16 inkers cover art by **KENNETH ROCAFORT**

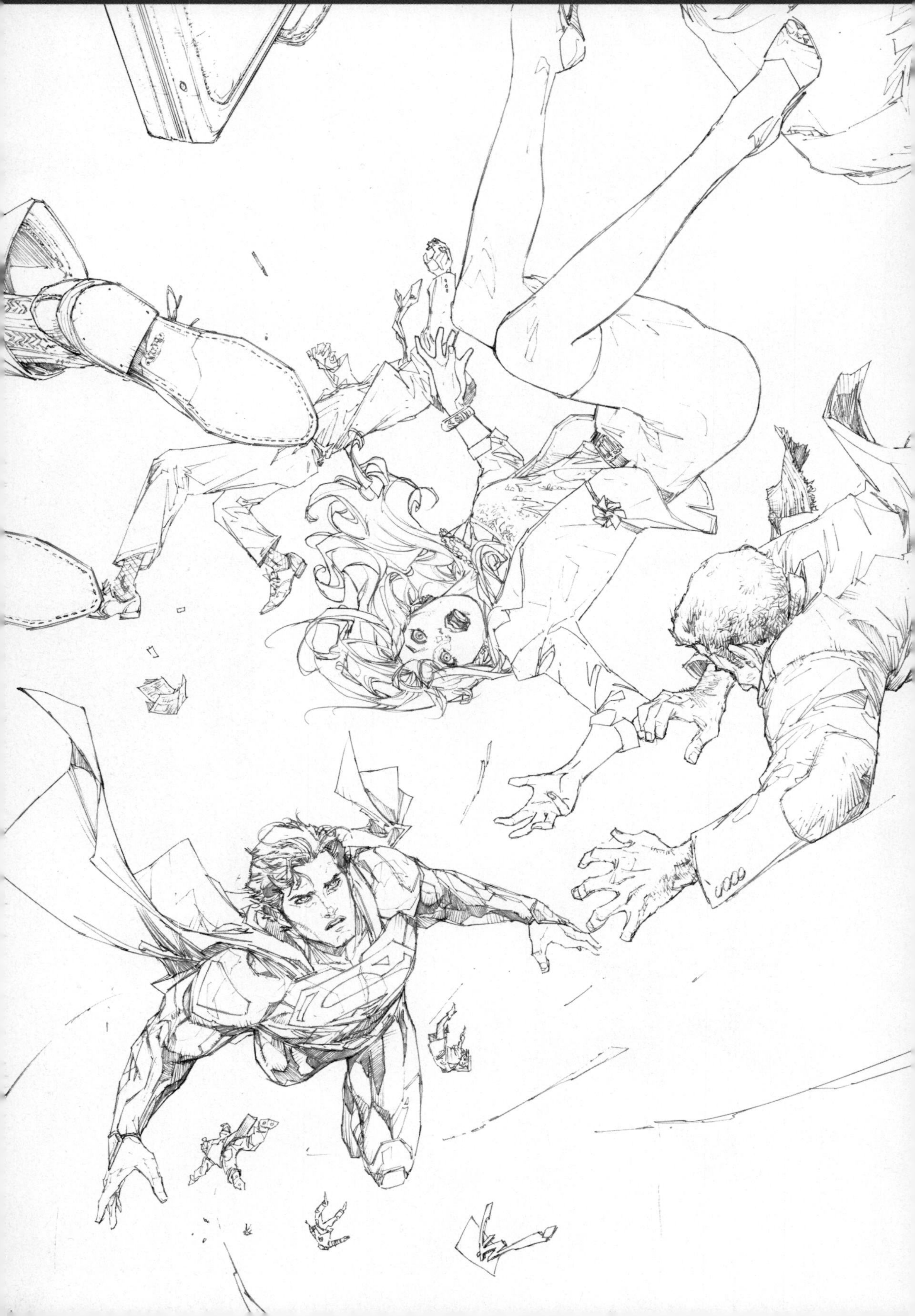

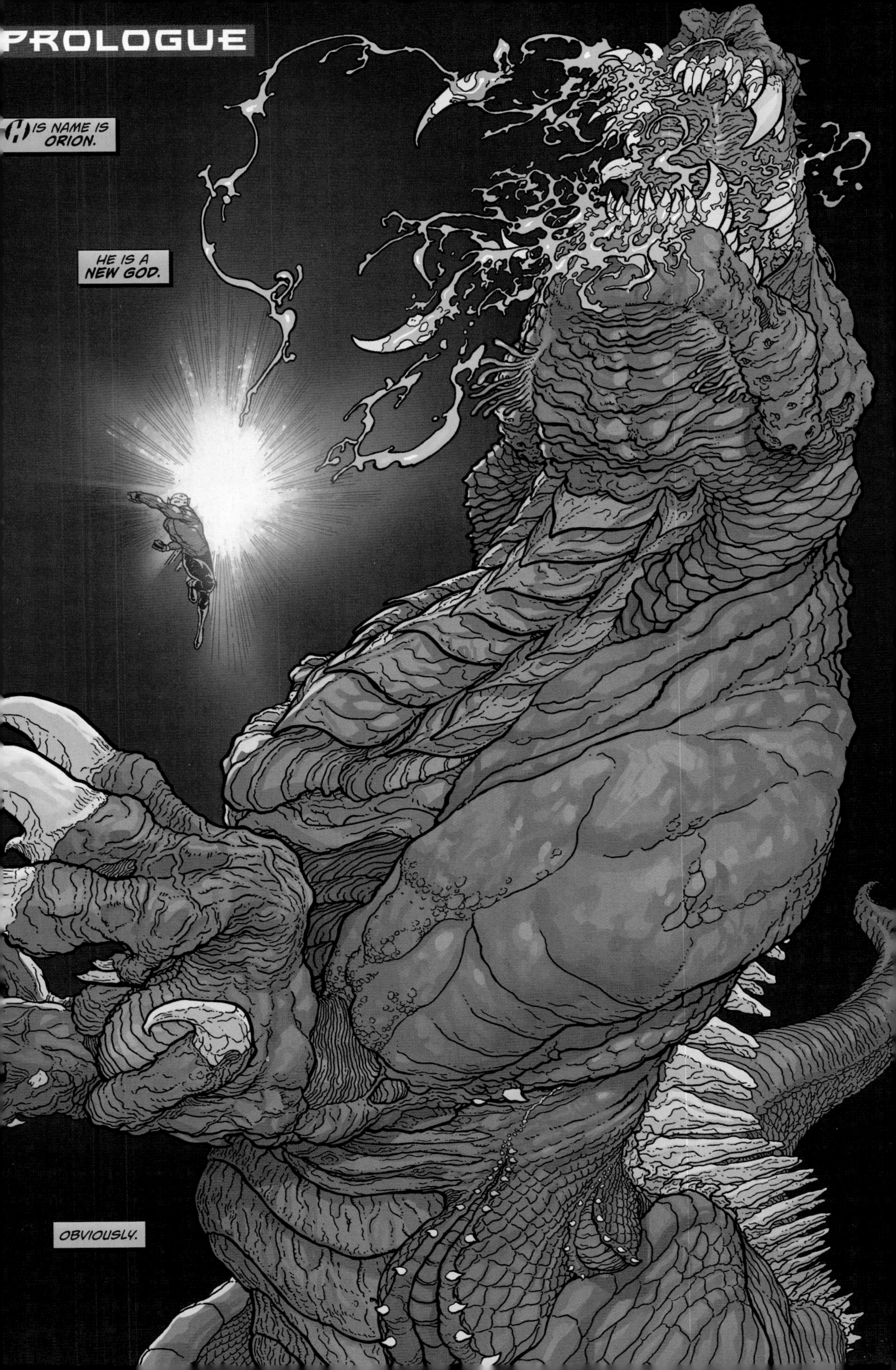
PROLOGUE
HIS NAME IS ORION.
HE IS A NEW GOD.
OBVIOUSLY.

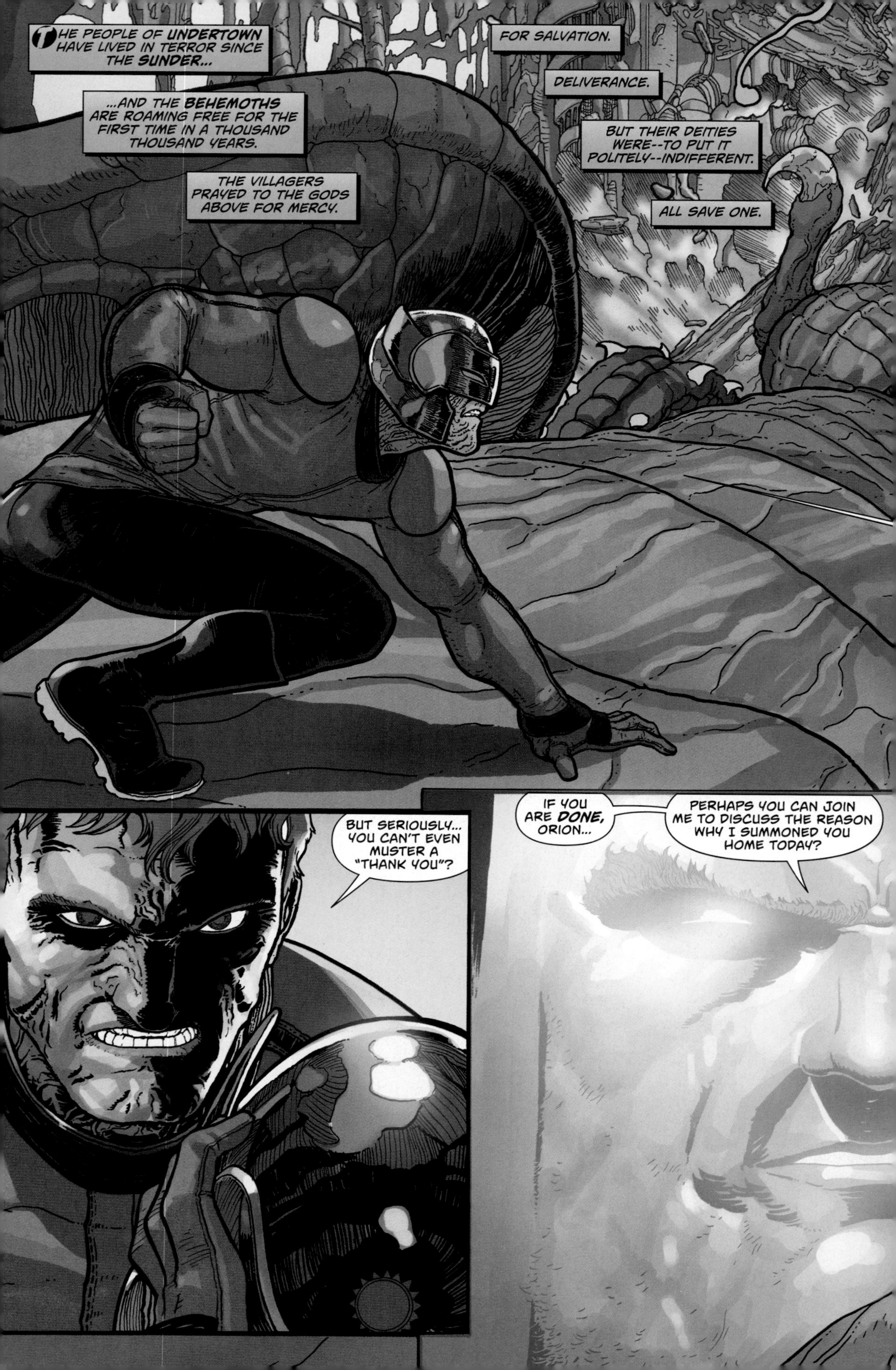
THE PEOPLE OF UNDERTOWN HAVE LIVED IN TERROR SINCE THE SUNDER...
...AND THE BEHEMOTHS ARE ROAMING FREE FOR THE FIRST TIME IN A THOUSAND THOUSAND YEARS.
THE VILLAGERS PRAYED TO THE GODS ABOVE FOR MERCY.
FOR SALVATION.
DELIVERANCE.
BUT THEIR DEITIES WERE--TO PUT IT POLITELY--INDIFFERENT.
ALL SAVE ONE.
BUT SERIOUSLY... YOU CAN'T EVEN MUSTER A "THANK YOU"?
IF YOU ARE DONE, ORION...
PERHAPS YOU CAN JOIN ME TO DISCUSS THE REASON WHY I SUMMONED YOU HOME TODAY?

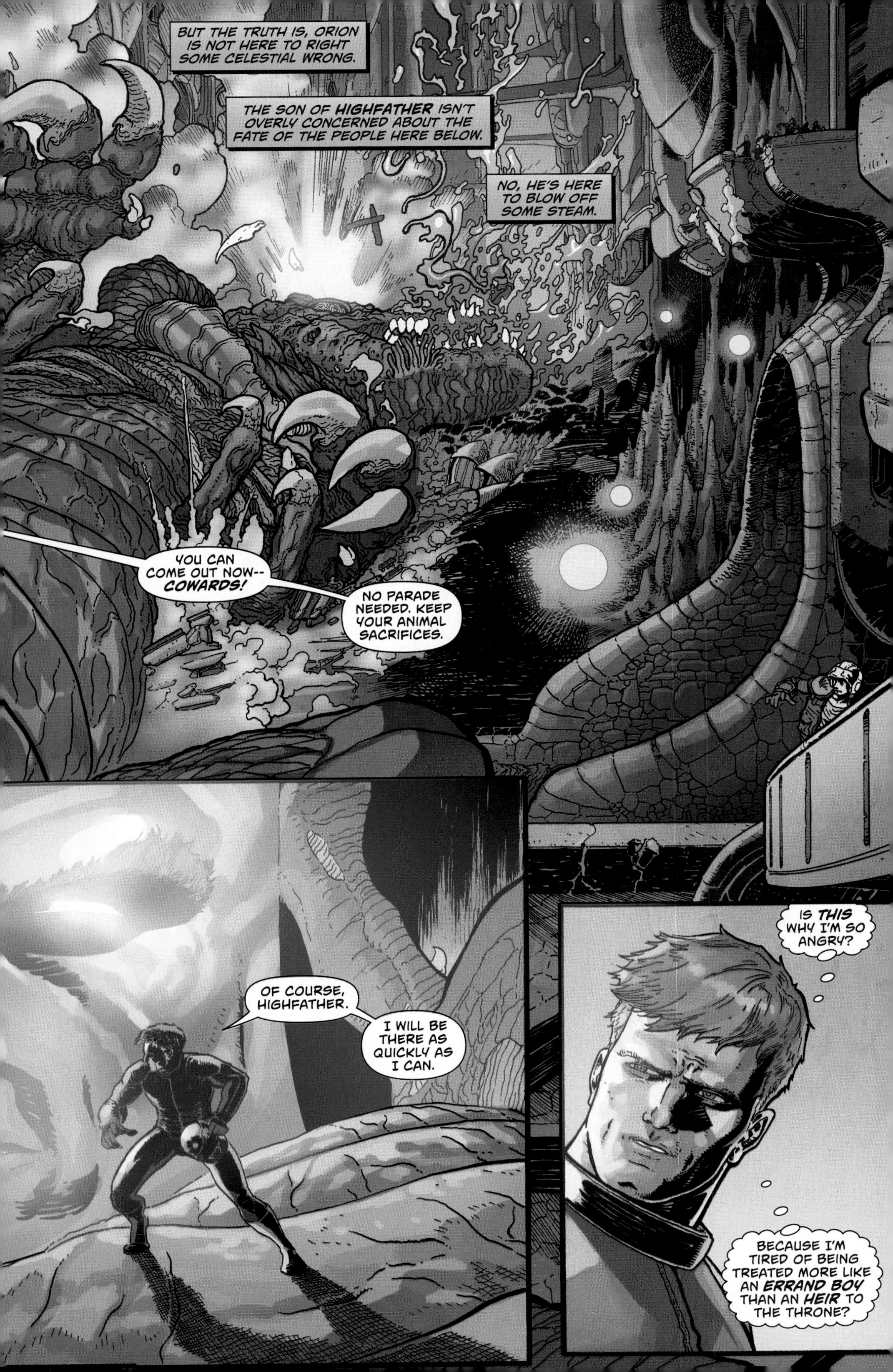
BUT THE TRUTH IS, ORION IS NOT HERE TO RIGHT SOME CELESTIAL WRONG.
THE SON OF HIGHFATHER ISN'T OVERLY CONCERNED ABOUT THE FATE OF THE PEOPLE HERE BELOW.
NO, HE'S HERE TO BLOW OFF SOME STEAM.
YOU CAN COME OUT NOW-- COWARDS!
NO PARADE NEEDED. KEEP YOUR ANIMAL SACRIFICES.
OF COURSE, HIGHFATHER.
I WILL BE THERE AS QUICKLY AS I CAN.
IS THIS WHY I'M SO ANGRY?
BECAUSE I'M TIRED OF BEING TREATED MORE LIKE AN ERRAND BOY THAN AN HEIR TO THE THRONE?

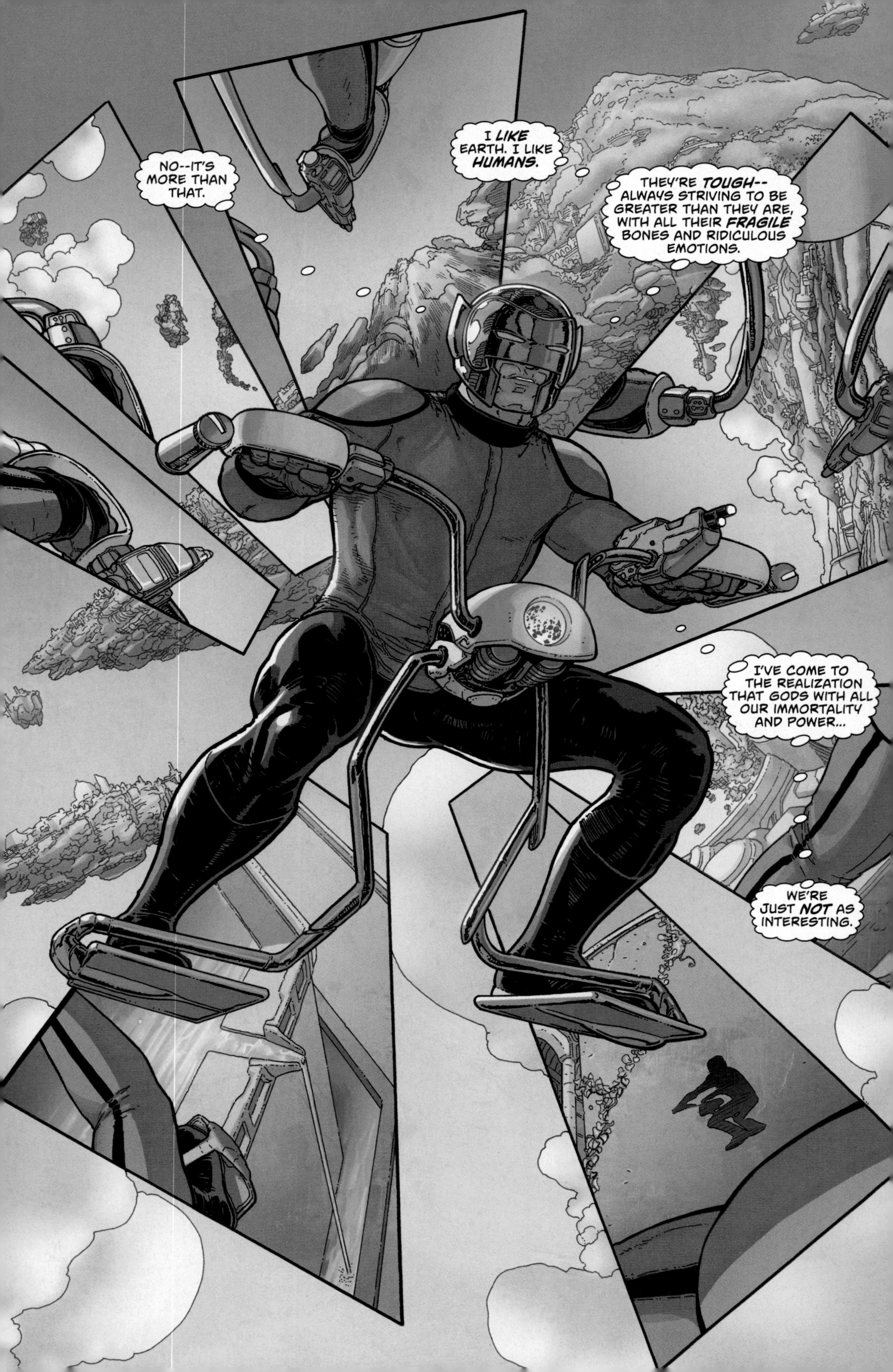

NO--IT'S MORE THAN THAT.
I LIKE EARTH. I LIKE HUMANS.
THEY'RE TOUGH-- ALWAYS STRIVING TO BE GREATER THAN THEY ARE, WITH ALL THEIR FRAGILE BONES AND RIDICULOUS EMOTIONS.
I'VE COME TO THE REALIZATION THAT GODS WITH ALL OUR IMMORTALITY AND POWER...
WE'RE JUST NOT AS INTERESTING.

CHAPTER ONE

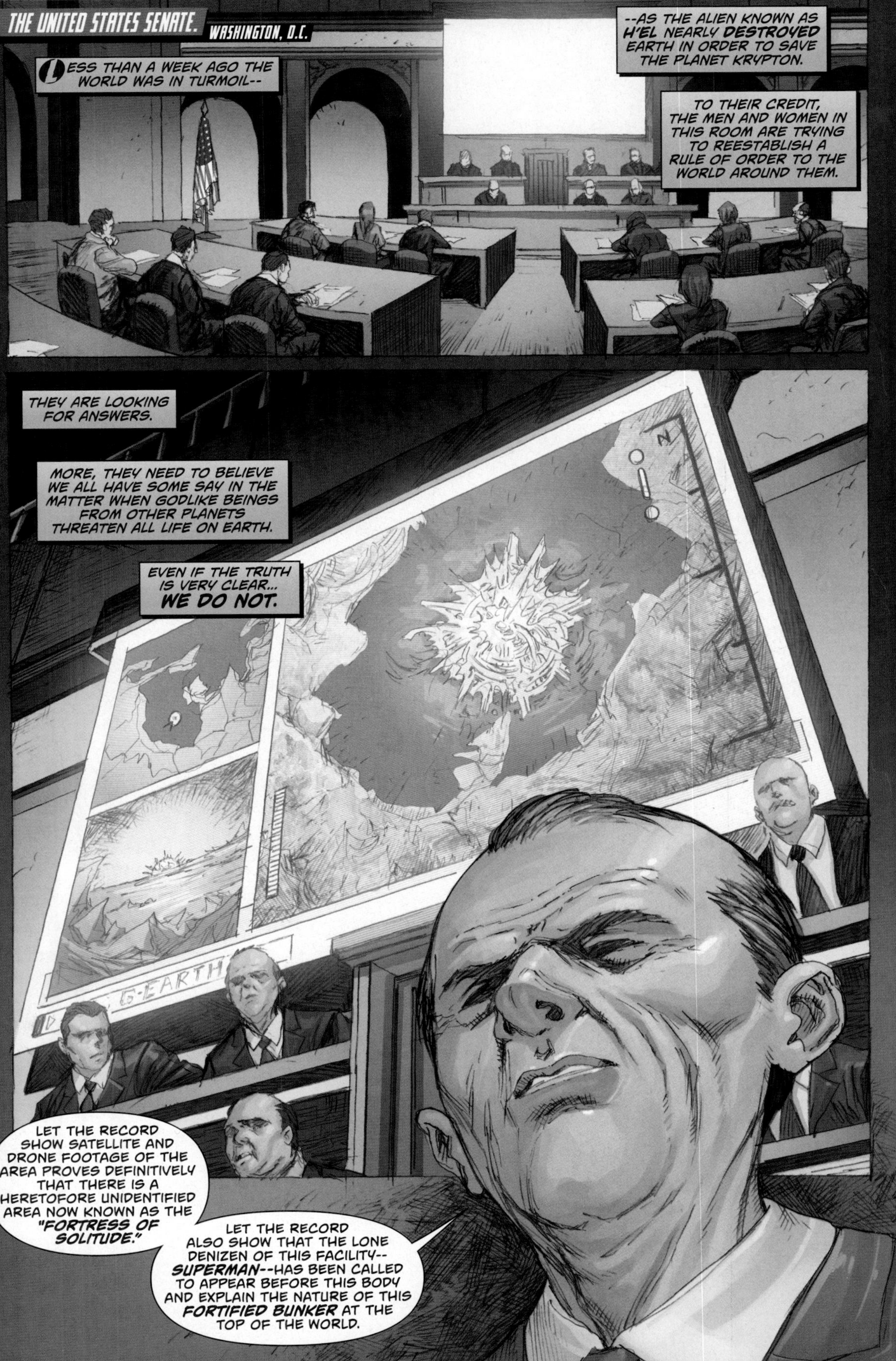
THE UNITED STATES SENATE.
WASHINGTON, D.C.
LESS THAN A WEEK AGO THE WORLD WAS IN TURMOIL--
--AS THE ALIEN KNOWN AS H'EL NEARLY DESTROYED EARTH IN ORDER TO SAVE THE PLANET KRYPTON.
TO THEIR CREDIT, THE MEN AND WOMEN IN THIS ROOM ARE TRYING TO REESTABLISH A RULE OF ORDER TO THE WORLD AROUND THEM.
THEY ARE LOOKING FOR ANSWERS.
MORE, THEY NEED TO BELIEVE WE ALL HAVE SOME SAY IN THE MATTER WHEN GODLIKE BEINGS FROM OTHER PLANETS THREATEN ALL LIFE ON EARTH.
EVEN IF THE TRUTH IS VERY CLEAR... WE DO NOT.
LET THE RECORD SHOW SATELLITE AND DRONE FOOTAGE OF THE AREA PROVES DEFINITIVELY THAT THERE IS A HERETOFORE UNIDENTIFIED AREA NOW KNOWN AS THE "FORTRESS OF SOLITUDE."
LET THE RECORD ALSO SHOW THAT THE LONE DENIZEN OF THIS FACILITY--SUPERMAN--HAS BEEN CALLED TO APPEAR BEFORE THIS BODY AND EXPLAIN THE NATURE OF THIS FORTIFIED BUNKER AT THE TOP OF THE WORLD.

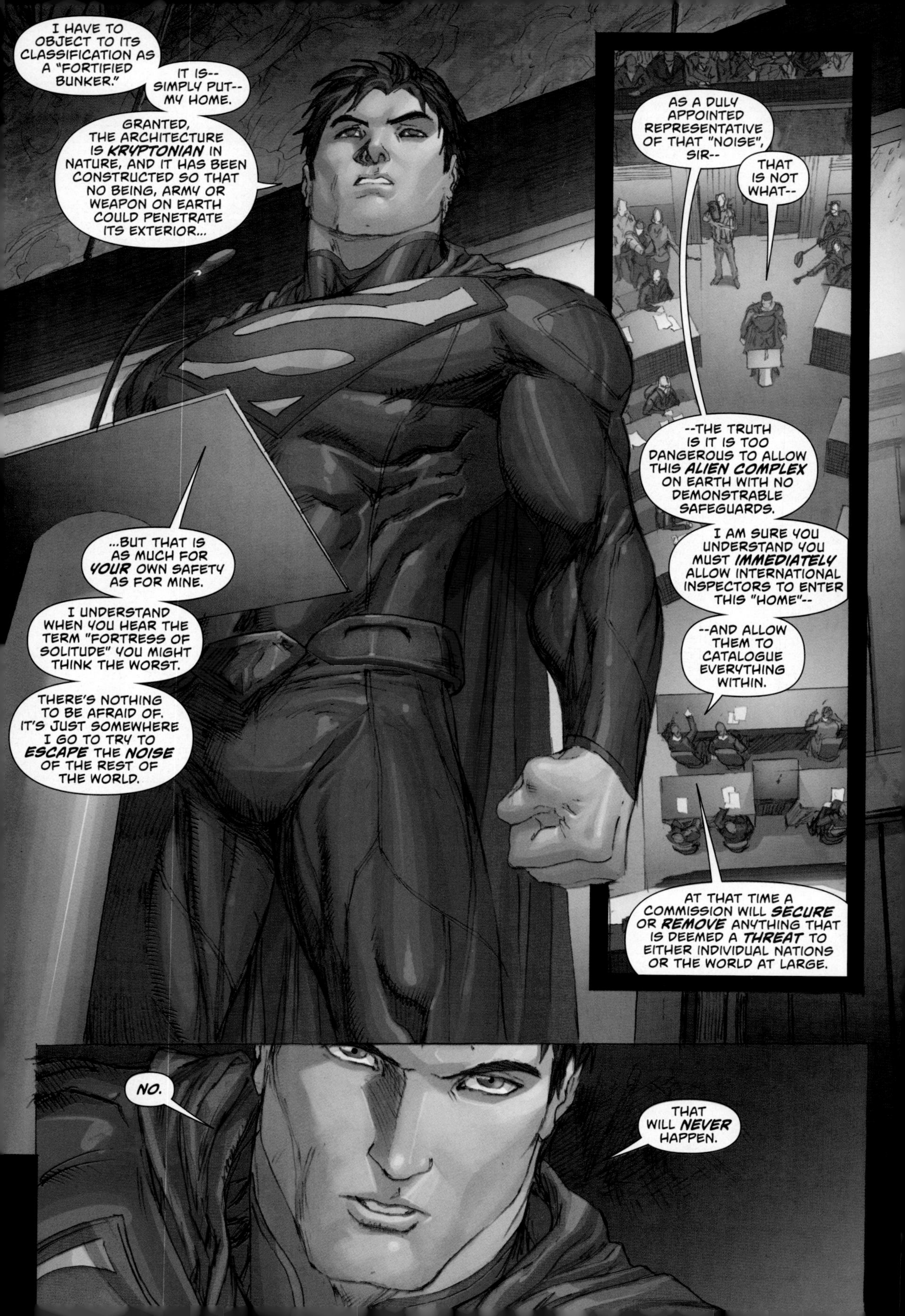

I HAVE TO OBJECT TO ITS CLASSIFICATION AS A "FORTIFIED BUNKER."
IT IS-- SIMPLY PUT-- MY HOME.
GRANTED, THE ARCHITECTURE IS **KRYPTONIAN** IN NATURE, AND IT HAS BEEN CONSTRUCTED SO THAT NO BEING, ARMY OR WEAPON ON EARTH COULD PENETRATE ITS EXTERIOR...
...BUT THAT IS AS MUCH FOR **YOUR** OWN SAFETY AS FOR MINE.
I UNDERSTAND WHEN YOU HEAR THE TERM "FORTRESS OF SOLITUDE" YOU MIGHT THINK THE WORST.
THERE'S NOTHING TO BE AFRAID OF. IT'S JUST SOMEWHERE I GO TO TRY TO **ESCAPE** THE **NOISE** OF THE REST OF THE WORLD.
AS A DULY APPOINTED REPRESENTATIVE OF THAT "NOISE", SIR--
THAT IS NOT WHAT--
--THE TRUTH IS IT IS TOO DANGEROUS TO ALLOW THIS **ALIEN COMPLEX** ON EARTH WITH NO DEMONSTRABLE SAFEGUARDS.
I AM SURE YOU UNDERSTAND YOU MUST **IMMEDIATELY** ALLOW INTERNATIONAL INSPECTORS TO ENTER THIS "HOME"--
--AND ALLOW THEM TO CATALOGUE EVERYTHING WITHIN.
AT THAT TIME A COMMISSION WILL **SECURE** OR **REMOVE** ANYTHING THAT IS DEEMED A **THREAT** TO EITHER INDIVIDUAL NATIONS OR THE WORLD AT LARGE.
NO.
THAT WILL **NEVER** HAPPEN.

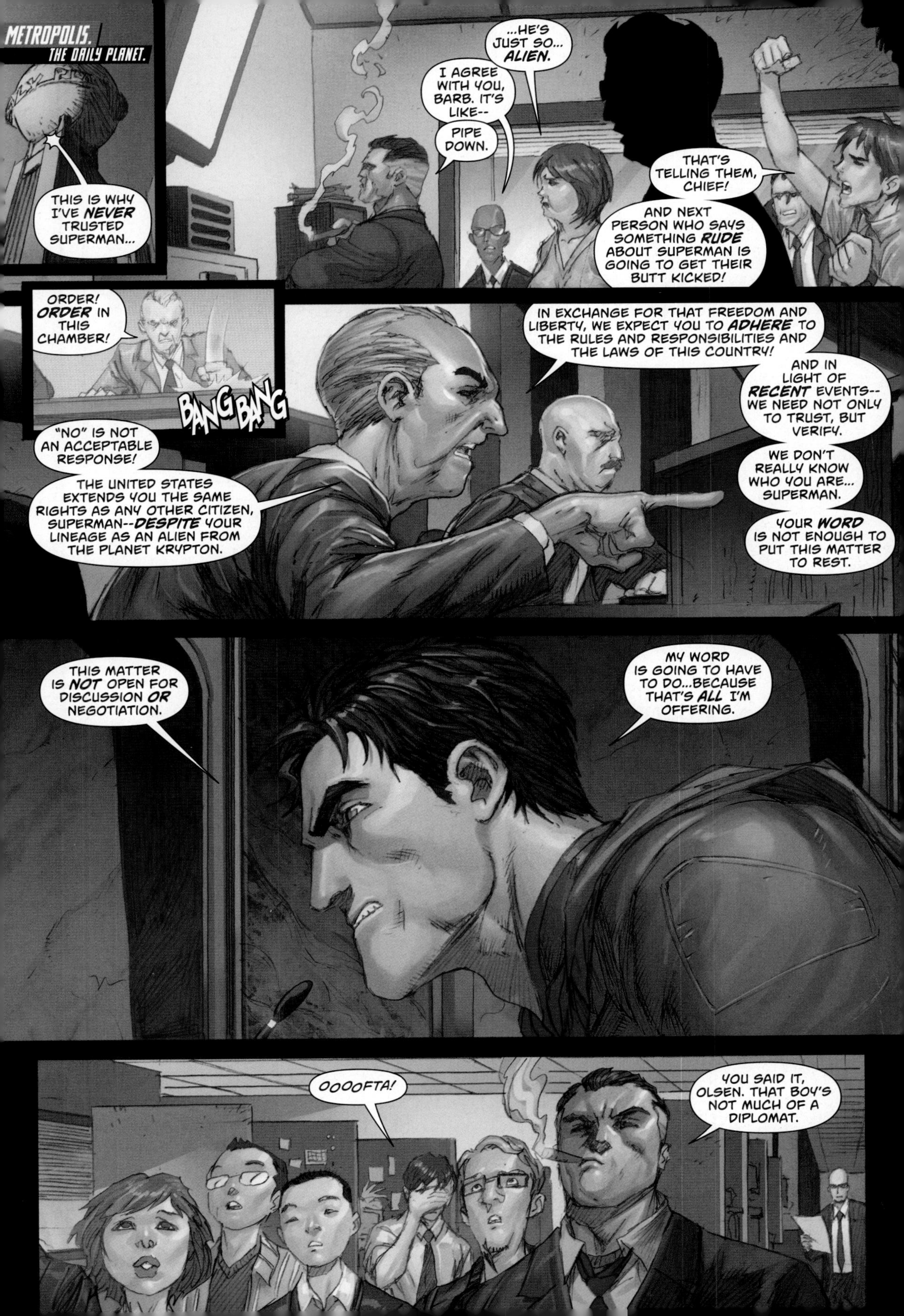
METROPOLIS.
THE DAILY PLANET.
THIS IS WHY I'VE NEVER TRUSTED SUPERMAN...
...HE'S JUST SO... ALIEN.
I AGREE WITH YOU, BARB. IT'S LIKE--
PIPE DOWN.
THAT'S TELLING THEM, CHIEF!
AND NEXT PERSON WHO SAYS SOMETHING RUDE ABOUT SUPERMAN IS GOING TO GET THEIR BUTT KICKED!
ORDER! ORDER IN THIS CHAMBER!
BANG BANG
"NO" IS NOT AN ACCEPTABLE RESPONSE!
THE UNITED STATES EXTENDS YOU THE SAME RIGHTS AS ANY OTHER CITIZEN, SUPERMAN--DESPITE YOUR LINEAGE AS AN ALIEN FROM THE PLANET KRYPTON.
IN EXCHANGE FOR THAT FREEDOM AND LIBERTY, WE EXPECT YOU TO ADHERE TO THE RULES AND RESPONSIBILITIES AND THE LAWS OF THIS COUNTRY!
AND IN LIGHT OF RECENT EVENTS-- WE NEED NOT ONLY TO TRUST, BUT VERIFY.
WE DON'T REALLY KNOW WHO YOU ARE... SUPERMAN.
YOUR WORD IS NOT ENOUGH TO PUT THIS MATTER TO REST.
THIS MATTER IS NOT OPEN FOR DISCUSSION OR NEGOTIATION.
MY WORD IS GOING TO HAVE TO DO...BECAUSE THAT'S ALL I'M OFFERING.
OOOOFTA!
YOU SAID IT, OLSEN. THAT BOY'S NOT MUCH OF A DIPLOMAT.

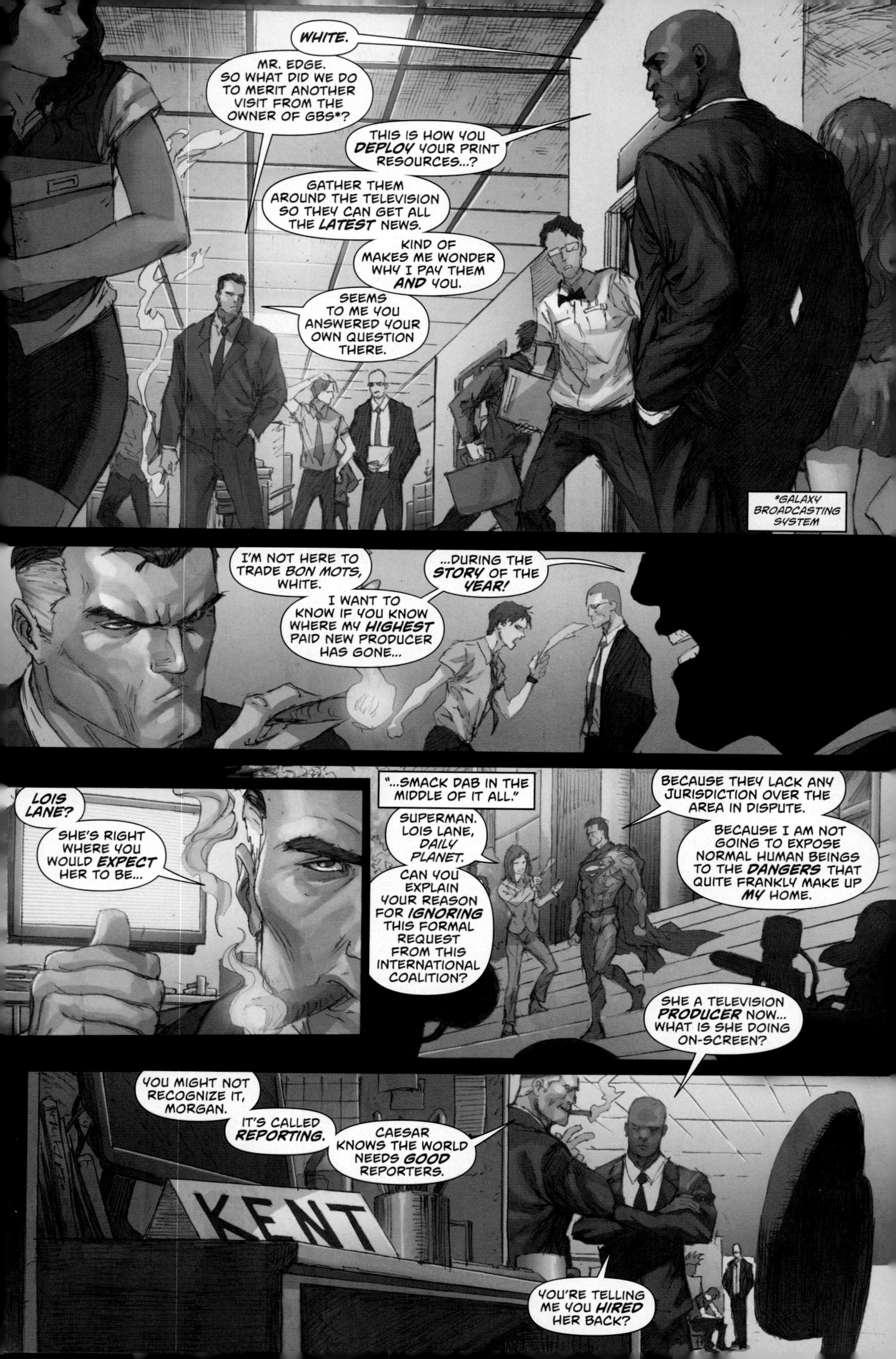
WHITE.
MR. EDGE. SO WHAT DID WE DO TO MERIT ANOTHER VISIT FROM THE OWNER OF GBS*?
THIS IS HOW YOU DEPLOY YOUR PRINT RESOURCES...?
GATHER THEM AROUND THE TELEVISION SO THEY CAN GET ALL THE LATEST NEWS.
KIND OF MAKES ME WONDER WHY I PAY THEM AND YOU.
SEEMS TO ME YOU ANSWERED YOUR OWN QUESTION THERE.
*GALAXY BROADCASTING SYSTEM
I'M NOT HERE TO TRADE BON MOTS, WHITE.
I WANT TO KNOW IF YOU KNOW WHERE MY HIGHEST PAID NEW PRODUCER HAS GONE...
...DURING THE STORY OF THE YEAR!
LOIS LANE?
SHE'S RIGHT WHERE YOU WOULD EXPECT HER TO BE...
"...SMACK DAB IN THE MIDDLE OF IT ALL."
SUPERMAN. LOIS LANE, DAILY PLANET.
CAN YOU EXPLAIN YOUR REASON FOR IGNORING THIS FORMAL REQUEST FROM THIS INTERNATIONAL COALITION?
BECAUSE THEY LACK ANY JURISDICTION OVER THE AREA IN DISPUTE.
BECAUSE I AM NOT GOING TO EXPOSE NORMAL HUMAN BEINGS TO THE DANGERS THAT QUITE FRANKLY MAKE UP MY HOME.
SHE A TELEVISION PRODUCER NOW... WHAT IS SHE DOING ON-SCREEN?
YOU MIGHT NOT RECOGNIZE IT, MORGAN.
IT'S CALLED REPORTING.
CAESAR KNOWS THE WORLD NEEDS GOOD REPORTERS.
KENT
YOU'RE TELLING ME YOU HIRED HER BACK?

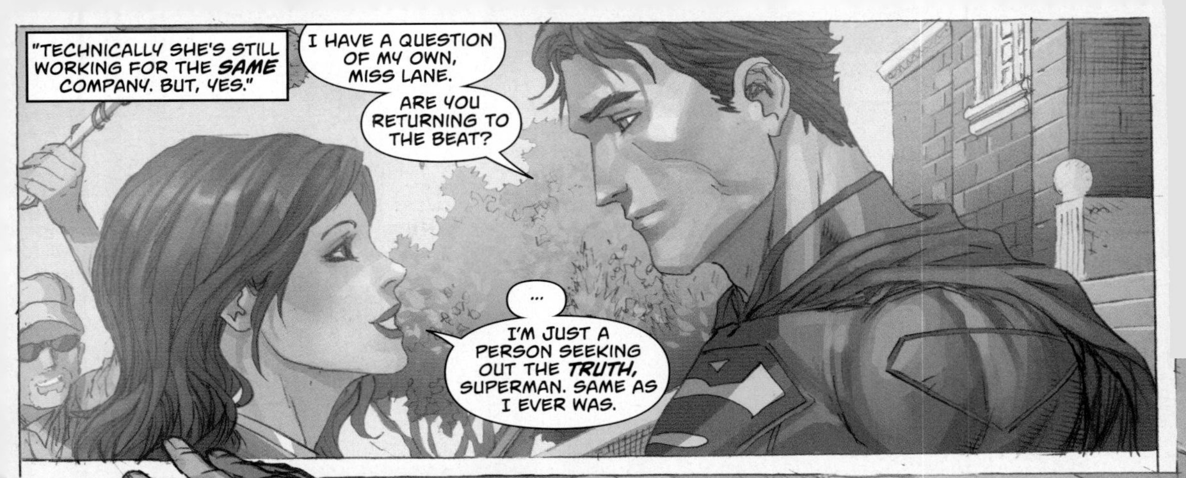
"TECHNICALLY SHE'S STILL WORKING FOR THE *SAME* COMPANY. BUT, YES."
I HAVE A QUESTION OF MY OWN, MISS LANE.
ARE YOU RETURNING TO THE BEAT?
...
I'M JUST A PERSON SEEKING OUT THE *TRUTH,* SUPERMAN. SAME AS I EVER WAS.

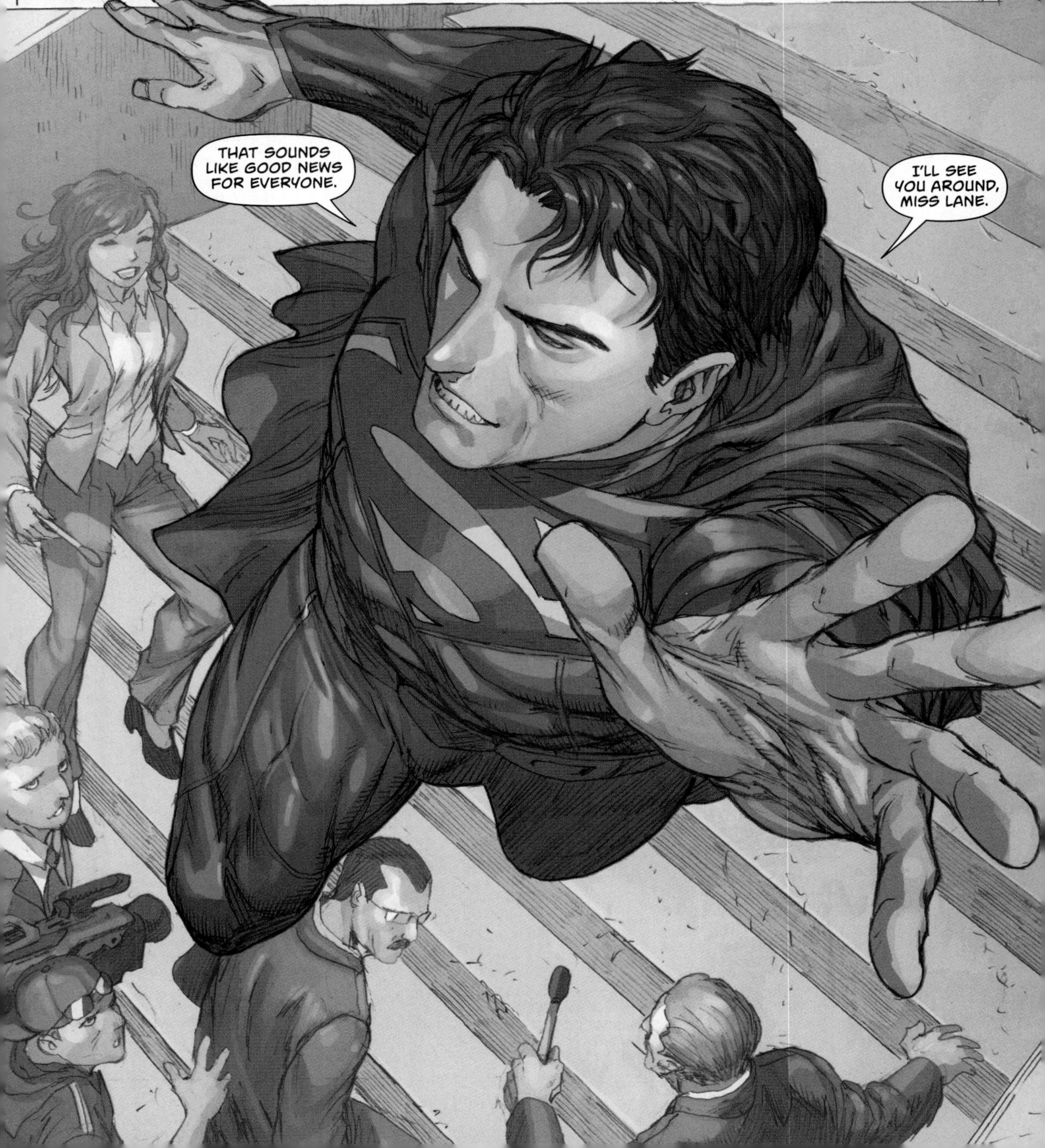
THAT SOUNDS LIKE GOOD NEWS FOR EVERYONE.
I'LL SEE YOU AROUND, MISS LANE.

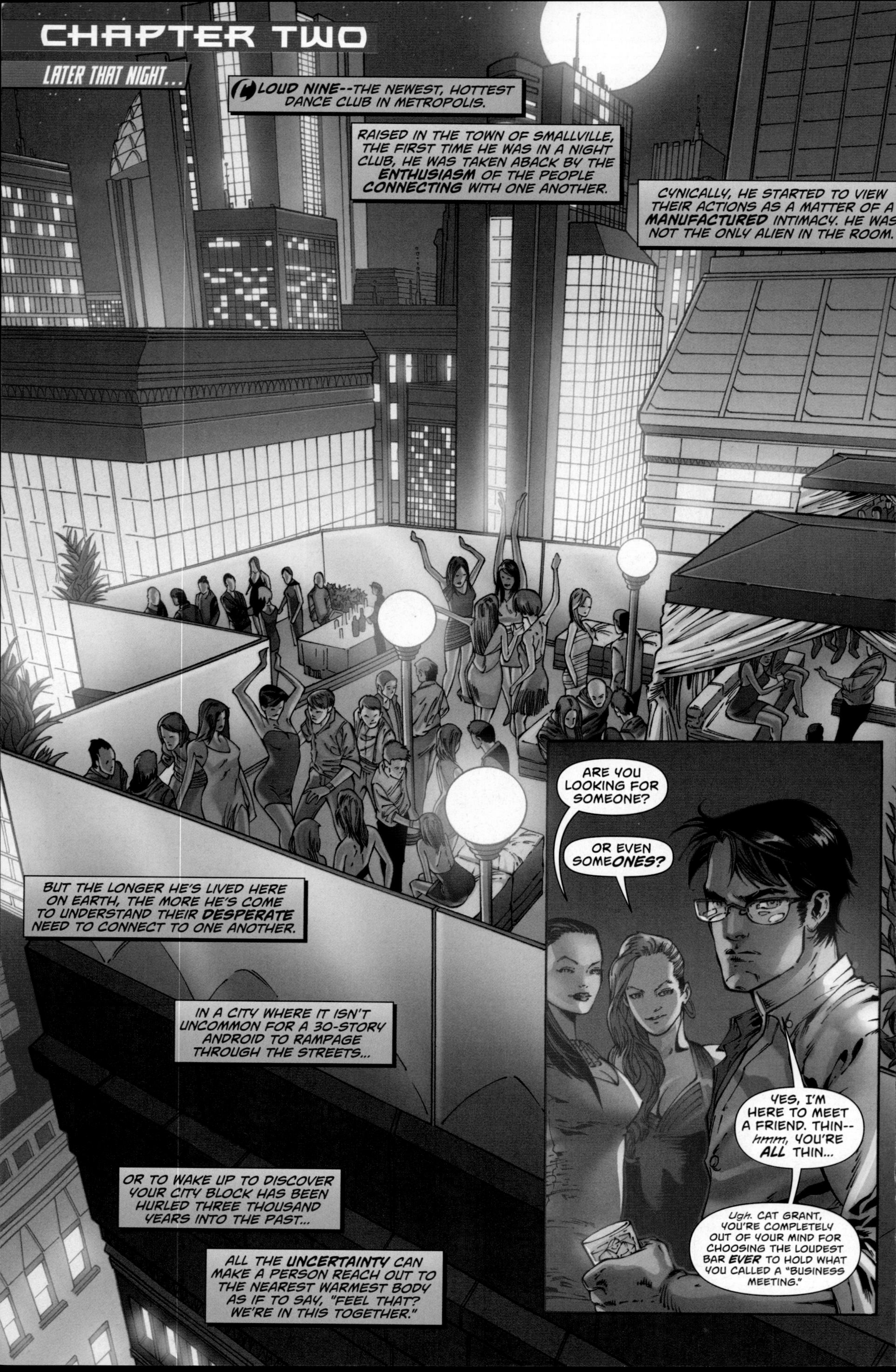
CHAPTER TWO
LATER THAT NIGHT...
CLOUD NINE--THE NEWEST, HOTTEST DANCE CLUB IN METROPOLIS.
RAISED IN THE TOWN OF SMALLVILLE, THE FIRST TIME HE WAS IN A NIGHT CLUB, HE WAS TAKEN ABACK BY THE ENTHUSIASM OF THE PEOPLE CONNECTING WITH ONE ANOTHER.
CYNICALLY, HE STARTED TO VIEW THEIR ACTIONS AS A MATTER OF A MANUFACTURED INTIMACY. HE WAS NOT THE ONLY ALIEN IN THE ROOM.
BUT THE LONGER HE'S LIVED HERE ON EARTH, THE MORE HE'S COME TO UNDERSTAND THEIR DESPERATE NEED TO CONNECT TO ONE ANOTHER.
IN A CITY WHERE IT ISN'T UNCOMMON FOR A 30-STORY ANDROID TO RAMPAGE THROUGH THE STREETS...
OR TO WAKE UP TO DISCOVER YOUR CITY BLOCK HAS BEEN HURLED THREE THOUSAND YEARS INTO THE PAST...
ALL THE UNCERTAINTY CAN MAKE A PERSON REACH OUT TO THE NEAREST WARMEST BODY AS IF TO SAY, "FEEL THAT? WE'RE IN THIS TOGETHER."
ARE YOU LOOKING FOR SOMEONE?
OR EVEN SOMEONES?
YES, I'M HERE TO MEET A FRIEND. THIN-- hmm, YOU'RE ALL THIN...
Ugh. CAT GRANT, YOU'RE COMPLETELY OUT OF YOUR MIND FOR CHOOSING THE LOUDEST BAR EVER TO HOLD WHAT YOU CALLED A "BUSINESS MEETING."

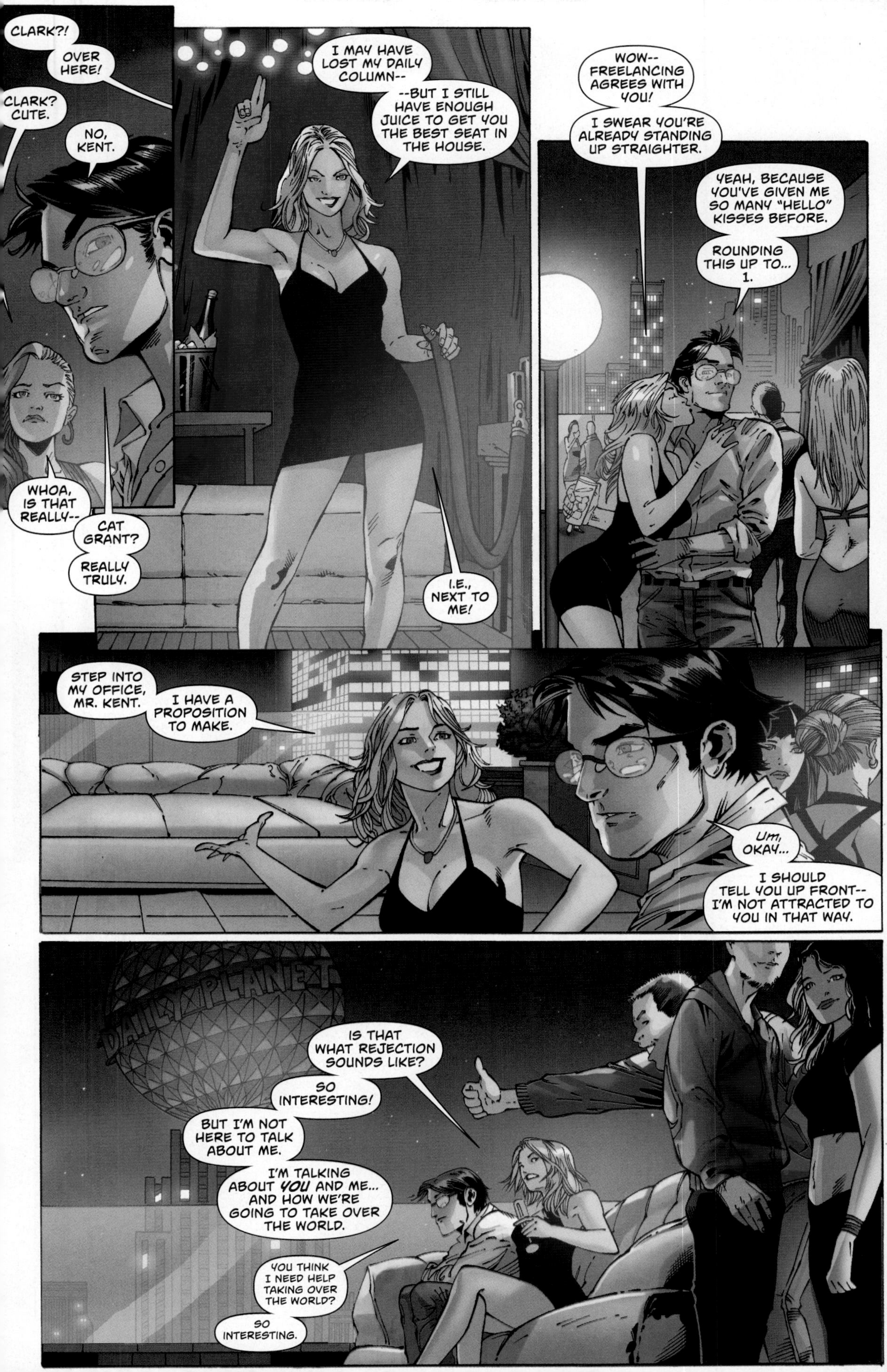
CLARK?!
OVER HERE!
CLARK? CUTE.
NO, KENT.
WHOA, IS THAT REALLY--
CAT GRANT?
REALLY TRULY.
I MAY HAVE LOST MY DAILY COLUMN--
--BUT I STILL HAVE ENOUGH JUICE TO GET YOU THE BEST SEAT IN THE HOUSE.
I.E., NEXT TO ME!
WOW--FREELANCING AGREES WITH YOU!
I SWEAR YOU'RE ALREADY STANDING UP STRAIGHTER.
YEAH, BECAUSE YOU'VE GIVEN ME SO MANY "HELLO" KISSES BEFORE.
ROUNDING THIS UP TO... 1.
STEP INTO MY OFFICE, MR. KENT.
I HAVE A PROPOSITION TO MAKE.
UM, OKAY...
I SHOULD TELL YOU UP FRONT-- I'M NOT ATTRACTED TO YOU IN THAT WAY.
DAILY PLANET
IS THAT WHAT REJECTION SOUNDS LIKE?
SO INTERESTING!
BUT I'M NOT HERE TO TALK ABOUT ME.
I'M TALKING ABOUT YOU AND ME... AND HOW WE'RE GOING TO TAKE OVER THE WORLD.
YOU THINK I NEED HELP TAKING OVER THE WORLD?
SO INTERESTING.

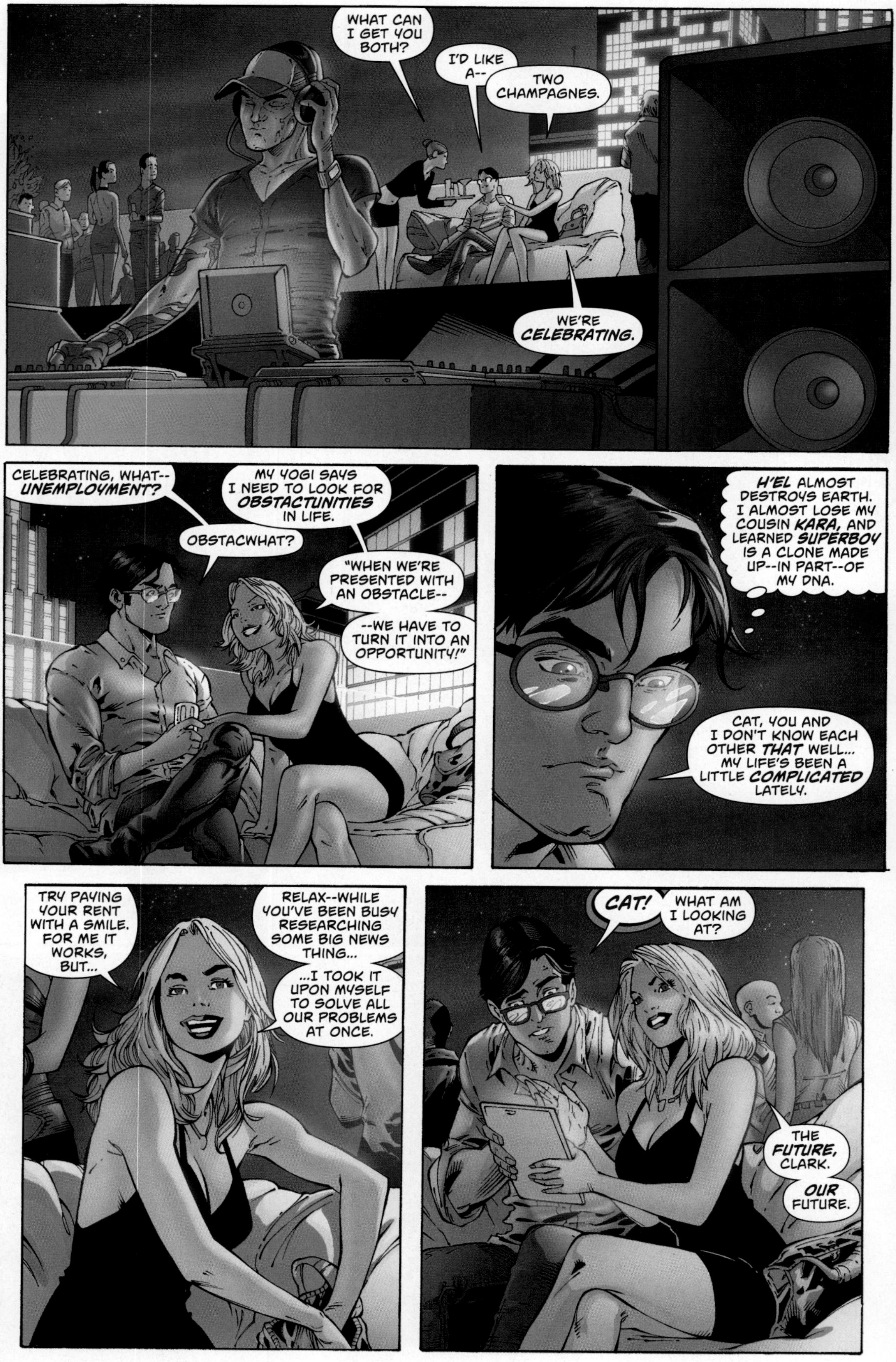
WHAT CAN I GET YOU BOTH?
I'D LIKE A--
TWO CHAMPAGNES.
WE'RE *CELEBRATING.*
CELEBRATING, WHAT-- *UNEMPLOYMENT?*
MY YOGI SAYS I NEED TO LOOK FOR *OBSTACTUNITIES* IN LIFE.
OBSTACWHAT?
"WHEN WE'RE PRESENTED WITH AN OBSTACLE--
--WE HAVE TO TURN IT INTO AN OPPORTUNITY!"
H'EL ALMOST DESTROYS EARTH. I ALMOST LOSE MY COUSIN *KARA,* AND LEARNED *SUPERBOY* IS A CLONE MADE UP--IN PART--OF MY DNA.
CAT, YOU AND I DON'T KNOW EACH OTHER *THAT* WELL... MY LIFE'S BEEN A LITTLE *COMPLICATED* LATELY.
TRY PAYING YOUR RENT WITH A SMILE. FOR ME IT WORKS, BUT...
RELAX--WHILE YOU'VE BEEN BUSY RESEARCHING SOME BIG NEWS THING...
...I TOOK IT UPON MYSELF TO SOLVE ALL OUR PROBLEMS AT ONCE.
CAT!
WHAT AM I LOOKING AT?
THE *FUTURE,* CLARK.
OUR FUTURE.

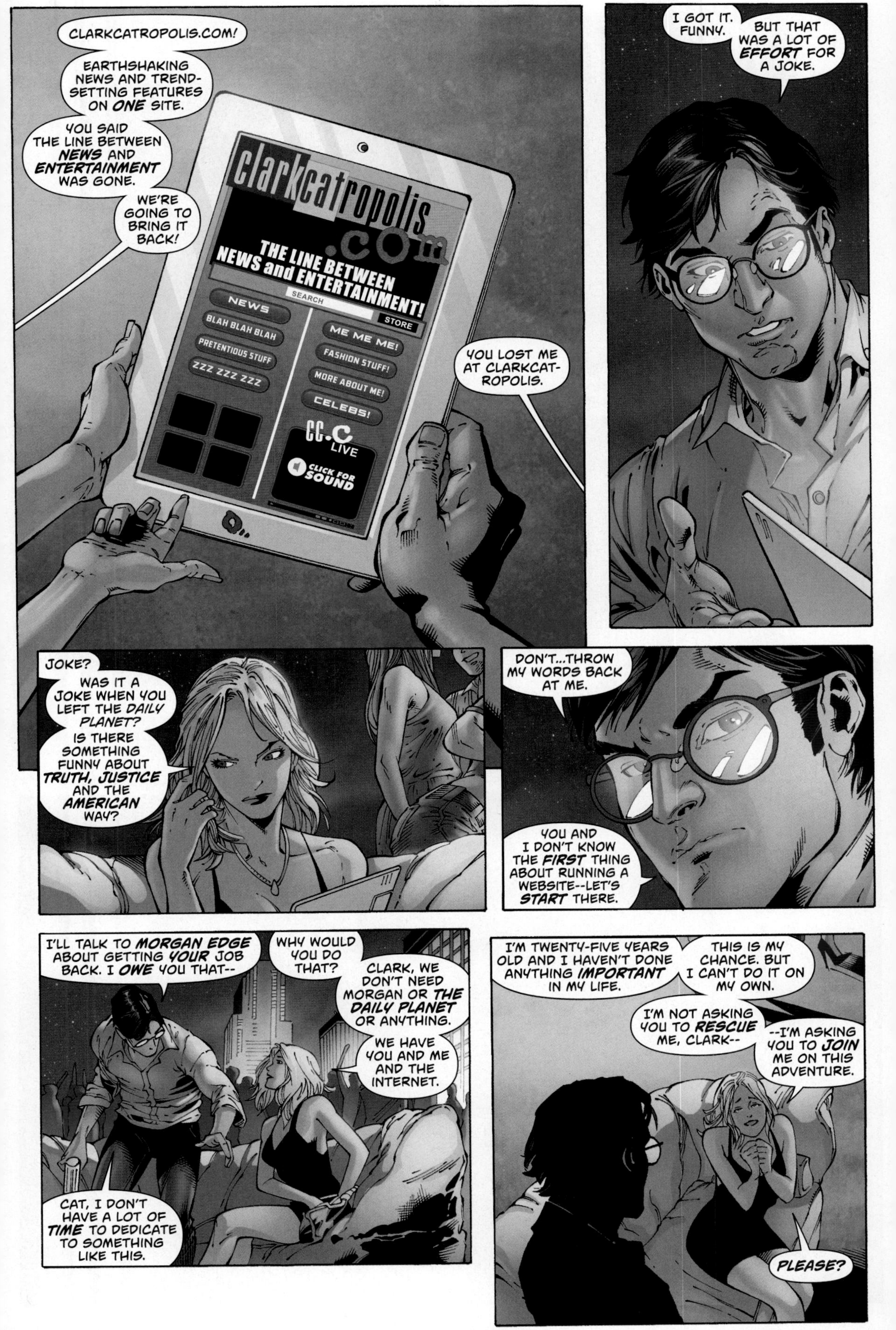
CLARKCATROPOLIS.COM!
EARTHSHAKING NEWS AND TREND-SETTING FEATURES ON *ONE* SITE.
YOU SAID THE LINE BETWEEN *NEWS* AND *ENTERTAINMENT* WAS GONE.
WE'RE GOING TO BRING IT BACK!
clarkcatropolis.com
THE LINE BETWEEN NEWS and ENTERTAINMENT!
SEARCH
STORE
NEWS
BLAH BLAH BLAH
PRETENTIOUS STUFF
ZZZ ZZZ ZZZ
ME ME ME!
FASHION STUFF!
MORE ABOUT ME!
CELEBS!
CC.C LIVE
CLICK FOR SOUND
YOU LOST ME AT CLARKCAT-ROPOLIS.
I GOT IT. FUNNY.
BUT THAT WAS A LOT OF *EFFORT* FOR A JOKE.
JOKE?
WAS IT A JOKE WHEN YOU LEFT THE *DAILY PLANET*?
IS THERE SOMETHING FUNNY ABOUT *TRUTH, JUSTICE* AND THE *AMERICAN* WAY?
DON'T...THROW MY WORDS BACK AT ME.
YOU AND I DON'T KNOW THE *FIRST* THING ABOUT RUNNING A WEBSITE--LET'S *START* THERE.
I'LL TALK TO *MORGAN EDGE* ABOUT GETTING *YOUR* JOB BACK. I *OWE* YOU THAT--
WHY WOULD YOU DO THAT?
CLARK, WE DON'T NEED MORGAN OR *THE DAILY PLANET* OR ANYTHING.
WE HAVE YOU AND ME AND THE INTERNET.
CAT, I DON'T HAVE A LOT OF *TIME* TO DEDICATE TO SOMETHING LIKE THIS.
I'M TWENTY-FIVE YEARS OLD AND I HAVEN'T DONE ANYTHING *IMPORTANT* IN MY LIFE.
THIS IS MY CHANCE. BUT I CAN'T DO IT ON MY OWN.
I'M NOT ASKING YOU TO *RESCUE* ME, CLARK--
--I'M ASKING YOU TO *JOIN* ME ON THIS ADVENTURE.
PLEASE?

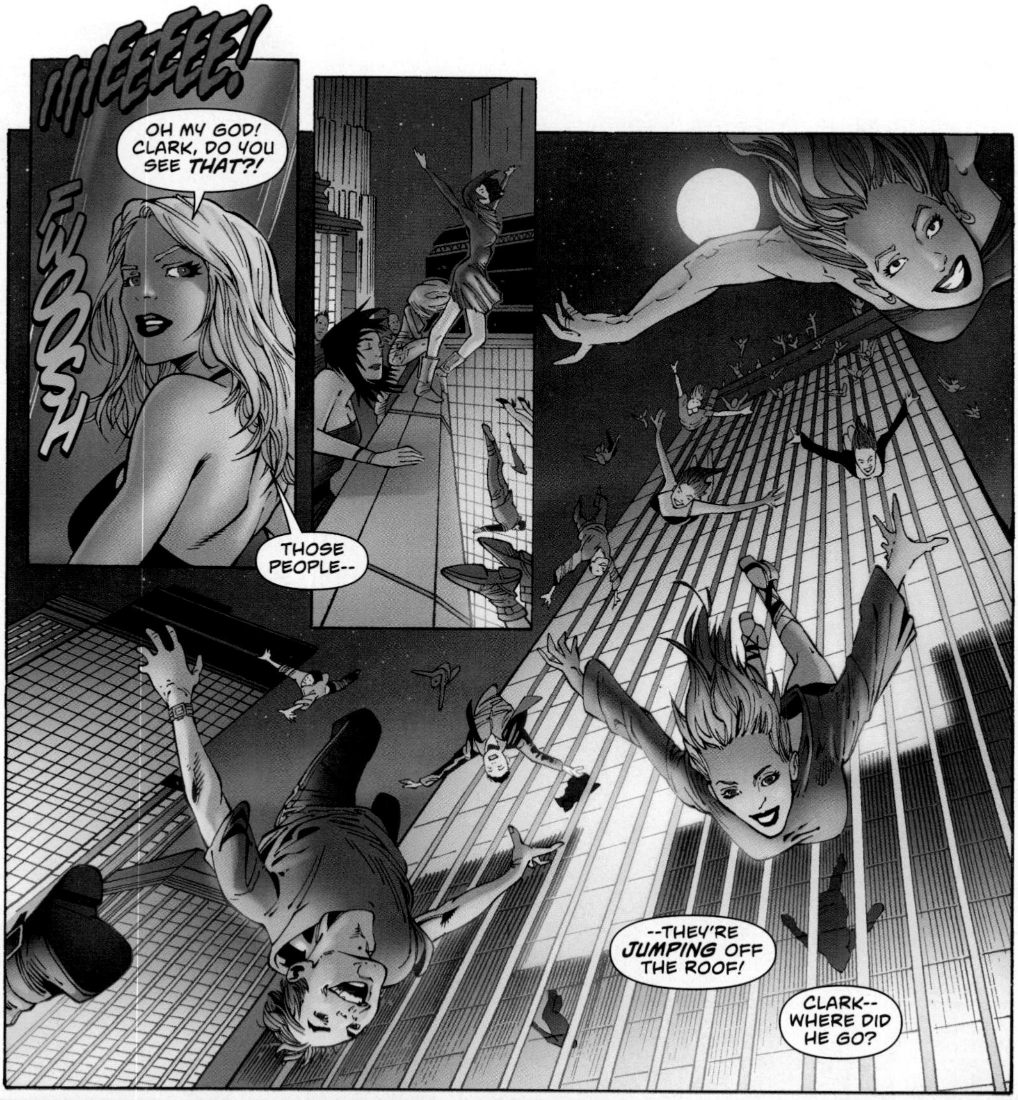

IIIIEEEEEE!
OH MY GOD! CLARK, DO YOU SEE THAT?!
FWOOSH
THOSE PEOPLE--
--THEY'RE JUMPING OFF THE ROOF!
CLARK-- WHERE DID HE GO?

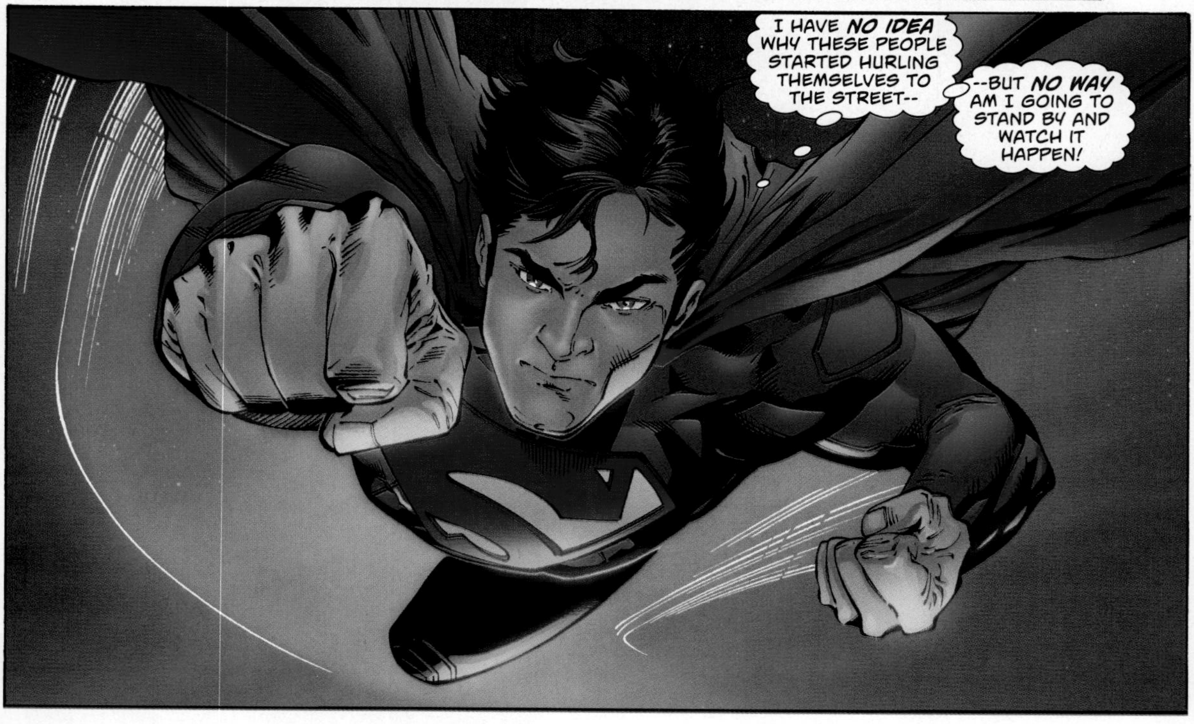

I HAVE NO IDEA WHY THESE PEOPLE STARTED HURLING THEMSELVES TO THE STREET--
--BUT NO WAY AM I GOING TO STAND BY AND WATCH IT HAPPEN!

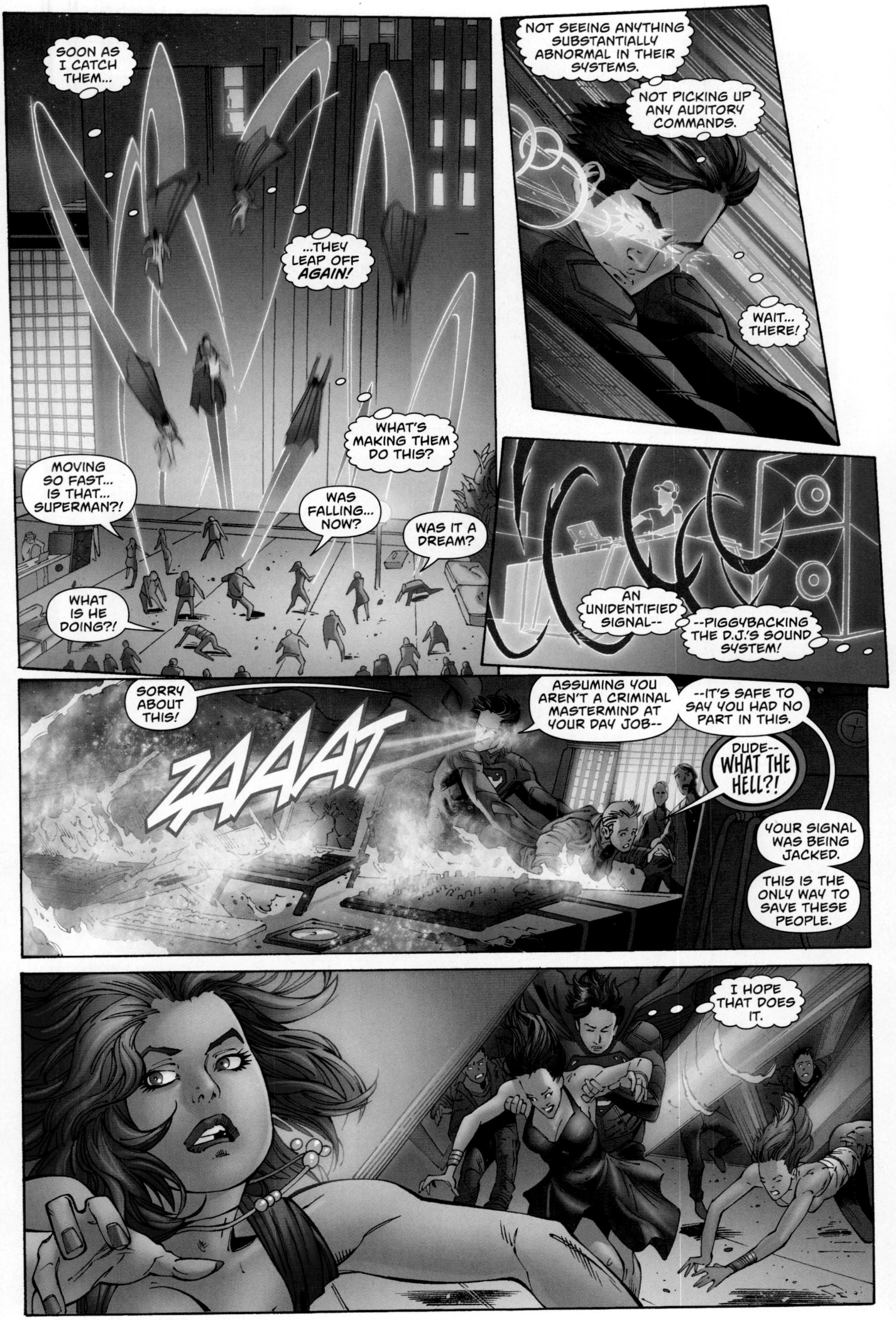
SOON AS I CATCH THEM...
...THEY LEAP OFF AGAIN!
WHAT'S MAKING THEM DO THIS?
MOVING SO FAST... IS THAT... SUPERMAN?!
WAS FALLING... NOW?
WAS IT A DREAM?
WHAT IS HE DOING?!
NOT SEEING ANYTHING SUBSTANTIALLY ABNORMAL IN THEIR SYSTEMS.
NOT PICKING UP ANY AUDITORY COMMANDS.
WAIT... THERE!
AN UNIDENTIFIED SIGNAL--
--PIGGYBACKING THE D.J.'S SOUND SYSTEM!
SORRY ABOUT THIS!
ZAAAT
ASSUMING YOU AREN'T A CRIMINAL MASTERMIND AT YOUR DAY JOB--
--IT'S SAFE TO SAY YOU HAD NO PART IN THIS.
DUDE-- WHAT THE HELL?!
YOUR SIGNAL WAS BEING JACKED.
THIS IS THE ONLY WAY TO SAVE THESE PEOPLE.
I HOPE THAT DOES IT.

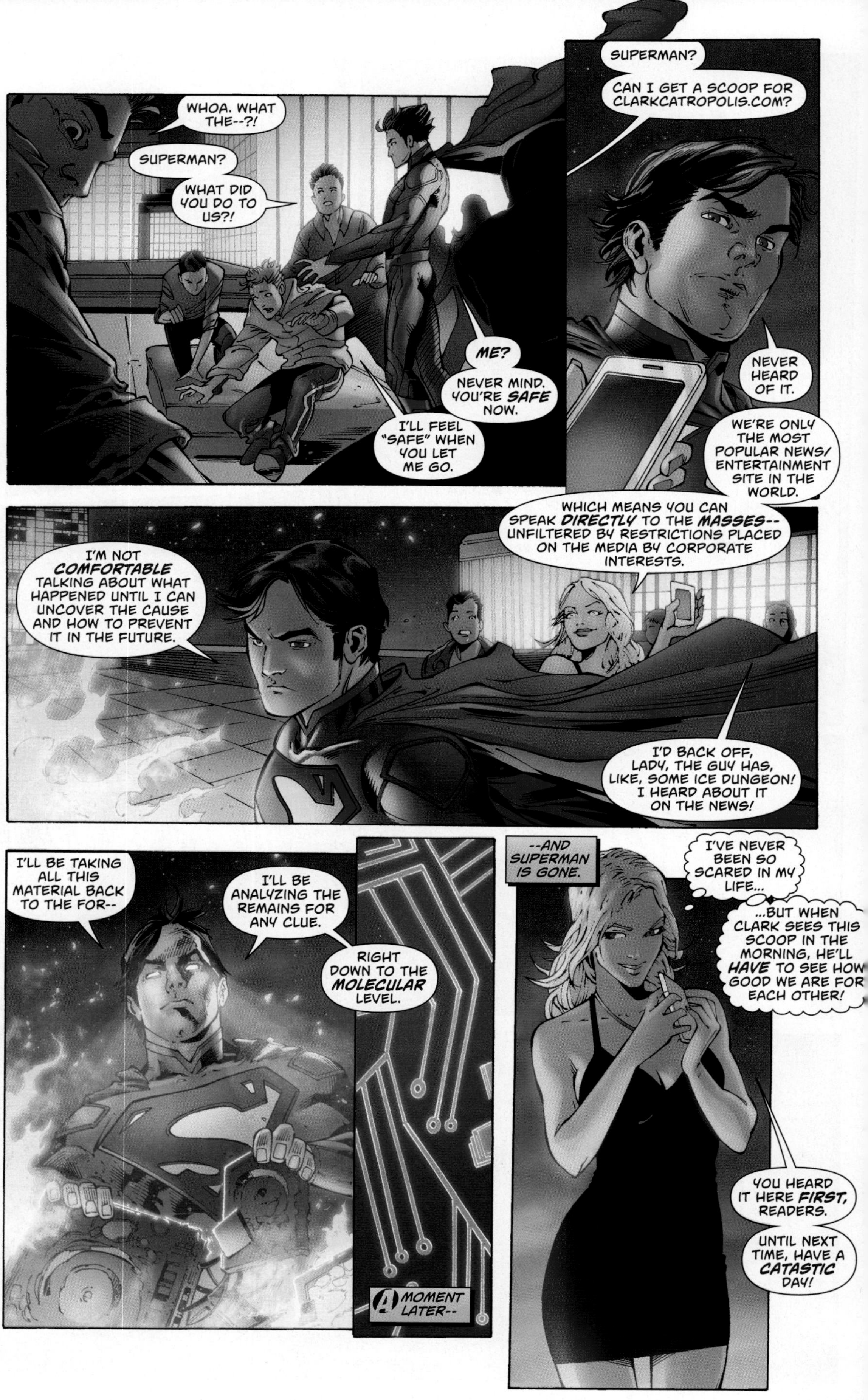
WHOA. WHAT THE--?!
SUPERMAN?
WHAT DID YOU DO TO US?!
ME?
NEVER MIND. YOU'RE SAFE NOW.
I'LL FEEL "SAFE" WHEN YOU LET ME GO.
SUPERMAN?
CAN I GET A SCOOP FOR CLARKCATROPOLIS.COM?
NEVER HEARD OF IT.
WE'RE ONLY THE MOST POPULAR NEWS/ ENTERTAINMENT SITE IN THE WORLD.
WHICH MEANS YOU CAN SPEAK DIRECTLY TO THE MASSES-- UNFILTERED BY RESTRICTIONS PLACED ON THE MEDIA BY CORPORATE INTERESTS.
I'M NOT COMFORTABLE TALKING ABOUT WHAT HAPPENED UNTIL I CAN UNCOVER THE CAUSE AND HOW TO PREVENT IT IN THE FUTURE.
I'D BACK OFF, LADY, THE GUY HAS, LIKE, SOME ICE DUNGEON! I HEARD ABOUT IT ON THE NEWS!
I'LL BE TAKING ALL THIS MATERIAL BACK TO THE FOR--
I'LL BE ANALYZING THE REMAINS FOR ANY CLUE.
RIGHT DOWN TO THE MOLECULAR LEVEL.
A MOMENT LATER--
--AND SUPERMAN IS GONE.
I'VE NEVER BEEN SO SCARED IN MY LIFE...
...BUT WHEN CLARK SEES THIS SCOOP IN THE MORNING, HE'LL HAVE TO SEE HOW GOOD WE ARE FOR EACH OTHER!
YOU HEARD IT HERE FIRST, READERS.
UNTIL NEXT TIME, HAVE A CATASTIC DAY!

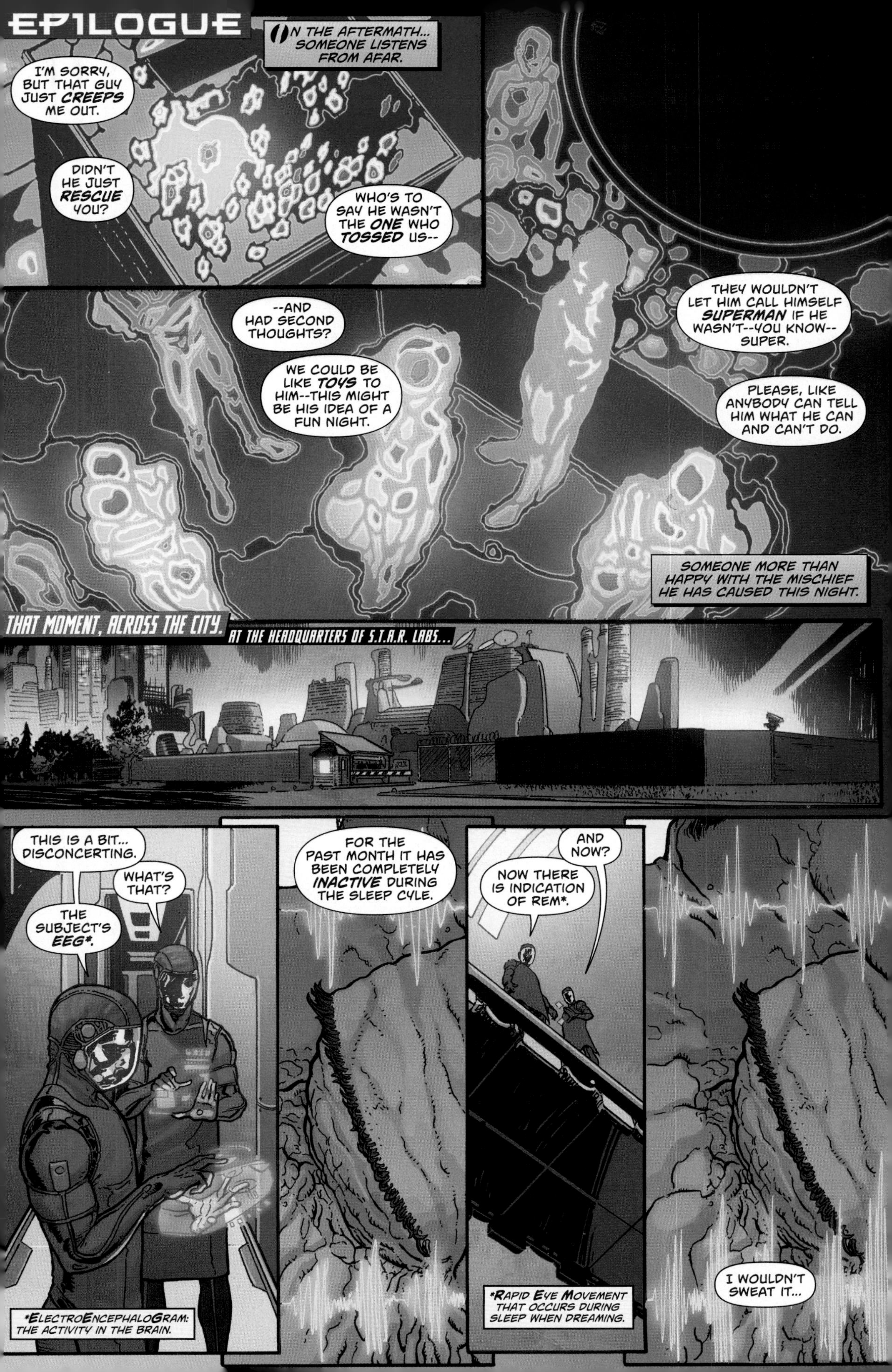

EPILOGUE
IN THE AFTERMATH... SOMEONE LISTENS FROM AFAR.
I'M SORRY, BUT THAT GUY JUST CREEPS ME OUT.
DIDN'T HE JUST RESCUE YOU?
WHO'S TO SAY HE WASN'T THE ONE WHO TOSSED US--
--AND HAD SECOND THOUGHTS?
WE COULD BE LIKE TOYS TO HIM--THIS MIGHT BE HIS IDEA OF A FUN NIGHT.
THEY WOULDN'T LET HIM CALL HIMSELF SUPERMAN IF HE WASN'T--YOU KNOW--SUPER.
PLEASE, LIKE ANYBODY CAN TELL HIM WHAT HE CAN AND CAN'T DO.
SOMEONE MORE THAN HAPPY WITH THE MISCHIEF HE HAS CAUSED THIS NIGHT.
THAT MOMENT, ACROSS THE CITY.
AT THE HEADQUARTERS OF S.T.A.R. LABS...
THIS IS A BIT... DISCONCERTING.
WHAT'S THAT?
THE SUBJECT'S EEG*.
*ELECTROENCEPHALOGRAM: THE ACTIVITY IN THE BRAIN.
FOR THE PAST MONTH IT HAS BEEN COMPLETELY INACTIVE DURING THE SLEEP CYLE.
AND NOW?
NOW THERE IS INDICATION OF REM*.
*RAPID EYE MOVEMENT THAT OCCURS DURING SLEEP WHEN DREAMING.
I WOULDN'T SWEAT IT...

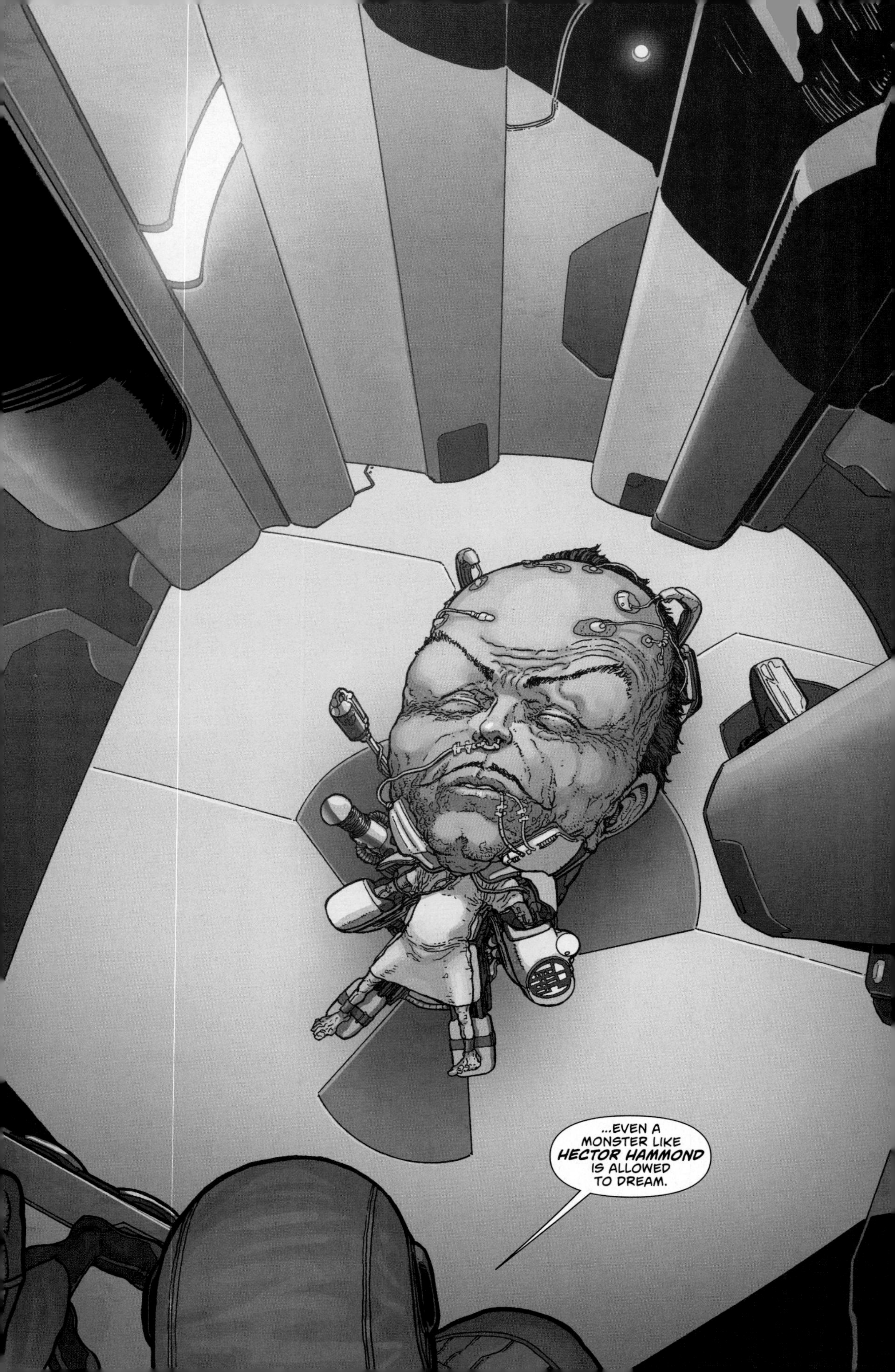
...EVEN A MONSTER LIKE HECTOR HAMMOND IS ALLOWED TO DREAM.

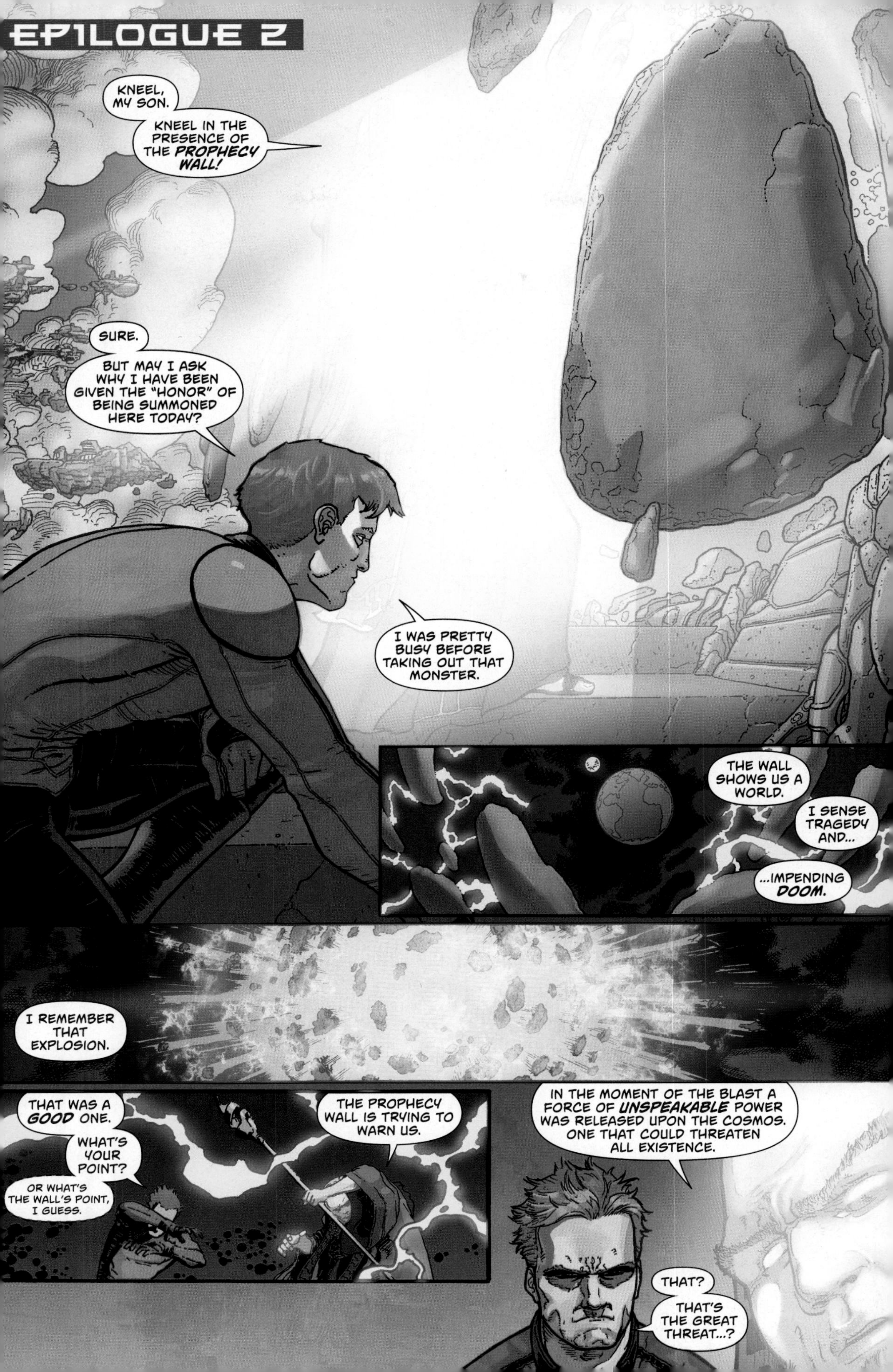
EPILOGUE 2
KNEEL, MY SON.
KNEEL IN THE PRESENCE OF THE PROPHECY WALL!
SURE.
BUT MAY I ASK WHY I HAVE BEEN GIVEN THE "HONOR" OF BEING SUMMONED HERE TODAY?
I WAS PRETTY BUSY BEFORE TAKING OUT THAT MONSTER.
THE WALL SHOWS US A WORLD.
I SENSE TRAGEDY AND...
...IMPENDING DOOM.
I REMEMBER THAT EXPLOSION.
THAT WAS A GOOD ONE.
WHAT'S YOUR POINT?
OR WHAT'S THE WALL'S POINT, I GUESS.
THE PROPHECY WALL IS TRYING TO WARN US.
IN THE MOMENT OF THE BLAST A FORCE OF UNSPEAKABLE POWER WAS RELEASED UPON THE COSMOS. ONE THAT COULD THREATEN ALL EXISTENCE.
THAT?
THAT'S THE GREAT THREAT...?

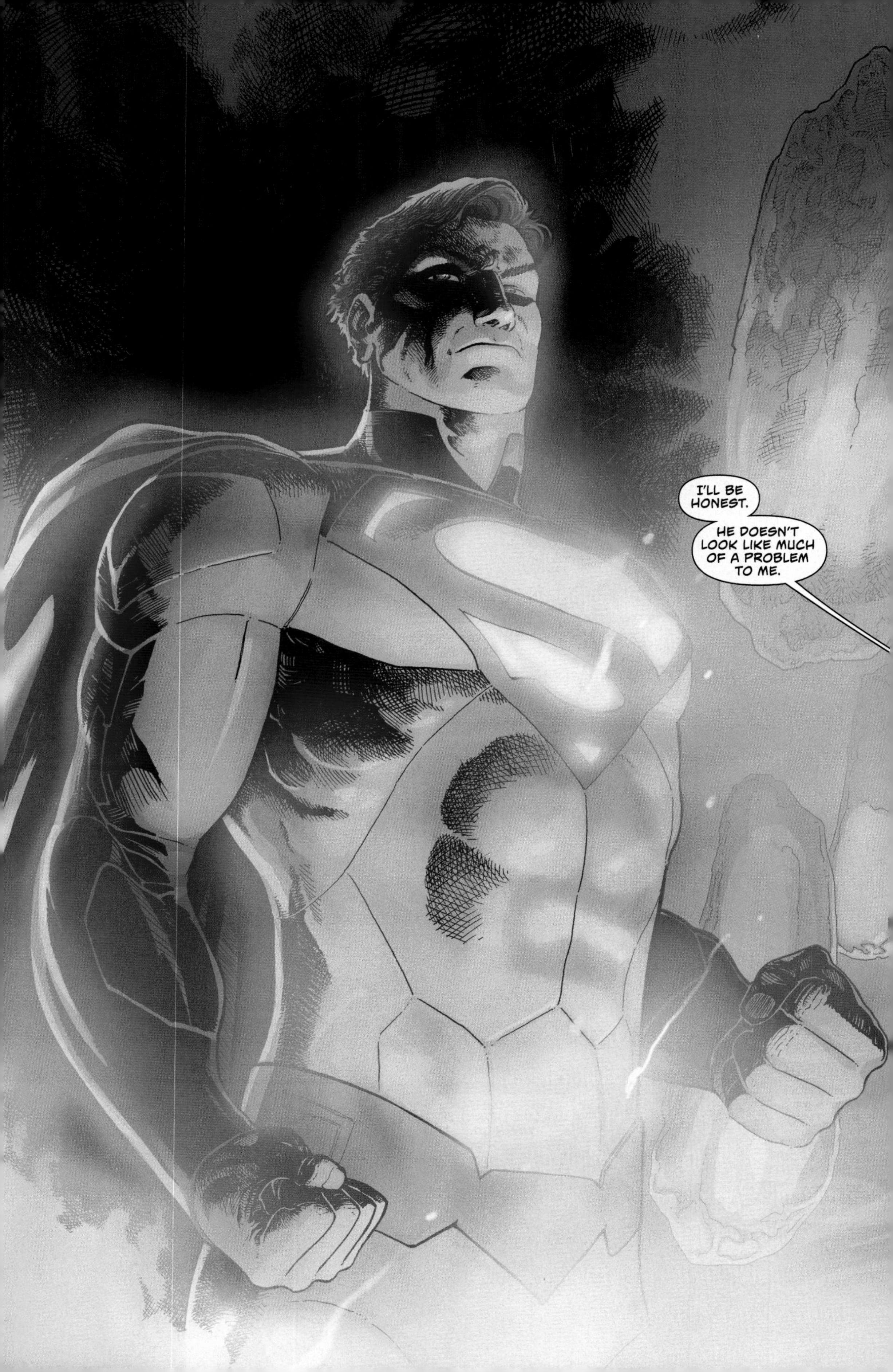
I'LL BE HONEST.
HE DOESN'T LOOK LIKE MUCH OF A PROBLEM TO ME.

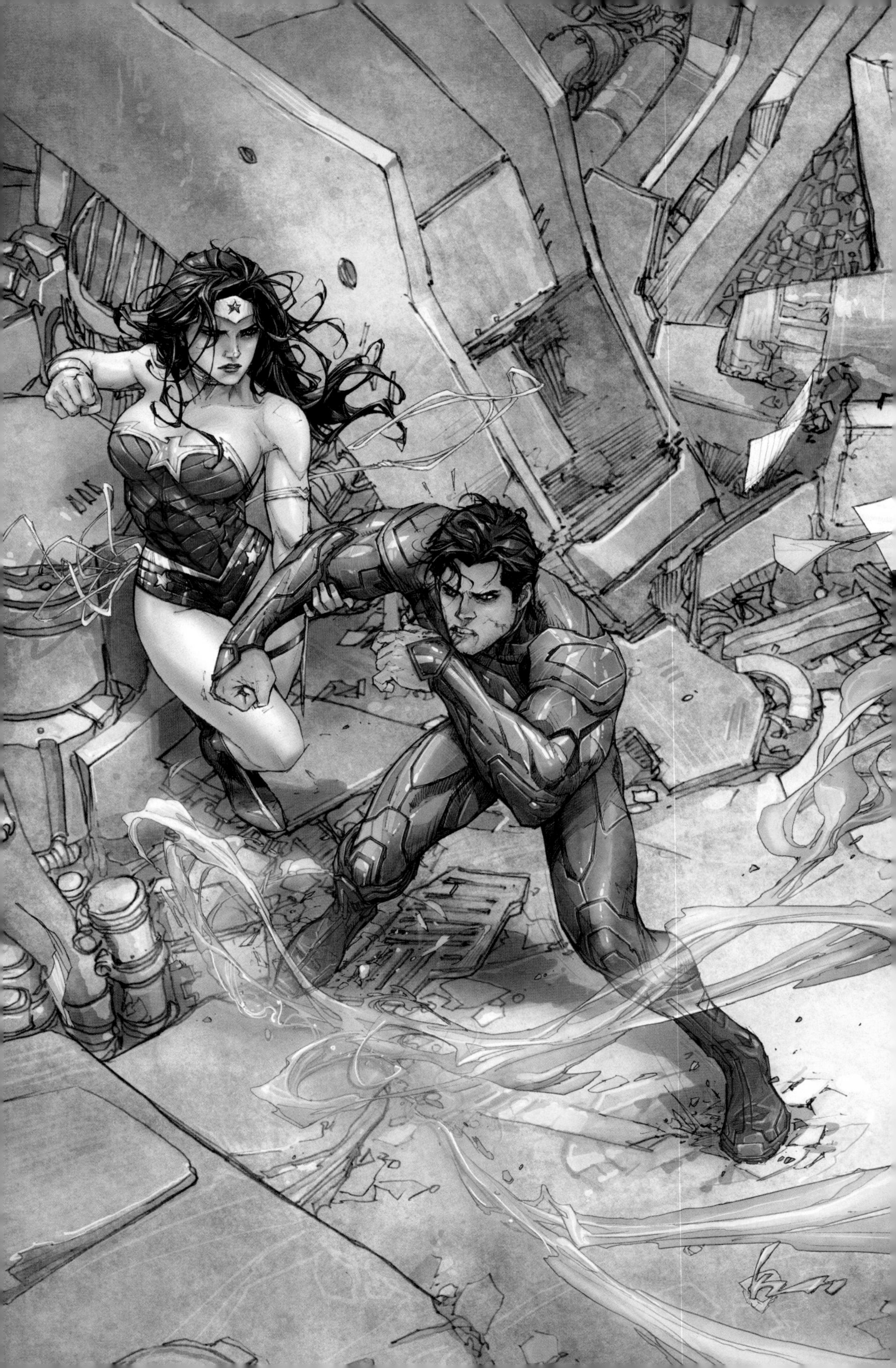

LOOK WHO'S FLYING TO DINNER

SCOTT LOBDELL writer **KENNETH ROCAFORT** artist cover art by **KENNETH ROCAFORT**

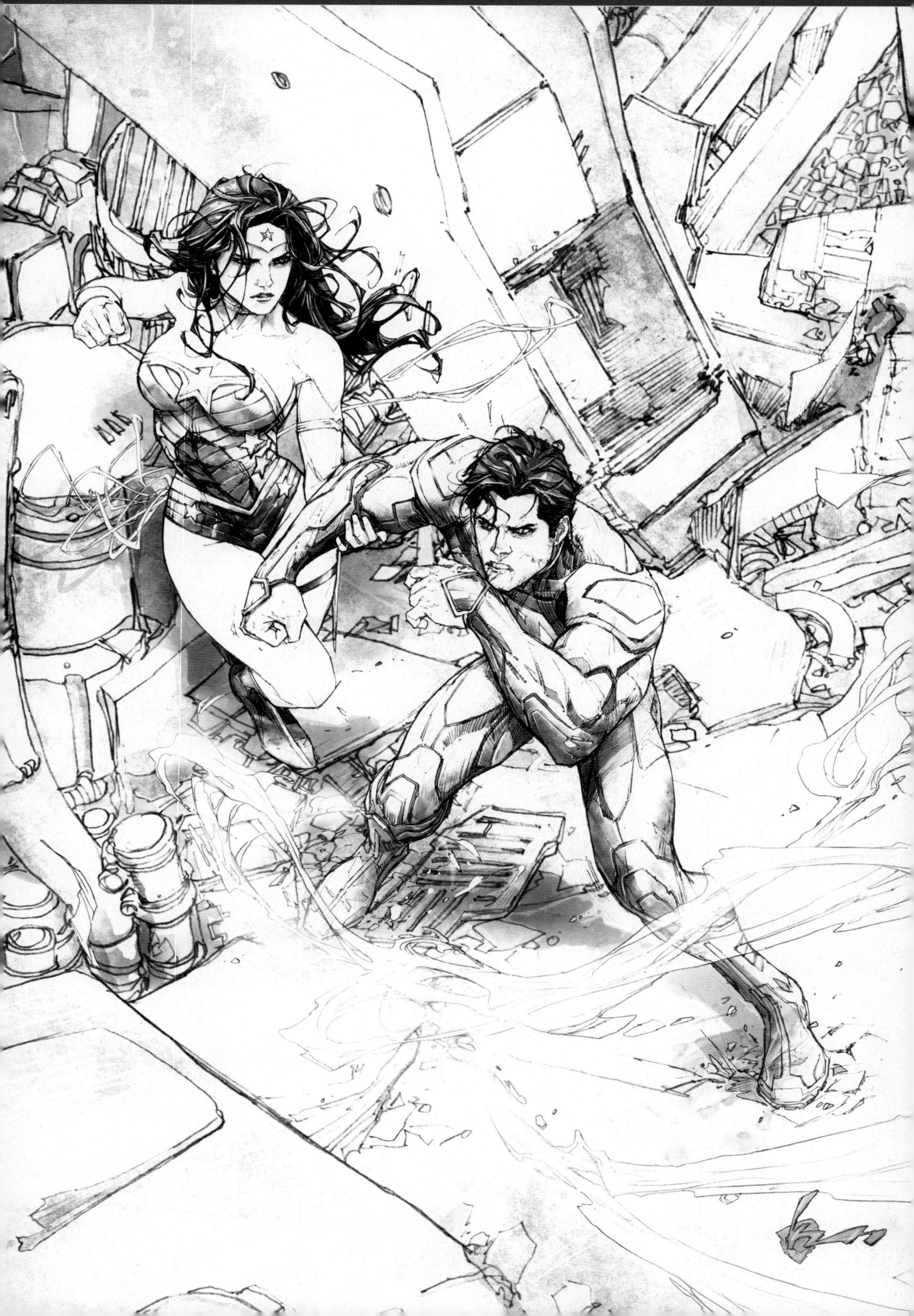

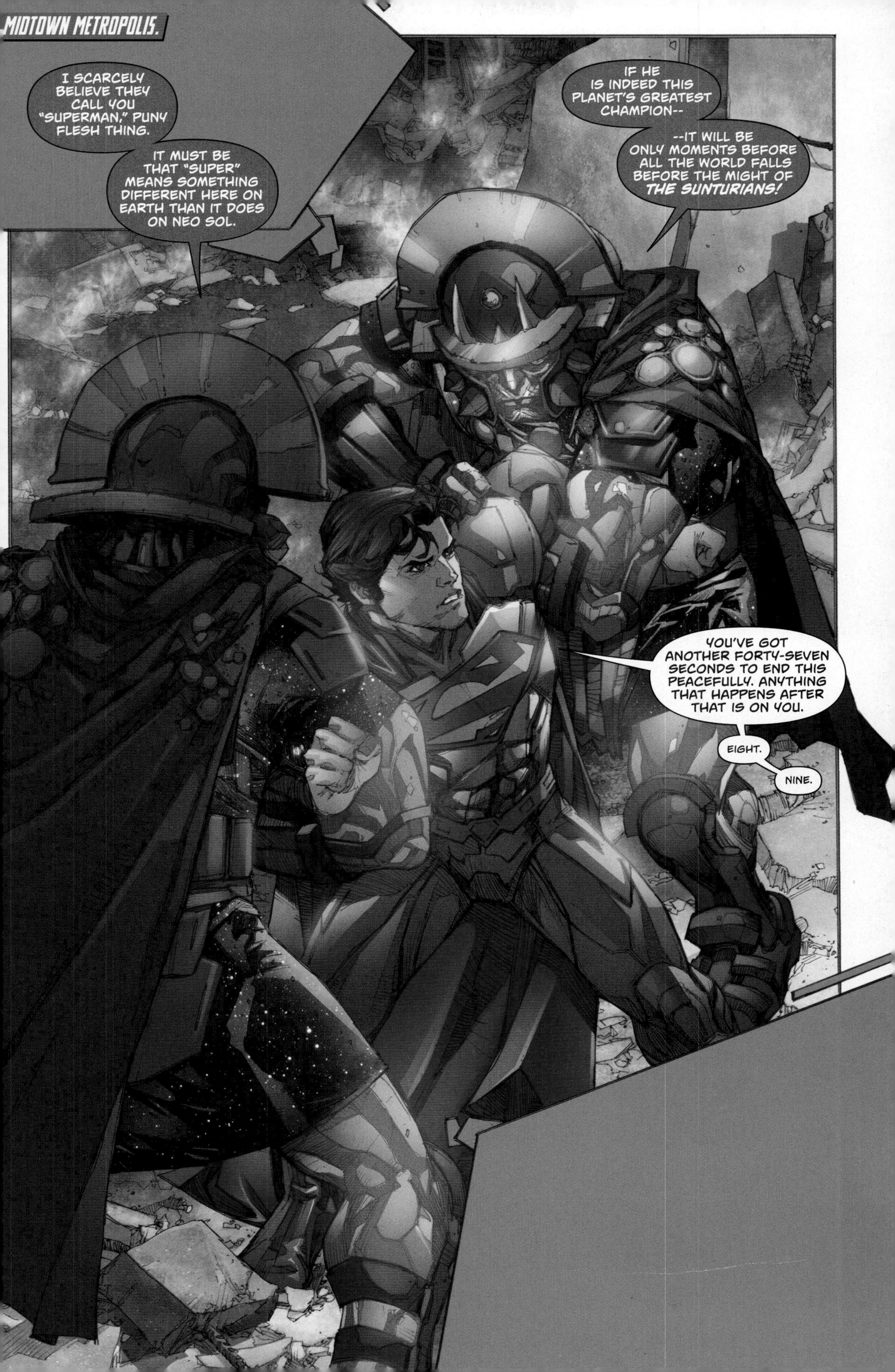
MIDTOWN METROPOLIS.
I SCARCELY BELIEVE THEY CALL YOU "SUPERMAN," PUNY FLESH THING.
IT MUST BE THAT "SUPER" MEANS SOMETHING DIFFERENT HERE ON EARTH THAN IT DOES ON NEO SOL.
IF HE IS INDEED THIS PLANET'S GREATEST CHAMPION--
--IT WILL BE ONLY MOMENTS BEFORE ALL THE WORLD FALLS BEFORE THE MIGHT OF *THE SUNTURIANS!*
YOU'VE GOT ANOTHER FORTY-SEVEN SECONDS TO END THIS PEACEFULLY. ANYTHING THAT HAPPENS AFTER THAT IS ON YOU.
EIGHT.
NINE.

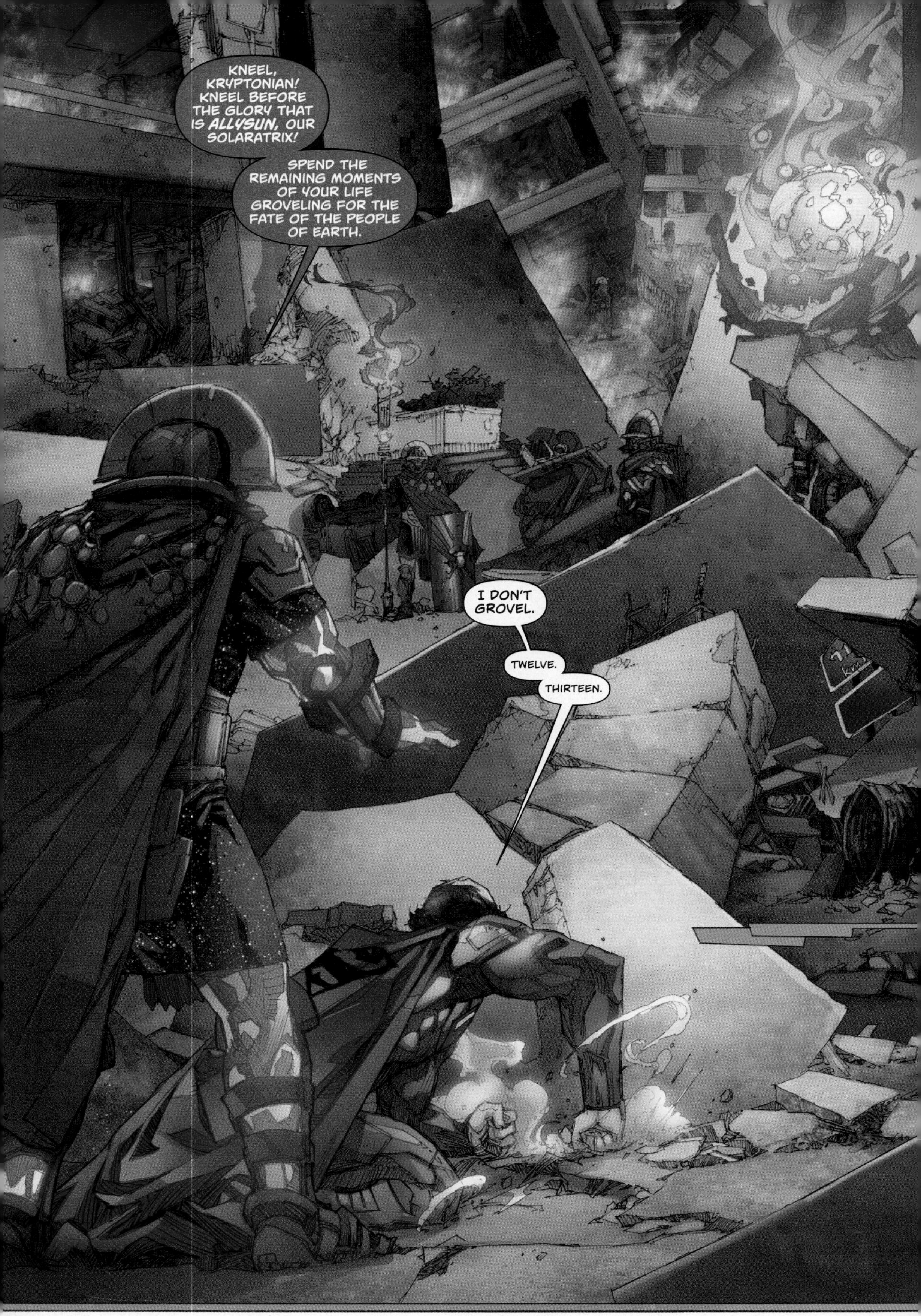
KNEEL, KRYPTONIAN! KNEEL BEFORE THE GLORY THAT IS ALLYSUN, OUR SOLARATRIX!
SPEND THE REMAINING MOMENTS OF YOUR LIFE GROVELING FOR THE FATE OF THE PEOPLE OF EARTH.
I DON'T GROVEL.
TWELVE.
THIRTEEN.

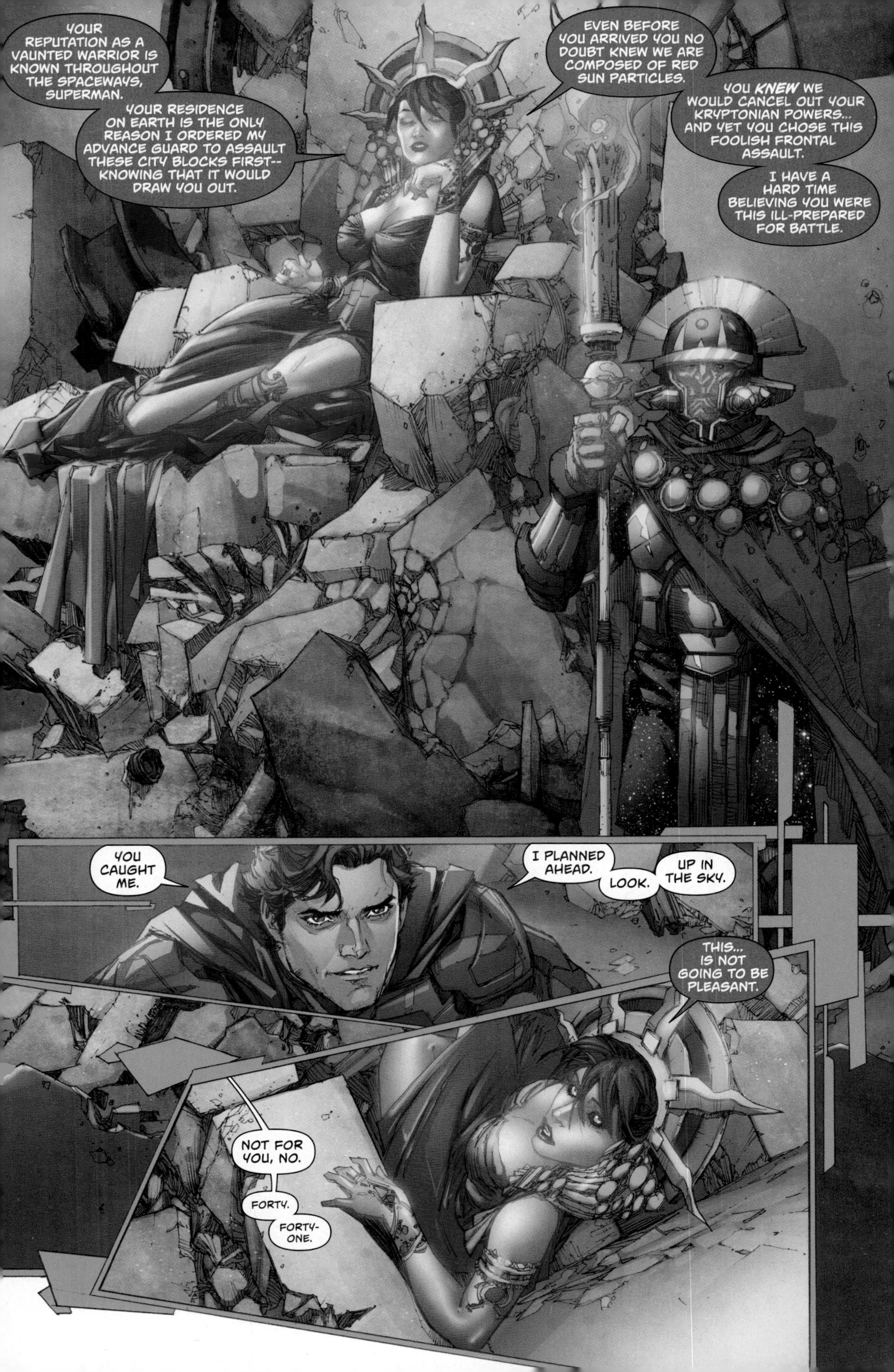
YOUR REPUTATION AS A VAUNTED WARRIOR IS KNOWN THROUGHOUT THE SPACEWAYS, SUPERMAN.
YOUR RESIDENCE ON EARTH IS THE ONLY REASON I ORDERED MY ADVANCE GUARD TO ASSAULT THESE CITY BLOCKS FIRST-- KNOWING THAT IT WOULD DRAW YOU OUT.
EVEN BEFORE YOU ARRIVED YOU NO DOUBT KNEW WE ARE COMPOSED OF RED SUN PARTICLES.
YOU *KNEW* WE WOULD CANCEL OUT YOUR KRYPTONIAN POWERS... AND YET YOU CHOSE THIS FOOLISH FRONTAL ASSAULT.
I HAVE A HARD TIME BELIEVING YOU WERE THIS ILL-PREPARED FOR BATTLE.
YOU CAUGHT ME.
I PLANNED AHEAD.
LOOK.
UP IN THE SKY.
THIS... IS NOT GOING TO BE PLEASANT.
NOT FOR YOU, NO.
FORTY.
FORTY-ONE.

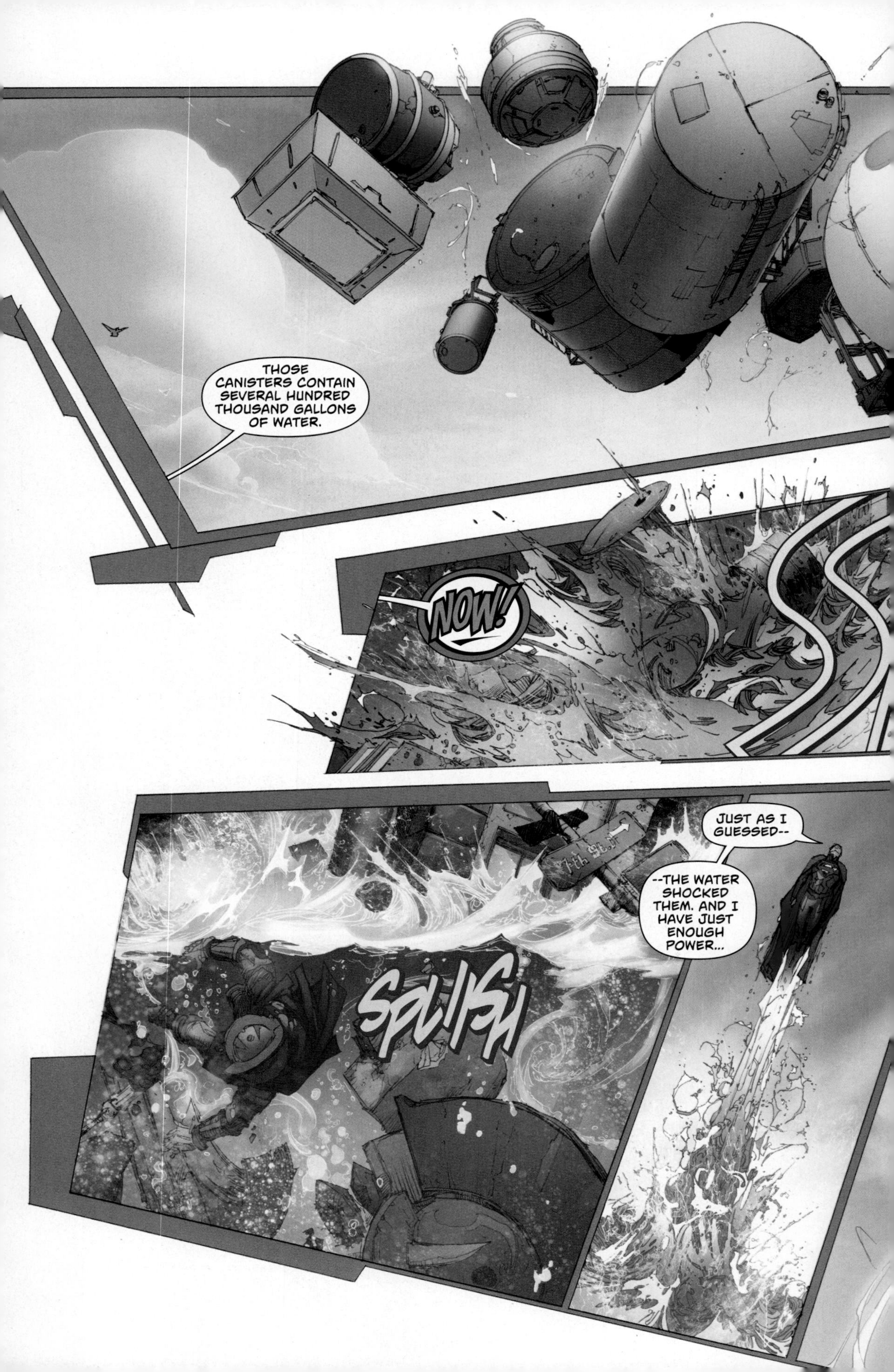
THOSE CANISTERS CONTAIN SEVERAL HUNDRED THOUSAND GALLONS OF WATER.
NOW!
JUST AS I GUESSED--
--THE WATER SHOCKED THEM. AND I HAVE JUST ENOUGH POWER...
SPLISH

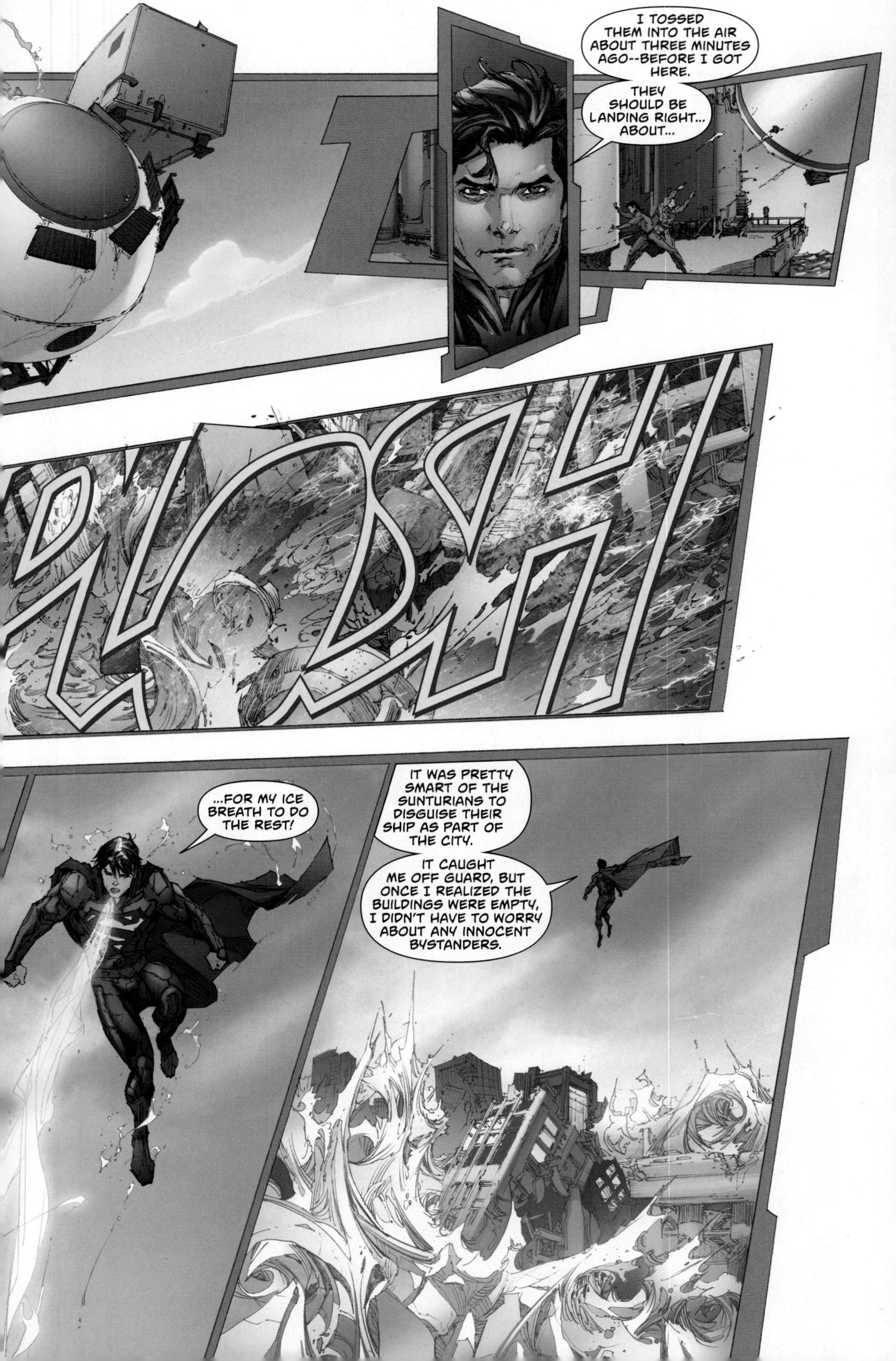
I TOSSED THEM INTO THE AIR ABOUT THREE MINUTES AGO--BEFORE I GOT HERE.
THEY SHOULD BE LANDING RIGHT... ABOUT...
...FOR MY ICE BREATH TO DO THE REST!
IT WAS PRETTY SMART OF THE SUNTURIANS TO DISGUISE THEIR SHIP AS PART OF THE CITY.
IT CAUGHT ME OFF GUARD, BUT ONCE I REALIZED THE BUILDINGS WERE EMPTY, I DIDN'T HAVE TO WORRY ABOUT ANY INNOCENT BYSTANDERS.

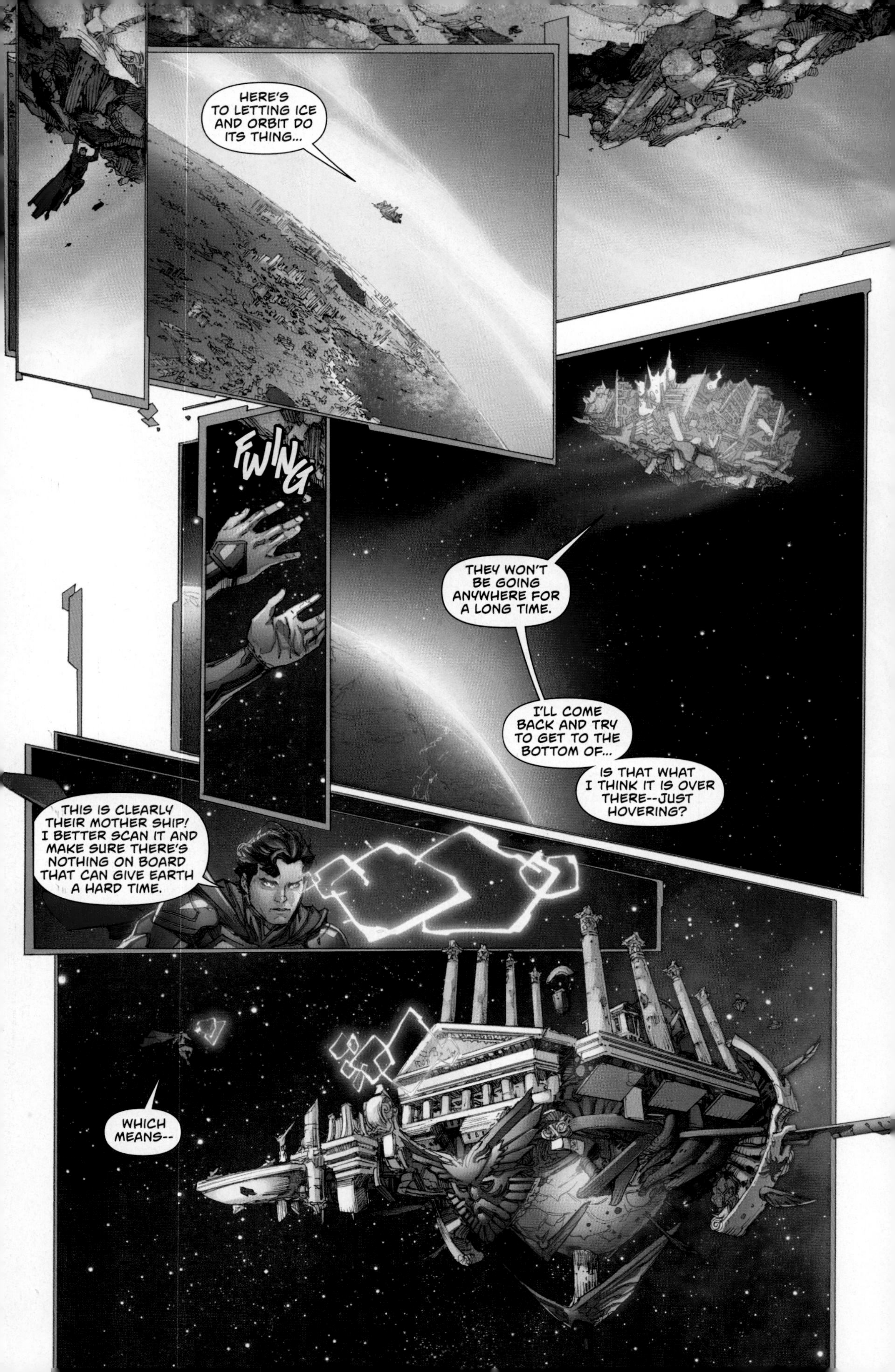
HERE'S TO LETTING ICE AND ORBIT DO ITS THING...
FWING
THEY WON'T BE GOING ANYWHERE FOR A LONG TIME.
I'LL COME BACK AND TRY TO GET TO THE BOTTOM OF...
IS THAT WHAT I THINK IT IS OVER THERE--JUST HOVERING?
THIS IS CLEARLY THEIR MOTHER SHIP! I BETTER SCAN IT AND MAKE SURE THERE'S NOTHING ON BOARD THAT CAN GIVE EARTH A HARD TIME.
WHICH MEANS--

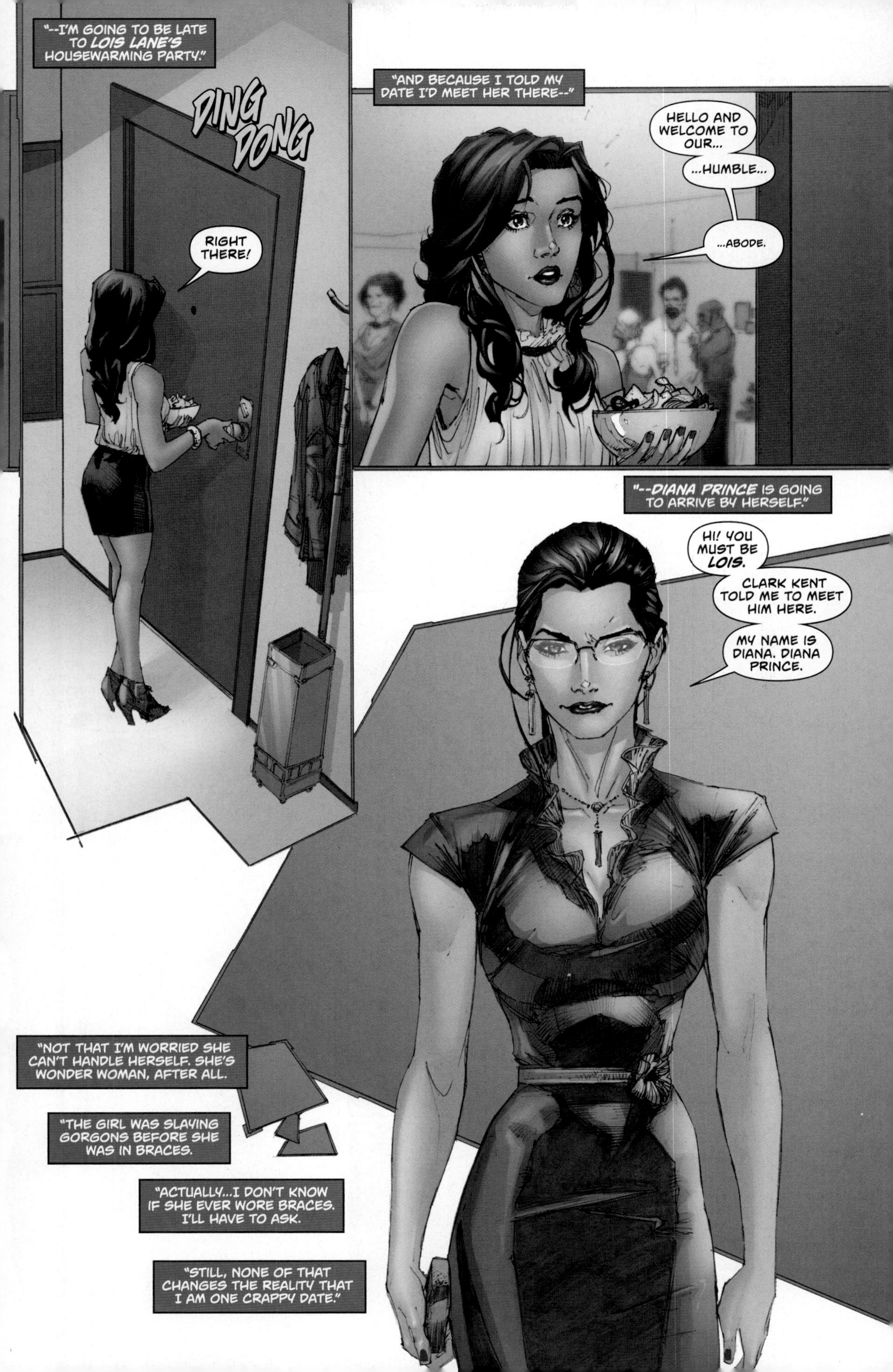
"--I'M GOING TO BE LATE TO LOIS LANE'S HOUSEWARMING PARTY."
DING DONG
RIGHT THERE!
"AND BECAUSE I TOLD MY DATE I'D MEET HER THERE--"
HELLO AND WELCOME TO OUR...
...HUMBLE...
...ABODE.
"--DIANA PRINCE IS GOING TO ARRIVE BY HERSELF."
HI! YOU MUST BE LOIS.
CLARK KENT TOLD ME TO MEET HIM HERE.
MY NAME IS DIANA. DIANA PRINCE.
"NOT THAT I'M WORRIED SHE CAN'T HANDLE HERSELF. SHE'S WONDER WOMAN, AFTER ALL.
"THE GIRL WAS SLAYING GORGONS BEFORE SHE WAS IN BRACES.
"ACTUALLY...I DON'T KNOW IF SHE EVER WORE BRACES. I'LL HAVE TO ASK.
"STILL, NONE OF THAT CHANGES THE REALITY THAT I AM ONE CRAPPY DATE."

Um.

THERE ARE THE CHIPS!

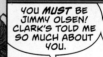

Um.

RIGHT?

YOU *MUST* BE JIMMY OLSEN! CLARK'S TOLD ME SO MUCH ABOUT YOU.

ABOUT ALL OF YOU, AS A MATTER OF FACT. IT'S GREAT TO FINALLY PUT THE FACES TO THE NAMES!

HEY, GUYS! WHAT'S WITH THE GAWK-A-THON?

ARE YOU GOING TO INVITE OUR...

Um.

REALLY, JON? Um?

DON'T TAKE THIS THE WRONG WAY.

BUT CAN I HAVE YOUR BABIES?

JAB

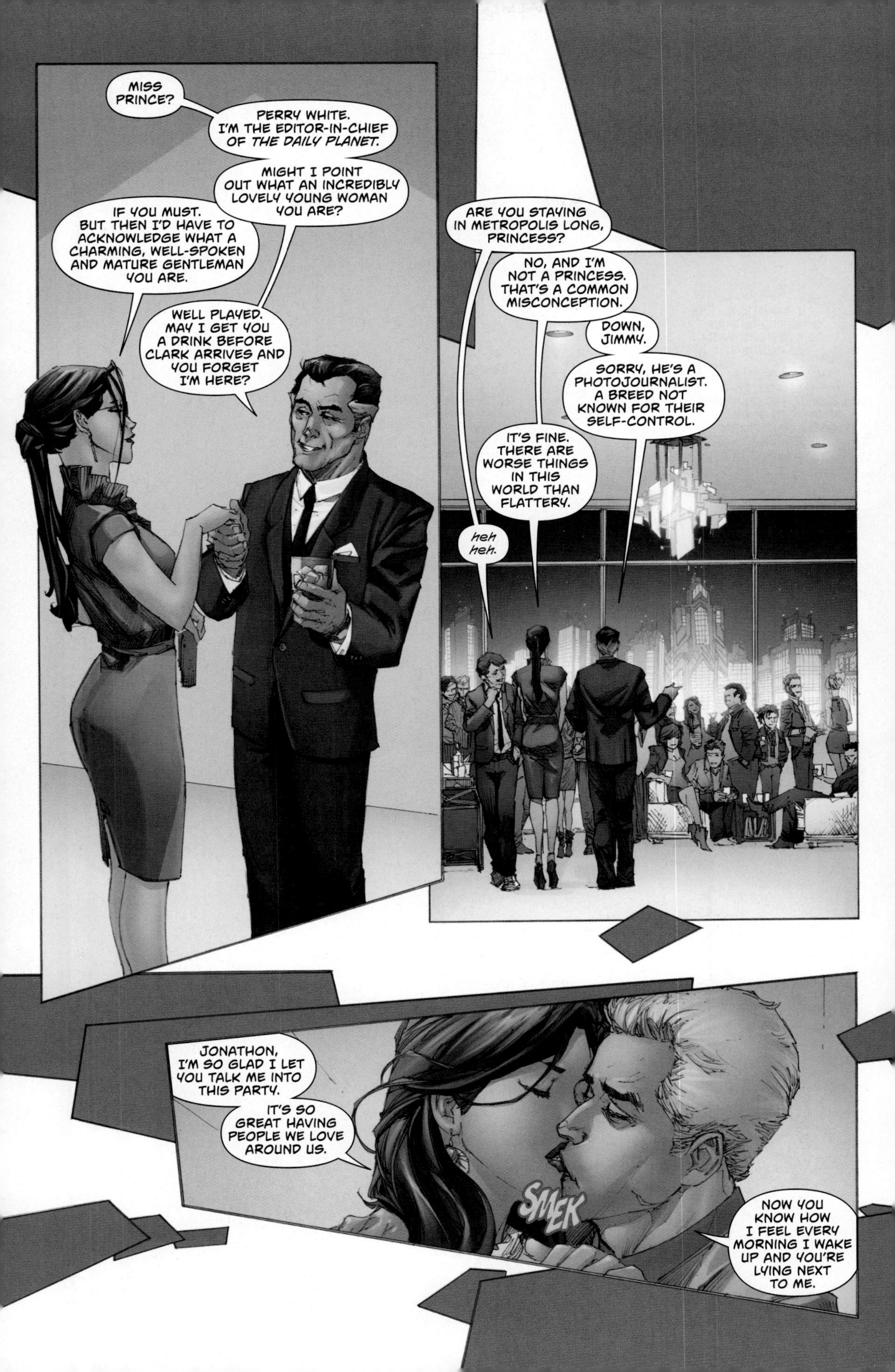
MISS PRINCE?
PERRY WHITE. I'M THE EDITOR-IN-CHIEF OF *THE DAILY PLANET.*
MIGHT I POINT OUT WHAT AN INCREDIBLY LOVELY YOUNG WOMAN YOU ARE?
IF YOU MUST. BUT THEN I'D HAVE TO ACKNOWLEDGE WHAT A CHARMING, WELL-SPOKEN AND MATURE GENTLEMAN YOU ARE.
WELL PLAYED. MAY I GET YOU A DRINK BEFORE CLARK ARRIVES AND YOU FORGET I'M HERE?
ARE YOU STAYING IN METROPOLIS LONG, PRINCESS?
NO, AND I'M NOT A PRINCESS. THAT'S A COMMON MISCONCEPTION.
DOWN, JIMMY.
SORRY, HE'S A PHOTOJOURNALIST. A BREED NOT KNOWN FOR THEIR SELF-CONTROL.
IT'S FINE. THERE ARE WORSE THINGS IN THIS WORLD THAN FLATTERY.
heh heh.
JONATHON, I'M SO GLAD I LET YOU TALK ME INTO THIS PARTY.
IT'S SO GREAT HAVING PEOPLE WE LOVE AROUND US.
SMEK
NOW YOU KNOW HOW I FEEL EVERY MORNING I WAKE UP AND YOU'RE LYING NEXT TO ME.

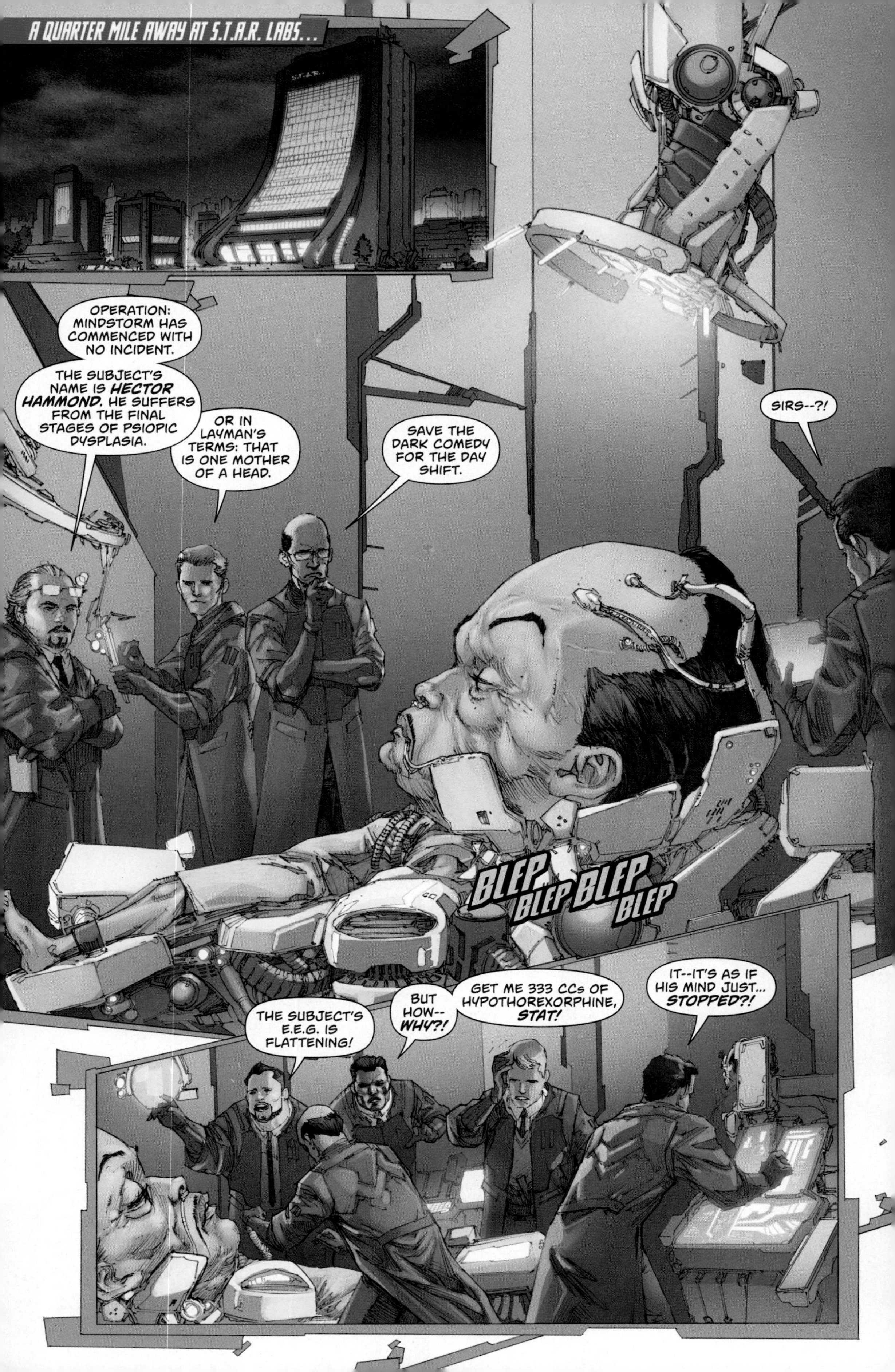
A QUARTER MILE AWAY AT S.T.A.R. LABS...
S.T.A.R.
OPERATION: MINDSTORM HAS COMMENCED WITH NO INCIDENT.
THE SUBJECT'S NAME IS HECTOR HAMMOND. HE SUFFERS FROM THE FINAL STAGES OF PSIOPIC DYSPLASIA.
OR IN LAYMAN'S TERMS: THAT IS ONE MOTHER OF A HEAD.
SAVE THE DARK COMEDY FOR THE DAY SHIFT.
SIRS--?!
BLEP BLEP BLEP BLEP
THE SUBJECT'S E.E.G. IS FLATTENING!
BUT HOW--WHY?!
GET ME 333 CCs OF HYPOTHOREXORPHINE, STAT!
IT--IT'S AS IF HIS MIND JUST... STOPPED?!

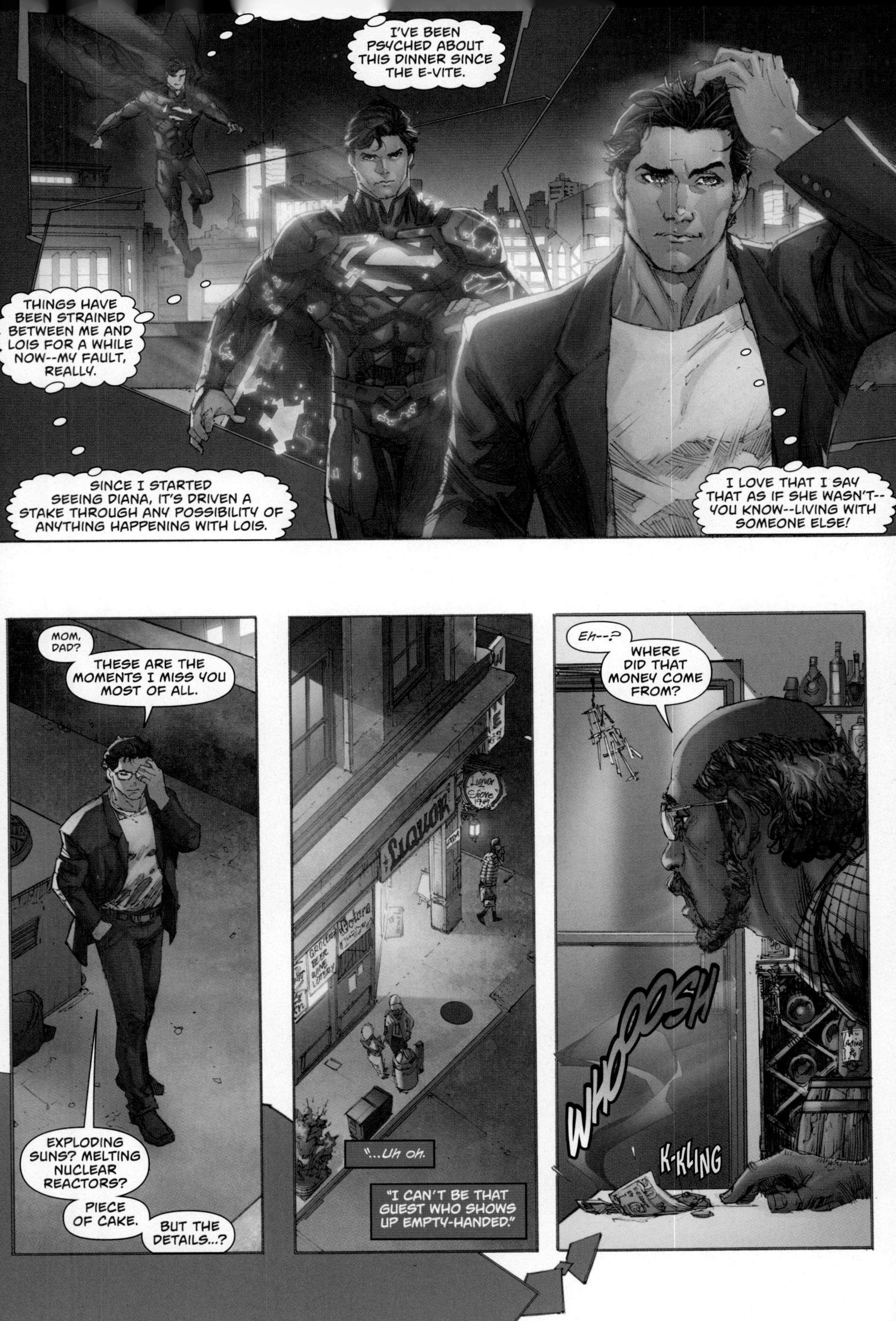
I'VE BEEN PSYCHED ABOUT THIS DINNER SINCE THE E-VITE.
THINGS HAVE BEEN STRAINED BETWEEN ME AND LOIS FOR A WHILE NOW--MY FAULT, REALLY.
SINCE I STARTED SEEING DIANA, IT'S DRIVEN A STAKE THROUGH ANY POSSIBILITY OF ANYTHING HAPPENING WITH LOIS.
I LOVE THAT I SAY THAT AS IF SHE WASN'T--YOU KNOW--LIVING WITH SOMEONE ELSE!
MOM, DAD?
THESE ARE THE MOMENTS I MISS YOU MOST OF ALL.
EXPLODING SUNS? MELTING NUCLEAR REACTORS?
PIECE OF CAKE.
BUT THE DETAILS...?
LIQUOR
"...Uh oh.
"I CAN'T BE THAT GUEST WHO SHOWS UP EMPTY-HANDED."
Eh--?
WHERE DID THAT MONEY COME FROM?
WHOOOSH
K-KLING

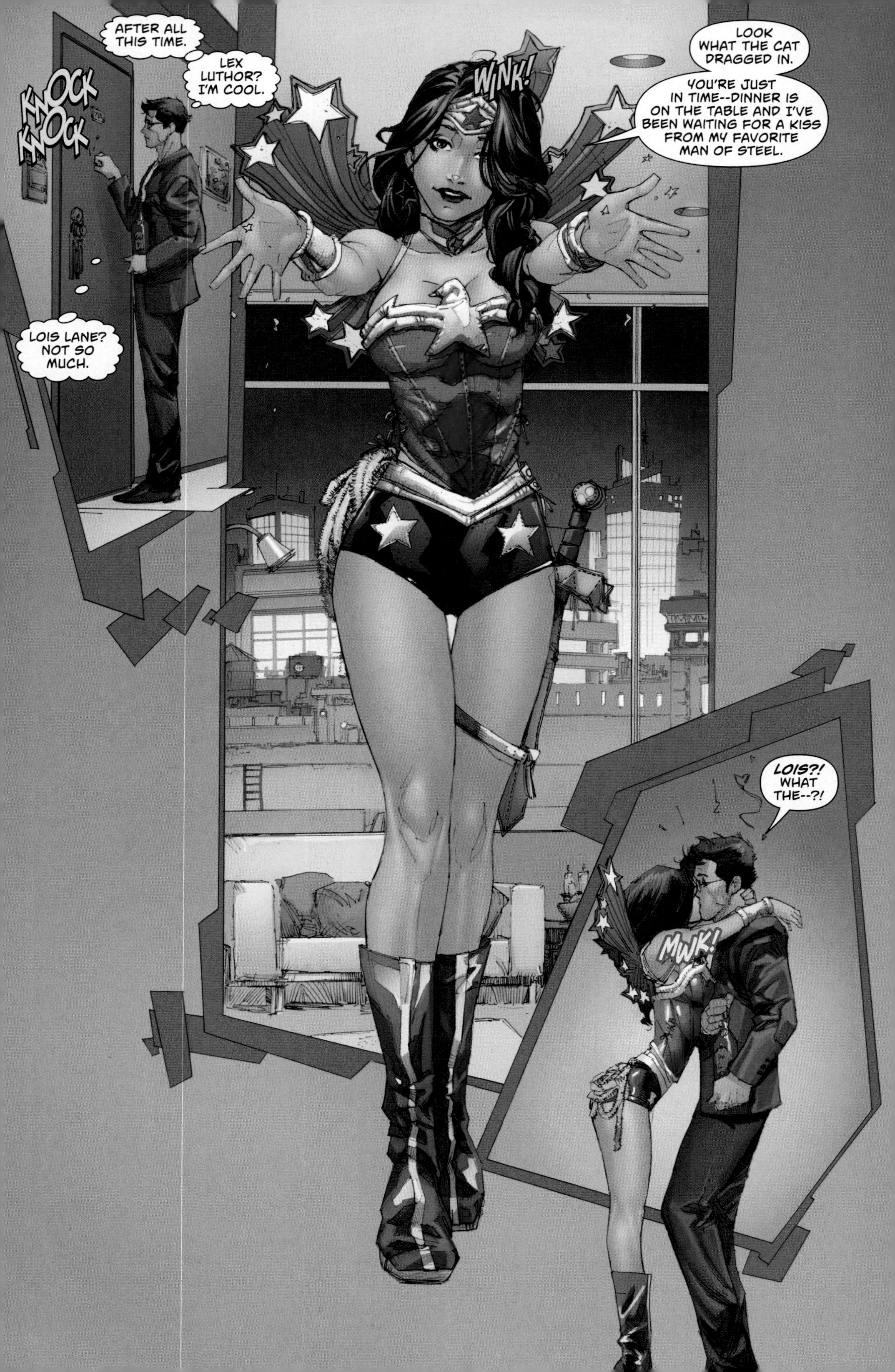
KNOCK KNOCK
AFTER ALL THIS TIME.
LEX LUTHOR? I'M COOL.
LOIS LANE? NOT SO MUCH.
WINK!
LOOK WHAT THE CAT DRAGGED IN.
YOU'RE JUST IN TIME--DINNER IS ON THE TABLE AND I'VE BEEN WAITING FOR A KISS FROM MY FAVORITE MAN OF STEEL.
LOIS?! WHAT THE--?!
MWK!

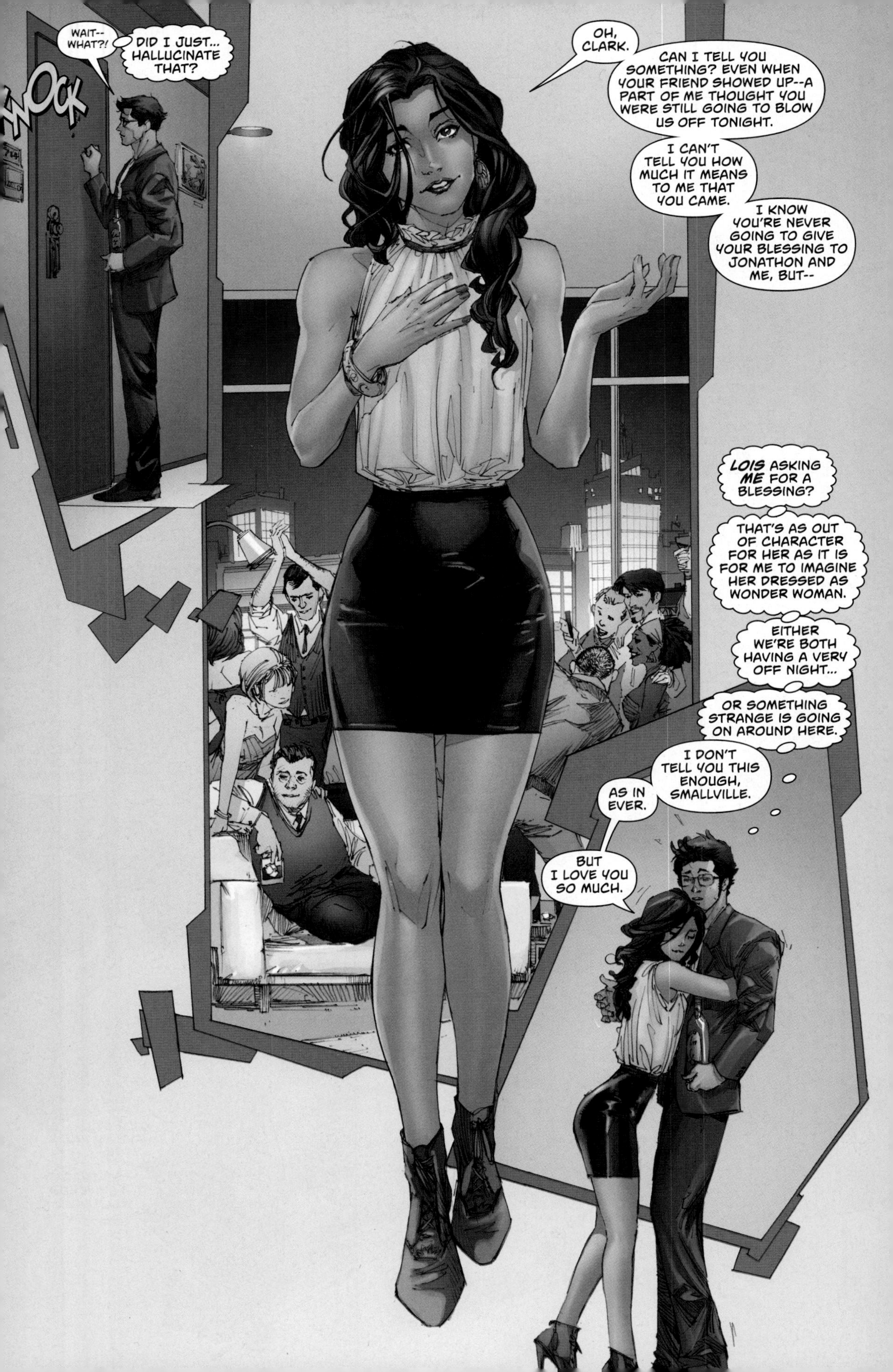
KNOCK
WAIT-- WHAT?!
DID I JUST... HALLUCINATE THAT?
OH, CLARK.
CAN I TELL YOU SOMETHING? EVEN WHEN YOUR FRIEND SHOWED UP--A PART OF ME THOUGHT YOU WERE STILL GOING TO BLOW US OFF TONIGHT.
I CAN'T TELL YOU HOW MUCH IT MEANS TO ME THAT YOU CAME.
I KNOW YOU'RE NEVER GOING TO GIVE YOUR BLESSING TO JONATHON AND ME, BUT--
LOIS ASKING ME FOR A BLESSING?
THAT'S AS OUT OF CHARACTER FOR HER AS IT IS FOR ME TO IMAGINE HER DRESSED AS WONDER WOMAN.
EITHER WE'RE BOTH HAVING A VERY OFF NIGHT...
OR SOMETHING STRANGE IS GOING ON AROUND HERE.
I DON'T TELL YOU THIS ENOUGH, SMALLVILLE.
AS IN EVER.
BUT I LOVE YOU SO MUCH.

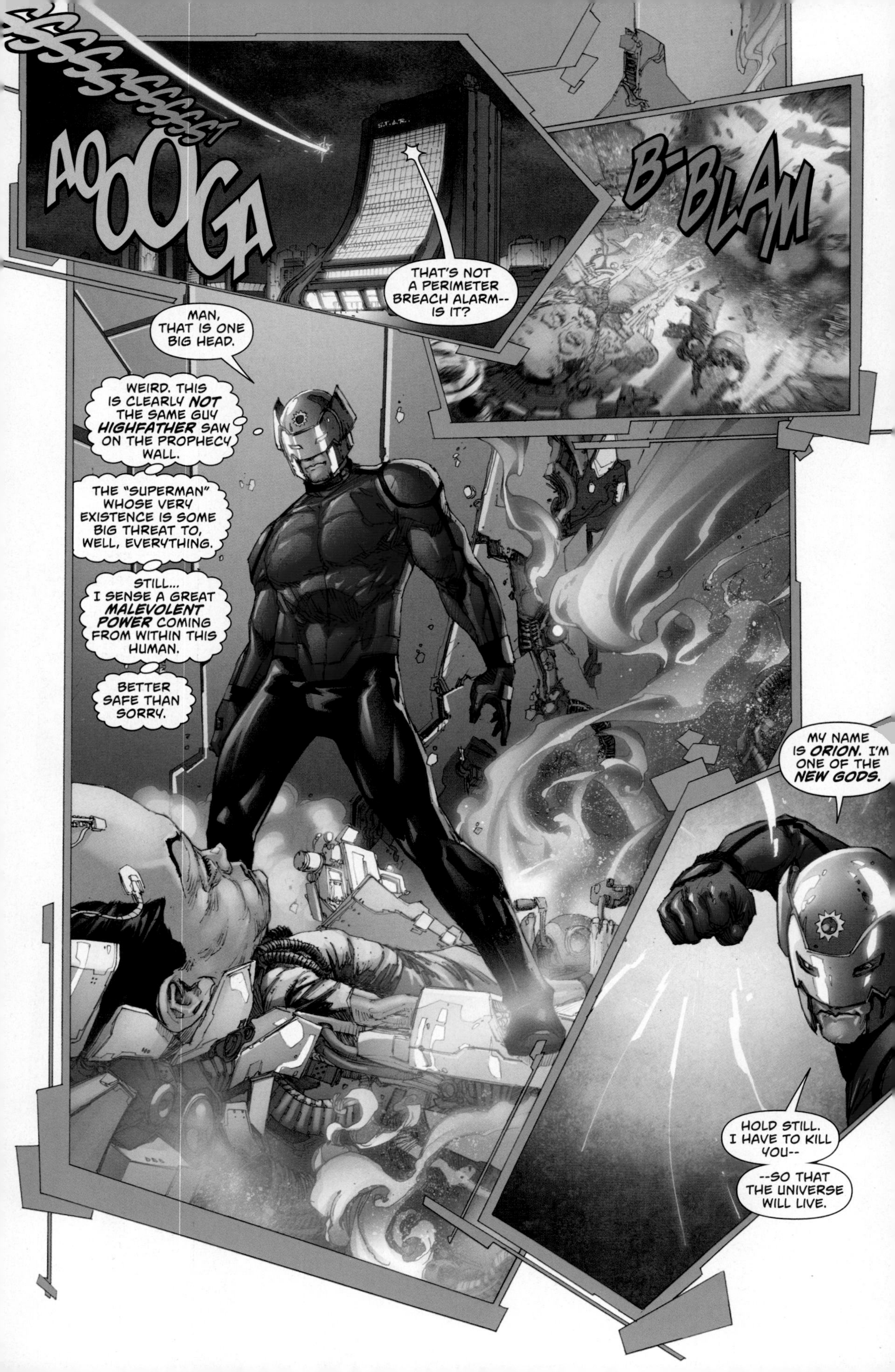
SSSSSSSSSST
AOOOGA
THAT'S NOT A PERIMETER BREACH ALARM-- IS IT?
B-BLAM
MAN, THAT IS ONE BIG HEAD.
WEIRD. THIS IS CLEARLY NOT THE SAME GUY HIGHFATHER SAW ON THE PROPHECY WALL.
THE "SUPERMAN" WHOSE VERY EXISTENCE IS SOME BIG THREAT TO, WELL, EVERYTHING.
STILL... I SENSE A GREAT MALEVOLENT POWER COMING FROM WITHIN THIS HUMAN.
BETTER SAFE THAN SORRY.
MY NAME IS ORION. I'M ONE OF THE NEW GODS.
HOLD STILL. I HAVE TO KILL YOU--
--SO THAT THE UNIVERSE WILL LIVE.

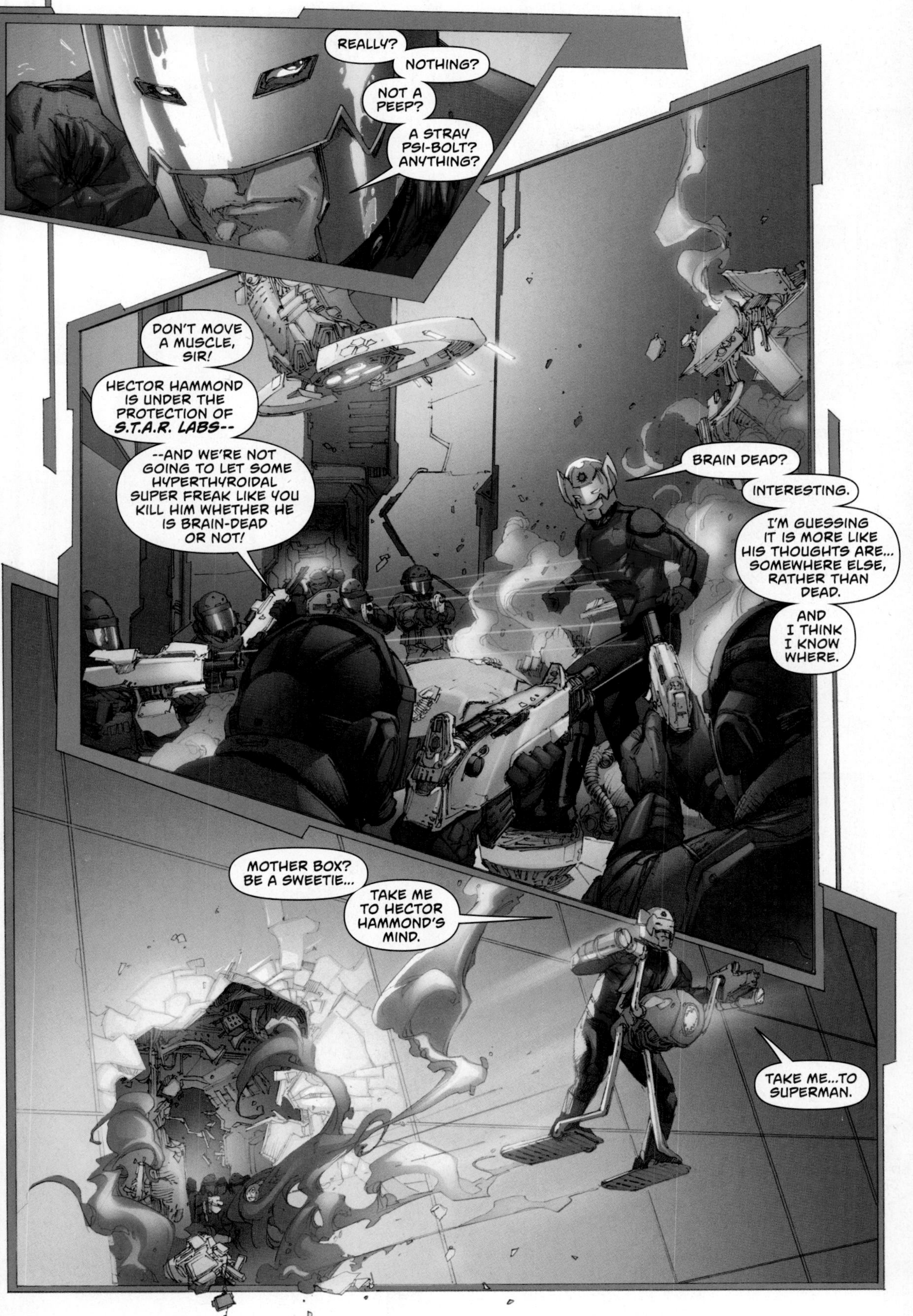
REALLY?
NOTHING?
NOT A PEEP?
A STRAY PSI-BOLT? ANYTHING?
DON'T MOVE A MUSCLE, SIR!
HECTOR HAMMOND IS UNDER THE PROTECTION OF S.T.A.R. LABS--
--AND WE'RE NOT GOING TO LET SOME HYPERTHYROIDAL SUPER FREAK LIKE YOU KILL HIM WHETHER HE IS BRAIN-DEAD OR NOT!
BRAIN DEAD?
INTERESTING.
I'M GUESSING IT IS MORE LIKE HIS THOUGHTS ARE... SOMEWHERE ELSE, RATHER THAN DEAD.
AND I THINK I KNOW WHERE.
MOTHER BOX? BE A SWEETIE...
TAKE ME TO HECTOR HAMMOND'S MIND.
TAKE ME...TO SUPERMAN.

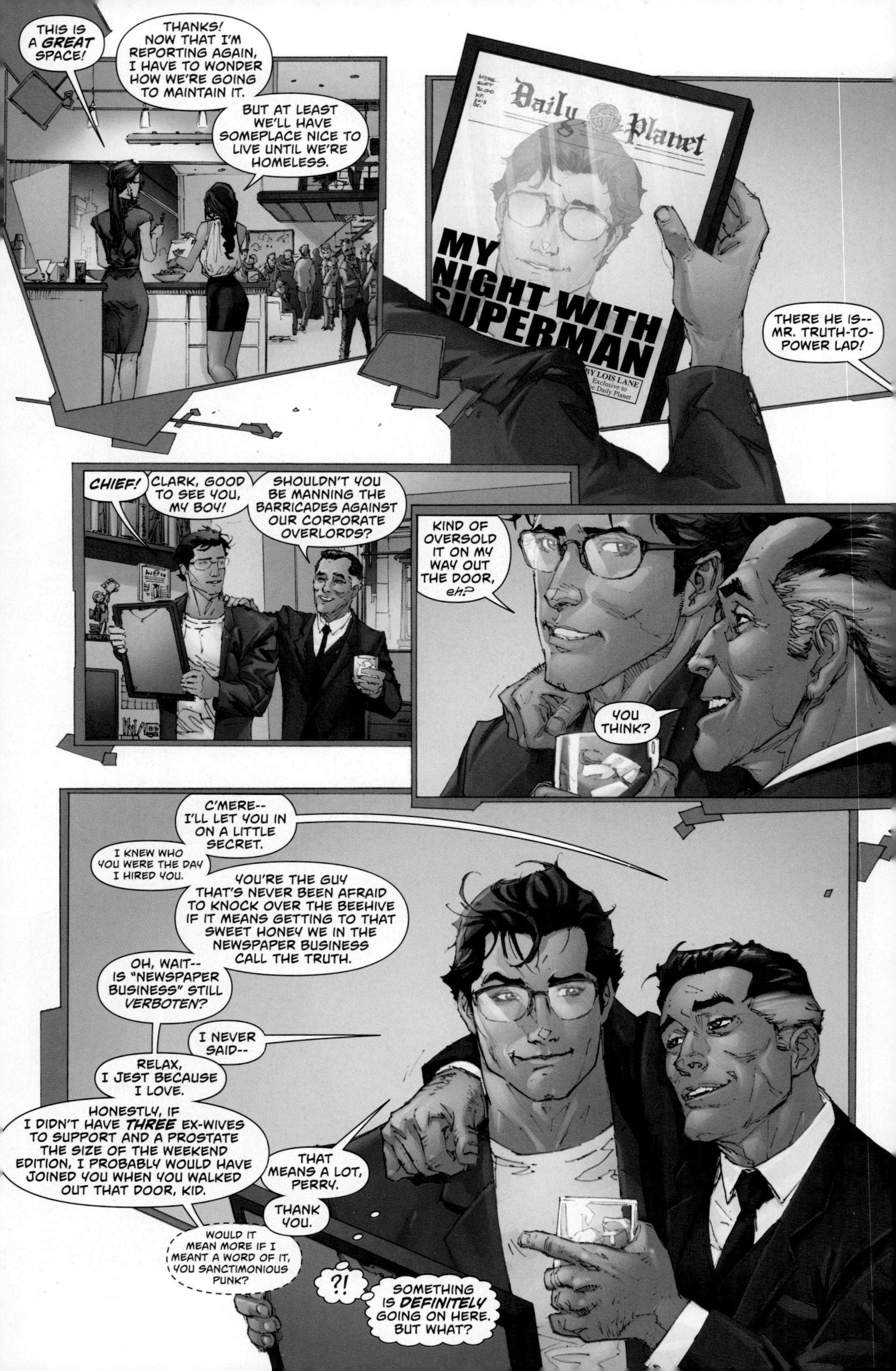

THIS IS A GREAT SPACE!
THANKS! NOW THAT I'M REPORTING AGAIN, I HAVE TO WONDER HOW WE'RE GOING TO MAINTAIN IT.
BUT AT LEAST WE'LL HAVE SOMEPLACE NICE TO LIVE UNTIL WE'RE HOMELESS.
Daily Planet
MY NIGHT WITH SUPERMAN
BY LOIS LANE
Exclusive to the Daily Planet
THERE HE IS-- MR. TRUTH-TO-POWER LAD!
CHIEF!
CLARK, GOOD TO SEE YOU, MY BOY!
SHOULDN'T YOU BE MANNING THE BARRICADES AGAINST OUR CORPORATE OVERLORDS?
KIND OF OVERSOLD IT ON MY WAY OUT THE DOOR, eh?
YOU THINK?
C'MERE-- I'LL LET YOU IN ON A LITTLE SECRET.
I KNEW WHO YOU WERE THE DAY I HIRED YOU.
YOU'RE THE GUY THAT'S NEVER BEEN AFRAID TO KNOCK OVER THE BEEHIVE IF IT MEANS GETTING TO THAT SWEET HONEY WE IN THE NEWSPAPER BUSINESS CALL THE TRUTH.
OH, WAIT-- IS "NEWSPAPER BUSINESS" STILL VERBOTEN?
I NEVER SAID--
RELAX, I JEST BECAUSE I LOVE.
HONESTLY, IF I DIDN'T HAVE THREE EX-WIVES TO SUPPORT AND A PROSTATE THE SIZE OF THE WEEKEND EDITION, I PROBABLY WOULD HAVE JOINED YOU WHEN YOU WALKED OUT THAT DOOR, KID.
THAT MEANS A LOT, PERRY.
THANK YOU.
WOULD IT MEAN MORE IF I MEANT A WORD OF IT, YOU SANCTIMONIOUS PUNK?
?!
SOMETHING IS DEFINITELY GOING ON HERE. BUT WHAT?

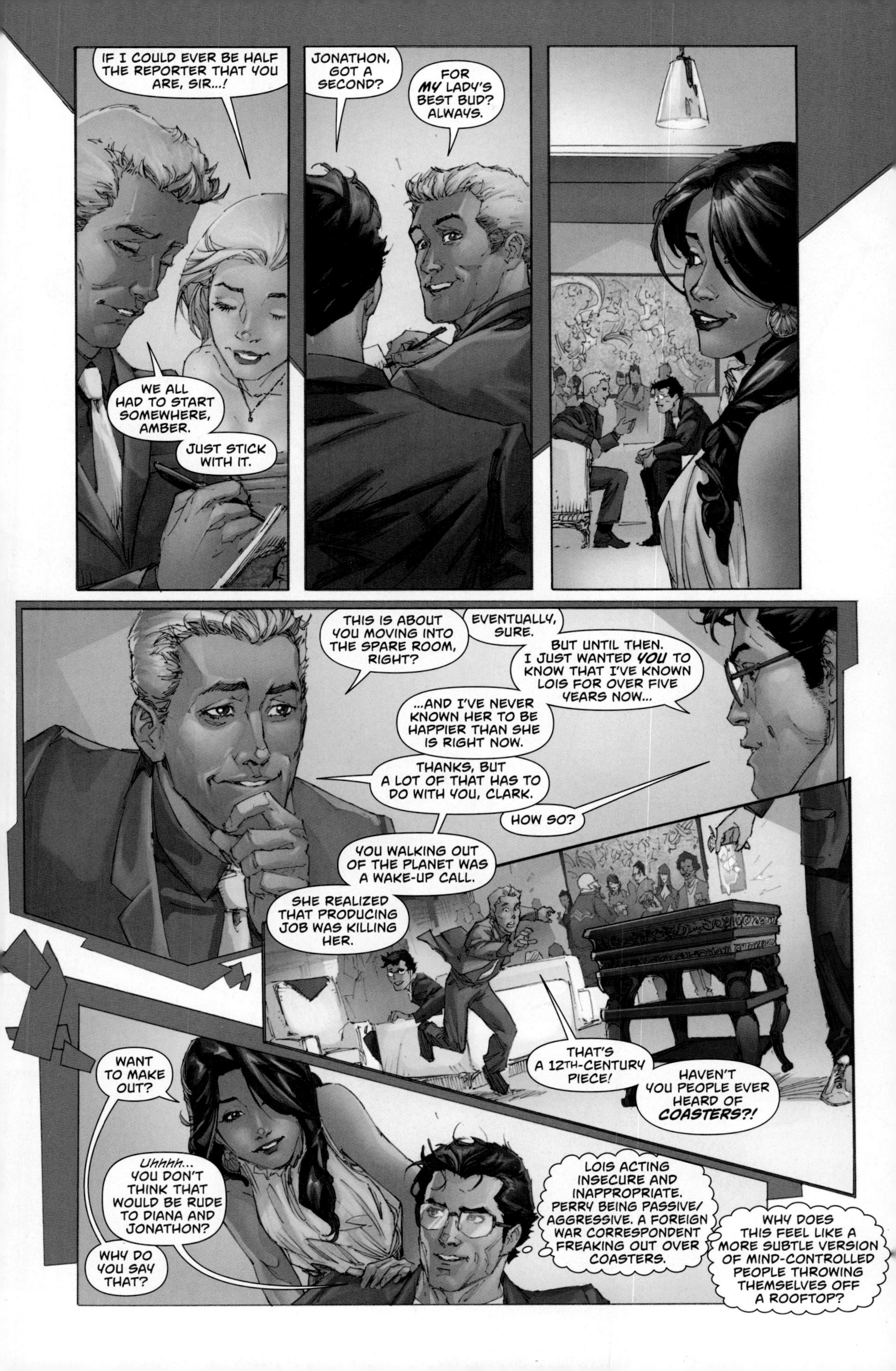
IF I COULD EVER BE HALF THE REPORTER THAT YOU ARE, SIR...!
WE ALL HAD TO START SOMEWHERE, AMBER.
JUST STICK WITH IT.
JONATHON, GOT A SECOND?
FOR MY LADY'S BEST BUD? ALWAYS.
THIS IS ABOUT YOU MOVING INTO THE SPARE ROOM, RIGHT?
EVENTUALLY, SURE.
BUT UNTIL THEN. I JUST WANTED YOU TO KNOW THAT I'VE KNOWN LOIS FOR OVER FIVE YEARS NOW...
...AND I'VE NEVER KNOWN HER TO BE HAPPIER THAN SHE IS RIGHT NOW.
THANKS, BUT A LOT OF THAT HAS TO DO WITH YOU, CLARK.
HOW SO?
YOU WALKING OUT OF THE PLANET WAS A WAKE-UP CALL.
SHE REALIZED THAT PRODUCING JOB WAS KILLING HER.
THAT'S A 12TH-CENTURY PIECE!
HAVEN'T YOU PEOPLE EVER HEARD OF COASTERS?!
WANT TO MAKE OUT?
Uhhhh... YOU DON'T THINK THAT WOULD BE RUDE TO DIANA AND JONATHON?
WHY DO YOU SAY THAT?
LOIS ACTING INSECURE AND INAPPROPRIATE. PERRY BEING PASSIVE/ AGGRESSIVE. A FOREIGN WAR CORRESPONDENT FREAKING OUT OVER COASTERS.
WHY DOES THIS FEEL LIKE A MORE SUBTLE VERSION OF MIND-CONTROLLED PEOPLE THROWING THEMSELVES OFF A ROOFTOP?

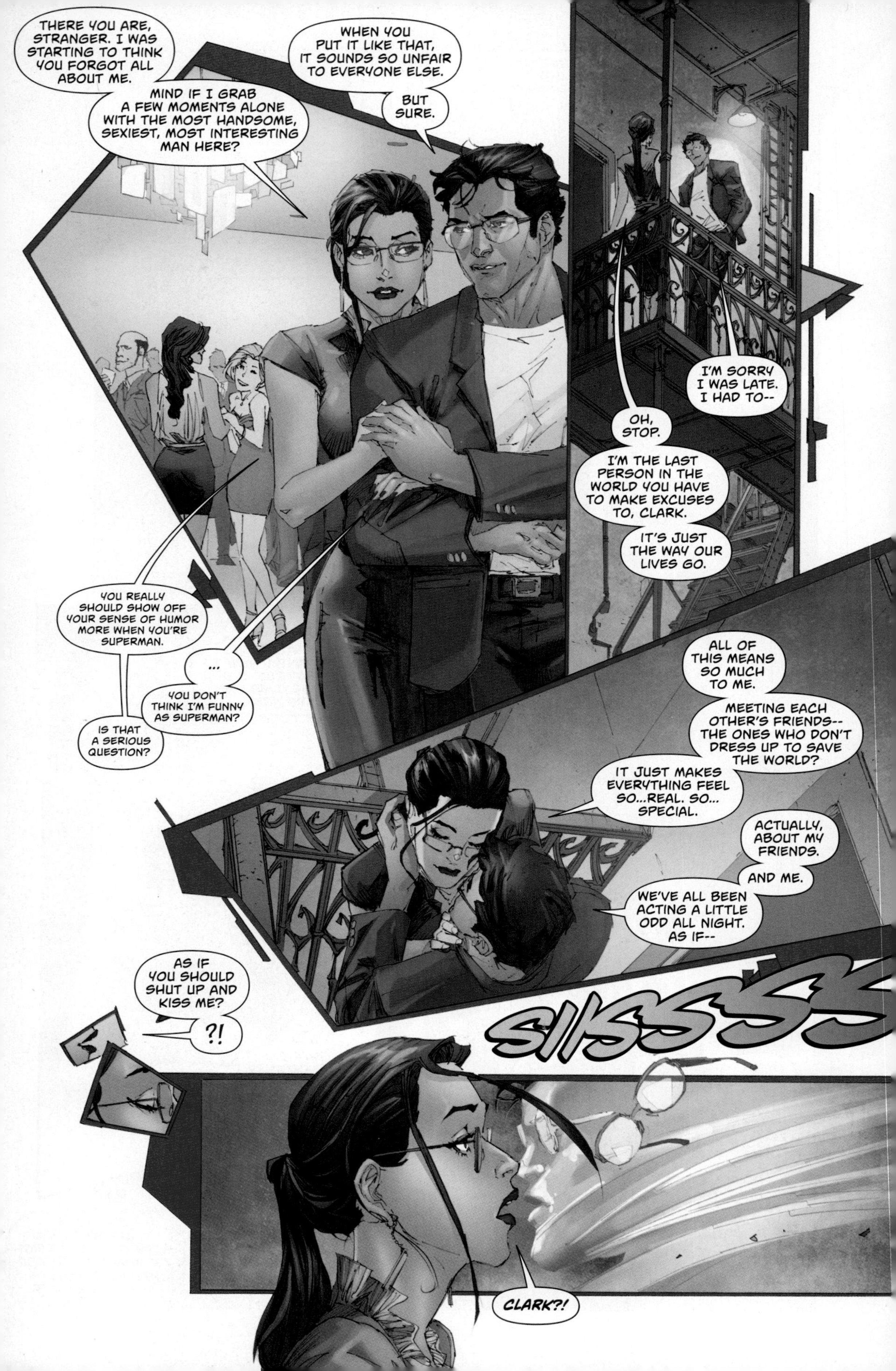
THERE YOU ARE, STRANGER. I WAS STARTING TO THINK YOU FORGOT ALL ABOUT ME.
MIND IF I GRAB A FEW MOMENTS ALONE WITH THE MOST HANDSOME, SEXIEST, MOST INTERESTING MAN HERE?
WHEN YOU PUT IT LIKE THAT, IT SOUNDS SO UNFAIR TO EVERYONE ELSE.
BUT SURE.
YOU REALLY SHOULD SHOW OFF YOUR SENSE OF HUMOR MORE WHEN YOU'RE SUPERMAN.
...
YOU DON'T THINK I'M FUNNY AS SUPERMAN?
IS THAT A SERIOUS QUESTION?
I'M SORRY I WAS LATE. I HAD TO--
OH, STOP.
I'M THE LAST PERSON IN THE WORLD YOU HAVE TO MAKE EXCUSES TO, CLARK.
IT'S JUST THE WAY OUR LIVES GO.
ALL OF THIS MEANS SO MUCH TO ME.
MEETING EACH OTHER'S FRIENDS-- THE ONES WHO DON'T DRESS UP TO SAVE THE WORLD?
IT JUST MAKES EVERYTHING FEEL SO...REAL. SO... SPECIAL.
ACTUALLY, ABOUT MY FRIENDS.
AND ME.
WE'VE ALL BEEN ACTING A LITTLE ODD ALL NIGHT. AS IF--
AS IF YOU SHOULD SHUT UP AND KISS ME?
?!
SIISSSS
CLARK?!

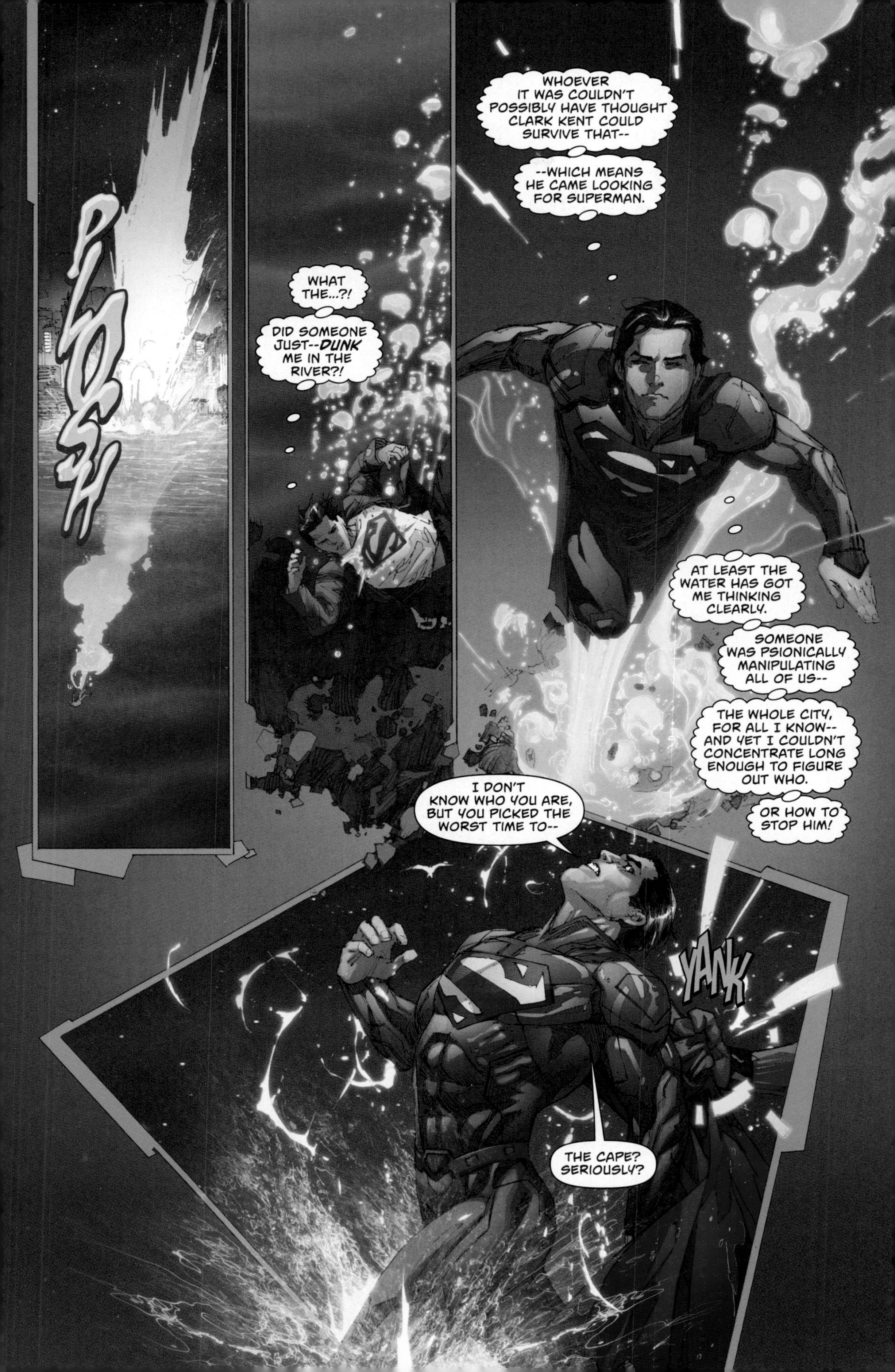
PLOOSH
WHAT THE...?!
DID SOMEONE JUST--DUNK ME IN THE RIVER?!
WHOEVER IT WAS COULDN'T POSSIBLY HAVE THOUGHT CLARK KENT COULD SURVIVE THAT--
--WHICH MEANS HE CAME LOOKING FOR SUPERMAN.
AT LEAST THE WATER HAS GOT ME THINKING CLEARLY.
SOMEONE WAS PSIONICALLY MANIPULATING ALL OF US--
THE WHOLE CITY, FOR ALL I KNOW--AND YET I COULDN'T CONCENTRATE LONG ENOUGH TO FIGURE OUT WHO.
OR HOW TO STOP HIM!
I DON'T KNOW WHO YOU ARE, BUT YOU PICKED THE WORST TIME TO--
YANK
THE CAPE? SERIOUSLY?

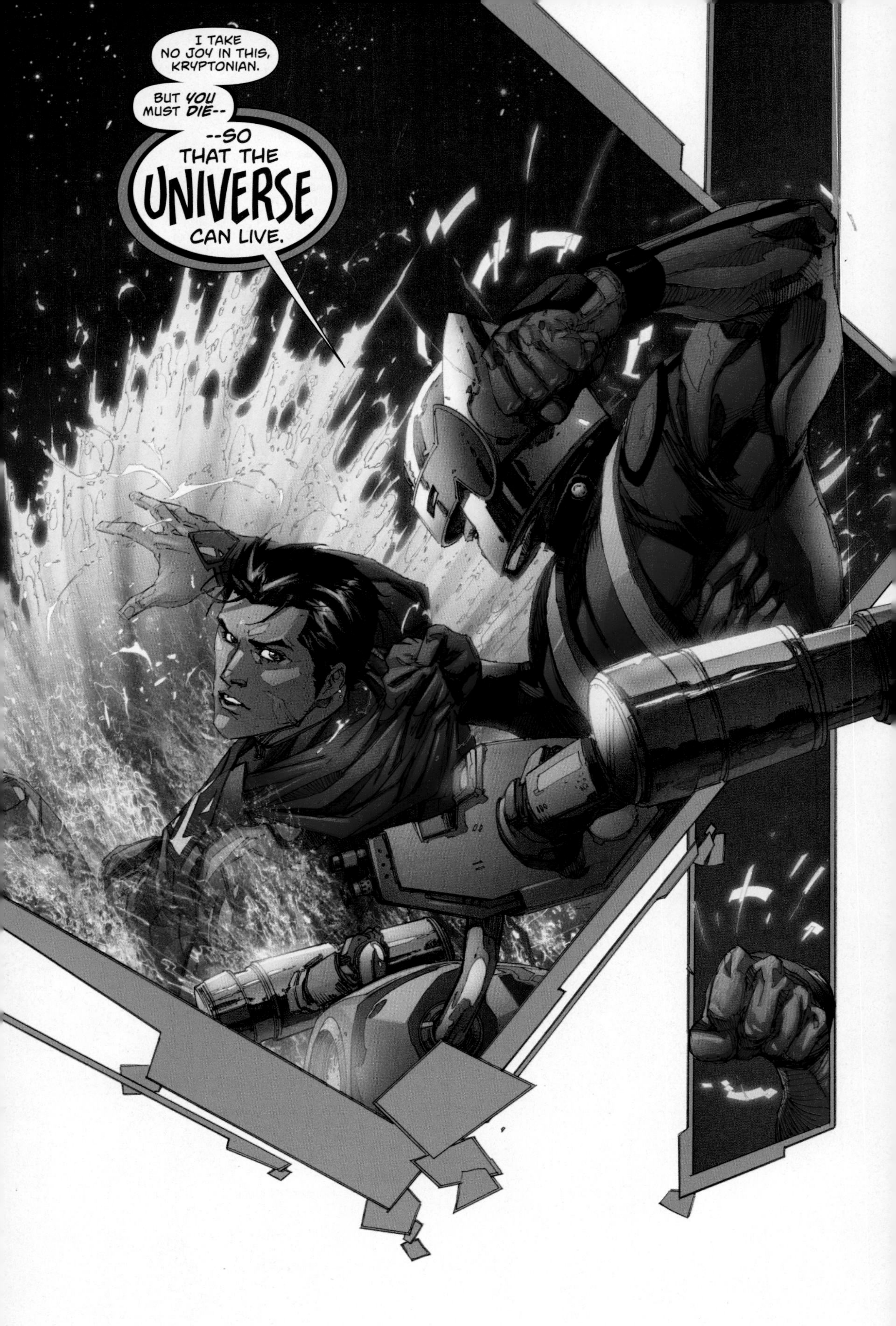
I TAKE NO JOY IN THIS, KRYPTONIAN.
BUT YOU MUST DIE--
--SO THAT THE UNIVERSE CAN LIVE.

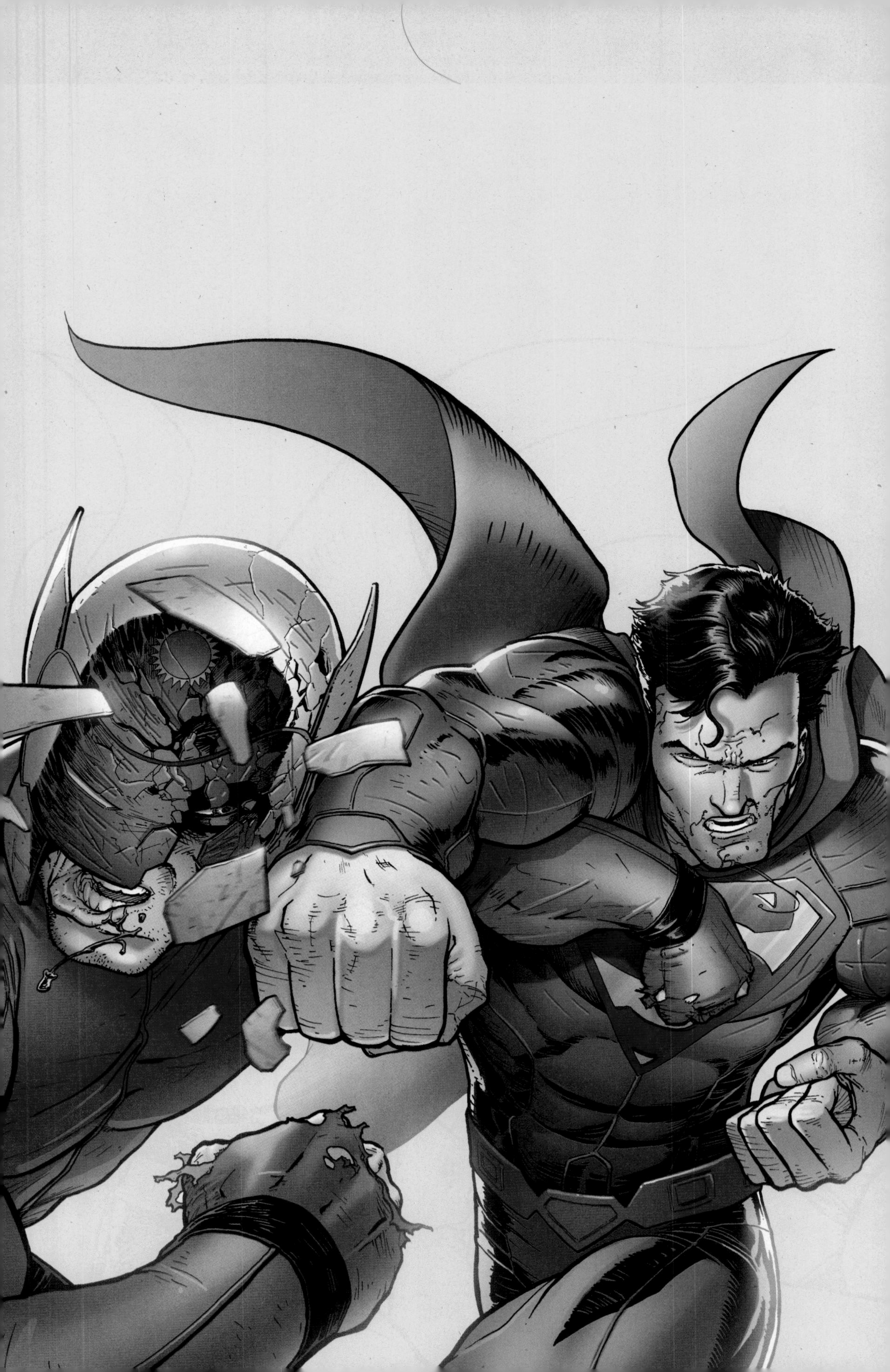

WHAM!

SCOTT LOBDELL writer **AARON KUDER** artist cover art by **AARON KUDER & QUINTANA**

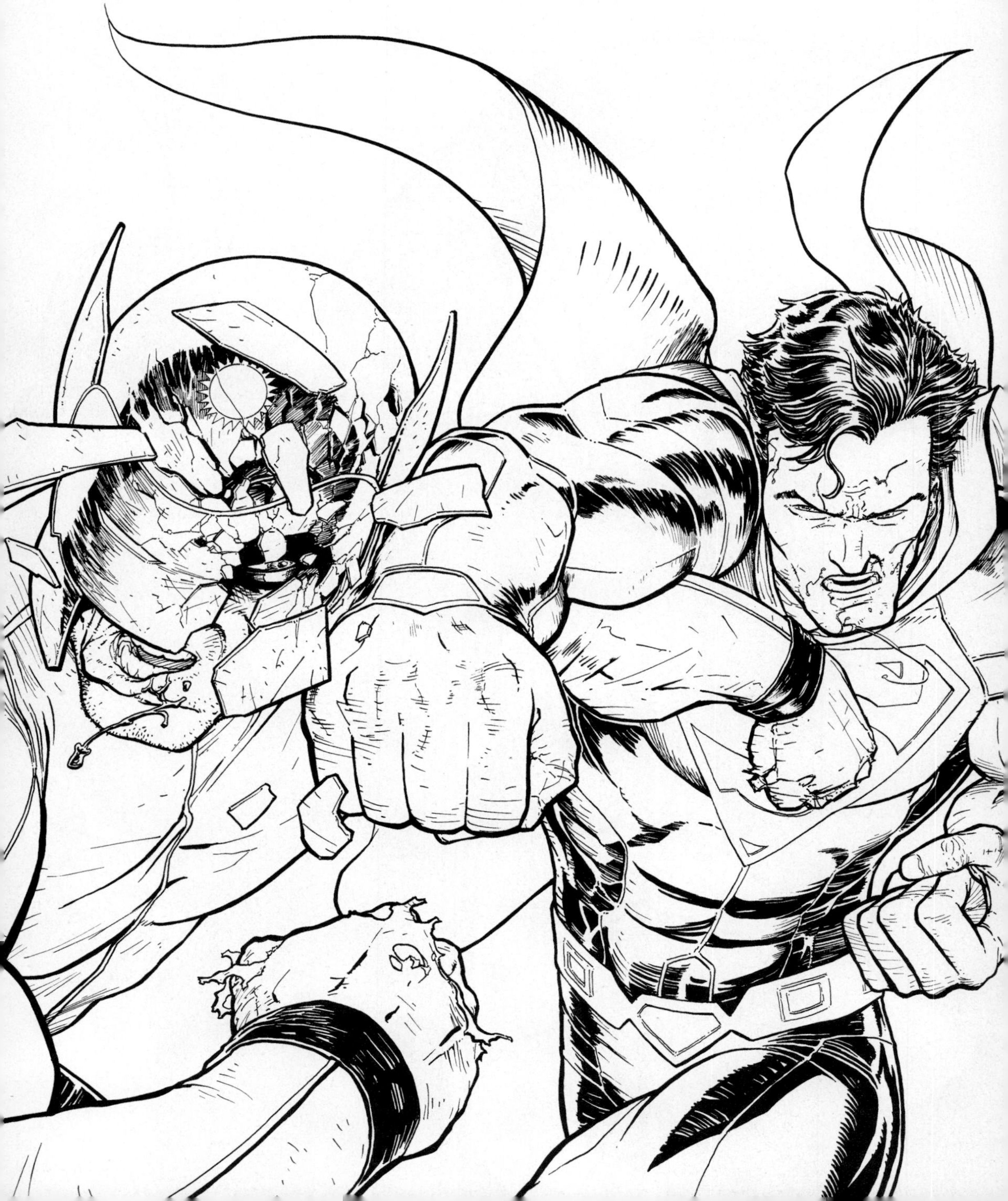

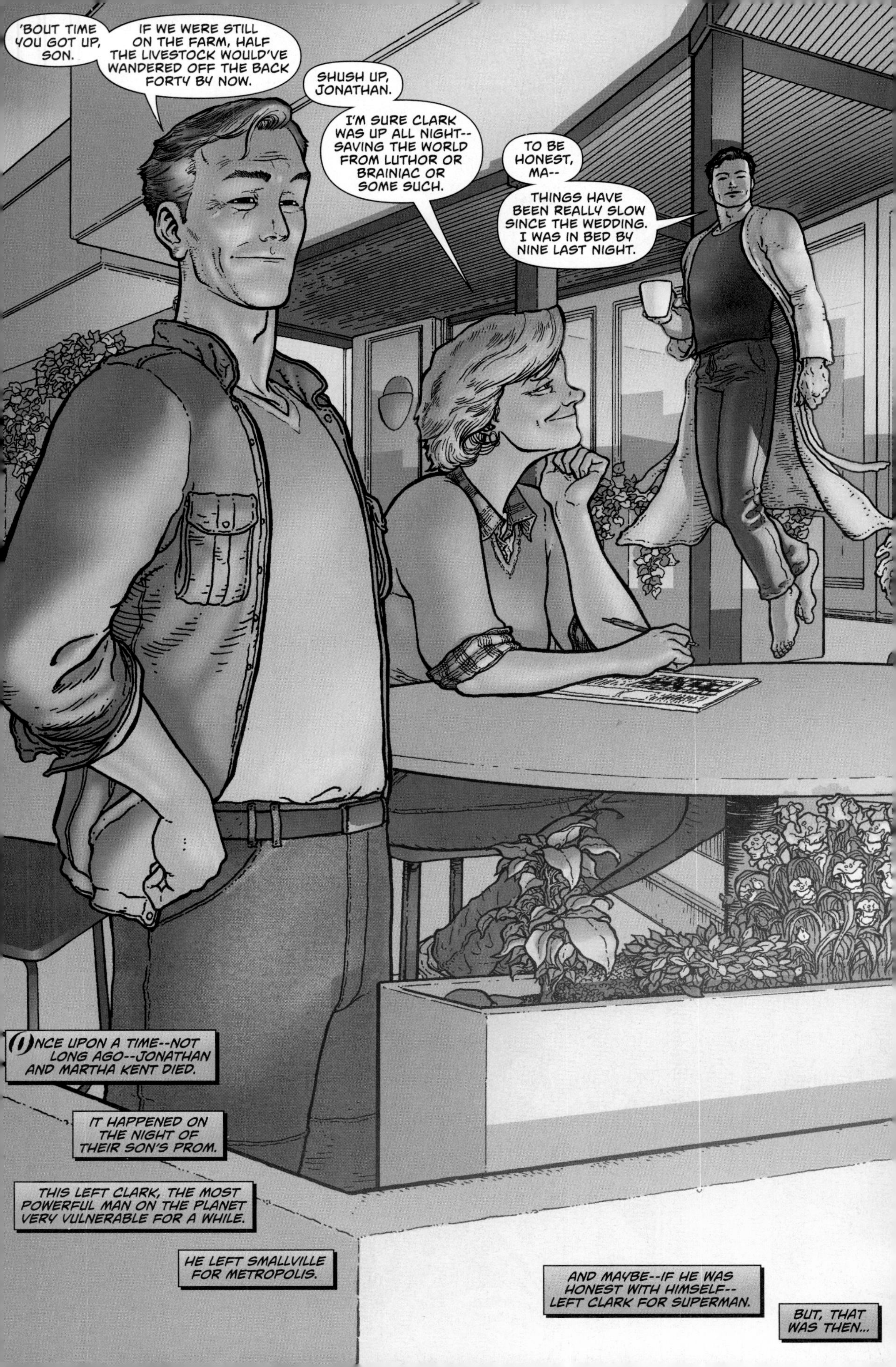
'BOUT TIME YOU GOT UP, SON.
IF WE WERE STILL ON THE FARM, HALF THE LIVESTOCK WOULD'VE WANDERED OFF THE BACK FORTY BY NOW.
SHUSH UP, JONATHAN.
I'M SURE CLARK WAS UP ALL NIGHT--SAVING THE WORLD FROM LUTHOR OR BRAINIAC OR SOME SUCH.
TO BE HONEST, MA--
THINGS HAVE BEEN REALLY SLOW SINCE THE WEDDING. I WAS IN BED BY NINE LAST NIGHT.
ONCE UPON A TIME--NOT LONG AGO--JONATHAN AND MARTHA KENT DIED.
IT HAPPENED ON THE NIGHT OF THEIR SON'S PROM.
THIS LEFT CLARK, THE MOST POWERFUL MAN ON THE PLANET VERY VULNERABLE FOR A WHILE.
HE LEFT SMALLVILLE FOR METROPOLIS.
AND MAYBE--IF HE WAS HONEST WITH HIMSELF--LEFT CLARK FOR SUPERMAN.
BUT, THAT WAS THEN...

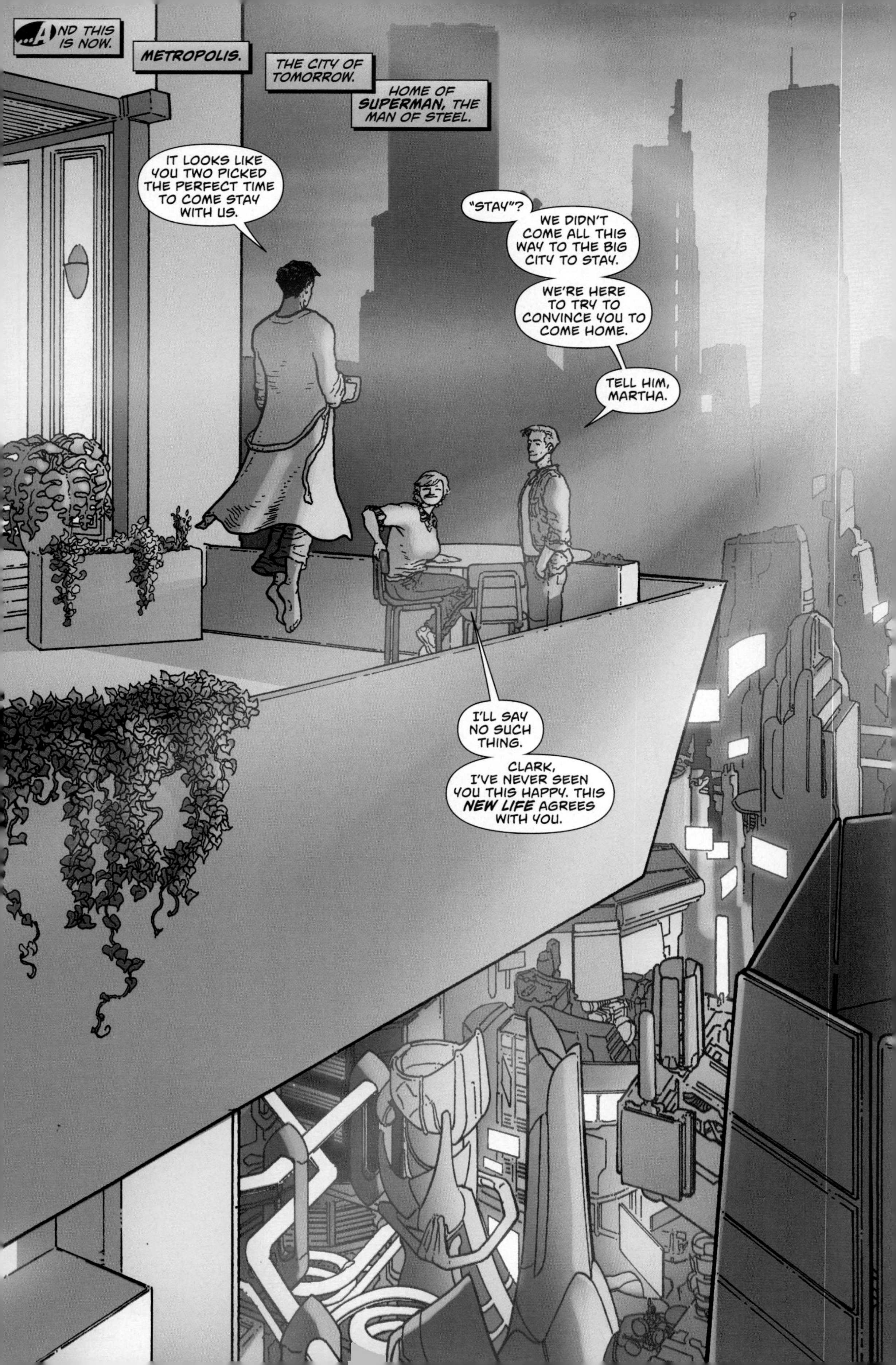
...AND THIS IS NOW.
METROPOLIS.
THE CITY OF TOMORROW.
HOME OF SUPERMAN, THE MAN OF STEEL.
IT LOOKS LIKE YOU TWO PICKED THE PERFECT TIME TO COME STAY WITH US.
"STAY"?
WE DIDN'T COME ALL THIS WAY TO THE BIG CITY TO STAY.
WE'RE HERE TO TRY TO CONVINCE YOU TO COME HOME.
TELL HIM, MARTHA.
I'LL SAY NO SUCH THING.
CLARK, I'VE NEVER SEEN YOU THIS HAPPY. THIS NEW LIFE AGREES WITH YOU.

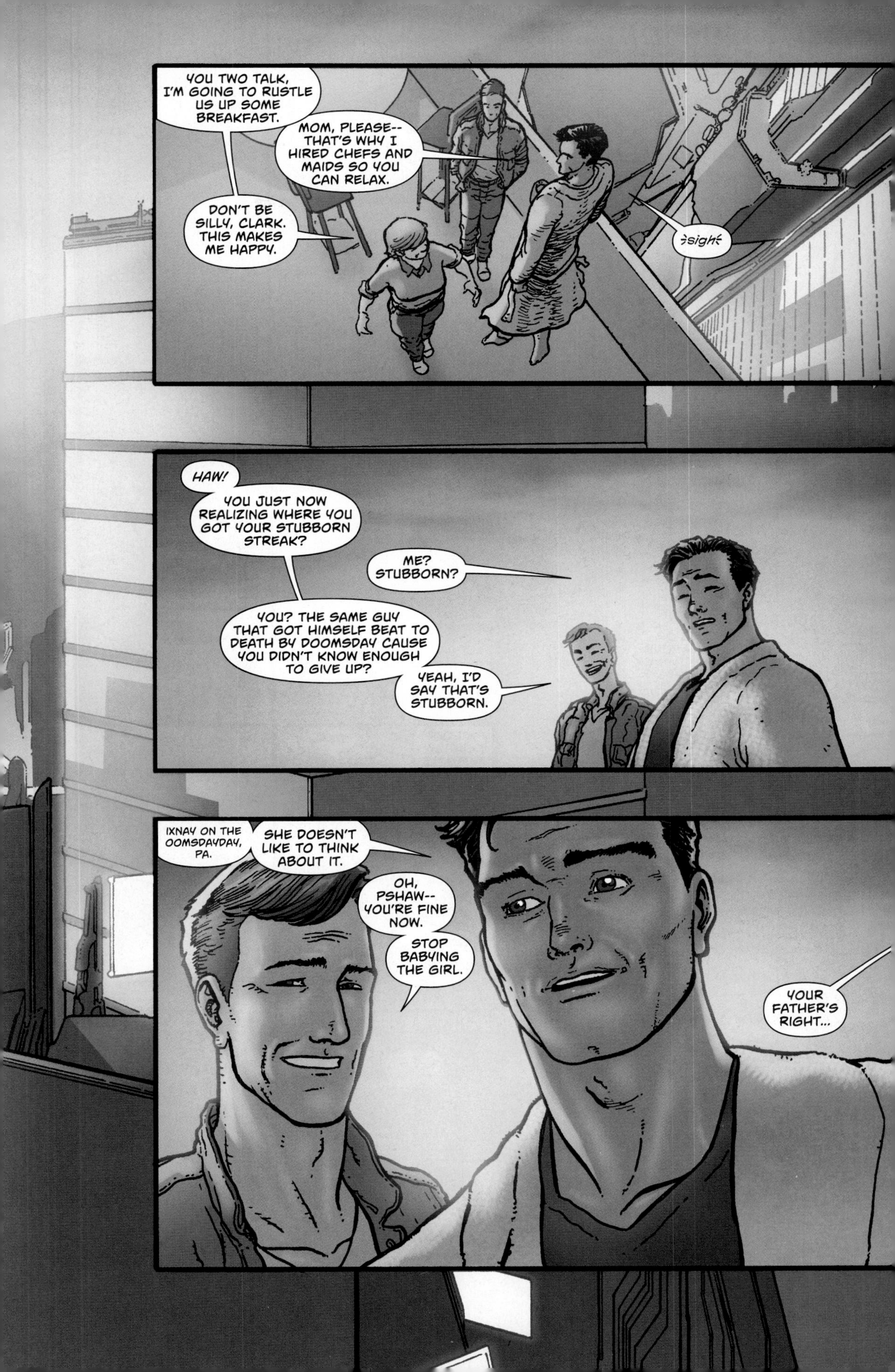
YOU TWO TALK, I'M GOING TO RUSTLE US UP SOME BREAKFAST.
MOM, PLEASE-- THAT'S WHY I HIRED CHEFS AND MAIDS SO YOU CAN RELAX.
DON'T BE SILLY, CLARK. THIS MAKES ME HAPPY.
sigh
HAW!
YOU JUST NOW REALIZING WHERE YOU GOT YOUR STUBBORN STREAK?
ME? STUBBORN?
YOU? THE SAME GUY THAT GOT HIMSELF BEAT TO DEATH BY DOOMSDAY CAUSE YOU DIDN'T KNOW ENOUGH TO GIVE UP?
YEAH, I'D SAY THAT'S STUBBORN.
IXNAY ON THE OOMSDAYDAY, PA.
SHE DOESN'T LIKE TO THINK ABOUT IT.
OH, PSHAW-- YOU'RE FINE NOW.
STOP BABYING THE GIRL.
YOUR FATHER'S RIGHT...

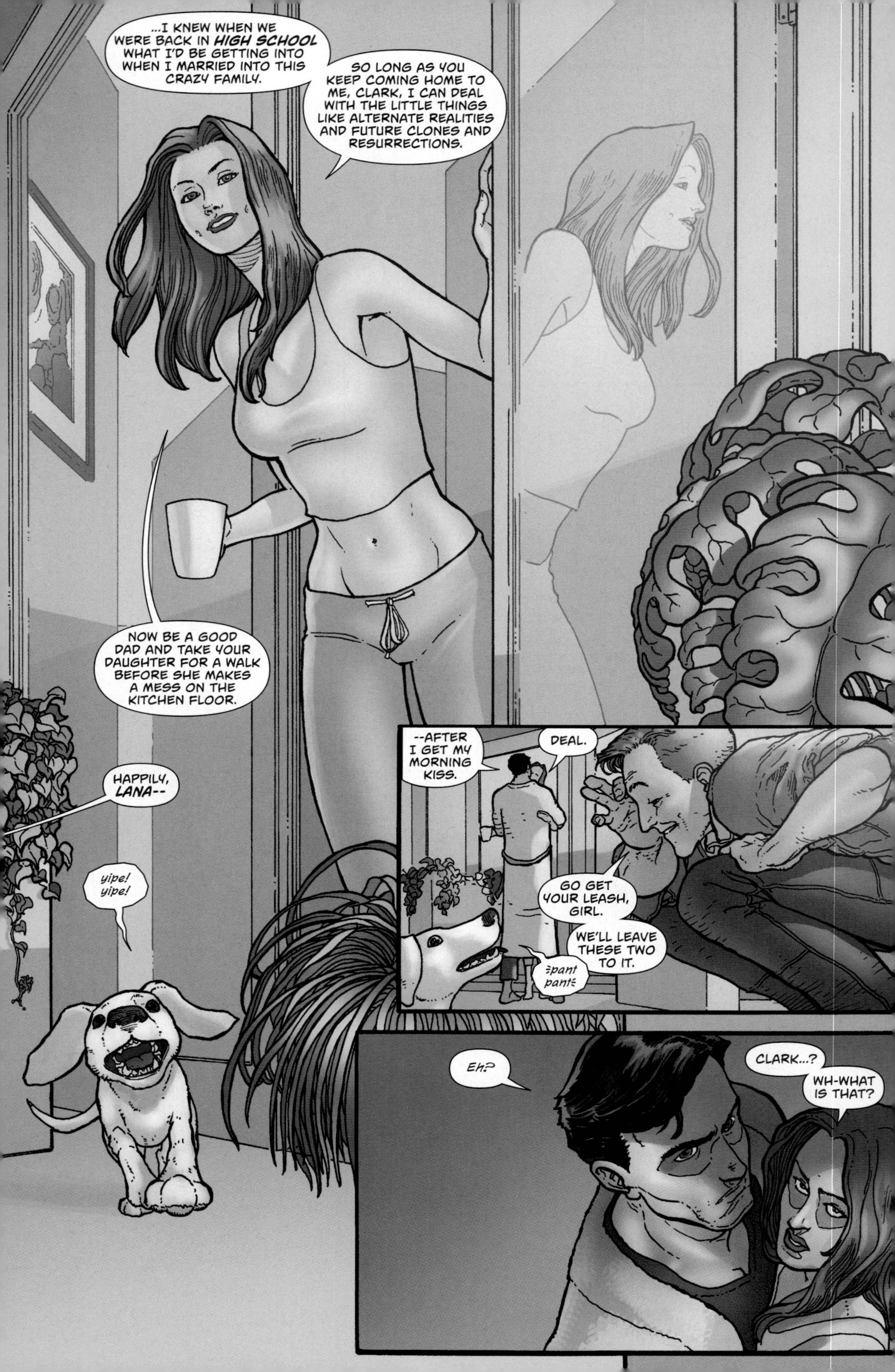
...I KNEW WHEN WE WERE BACK IN HIGH SCHOOL WHAT I'D BE GETTING INTO WHEN I MARRIED INTO THIS CRAZY FAMILY.
SO LONG AS YOU KEEP COMING HOME TO ME, CLARK, I CAN DEAL WITH THE LITTLE THINGS LIKE ALTERNATE REALITIES AND FUTURE CLONES AND RESURRECTIONS.
NOW BE A GOOD DAD AND TAKE YOUR DAUGHTER FOR A WALK BEFORE SHE MAKES A MESS ON THE KITCHEN FLOOR.
HAPPILY, LANA--
yipe! yipe!
--AFTER I GET MY MORNING KISS.
DEAL.
GO GET YOUR LEASH, GIRL.
WE'LL LEAVE THESE TWO TO IT.
pant pant
Eh?
CLARK...?
WH-WHAT IS THAT?

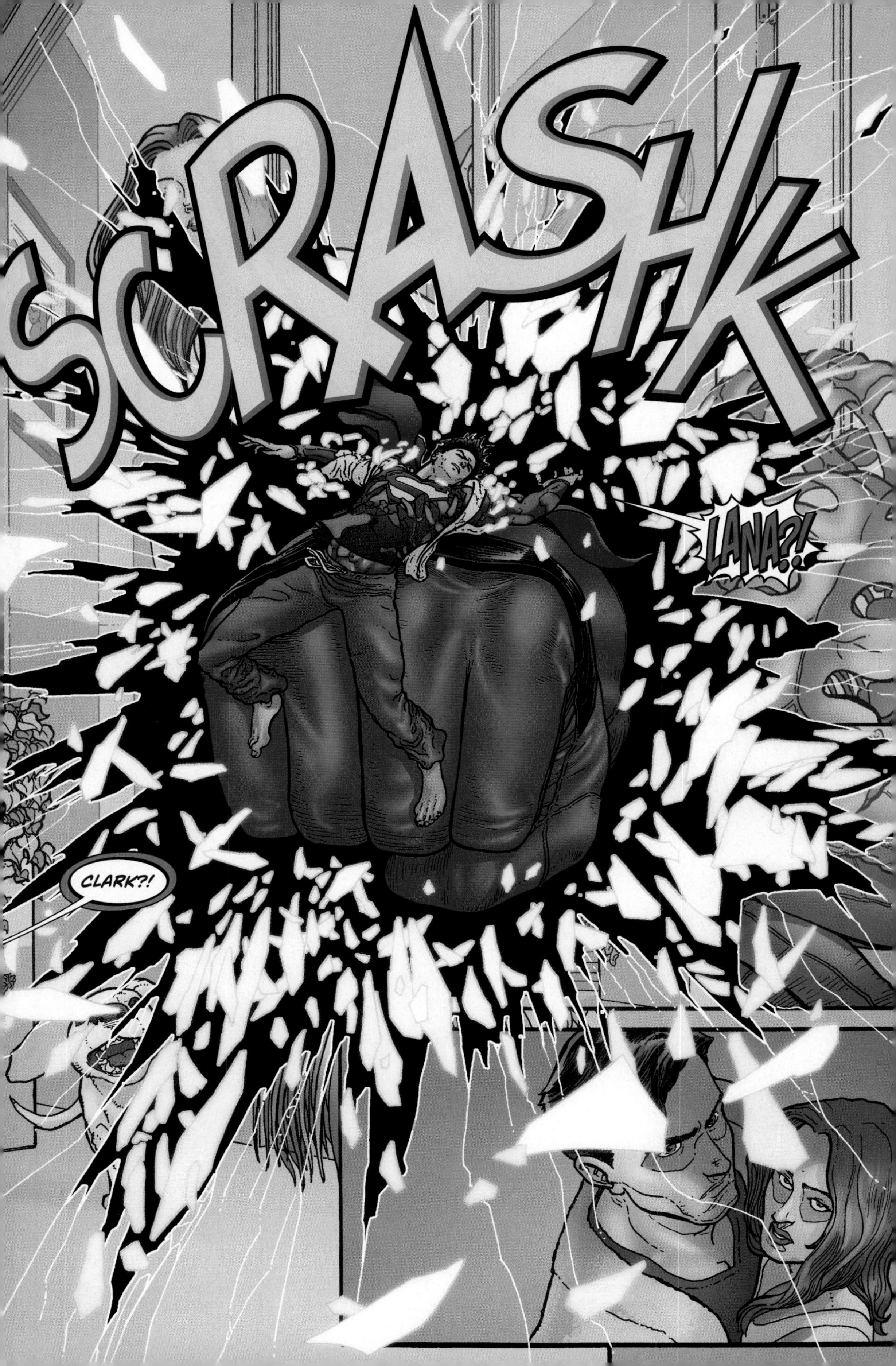
SCRASHK
LANA?!
CLARK?!

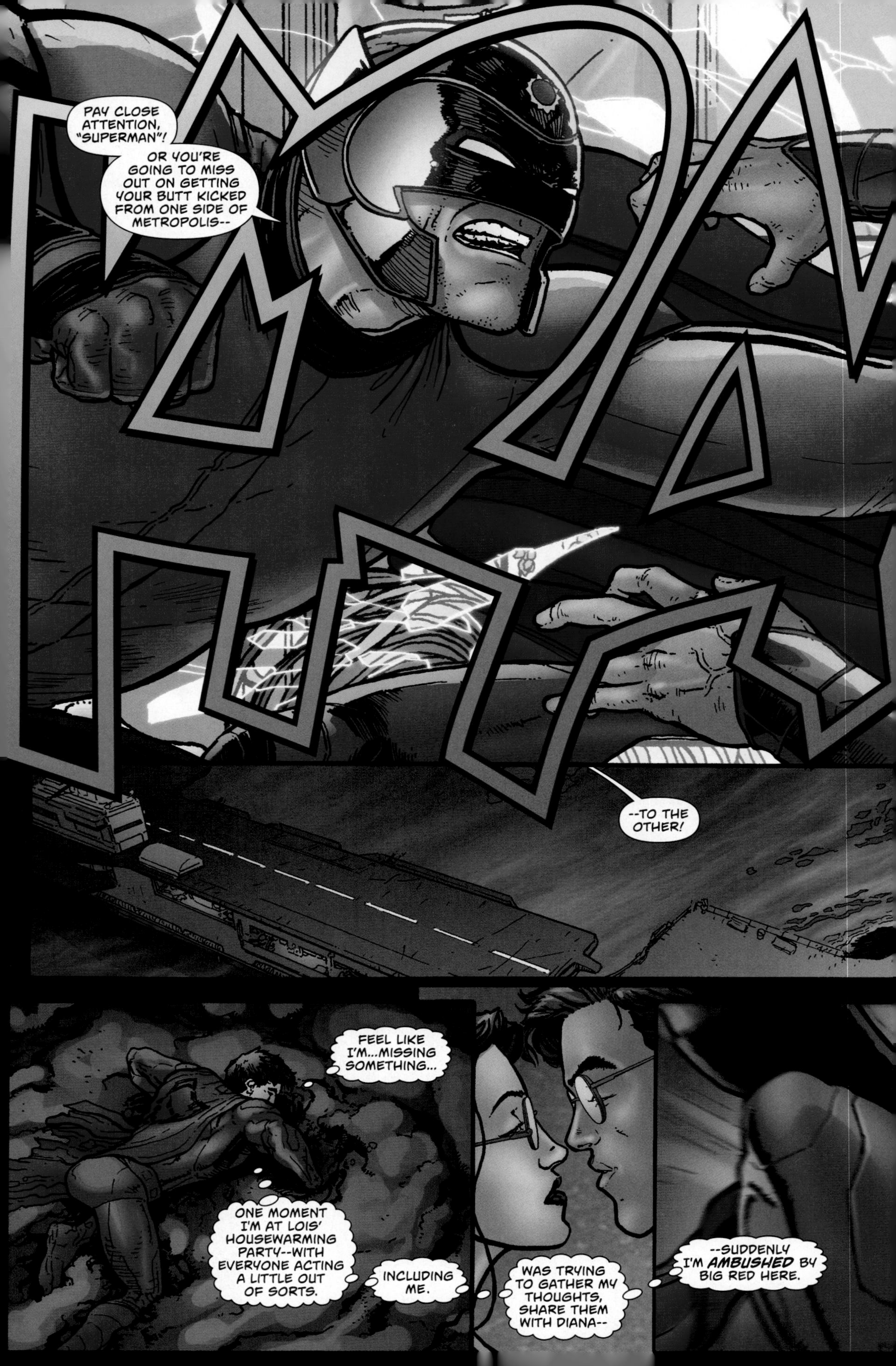
PAY CLOSE ATTENTION, "SUPERMAN"!
OR YOU'RE GOING TO MISS OUT ON GETTING YOUR BUTT KICKED FROM ONE SIDE OF METROPOLIS--
--TO THE OTHER!
FEEL LIKE I'M...MISSING SOMETHING...
ONE MOMENT I'M AT LOIS' HOUSEWARMING PARTY--WITH EVERYONE ACTING A LITTLE OUT OF SORTS.
INCLUDING ME.
WAS TRYING TO GATHER MY THOUGHTS, SHARE THEM WITH DIANA--
--SUDDENLY I'M AMBUSHED BY BIG RED HERE.

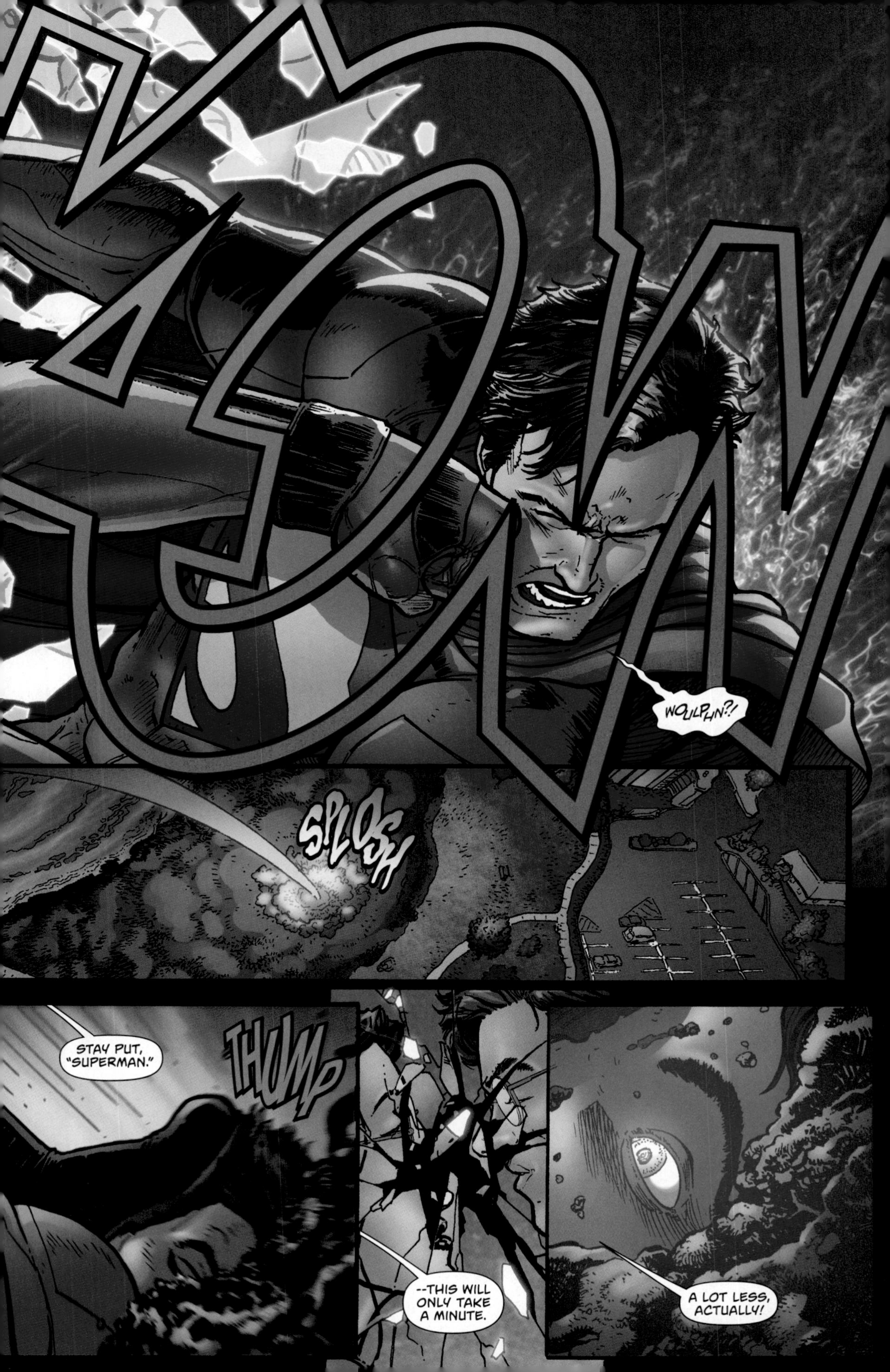
WOULPHN?!
SPLOOSH
STAY PUT, "SUPERMAN."
THUMP
--THIS WILL ONLY TAKE A MINUTE.
A LOT LESS, ACTUALLY!

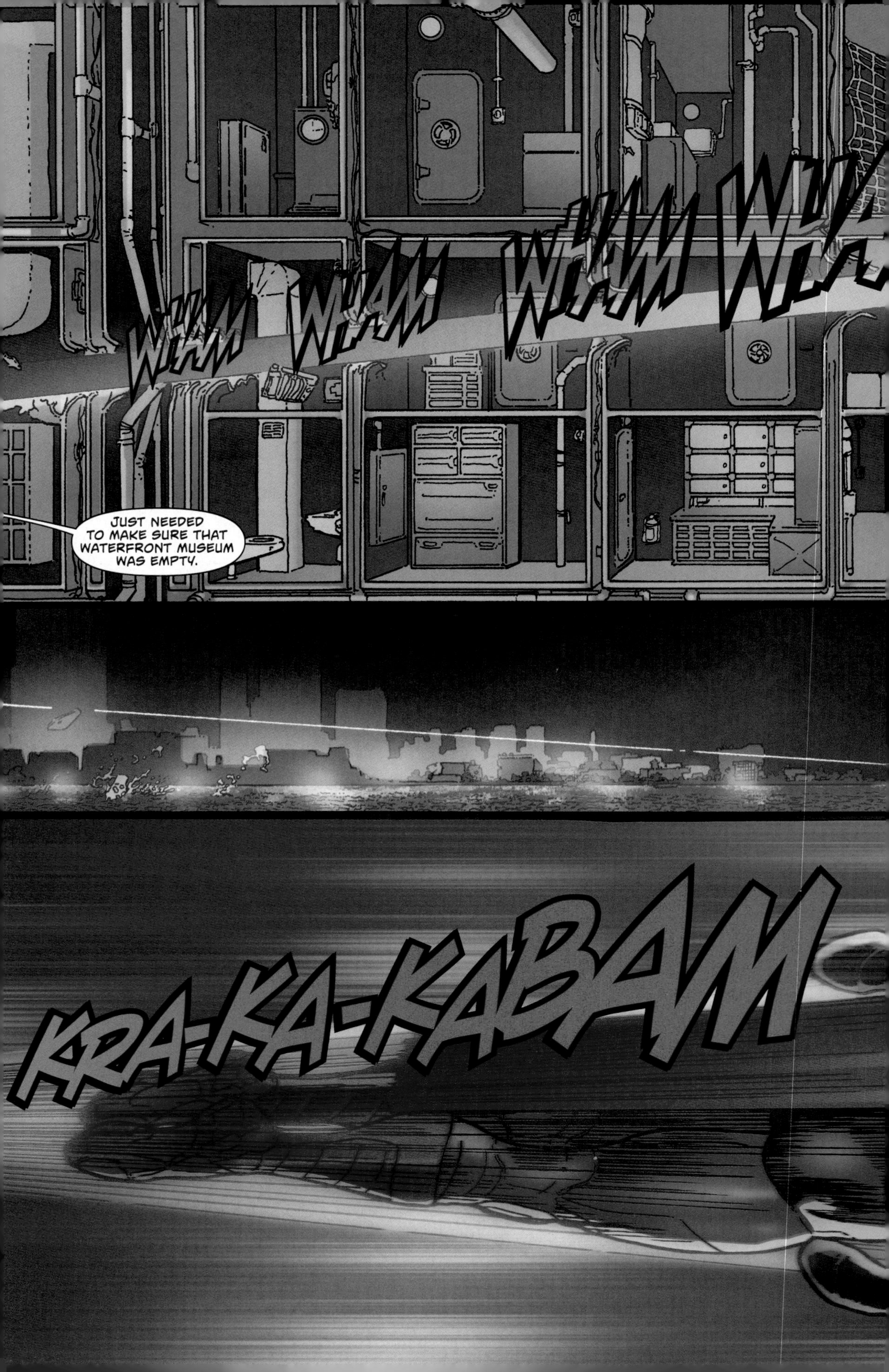
WHAM WHAM WHAM WHA
JUST NEEDED TO MAKE SURE THAT WATERFRONT MUSEUM WAS EMPTY.
KRA-KA-KABAM

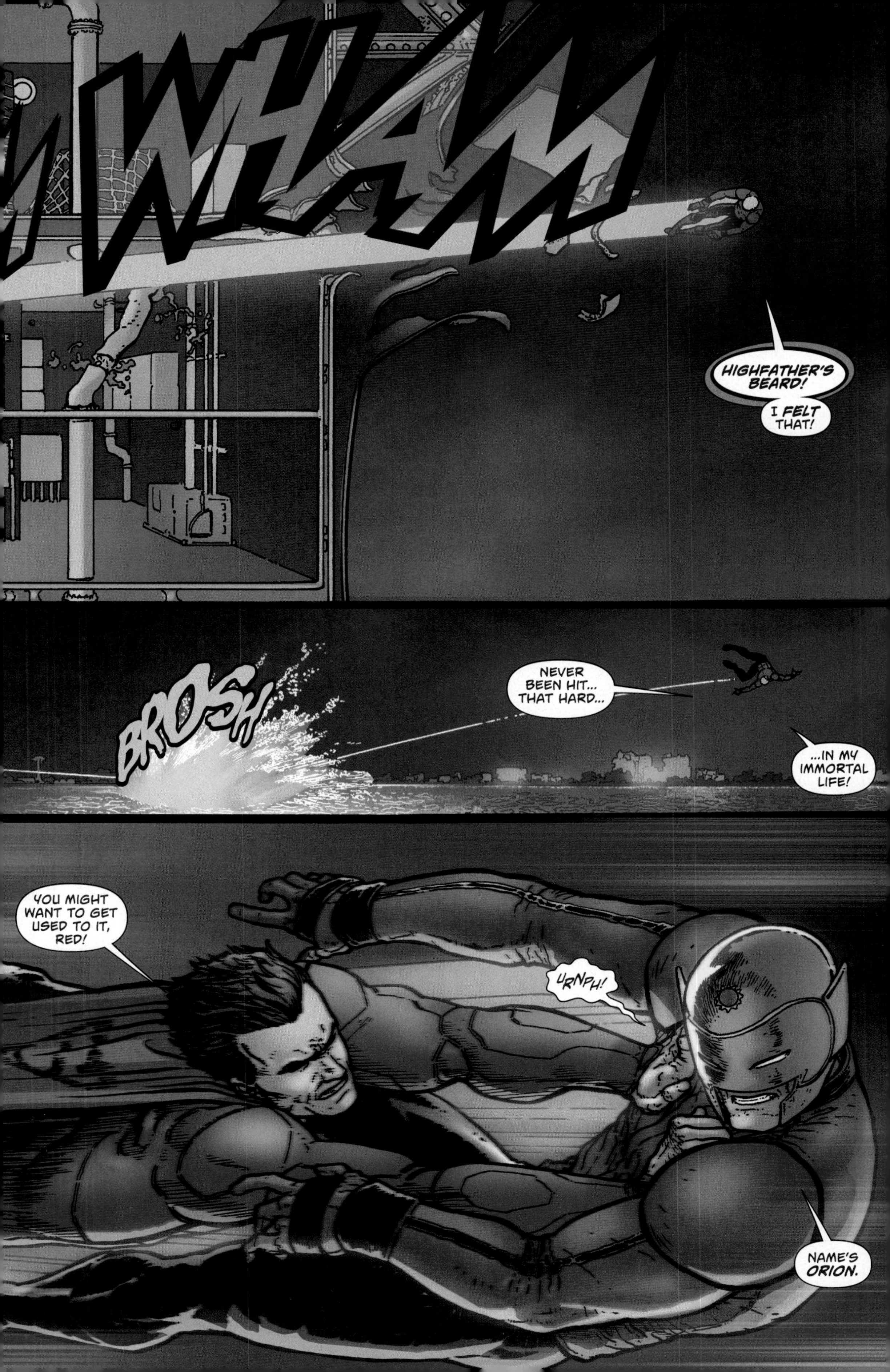
WHAM
HIGHFATHER'S BEARD!
I FELT THAT!
BROSH
NEVER BEEN HIT... THAT HARD...
...IN MY IMMORTAL LIFE!
YOU MIGHT WANT TO GET USED TO IT, RED!
URNPH!
NAME'S ORION.

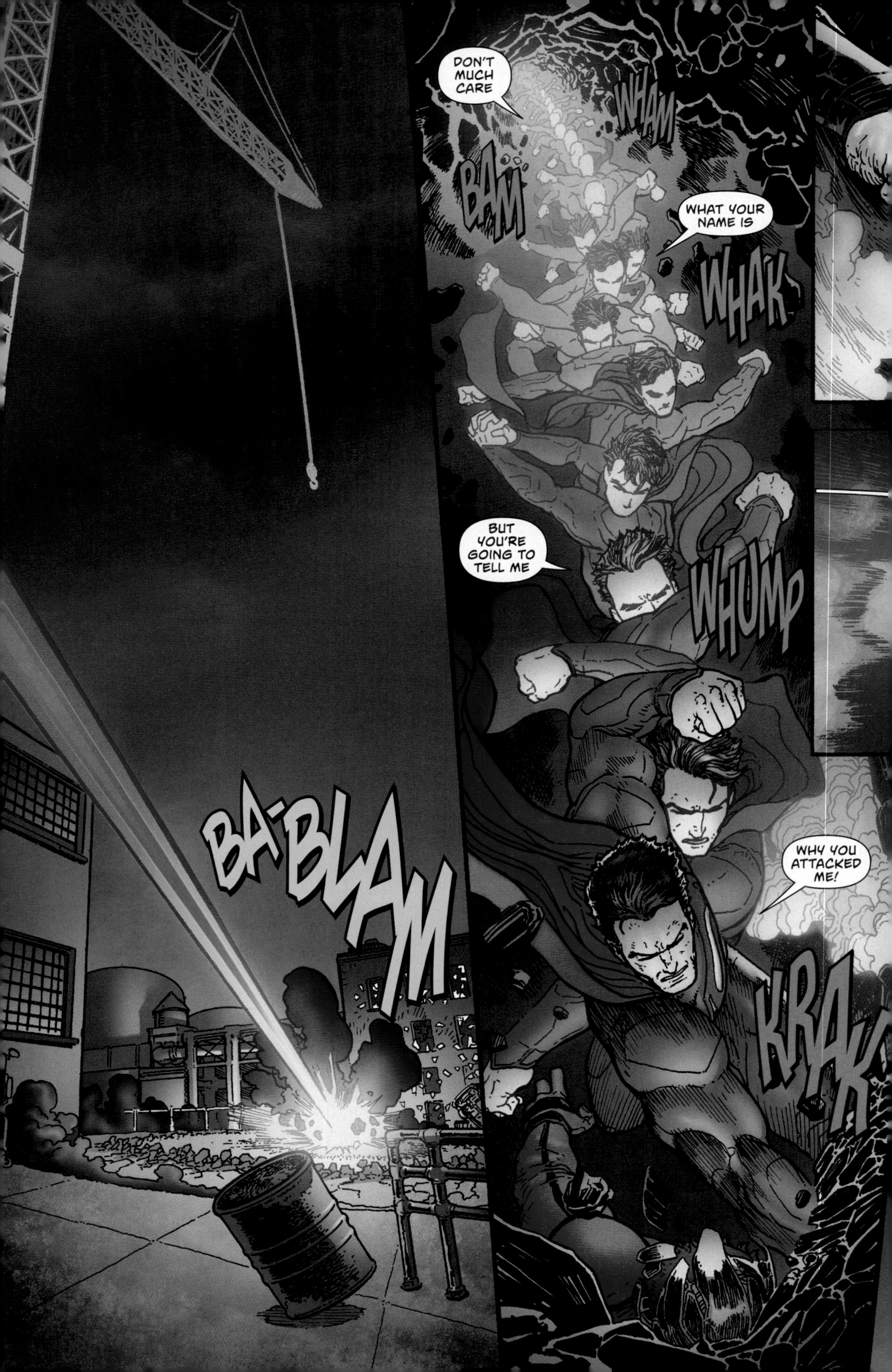
BA-BLAM
DON'T MUCH CARE
WHAM
BAM
WHAT YOUR NAME IS
WHAK
BUT YOU'RE GOING TO TELL ME
WHUMP
WHY YOU ATTACKED ME!
KRAK

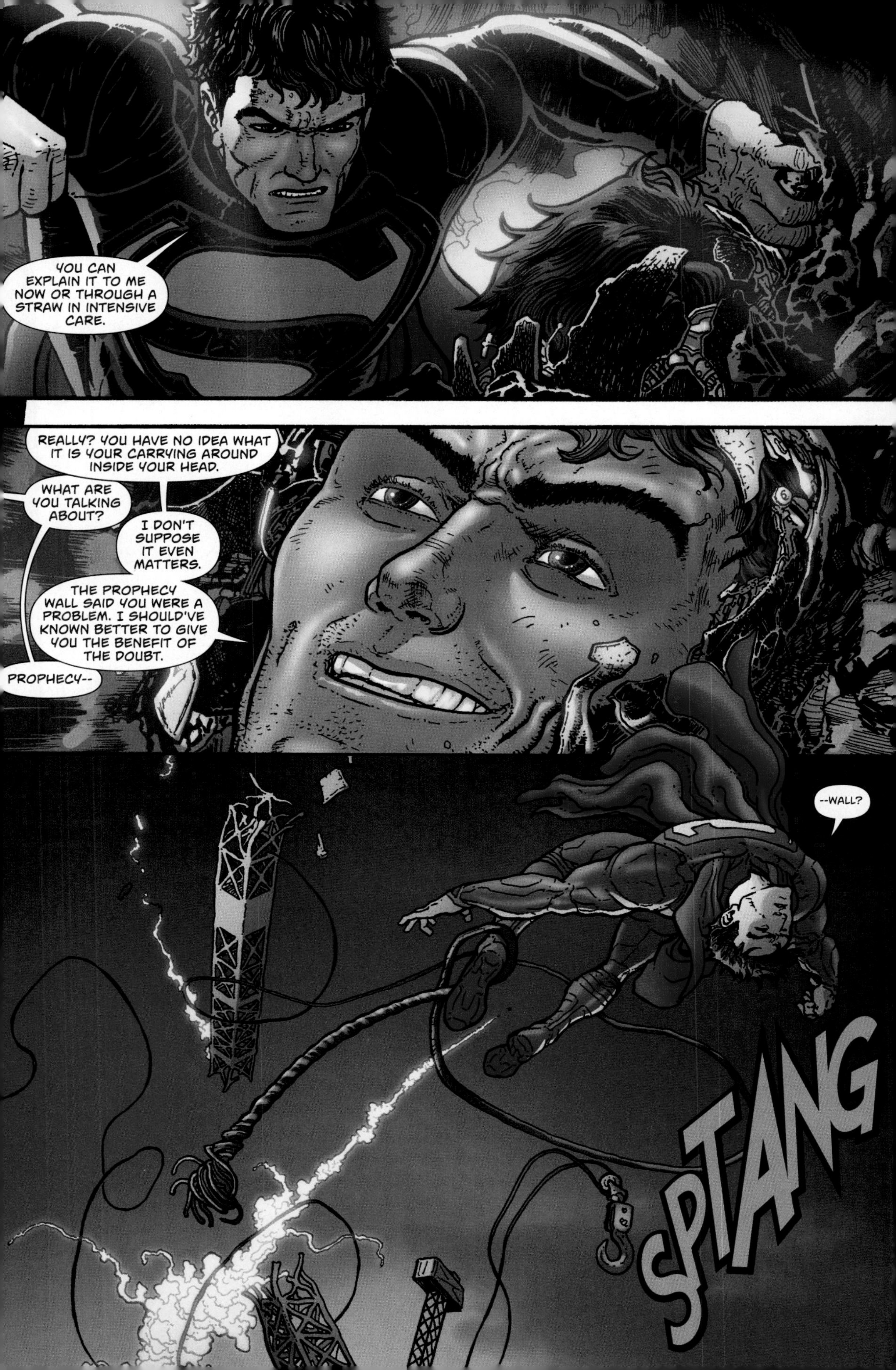
YOU CAN EXPLAIN IT TO ME NOW OR THROUGH A STRAW IN INTENSIVE CARE.
REALLY? YOU HAVE NO IDEA WHAT IT IS YOUR CARRYING AROUND INSIDE YOUR HEAD.
WHAT ARE YOU TALKING ABOUT?
I DON'T SUPPOSE IT EVEN MATTERS.
THE PROPHECY WALL SAID YOU WERE A PROBLEM. I SHOULD'VE KNOWN BETTER TO GIVE YOU THE BENEFIT OF THE DOUBT.
PROPHECY--
--WALL?
SPTANG

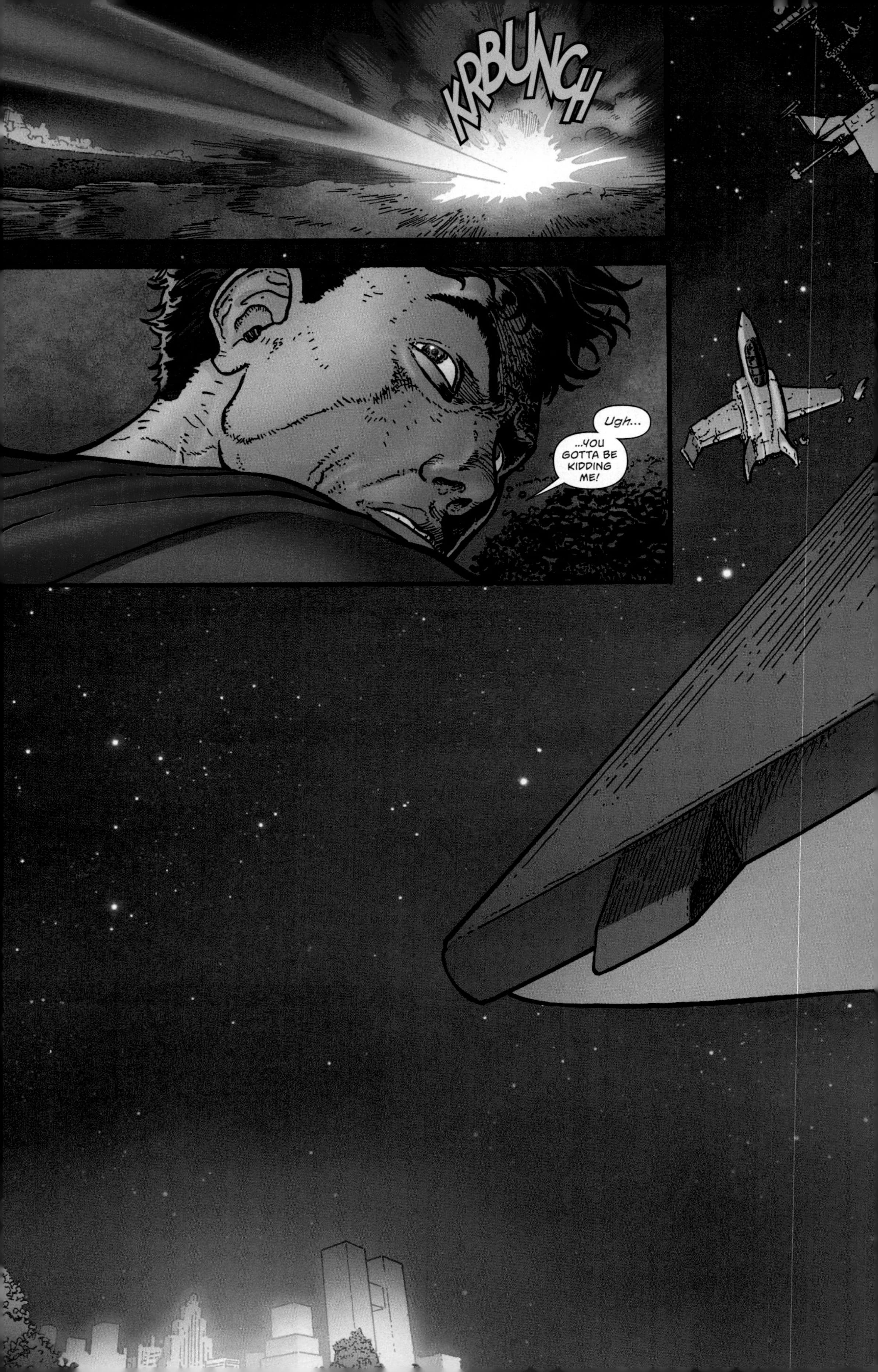
KRBUNCH
Ugh...
...YOU GOTTA BE KIDDING ME!

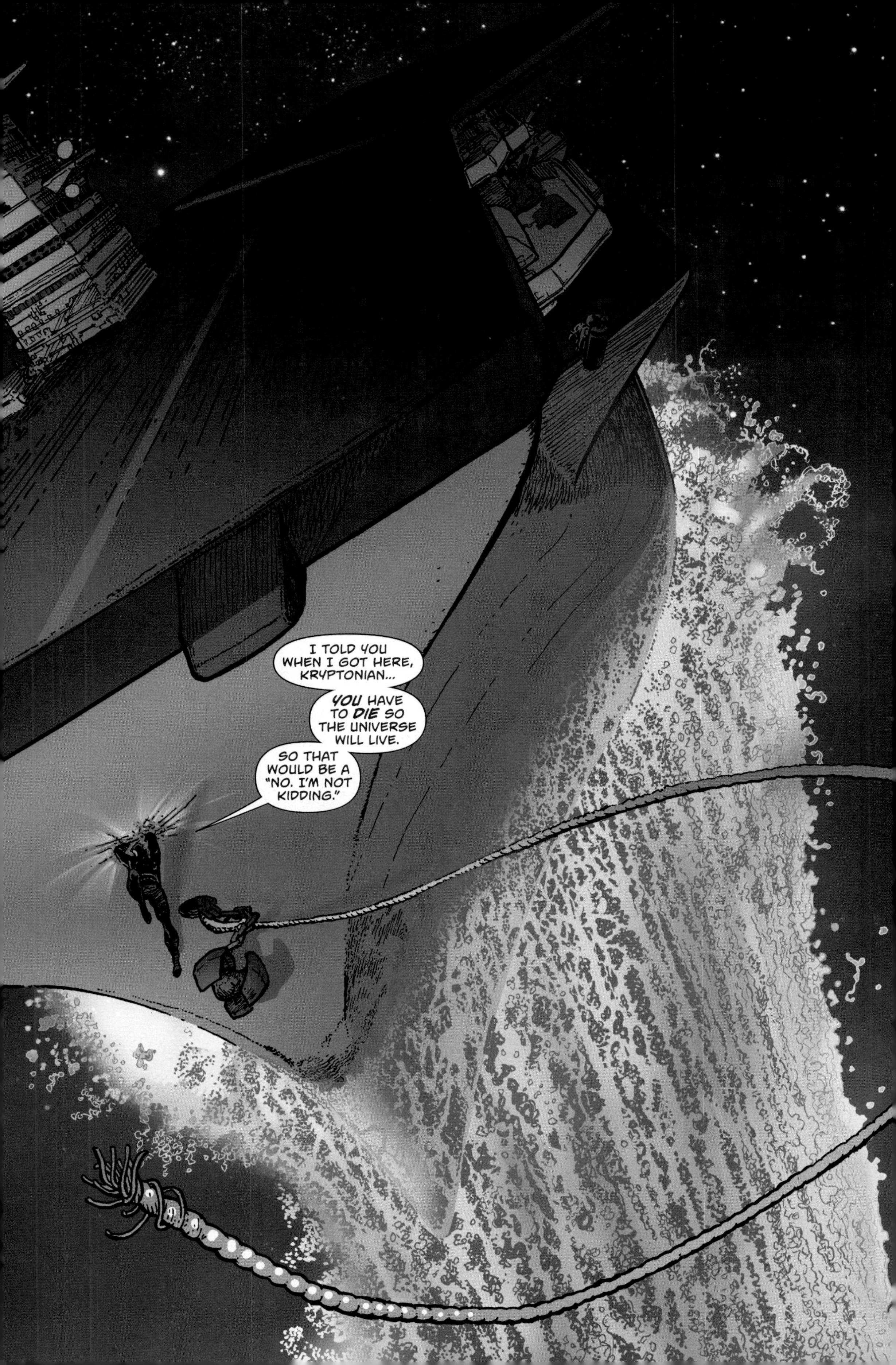
I TOLD YOU WHEN I GOT HERE, KRYPTONIAN...
YOU HAVE TO DIE SO THE UNIVERSE WILL LIVE.
SO THAT WOULD BE A "NO. I'M NOT KIDDING."

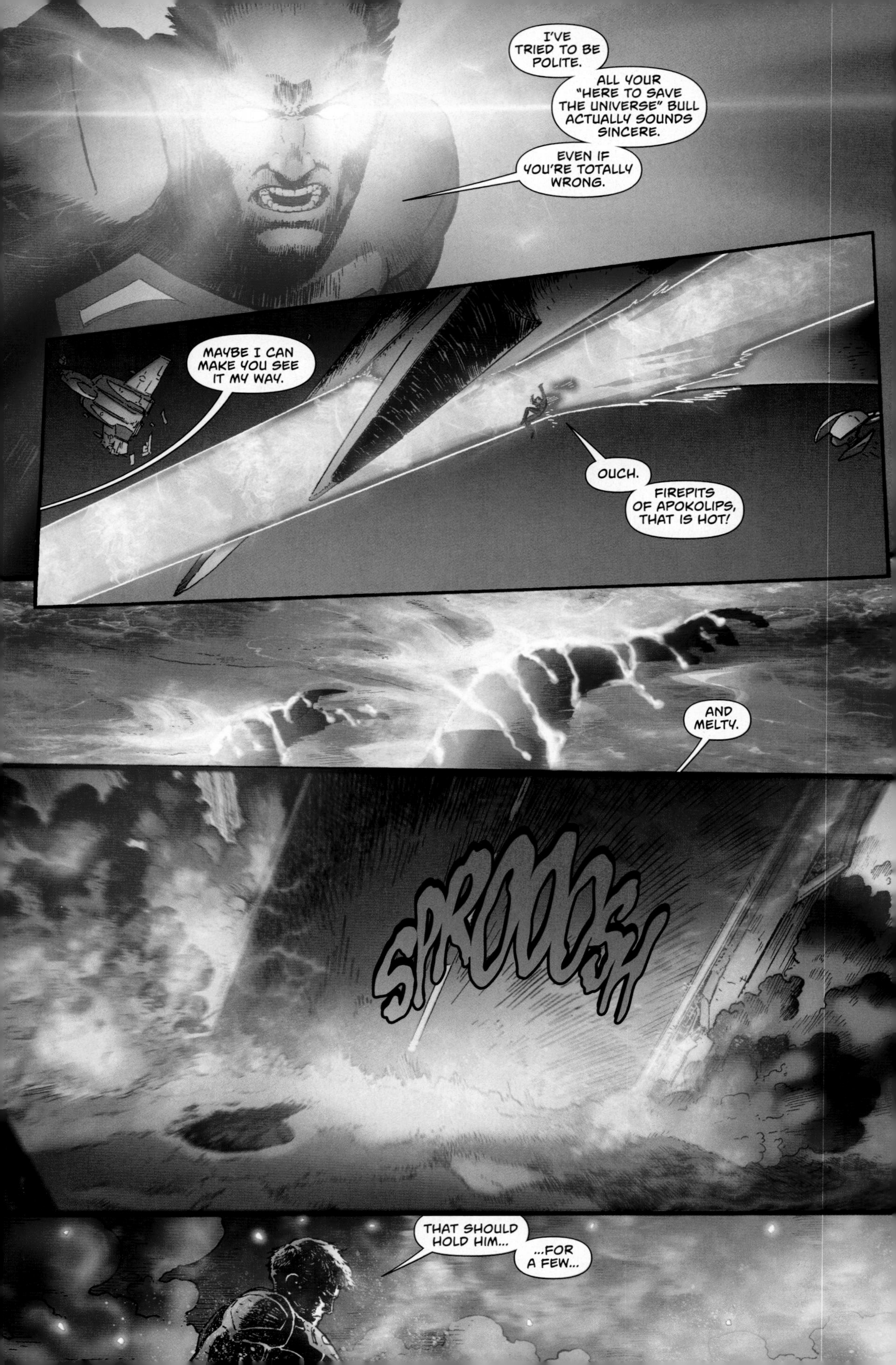

I'VE TRIED TO BE POLITE.
ALL YOUR "HERE TO SAVE THE UNIVERSE" BULL ACTUALLY SOUNDS SINCERE.
EVEN IF YOU'RE TOTALLY WRONG.
MAYBE I CAN MAKE YOU SEE IT MY WAY.
OUCH.
FIREPITS OF APOKOLIPS, THAT IS HOT!
AND MELTY.
SPROOSH
THAT SHOULD HOLD HIM...
...FOR A FEW...

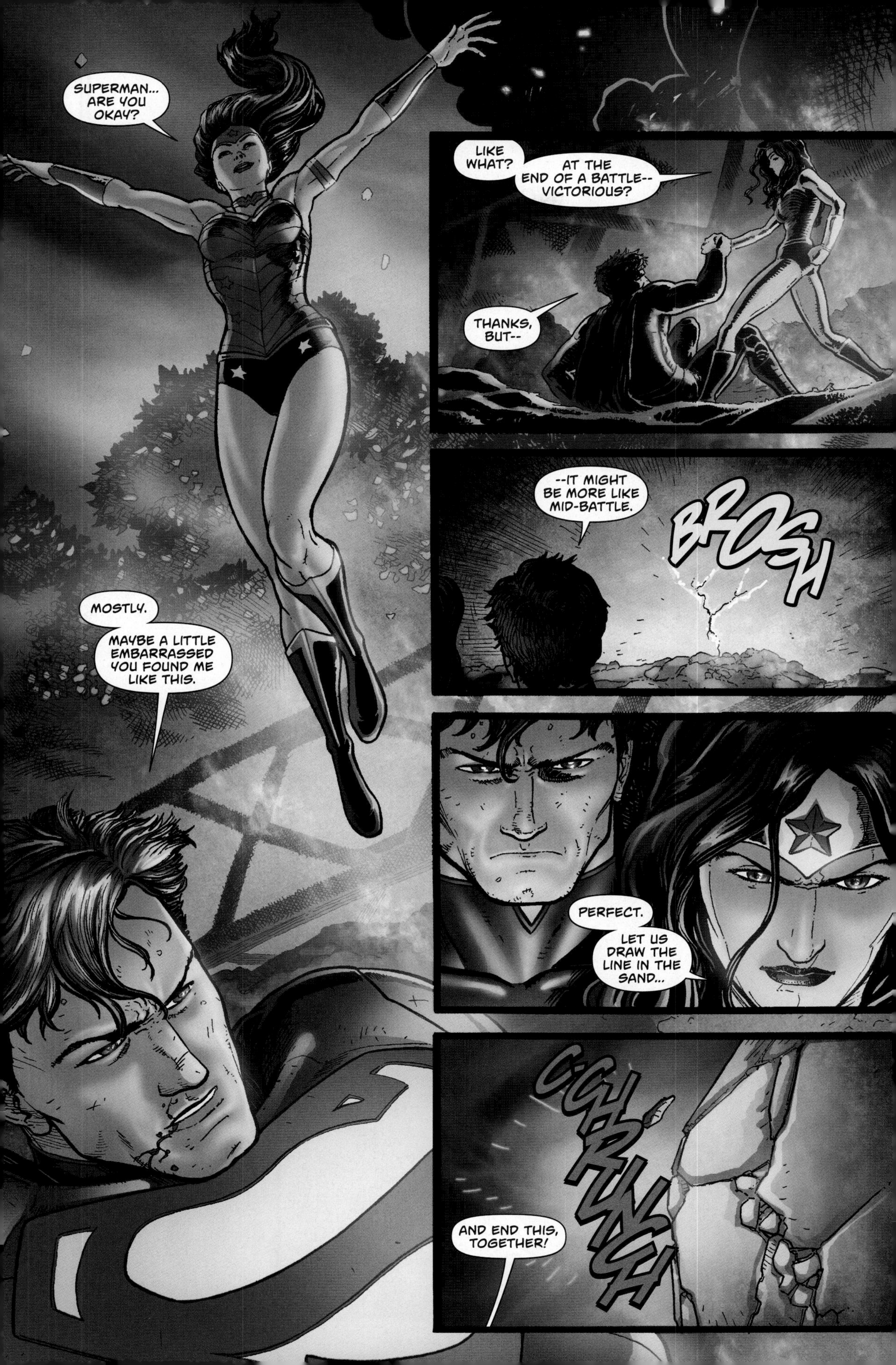
SUPERMAN... ARE YOU OKAY?
MOSTLY.
MAYBE A LITTLE EMBARRASSED YOU FOUND ME LIKE THIS.
LIKE WHAT?
AT THE END OF A BATTLE-- VICTORIOUS?
THANKS, BUT--
--IT MIGHT BE MORE LIKE MID-BATTLE.
BROSH
PERFECT.
LET US DRAW THE LINE IN THE SAND...
C-CRUNCH
AND END THIS, TOGETHER!

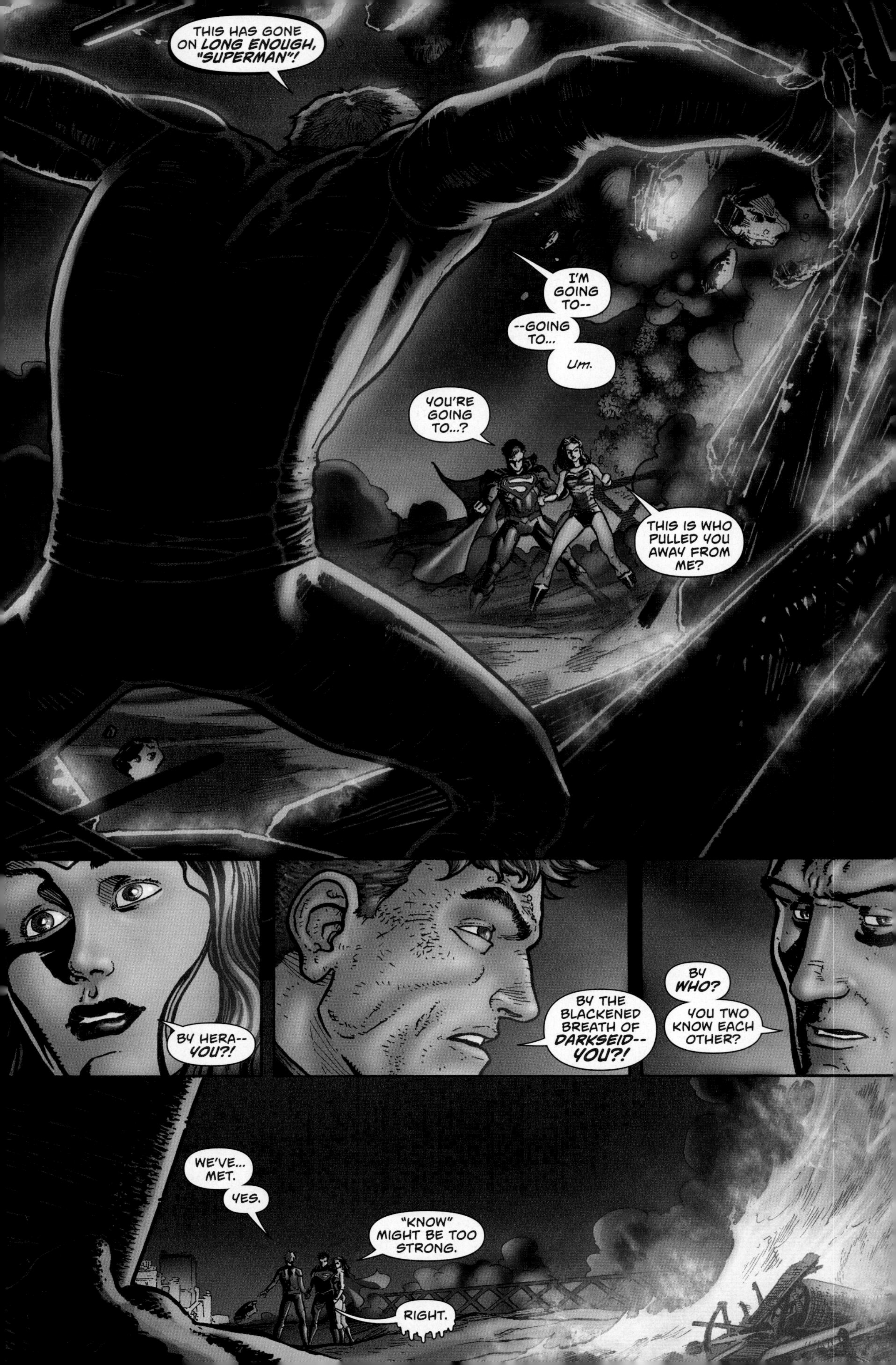
THIS HAS GONE ON LONG ENOUGH, "SUPERMAN"!
I'M GOING TO--
--GOING TO...
Um.
YOU'RE GOING TO...?
THIS IS WHO PULLED YOU AWAY FROM ME?
BY HERA-- YOU?!
BY THE BLACKENED BREATH OF DARKSEID-- YOU?!
BY WHO?
YOU TWO KNOW EACH OTHER?
WE'VE... MET.
YES.
"KNOW" MIGHT BE TOO STRONG.
RIGHT.

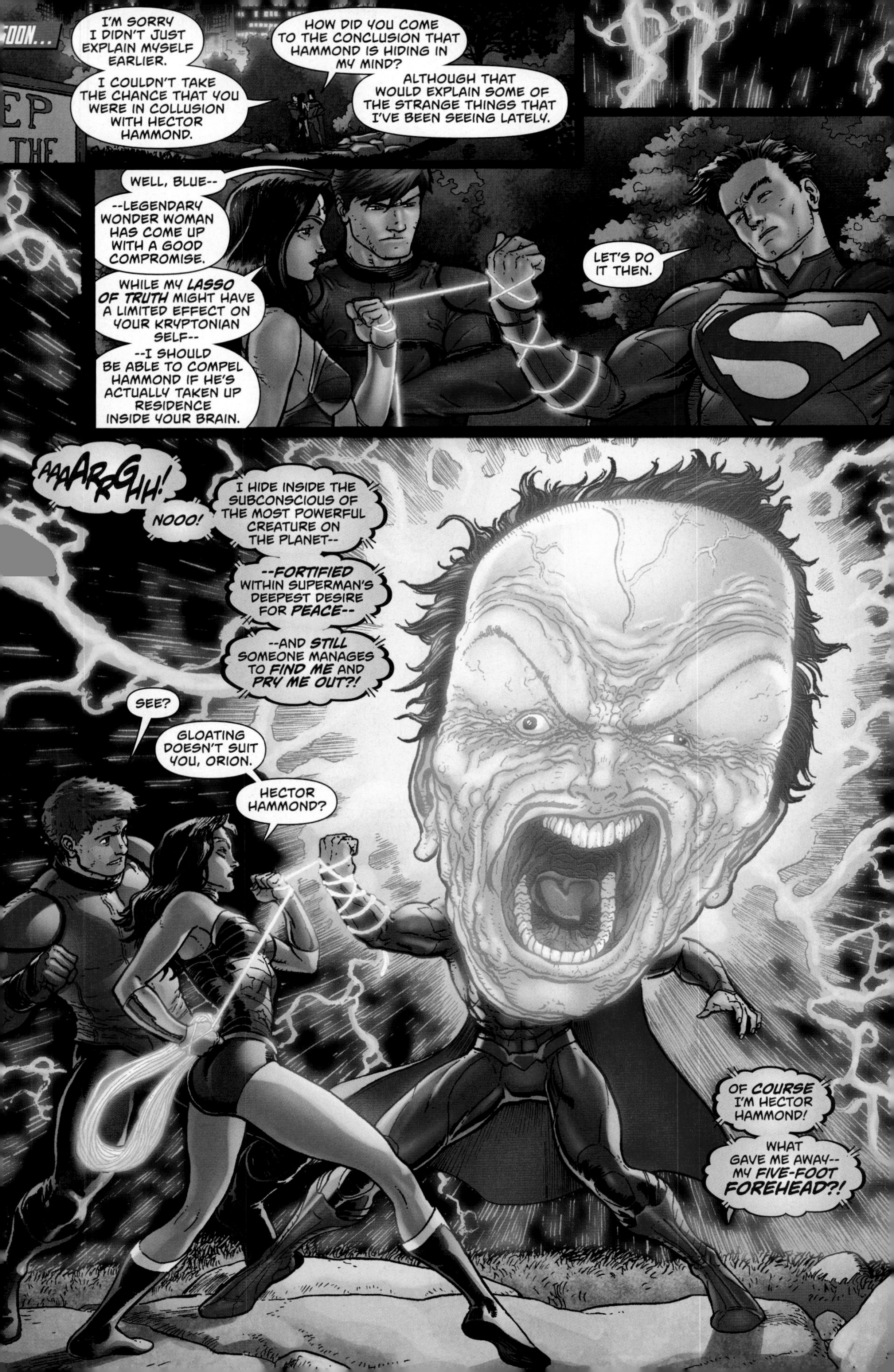
SOON...
I'M SORRY I DIDN'T JUST EXPLAIN MYSELF EARLIER.
I COULDN'T TAKE THE CHANCE THAT YOU WERE IN COLLUSION WITH HECTOR HAMMOND.
HOW DID YOU COME TO THE CONCLUSION THAT HAMMOND IS HIDING IN MY MIND?
ALTHOUGH THAT WOULD EXPLAIN SOME OF THE STRANGE THINGS THAT I'VE BEEN SEEING LATELY.
WELL, BLUE--
--LEGENDARY WONDER WOMAN HAS COME UP WITH A GOOD COMPROMISE.
WHILE MY LASSO OF TRUTH MIGHT HAVE A LIMITED EFFECT ON YOUR KRYPTONIAN SELF--
--I SHOULD BE ABLE TO COMPEL HAMMOND IF HE'S ACTUALLY TAKEN UP RESIDENCE INSIDE YOUR BRAIN.
LET'S DO IT THEN.
AAAARRGHH!
NOOO!
I HIDE INSIDE THE SUBCONSCIOUS OF THE MOST POWERFUL CREATURE ON THE PLANET--
--FORTIFIED WITHIN SUPERMAN'S DEEPEST DESIRE FOR PEACE--
--AND STILL SOMEONE MANAGES TO FIND ME AND PRY ME OUT?!
SEE?
GLOATING DOESN'T SUIT YOU, ORION.
HECTOR HAMMOND?
OF COURSE I'M HECTOR HAMMOND!
WHAT GAVE ME AWAY-- MY FIVE-FOOT FOREHEAD?!

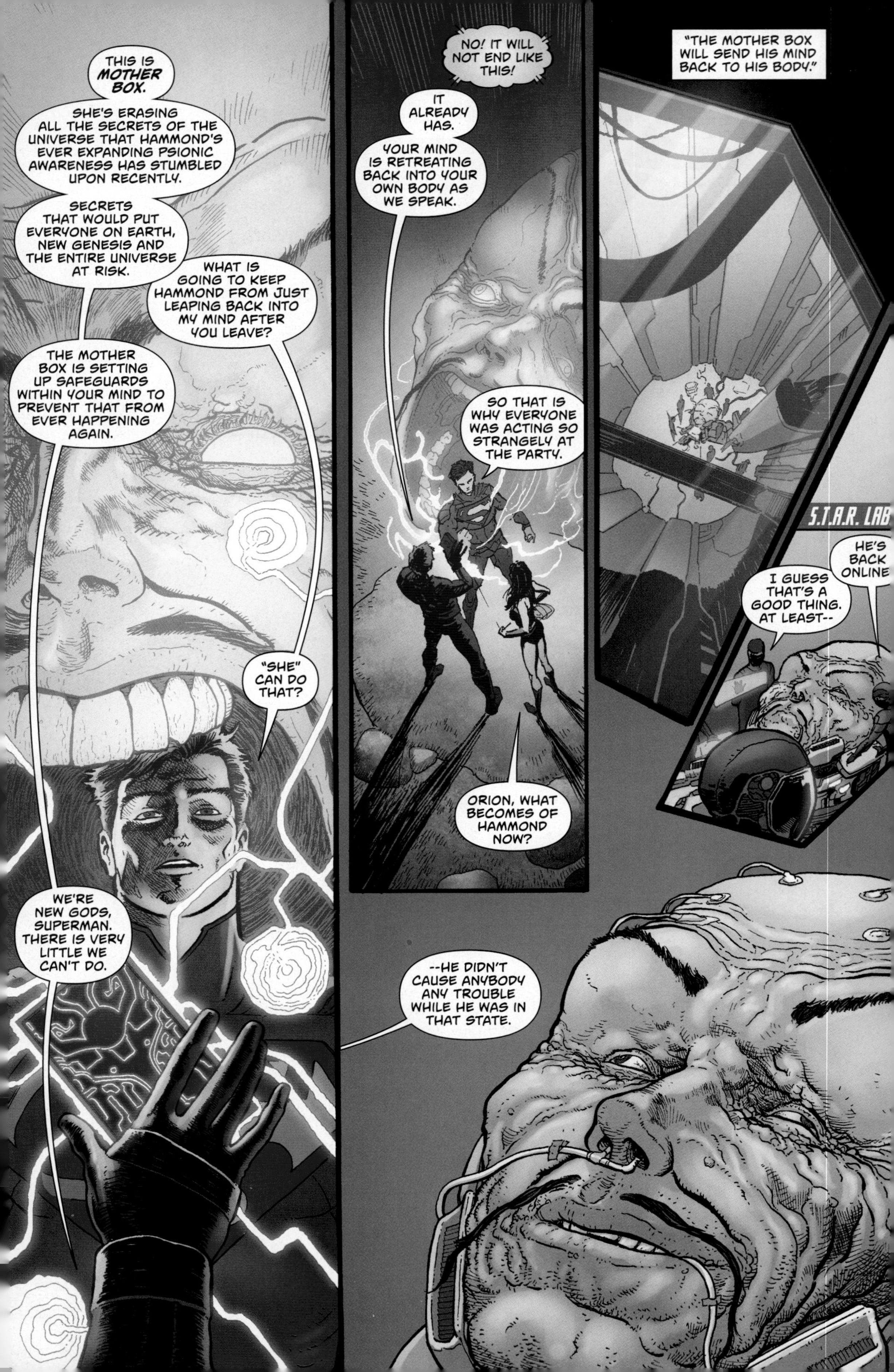
THIS IS MOTHER BOX.
SHE'S ERASING ALL THE SECRETS OF THE UNIVERSE THAT HAMMOND'S EVER EXPANDING PSIONIC AWARENESS HAS STUMBLED UPON RECENTLY.
SECRETS THAT WOULD PUT EVERYONE ON EARTH, NEW GENESIS AND THE ENTIRE UNIVERSE AT RISK.
WHAT IS GOING TO KEEP HAMMOND FROM JUST LEAPING BACK INTO MY MIND AFTER YOU LEAVE?
THE MOTHER BOX IS SETTING UP SAFEGUARDS WITHIN YOUR MIND TO PREVENT THAT FROM EVER HAPPENING AGAIN.
"SHE" CAN DO THAT?
WE'RE NEW GODS, SUPERMAN. THERE IS VERY LITTLE WE CAN'T DO.
NO! IT WILL NOT END LIKE THIS!
IT ALREADY HAS.
YOUR MIND IS RETREATING BACK INTO YOUR OWN BODY AS WE SPEAK.
SO THAT IS WHY EVERYONE WAS ACTING SO STRANGELY AT THE PARTY.
ORION, WHAT BECOMES OF HAMMOND NOW?
"THE MOTHER BOX WILL SEND HIS MIND BACK TO HIS BODY."
S.T.A.R. LAB
HE'S BACK ONLINE
I GUESS THAT'S A GOOD THING. AT LEAST--
--HE DIDN'T CAUSE ANYBODY ANY TROUBLE WHILE HE WAS IN THAT STATE.

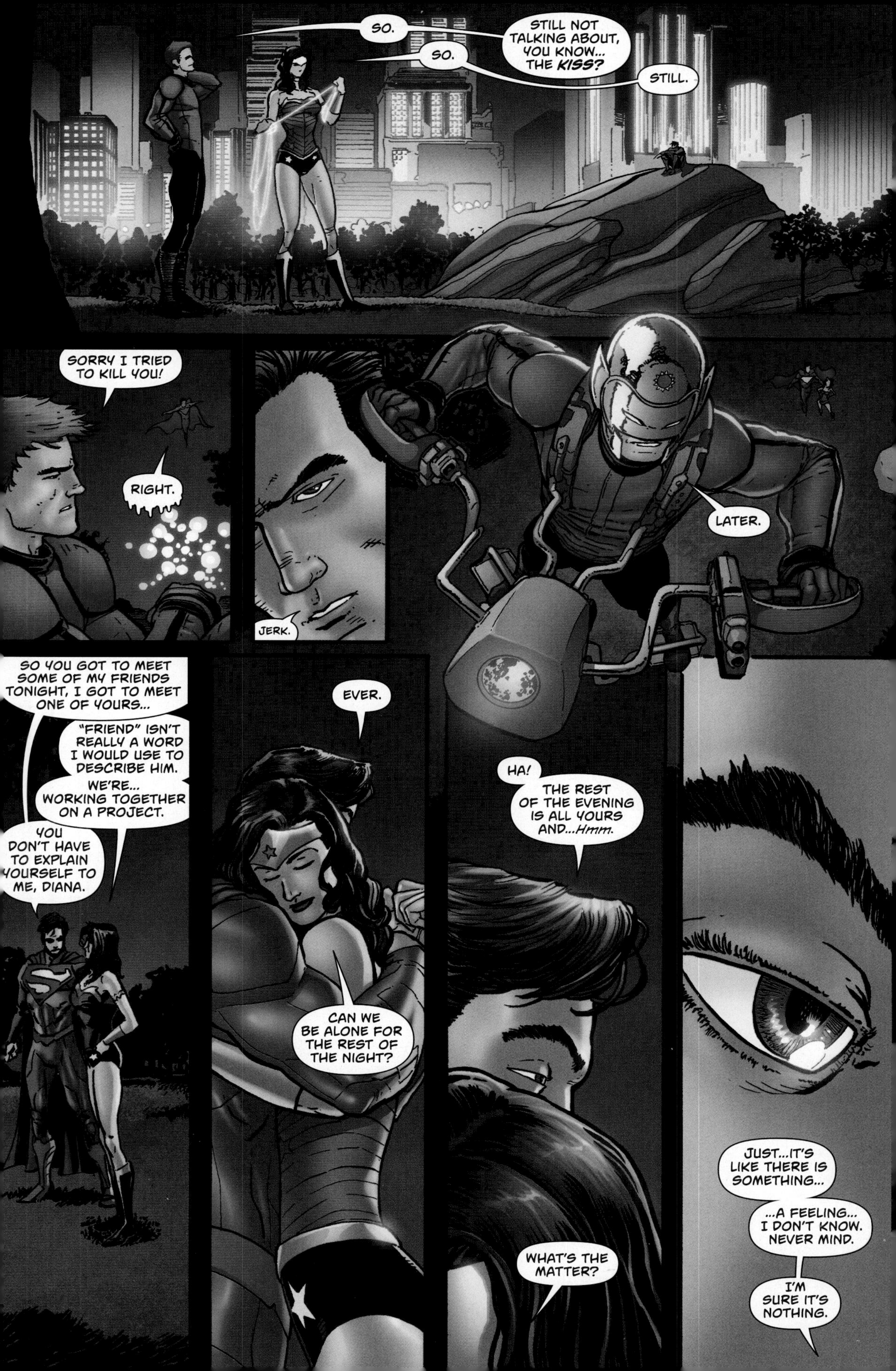
SO.
STILL NOT TALKING ABOUT, YOU KNOW... THE KISS?
SO.
STILL.
SORRY I TRIED TO KILL YOU!
RIGHT.
JERK.
LATER.
SO YOU GOT TO MEET SOME OF MY FRIENDS TONIGHT, I GOT TO MEET ONE OF YOURS...
"FRIEND" ISN'T REALLY A WORD I WOULD USE TO DESCRIBE HIM.
WE'RE... WORKING TOGETHER ON A PROJECT.
YOU DON'T HAVE TO EXPLAIN YOURSELF TO ME, DIANA.
EVER.
CAN WE BE ALONE FOR THE REST OF THE NIGHT?
HA!
THE REST OF THE EVENING IS ALL YOURS AND...Hmm.
WHAT'S THE MATTER?
JUST...IT'S LIKE THERE IS SOMETHING...
...A FEELING... I DON'T KNOW. NEVER MIND.
I'M SURE IT'S NOTHING.

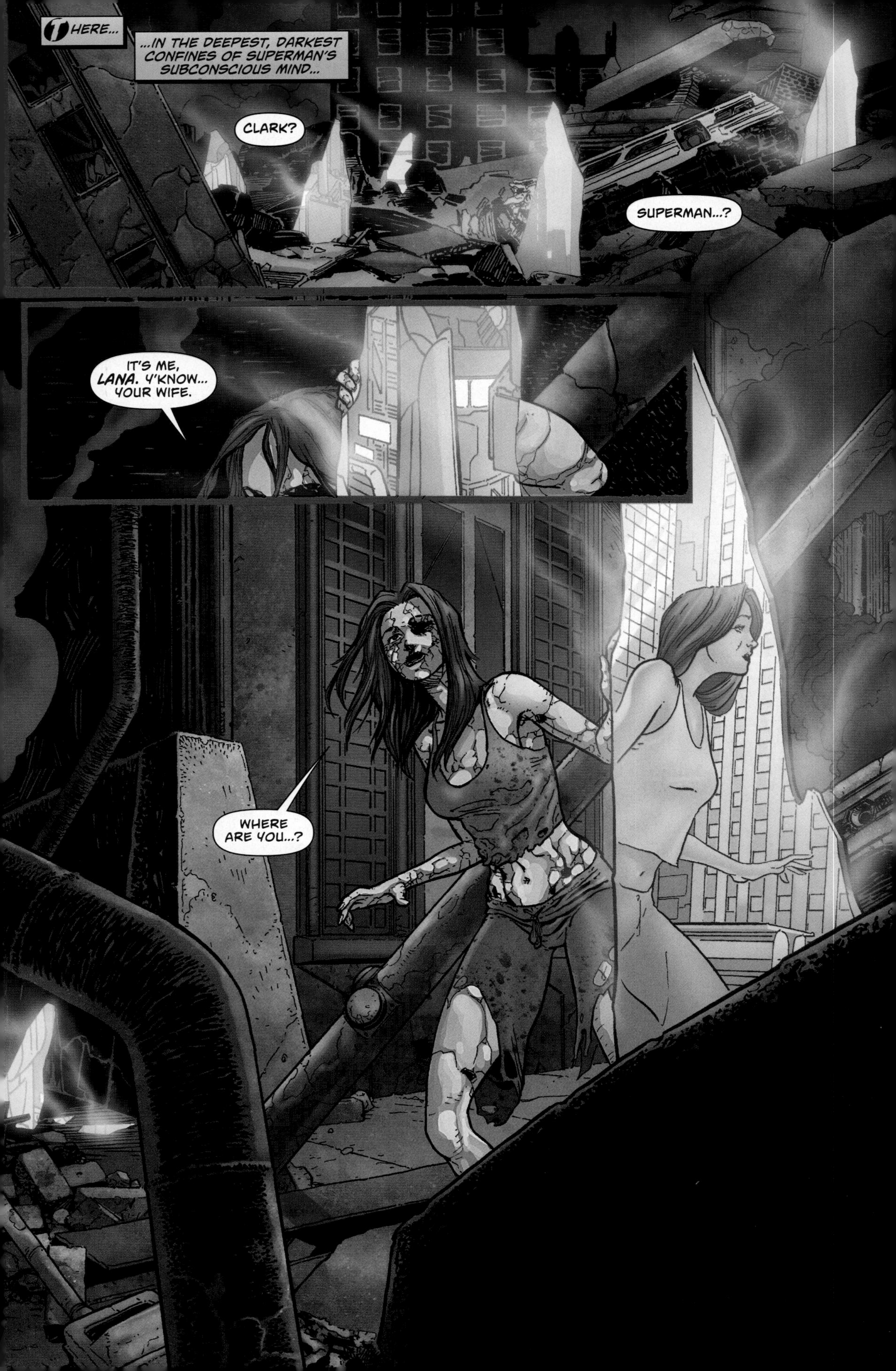
THERE...
...IN THE DEEPEST, DARKEST CONFINES OF SUPERMAN'S SUBCONSCIOUS MIND...
CLARK?
SUPERMAN...?
IT'S ME, LANA. Y'KNOW... YOUR WIFE.
WHERE ARE YOU...?

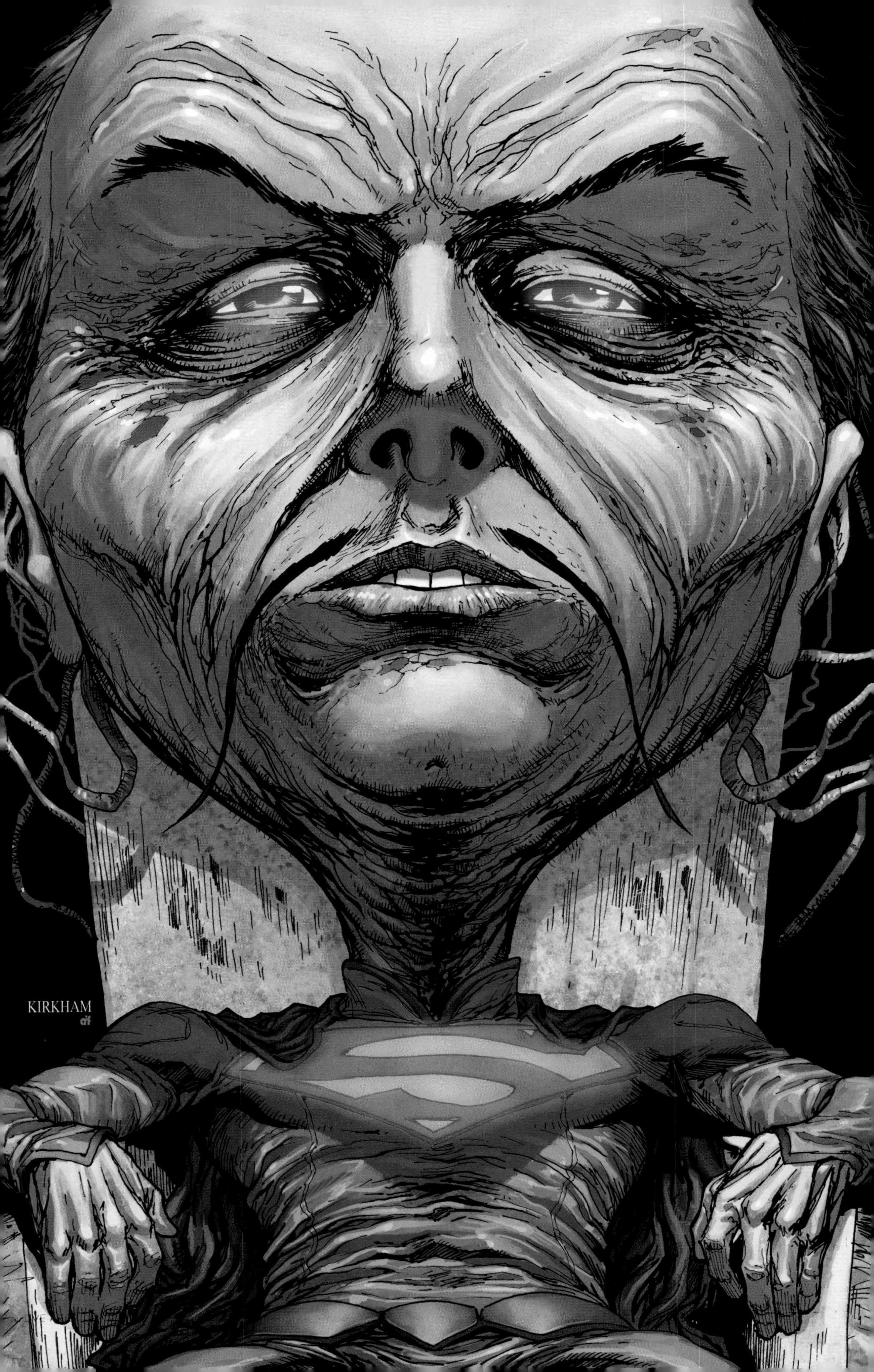
KIRKHAM
art

DON'T MIND IF I DO...

SCOTT LOBDELL writer **KENNETH ROCAFORT** artist cover art by **TYLER KIRKHAM & ARIF PRIANTO**

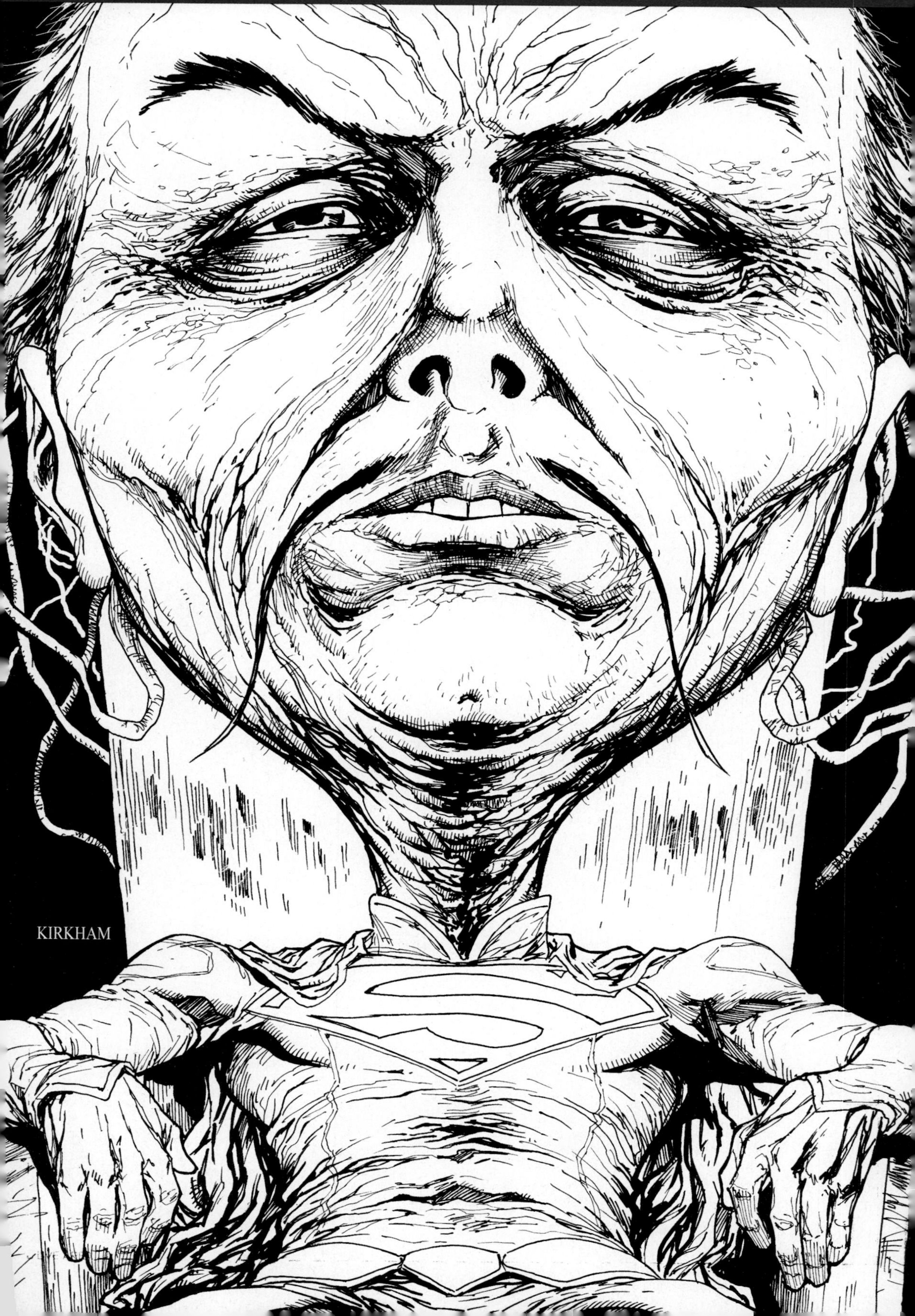
KIRKHAM

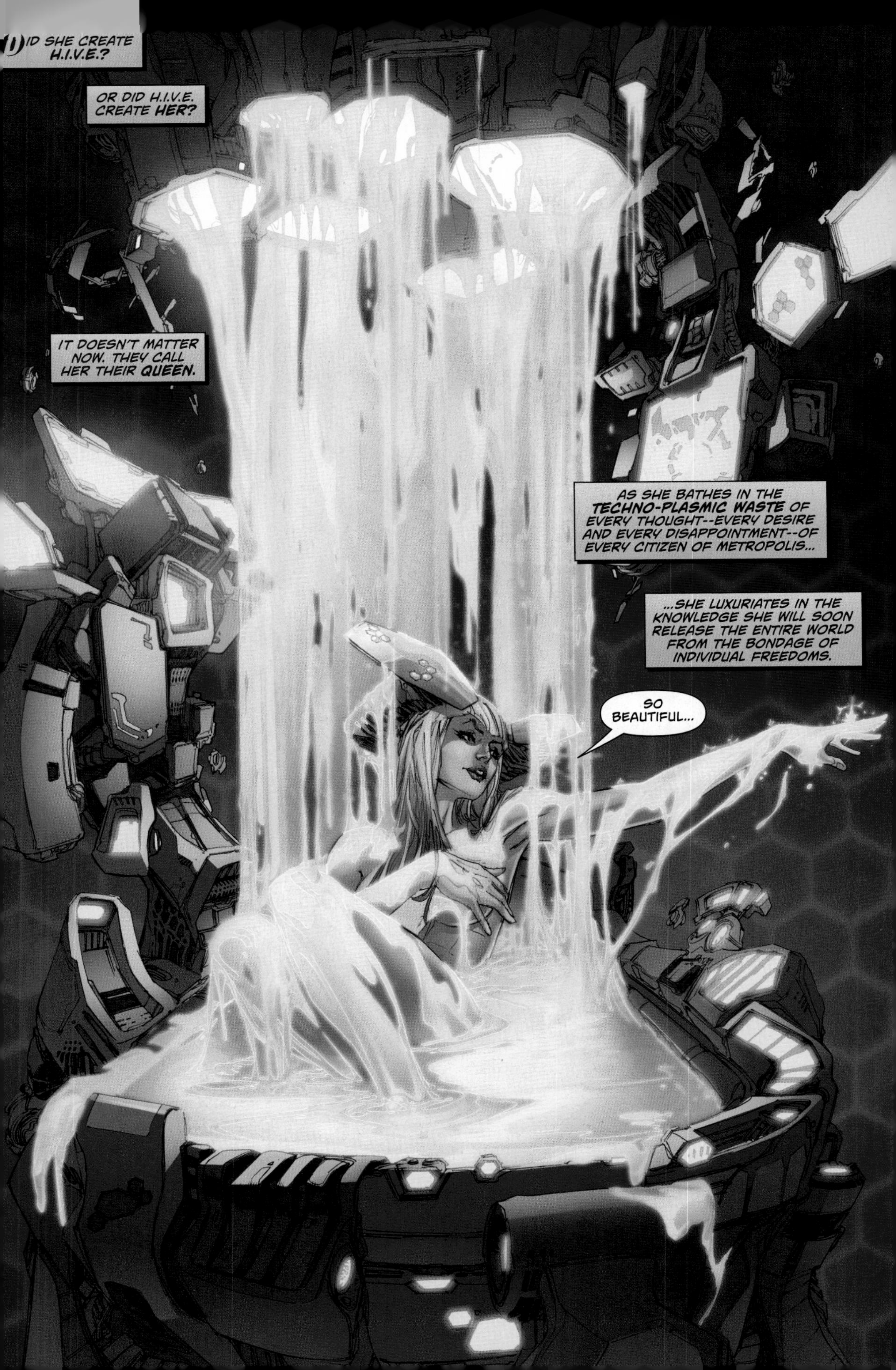
DID SHE CREATE H.I.V.E.?
OR DID H.I.V.E. CREATE HER?
IT DOESN'T MATTER NOW. THEY CALL HER THEIR QUEEN.
AS SHE BATHES IN THE TECHNO-PLASMIC WASTE OF EVERY THOUGHT--EVERY DESIRE AND EVERY DISAPPOINTMENT--OF EVERY CITIZEN OF METROPOLIS...
...SHE LUXURIATES IN THE KNOWLEDGE SHE WILL SOON RELEASE THE ENTIRE WORLD FROM THE BONDAGE OF INDIVIDUAL FREEDOMS.
SO BEAUTIFUL...

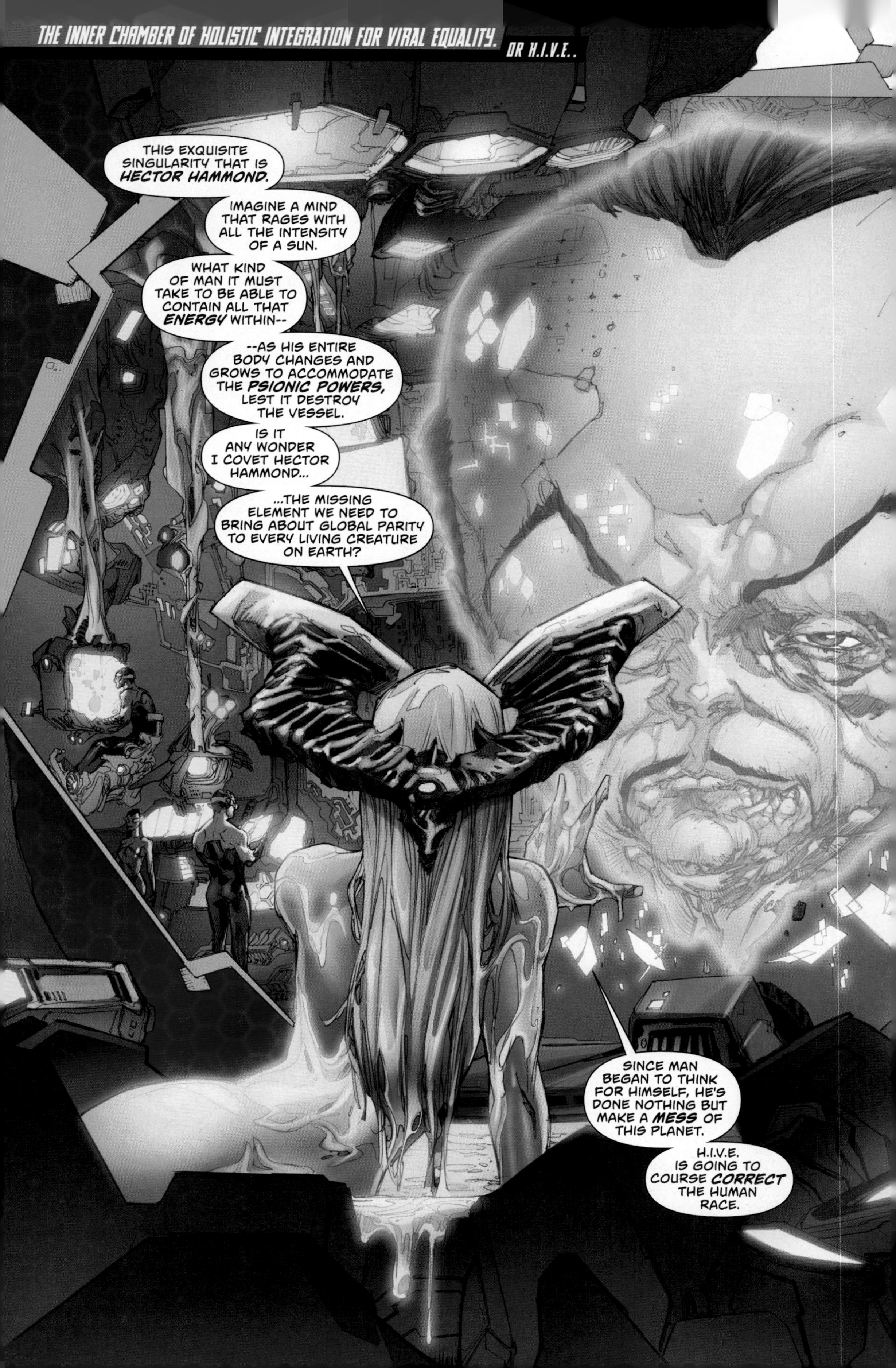
THE INNER CHAMBER OF HOLISTIC INTEGRATION FOR VIRAL EQUALITY.
OR H.I.V.E..
THIS EXQUISITE SINGULARITY THAT IS HECTOR HAMMOND.
IMAGINE A MIND THAT RAGES WITH ALL THE INTENSITY OF A SUN.
WHAT KIND OF MAN IT MUST TAKE TO BE ABLE TO CONTAIN ALL THAT ENERGY WITHIN--
--AS HIS ENTIRE BODY CHANGES AND GROWS TO ACCOMMODATE THE PSIONIC POWERS, LEST IT DESTROY THE VESSEL.
IS IT ANY WONDER I COVET HECTOR HAMMOND...
...THE MISSING ELEMENT WE NEED TO BRING ABOUT GLOBAL PARITY TO EVERY LIVING CREATURE ON EARTH?
SINCE MAN BEGAN TO THINK FOR HIMSELF, HE'S DONE NOTHING BUT MAKE A MESS OF THIS PLANET.
H.I.V.E. IS GOING TO COURSE CORRECT THE HUMAN RACE.

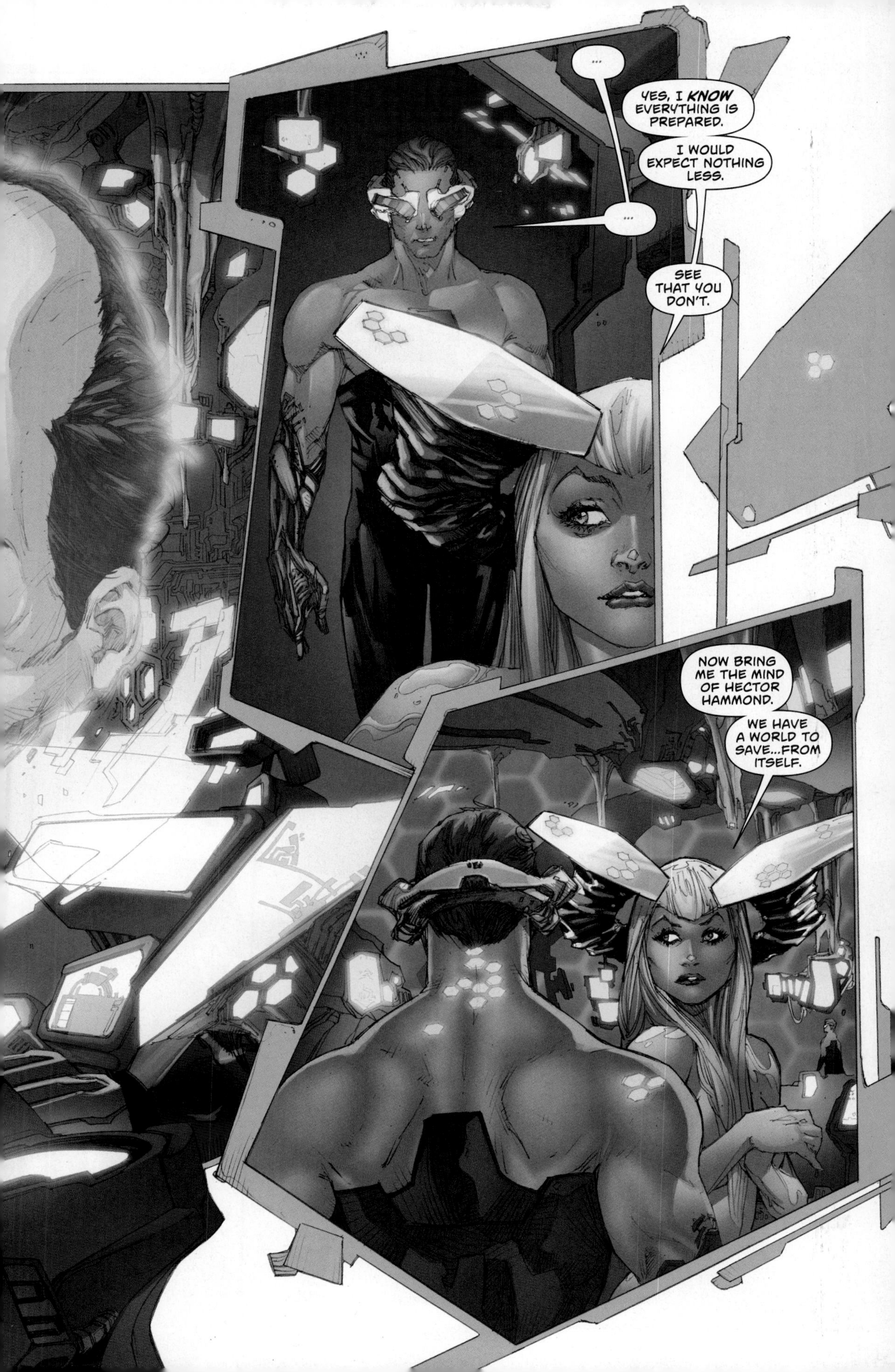
...
YES, I KNOW EVERYTHING IS PREPARED.
I WOULD EXPECT NOTHING LESS.
...
SEE THAT YOU DON'T.
NOW BRING ME THE MIND OF HECTOR HAMMOND.
WE HAVE A WORLD TO SAVE...FROM ITSELF.

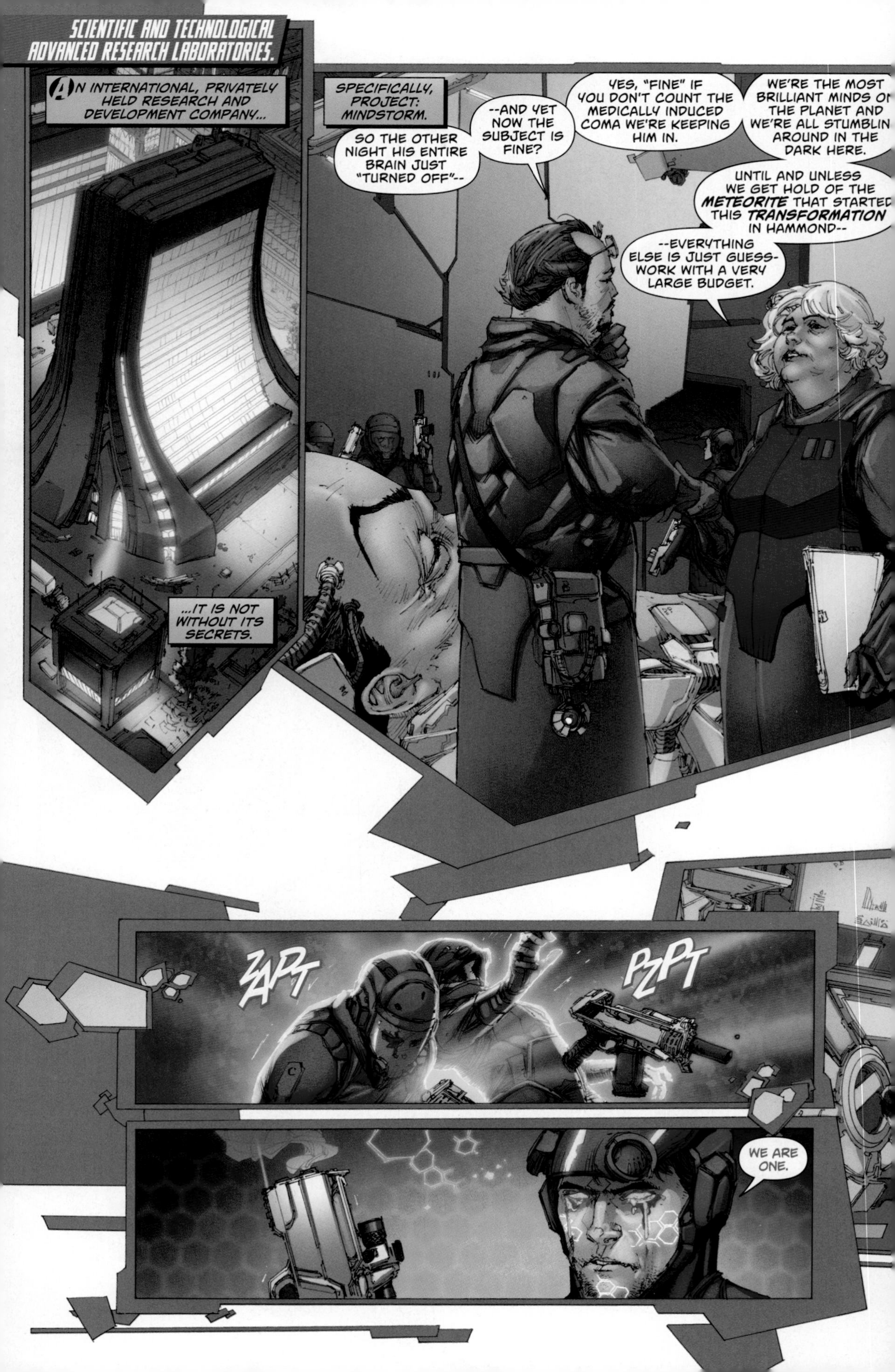

SCIENTIFIC AND TECHNOLOGICAL ADVANCED RESEARCH LABORATORIES.
AN INTERNATIONAL, PRIVATELY HELD RESEARCH AND DEVELOPMENT COMPANY...
...IT IS NOT WITHOUT ITS SECRETS.
SPECIFICALLY, PROJECT: MINDSTORM.
SO THE OTHER NIGHT HIS ENTIRE BRAIN JUST "TURNED OFF"--
--AND YET NOW THE SUBJECT IS FINE?
YES, "FINE" IF YOU DON'T COUNT THE MEDICALLY INDUCED COMA WE'RE KEEPING HIM IN.
WE'RE THE MOST BRILLIANT MINDS ON THE PLANET AND WE'RE ALL STUMBLING AROUND IN THE DARK HERE.
UNTIL AND UNLESS WE GET HOLD OF THE METEORITE THAT STARTED THIS TRANSFORMATION IN HAMMOND--
--EVERYTHING ELSE IS JUST GUESS-WORK WITH A VERY LARGE BUDGET.
ZAPT
PZPT
WE ARE ONE.

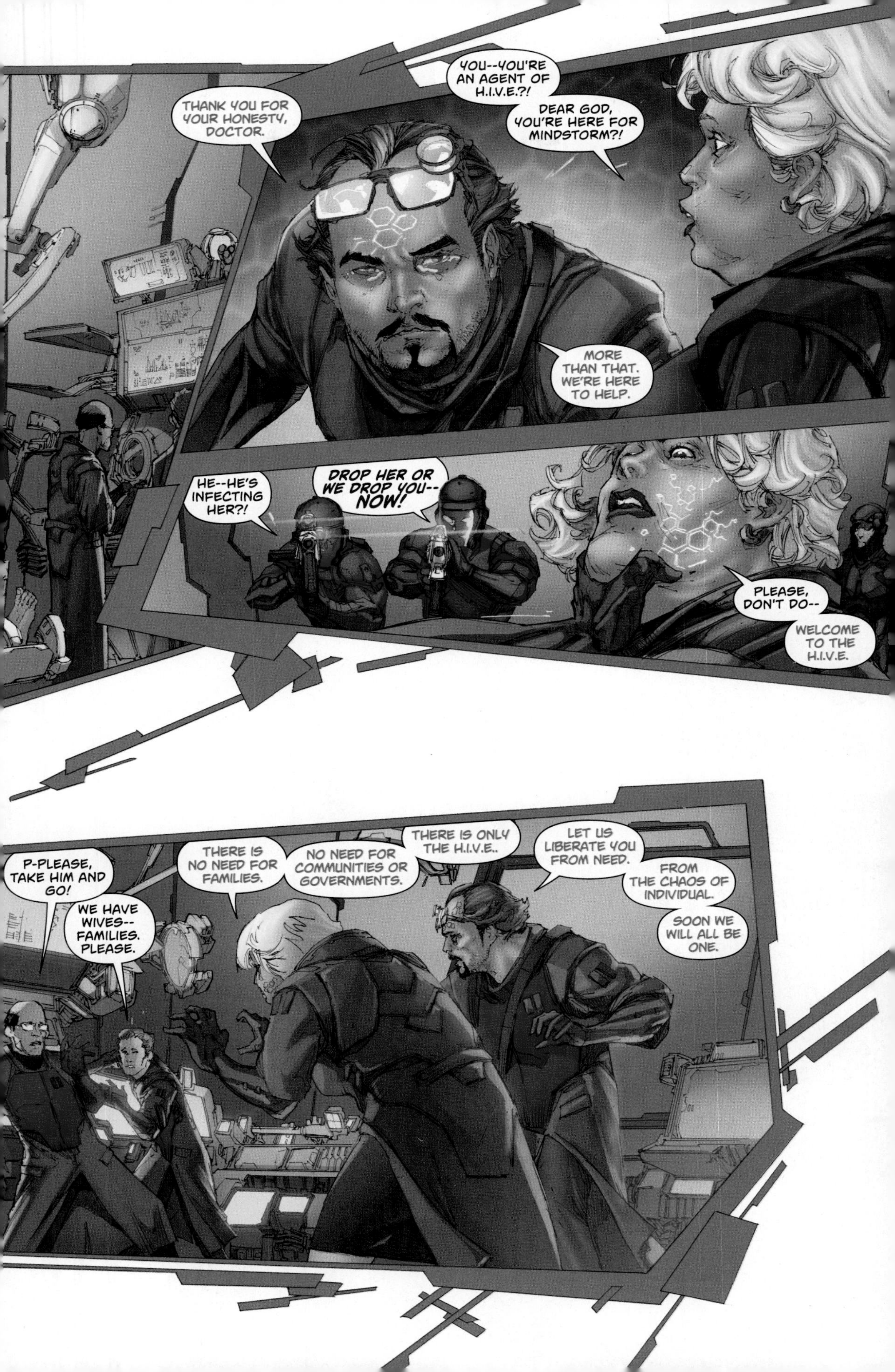
THANK YOU FOR YOUR HONESTY, DOCTOR.
YOU--YOU'RE AN AGENT OF H.I.V.E.?!
DEAR GOD, YOU'RE HERE FOR MINDSTORM?!
MORE THAN THAT. WE'RE HERE TO HELP.
HE--HE'S INFECTING HER?!
DROP HER OR WE DROP YOU-- NOW!
PLEASE, DON'T DO--
WELCOME TO THE H.I.V.E.
P-PLEASE, TAKE HIM AND GO!
WE HAVE WIVES-- FAMILIES. PLEASE.
THERE IS NO NEED FOR FAMILIES.
NO NEED FOR COMMUNITIES OR GOVERNMENTS.
THERE IS ONLY THE H.I.V.E..
LET US LIBERATE YOU FROM NEED.
FROM THE CHAOS OF INDIVIDUAL.
SOON WE WILL ALL BE ONE.

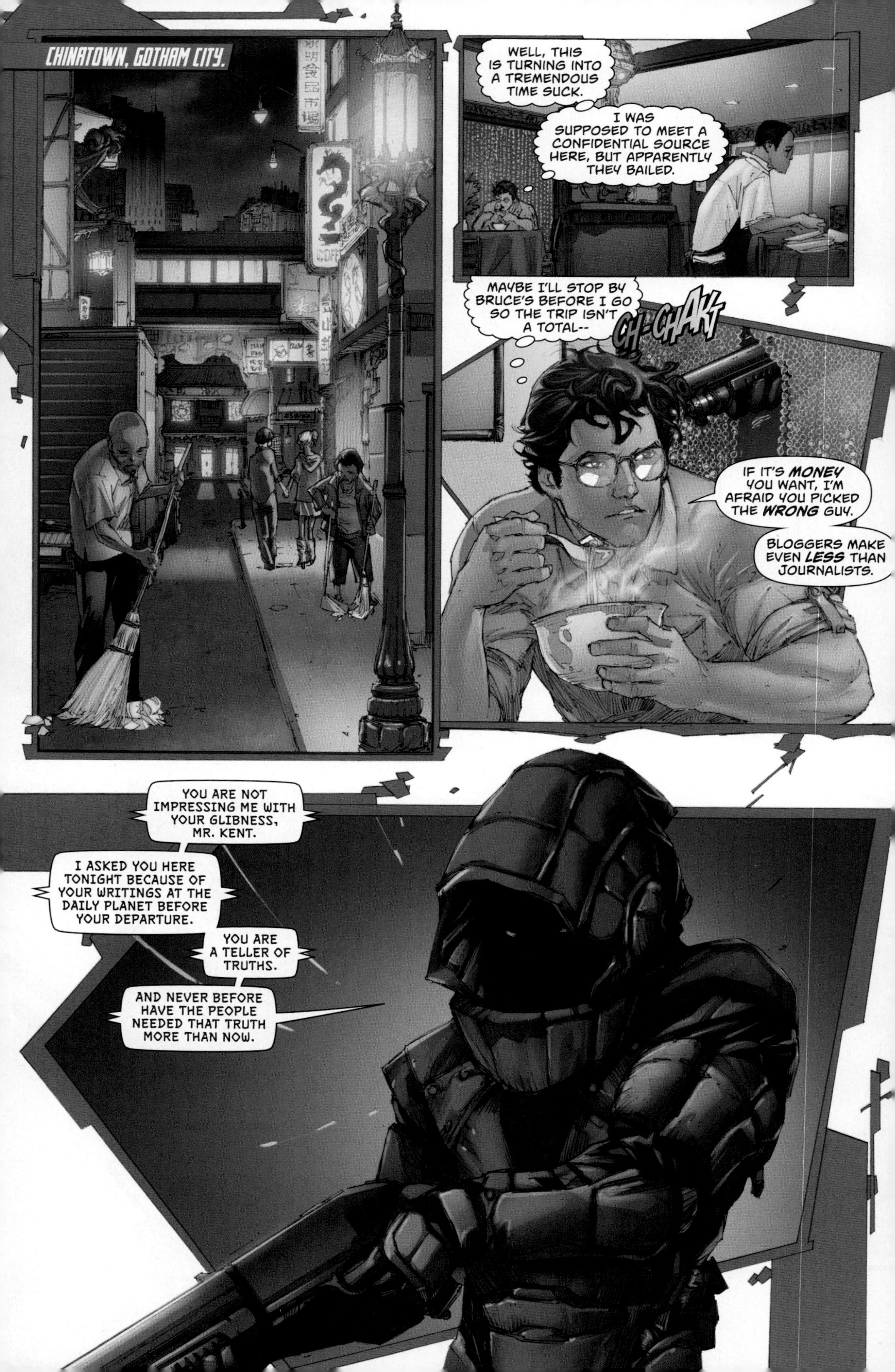
CHINATOWN, GOTHAM CITY.
WELL, THIS IS TURNING INTO A TREMENDOUS TIME SUCK.
I WAS SUPPOSED TO MEET A CONFIDENTIAL SOURCE HERE, BUT APPARENTLY THEY BAILED.
MAYBE I'LL STOP BY BRUCE'S BEFORE I GO SO THE TRIP ISN'T A TOTAL--
CH-CHAK!
IF IT'S MONEY YOU WANT, I'M AFRAID YOU PICKED THE WRONG GUY.
BLOGGERS MAKE EVEN LESS THAN JOURNALISTS.
YOU ARE NOT IMPRESSING ME WITH YOUR GLIBNESS, MR. KENT.
I ASKED YOU HERE TONIGHT BECAUSE OF YOUR WRITINGS AT THE DAILY PLANET BEFORE YOUR DEPARTURE.
YOU ARE A TELLER OF TRUTHS.
AND NEVER BEFORE HAVE THE PEOPLE NEEDED THAT TRUTH MORE THAN NOW.

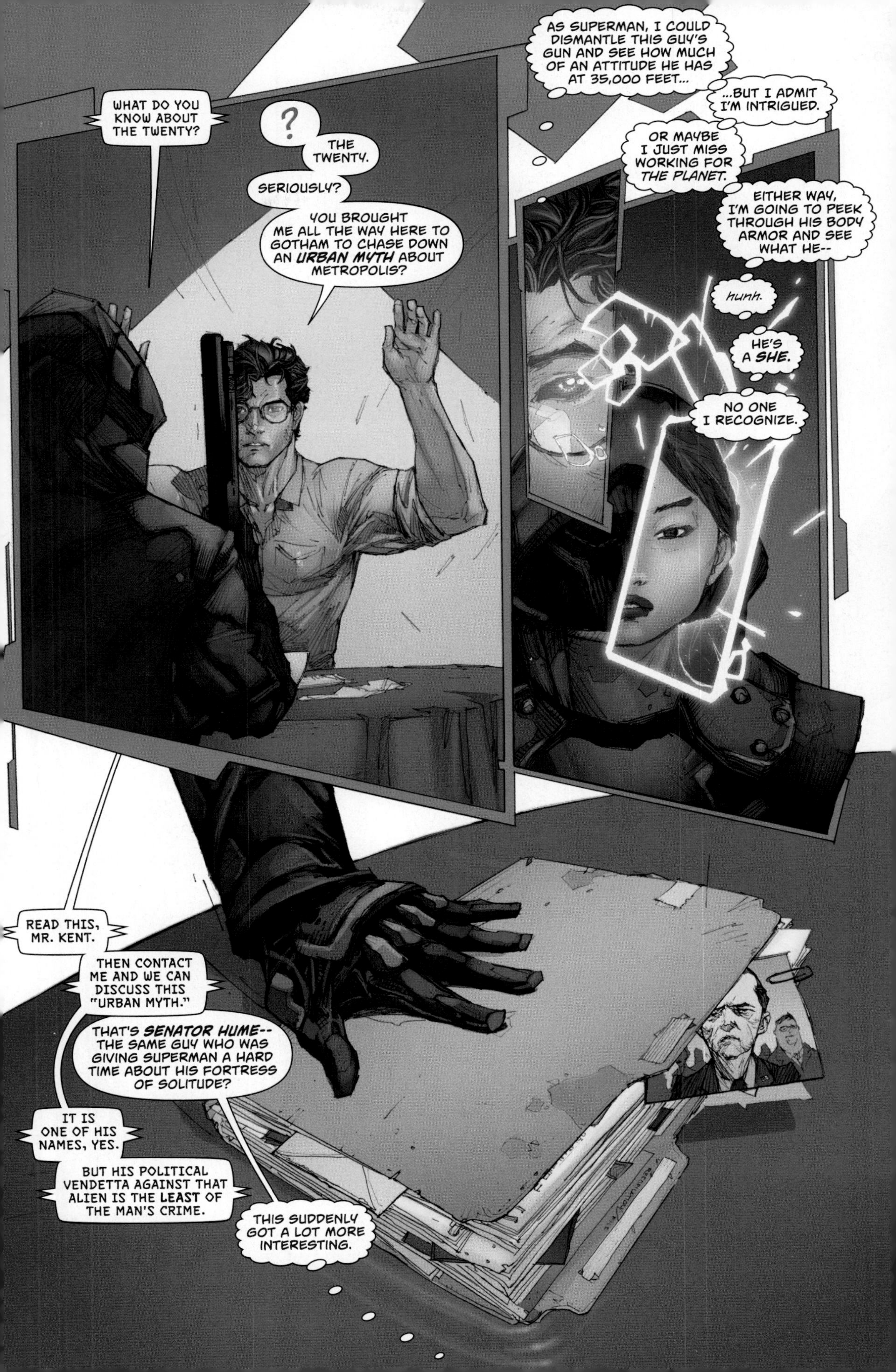

WHAT DO YOU KNOW ABOUT THE TWENTY?
?
THE TWENTY.
SERIOUSLY?
YOU BROUGHT ME ALL THE WAY HERE TO GOTHAM TO CHASE DOWN AN URBAN MYTH ABOUT METROPOLIS?
AS SUPERMAN, I COULD DISMANTLE THIS GUY'S GUN AND SEE HOW MUCH OF AN ATTITUDE HE HAS AT 35,000 FEET...
...BUT I ADMIT I'M INTRIGUED.
OR MAYBE I JUST MISS WORKING FOR THE PLANET.
EITHER WAY, I'M GOING TO PEEK THROUGH HIS BODY ARMOR AND SEE WHAT HE--
hunh.
HE'S A SHE.
NO ONE I RECOGNIZE.
READ THIS, MR. KENT.
THEN CONTACT ME AND WE CAN DISCUSS THIS "URBAN MYTH."
THAT'S SENATOR HUME-- THE SAME GUY WHO WAS GIVING SUPERMAN A HARD TIME ABOUT HIS FORTRESS OF SOLITUDE?
IT IS ONE OF HIS NAMES, YES.
BUT HIS POLITICAL VENDETTA AGAINST THAT ALIEN IS THE LEAST OF THE MAN'S CRIME.
THIS SUDDENLY GOT A LOT MORE INTERESTING.

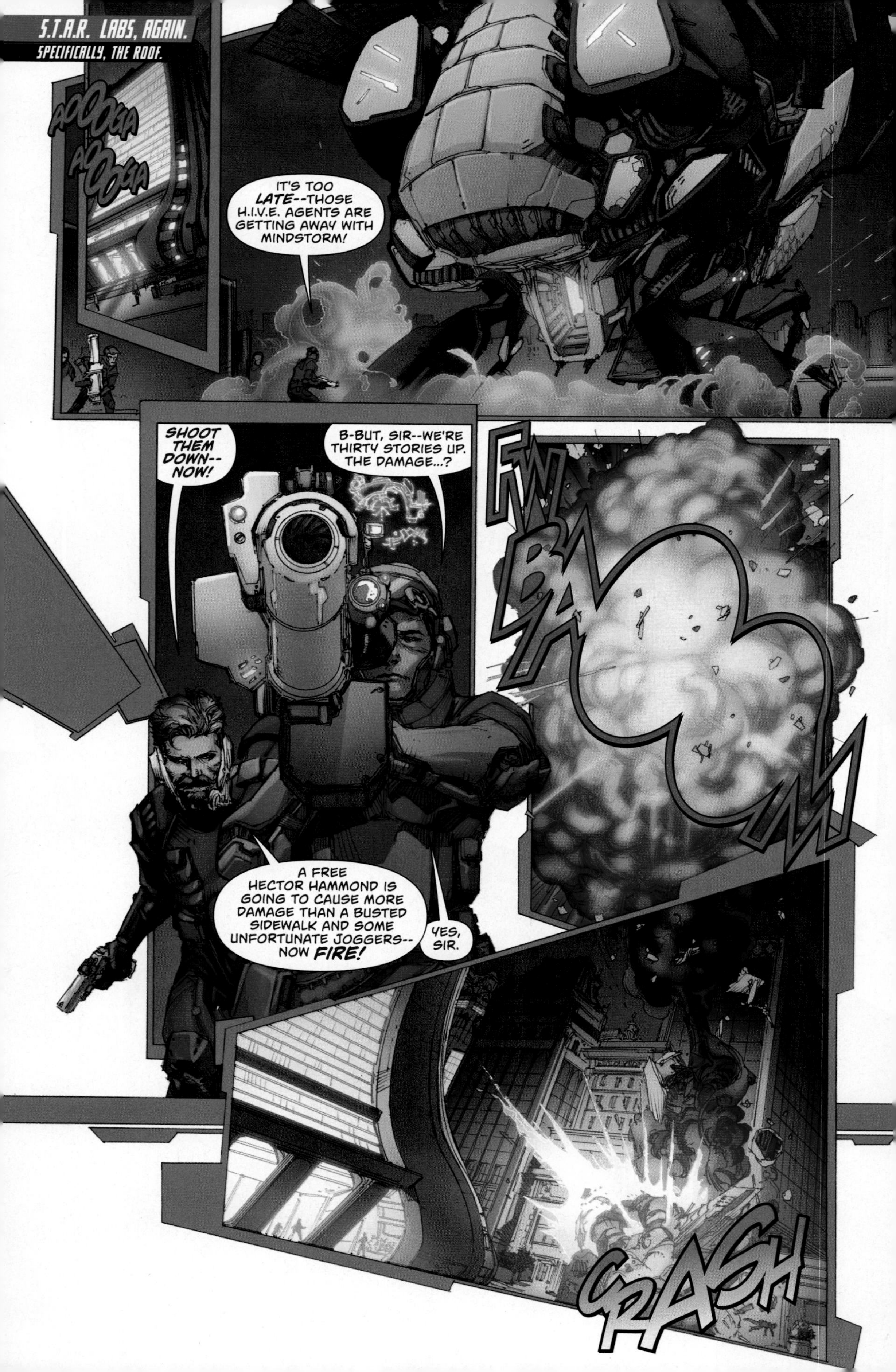
S.T.A.R. LABS, AGAIN.
SPECIFICALLY, THE ROOF.
AOOOGA
AOOOGA
IT'S TOO LATE--THOSE H.I.V.E. AGENTS ARE GETTING AWAY WITH MINDSTORM!
SHOOT THEM DOWN--NOW!
B-BUT, SIR--WE'RE THIRTY STORIES UP. THE DAMAGE...?
A FREE HECTOR HAMMOND IS GOING TO CAUSE MORE DAMAGE THAN A BUSTED SIDEWALK AND SOME UNFORTUNATE JOGGERS--NOW FIRE!
YES, SIR.
FWBAOOM
CRASH

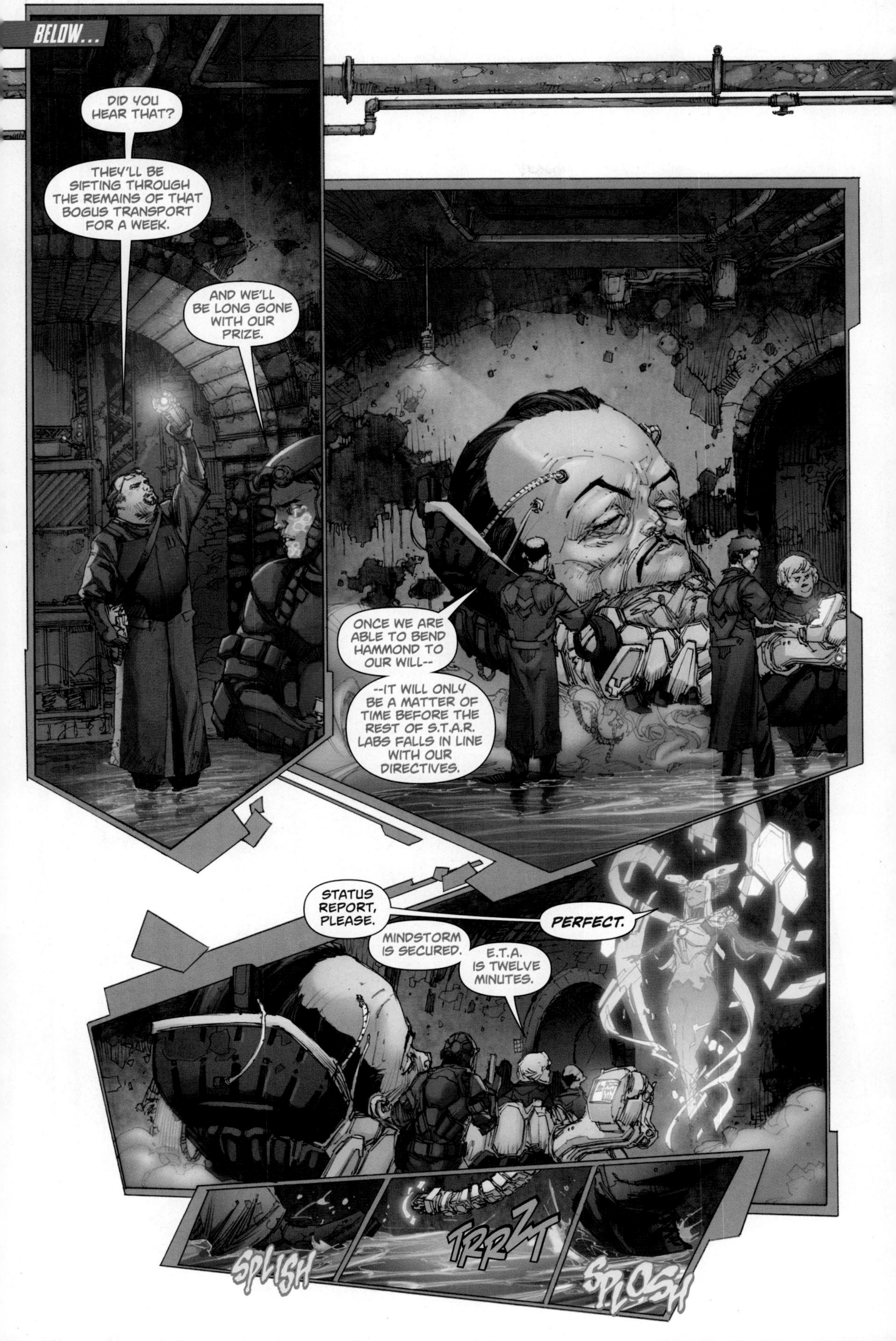
BELOW...
DID YOU HEAR THAT?
THEY'LL BE SIFTING THROUGH THE REMAINS OF THAT BOGUS TRANSPORT FOR A WEEK.
AND WE'LL BE LONG GONE WITH OUR PRIZE.
ONCE WE ARE ABLE TO BEND HAMMOND TO OUR WILL--
--IT WILL ONLY BE A MATTER OF TIME BEFORE THE REST OF S.T.A.R. LABS FALLS IN LINE WITH OUR DIRECTIVES.
STATUS REPORT, PLEASE.
MINDSTORM IS SECURED.
E.T.A. IS TWELVE MINUTES.
PERFECT.
SPLISH
TRRZT
SPLOSH

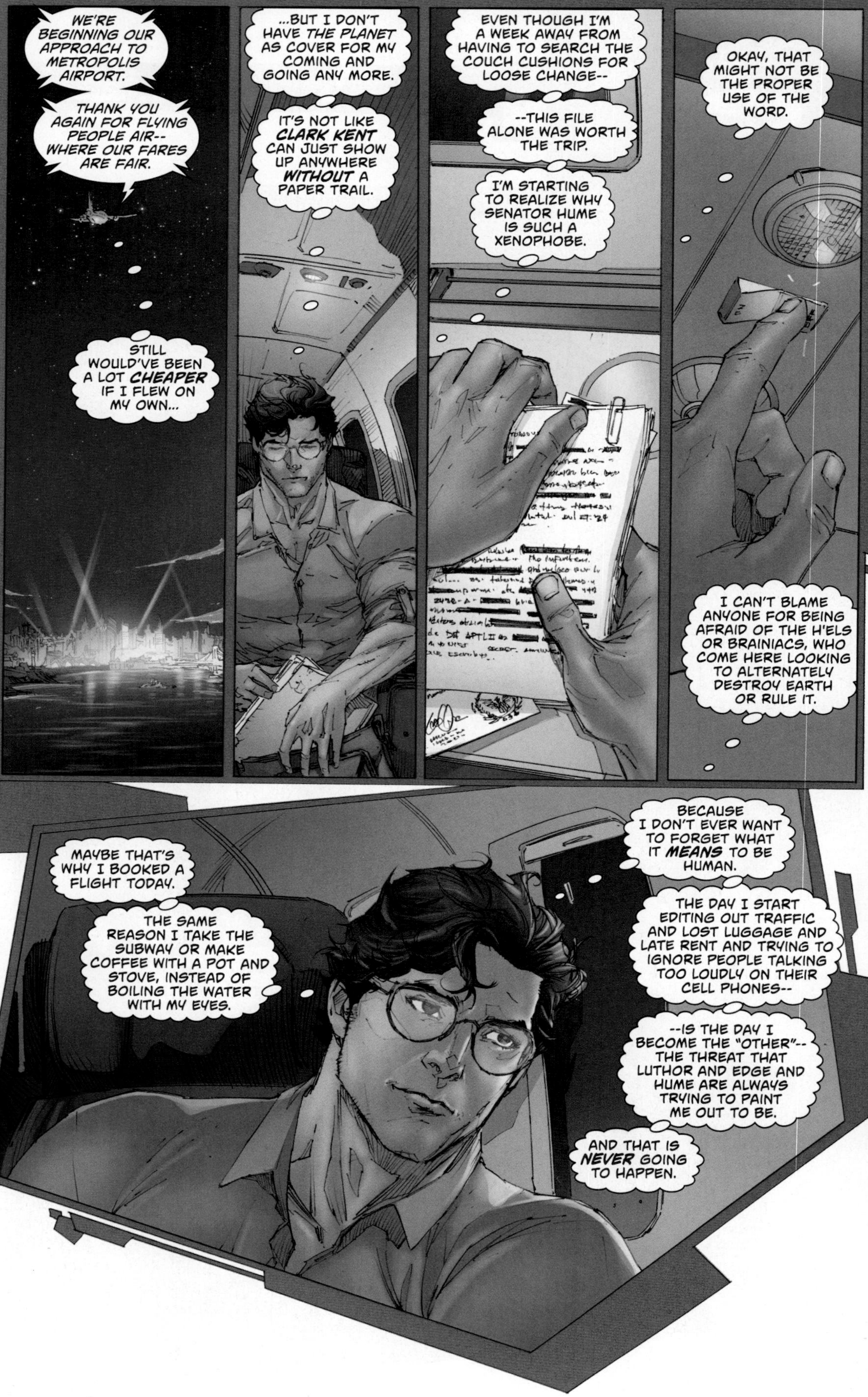
WE'RE BEGINNING OUR APPROACH TO METROPOLIS AIRPORT.
THANK YOU AGAIN FOR FLYING PEOPLE AIR--WHERE OUR FARES ARE FAIR.
STILL WOULD'VE BEEN A LOT CHEAPER IF I FLEW ON MY OWN...
...BUT I DON'T HAVE THE PLANET AS COVER FOR MY COMING AND GOING ANY MORE.
IT'S NOT LIKE CLARK KENT CAN JUST SHOW UP ANYWHERE WITHOUT A PAPER TRAIL.
EVEN THOUGH I'M A WEEK AWAY FROM HAVING TO SEARCH THE COUCH CUSHIONS FOR LOOSE CHANGE--
--THIS FILE ALONE WAS WORTH THE TRIP.
I'M STARTING TO REALIZE WHY SENATOR HUME IS SUCH A XENOPHOBE.
OKAY, THAT MIGHT NOT BE THE PROPER USE OF THE WORD.
I CAN'T BLAME ANYONE FOR BEING AFRAID OF THE H'ELS OR BRAINIACS, WHO COME HERE LOOKING TO ALTERNATELY DESTROY EARTH OR RULE IT.
MAYBE THAT'S WHY I BOOKED A FLIGHT TODAY.
THE SAME REASON I TAKE THE SUBWAY OR MAKE COFFEE WITH A POT AND STOVE, INSTEAD OF BOILING THE WATER WITH MY EYES.
BECAUSE I DON'T EVER WANT TO FORGET WHAT IT MEANS TO BE HUMAN.
THE DAY I START EDITING OUT TRAFFIC AND LOST LUGGAGE AND LATE RENT AND TRYING TO IGNORE PEOPLE TALKING TOO LOUDLY ON THEIR CELL PHONES--
--IS THE DAY I BECOME THE "OTHER"--THE THREAT THAT LUTHOR AND EDGE AND HUME ARE ALWAYS TRYING TO PAINT ME OUT TO BE.
AND THAT IS NEVER GOING TO HAPPEN.

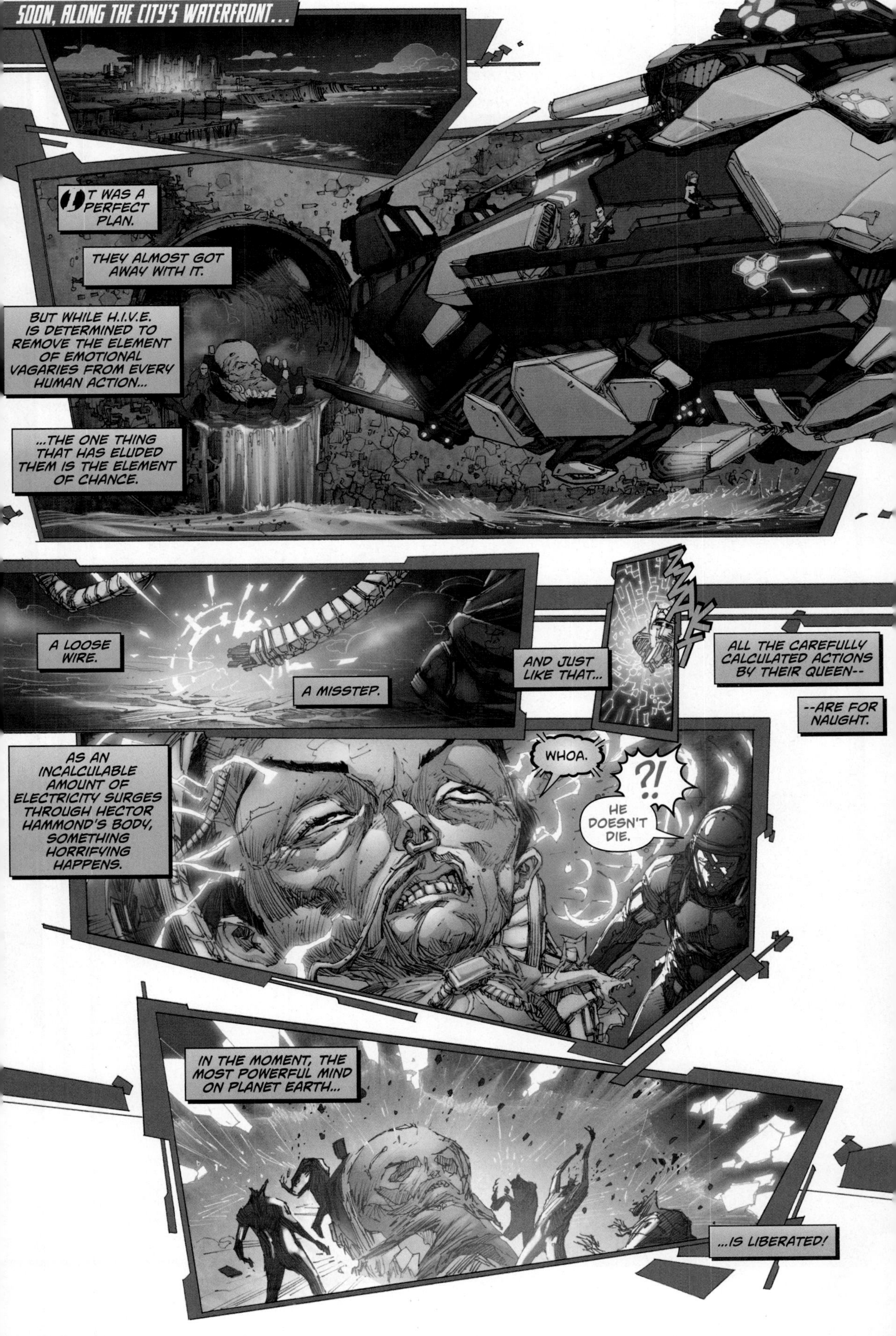
SOON, ALONG THE CITY'S WATERFRONT...
IT WAS A PERFECT PLAN.
THEY ALMOST GOT AWAY WITH IT.
BUT WHILE H.I.V.E. IS DETERMINED TO REMOVE THE ELEMENT OF EMOTIONAL VAGARIES FROM EVERY HUMAN ACTION...
...THE ONE THING THAT HAS ELUDED THEM IS THE ELEMENT OF CHANCE.
A LOOSE WIRE.
A MISSTEP.
AND JUST LIKE THAT...
ALL THE CAREFULLY CALCULATED ACTIONS BY THEIR QUEEN--
--ARE FOR NAUGHT.
AS AN INCALCULABLE AMOUNT OF ELECTRICITY SURGES THROUGH HECTOR HAMMOND'S BODY, SOMETHING HORRIFYING HAPPENS.
WHOA.
?!
HE DOESN'T DIE.
IN THE MOMENT, THE MOST POWERFUL MIND ON PLANET EARTH...
...IS LIBERATED!

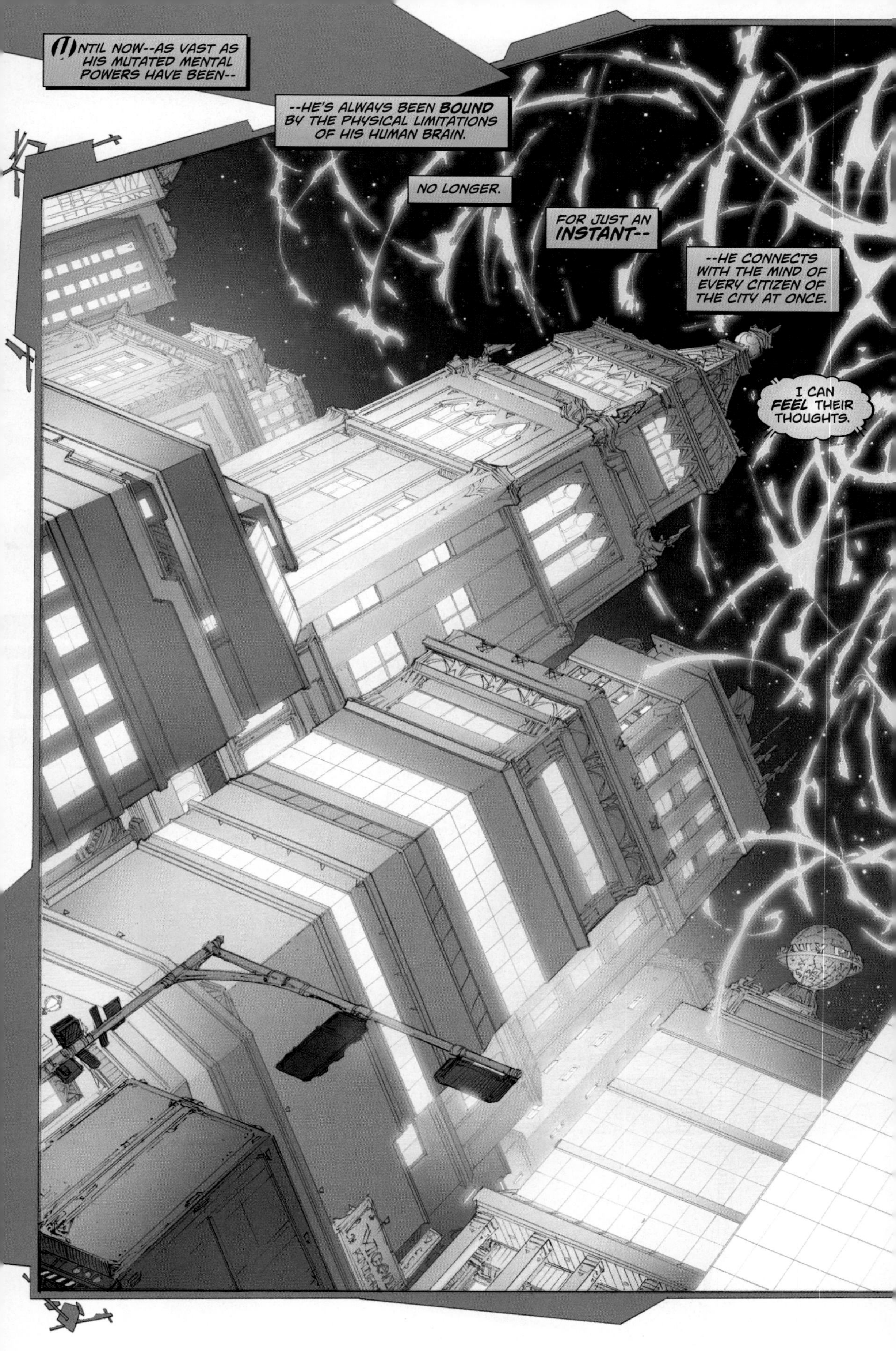
UNTIL NOW--AS VAST AS HIS MUTATED MENTAL POWERS HAVE BEEN--
--HE'S ALWAYS BEEN BOUND BY THE PHYSICAL LIMITATIONS OF HIS HUMAN BRAIN.
NO LONGER.
FOR JUST AN INSTANT--
--HE CONNECTS WITH THE MIND OF EVERY CITIZEN OF THE CITY AT ONCE.
I CAN FEEL THEIR THOUGHTS.

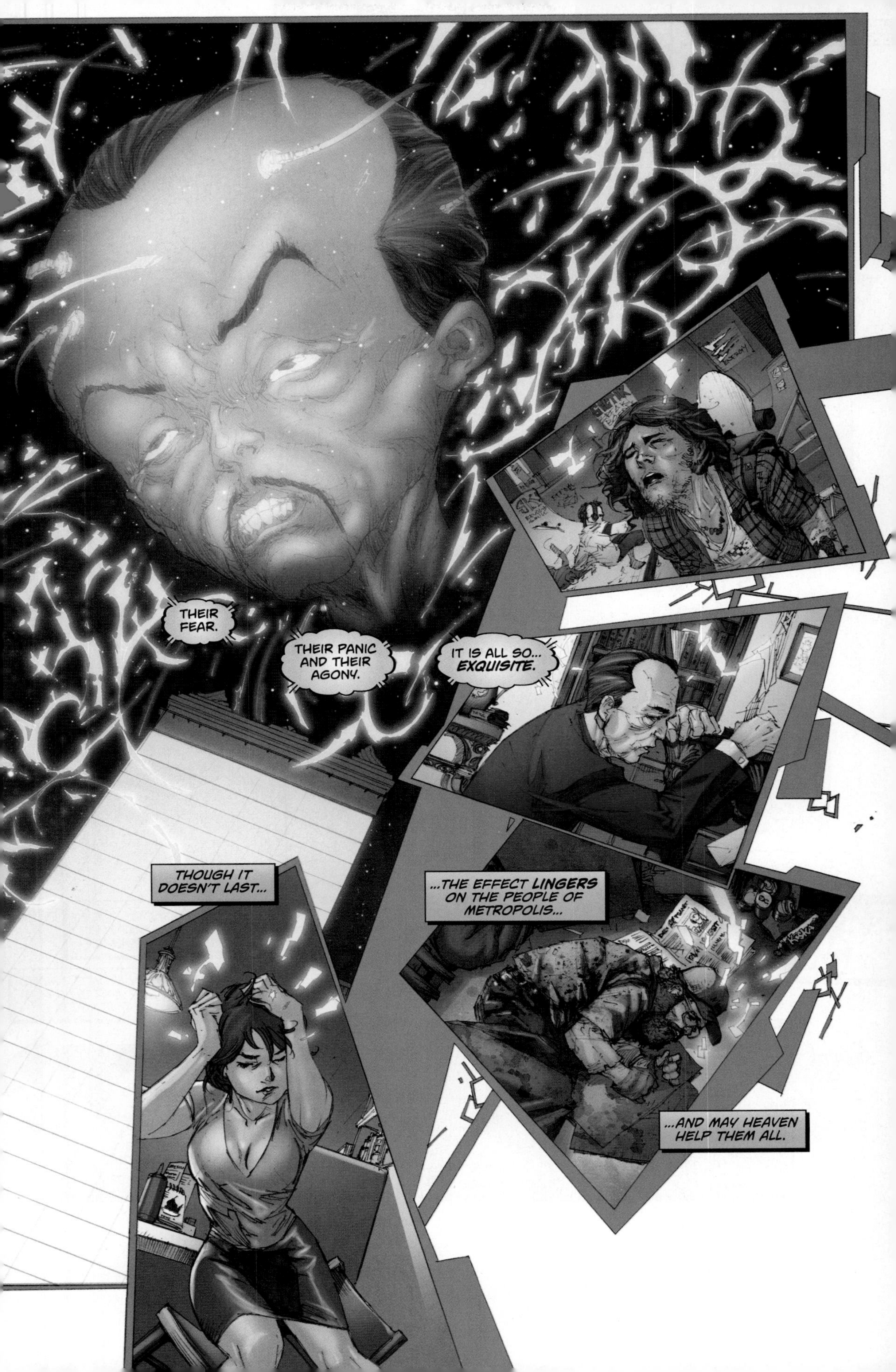
THEIR FEAR.
THEIR PANIC AND THEIR AGONY.
IT IS ALL SO... EXQUISITE.
THOUGH IT DOESN'T LAST...
...THE EFFECT LINGERS ON THE PEOPLE OF METROPOLIS...
...AND MAY HEAVEN HELP THEM ALL.

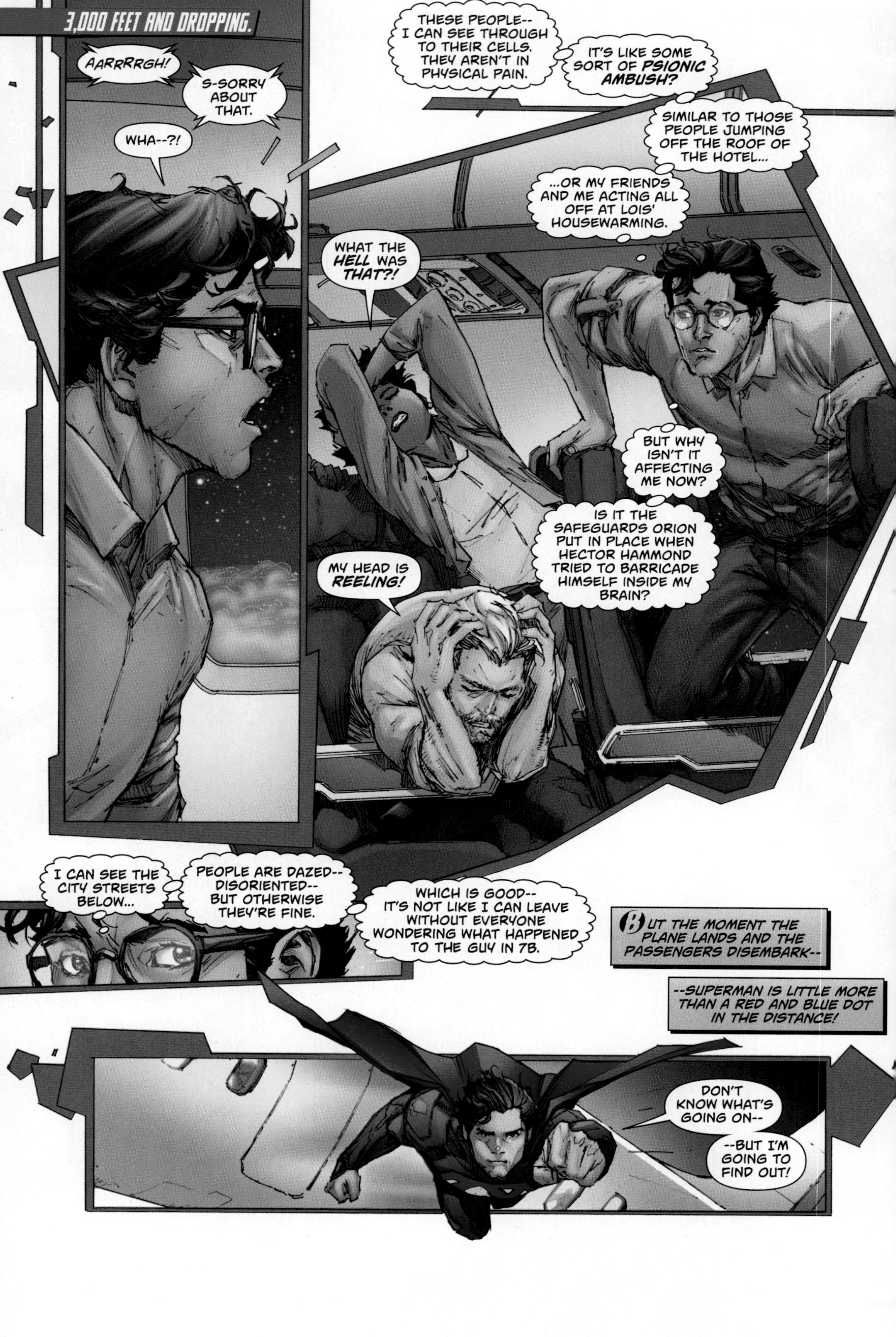
3,000 FEET AND DROPPING.
AARRRRGH!
S-SORRY ABOUT THAT.
WHA--?!
THESE PEOPLE-- I CAN SEE THROUGH TO THEIR CELLS. THEY AREN'T IN PHYSICAL PAIN.
IT'S LIKE SOME SORT OF PSIONIC AMBUSH?
SIMILAR TO THOSE PEOPLE JUMPING OFF THE ROOF OF THE HOTEL...
...OR MY FRIENDS AND ME ACTING ALL OFF AT LOIS' HOUSEWARMING.
WHAT THE HELL WAS THAT?!
BUT WHY ISN'T IT AFFECTING ME NOW?
IS IT THE SAFEGUARDS ORION PUT IN PLACE WHEN HECTOR HAMMOND TRIED TO BARRICADE HIMSELF INSIDE MY BRAIN?
MY HEAD IS REELING!
I CAN SEE THE CITY STREETS BELOW...
PEOPLE ARE DAZED-- DISORIENTED-- BUT OTHERWISE THEY'RE FINE.
WHICH IS GOOD-- IT'S NOT LIKE I CAN LEAVE WITHOUT EVERYONE WONDERING WHAT HAPPENED TO THE GUY IN 7B.
BUT THE MOMENT THE PLANE LANDS AND THE PASSENGERS DISEMBARK--
--SUPERMAN IS LITTLE MORE THAN A RED AND BLUE DOT IN THE DISTANCE!
DON'T KNOW WHAT'S GOING ON--
--BUT I'M GOING TO FIND OUT!

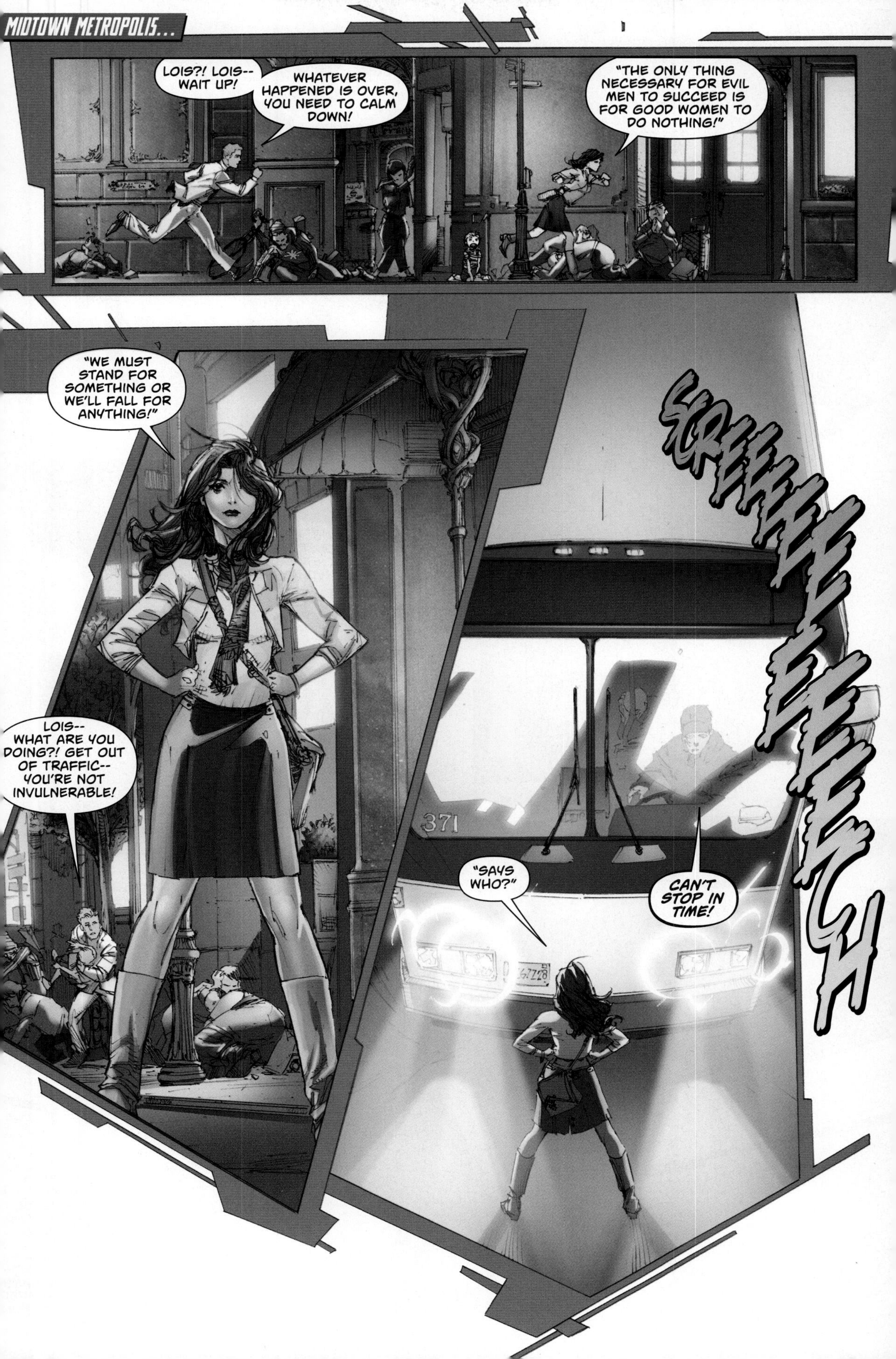
MIDTOWN METROPOLIS...
LOIS?! LOIS-- WAIT UP!
WHATEVER HAPPENED IS OVER, YOU NEED TO CALM DOWN!
"THE ONLY THING NECESSARY FOR EVIL MEN TO SUCCEED IS FOR GOOD WOMEN TO DO NOTHING!"
"WE MUST STAND FOR SOMETHING OR WE'LL FALL FOR ANYTHING!"
LOIS-- WHAT ARE YOU DOING?! GET OUT OF TRAFFIC-- YOU'RE NOT INVULNERABLE!
SCREEEEEEEECH
371
"SAYS WHO?"
CAN'T STOP IN TIME!

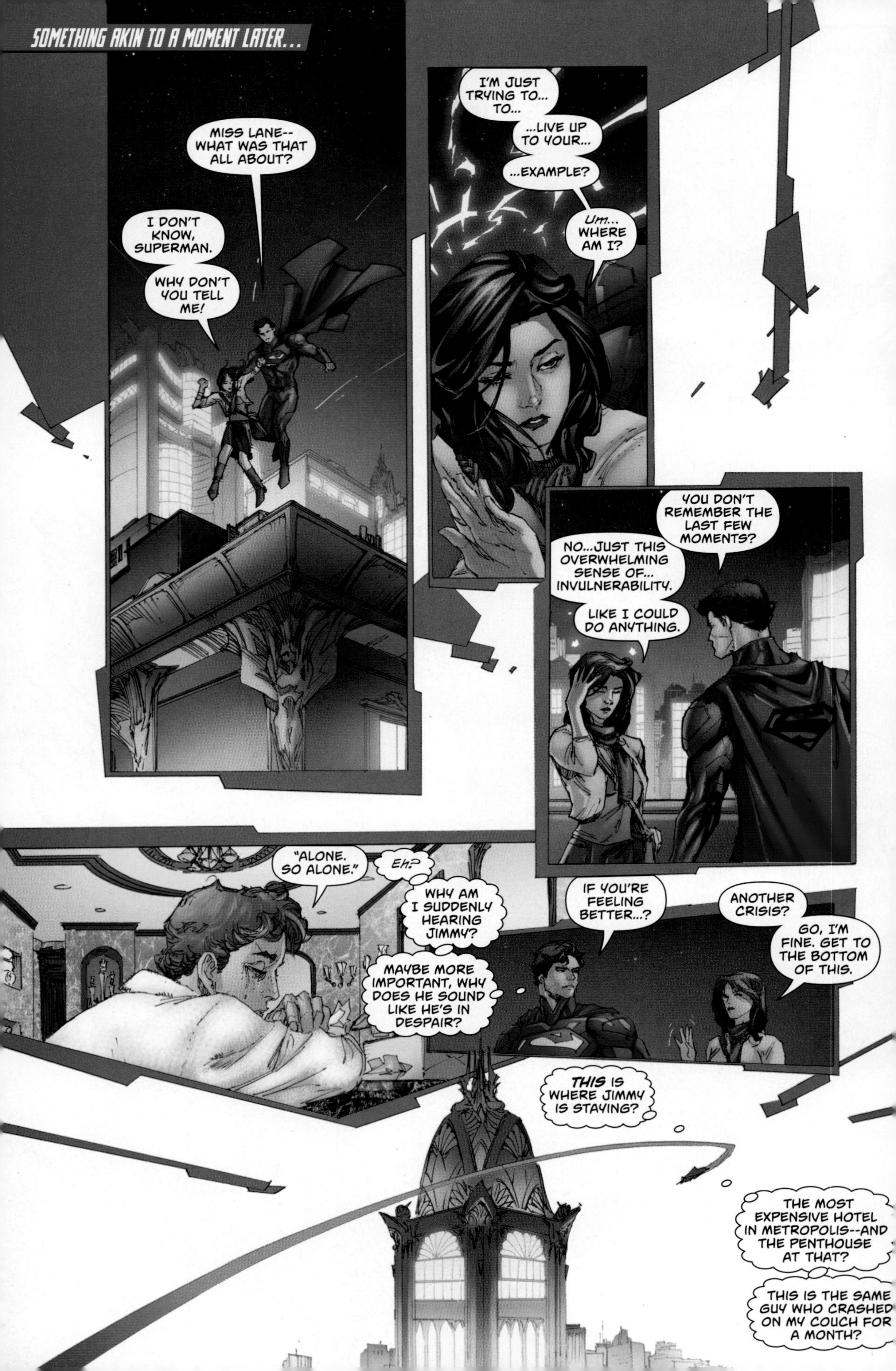

SOMETHING AKIN TO A MOMENT LATER...
MISS LANE--WHAT WAS THAT ALL ABOUT?
I DON'T KNOW, SUPERMAN.
WHY DON'T YOU TELL ME!
I'M JUST TRYING TO... TO...
...LIVE UP TO YOUR...
...EXAMPLE?
Um... WHERE AM I?
YOU DON'T REMEMBER THE LAST FEW MOMENTS?
NO...JUST THIS OVERWHELMING SENSE OF... INVULNERABILITY.
LIKE I COULD DO ANYTHING.
"ALONE. SO ALONE."
Eh?
WHY AM I SUDDENLY HEARING JIMMY?
MAYBE MORE IMPORTANT, WHY DOES HE SOUND LIKE HE'S IN DESPAIR?
IF YOU'RE FEELING BETTER...?
ANOTHER CRISIS?
GO, I'M FINE. GET TO THE BOTTOM OF THIS.
THIS IS WHERE JIMMY IS STAYING?
THE MOST EXPENSIVE HOTEL IN METROPOLIS--AND THE PENTHOUSE AT THAT?
THIS IS THE SAME GUY WHO CRASHED ON MY COUCH FOR A MONTH?

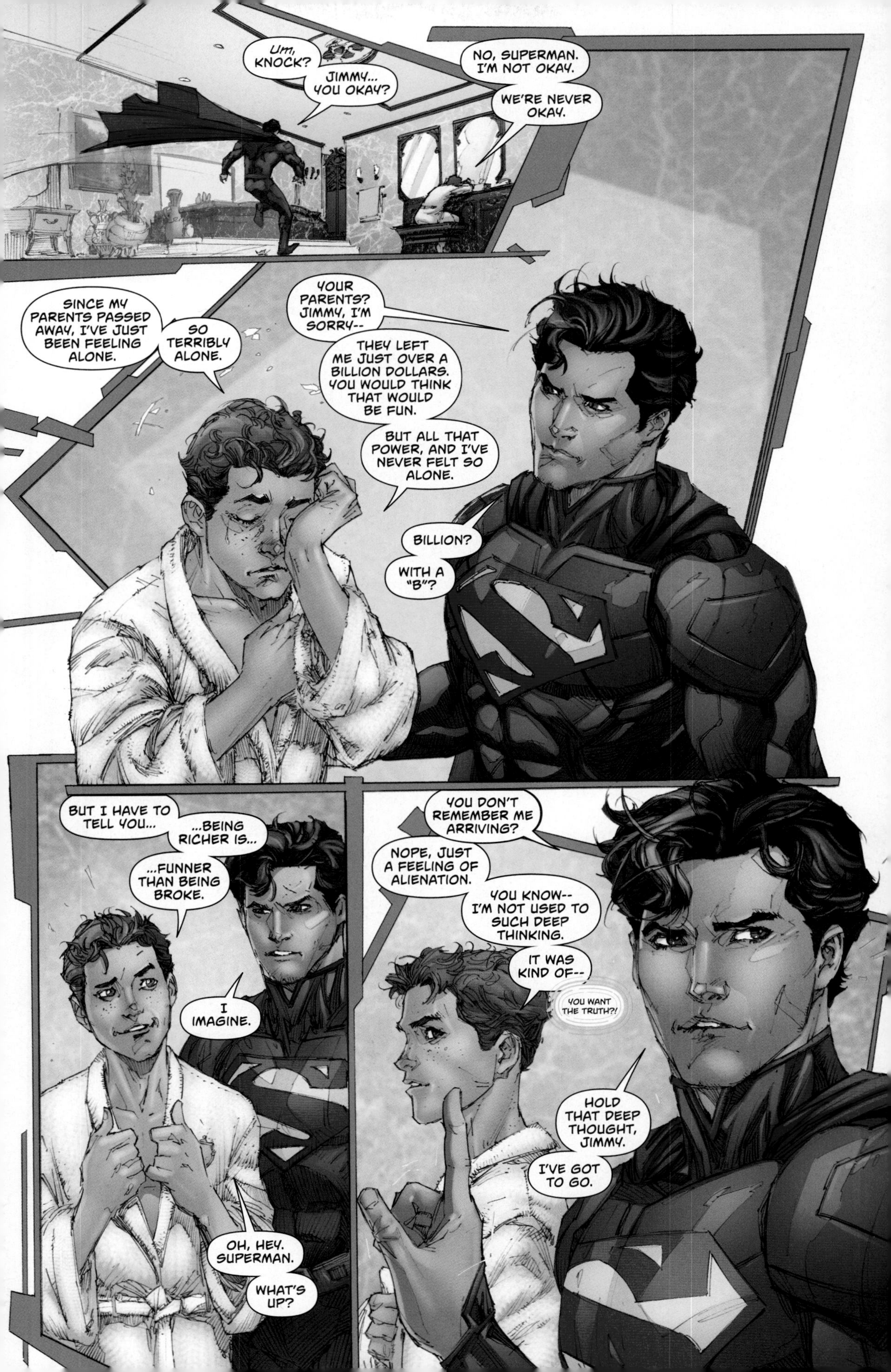
UM, KNOCK?
JIMMY... YOU OKAY?
NO, SUPERMAN. I'M NOT OKAY.
WE'RE NEVER OKAY.
SINCE MY PARENTS PASSED AWAY, I'VE JUST BEEN FEELING ALONE.
SO TERRIBLY ALONE.
YOUR PARENTS? JIMMY, I'M SORRY--
THEY LEFT ME JUST OVER A BILLION DOLLARS. YOU WOULD THINK THAT WOULD BE FUN.
BUT ALL THAT POWER, AND I'VE NEVER FELT SO ALONE.
BILLION?
WITH A "B"?
BUT I HAVE TO TELL YOU...
...BEING RICHER IS...
...FUNNER THAN BEING BROKE.
I IMAGINE.
OH, HEY. SUPERMAN.
WHAT'S UP?
YOU DON'T REMEMBER ME ARRIVING?
NOPE, JUST A FEELING OF ALIENATION.
YOU KNOW-- I'M NOT USED TO SUCH DEEP THINKING.
IT WAS KIND OF--
YOU WANT THE TRUTH?!
HOLD THAT DEEP THOUGHT, JIMMY.
I'VE GOT TO GO.

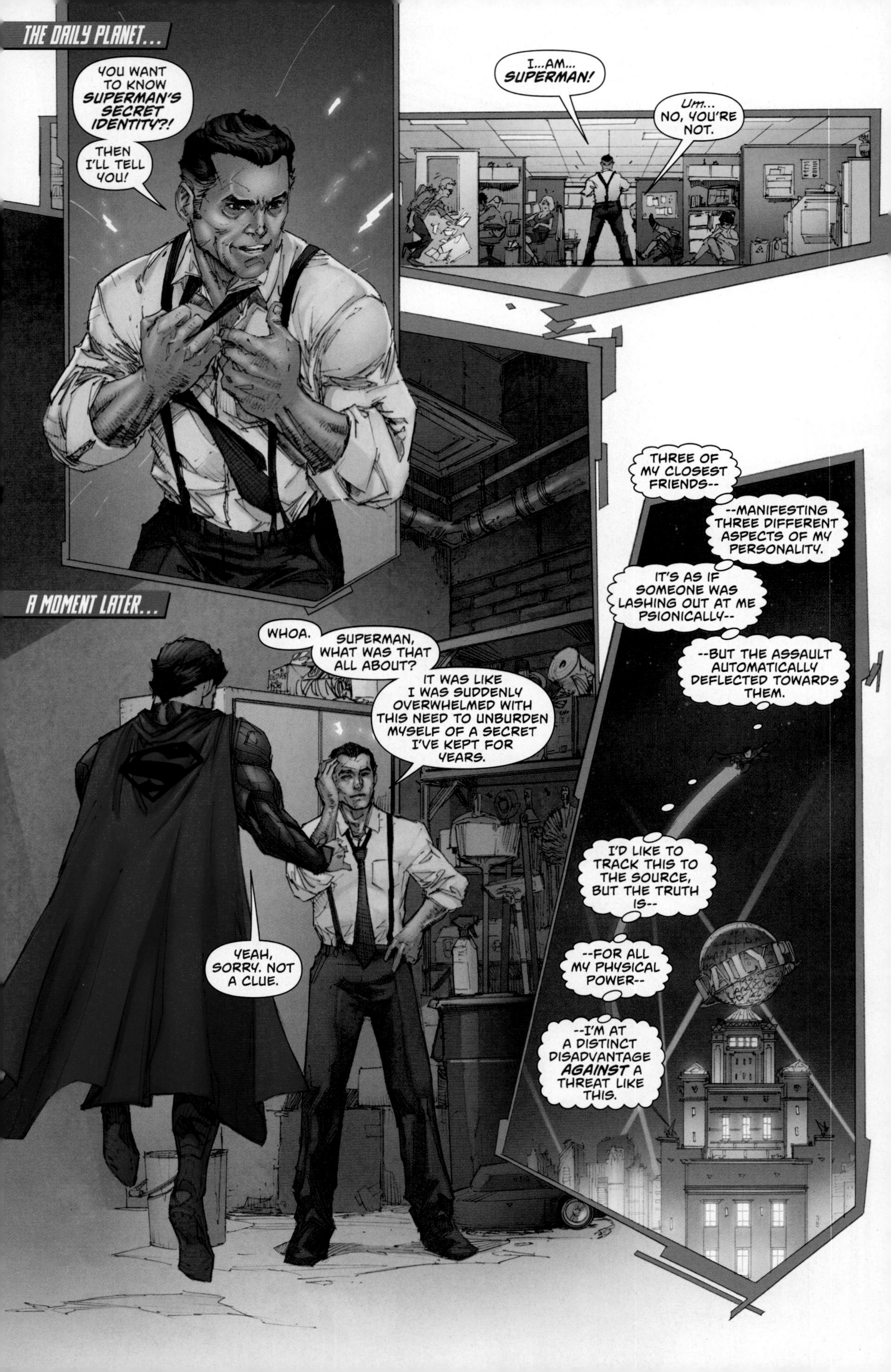
THE DAILY PLANET...
YOU WANT TO KNOW SUPERMAN'S SECRET IDENTITY?!
THEN I'LL TELL YOU!
I...AM... SUPERMAN!
Um... NO, YOU'RE NOT.
A MOMENT LATER...
WHOA.
SUPERMAN, WHAT WAS THAT ALL ABOUT?
IT WAS LIKE I WAS SUDDENLY OVERWHELMED WITH THIS NEED TO UNBURDEN MYSELF OF A SECRET I'VE KEPT FOR YEARS.
YEAH, SORRY. NOT A CLUE.
THREE OF MY CLOSEST FRIENDS--
--MANIFESTING THREE DIFFERENT ASPECTS OF MY PERSONALITY.
IT'S AS IF SOMEONE WAS LASHING OUT AT ME PSIONICALLY--
--BUT THE ASSAULT AUTOMATICALLY DEFLECTED TOWARDS THEM.
I'D LIKE TO TRACK THIS TO THE SOURCE, BUT THE TRUTH IS--
--FOR ALL MY PHYSICAL POWER--
--I'M AT A DISTINCT DISADVANTAGE AGAINST A THREAT LIKE THIS.

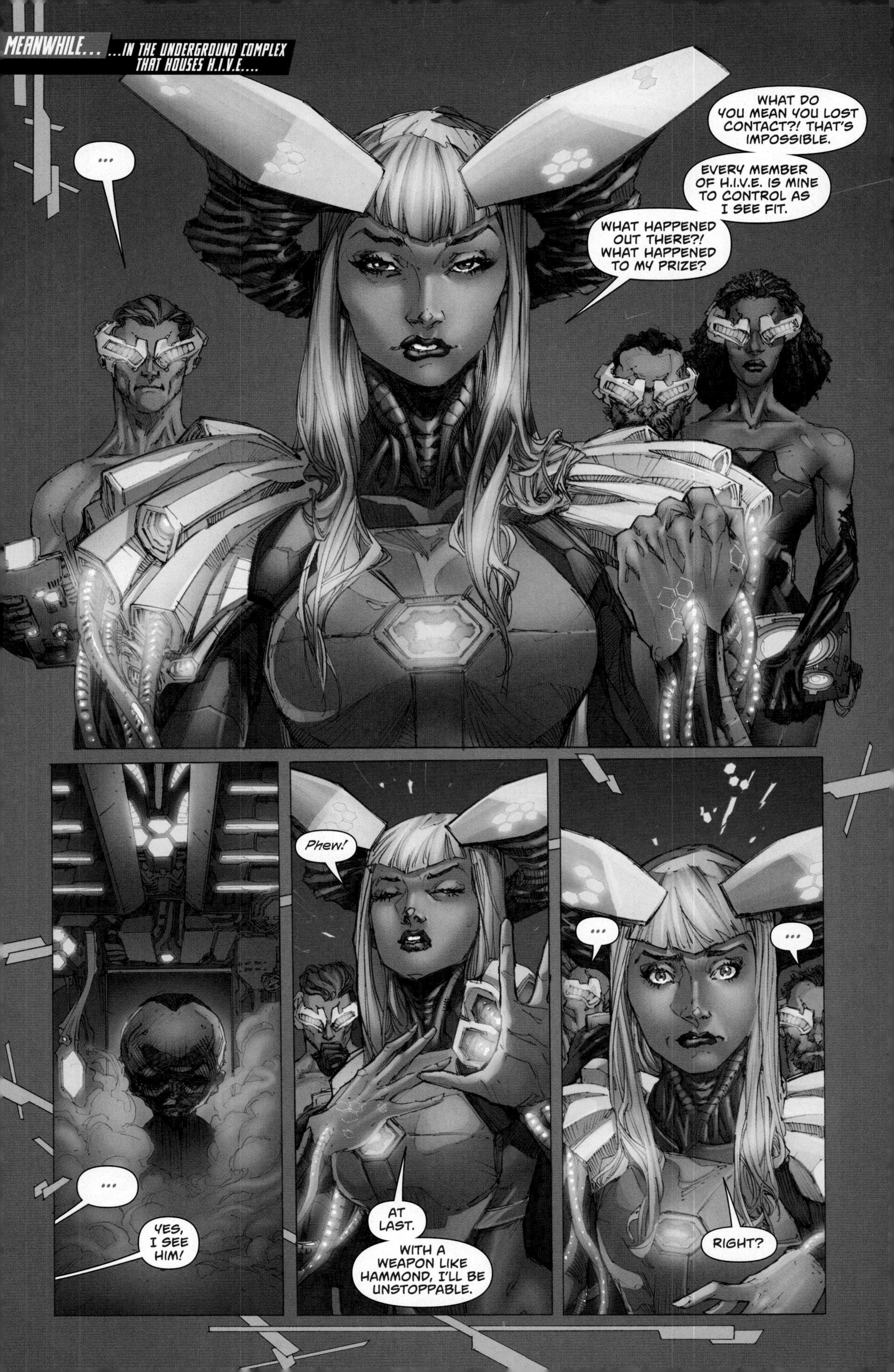
MEANWHILE...
...IN THE UNDERGROUND COMPLEX THAT HOUSES H.I.V.E....
...
WHAT DO YOU MEAN YOU LOST CONTACT?! THAT'S IMPOSSIBLE.
EVERY MEMBER OF H.I.V.E. IS MINE TO CONTROL AS I SEE FIT.
WHAT HAPPENED OUT THERE?! WHAT HAPPENED TO MY PRIZE?
...
YES, I SEE HIM!
Phew!
AT LAST.
WITH A WEAPON LIKE HAMMOND, I'LL BE UNSTOPPABLE.
...
...
RIGHT?

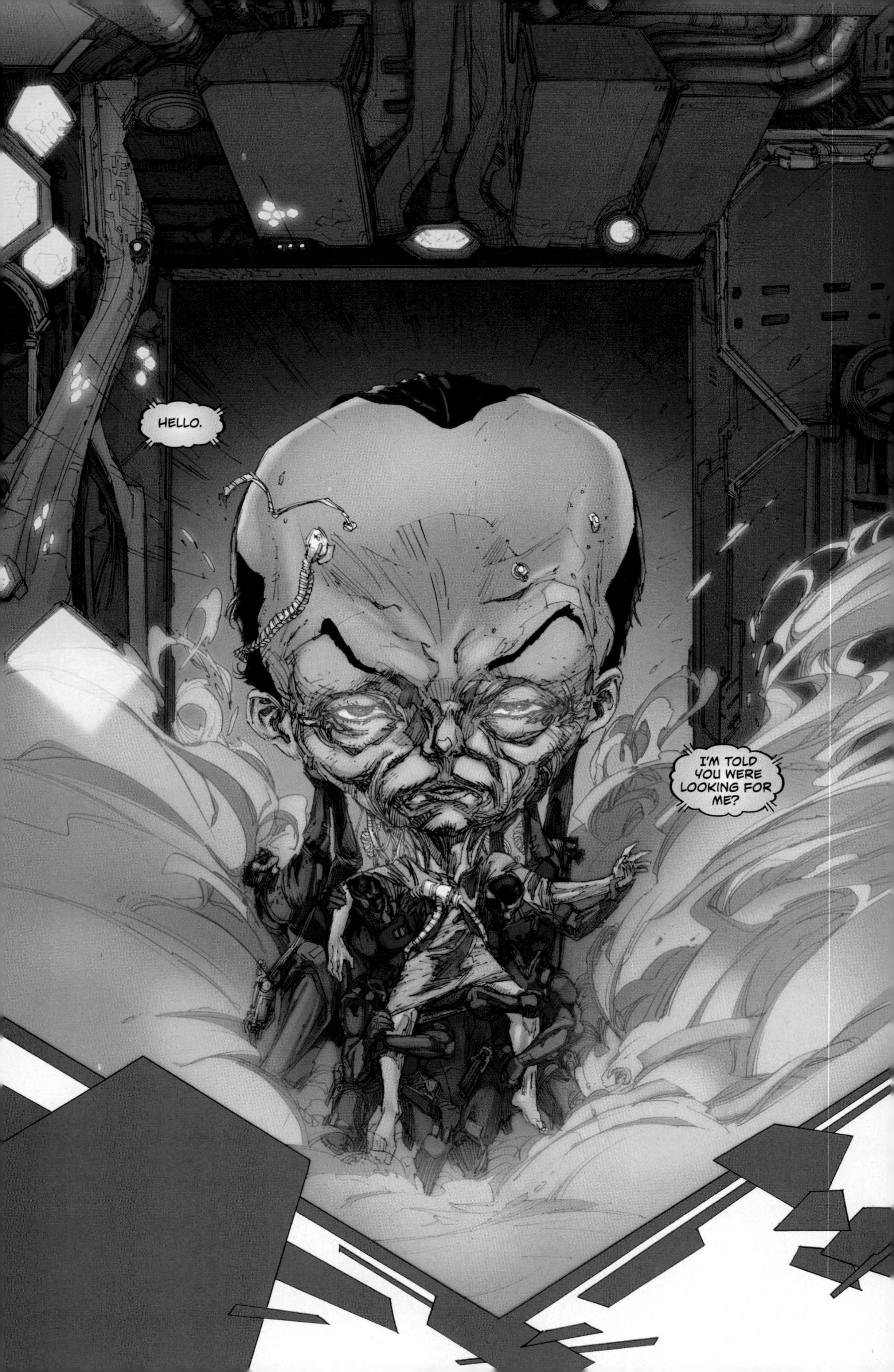
HELLO.
I'M TOLD YOU WERE LOOKING FOR ME?

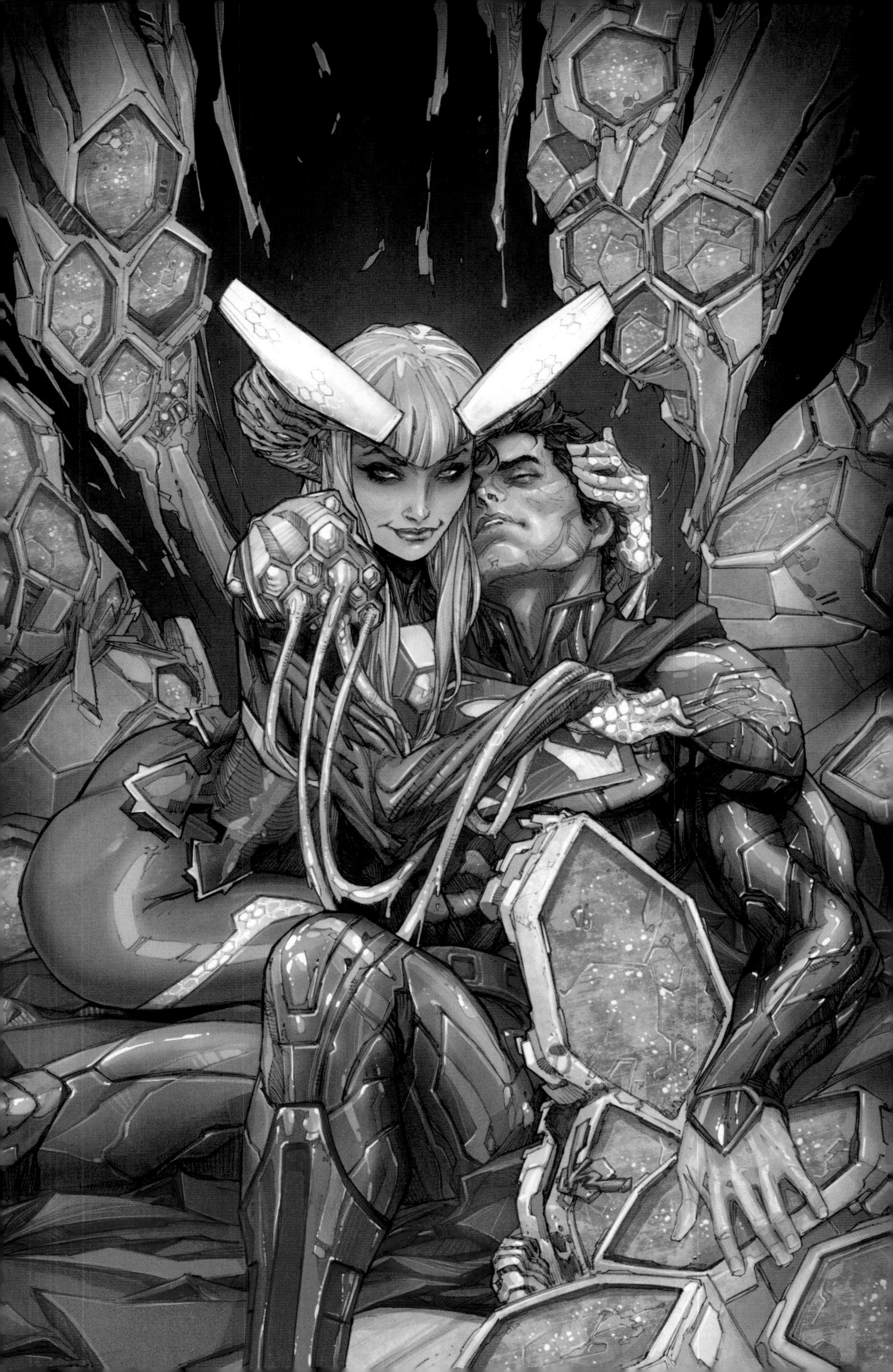

HEADACHES

SCOTT LOBDELL writer **EDDY BARROWS DANIEL HDR GERALDO BORGES** pencillers
EBER FERREIRA DANIEL HDR GERALDO BORGES inkers cover art by **KENNETH ROCAFORT**

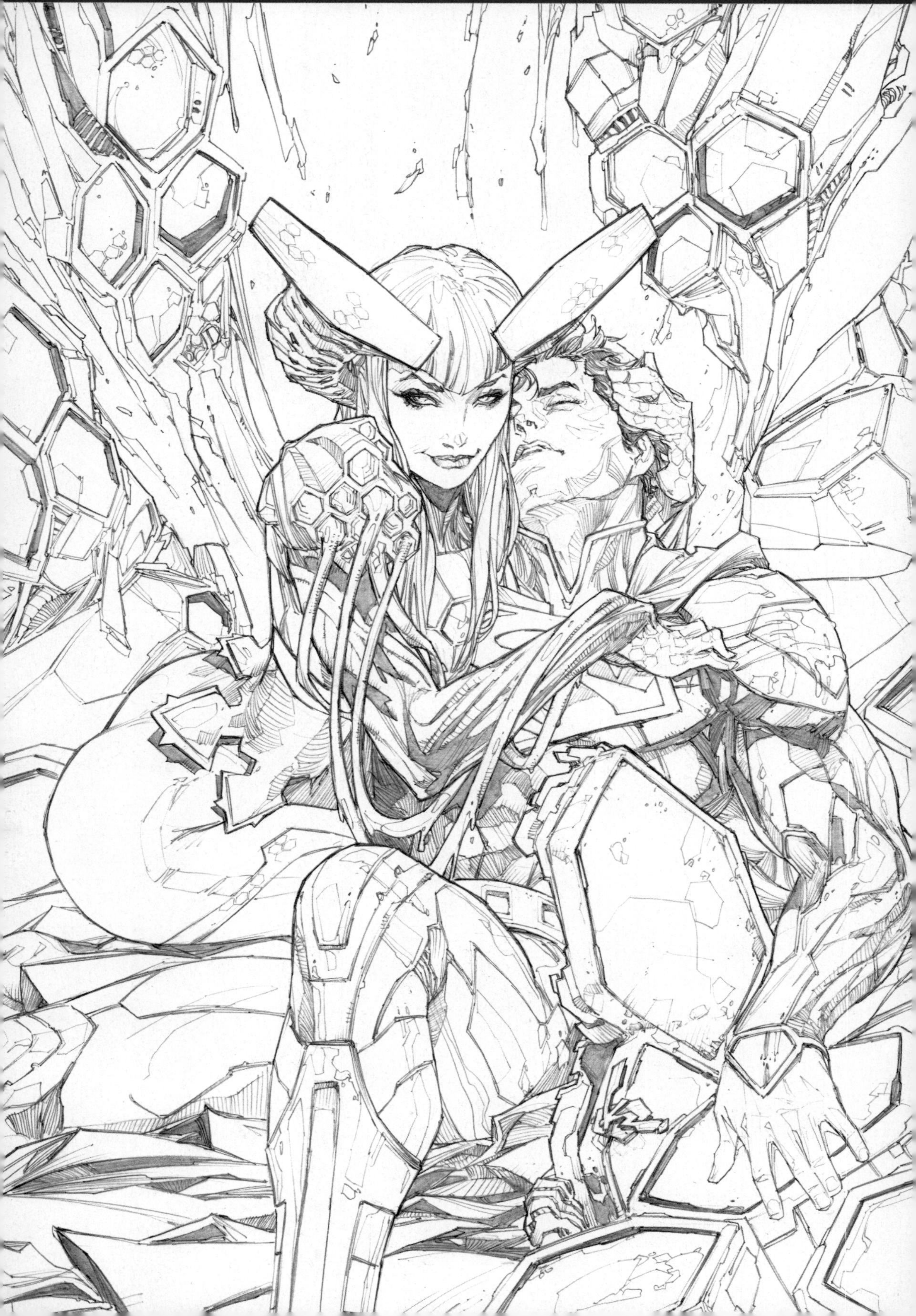

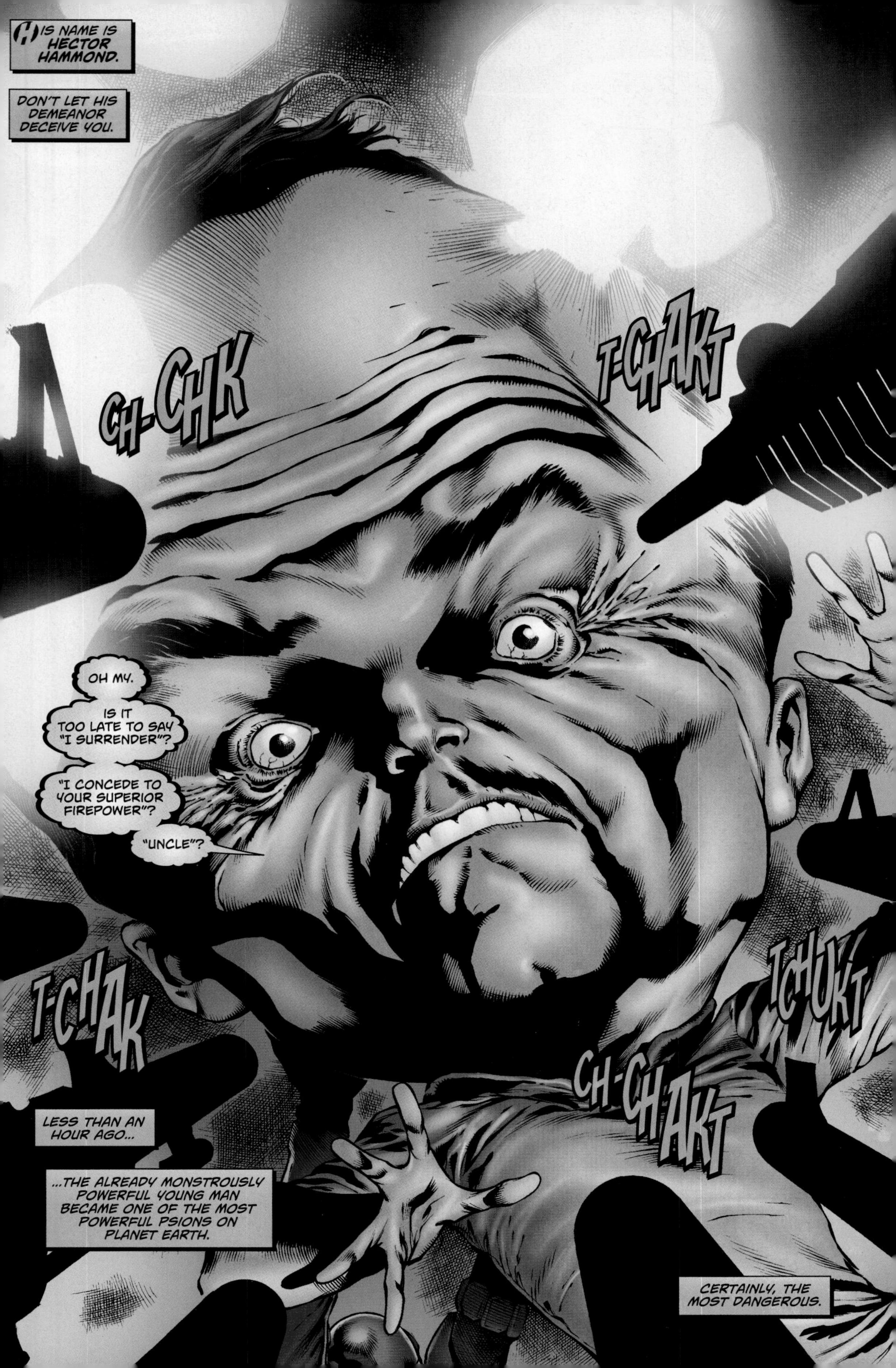
HIS NAME IS HECTOR HAMMOND.
DON'T LET HIS DEMEANOR DECEIVE YOU.
CH-CHK
T-CHAKT
OH MY.
IS IT TOO LATE TO SAY "I SURRENDER"?
"I CONCEDE TO YOUR SUPERIOR FIREPOWER"?
"UNCLE"?
T-CHAK
TCHUKT
CH-CHAKT
LESS THAN AN HOUR AGO...
...THE ALREADY MONSTROUSLY POWERFUL YOUNG MAN BECAME ONE OF THE MOST POWERFUL PSIONS ON PLANET EARTH.
CERTAINLY, THE MOST DANGEROUS.

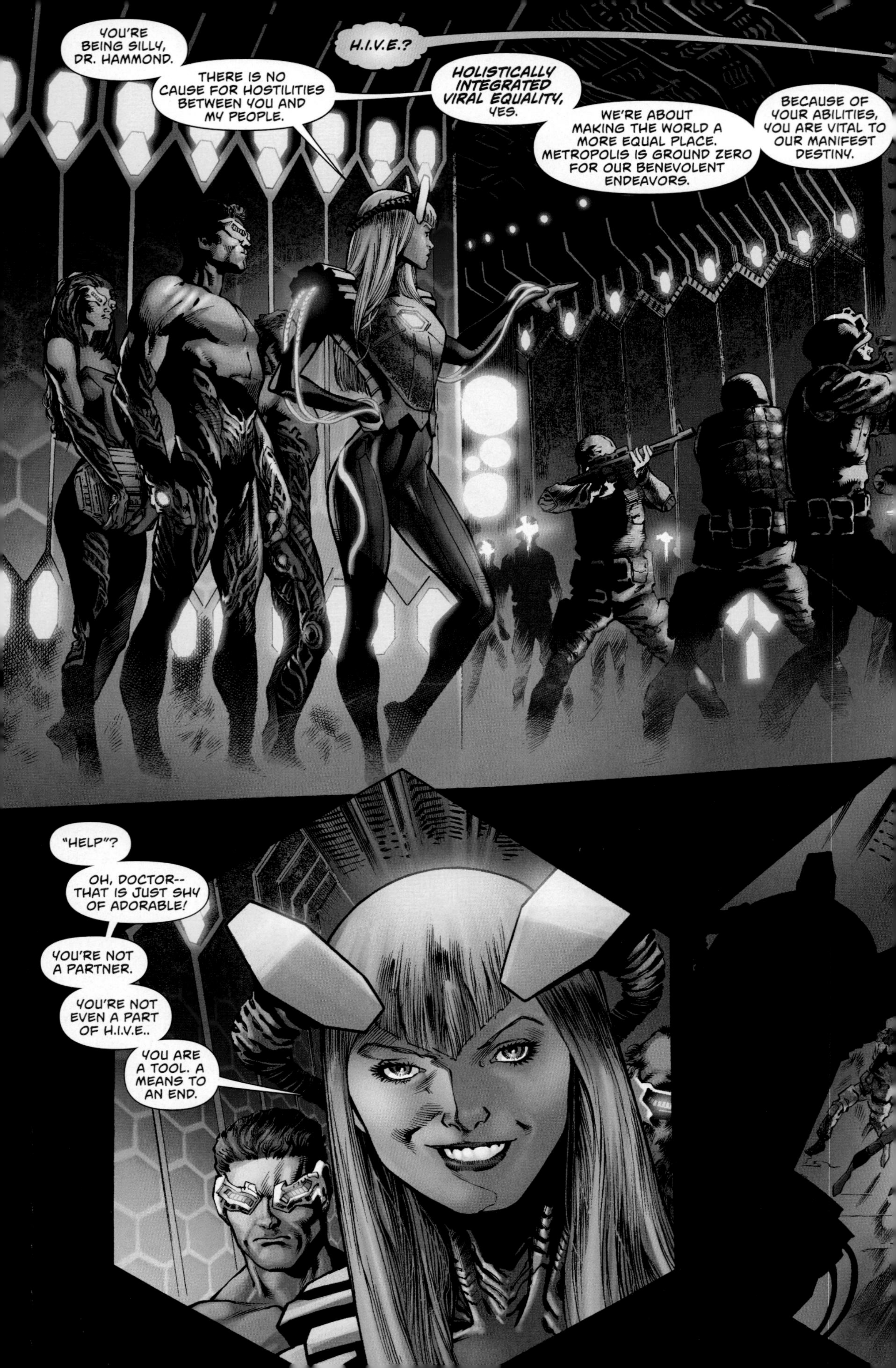
YOU'RE BEING SILLY, DR. HAMMOND.
THERE IS NO CAUSE FOR HOSTILITIES BETWEEN YOU AND MY PEOPLE.
H.I.V.E.?
HOLISTICALLY INTEGRATED VIRAL EQUALITY, YES.
WE'RE ABOUT MAKING THE WORLD A MORE EQUAL PLACE. METROPOLIS IS GROUND ZERO FOR OUR BENEVOLENT ENDEAVORS.
BECAUSE OF YOUR ABILITIES, YOU ARE VITAL TO OUR MANIFEST DESTINY.
"HELP"?
OH, DOCTOR-- THAT IS JUST SHY OF ADORABLE!
YOU'RE NOT A PARTNER.
YOU'RE NOT EVEN A PART OF H.I.V.E..
YOU ARE A TOOL. A MEANS TO AN END.

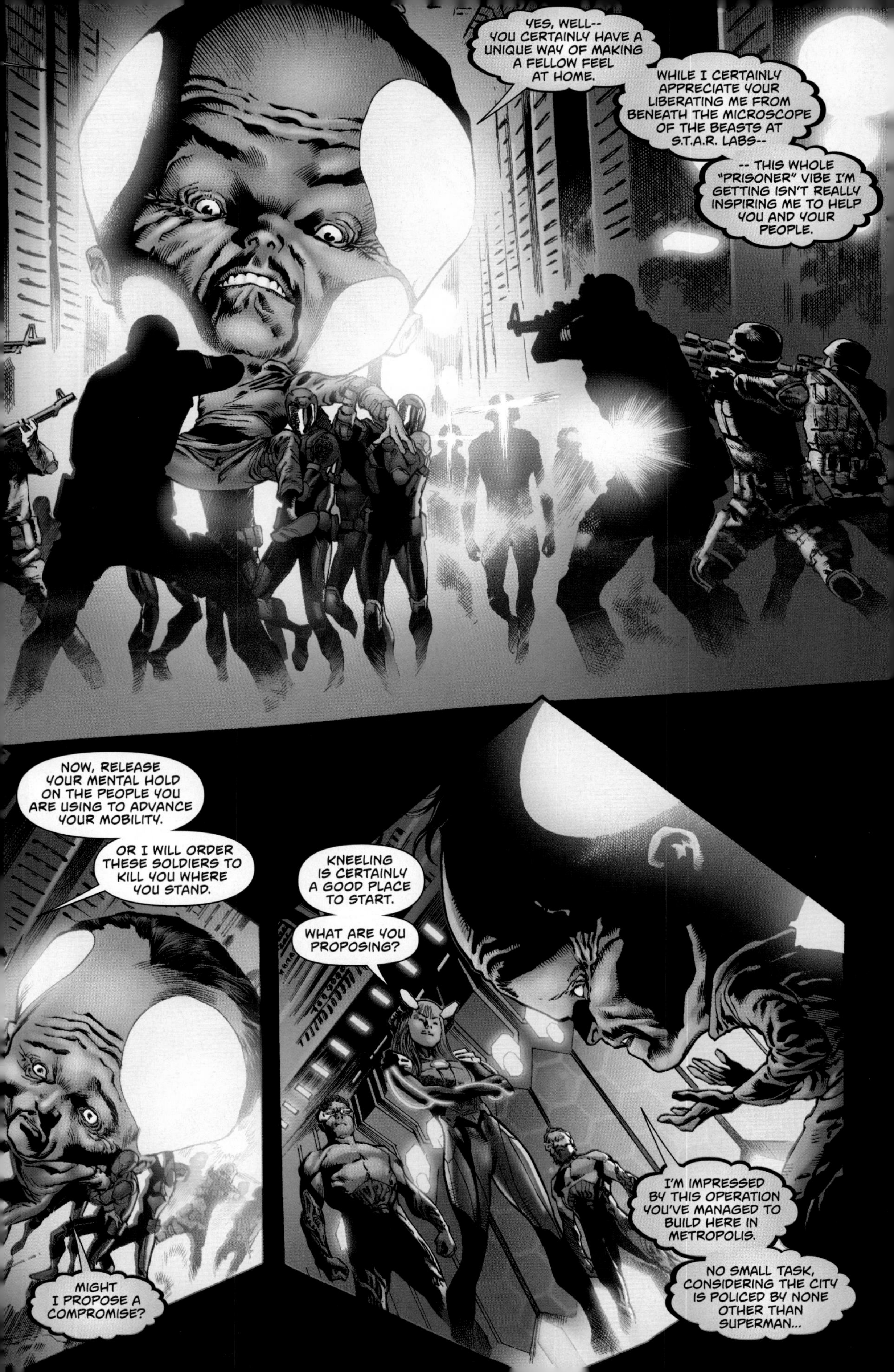
YES, WELL-- YOU CERTAINLY HAVE A UNIQUE WAY OF MAKING A FELLOW FEEL AT HOME.
WHILE I CERTAINLY APPRECIATE YOUR LIBERATING ME FROM BENEATH THE MICROSCOPE OF THE BEASTS AT S.T.A.R. LABS--
-- THIS WHOLE "PRISONER" VIBE I'M GETTING ISN'T REALLY INSPIRING ME TO HELP YOU AND YOUR PEOPLE.
NOW, RELEASE YOUR MENTAL HOLD ON THE PEOPLE YOU ARE USING TO ADVANCE YOUR MOBILITY.
OR I WILL ORDER THESE SOLDIERS TO KILL YOU WHERE YOU STAND.
MIGHT I PROPOSE A COMPROMISE?
KNEELING IS CERTAINLY A GOOD PLACE TO START.
WHAT ARE YOU PROPOSING?
I'M IMPRESSED BY THIS OPERATION YOU'VE MANAGED TO BUILD HERE IN METROPOLIS.
NO SMALL TASK, CONSIDERING THE CITY IS POLICED BY NONE OTHER THAN SUPERMAN...

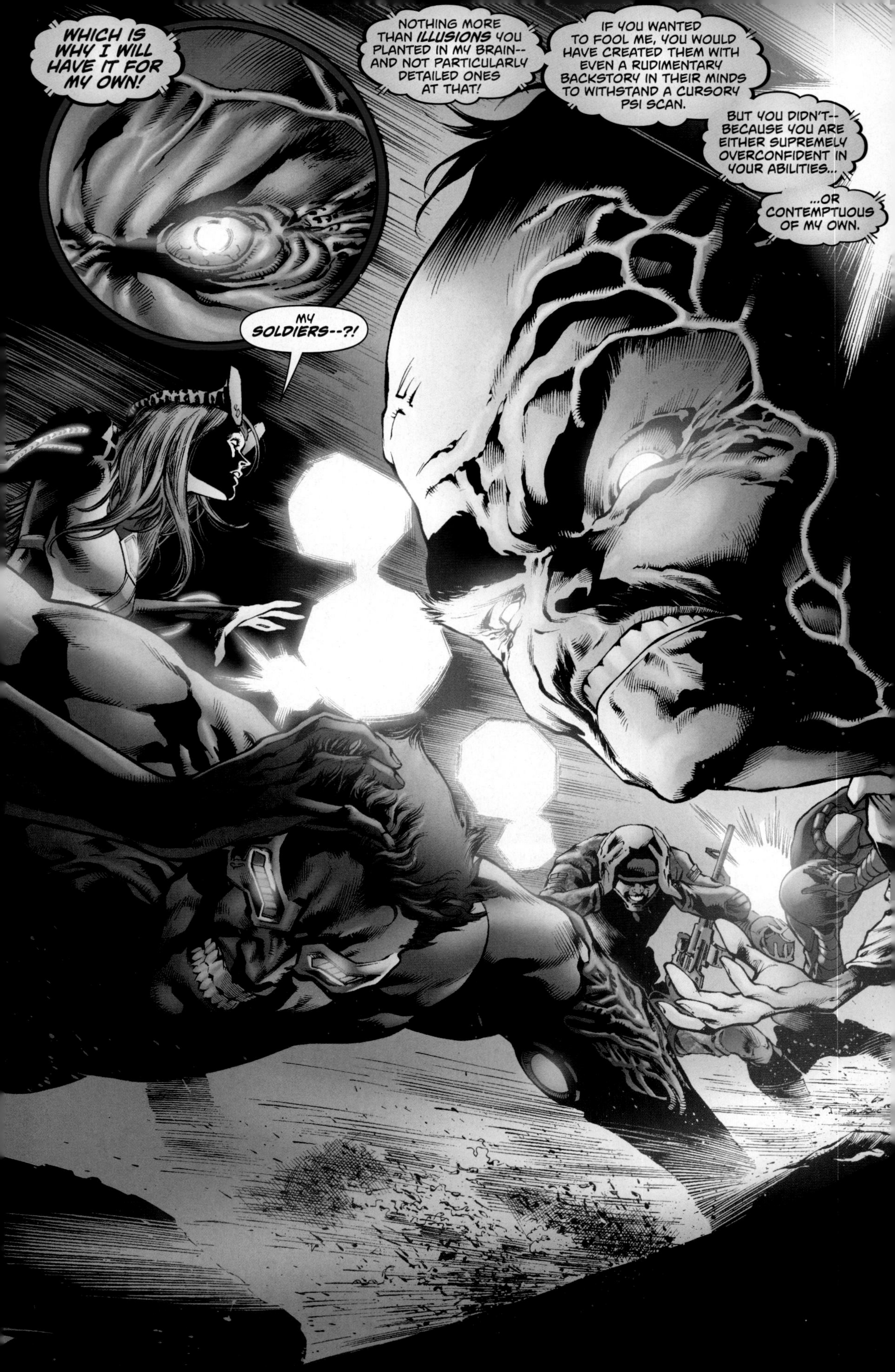
WHICH IS WHY I WILL HAVE IT FOR MY OWN!
NOTHING MORE THAN ILLUSIONS YOU PLANTED IN MY BRAIN-- AND NOT PARTICULARLY DETAILED ONES AT THAT!
IF YOU WANTED TO FOOL ME, YOU WOULD HAVE CREATED THEM WITH EVEN A RUDIMENTARY BACKSTORY IN THEIR MINDS TO WITHSTAND A CURSORY PSI SCAN.
BUT YOU DIDN'T-- BECAUSE YOU ARE EITHER SUPREMELY OVERCONFIDENT IN YOUR ABILITIES...
...OR CONTEMPTUOUS OF MY OWN.
MY SOLDIERS--?!

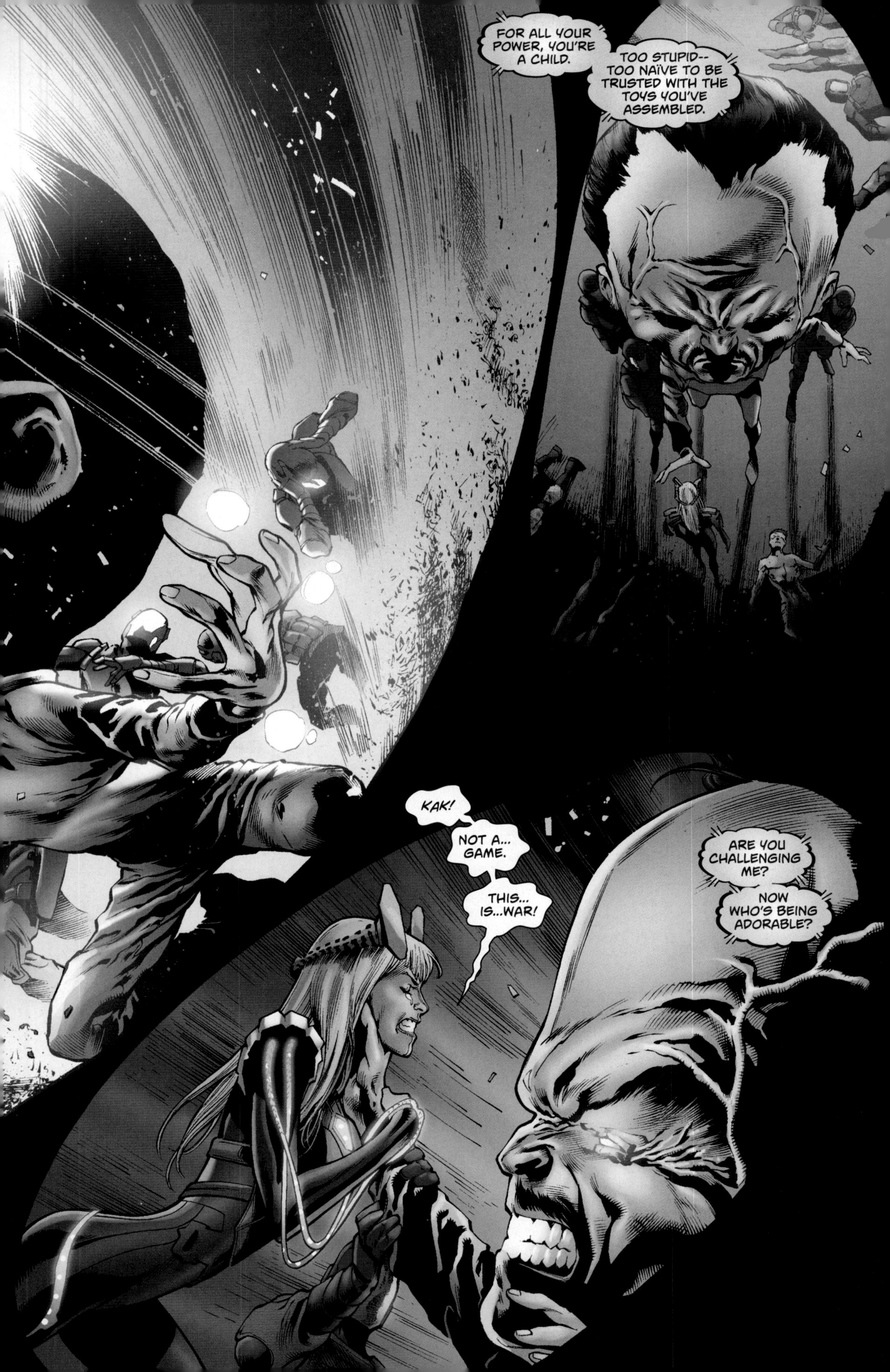

FOR ALL YOUR POWER, YOU'RE A CHILD.
TOO STUPID-- TOO NAÏVE TO BE TRUSTED WITH THE TOYS YOU'VE ASSEMBLED.
KAK!
NOT A... GAME.
THIS... IS...WAR!
ARE YOU CHALLENGING ME?
NOW WHO'S BEING ADORABLE?

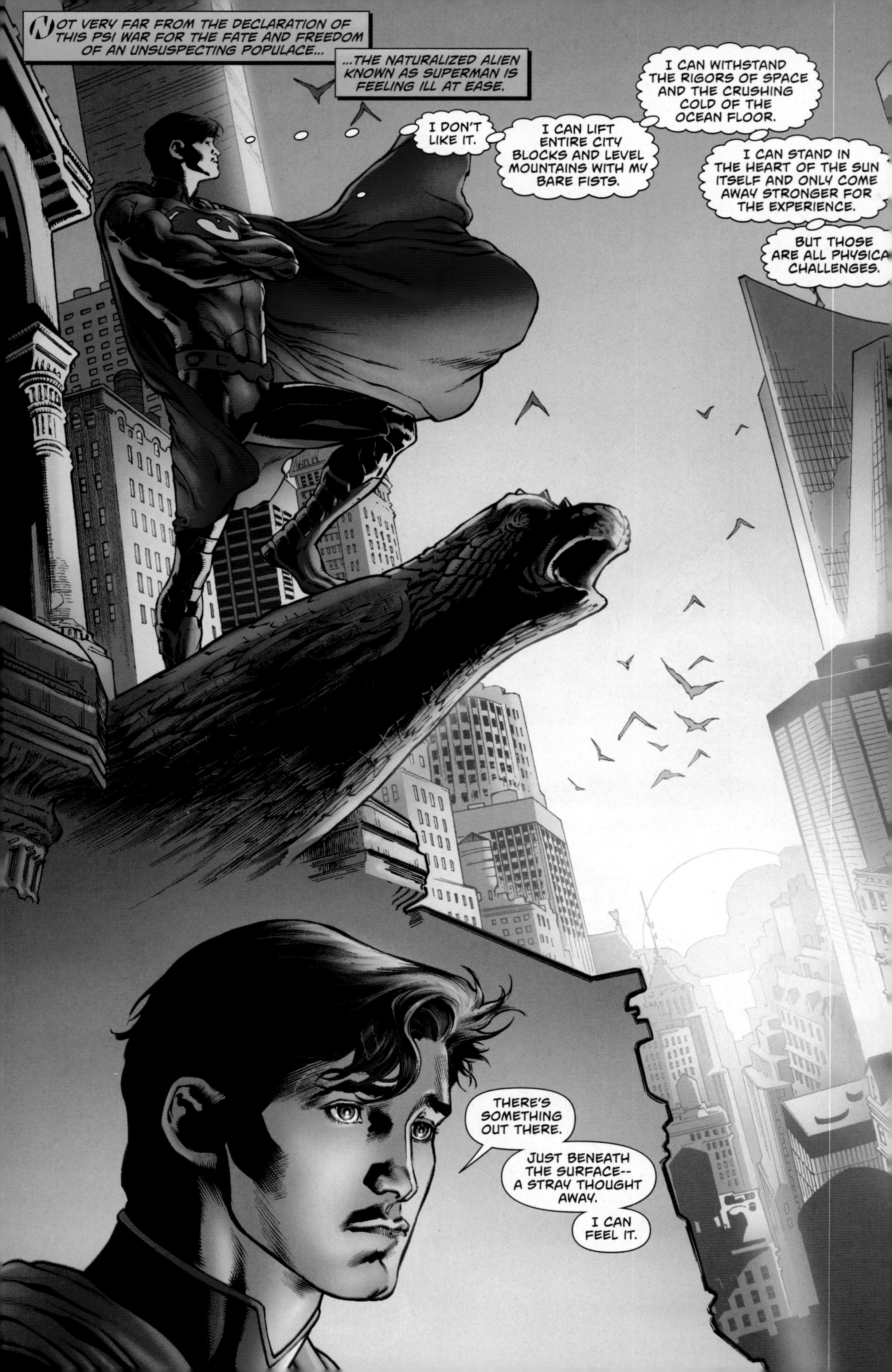
NOT VERY FAR FROM THE DECLARATION OF THIS PSI WAR FOR THE FATE AND FREEDOM OF AN UNSUSPECTING POPULACE...
...THE NATURALIZED ALIEN KNOWN AS SUPERMAN IS FEELING ILL AT EASE.
I DON'T LIKE IT.
I CAN LIFT ENTIRE CITY BLOCKS AND LEVEL MOUNTAINS WITH MY BARE FISTS.
I CAN WITHSTAND THE RIGORS OF SPACE AND THE CRUSHING COLD OF THE OCEAN FLOOR.
I CAN STAND IN THE HEART OF THE SUN ITSELF AND ONLY COME AWAY STRONGER FOR THE EXPERIENCE.
BUT THOSE ARE ALL PHYSICA CHALLENGES.
THERE'S SOMETHING OUT THERE.
JUST BENEATH THE SURFACE-- A STRAY THOUGHT AWAY.
I CAN FEEL IT.

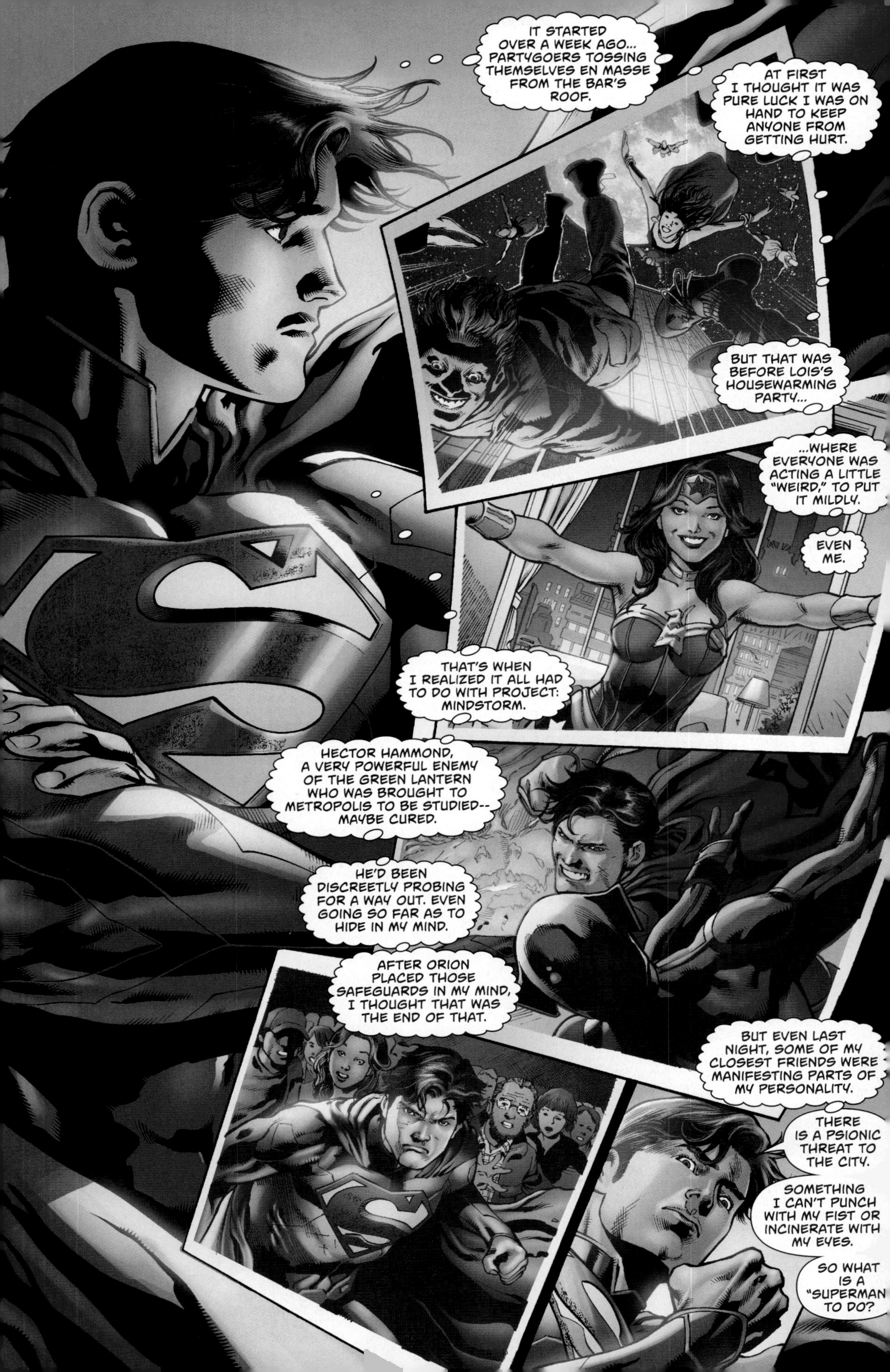
IT STARTED OVER A WEEK AGO... PARTYGOERS TOSSING THEMSELVES EN MASSE FROM THE BAR'S ROOF.
AT FIRST I THOUGHT IT WAS PURE LUCK I WAS ON HAND TO KEEP ANYONE FROM GETTING HURT.
BUT THAT WAS BEFORE LOIS'S HOUSEWARMING PARTY...
...WHERE EVERYONE WAS ACTING A LITTLE "WEIRD," TO PUT IT MILDLY.
EVEN ME.
THAT'S WHEN I REALIZED IT ALL HAD TO DO WITH PROJECT: MINDSTORM.
HECTOR HAMMOND, A VERY POWERFUL ENEMY OF THE GREEN LANTERN WHO WAS BROUGHT TO METROPOLIS TO BE STUDIED-- MAYBE CURED.
HE'D BEEN DISCREETLY PROBING FOR A WAY OUT. EVEN GOING SO FAR AS TO HIDE IN MY MIND.
AFTER ORION PLACED THOSE SAFEGUARDS IN MY MIND, I THOUGHT THAT WAS THE END OF THAT.
BUT EVEN LAST NIGHT, SOME OF MY CLOSEST FRIENDS WERE MANIFESTING PARTS OF MY PERSONALITY.
THERE IS A PSIONIC THREAT TO THE CITY.
SOMETHING I CAN'T PUNCH WITH MY FIST OR INCINERATE WITH MY EYES.
SO WHAT IS A "SUPERMAN" TO DO?

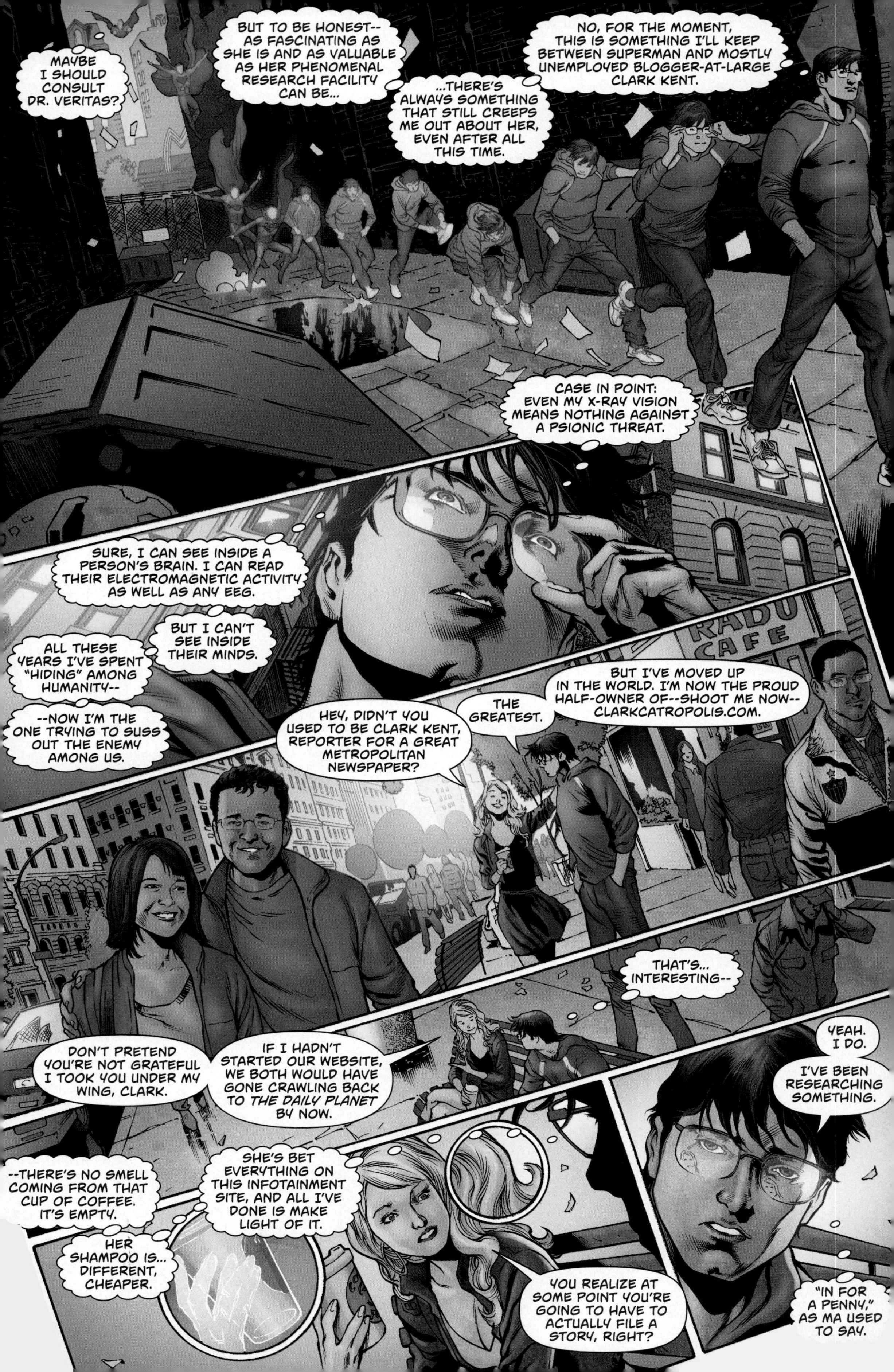
MAYBE I SHOULD CONSULT DR. VERITAS?
BUT TO BE HONEST--AS FASCINATING AS SHE IS AND AS VALUABLE AS HER PHENOMENAL RESEARCH FACILITY CAN BE...
...THERE'S ALWAYS SOMETHING THAT STILL CREEPS ME OUT ABOUT HER, EVEN AFTER ALL THIS TIME.
NO, FOR THE MOMENT, THIS IS SOMETHING I'LL KEEP BETWEEN SUPERMAN AND MOSTLY UNEMPLOYED BLOGGER-AT-LARGE CLARK KENT.
CASE IN POINT: EVEN MY X-RAY VISION MEANS NOTHING AGAINST A PSIONIC THREAT.
SURE, I CAN SEE INSIDE A PERSON'S BRAIN. I CAN READ THEIR ELECTROMAGNETIC ACTIVITY AS WELL AS ANY EEG.
BUT I CAN'T SEE INSIDE THEIR MINDS.
ALL THESE YEARS I'VE SPENT "HIDING" AMONG HUMANITY--
--NOW I'M THE ONE TRYING TO SUSS OUT THE ENEMY AMONG US.
RADU CAFE
HEY, DIDN'T YOU USED TO BE CLARK KENT, REPORTER FOR A GREAT METROPOLITAN NEWSPAPER?
THE GREATEST.
BUT I'VE MOVED UP IN THE WORLD. I'M NOW THE PROUD HALF-OWNER OF--SHOOT ME NOW--CLARKCATROPOLIS.COM.
THAT'S... INTERESTING--
DON'T PRETEND YOU'RE NOT GRATEFUL I TOOK YOU UNDER MY WING, CLARK.
IF I HADN'T STARTED OUR WEBSITE, WE BOTH WOULD HAVE GONE CRAWLING BACK TO THE DAILY PLANET BY NOW.
--THERE'S NO SMELL COMING FROM THAT CUP OF COFFEE. IT'S EMPTY.
HER SHAMPOO IS... DIFFERENT, CHEAPER.
SHE'S BET EVERYTHING ON THIS INFOTAINMENT SITE, AND ALL I'VE DONE IS MAKE LIGHT OF IT.
YOU REALIZE AT SOME POINT YOU'RE GOING TO HAVE TO ACTUALLY FILE A STORY, RIGHT?
YEAH. I DO.
I'VE BEEN RESEARCHING SOMETHING.
"IN FOR A PENNY," AS MA USED TO SAY.

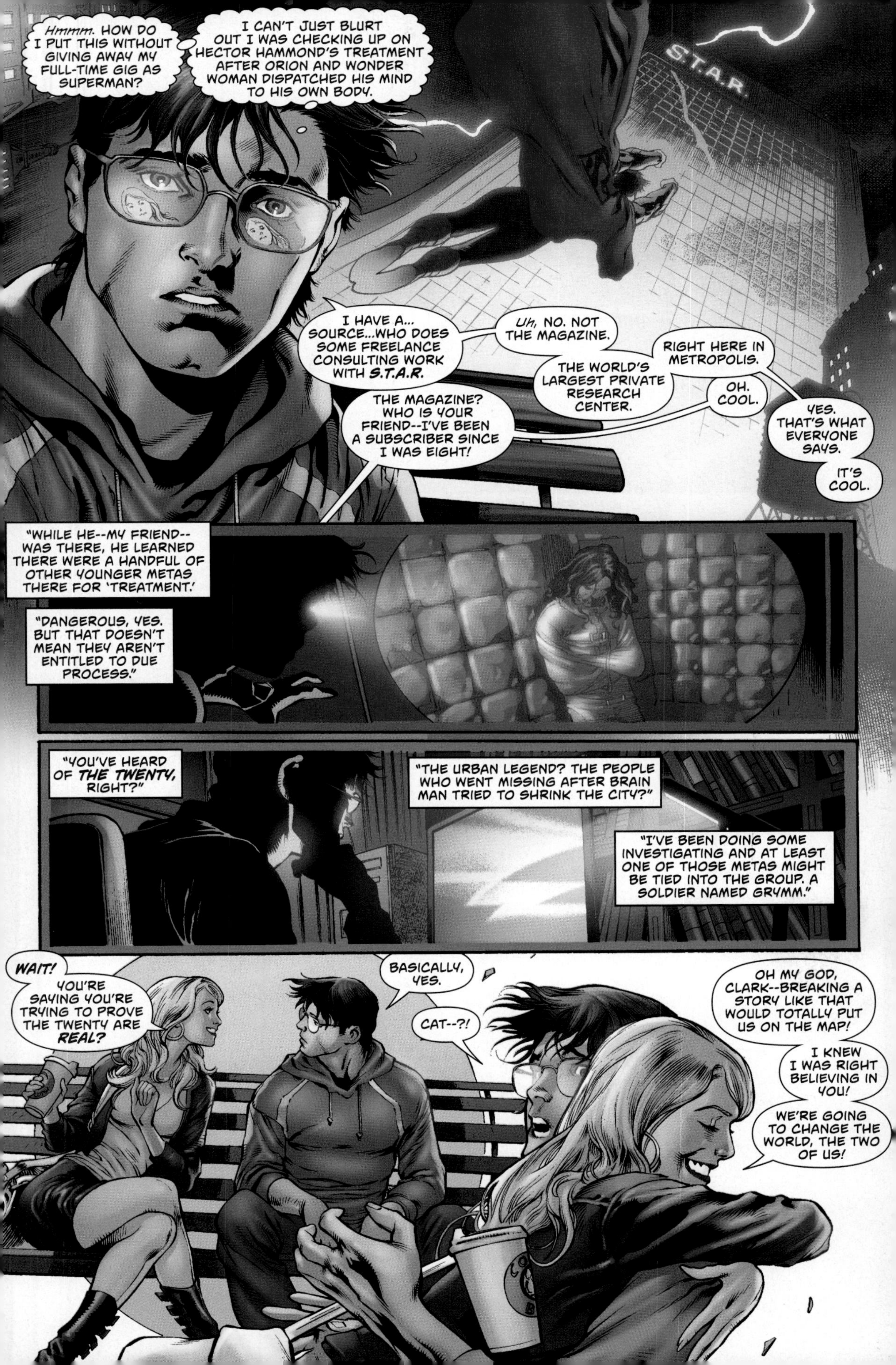
Hmmm. HOW DO I PUT THIS WITHOUT GIVING AWAY MY FULL-TIME GIG AS SUPERMAN?
I CAN'T JUST BLURT OUT I WAS CHECKING UP ON HECTOR HAMMOND'S TREATMENT AFTER ORION AND WONDER WOMAN DISPATCHED HIS MIND TO HIS OWN BODY.
S.T.A.R.
I HAVE A... SOURCE...WHO DOES SOME FREELANCE CONSULTING WORK WITH S.T.A.R.
THE MAGAZINE? WHO IS YOUR FRIEND--I'VE BEEN A SUBSCRIBER SINCE I WAS EIGHT!
Uh, NO. NOT THE MAGAZINE.
THE WORLD'S LARGEST PRIVATE RESEARCH CENTER.
RIGHT HERE IN METROPOLIS.
OH. COOL.
YES. THAT'S WHAT EVERYONE SAYS.
IT'S COOL.
"WHILE HE--MY FRIEND--WAS THERE, HE LEARNED THERE WERE A HANDFUL OF OTHER YOUNGER METAS THERE FOR 'TREATMENT.'
"DANGEROUS, YES. BUT THAT DOESN'T MEAN THEY AREN'T ENTITLED TO DUE PROCESS."
"YOU'VE HEARD OF THE TWENTY, RIGHT?"
"THE URBAN LEGEND? THE PEOPLE WHO WENT MISSING AFTER BRAIN MAN TRIED TO SHRINK THE CITY?"
"I'VE BEEN DOING SOME INVESTIGATING AND AT LEAST ONE OF THOSE METAS MIGHT BE TIED INTO THE GROUP. A SOLDIER NAMED GRYMM."
WAIT! YOU'RE SAYING YOU'RE TRYING TO PROVE THE TWENTY ARE REAL?
BASICALLY, YES.
CAT--?!
OH MY GOD, CLARK--BREAKING A STORY LIKE THAT WOULD TOTALLY PUT US ON THE MAP!
I KNEW I WAS RIGHT BELIEVING IN YOU!
WE'RE GOING TO CHANGE THE WORLD, THE TWO OF US!

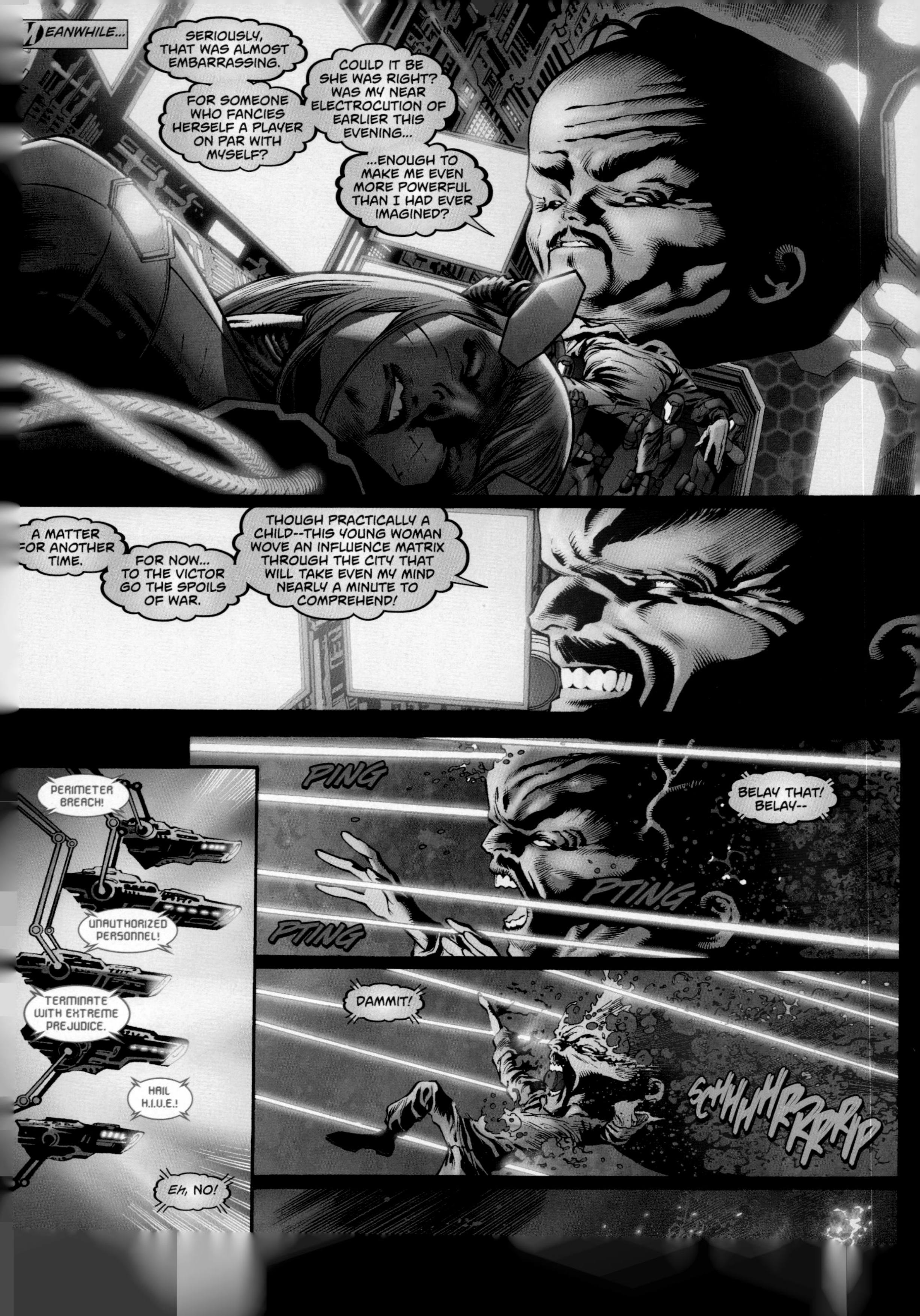
MEANWHILE...
SERIOUSLY, THAT WAS ALMOST EMBARRASSING.
FOR SOMEONE WHO FANCIES HERSELF A PLAYER ON PAR WITH MYSELF?
COULD IT BE SHE WAS RIGHT? WAS MY NEAR ELECTROCUTION OF EARLIER THIS EVENING...
...ENOUGH TO MAKE ME EVEN MORE POWERFUL THAN I HAD EVER IMAGINED?
A MATTER FOR ANOTHER TIME.
FOR NOW... TO THE VICTOR GO THE SPOILS OF WAR.
THOUGH PRACTICALLY A CHILD--THIS YOUNG WOMAN WOVE AN INFLUENCE MATRIX THROUGH THE CITY THAT WILL TAKE EVEN MY MIND NEARLY A MINUTE TO COMPREHEND!
PERIMETER BREACH!
UNAUTHORIZED PERSONNEL!
TERMINATE WITH EXTREME PREJUDICE.
HAIL H.I.V.E.!
EH, NO!
PING
BELAY THAT! BELAY--
PTING
PTING
DAMMIT!
SCHHHMRRRRIP

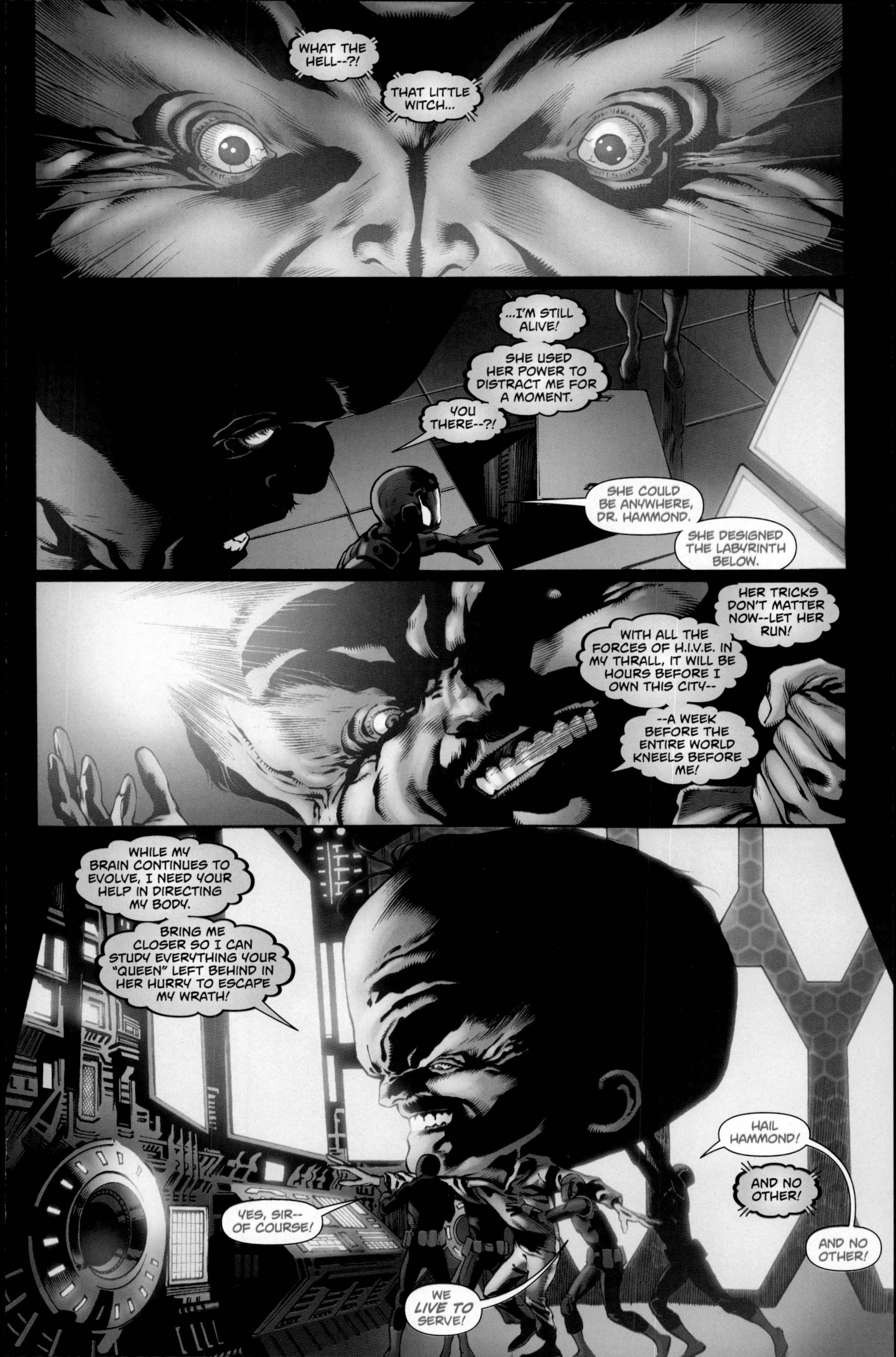
WHAT THE HELL--?!
THAT LITTLE WITCH...
...I'M STILL ALIVE!
SHE USED HER POWER TO DISTRACT ME FOR A MOMENT.
YOU THERE--?!
SHE COULD BE ANYWHERE, DR. HAMMOND.
SHE DESIGNED THE LABYRINTH BELOW.
HER TRICKS DON'T MATTER NOW--LET HER RUN!
WITH ALL THE FORCES OF H.I.V.E. IN MY THRALL, IT WILL BE HOURS BEFORE I OWN THIS CITY--
--A WEEK BEFORE THE ENTIRE WORLD KNEELS BEFORE ME!
WHILE MY BRAIN CONTINUES TO EVOLVE, I NEED YOUR HELP IN DIRECTING MY BODY.
BRING ME CLOSER SO I CAN STUDY EVERYTHING YOUR "QUEEN" LEFT BEHIND IN HER HURRY TO ESCAPE MY WRATH!
YES, SIR--OF COURSE!
WE *LIVE TO* SERVE!
HAIL HAMMOND!
AND NO OTHER!
AND NO OTHER!

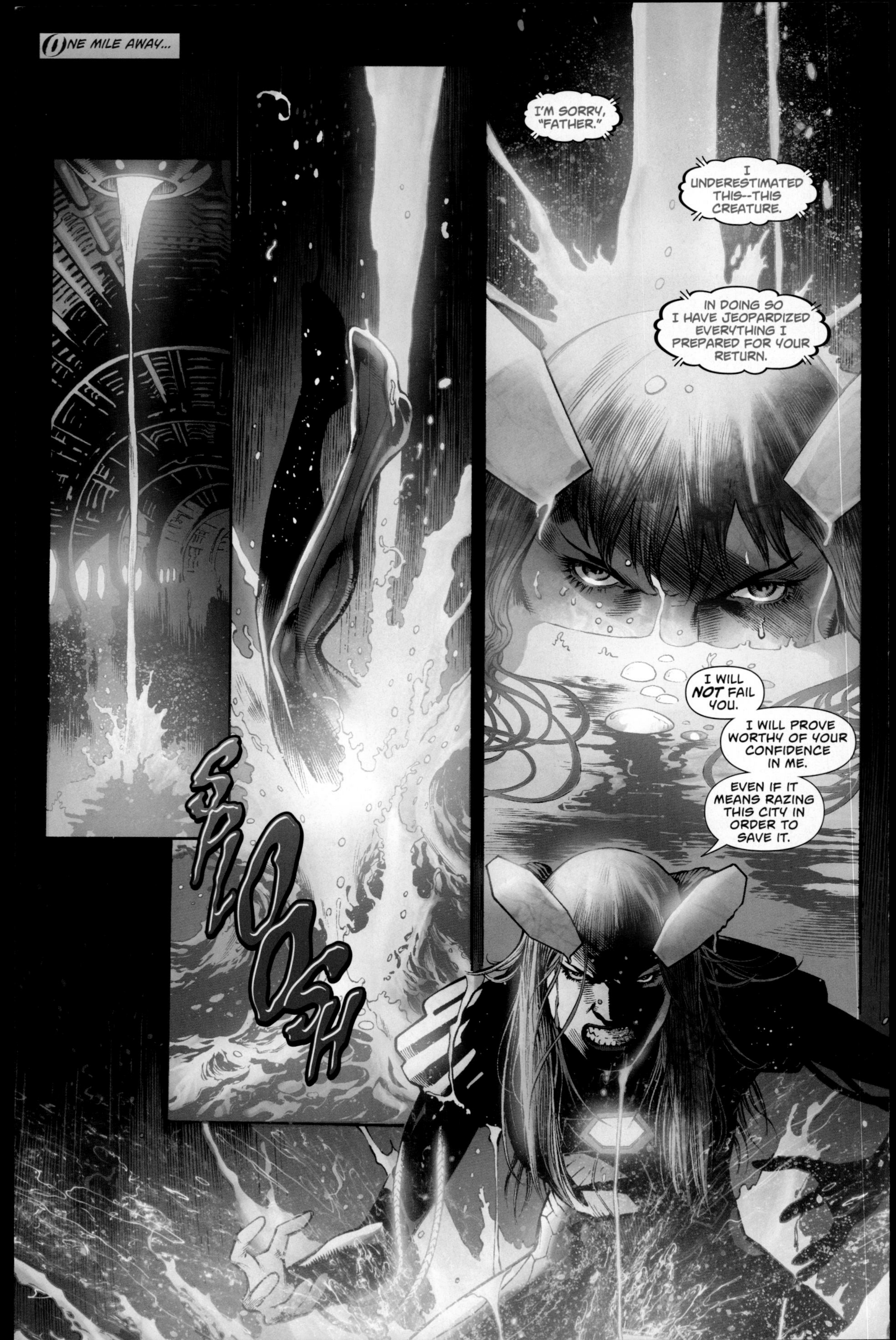
ONE MILE AWAY...
I'M SORRY, "FATHER."
I UNDERESTIMATED THIS--THIS CREATURE.
IN DOING SO I HAVE JEOPARDIZED EVERYTHING I PREPARED FOR YOUR RETURN.
I WILL **NOT** FAIL YOU.
I WILL PROVE WORTHY OF YOUR CONFIDENCE IN ME.
EVEN IF IT MEANS RAZING THIS CITY IN ORDER TO SAVE IT.
SPLOOSH

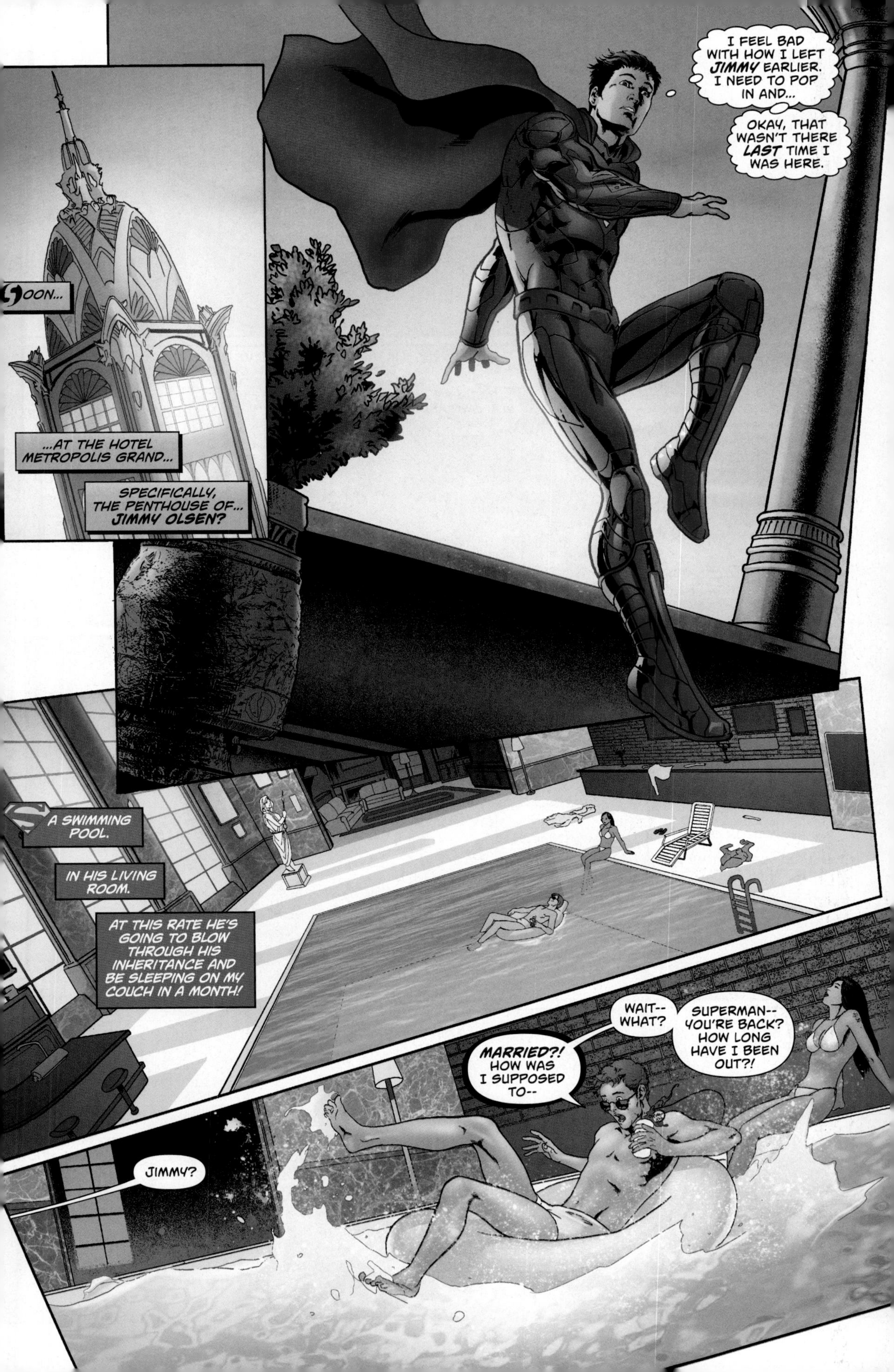
SOON...
...AT THE HOTEL METROPOLIS GRAND...
SPECIFICALLY, THE PENTHOUSE OF... JIMMY OLSEN?
I FEEL BAD WITH HOW I LEFT JIMMY EARLIER. I NEED TO POP IN AND...
OKAY, THAT WASN'T THERE LAST TIME I WAS HERE.
A SWIMMING POOL.
IN HIS LIVING ROOM.
AT THIS RATE HE'S GOING TO BLOW THROUGH HIS INHERITANCE AND BE SLEEPING ON MY COUCH IN A MONTH!
JIMMY?
MARRIED?! HOW WAS I SUPPOSED TO--
WAIT-- WHAT?
SUPERMAN-- YOU'RE BACK? HOW LONG HAVE I BEEN OUT?!

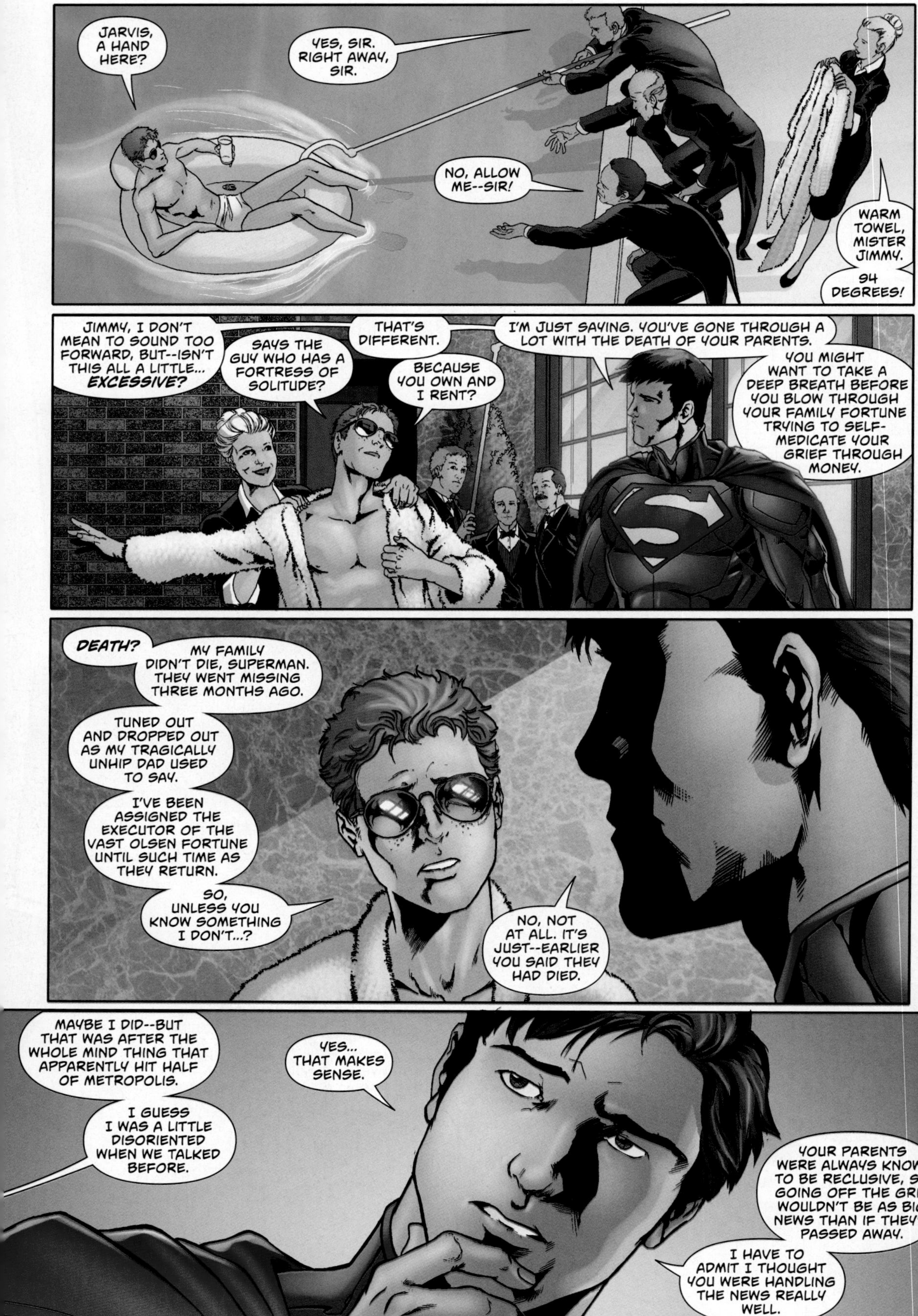
JARVIS, A HAND HERE?
YES, SIR. RIGHT AWAY, SIR.
NO, ALLOW ME--SIR!
WARM TOWEL, MISTER JIMMY.
94 DEGREES!
JIMMY, I DON'T MEAN TO SOUND TOO FORWARD, BUT--ISN'T THIS ALL A LITTLE... EXCESSIVE?
SAYS THE GUY WHO HAS A FORTRESS OF SOLITUDE?
THAT'S DIFFERENT.
BECAUSE YOU OWN AND I RENT?
I'M JUST SAYING. YOU'VE GONE THROUGH A LOT WITH THE DEATH OF YOUR PARENTS.
YOU MIGHT WANT TO TAKE A DEEP BREATH BEFORE YOU BLOW THROUGH YOUR FAMILY FORTUNE TRYING TO SELF-MEDICATE YOUR GRIEF THROUGH MONEY.
DEATH?
MY FAMILY DIDN'T DIE, SUPERMAN. THEY WENT MISSING THREE MONTHS AGO.
TUNED OUT AND DROPPED OUT AS MY TRAGICALLY UNHIP DAD USED TO SAY.
I'VE BEEN ASSIGNED THE EXECUTOR OF THE VAST OLSEN FORTUNE UNTIL SUCH TIME AS THEY RETURN.
SO, UNLESS YOU KNOW SOMETHING I DON'T...?
NO, NOT AT ALL. IT'S JUST--EARLIER YOU SAID THEY HAD DIED.
MAYBE I DID--BUT THAT WAS AFTER THE WHOLE MIND THING THAT APPARENTLY HIT HALF OF METROPOLIS.
I GUESS I WAS A LITTLE DISORIENTED WHEN WE TALKED BEFORE.
YES... THAT MAKES SENSE.
YOUR PARENTS WERE ALWAYS KNOWN TO BE RECLUSIVE, SO GOING OFF THE GRID WOULDN'T BE AS BIG NEWS THAN IF THEY'D PASSED AWAY.
I HAVE TO ADMIT I THOUGHT YOU WERE HANDLING THE NEWS REALLY WELL.

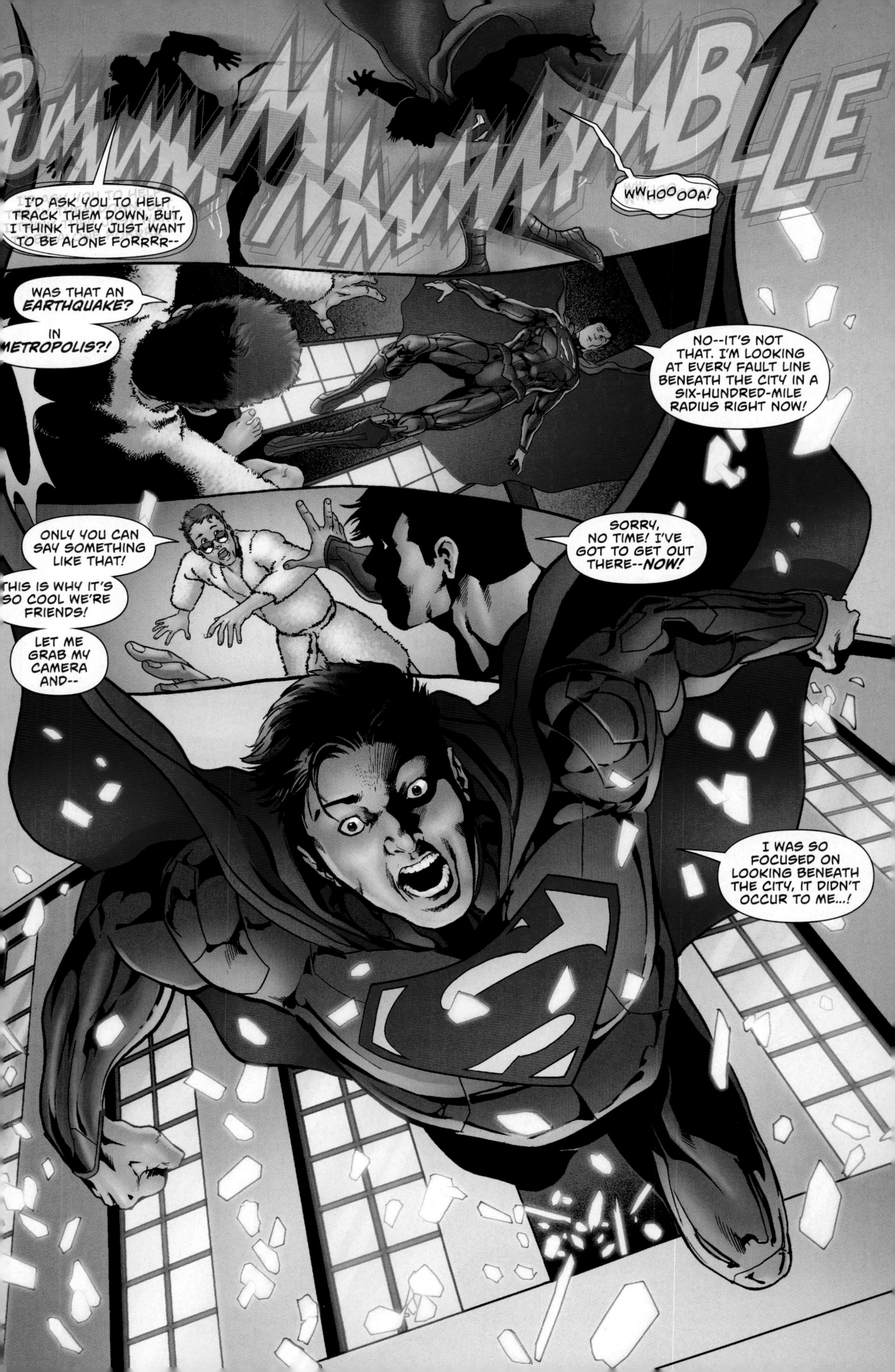
RUMMMMMMMMBLE
I'D ASK YOU TO HELP TRACK THEM DOWN, BUT, I THINK THEY JUST WANT TO BE ALONE FORRRR--
WWHOOOOA!
WAS THAT AN EARTHQUAKE?
IN METROPOLIS?!
NO--IT'S NOT THAT. I'M LOOKING AT EVERY FAULT LINE BENEATH THE CITY IN A SIX-HUNDRED-MILE RADIUS RIGHT NOW!
ONLY YOU CAN SAY SOMETHING LIKE THAT!
THIS IS WHY IT'S SO COOL WE'RE FRIENDS!
LET ME GRAB MY CAMERA AND--
SORRY, NO TIME! I'VE GOT TO GET OUT THERE--NOW!
I WAS SO FOCUSED ON LOOKING BENEATH THE CITY, IT DIDN'T OCCUR TO ME...!

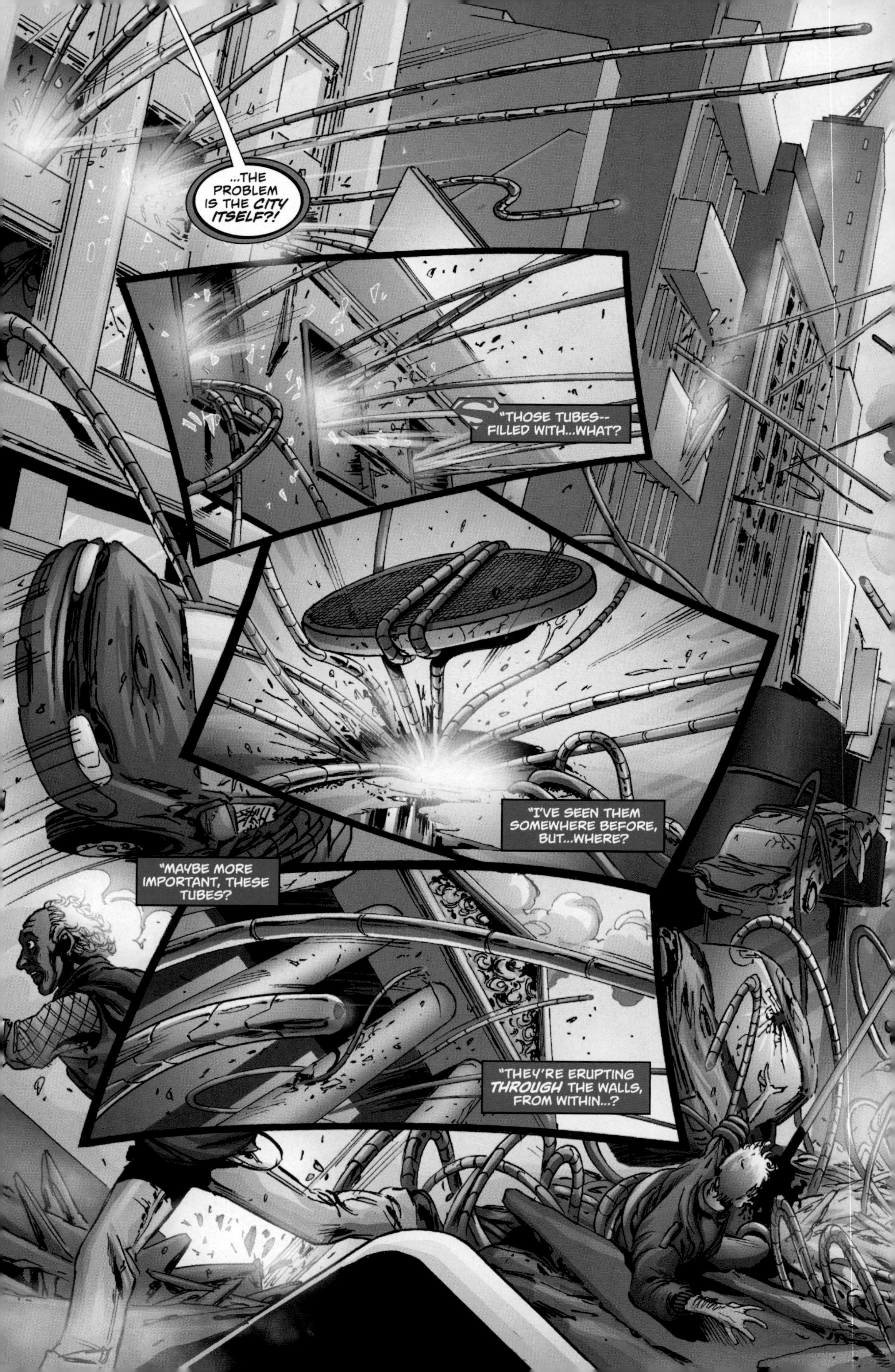
...THE PROBLEM IS THE CITY ITSELF?!
"THOSE TUBES-- FILLED WITH...WHAT?
"I'VE SEEN THEM SOMEWHERE BEFORE, BUT...WHERE?
"MAYBE MORE IMPORTANT, THESE TUBES?
"THEY'RE ERUPTING THROUGH THE WALLS, FROM WITHIN...?

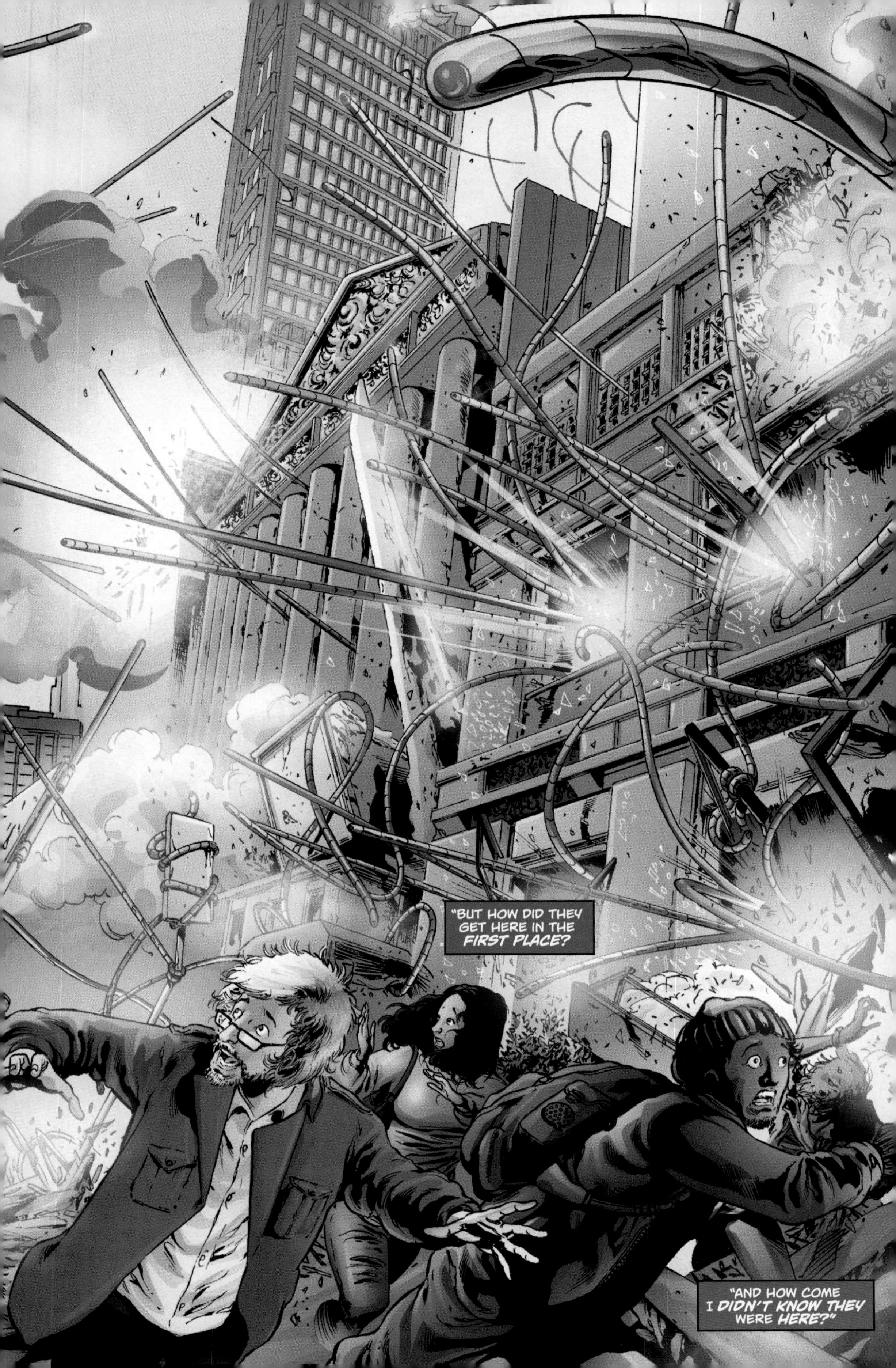
"BUT HOW DID THEY GET HERE IN THE FIRST PLACE?
"AND HOW COME I DIDN'T KNOW THEY WERE HERE?"

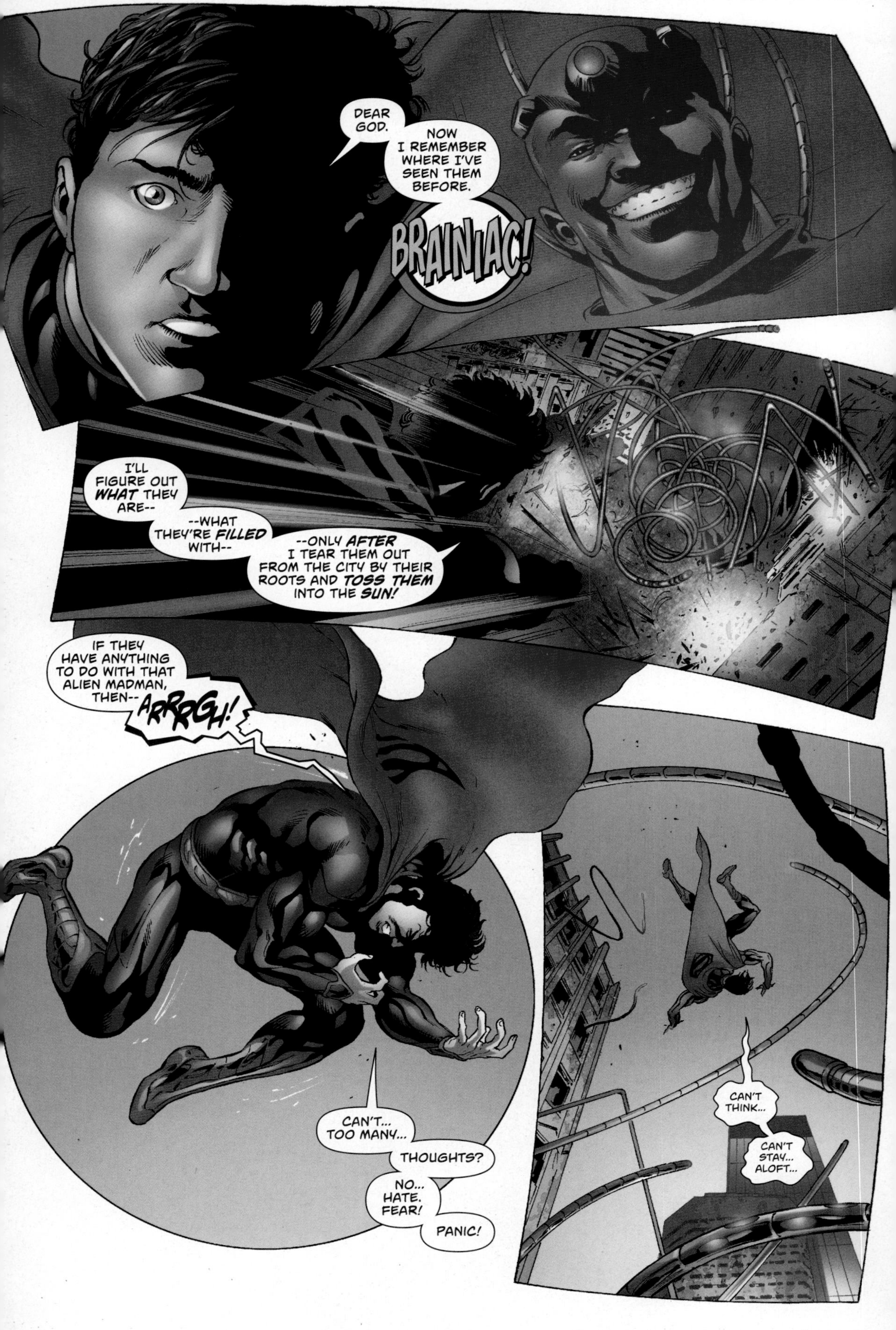
DEAR GOD.
NOW I REMEMBER WHERE I'VE SEEN THEM BEFORE.
BRAINIAC!
I'LL FIGURE OUT WHAT THEY ARE--
--WHAT THEY'RE FILLED WITH--
--ONLY AFTER I TEAR THEM OUT FROM THE CITY BY THEIR ROOTS AND TOSS THEM INTO THE SUN!
IF THEY HAVE ANYTHING TO DO WITH THAT ALIEN MADMAN, THEN--
ARRRGH!
CAN'T... TOO MANY...
THOUGHTS?
NO... HATE. FEAR!
PANIC!
CAN'T THINK...
CAN'T STAY... ALOFT...

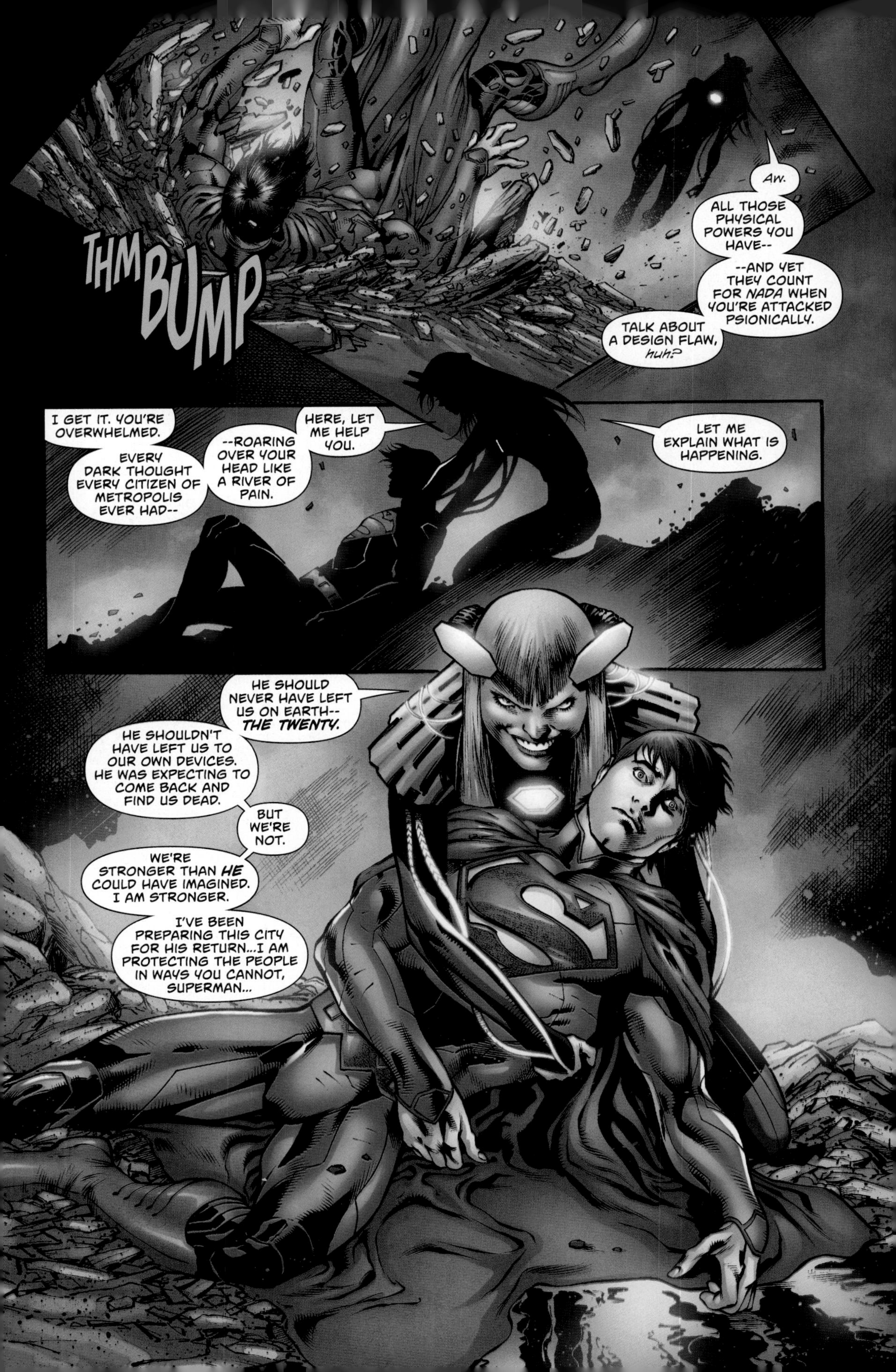
THM BUMP
Aw.
ALL THOSE PHYSICAL POWERS YOU HAVE--
--AND YET THEY COUNT FOR NADA WHEN YOU'RE ATTACKED PSIONICALLY.
TALK ABOUT A DESIGN FLAW, huh?
I GET IT. YOU'RE OVERWHELMED.
EVERY DARK THOUGHT EVERY CITIZEN OF METROPOLIS EVER HAD--
--ROARING OVER YOUR HEAD LIKE A RIVER OF PAIN.
HERE, LET ME HELP YOU.
LET ME EXPLAIN WHAT IS HAPPENING.
HE SHOULD NEVER HAVE LEFT US ON EARTH-- THE TWENTY.
HE SHOULDN'T HAVE LEFT US TO OUR OWN DEVICES. HE WAS EXPECTING TO COME BACK AND FIND US DEAD.
BUT WE'RE NOT.
WE'RE STRONGER THAN HE COULD HAVE IMAGINED. I AM STRONGER.
I'VE BEEN PREPARING THIS CITY FOR HIS RETURN...I AM PROTECTING THE PEOPLE IN WAYS YOU CANNOT, SUPERMAN...

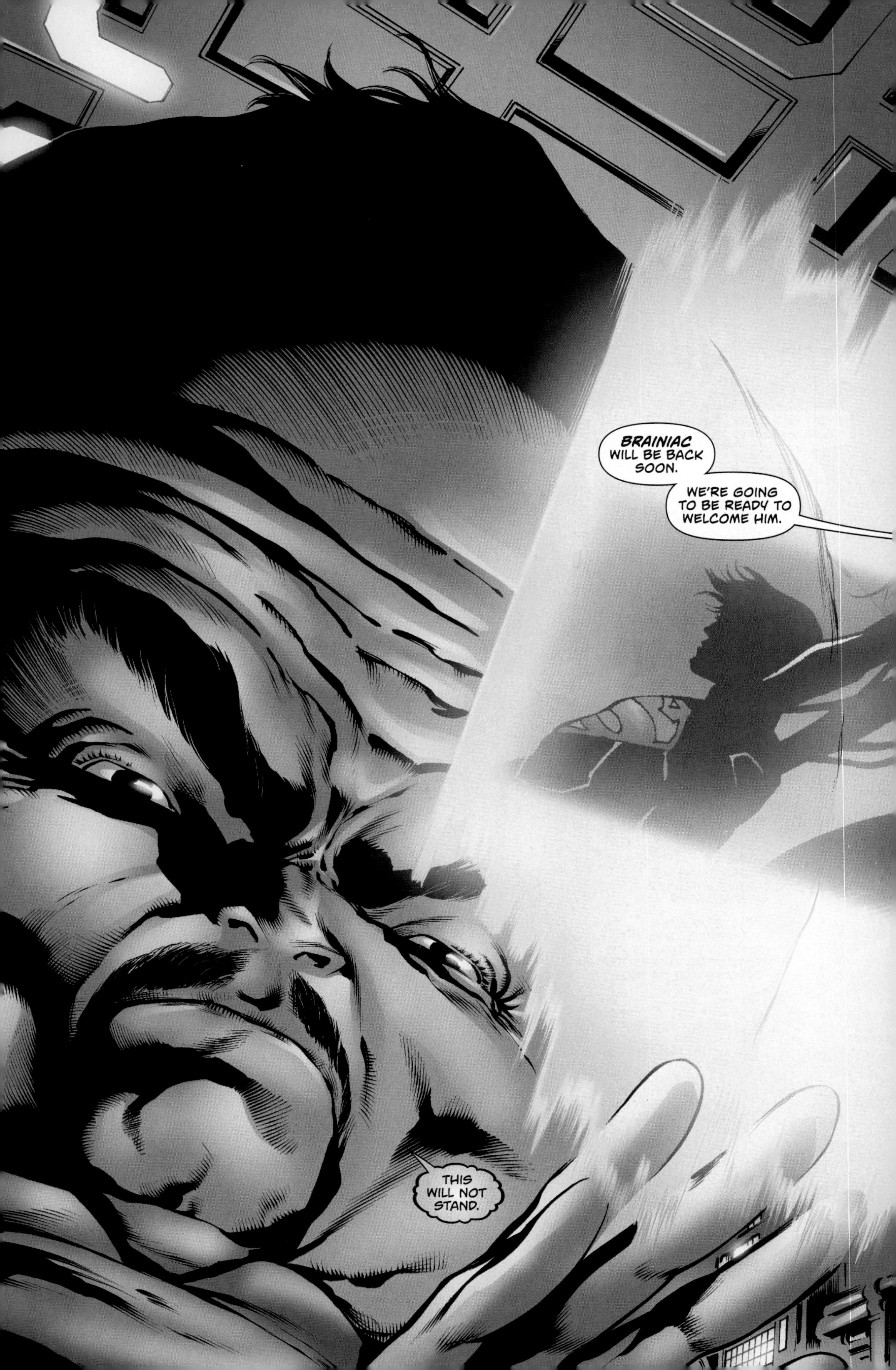
BRAINIAC WILL BE BACK SOON.
WE'RE GOING TO BE READY TO WELCOME HIM.
THIS WILL NOT STAND.

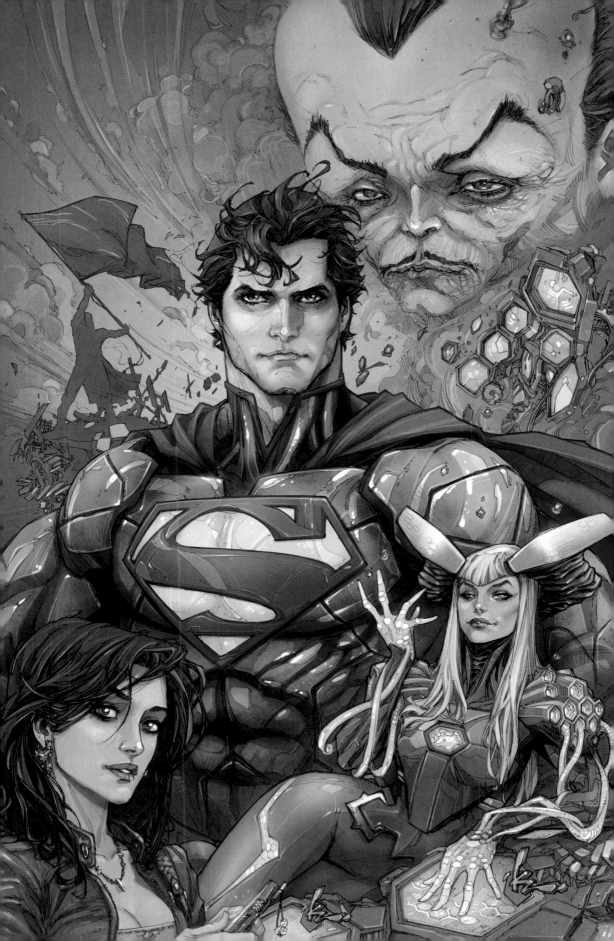

PSI WAR: PART ONE

MIKE JOHNSON writer **EDDY BARROWS** thumbnails **JESUS MERINO** artist cover art by **KENNETH ROCAFORT**

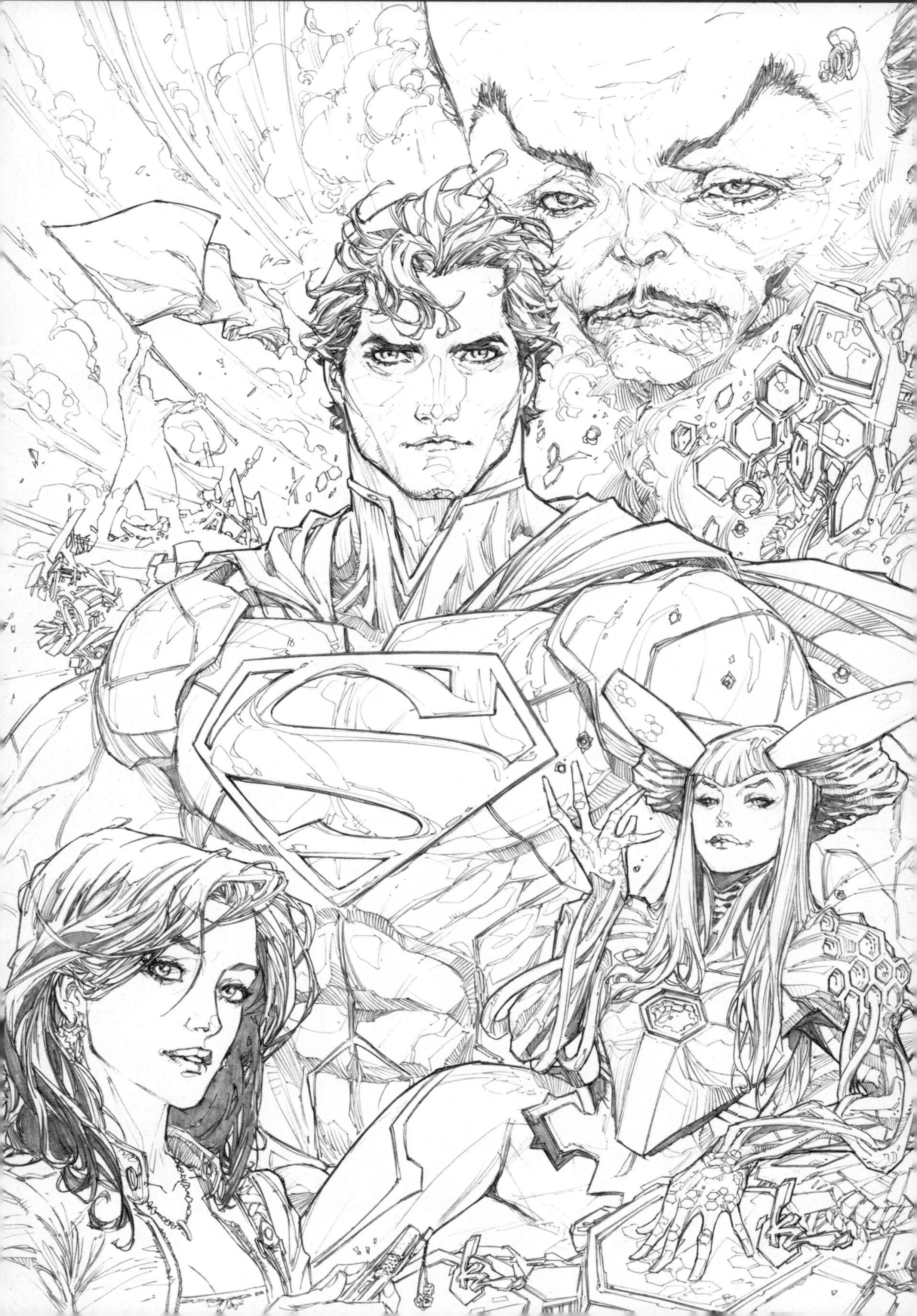

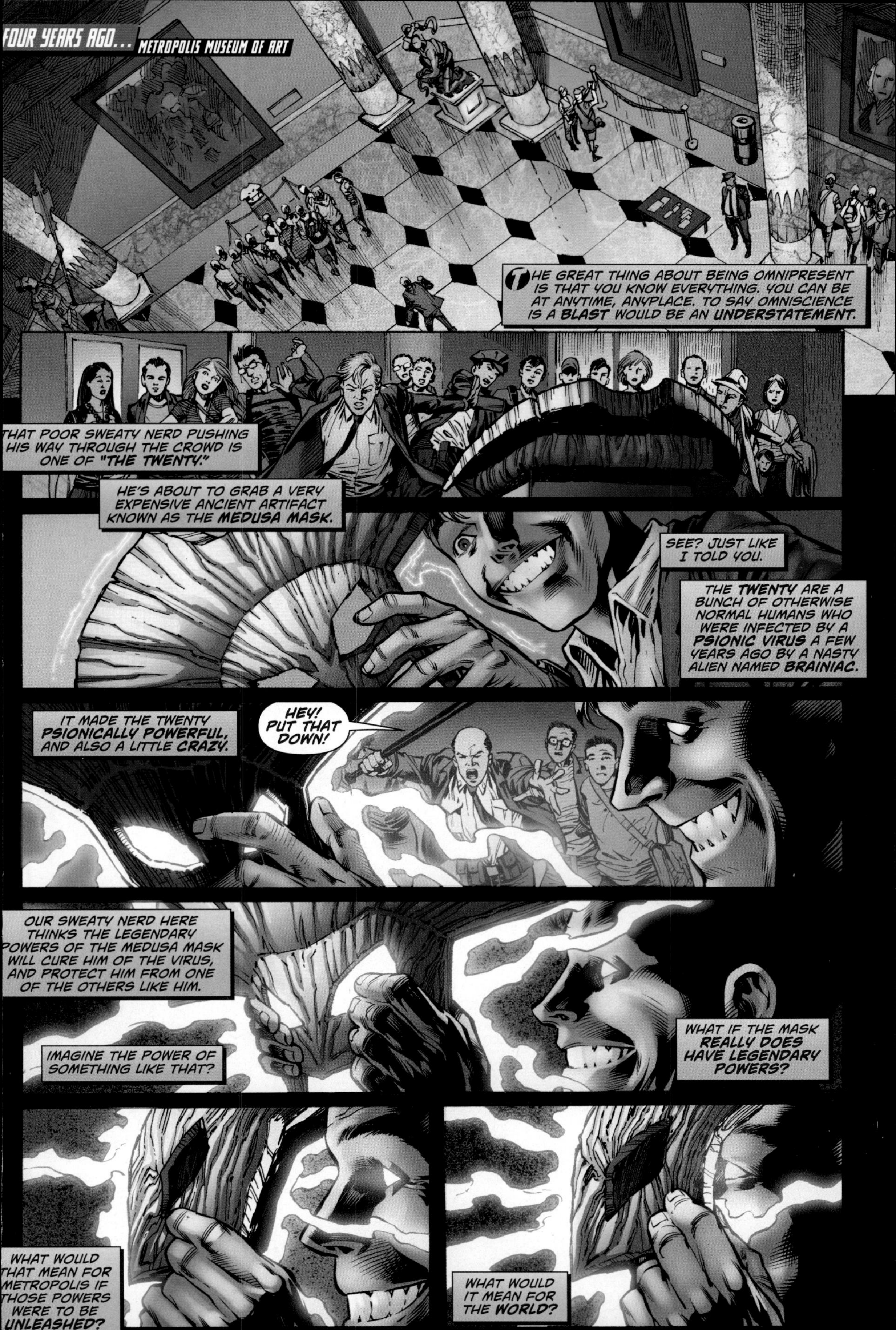
FOUR YEARS AGO... METROPOLIS MUSEUM OF ART
THE GREAT THING ABOUT BEING OMNIPRESENT IS THAT YOU KNOW EVERYTHING. YOU CAN BE AT ANYTIME, ANYPLACE. TO SAY OMNISCIENCE IS A BLAST WOULD BE AN UNDERSTATEMENT.
THAT POOR SWEATY NERD PUSHING HIS WAY THROUGH THE CROWD IS ONE OF "THE TWENTY."
HE'S ABOUT TO GRAB A VERY EXPENSIVE ANCIENT ARTIFACT KNOWN AS THE MEDUSA MASK.
SEE? JUST LIKE I TOLD YOU.
THE TWENTY ARE A BUNCH OF OTHERWISE NORMAL HUMANS WHO WERE INFECTED BY A PSIONIC VIRUS A FEW YEARS AGO BY A NASTY ALIEN NAMED BRAINIAC.
IT MADE THE TWENTY PSIONICALLY POWERFUL, AND ALSO A LITTLE CRAZY.
HEY! PUT THAT DOWN!
OUR SWEATY NERD HERE THINKS THE LEGENDARY POWERS OF THE MEDUSA MASK WILL CURE HIM OF THE VIRUS, AND PROTECT HIM FROM ONE OF THE OTHERS LIKE HIM.
IMAGINE THE POWER OF SOMETHING LIKE THAT?
WHAT IF THE MASK REALLY DOES HAVE LEGENDARY POWERS?
WHAT WOULD THAT MEAN FOR METROPOLIS IF THOSE POWERS WERE TO BE UNLEASHED?
WHAT WOULD IT MEAN FOR THE WORLD?

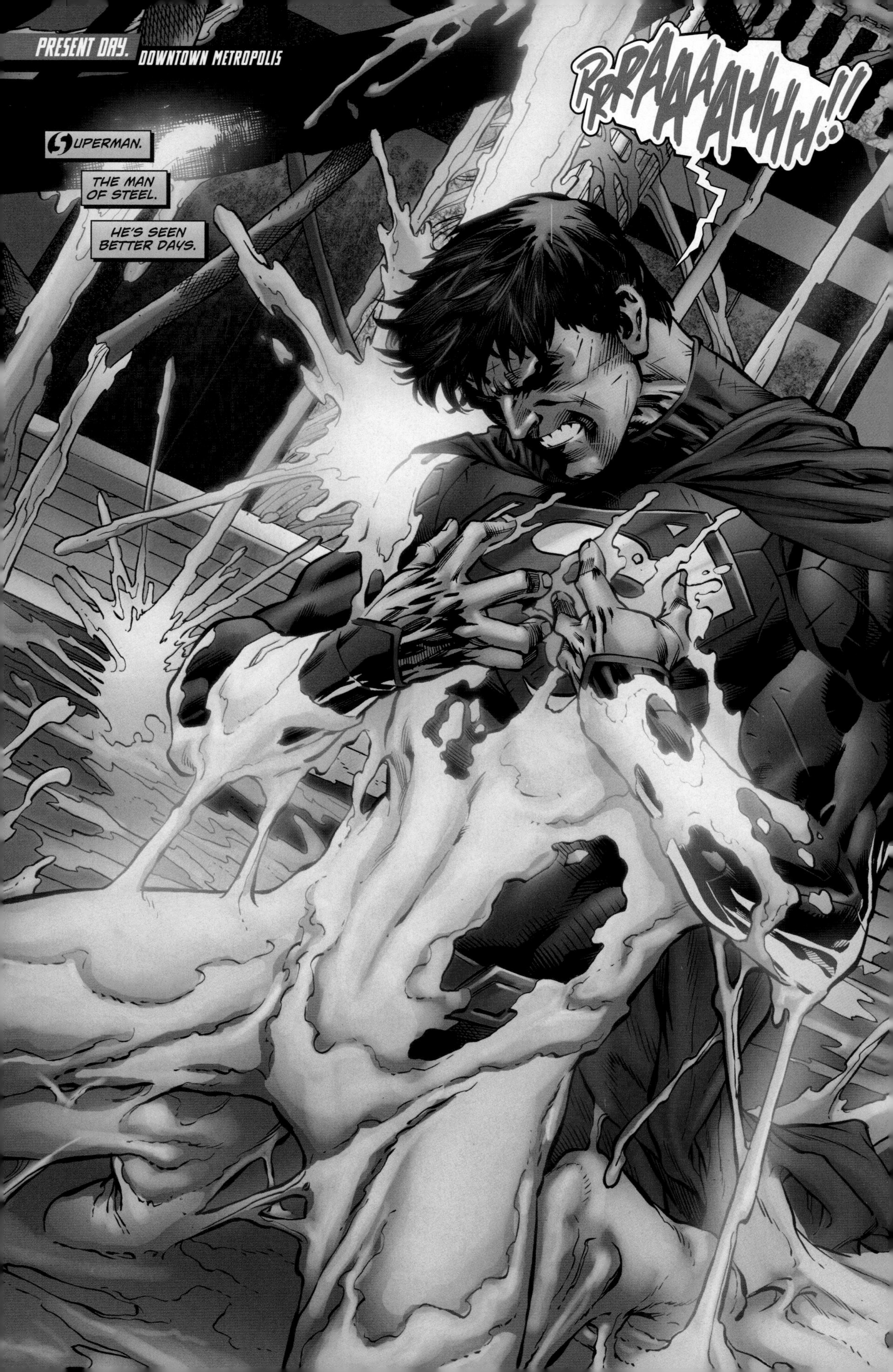
PRESENT DAY. DOWNTOWN METROPOLIS
SUPERMAN.
THE MAN OF STEEL.
HE'S SEEN BETTER DAYS.
RRRAAAAAAHHH!!

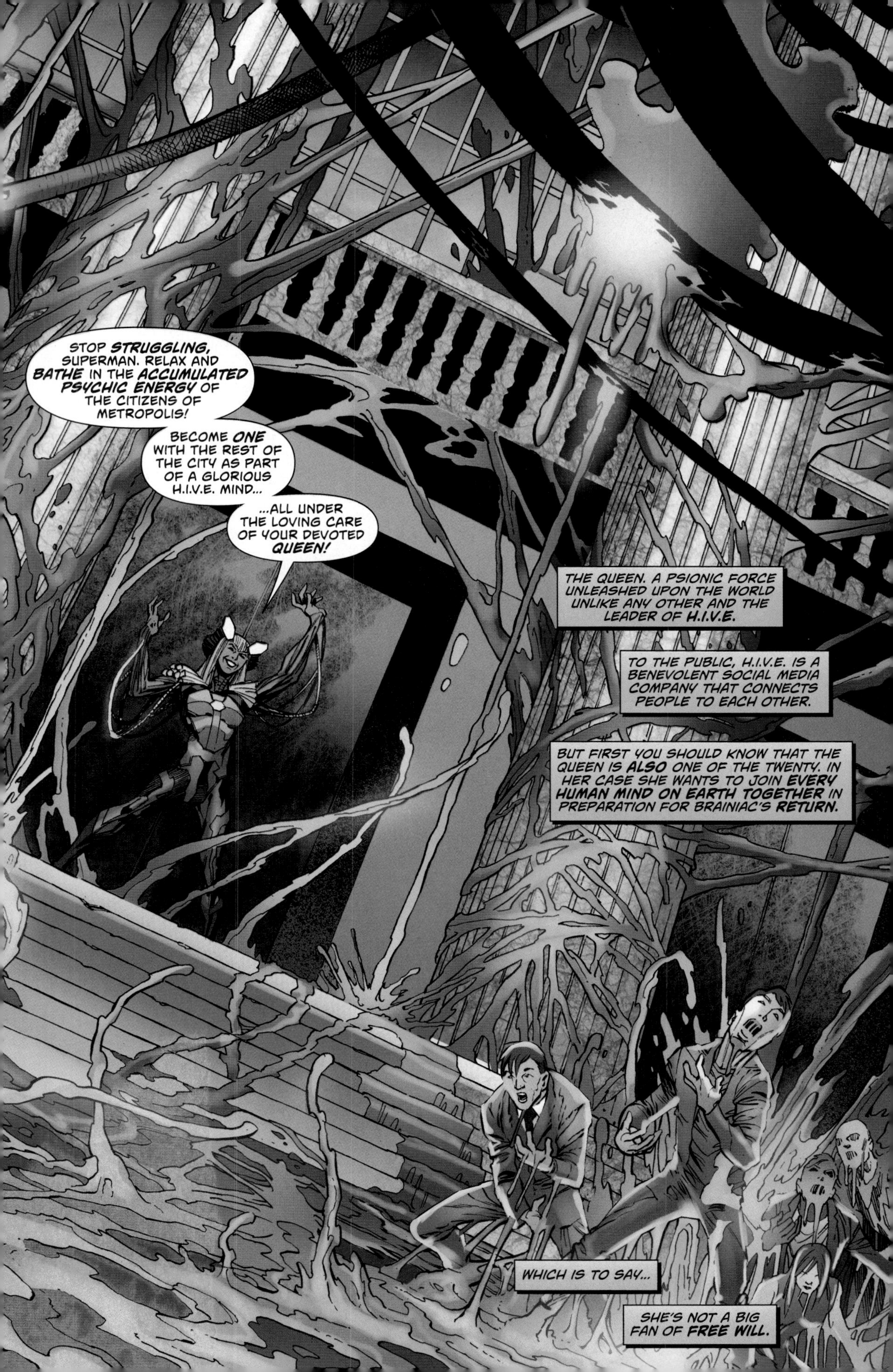
STOP STRUGGLING, SUPERMAN. RELAX AND BATHE IN THE ACCUMULATED PSYCHIC ENERGY OF THE CITIZENS OF METROPOLIS!
BECOME ONE WITH THE REST OF THE CITY AS PART OF A GLORIOUS H.I.V.E. MIND...
...ALL UNDER THE LOVING CARE OF YOUR DEVOTED QUEEN!
THE QUEEN. A PSIONIC FORCE UNLEASHED UPON THE WORLD UNLIKE ANY OTHER AND THE LEADER OF H.I.V.E.
TO THE PUBLIC, H.I.V.E. IS A BENEVOLENT SOCIAL MEDIA COMPANY THAT CONNECTS PEOPLE TO EACH OTHER.
BUT FIRST YOU SHOULD KNOW THAT THE QUEEN IS ALSO ONE OF THE TWENTY. IN HER CASE SHE WANTS TO JOIN EVERY HUMAN MIND ON EARTH TOGETHER IN PREPARATION FOR BRAINIAC'S RETURN.
WHICH IS TO SAY...
SHE'S NOT A BIG FAN OF FREE WILL.

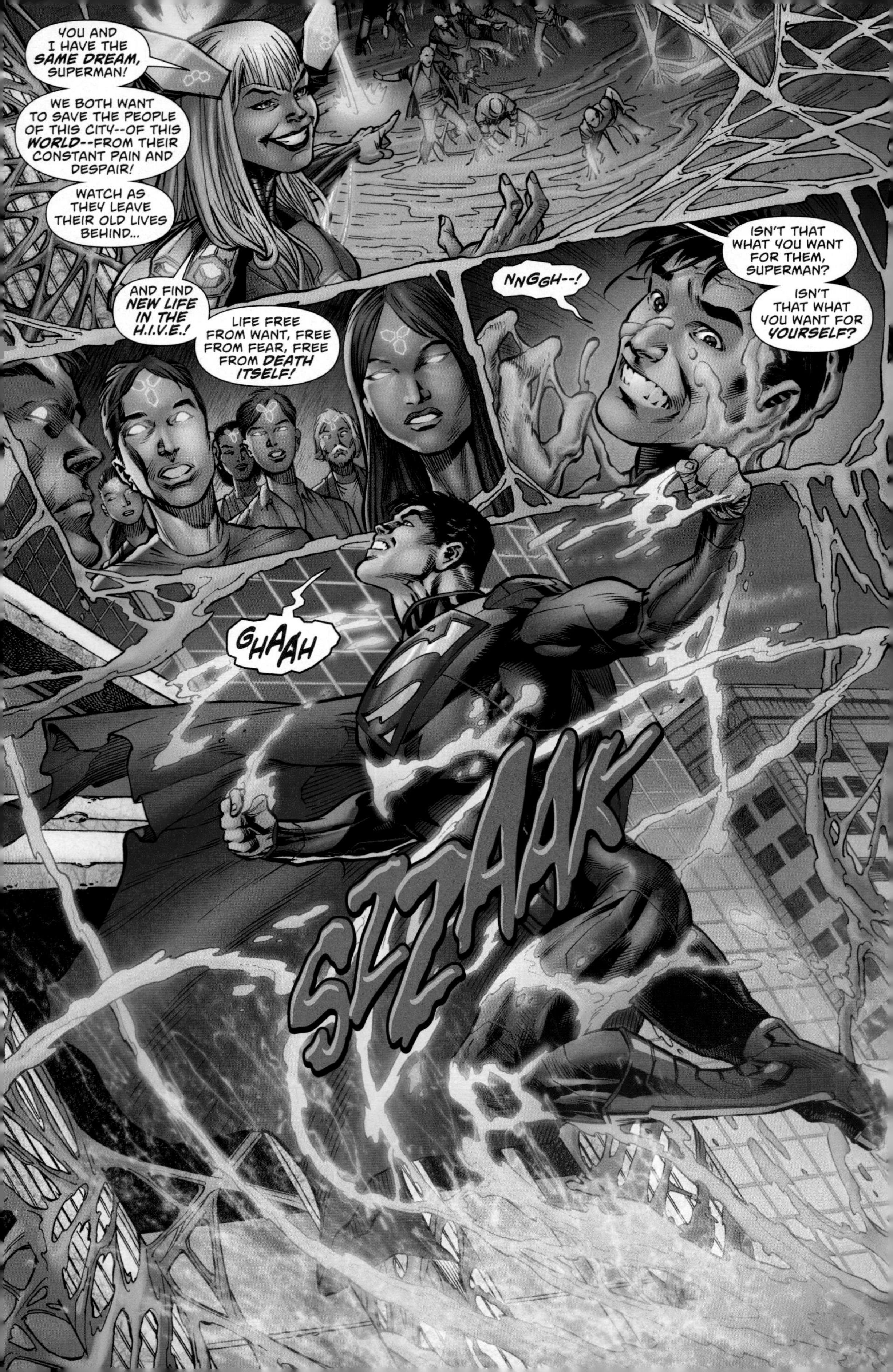

YOU AND I HAVE THE SAME DREAM, SUPERMAN!
WE BOTH WANT TO SAVE THE PEOPLE OF THIS CITY--OF THIS WORLD--FROM THEIR CONSTANT PAIN AND DESPAIR!
WATCH AS THEY LEAVE THEIR OLD LIVES BEHIND...
AND FIND NEW LIFE IN THE H.I.V.E.!
LIFE FREE FROM WANT, FREE FROM FEAR, FREE FROM DEATH ITSELF!
NNGGH--!
ISN'T THAT WHAT YOU WANT FOR THEM, SUPERMAN?
ISN'T THAT WHAT YOU WANT FOR YOURSELF?
GHAAAH
SZZAAK

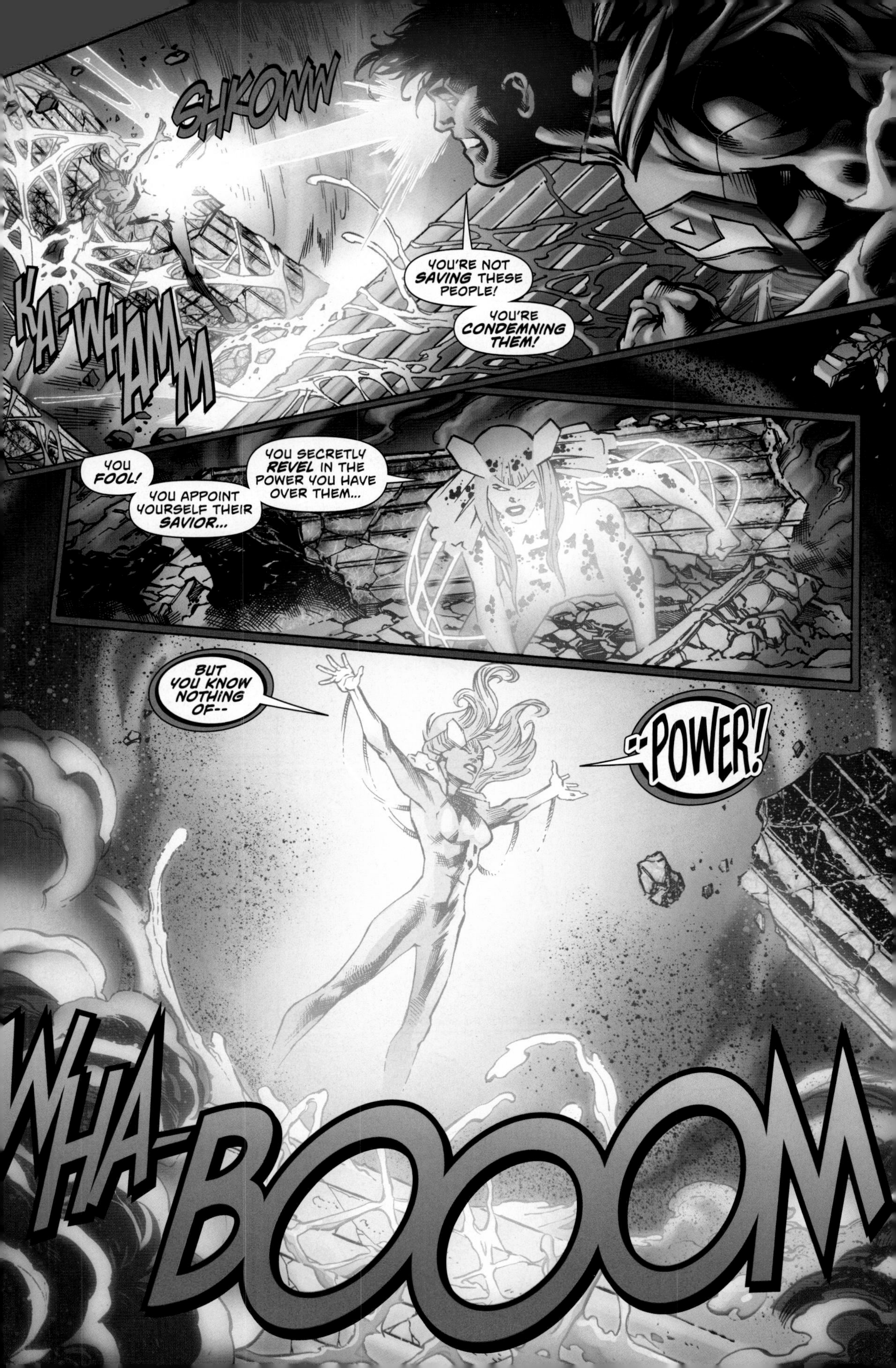
SHKOWW
KA-WHAMMM
YOU'RE NOT SAVING THESE PEOPLE!
YOU'RE CONDEMNING THEM!
YOU FOOL!
YOU APPOINT YOURSELF THEIR SAVIOR...
YOU SECRETLY REVEL IN THE POWER YOU HAVE OVER THEM...
BUT YOU KNOW NOTHING OF--
--POWER!
WHA-BOOOM

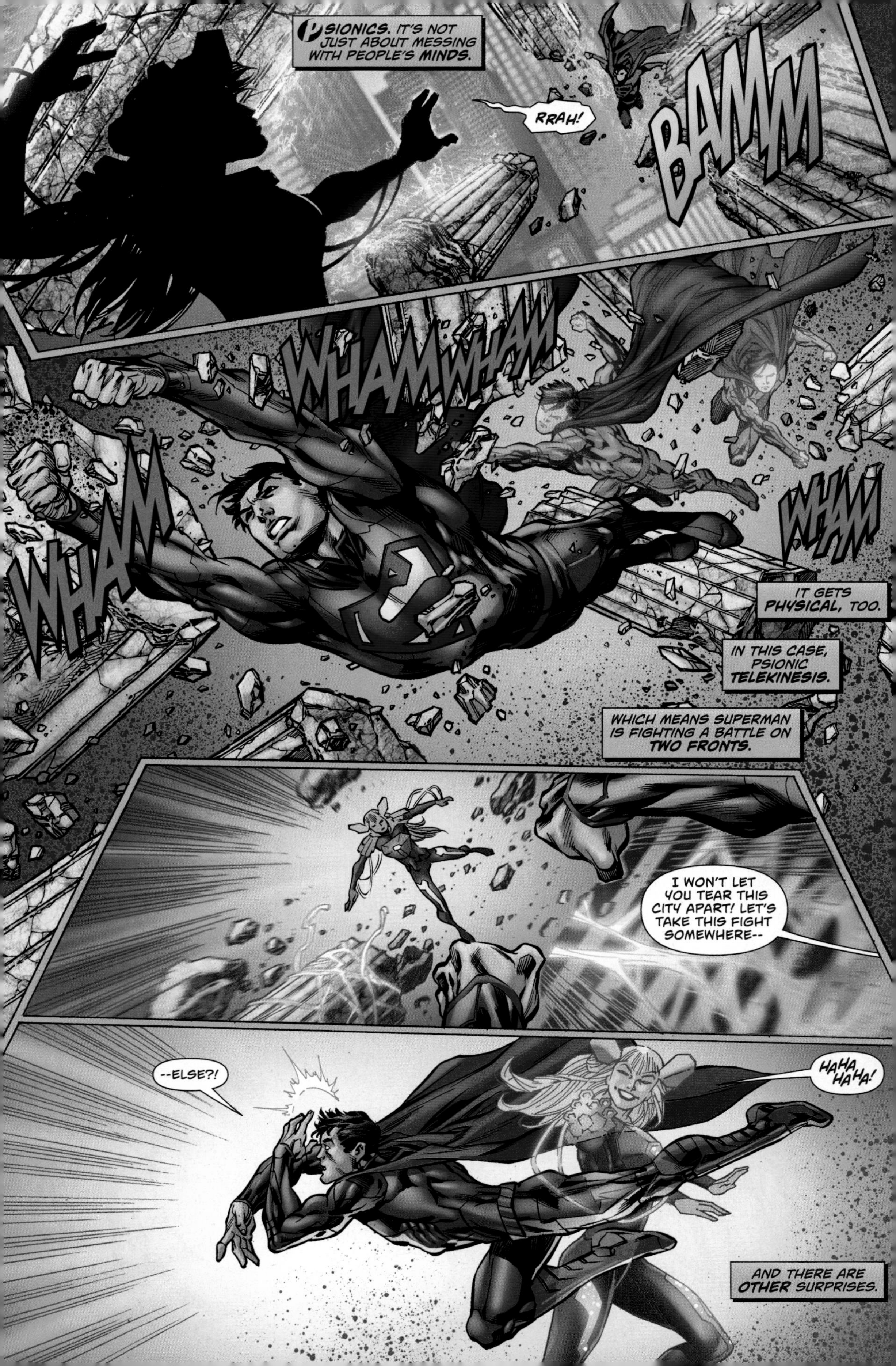
PSIONICS. IT'S NOT JUST ABOUT MESSING WITH PEOPLE'S MINDS.
RRAH!
BAMM
WHAMWHAM
WHAM
WHAM
IT GETS PHYSICAL, TOO.
IN THIS CASE, PSIONIC TELEKINESIS.
WHICH MEANS SUPERMAN IS FIGHTING A BATTLE ON TWO FRONTS.
I WON'T LET YOU TEAR THIS CITY APART! LET'S TAKE THIS FIGHT SOMEWHERE--
--ELSE?!
HAHA HAHA!
AND THERE ARE OTHER SURPRISES.

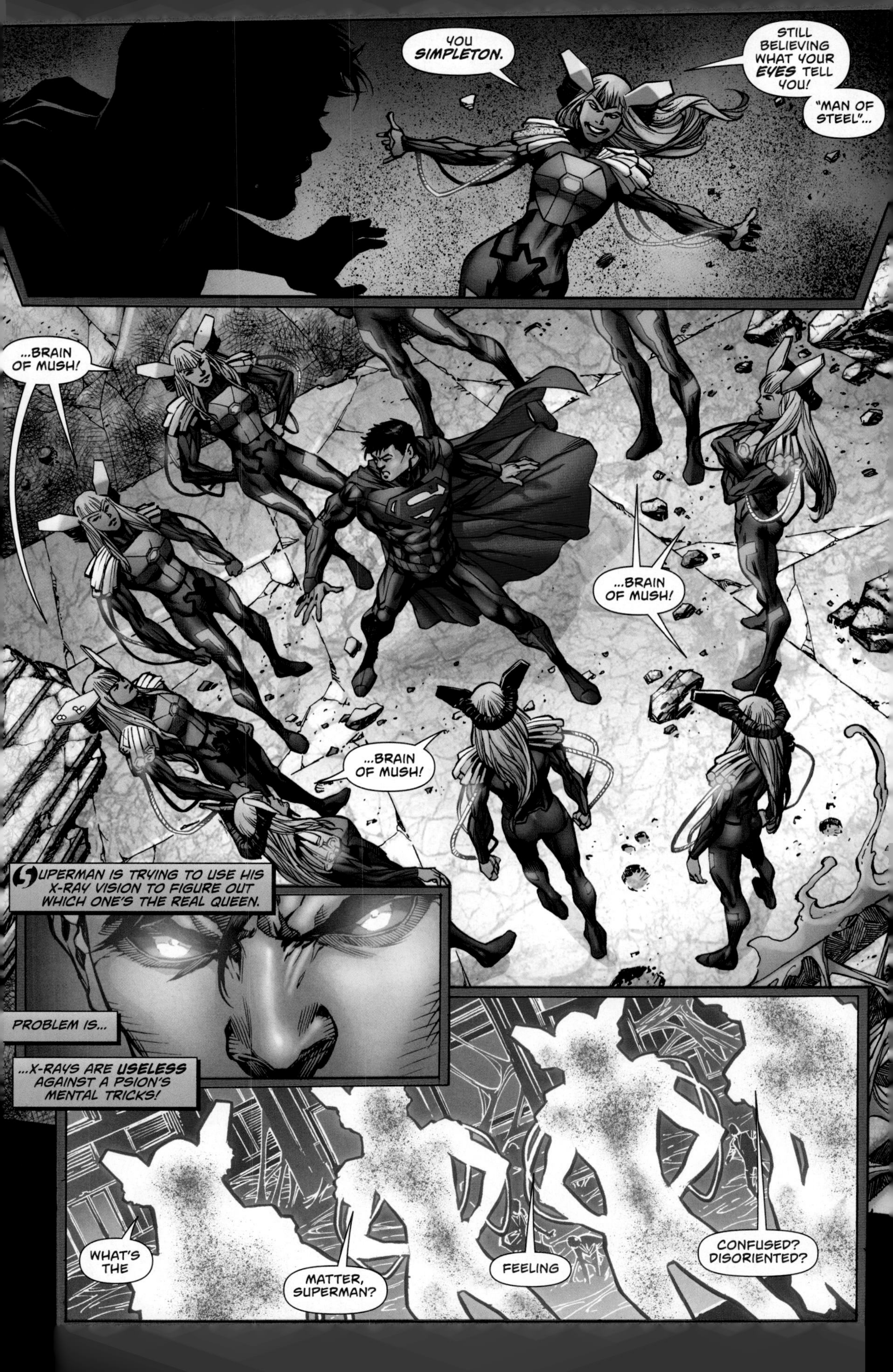
YOU SIMPLETON.
STILL BELIEVING WHAT YOUR EYES TELL YOU!
"MAN OF STEEL"...
...BRAIN OF MUSH!
...BRAIN OF MUSH!
...BRAIN OF MUSH!
SUPERMAN IS TRYING TO USE HIS X-RAY VISION TO FIGURE OUT WHICH ONE'S THE REAL QUEEN.
PROBLEM IS...
...X-RAYS ARE USELESS AGAINST A PSION'S MENTAL TRICKS!
WHAT'S THE
MATTER, SUPERMAN?
FEELING
CONFUSED? DISORIENTED?

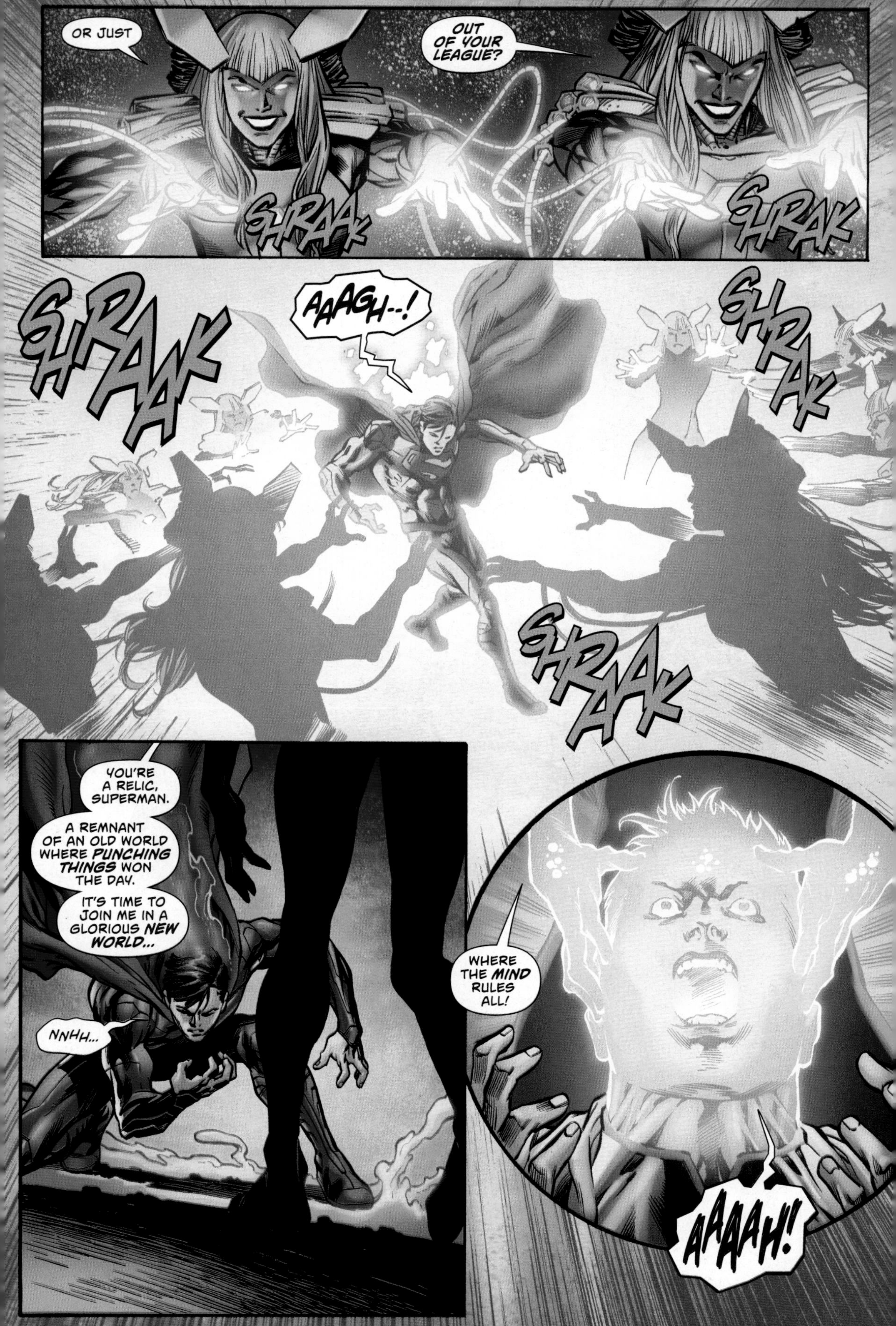
OR JUST
SHRAAK
OUT OF YOUR LEAGUE?
SHRAK
SHRAAK
AAAGH--!
SHRAK
SHRAAK
YOU'RE A RELIC, SUPERMAN.
A REMNANT OF AN OLD WORLD WHERE PUNCHING THINGS WON THE DAY.
IT'S TIME TO JOIN ME IN A GLORIOUS NEW WORLD...
NNHH...
WHERE THE MIND RULES ALL!
AAAAH!

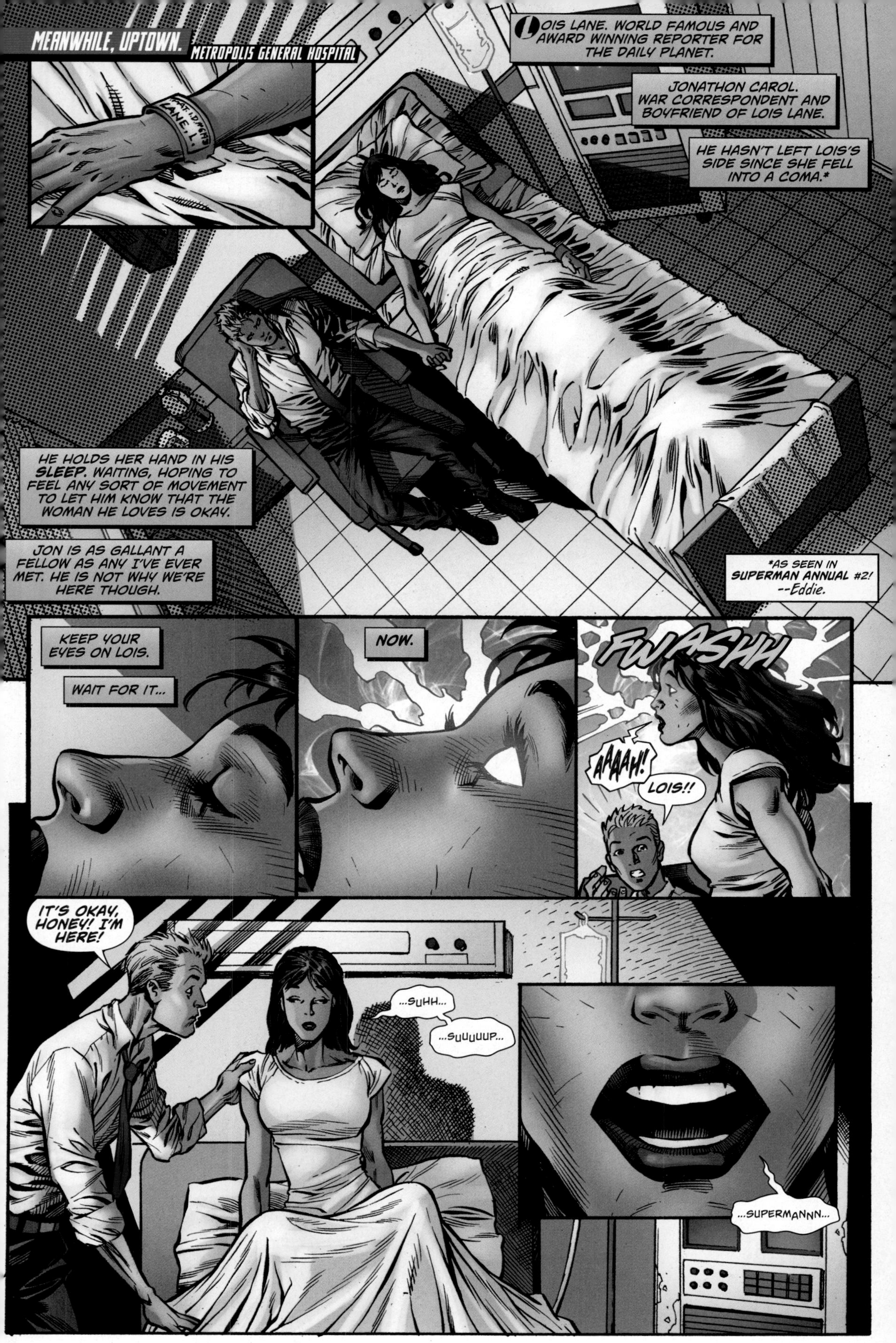
MEANWHILE, UPTOWN.
METROPOLIS GENERAL HOSPITAL
LANE, L.
LOIS LANE. WORLD FAMOUS AND AWARD WINNING REPORTER FOR THE DAILY PLANET.
JONATHON CAROL. WAR CORRESPONDENT AND BOYFRIEND OF LOIS LANE.
HE HASN'T LEFT LOIS'S SIDE SINCE SHE FELL INTO A COMA.*
HE HOLDS HER HAND IN HIS SLEEP. WAITING, HOPING TO FEEL ANY SORT OF MOVEMENT TO LET HIM KNOW THAT THE WOMAN HE LOVES IS OKAY.
JON IS AS GALLANT A FELLOW AS ANY I'VE EVER MET. HE IS NOT WHY WE'RE HERE THOUGH.
*AS SEEN IN SUPERMAN ANNUAL #2! --Eddie.
KEEP YOUR EYES ON LOIS.
WAIT FOR IT...
NOW.
FWASHH
AAAAH!
LOIS!!
IT'S OKAY, HONEY! I'M HERE!
...SUHH...
...SUUUUUP...
...SUPERMANNN...

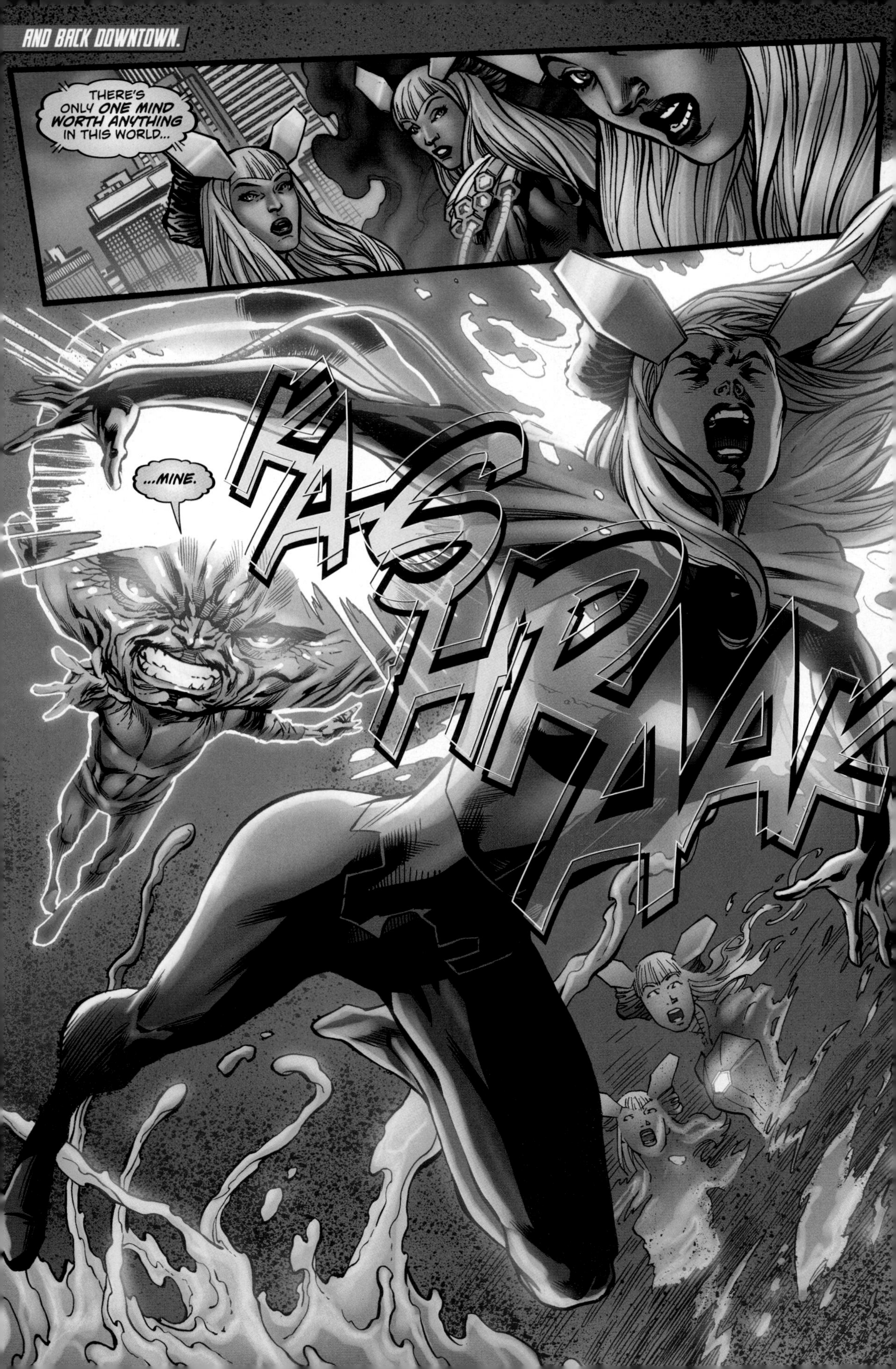
AND BACK DOWNTOWN.
THERE'S ONLY ONE MIND WORTH ANYTHING IN THIS WORLD...
...MINE.
KASHRAKK

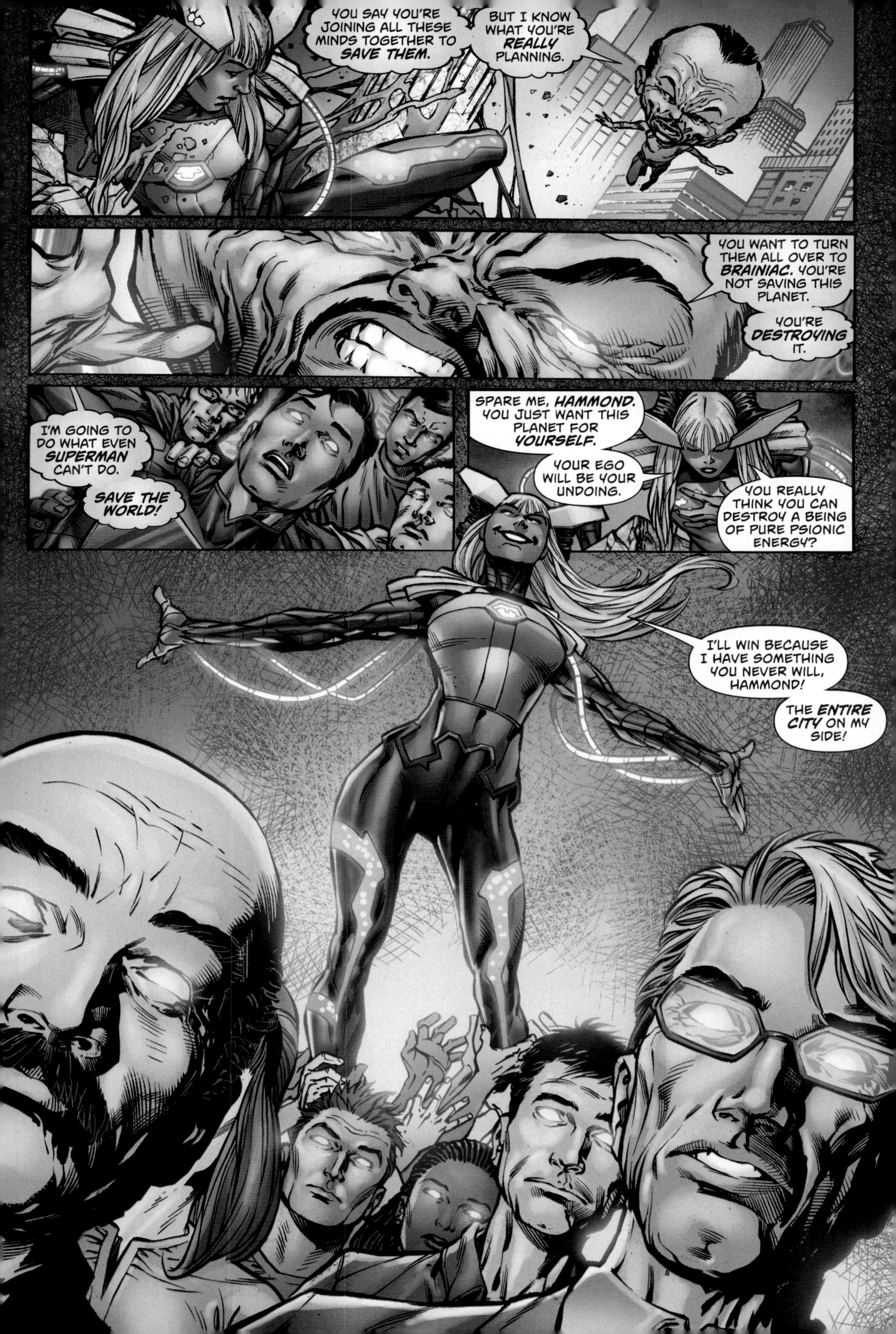
YOU SAY YOU'RE JOINING ALL THESE MINDS TOGETHER TO SAVE THEM.
BUT I KNOW WHAT YOU'RE REALLY PLANNING.
YOU WANT TO TURN THEM ALL OVER TO BRAINIAC. YOU'RE NOT SAVING THIS PLANET.
YOU'RE DESTROYING IT.
I'M GOING TO DO WHAT EVEN SUPERMAN CAN'T DO.
SAVE THE WORLD!
SPARE ME, HAMMOND. YOU JUST WANT THIS PLANET FOR YOURSELF.
YOUR EGO WILL BE YOUR UNDOING.
YOU REALLY THINK YOU CAN DESTROY A BEING OF PURE PSIONIC ENERGY?
I'LL WIN BECAUSE I HAVE SOMETHING YOU NEVER WILL, HAMMOND!
THE ENTIRE CITY ON MY SIDE!

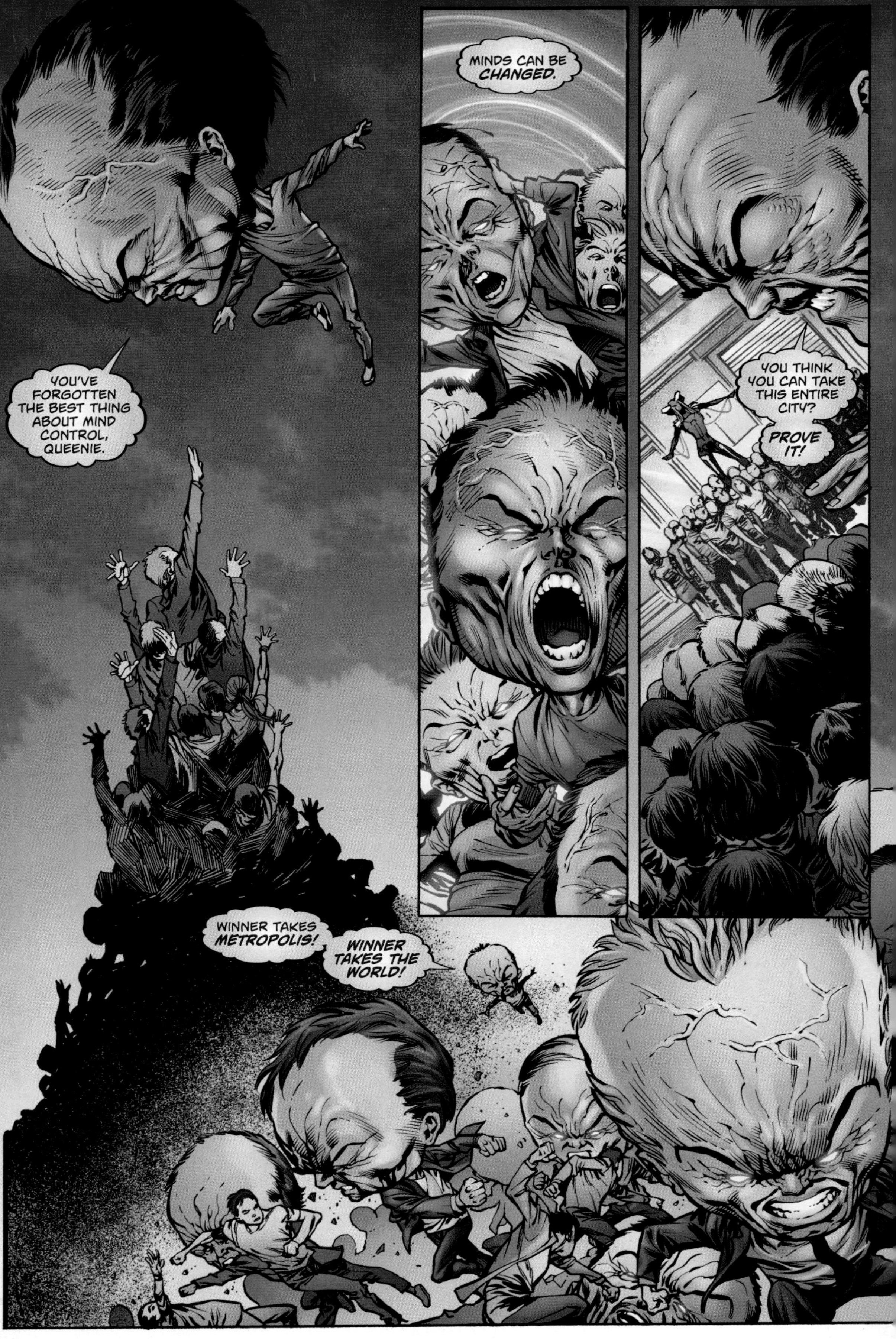

YOU'VE FORGOTTEN THE BEST THING ABOUT MIND CONTROL, QUEENIE.
MINDS CAN BE CHANGED.
YOU THINK YOU CAN TAKE THIS ENTIRE CITY?
PROVE IT!
WINNER TAKES METROPOLIS!
WINNER TAKES THE WORLD!

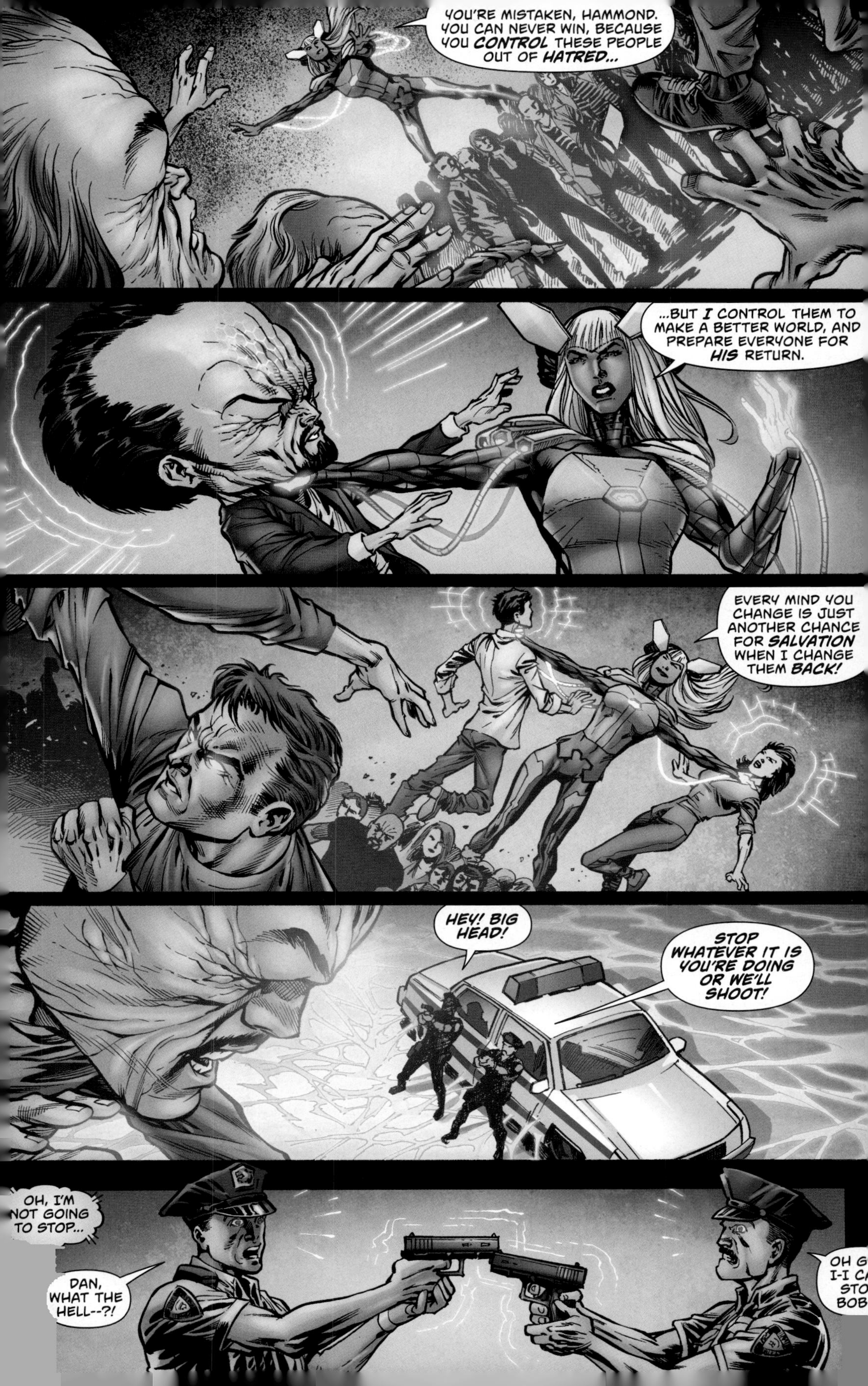

YOU'RE MISTAKEN, HAMMOND. YOU CAN NEVER WIN, BECAUSE YOU CONTROL THESE PEOPLE OUT OF HATRED...
...BUT I CONTROL THEM TO MAKE A BETTER WORLD, AND PREPARE EVERYONE FOR HIS RETURN.
EVERY MIND YOU CHANGE IS JUST ANOTHER CHANCE FOR SALVATION WHEN I CHANGE THEM BACK!
HEY! BIG HEAD!
STOP WHATEVER IT IS YOU'RE DOING OR WE'LL SHOOT!
OH, I'M NOT GOING TO STOP...
DAN, WHAT THE HELL--?!

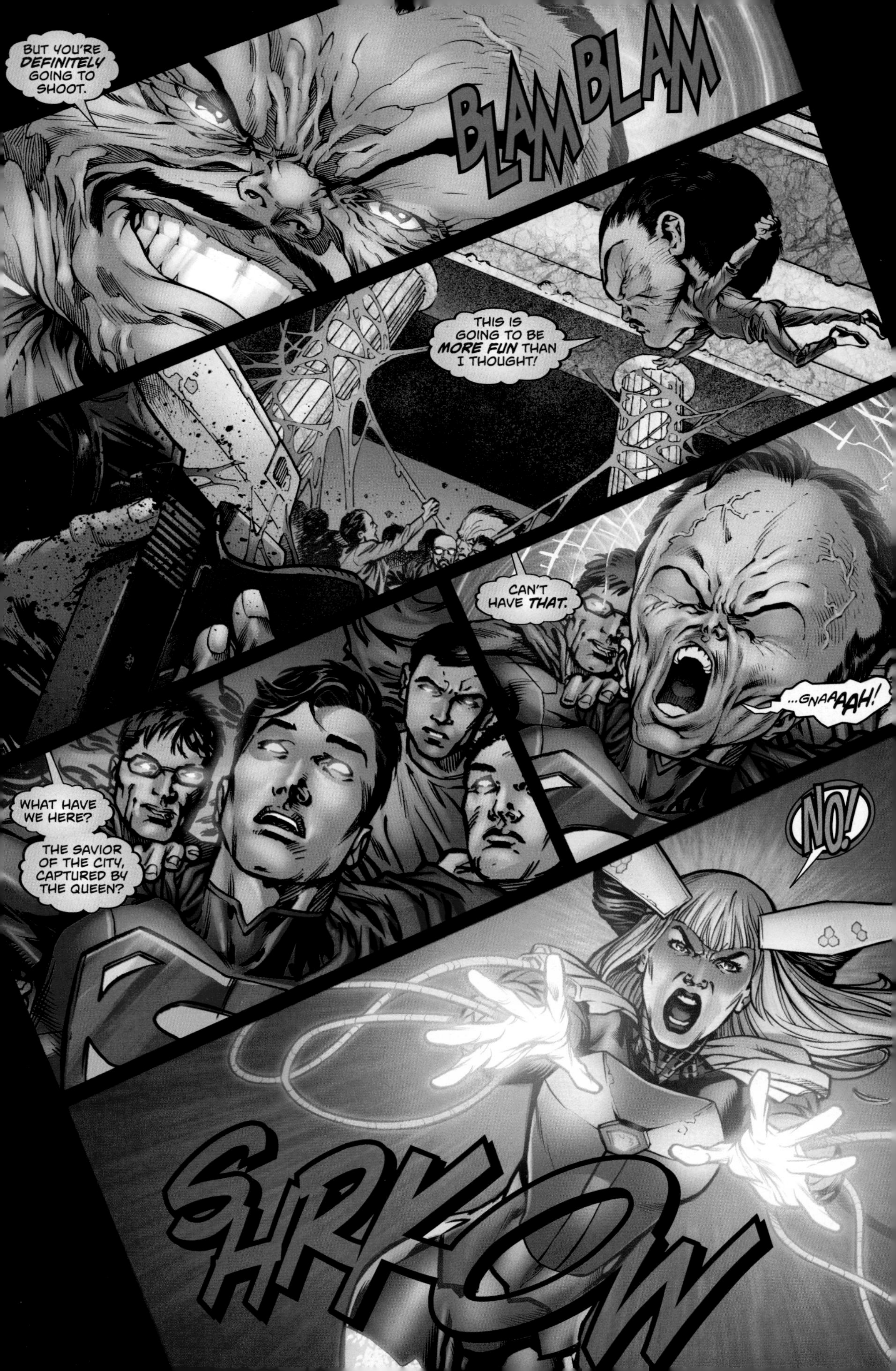
BUT YOU'RE DEFINITELY GOING TO SHOOT.
BLAM BLAM
THIS IS GOING TO BE MORE FUN THAN I THOUGHT!
CAN'T HAVE THAT.
...GNAAAAH!
WHAT HAVE WE HERE?
THE SAVIOR OF THE CITY, CAPTURED BY THE QUEEN?
NO!
SHRAKOW

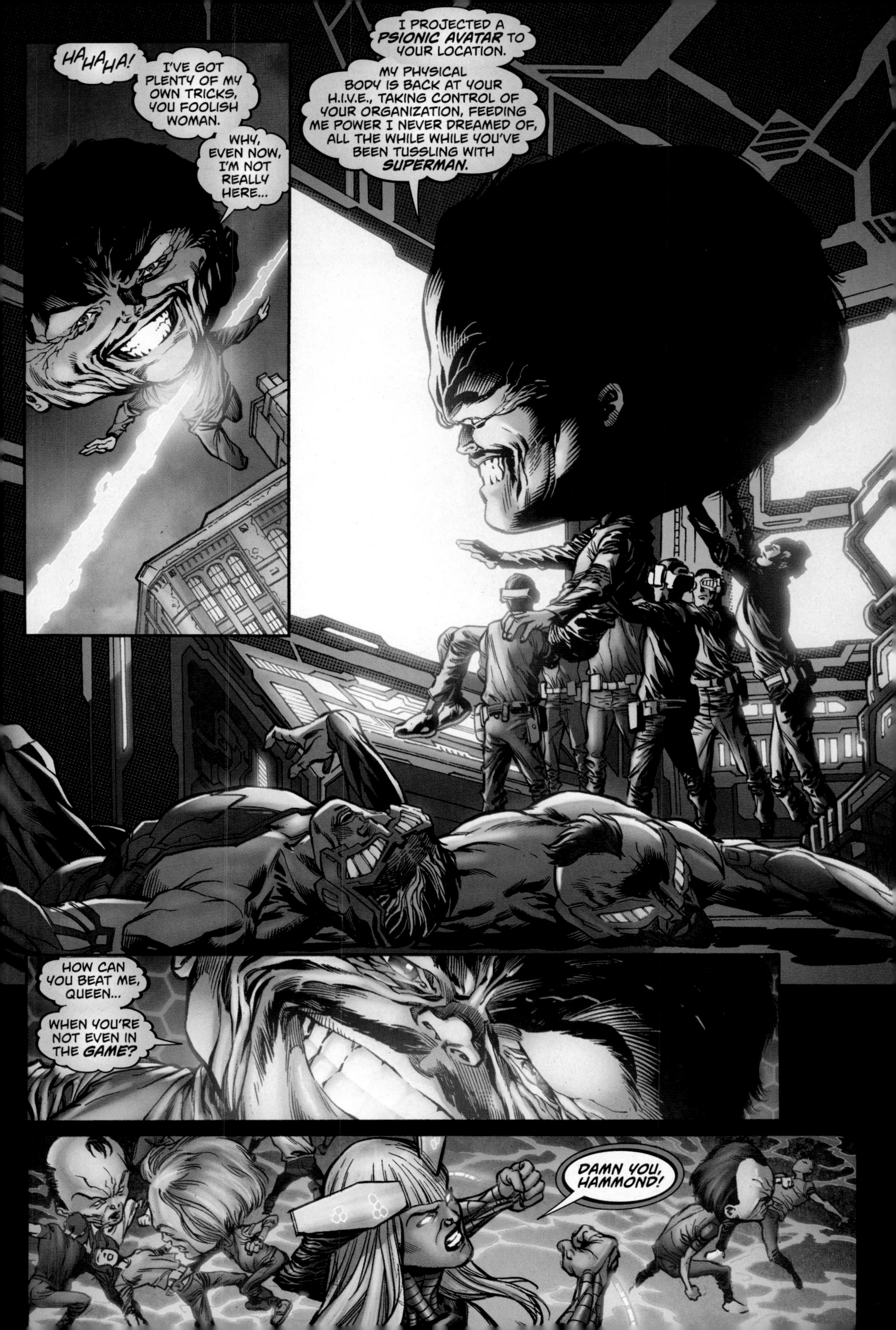
HA HA HA!
I'VE GOT PLENTY OF MY OWN TRICKS, YOU FOOLISH WOMAN.
WHY, EVEN NOW, I'M NOT REALLY HERE...
I PROJECTED A PSIONIC AVATAR TO YOUR LOCATION.
MY PHYSICAL BODY IS BACK AT YOUR H.I.V.E., TAKING CONTROL OF YOUR ORGANIZATION, FEEDING ME POWER I NEVER DREAMED OF, ALL THE WHILE WHILE YOU'VE BEEN TUSSLING WITH SUPERMAN.
HOW CAN YOU BEAT ME, QUEEN...
WHEN YOU'RE NOT EVEN IN THE GAME?
DAMN YOU, HAMMOND!

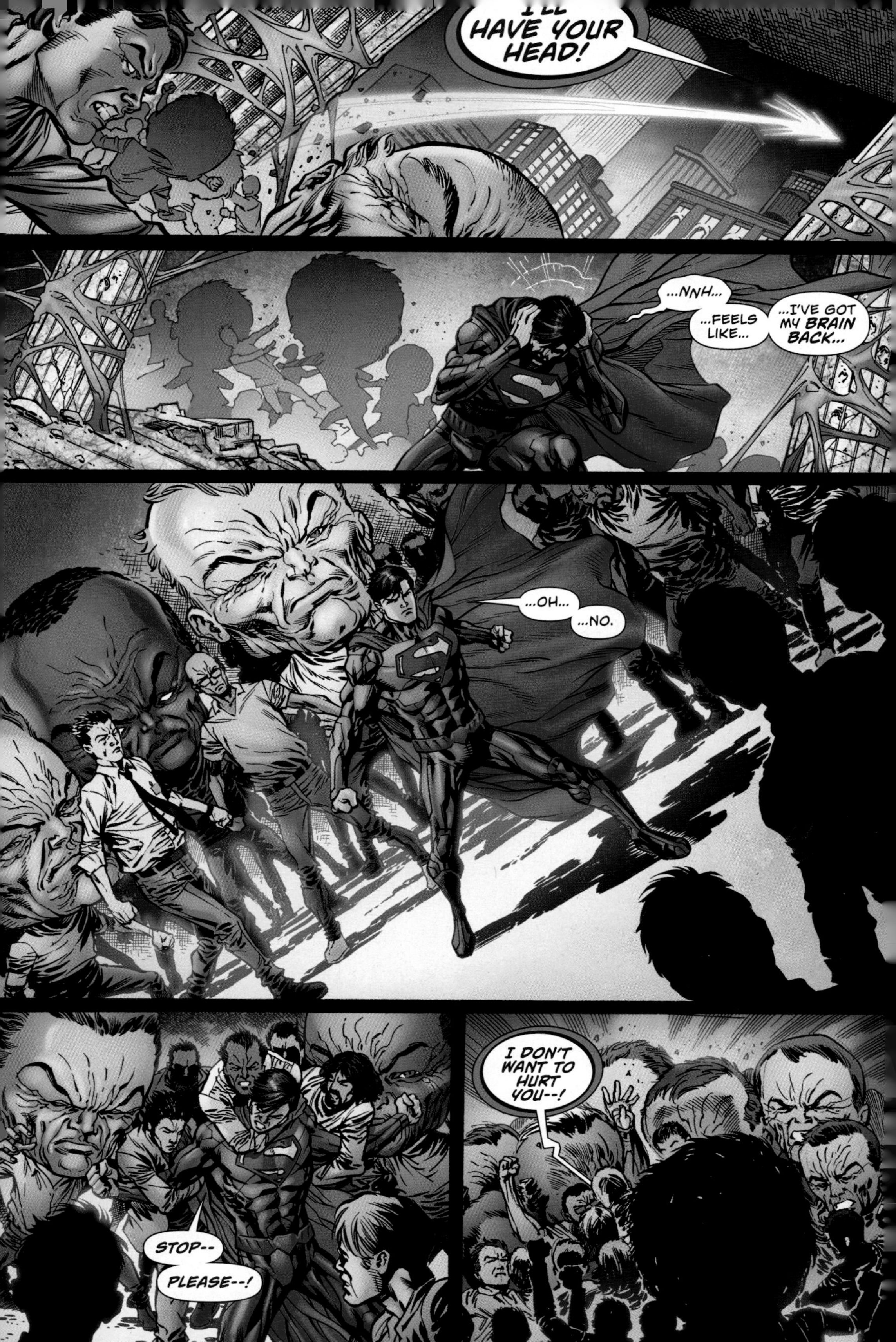
HAVE YOUR HEAD!
...NNH...
...FEELS LIKE...
...I'VE GOT MY BRAIN BACK...
...OH...
...NO.
STOP--
PLEASE--!
I DON'T WANT TO HURT YOU--!

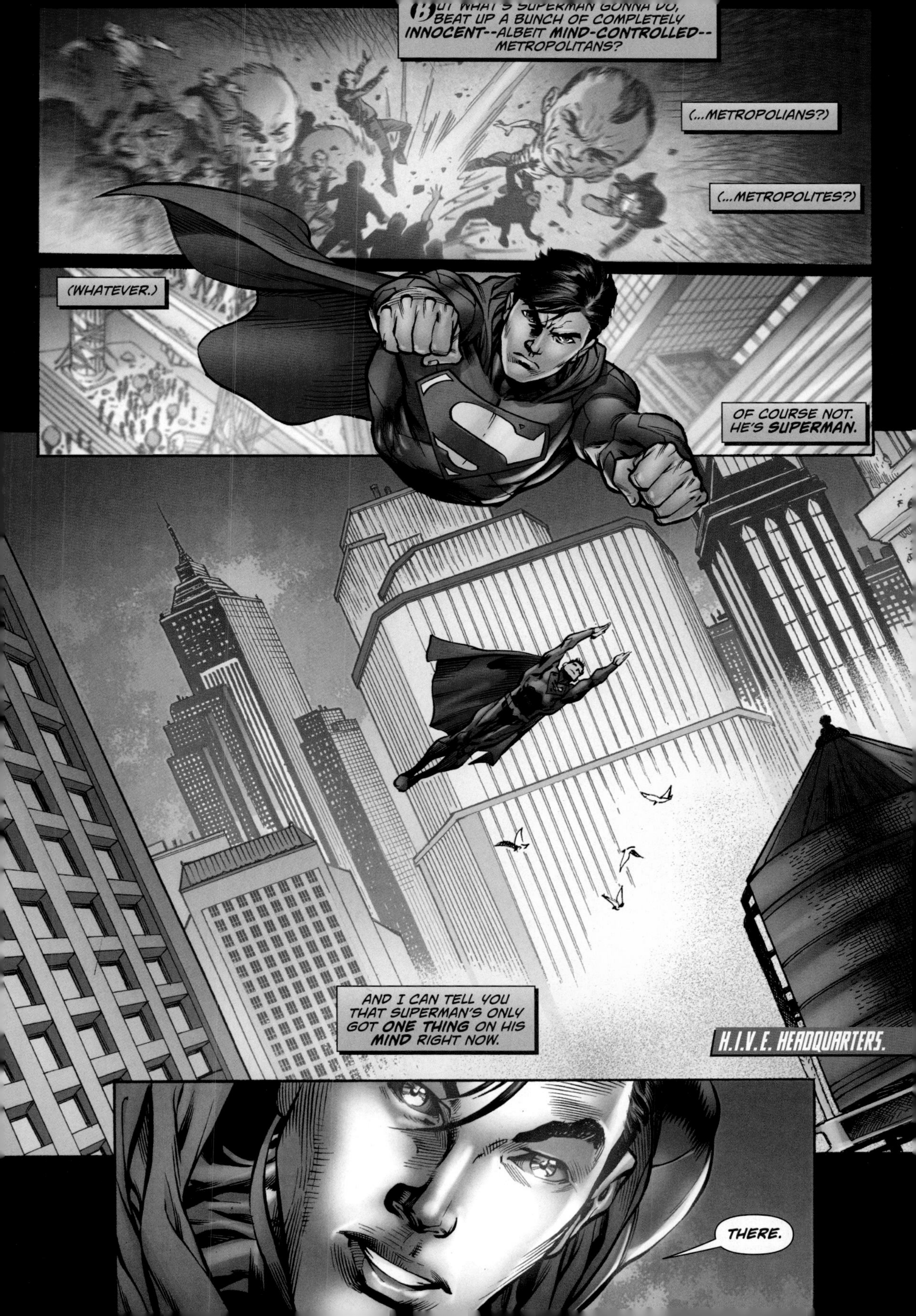
BUT WHAT'S SUPERMAN GONNA DO, BEAT UP A BUNCH OF COMPLETELY INNOCENT--ALBEIT MIND-CONTROLLED--METROPOLITANS?
(...METROPOLIANS?)
(...METROPOLITES?)
(WHATEVER.)
OF COURSE NOT. HE'S SUPERMAN.
AND I CAN TELL YOU THAT SUPERMAN'S ONLY GOT ONE THING ON HIS MIND RIGHT NOW.
H.I.V.E. HEADQUARTERS.
THERE.

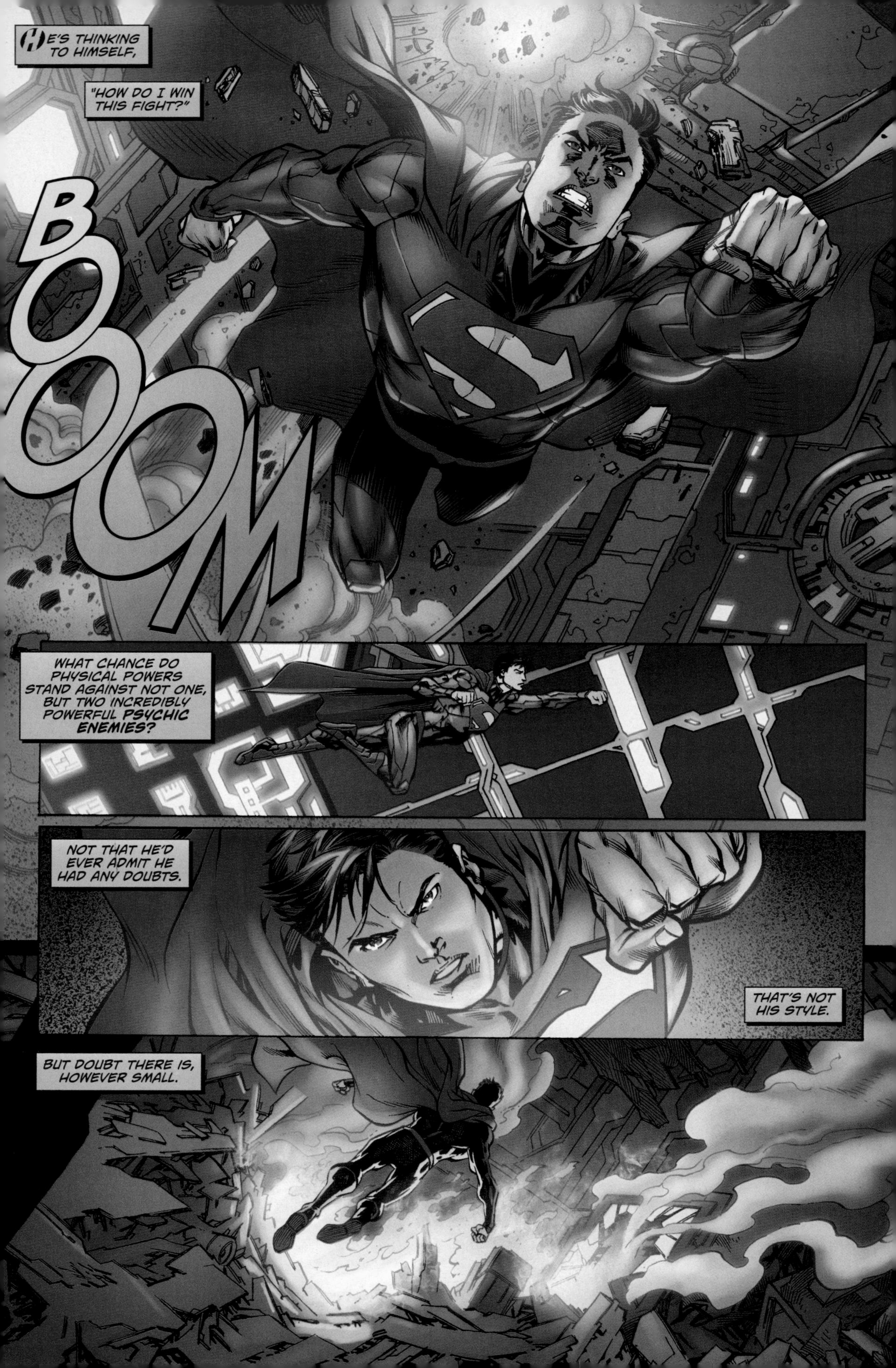
HE'S THINKING TO HIMSELF,
"HOW DO I WIN THIS FIGHT?"
BOOOM
WHAT CHANCE DO PHYSICAL POWERS STAND AGAINST NOT ONE, BUT TWO INCREDIBLY POWERFUL PSYCHIC ENEMIES?
NOT THAT HE'D EVER ADMIT HE HAD ANY DOUBTS.
THAT'S NOT HIS STYLE.
BUT DOUBT THERE IS, HOWEVER SMALL.

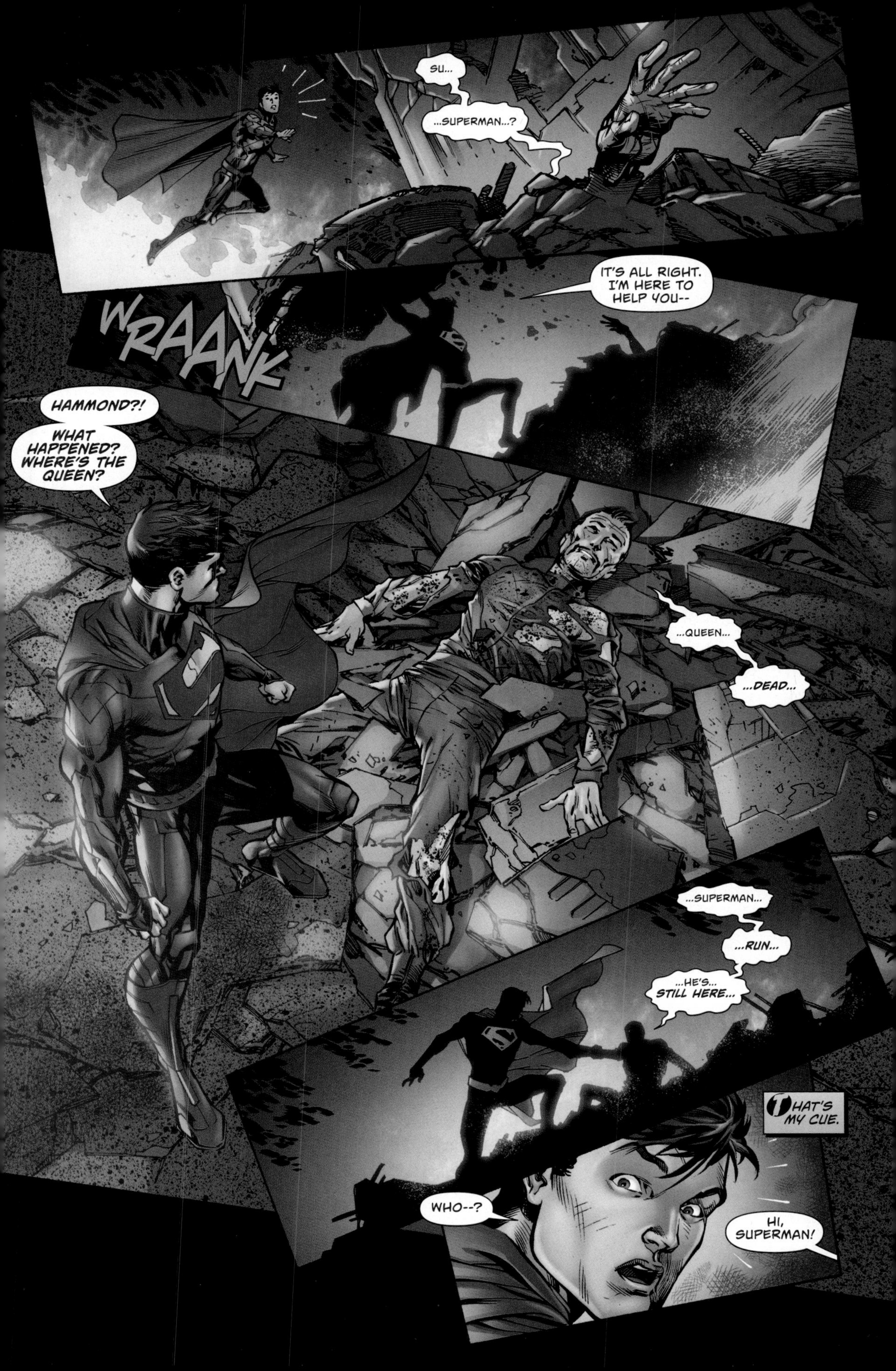
SU...
...SUPERMAN...?
IT'S ALL RIGHT. I'M HERE TO HELP YOU--
WRAANK
HAMMOND?!
WHAT HAPPENED? WHERE'S THE QUEEN?
...QUEEN...
...DEAD...
...SUPERMAN...
...RUN...
...HE'S... STILL HERE...
THAT'S MY CUE.
WHO--?
HI, SUPERMAN!

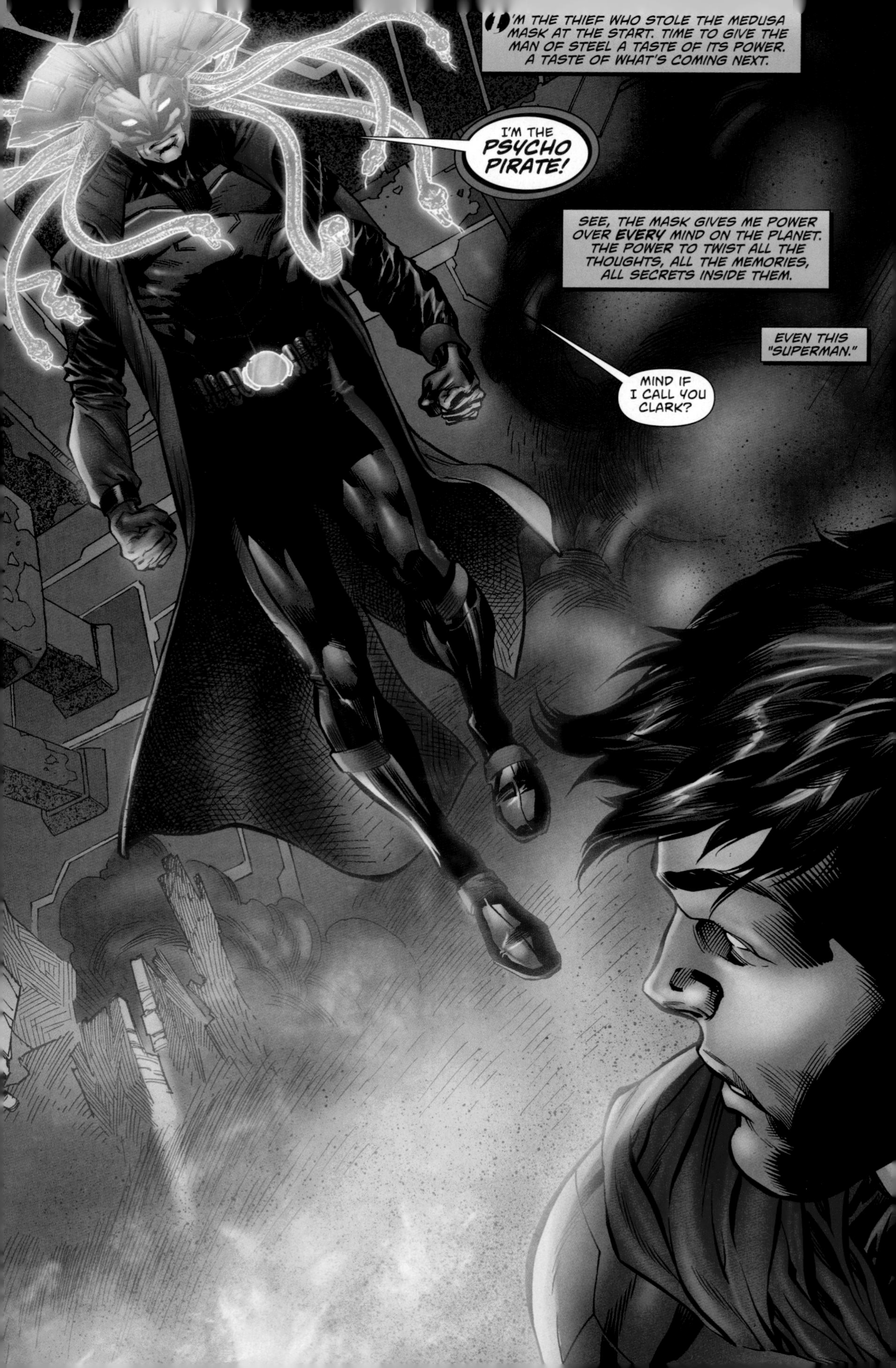
I'M THE THIEF WHO STOLE THE MEDUSA MASK AT THE START. TIME TO GIVE THE MAN OF STEEL A TASTE OF ITS POWER. A TASTE OF WHAT'S COMING NEXT.
I'M THE PSYCHO PIRATE!
SEE, THE MASK GIVES ME POWER OVER EVERY MIND ON THE PLANET. THE POWER TO TWIST ALL THE THOUGHTS, ALL THE MEMORIES, ALL SECRETS INSIDE THEM.
EVEN THIS "SUPERMAN."
MIND IF I CALL YOU CLARK?

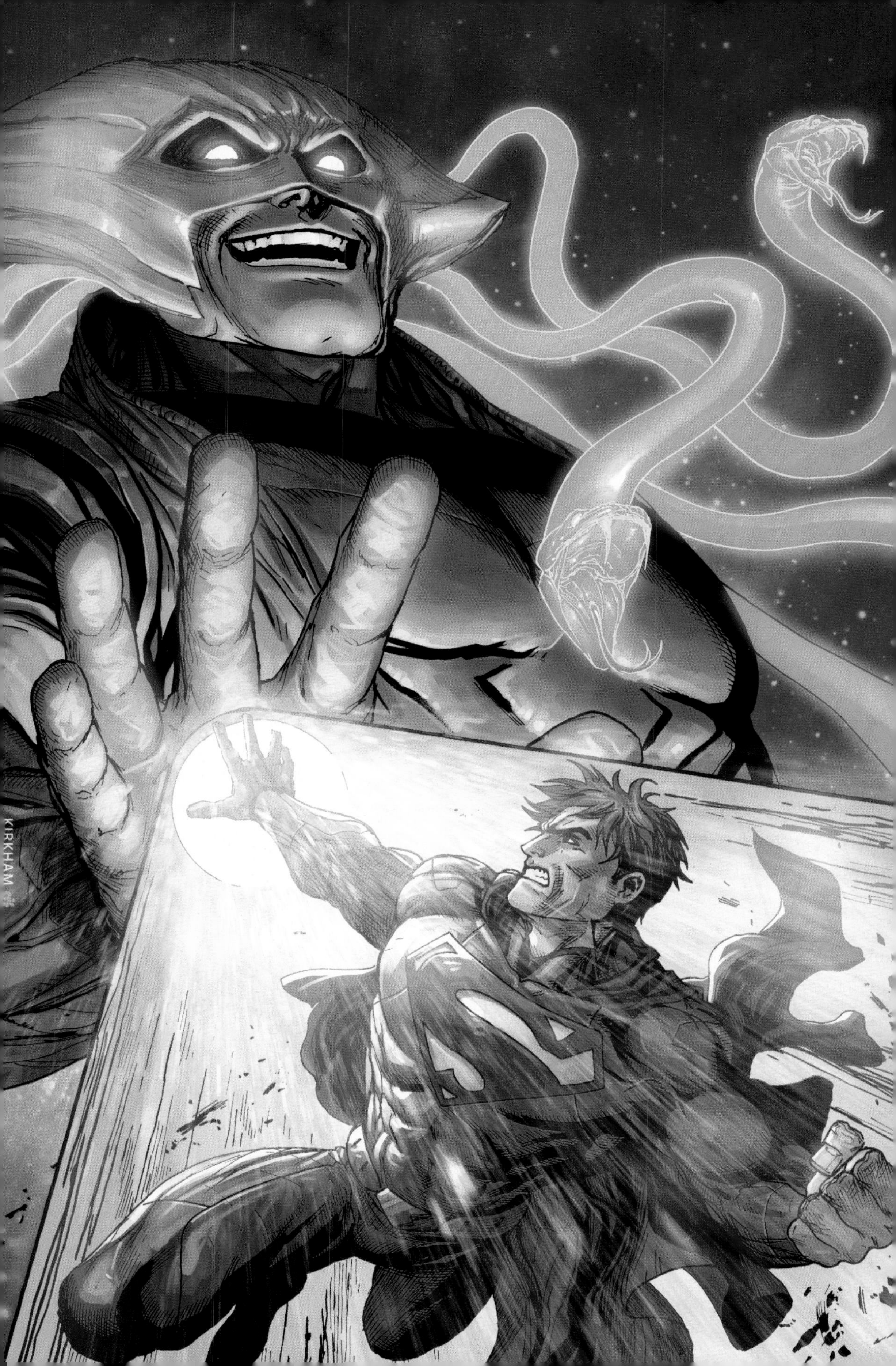
KIRKHAM

PSI WAR: PART TWO

MIKE JOHNSON writer TYLER KIRKHAM & JESUS MERINO artists cover art by TYLER KIRKHAM & ARIF PRIANTO

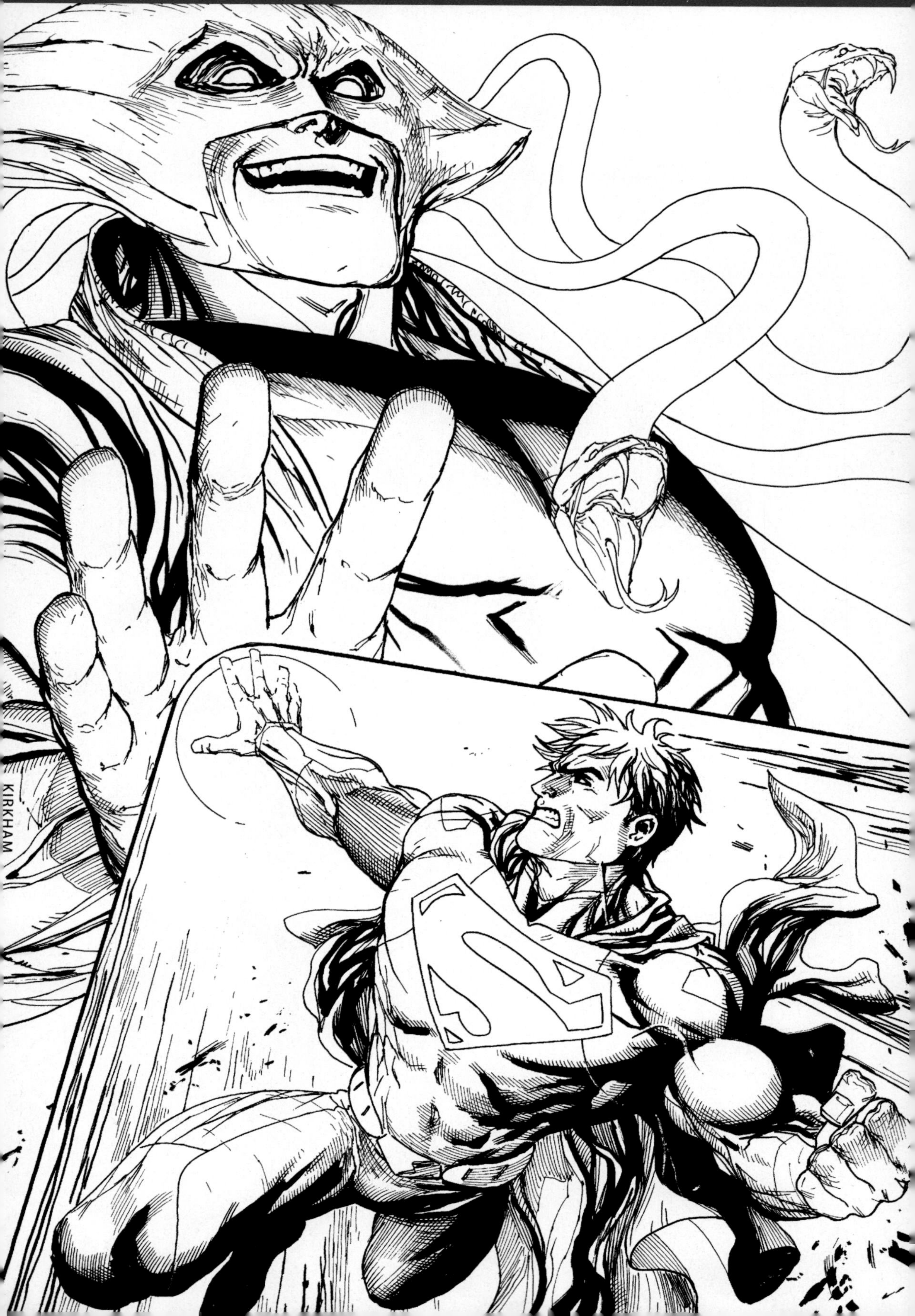
KIRKHAM

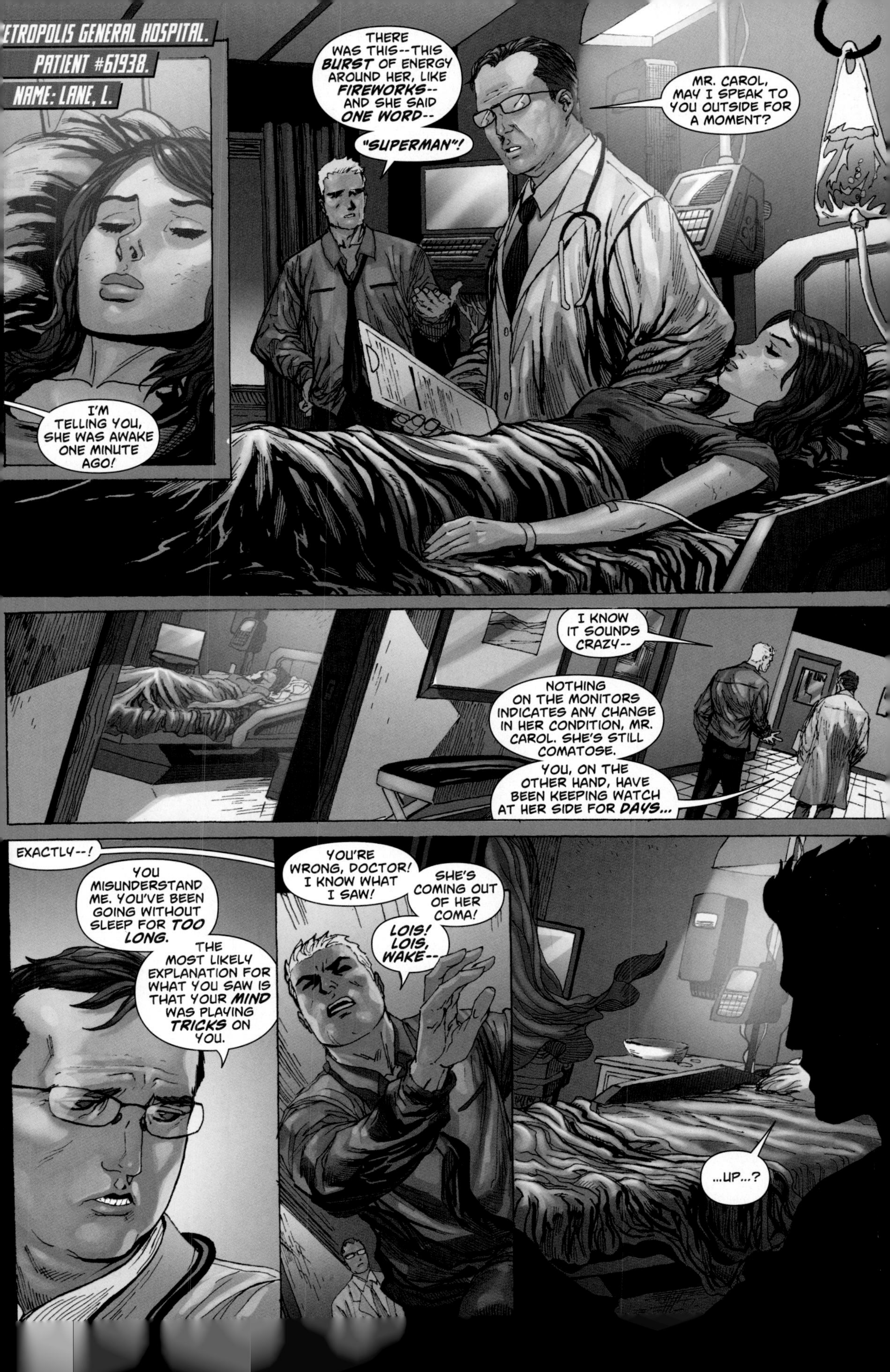
ETROPOLIS GENERAL HOSPITAL.
PATIENT #61938.
NAME: LANE, L.
I'M TELLING YOU, SHE WAS AWAKE ONE MINUTE AGO!
THERE WAS THIS--THIS BURST OF ENERGY AROUND HER, LIKE FIREWORKS-- AND SHE SAID ONE WORD--
"SUPERMAN"!
MR. CAROL, MAY I SPEAK TO YOU OUTSIDE FOR A MOMENT?
I KNOW IT SOUNDS CRAZY--
NOTHING ON THE MONITORS INDICATES ANY CHANGE IN HER CONDITION, MR. CAROL. SHE'S STILL COMATOSE.
YOU, ON THE OTHER HAND, HAVE BEEN KEEPING WATCH AT HER SIDE FOR DAYS...
EXACTLY--!
YOU MISUNDERSTAND ME. YOU'VE BEEN GOING WITHOUT SLEEP FOR TOO LONG.
THE MOST LIKELY EXPLANATION FOR WHAT YOU SAW IS THAT YOUR MIND WAS PLAYING TRICKS ON YOU.
YOU'RE WRONG, DOCTOR! I KNOW WHAT I SAW!
SHE'S COMING OUT OF HER COMA!
LOIS! LOIS, WAKE--
...UP...?

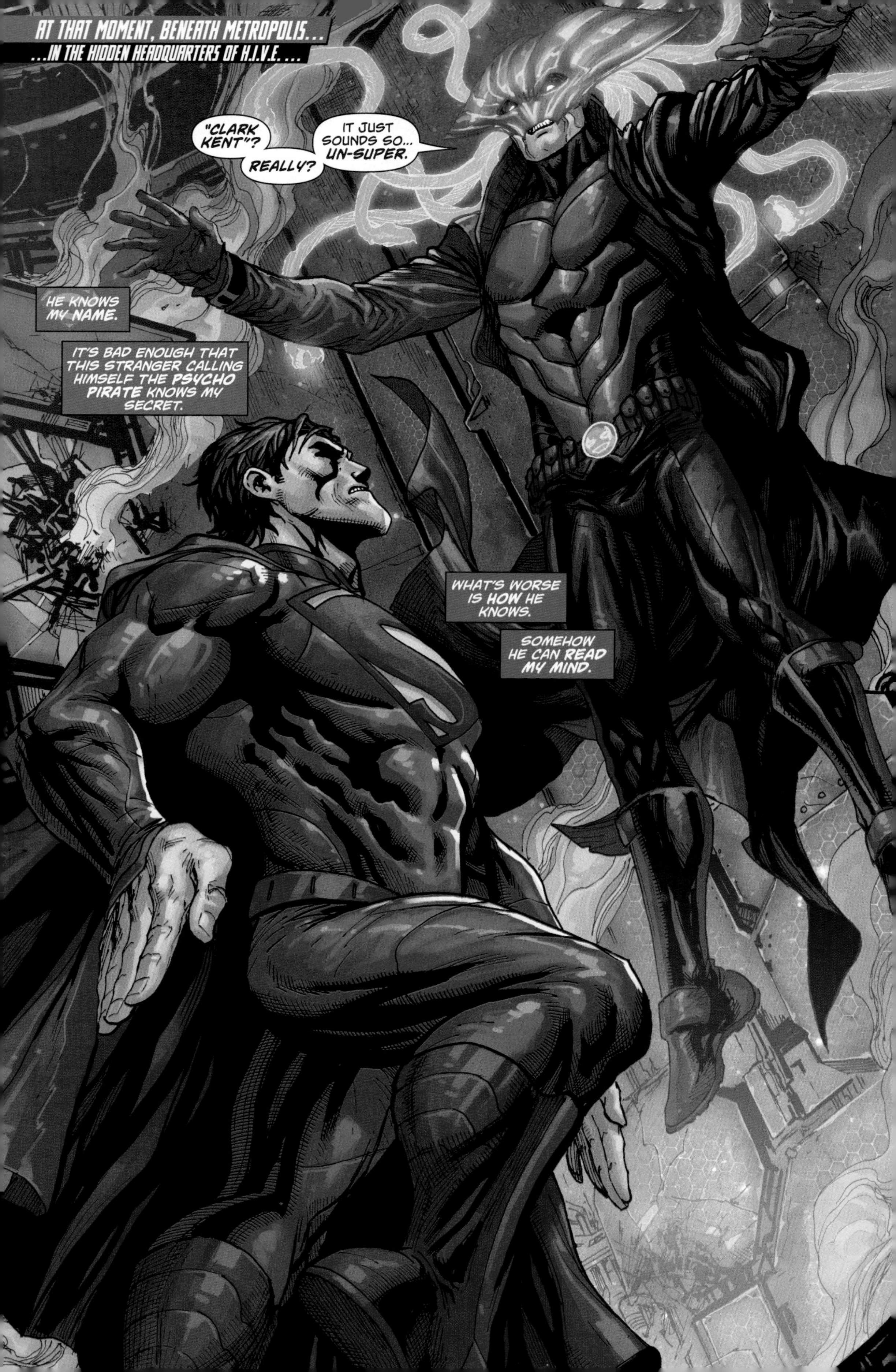
AT THAT MOMENT, BENEATH METROPOLIS...
...IN THE HIDDEN HEADQUARTERS OF H.I.V.E. ...
"CLARK KENT"? REALLY?
IT JUST SOUNDS SO... UN-SUPER.
HE KNOWS MY NAME.
IT'S BAD ENOUGH THAT THIS STRANGER CALLING HIMSELF THE PSYCHO PIRATE KNOWS MY SECRET.
WHAT'S WORSE IS HOW HE KNOWS.
SOMEHOW HE CAN READ MY MIND.

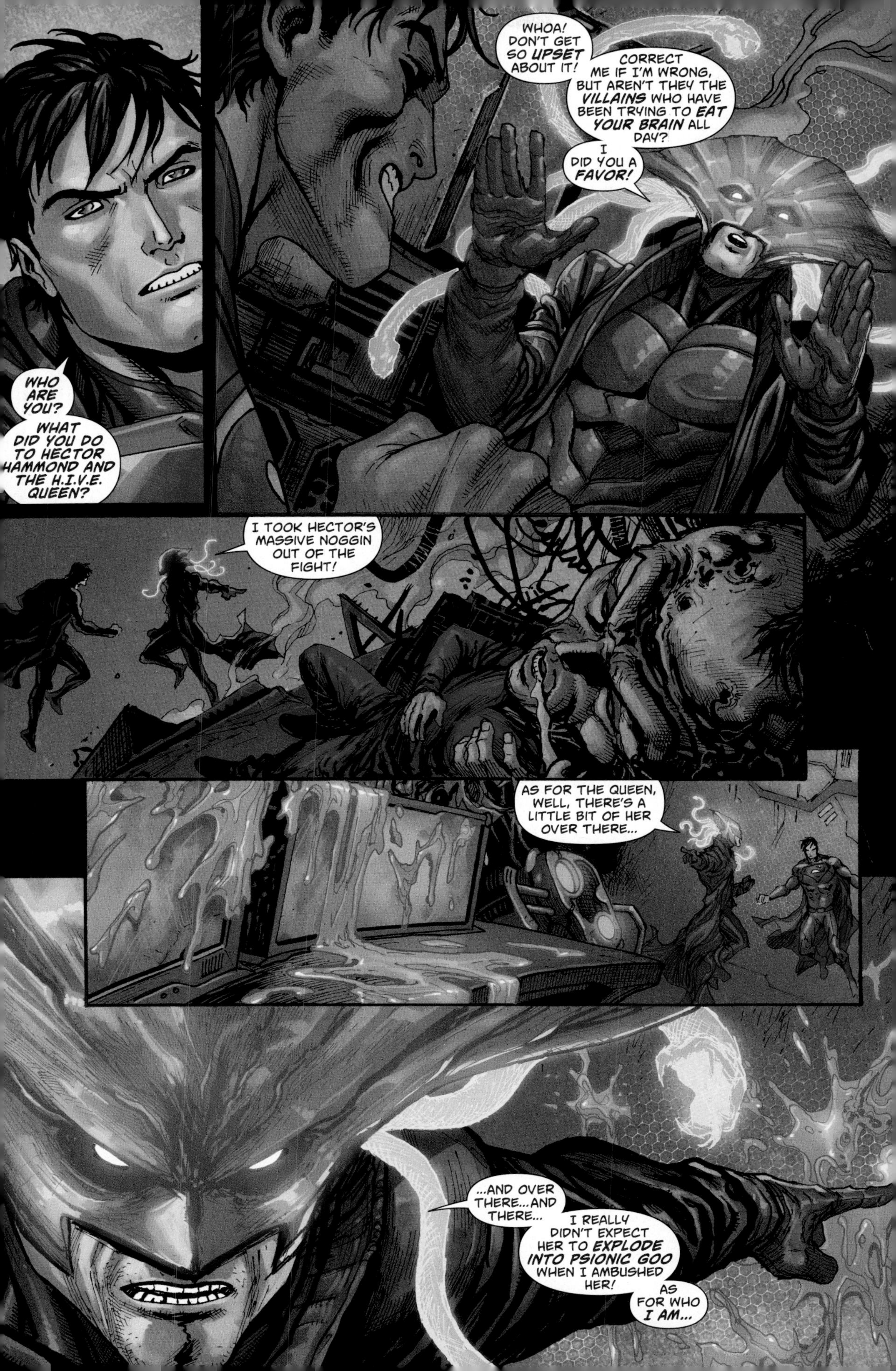
WHO ARE YOU?
WHAT DID YOU DO TO HECTOR HAMMOND AND THE H.I.V.E. QUEEN?
WHOA! DON'T GET SO UPSET ABOUT IT!
CORRECT ME IF I'M WRONG, BUT AREN'T THEY THE VILLAINS WHO HAVE BEEN TRYING TO EAT YOUR BRAIN ALL DAY?
I DID YOU A FAVOR!
I TOOK HECTOR'S MASSIVE NOGGIN OUT OF THE FIGHT!
AS FOR THE QUEEN, WELL, THERE'S A LITTLE BIT OF HER OVER THERE...
...AND OVER THERE...AND THERE...
I REALLY DIDN'T EXPECT HER TO EXPLODE INTO PSIONIC GOO WHEN I AMBUSHED HER!
AS FOR WHO I AM...

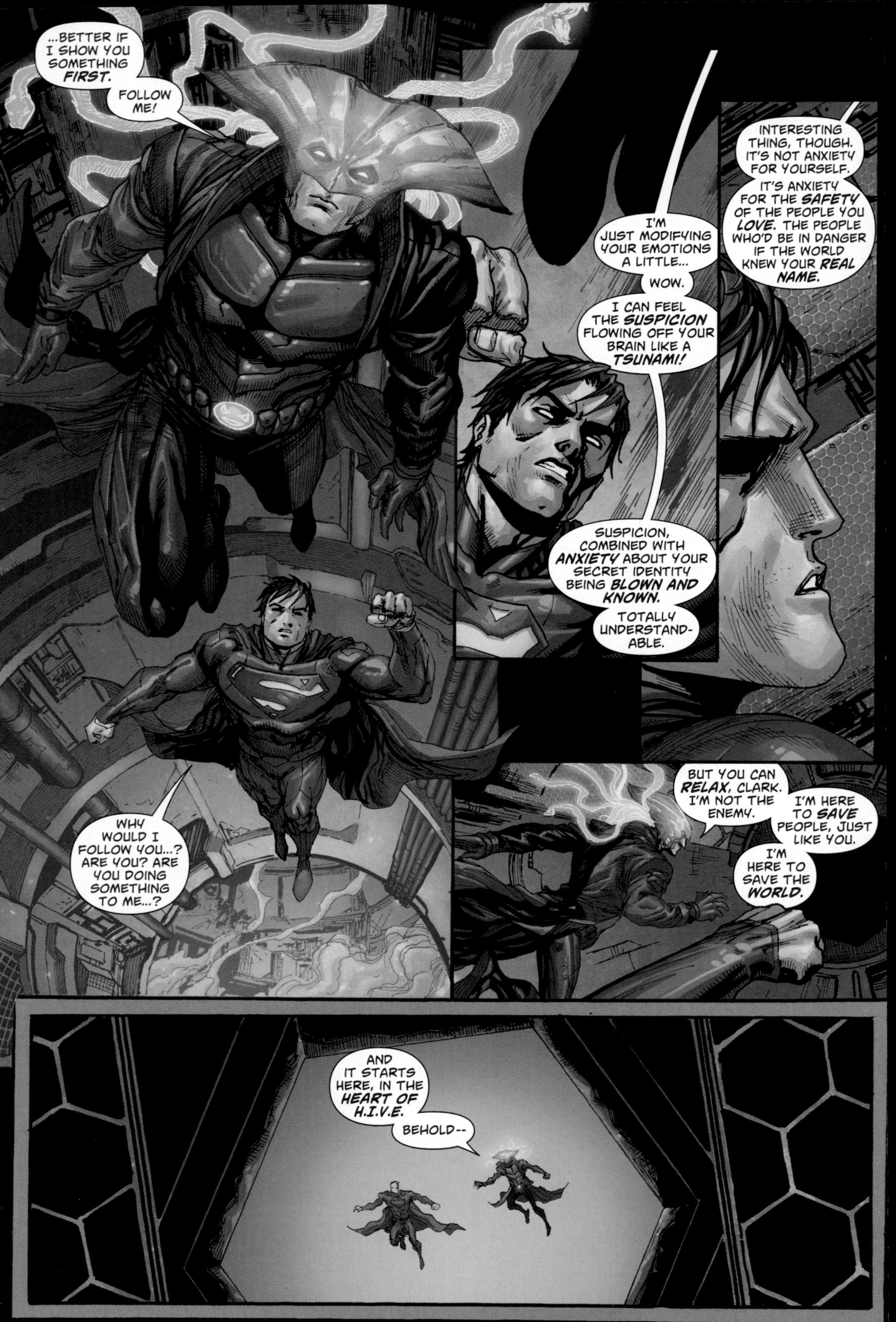

...BETTER IF I SHOW YOU SOMETHING *FIRST*.
FOLLOW ME!
I'M JUST MODIFYING YOUR EMOTIONS A LITTLE...
WOW.
I CAN FEEL THE *SUSPICION* FLOWING OFF YOUR BRAIN LIKE A *TSUNAMI!*
SUSPICION, COMBINED WITH *ANXIETY* ABOUT YOUR SECRET IDENTITY BEING *BLOWN AND KNOWN*.
TOTALLY UNDERSTANDABLE.
INTERESTING THING, THOUGH. IT'S NOT ANXIETY FOR YOURSELF.
IT'S ANXIETY FOR THE *SAFETY* OF THE PEOPLE YOU *LOVE*. THE PEOPLE WHO'D BE IN DANGER IF THE WORLD KNEW YOUR *REAL NAME*.
WHY WOULD I FOLLOW YOU...? ARE YOU? ARE YOU DOING SOMETHING TO ME...?
BUT YOU CAN *RELAX*, CLARK. I'M NOT THE ENEMY.
I'M HERE TO *SAVE* PEOPLE, JUST LIKE YOU.
I'M HERE TO SAVE THE *WORLD*.
AND IT STARTS HERE, IN THE *HEART OF H.I.V.E.*
BEHOLD--

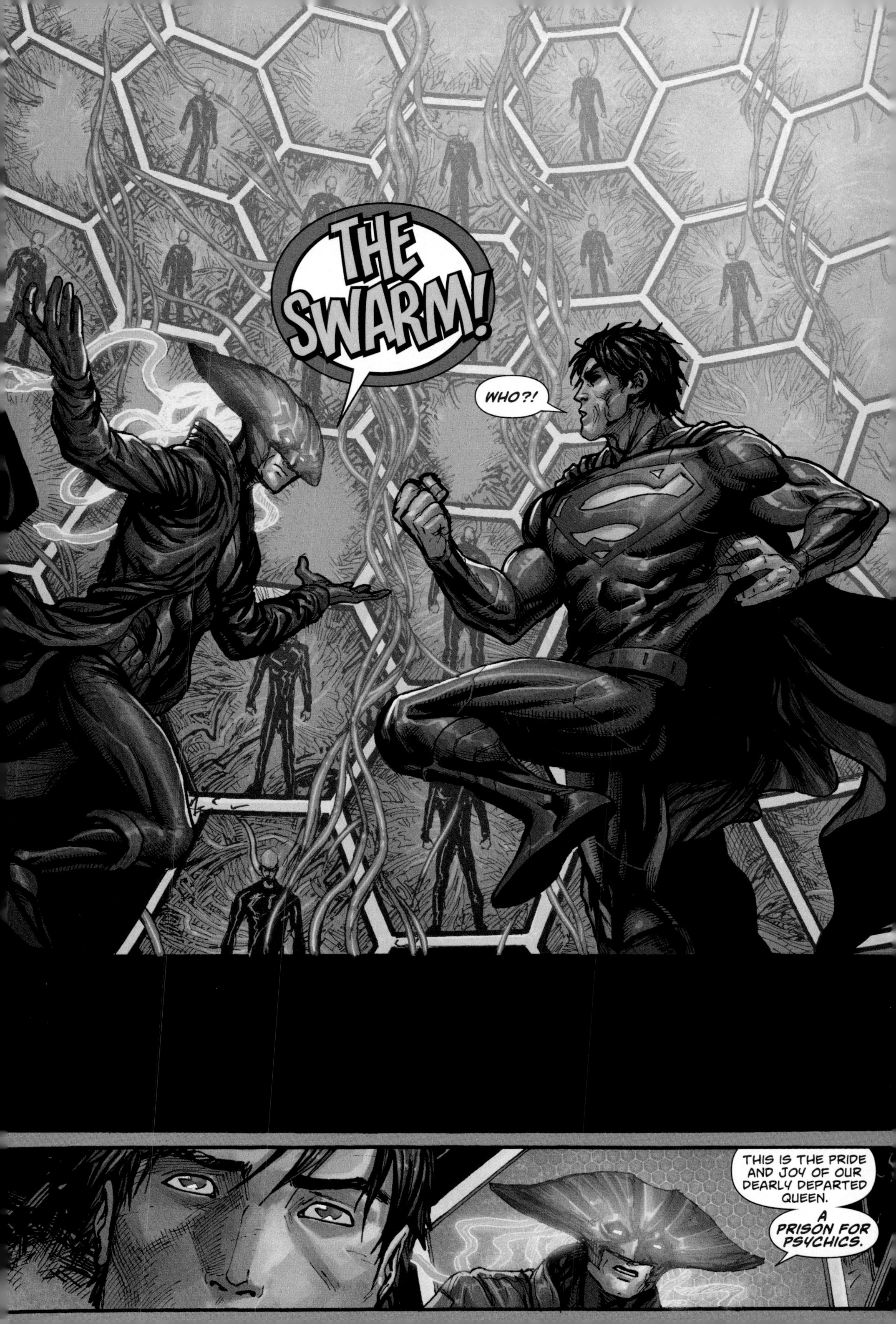
THE SWARM!
WHO?!
THIS IS THE PRIDE AND JOY OF OUR DEARLY DEPARTED QUEEN.
A PRISON FOR PSYCHICS.

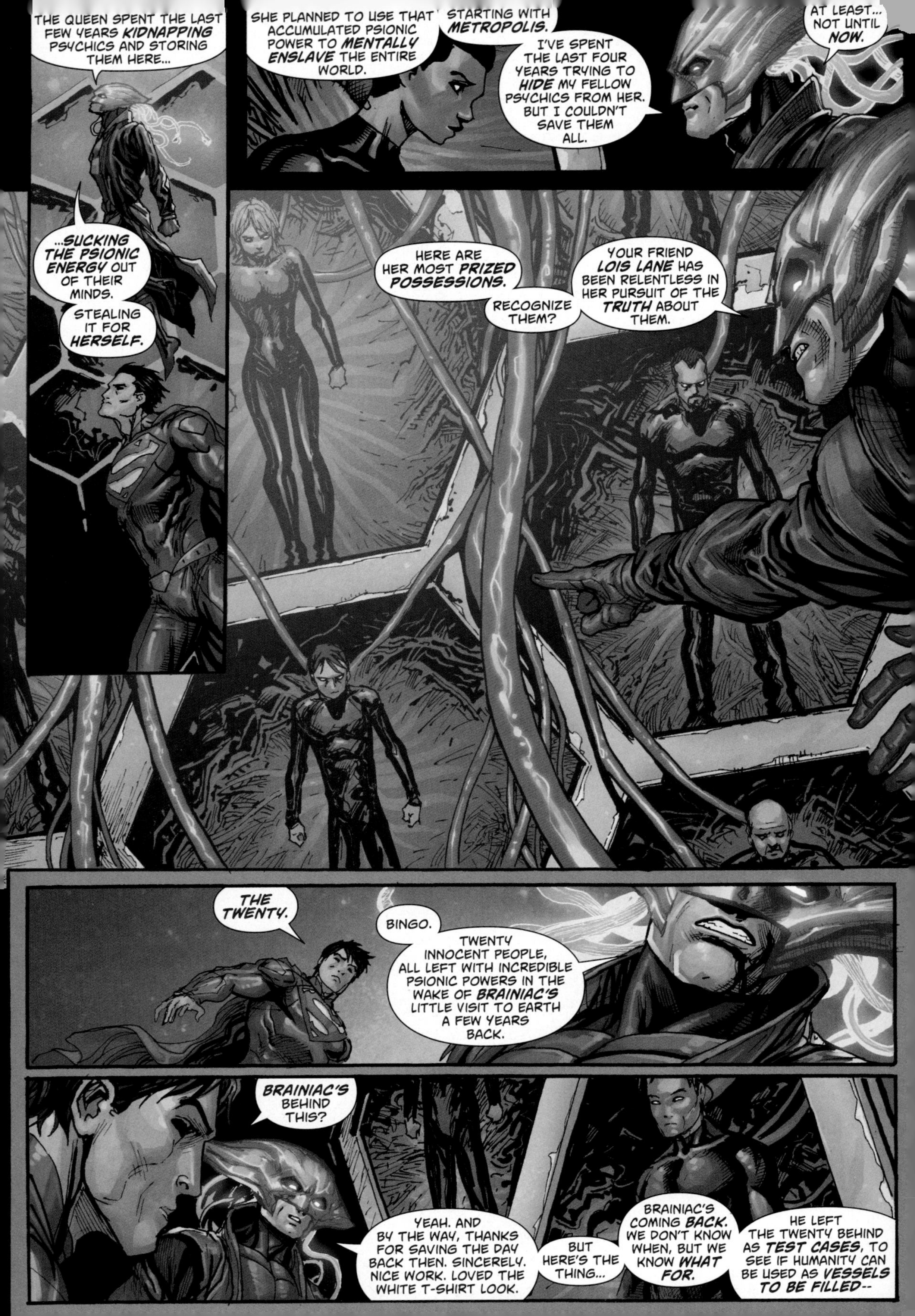

THE QUEEN SPENT THE LAST FEW YEARS KIDNAPPING PSYCHICS AND STORING THEM HERE...
SHE PLANNED TO USE THAT ACCUMULATED PSIONIC POWER TO MENTALLY ENSLAVE THE ENTIRE WORLD.
STARTING WITH METROPOLIS.
I'VE SPENT THE LAST FOUR YEARS TRYING TO HIDE MY FELLOW PSYCHICS FROM HER. BUT I COULDN'T SAVE THEM ALL.
AT LEAST... NOT UNTIL NOW.
...SUCKING THE PSIONIC ENERGY OUT OF THEIR MINDS.
STEALING IT FOR HERSELF.
HERE ARE HER MOST PRIZED POSSESSIONS.
RECOGNIZE THEM?
YOUR FRIEND LOIS LANE HAS BEEN RELENTLESS IN HER PURSUIT OF THE TRUTH ABOUT THEM.
THE TWENTY.
BINGO.
TWENTY INNOCENT PEOPLE, ALL LEFT WITH INCREDIBLE PSIONIC POWERS IN THE WAKE OF BRAINIAC'S LITTLE VISIT TO EARTH A FEW YEARS BACK.
BRAINIAC'S BEHIND THIS?
YEAH. AND BY THE WAY, THANKS FOR SAVING THE DAY BACK THEN. SINCERELY. NICE WORK. LOVED THE WHITE T-SHIRT LOOK.
BUT HERE'S THE THING...
BRAINIAC'S COMING BACK. WE DON'T KNOW WHEN, BUT WE KNOW WHAT FOR.
HE LEFT THE TWENTY BEHIND AS TEST CASES, TO SEE IF HUMANITY CAN BE USED AS VESSELS TO BE FILLED--

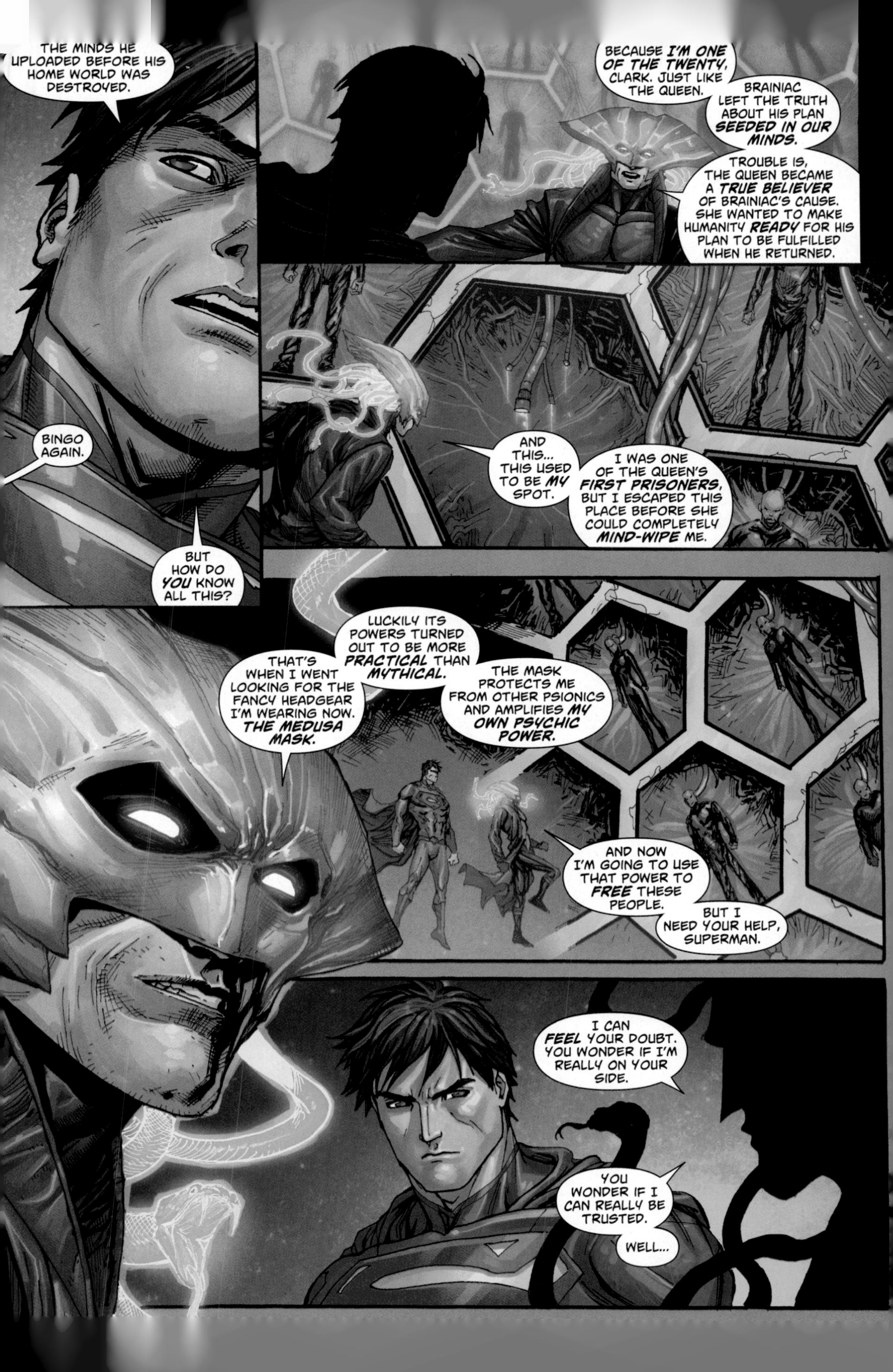
THE MINDS HE UPLOADED BEFORE HIS HOME WORLD WAS DESTROYED.
BECAUSE I'M ONE OF THE TWENTY, CLARK. JUST LIKE THE QUEEN.
BRAINIAC LEFT THE TRUTH ABOUT HIS PLAN SEEDED IN OUR MINDS.
TROUBLE IS, THE QUEEN BECAME A TRUE BELIEVER OF BRAINIAC'S CAUSE. SHE WANTED TO MAKE HUMANITY READY FOR HIS PLAN TO BE FULFILLED WHEN HE RETURNED.
BINGO AGAIN.
BUT HOW DO YOU KNOW ALL THIS?
AND THIS... THIS USED TO BE MY SPOT.
I WAS ONE OF THE QUEEN'S FIRST PRISONERS, BUT I ESCAPED THIS PLACE BEFORE SHE COULD COMPLETELY MIND-WIPE ME.
THAT'S WHEN I WENT LOOKING FOR THE FANCY HEADGEAR I'M WEARING NOW. THE MEDUSA MASK.
LUCKILY ITS POWERS TURNED OUT TO BE MORE PRACTICAL THAN MYTHICAL.
THE MASK PROTECTS ME FROM OTHER PSIONICS AND AMPLIFIES MY OWN PSYCHIC POWER.
AND NOW I'M GOING TO USE THAT POWER TO FREE THESE PEOPLE.
BUT I NEED YOUR HELP, SUPERMAN.
I CAN FEEL YOUR DOUBT. YOU WONDER IF I'M REALLY ON YOUR SIDE.
YOU WONDER IF I CAN REALLY BE TRUSTED.
WELL...

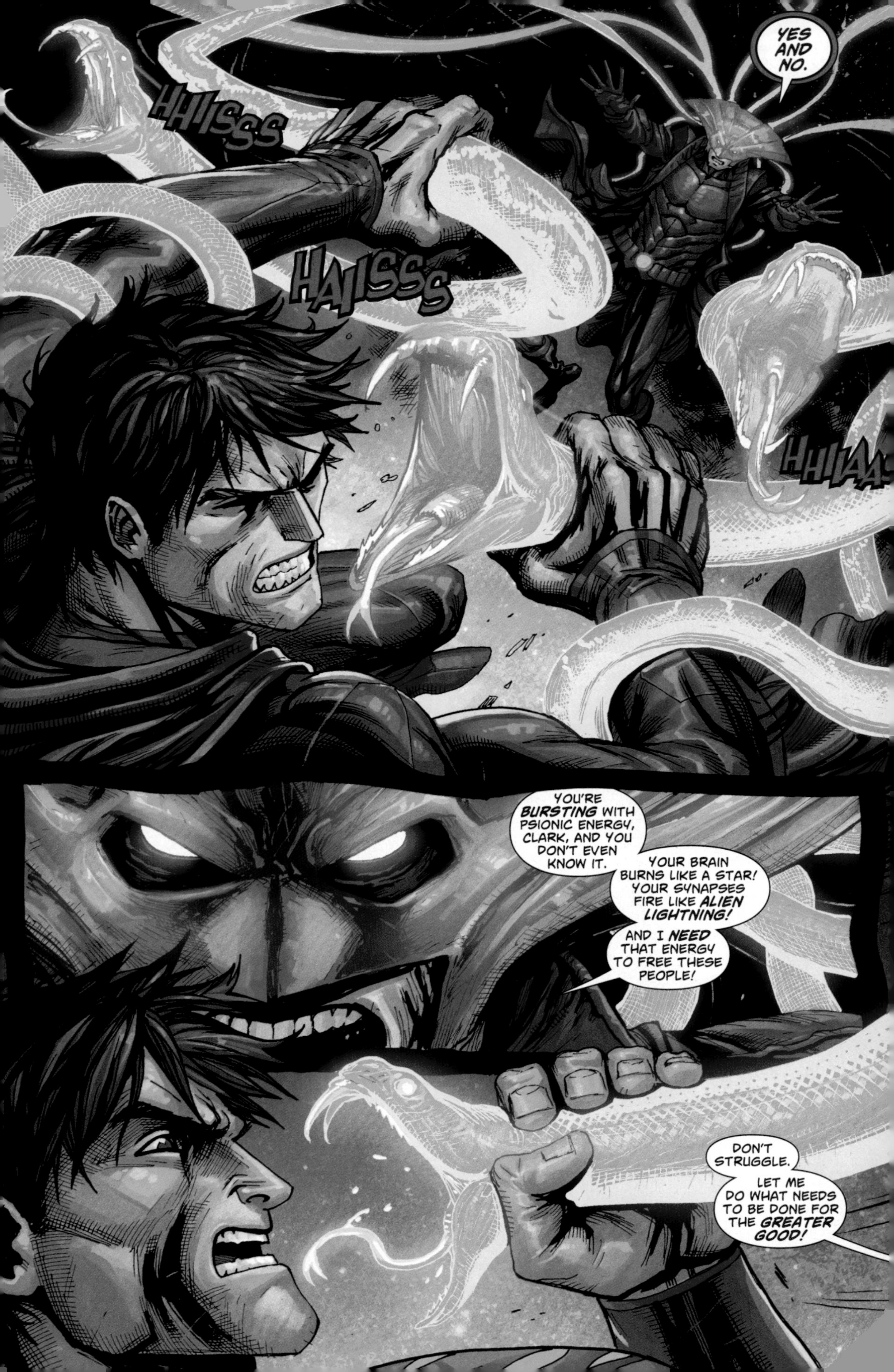
HHIISSS
HAIISSS
YES AND NO.
HHIIAA
YOU'RE BURSTING WITH PSIONIC ENERGY, CLARK, AND YOU DON'T EVEN KNOW IT.
YOUR BRAIN BURNS LIKE A STAR! YOUR SYNAPSES FIRE LIKE ALIEN LIGHTNING!
AND I NEED THAT ENERGY TO FREE THESE PEOPLE!
DON'T STRUGGLE.
LET ME DO WHAT NEEDS TO BE DONE FOR THE GREATER GOOD!

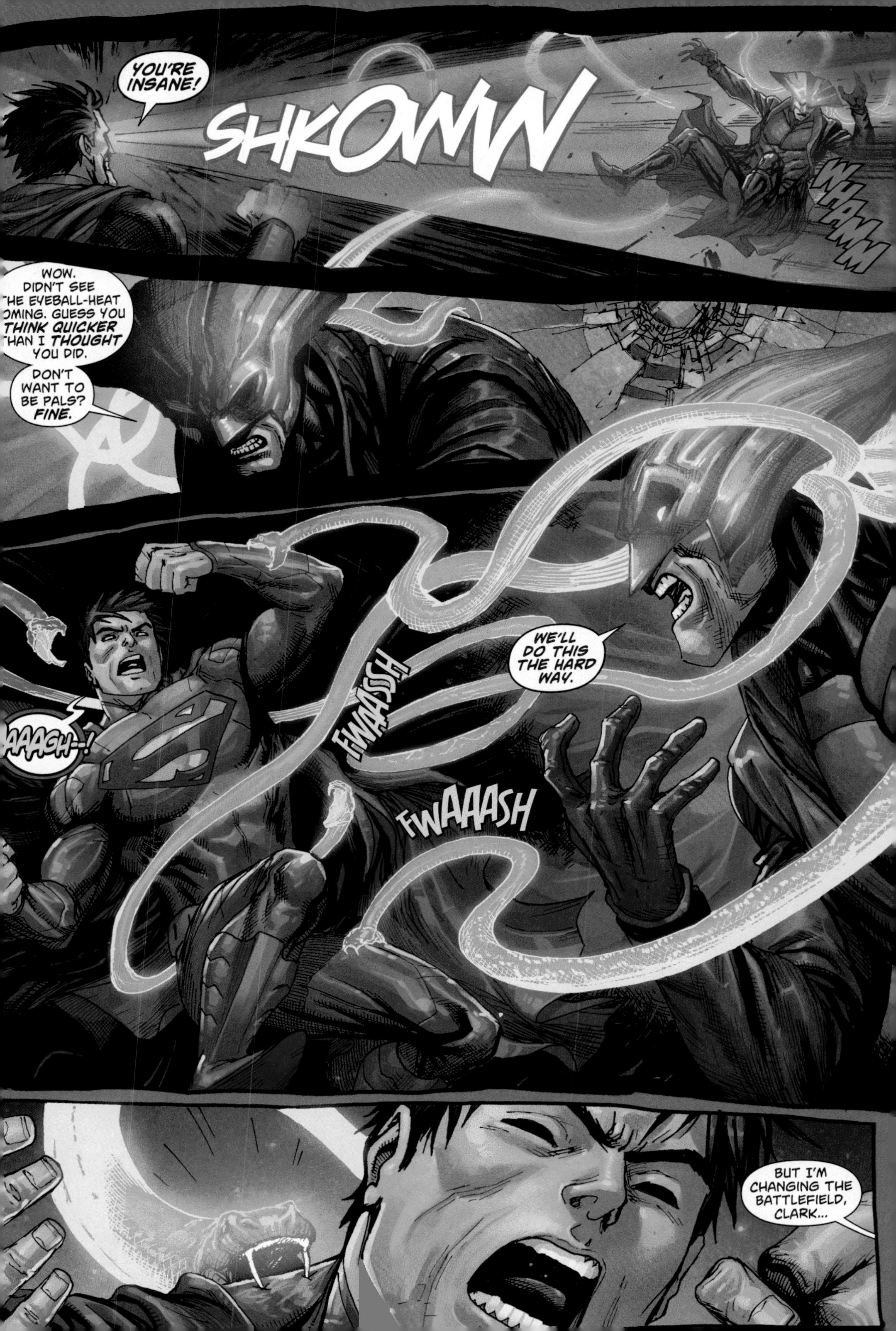

YOU'RE INSANE!
SHKOWW
WHAMM
WOW. DIDN'T SEE THE EYEBALL-HEAT COMING. GUESS YOU THINK QUICKER THAN I THOUGHT YOU DID.
DON'T WANT TO BE PALS? FINE.
WE'LL DO THIS THE HARD WAY.
FWAASSH
AAAGH--!
FWAAASH
BUT I'M CHANGING THE BATTLEFIELD, CLARK...

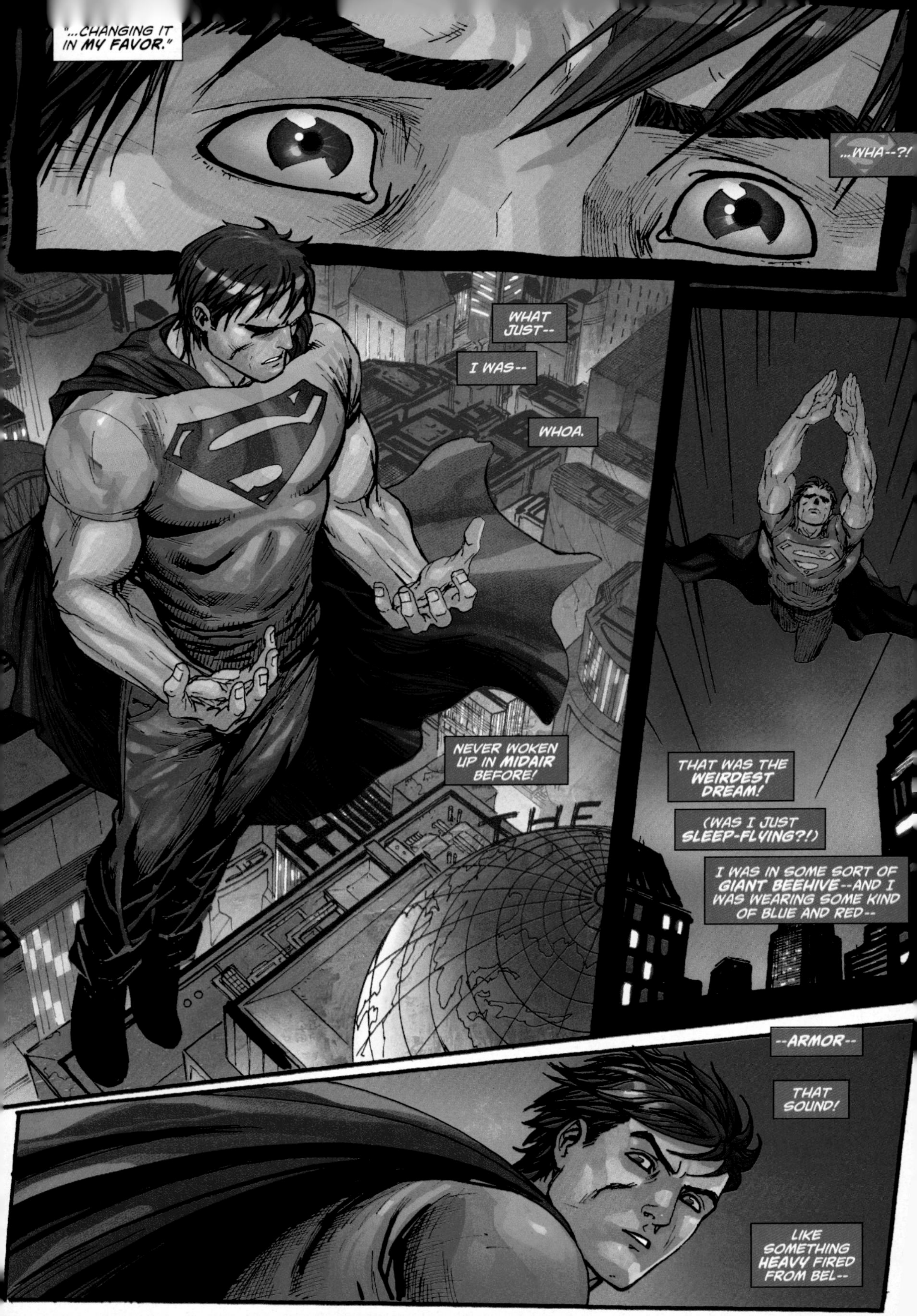

"...CHANGING IT IN MY FAVOR."
...WHA--?!
WHAT JUST--
I WAS--
WHOA.
NEVER WOKEN UP IN MIDAIR BEFORE!
THAT WAS THE WEIRDEST DREAM!
(WAS I JUST SLEEP-FLYING?!)
I WAS IN SOME SORT OF GIANT BEEHIVE--AND I WAS WEARING SOME KIND OF BLUE AND RED--
--ARMOR--
THAT SOUND!
LIKE SOMETHING HEAVY FIRED FROM BEL--

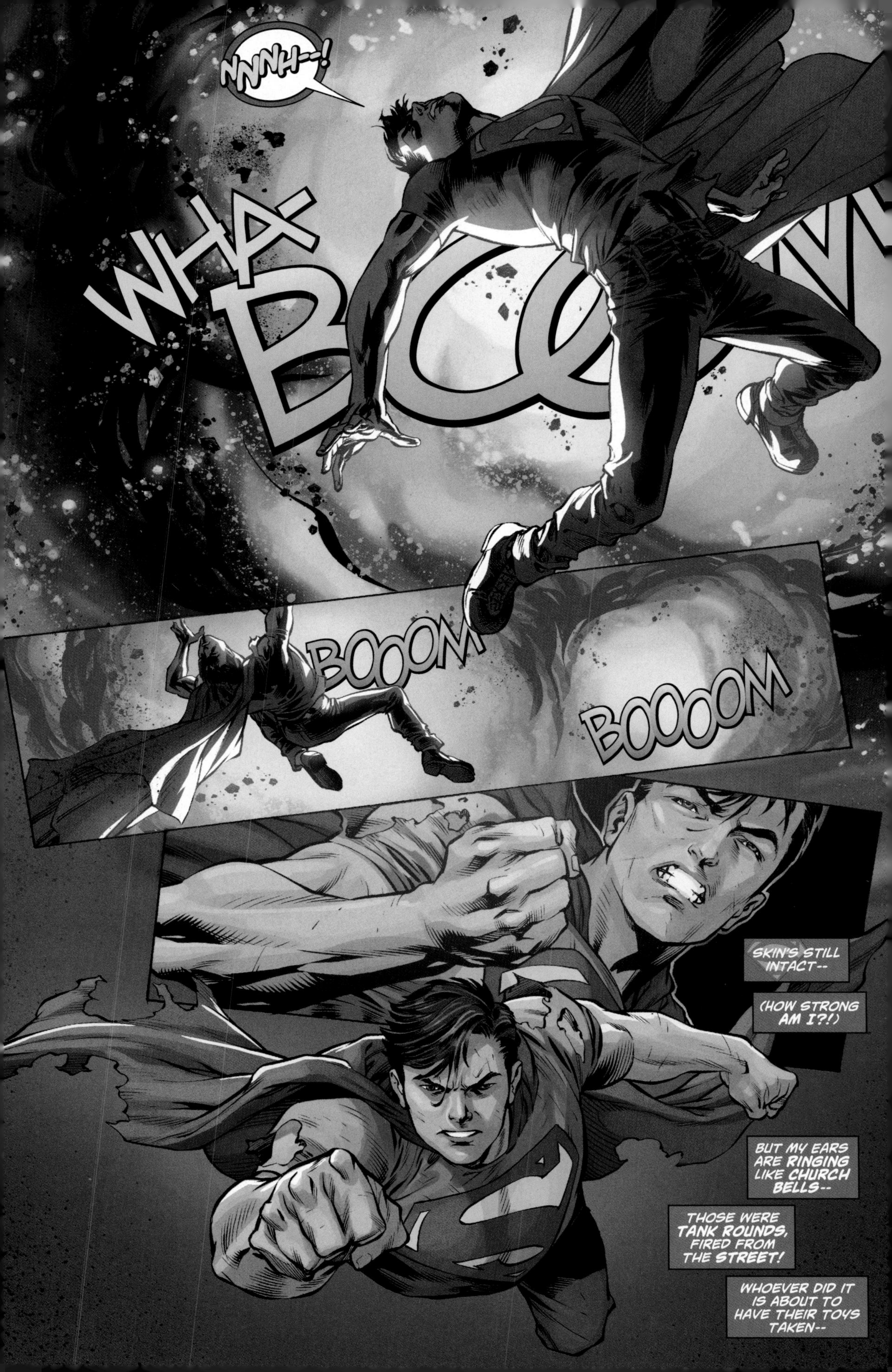
NNNH--!
WHA-BOOM
BOOOM
BOOOOM
SKIN'S STILL INTACT--
(HOW STRONG AM I?!)
BUT MY EARS ARE RINGING LIKE CHURCH BELLS--
THOSE WERE TANK ROUNDS, FIRED FROM THE STREET!
WHOEVER DID IT IS ABOUT TO HAVE THEIR TOYS TAKEN--

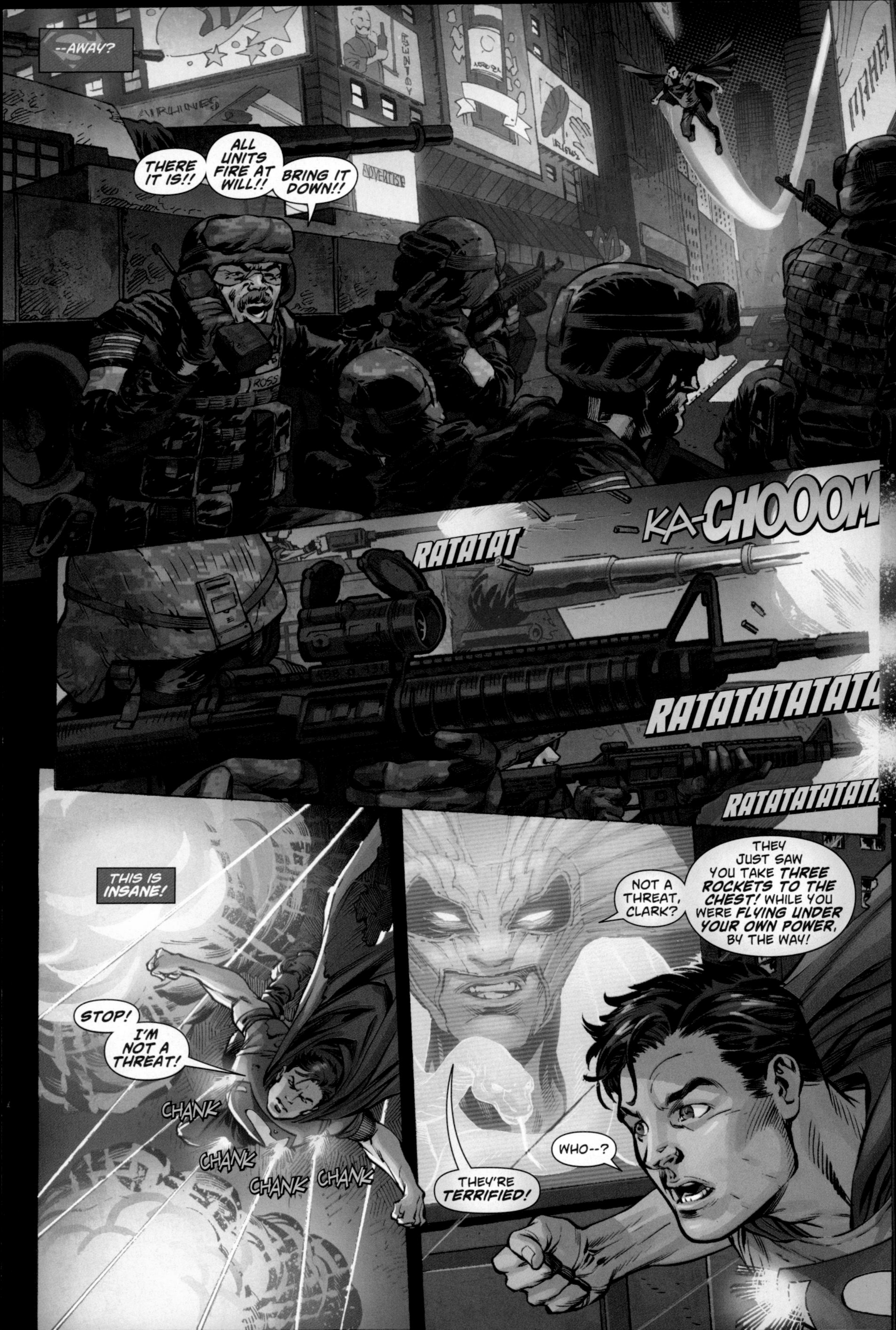
--AWAY?
THERE IT IS!!
ALL UNITS FIRE AT WILL!!
BRING IT DOWN!!
RATATAT
KA-CHOOOM
RATATATATATA
RATATATATATA
THIS IS INSANE!
STOP! I'M NOT A THREAT!
CHANK
CHANK
CHANK
CHANK
NOT A THREAT, CLARK?
THEY JUST SAW YOU TAKE THREE ROCKETS TO THE CHEST! WHILE YOU WERE FLYING UNDER YOUR OWN POWER, BY THE WAY!
WHO--?
THEY'RE TERRIFIED!

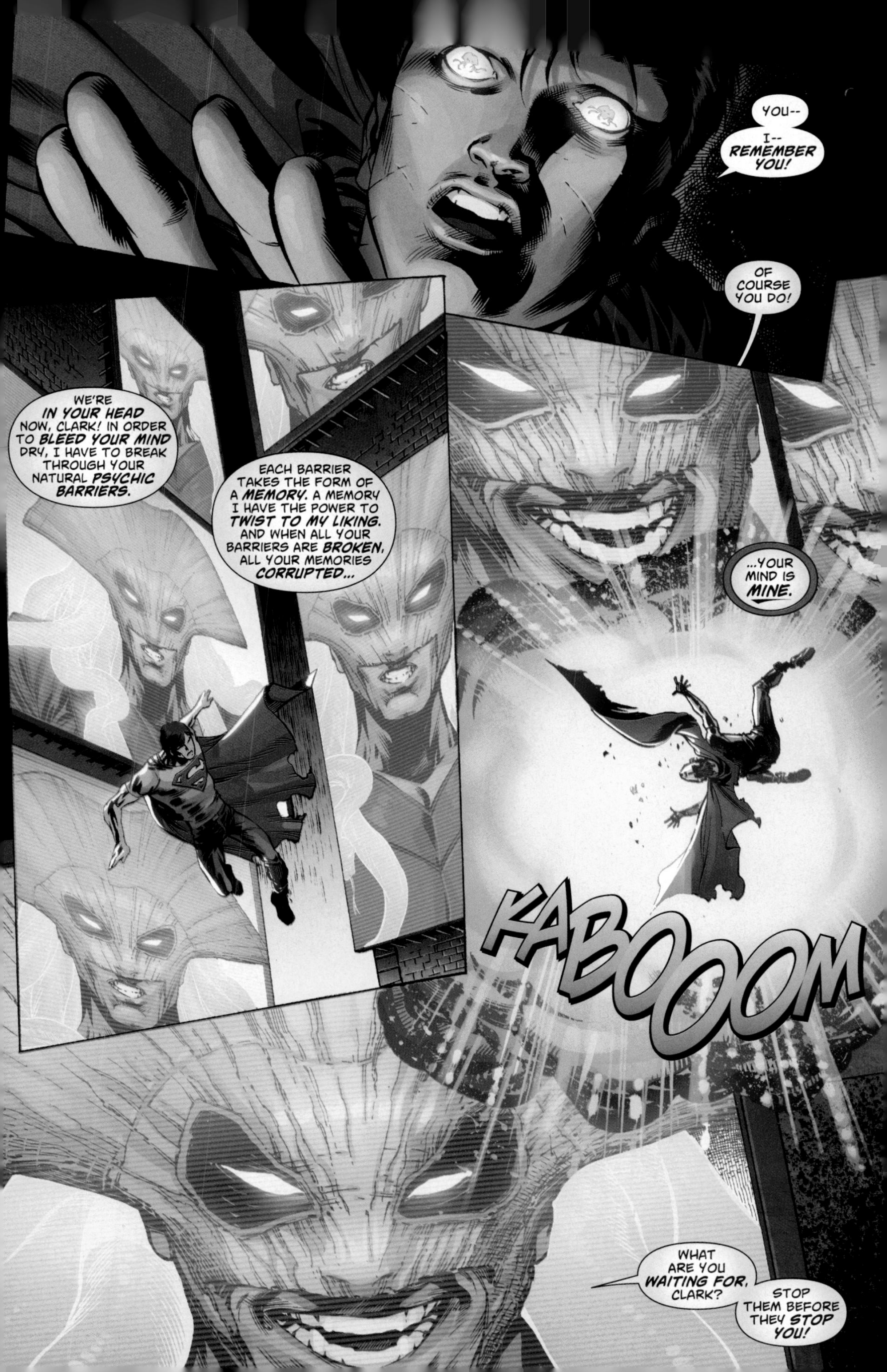
YOU--
I-- REMEMBER YOU!
OF COURSE YOU DO!
WE'RE IN YOUR HEAD NOW, CLARK! IN ORDER TO BLEED YOUR MIND DRY, I HAVE TO BREAK THROUGH YOUR NATURAL PSYCHIC BARRIERS.
EACH BARRIER TAKES THE FORM OF A MEMORY. A MEMORY I HAVE THE POWER TO TWIST TO MY LIKING. AND WHEN ALL YOUR BARRIERS ARE BROKEN, ALL YOUR MEMORIES CORRUPTED...
...YOUR MIND IS MINE.
KABOOOOM
WHAT ARE YOU WAITING FOR, CLARK?
STOP THEM BEFORE THEY STOP YOU!

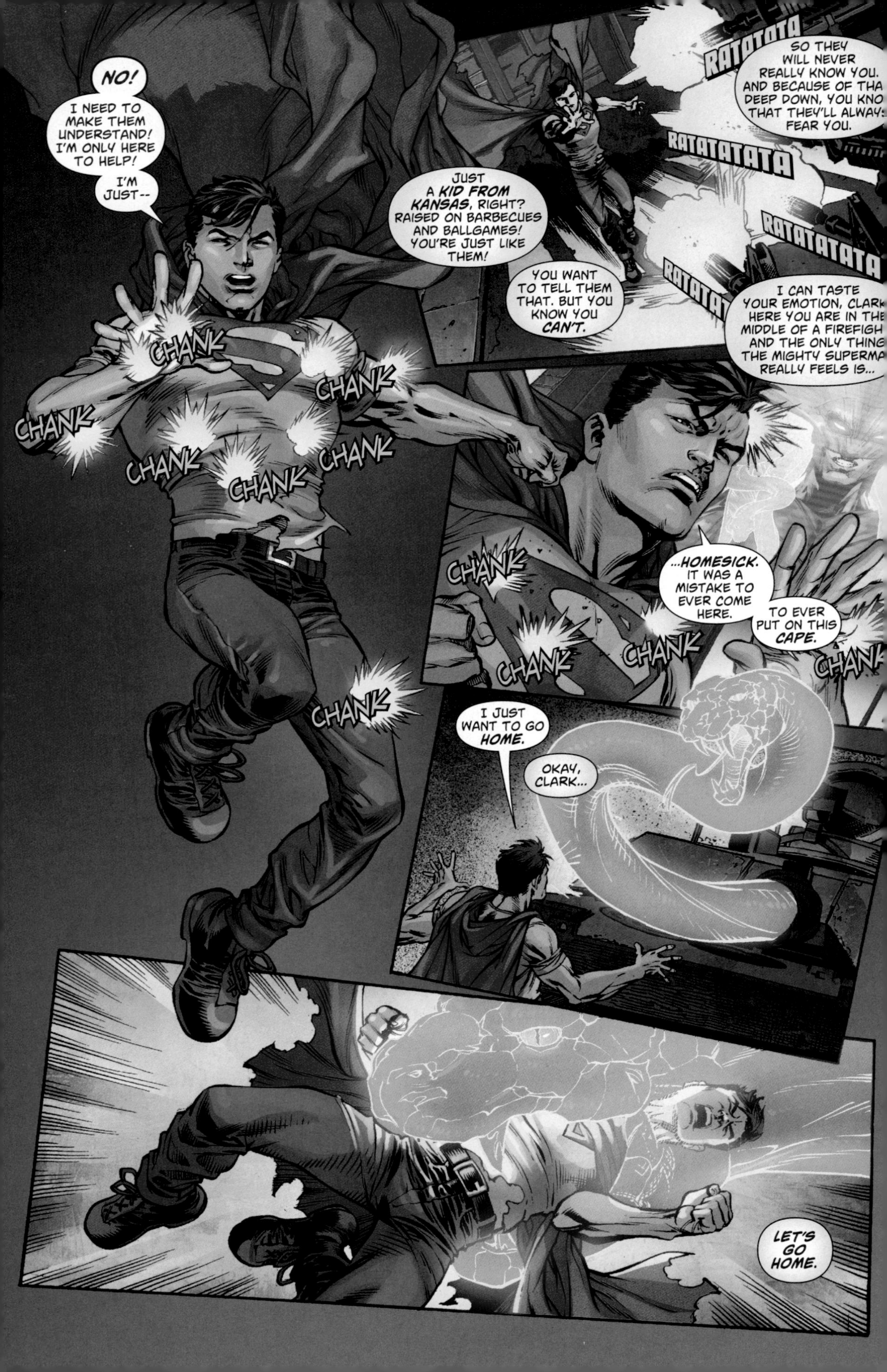

NO!
I NEED TO MAKE THEM UNDERSTAND! I'M ONLY HERE TO HELP!
I'M JUST--
JUST A KIDS FROM KANSAS, RIGHT? RAISED ON BARBECUES AND BALLGAMES! YOU'RE JUST LIKE THEM!
RATATATA
SO THEY WILL NEVER REALLY KNOW YOU. AND BECAUSE OF THA DEEP DOWN, YOU KNO THAT THEY'LL ALWAY FEAR YOU.
RATATATATA
RATATATATA
YOU WANT TO TELL THEM THAT. BUT YOU KNOW YOU CAN'T.
I CAN TASTE YOUR EMOTION, CLARK HERE YOU ARE IN THE MIDDLE OF A FIREFIGH AND THE ONLY THING THE MIGHTY SUPERMA REALLY FEELS IS...
CHANK
CHANK
CHANK
CHANK
CHANK
CHANK
CHANK
...HOMESICK. IT WAS A MISTAKE TO EVER COME HERE.
TO EVER PUT ON THIS CAPE.
CHANK
CHANK
CHANK
CHANK
I JUST WANT TO GO HOME.
OKAY, CLARK...
LET'S GO HOME.

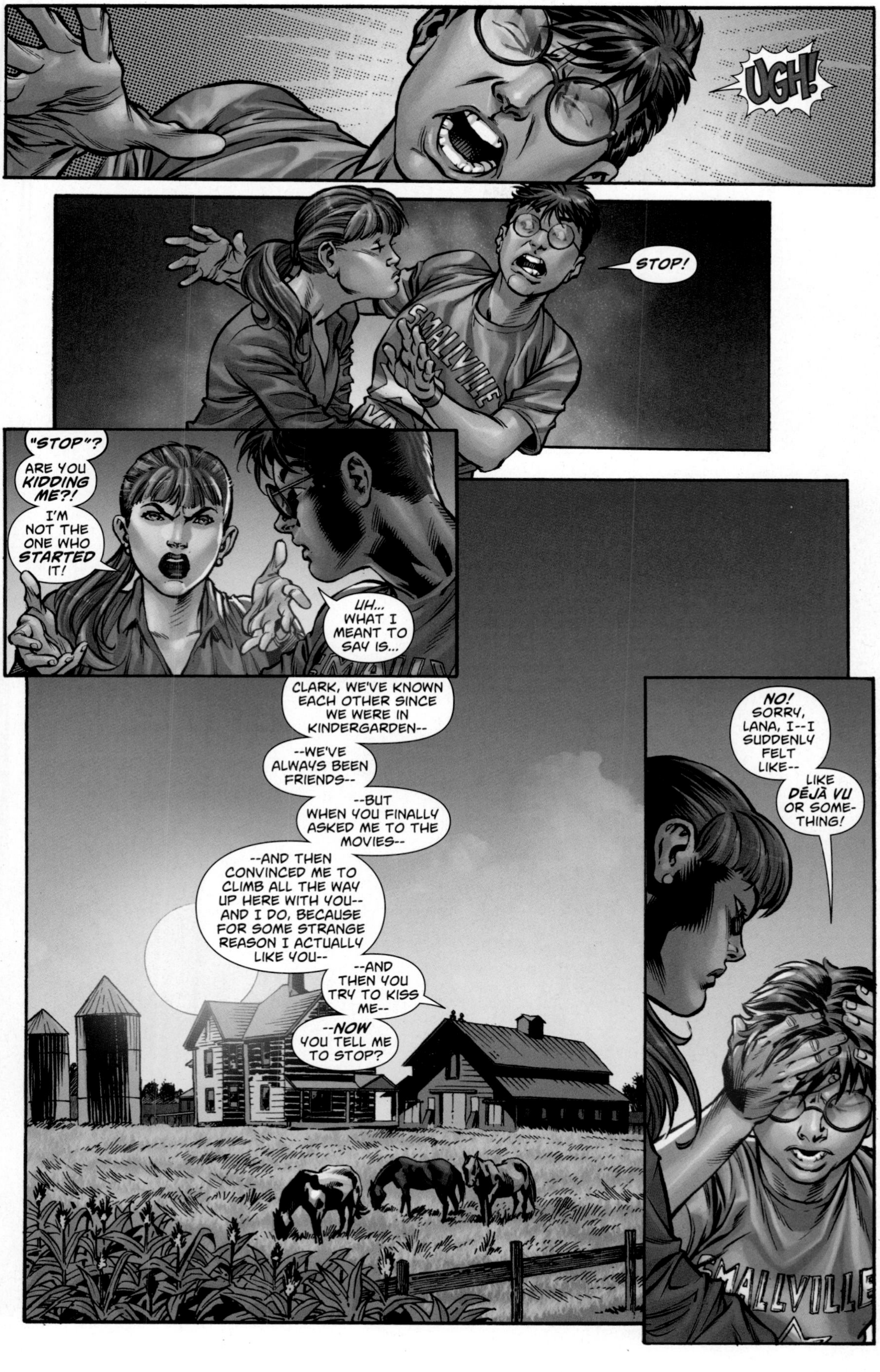
UGH!
STOP!
"STOP"?
ARE YOU KIDDING ME?!
I'M NOT THE ONE WHO STARTED IT!
UH... WHAT I MEANT TO SAY IS...
CLARK, WE'VE KNOWN EACH OTHER SINCE WE WERE IN KINDERGARDEN--
--WE'VE ALWAYS BEEN FRIENDS--
--BUT WHEN YOU FINALLY ASKED ME TO THE MOVIES--
--AND THEN CONVINCED ME TO CLIMB ALL THE WAY UP HERE WITH YOU-- AND I DO, BECAUSE FOR SOME STRANGE REASON I ACTUALLY LIKE YOU--
--AND THEN YOU TRY TO KISS ME--
--NOW YOU TELL ME TO STOP?
NO! SORRY, LANA, I--I SUDDENLY FELT LIKE--
LIKE DÉJÀ VU OR SOME-THING!

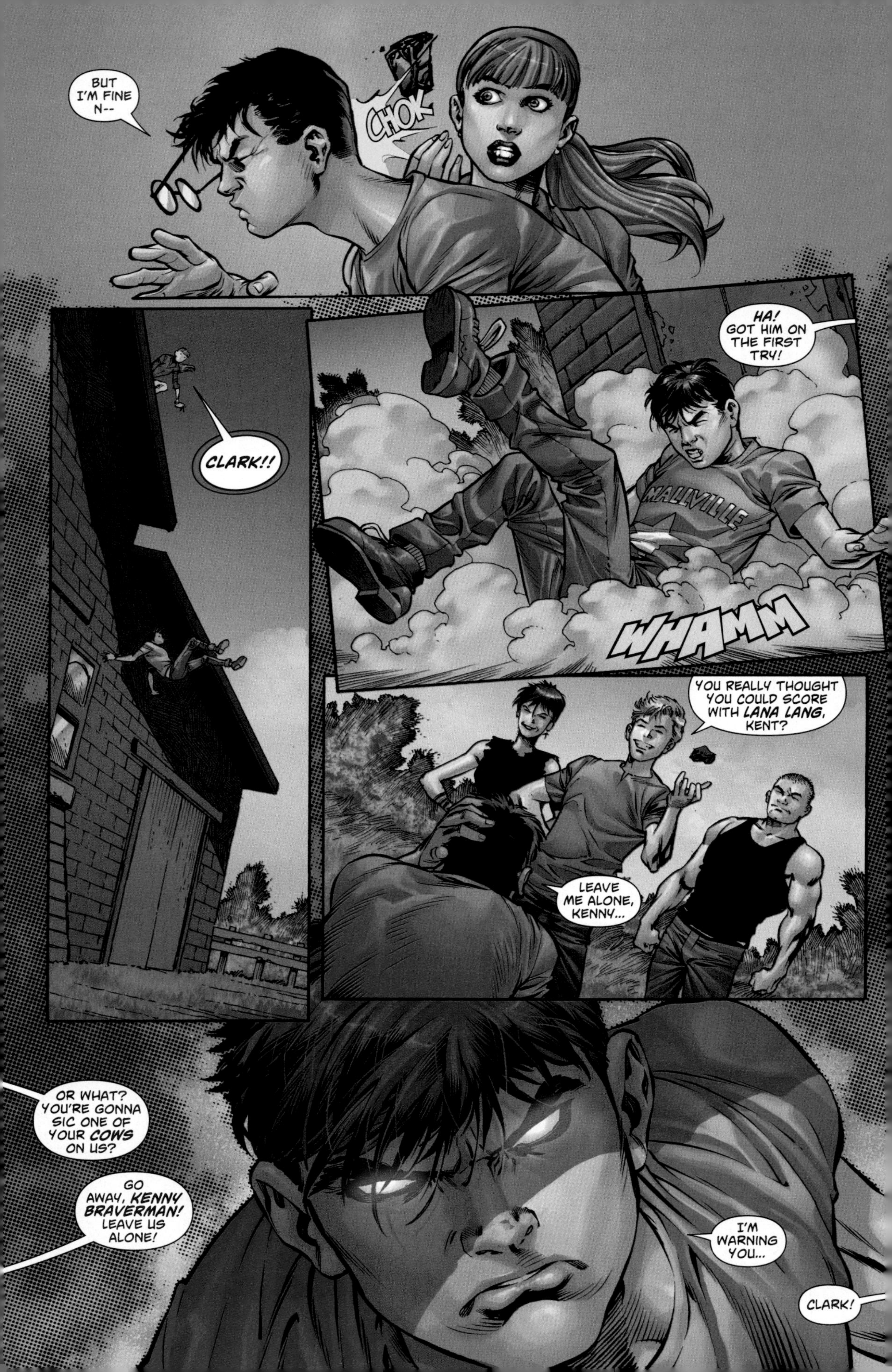
BUT I'M FINE N--
CHOK
CLARK!!
HA! GOT HIM ON THE FIRST TRY!
WHAMM
YOU REALLY THOUGHT YOU COULD SCORE WITH LANA LANG, KENT?
LEAVE ME ALONE, KENNY...
OR WHAT? YOU'RE GONNA SIC ONE OF YOUR COWS ON US?
GO AWAY, KENNY BRAVERMAN! LEAVE US ALONE!
I'M WARNING YOU...
CLARK!

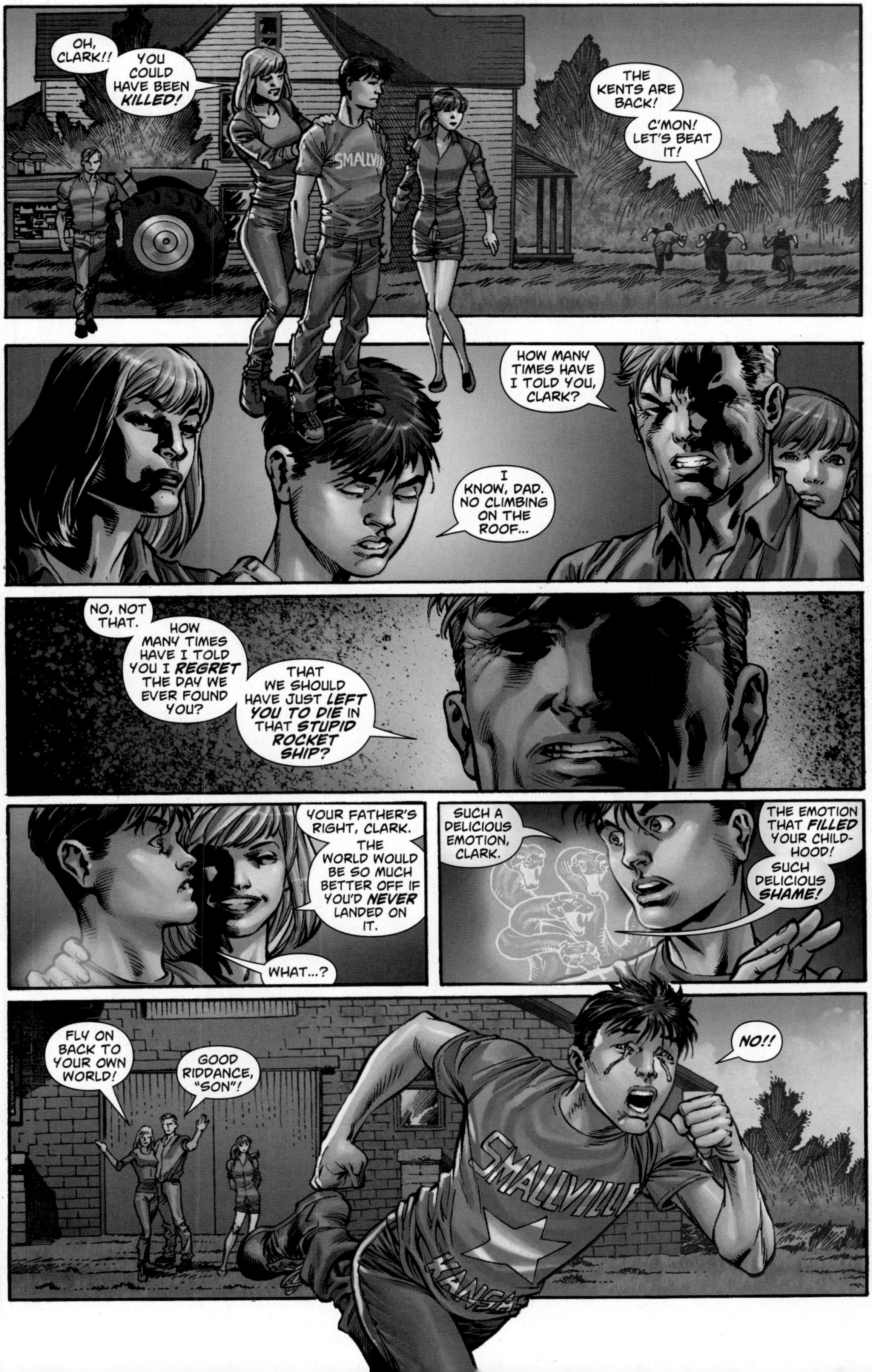
OH, CLARK!!
YOU COULD HAVE BEEN KILLED!
THE KENTS ARE BACK!
C'MON! LET'S BEAT IT!
SMALLVILLE
HOW MANY TIMES HAVE I TOLD YOU, CLARK?
I KNOW, DAD. NO CLIMBING ON THE ROOF...
NO, NOT THAT.
HOW MANY TIMES HAVE I TOLD YOU I REGRET THE DAY WE EVER FOUND YOU?
THAT WE SHOULD HAVE JUST LEFT YOU TO DIE IN THAT STUPID ROCKET SHIP?
YOUR FATHER'S RIGHT, CLARK.
THE WORLD WOULD BE SO MUCH BETTER OFF IF YOU'D NEVER LANDED ON IT.
WHAT...?
SUCH A DELICIOUS EMOTION, CLARK.
THE EMOTION THAT FILLED YOUR CHILDHOOD!
SUCH DELICIOUS SHAME!
FLY ON BACK TO YOUR OWN WORLD!
GOOD RIDDANCE, "SON"!
NO!!
SMALLVILLE

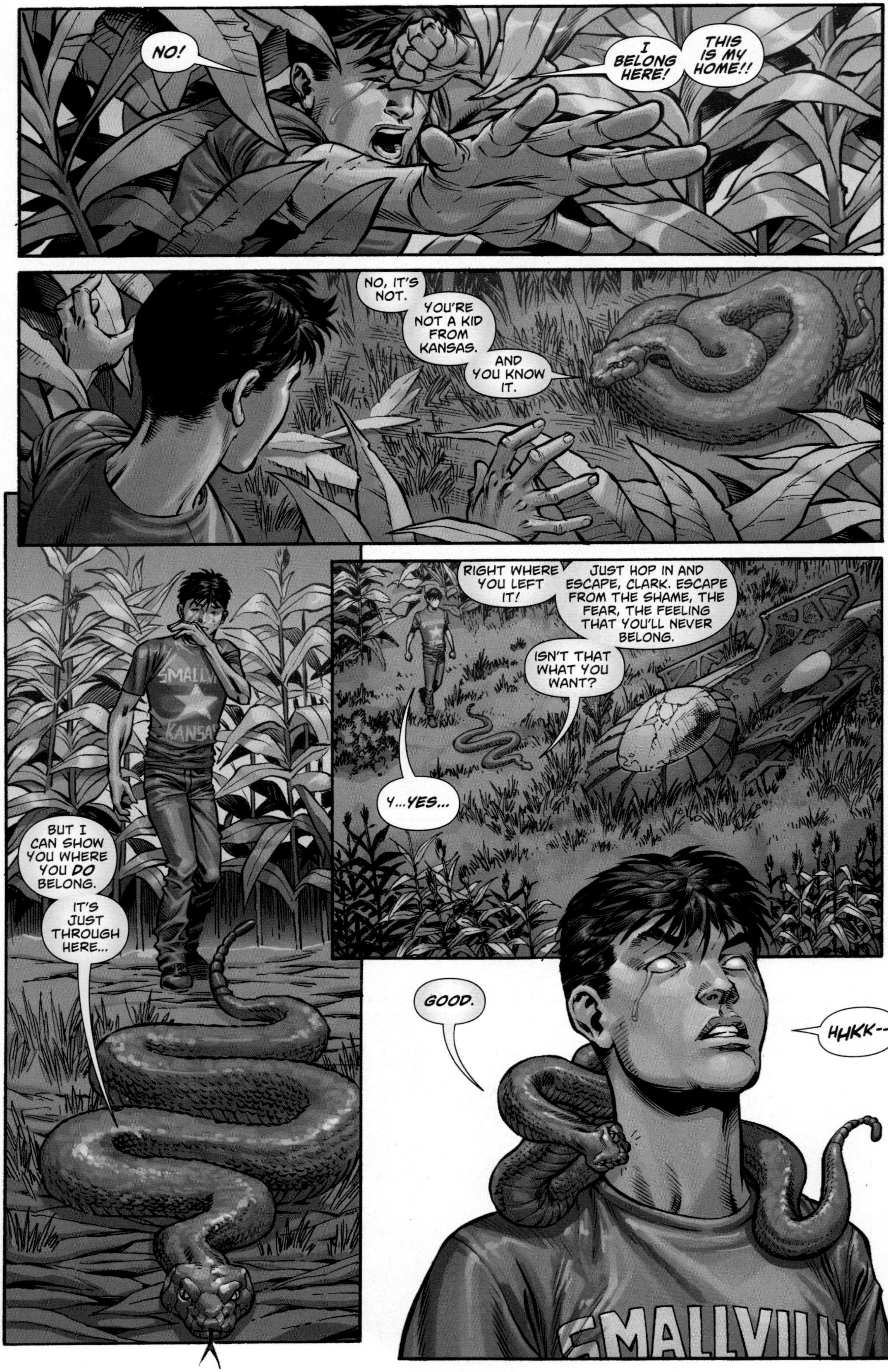
NO!
I BELONG HERE!
THIS IS MY HOME!!
NO, IT'S NOT.
YOU'RE NOT A KID FROM KANSAS.
AND YOU KNOW IT.
BUT I CAN SHOW YOU WHERE YOU *DO* BELONG.
IT'S JUST THROUGH HERE...
RIGHT WHERE YOU LEFT IT!
JUST HOP IN AND ESCAPE, CLARK. ESCAPE FROM THE SHAME, THE FEAR, THE FEELING THAT YOU'LL NEVER BELONG.
ISN'T THAT WHAT YOU WANT?
Y...*YES*...
GOOD.
HHKK--

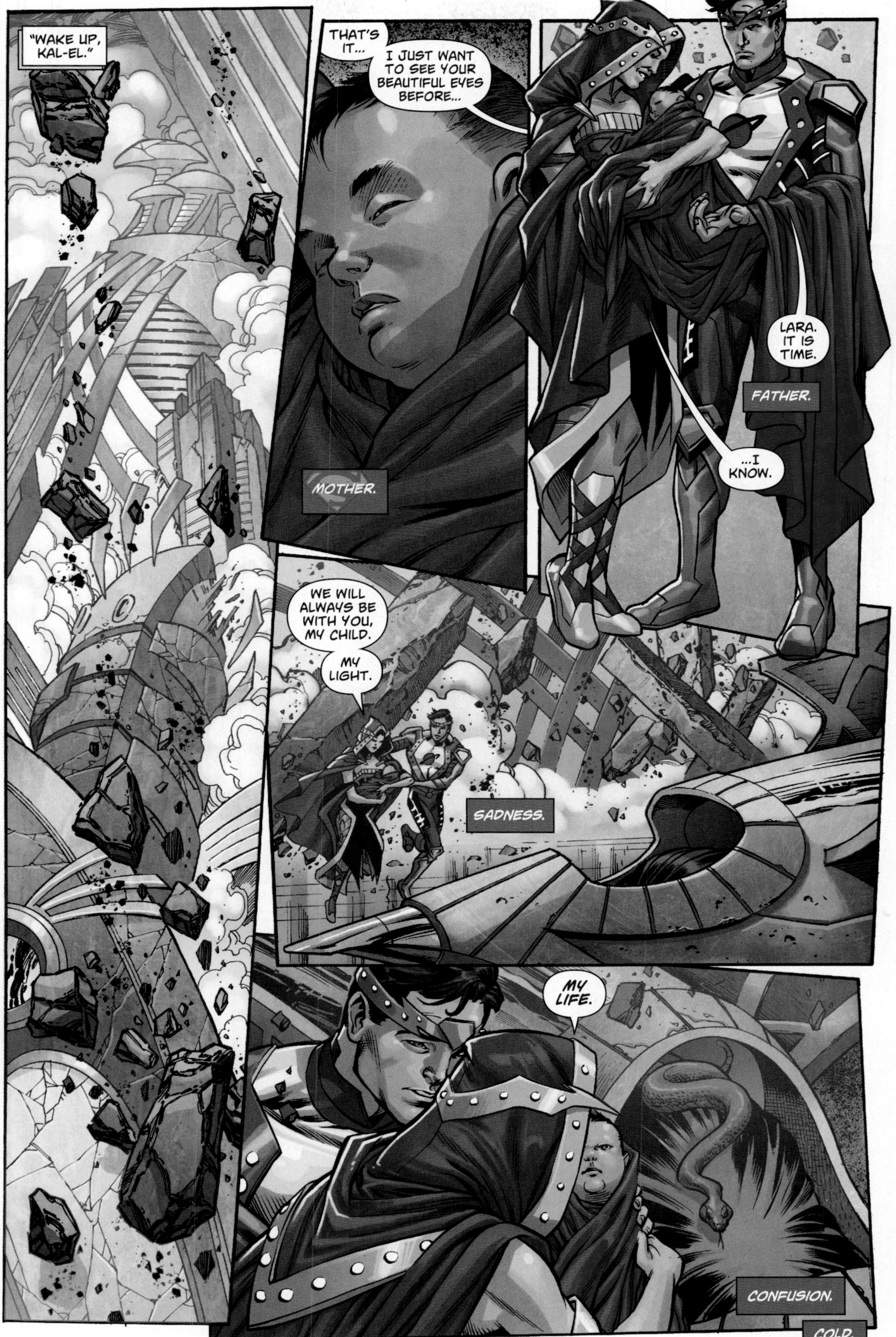
"WAKE UP, KAL-EL."
THAT'S IT...
I JUST WANT TO SEE YOUR BEAUTIFUL EYES BEFORE...
MOTHER.
LARA. IT IS TIME.
FATHER.
...I KNOW.
WE WILL ALWAYS BE WITH YOU, MY CHILD.
MY LIGHT.
SADNESS.
MY LIFE.
CONFUSION.
COLD.

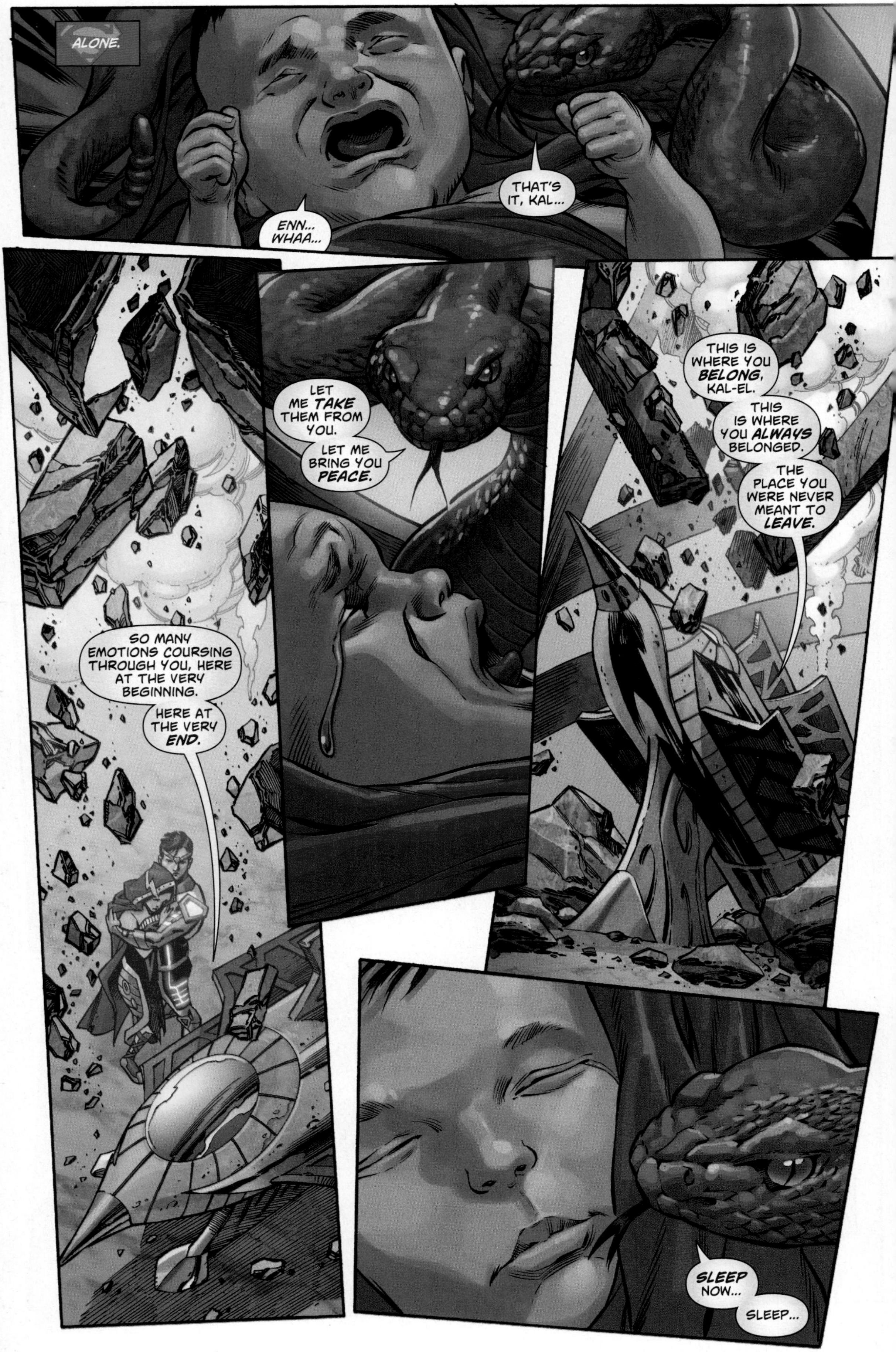
ALONE.
ENN... WHAA...
THAT'S IT, KAL...
SO MANY EMOTIONS COURSING THROUGH YOU, HERE AT THE VERY BEGINNING.
HERE AT THE VERY END.
LET ME TAKE THEM FROM YOU.
LET ME BRING YOU PEACE.
THIS IS WHERE YOU BELONG, KAL-EL.
THIS IS WHERE YOU ALWAYS BELONGED.
THE PLACE YOU WERE NEVER MEANT TO LEAVE.
SLEEP NOW...
SLEEP...

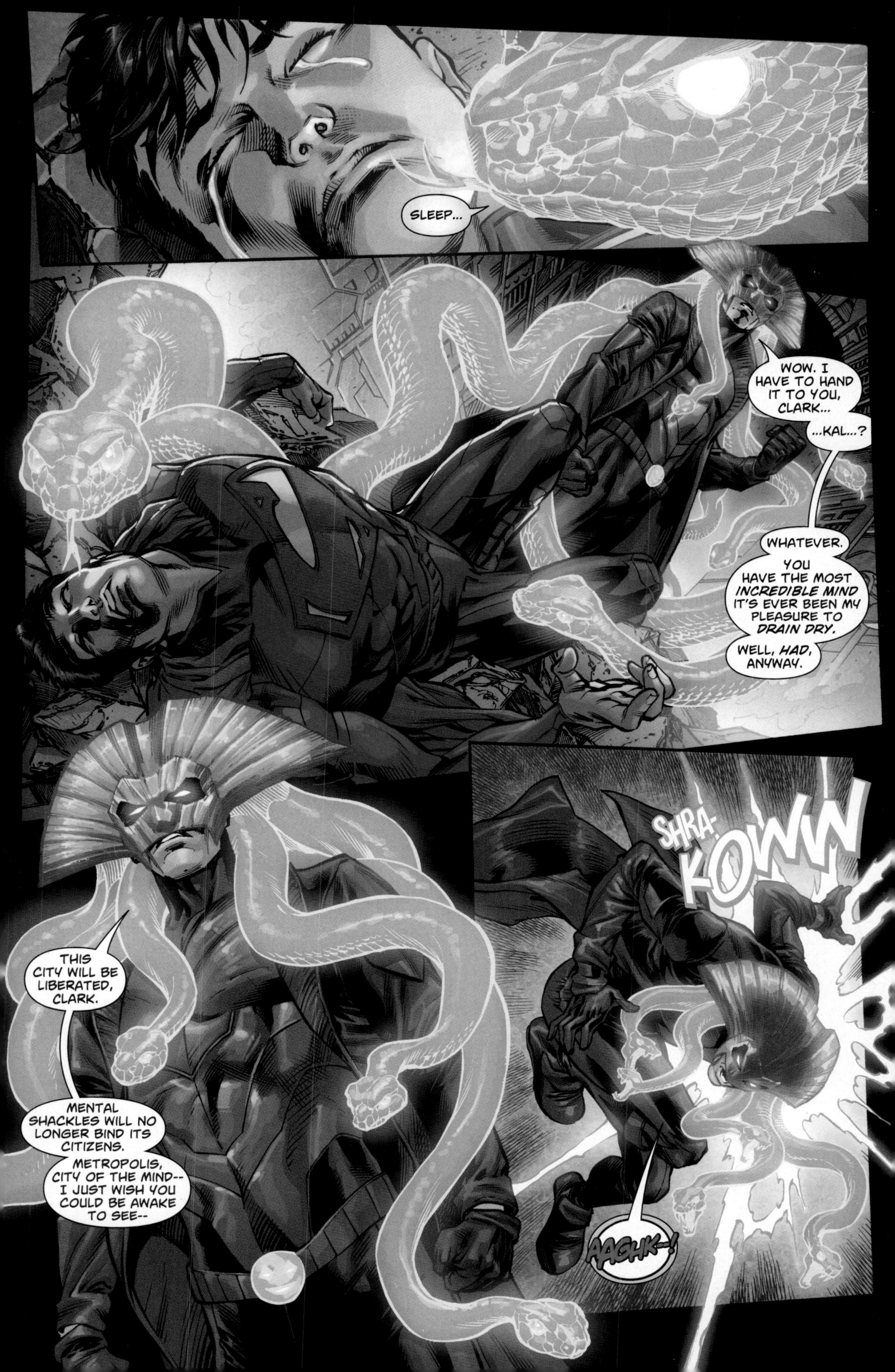
SLEEP...
WOW. I HAVE TO HAND IT TO YOU, CLARK...
...KAL...?
WHATEVER.
YOU HAVE THE MOST *INCREDIBLE MIND* IT'S EVER BEEN MY PLEASURE TO *DRAIN DRY.*
WELL, *HAD,* ANYWAY.
THIS CITY WILL BE LIBERATED, CLARK.
MENTAL SHACKLES WILL NO LONGER BIND ITS CITIZENS.
METROPOLIS, CITY OF THE MIND-- I JUST WISH YOU COULD BE AWAKE TO SEE--
SHRA-KOWW
AAGHK--!

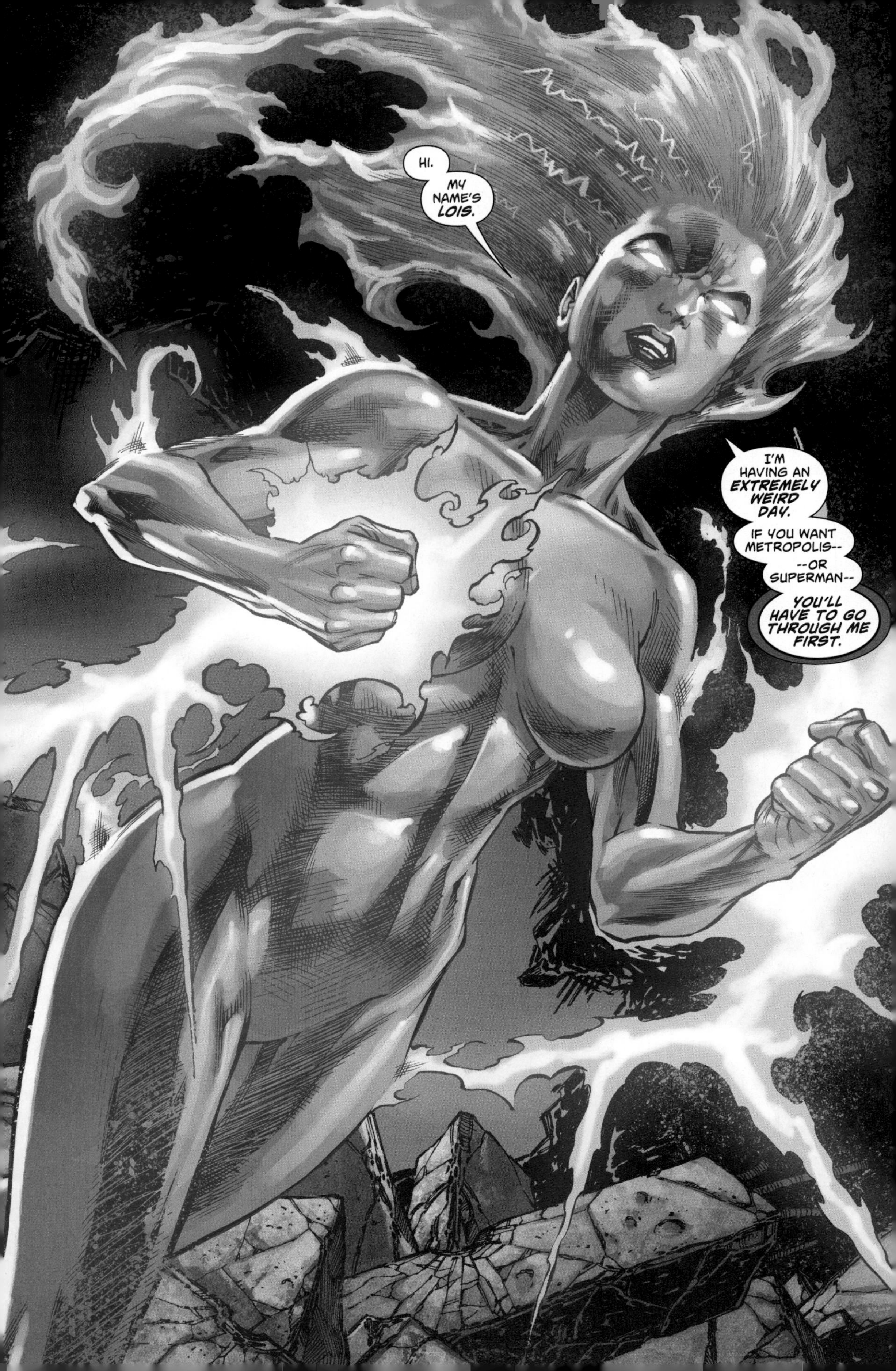
HI.
MY NAME'S LOIS.
I'M HAVING AN EXTREMELY WEIRD DAY.
IF YOU WANT METROPOLIS--
--OR SUPERMAN--
YOU'LL HAVE TO GO THROUGH ME FIRST.

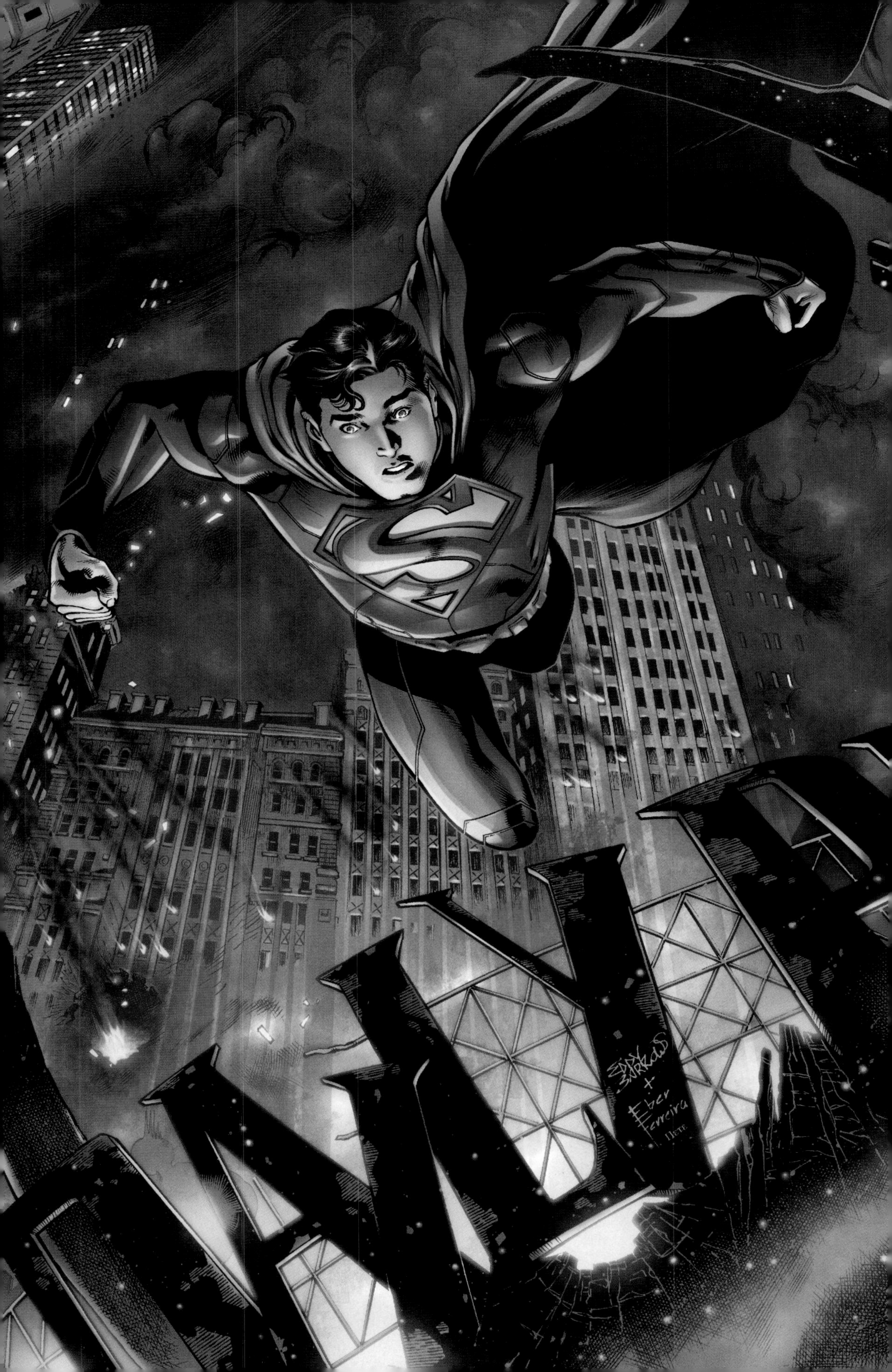

PSI WAR: PART THREE

MIKE JOHNSON writer **EDDY BARROWS** penciller **EBER FERREIRA** inker cover art by **EDDY BARROWS, EBER FERREIRA & PETE PANTAZIS**

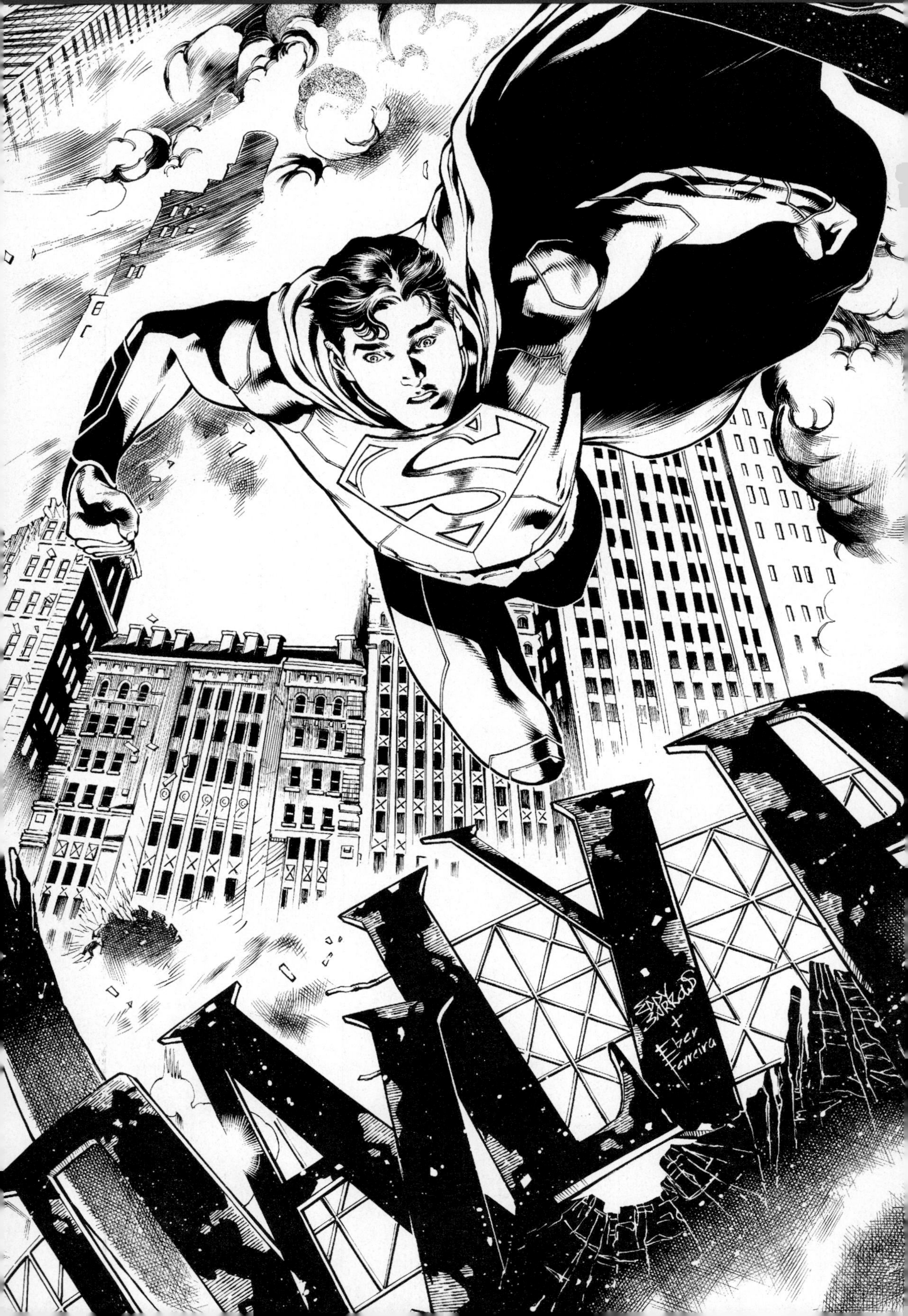
EDDY BARROWS + Eber Ferreira

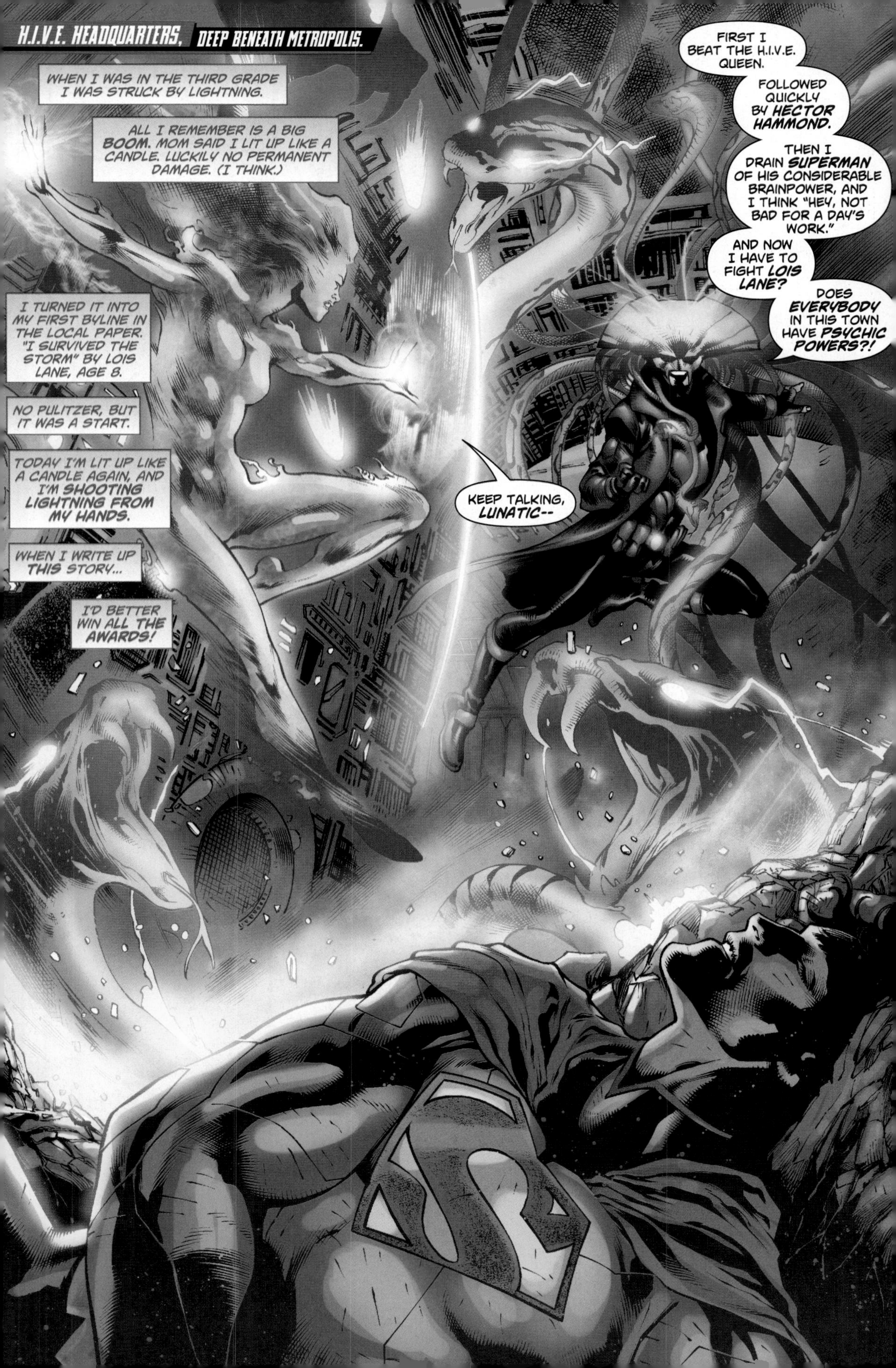
H.I.V.E. HEADQUARTERS, DEEP BENEATH METROPOLIS.
WHEN I WAS IN THE THIRD GRADE I WAS STRUCK BY LIGHTNING.
ALL I REMEMBER IS A BIG BOOM. MOM SAID I LIT UP LIKE A CANDLE. LUCKILY NO PERMANENT DAMAGE. (I THINK.)
FIRST I BEAT THE H.I.V.E. QUEEN.
FOLLOWED QUICKLY BY HECTOR HAMMOND.
THEN I DRAIN SUPERMAN OF HIS CONSIDERABLE BRAINPOWER, AND I THINK "HEY, NOT BAD FOR A DAY'S WORK."
AND NOW I HAVE TO FIGHT LOIS LANE?
DOES EVERYBODY IN THIS TOWN HAVE PSYCHIC POWERS?!
I TURNED IT INTO MY FIRST BYLINE IN THE LOCAL PAPER. "I SURVIVED THE STORM" BY LOIS LANE, AGE 8.
NO PULITZER, BUT IT WAS A START.
TODAY I'M LIT UP LIKE A CANDLE AGAIN, AND I'M SHOOTING LIGHTNING FROM MY HANDS.
KEEP TALKING, LUNATIC--
WHEN I WRITE UP THIS STORY...
I'D BETTER WIN ALL THE AWARDS!

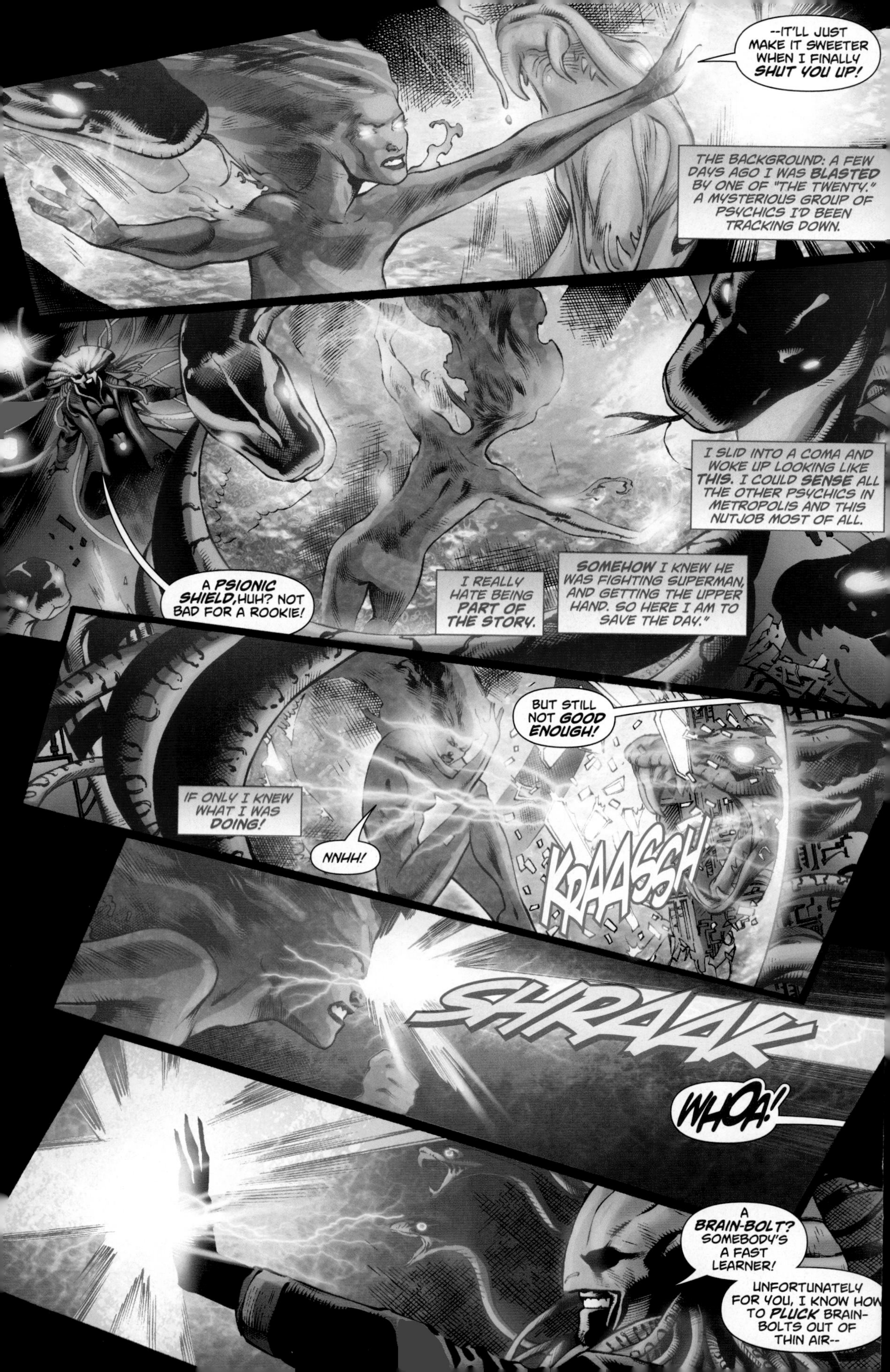
--IT'LL JUST MAKE IT SWEETER WHEN I FINALLY SHUT YOU UP!
THE BACKGROUND: A FEW DAYS AGO I WAS BLASTED BY ONE OF "THE TWENTY." A MYSTERIOUS GROUP OF PSYCHICS I'D BEEN TRACKING DOWN.
I SLID INTO A COMA AND WOKE UP LOOKING LIKE THIS. I COULD SENSE ALL THE OTHER PSYCHICS IN METROPOLIS AND THIS NUTJOB MOST OF ALL.
A PSIONIC SHIELD, HUH? NOT BAD FOR A ROOKIE!
I REALLY HATE BEING PART OF THE STORY.
SOMEHOW I KNEW HE WAS FIGHTING SUPERMAN, AND GETTING THE UPPER HAND. SO HERE I AM TO SAVE THE DAY."
BUT STILL NOT GOOD ENOUGH!
IF ONLY I KNEW WHAT I WAS DOING!
NNHH!
KRAASSH
SHRAAK
WHOA!
A BRAIN-BOLT? SOMEBODY'S A FAST LEARNER!
UNFORTUNATELY FOR YOU, I KNOW HOW TO PLUCK BRAIN-BOLTS OUT OF THIN AIR--

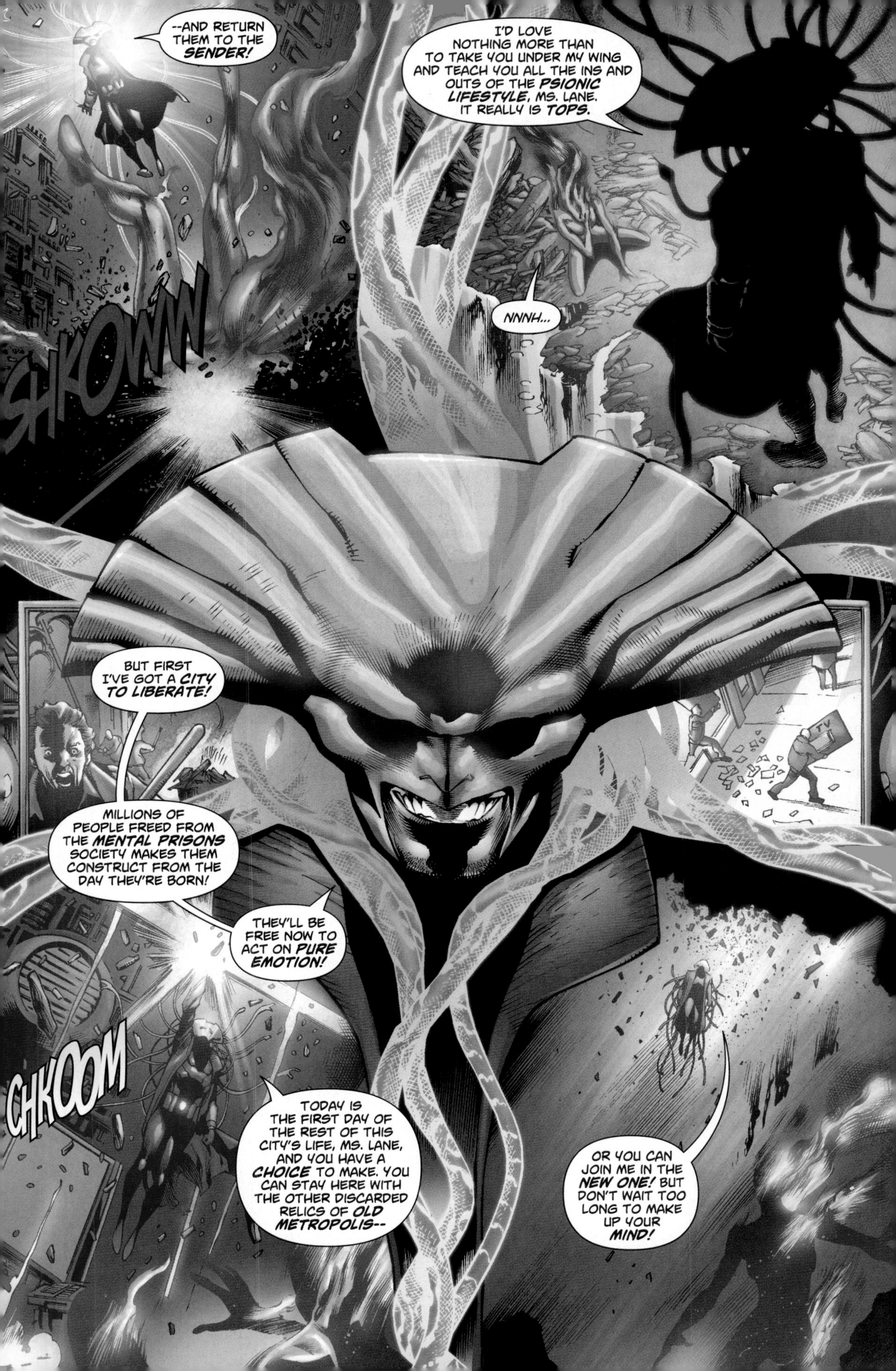
--AND RETURN THEM TO THE SENDER!
I'D LOVE NOTHING MORE THAN TO TAKE YOU UNDER MY WING AND TEACH YOU ALL THE INS AND OUTS OF THE PSIONIC LIFESTYLE, MS. LANE. IT REALLY IS TOPS.
SHKOWW
NNNH...
BUT FIRST I'VE GOT A CITY TO LIBERATE!
MILLIONS OF PEOPLE FREED FROM THE MENTAL PRISONS SOCIETY MAKES THEM CONSTRUCT FROM THE DAY THEY'RE BORN!
THEY'LL BE FREE NOW TO ACT ON PURE EMOTION!
CHKOOM
TODAY IS THE FIRST DAY OF THE REST OF THIS CITY'S LIFE, MS. LANE, AND YOU HAVE A CHOICE TO MAKE. YOU CAN STAY HERE WITH THE OTHER DISCARDED RELICS OF OLD METROPOLIS--
OR YOU CAN JOIN ME IN THE NEW ONE! BUT DON'T WAIT TOO LONG TO MAKE UP YOUR MIND!

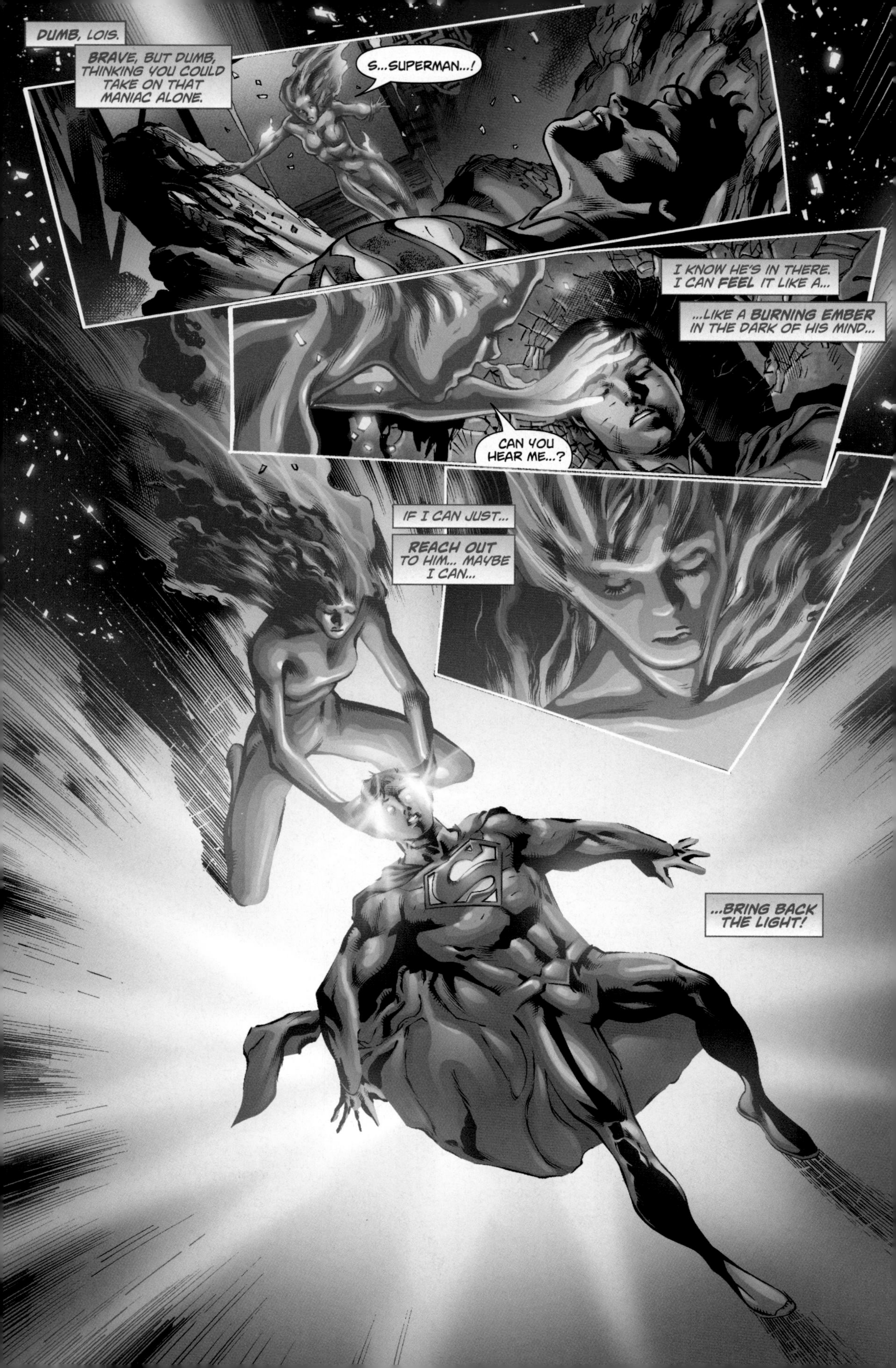
DUMB, LOIS.
BRAVE, BUT DUMB, THINKING YOU COULD TAKE ON THAT MANIAC ALONE.
S...SUPERMAN...!
I KNOW HE'S IN THERE. I CAN FEEL IT LIKE A...
...LIKE A BURNING EMBER IN THE DARK OF HIS MIND...
CAN YOU HEAR ME...?
IF I CAN JUST...
REACH OUT TO HIM... MAYBE I CAN...
...BRING BACK THE LIGHT!

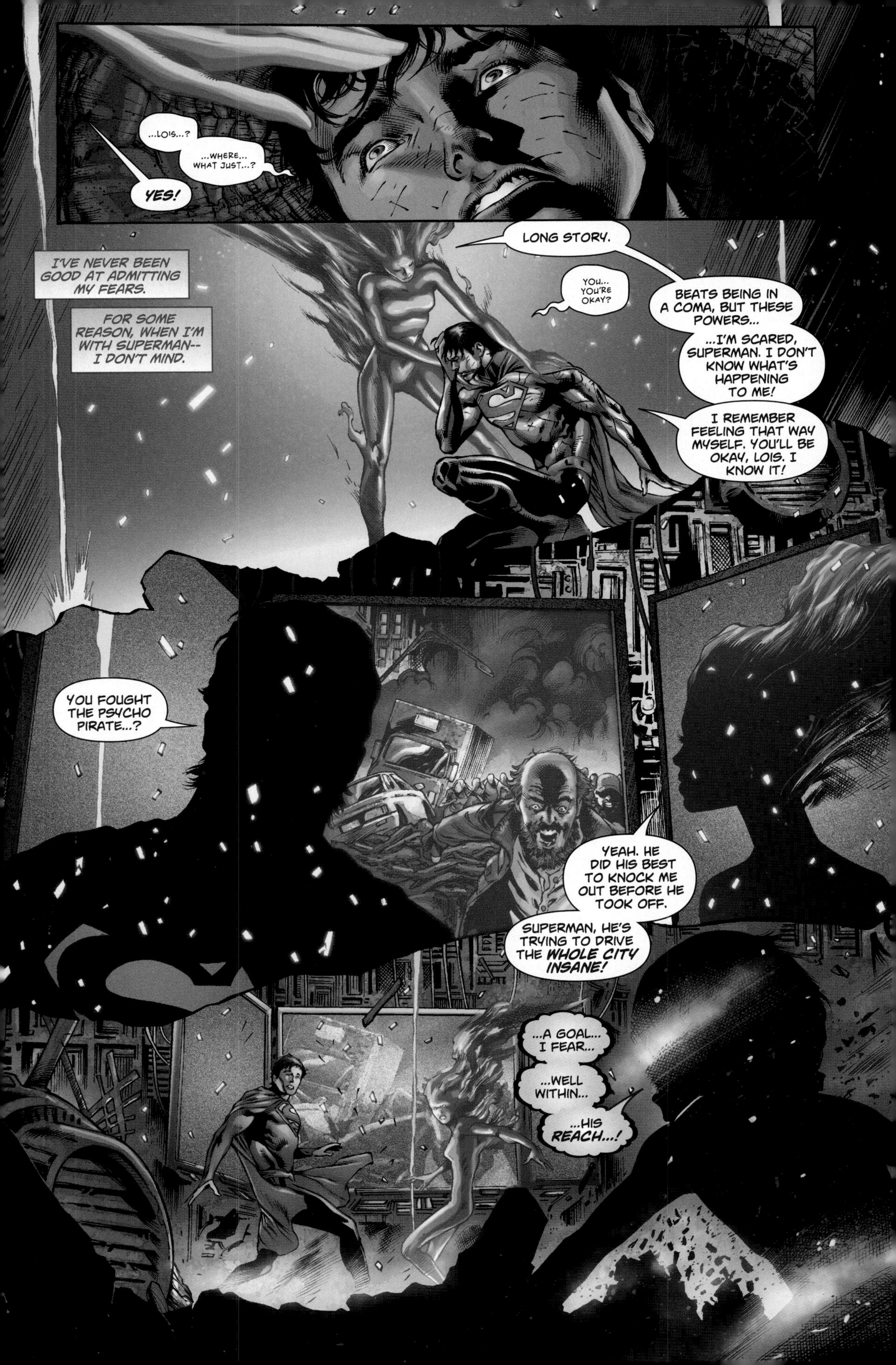
...LOIS...?
...WHERE... WHAT JUST...?
YES!
I'VE NEVER BEEN GOOD AT ADMITTING MY FEARS.
FOR SOME REASON, WHEN I'M WITH SUPERMAN-- I DON'T MIND.
LONG STORY.
YOU... YOU'RE OKAY?
BEATS BEING IN A COMA, BUT THESE POWERS...
...I'M SCARED, SUPERMAN. I DON'T KNOW WHAT'S HAPPENING TO ME!
I REMEMBER FEELING THAT WAY MYSELF. YOU'LL BE OKAY, LOIS. I KNOW IT!
YOU FOUGHT THE PSYCHO PIRATE...?
YEAH. HE DID HIS BEST TO KNOCK ME OUT BEFORE HE TOOK OFF.
SUPERMAN, HE'S TRYING TO DRIVE THE WHOLE CITY INSANE!
...A GOAL... I FEAR...
...WELL WITHIN...
...HIS REACH...!

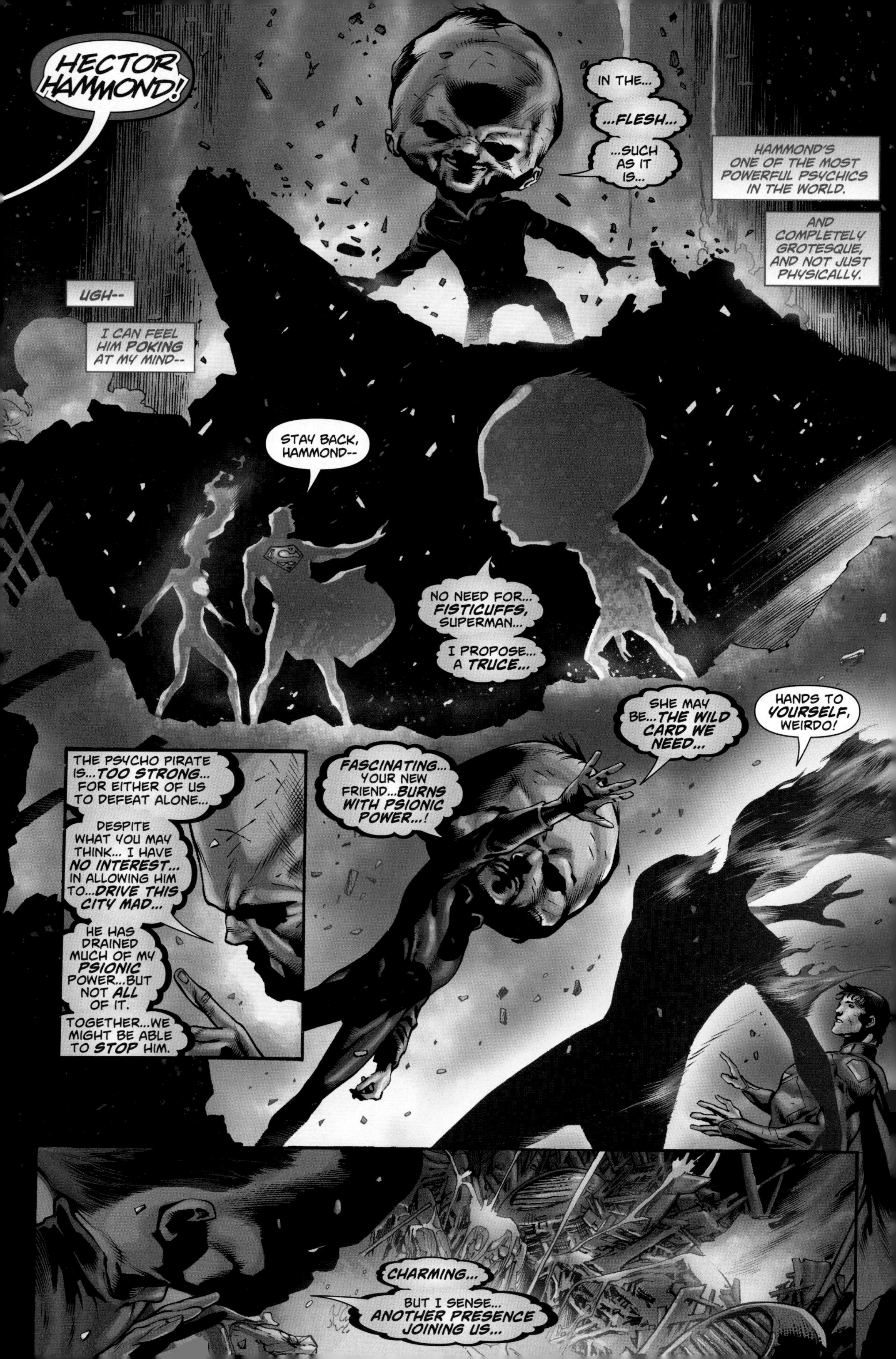
HECTOR HAMMOND!
IN THE...
...FLESH...
...SUCH AS IT IS...
HAMMOND'S ONE OF THE MOST POWERFUL PSYCHICS IN THE WORLD.
AND COMPLETELY GROTESQUE, AND NOT JUST PHYSICALLY.
UGH--
I CAN FEEL HIM POKING AT MY MIND--
STAY BACK, HAMMOND--
NO NEED FOR... FISTICUFFS, SUPERMAN...
I PROPOSE... A TRUCE...
THE PSYCHO PIRATE IS...TOO STRONG... FOR EITHER OF US TO DEFEAT ALONE...
DESPITE WHAT YOU MAY THINK... I HAVE NO INTEREST... IN ALLOWING HIM TO...DRIVE THIS CITY MAD...
HE HAS DRAINED MUCH OF MY PSIONIC POWER...BUT NOT ALL OF IT.
TOGETHER...WE MIGHT BE ABLE TO STOP HIM.
FASCINATING... YOUR NEW FRIEND...BURNS WITH PSIONIC POWER...!
SHE MAY BE...THE WILD CARD WE NEED...
HANDS TO YOURSELF, WEIRDO!
CHARMING...
BUT I SENSE... ANOTHER PRESENCE JOINING US...

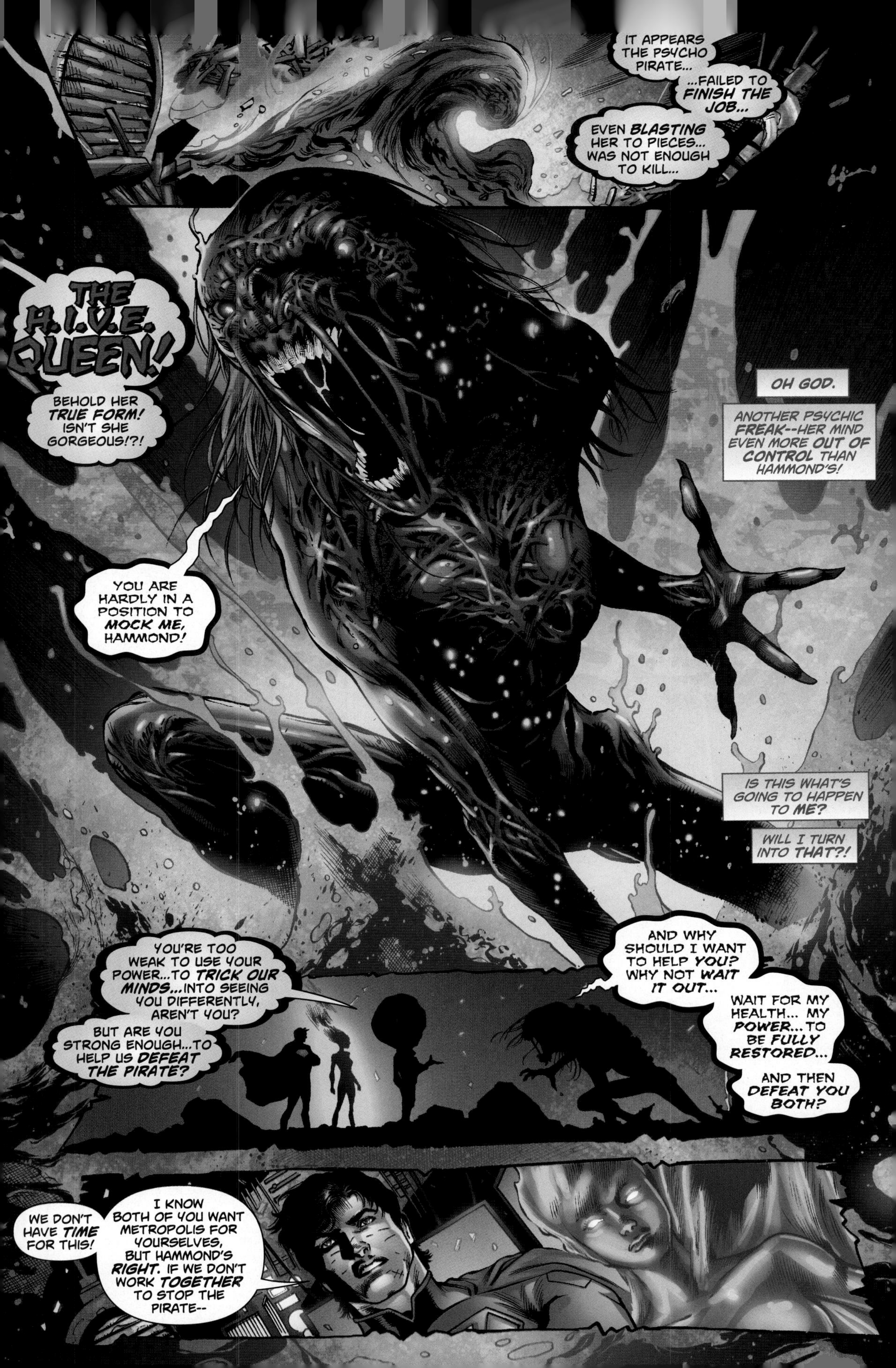
IT APPEARS THE PSYCHO PIRATE...
...FAILED TO FINISH THE JOB...
EVEN BLASTING HER TO PIECES... WAS NOT ENOUGH TO KILL...
THE H.I.V.E. QUEEN!
BEHOLD HER TRUE FORM! ISN'T SHE GORGEOUS!?!
OH GOD.
ANOTHER PSYCHIC FREAK--HER MIND EVEN MORE OUT OF CONTROL THAN HAMMOND'S!
YOU ARE HARDLY IN A POSITION TO MOCK ME, HAMMOND!
IS THIS WHAT'S GOING TO HAPPEN TO ME?
WILL I TURN INTO THAT?!
YOU'RE TOO WEAK TO USE YOUR POWER...TO TRICK OUR MINDS...INTO SEEING YOU DIFFERENTLY, AREN'T YOU?
BUT ARE YOU STRONG ENOUGH...TO HELP US DEFEAT THE PIRATE?
AND WHY SHOULD I WANT TO HELP YOU? WHY NOT WAIT IT OUT...
WAIT FOR MY HEALTH... MY POWER...TO BE FULLY RESTORED...
AND THEN DEFEAT YOU BOTH?
WE DON'T HAVE TIME FOR THIS!
I KNOW BOTH OF YOU WANT METROPOLIS FOR YOURSELVES, BUT HAMMOND'S RIGHT. IF WE DON'T WORK TOGETHER TO STOP THE PIRATE--

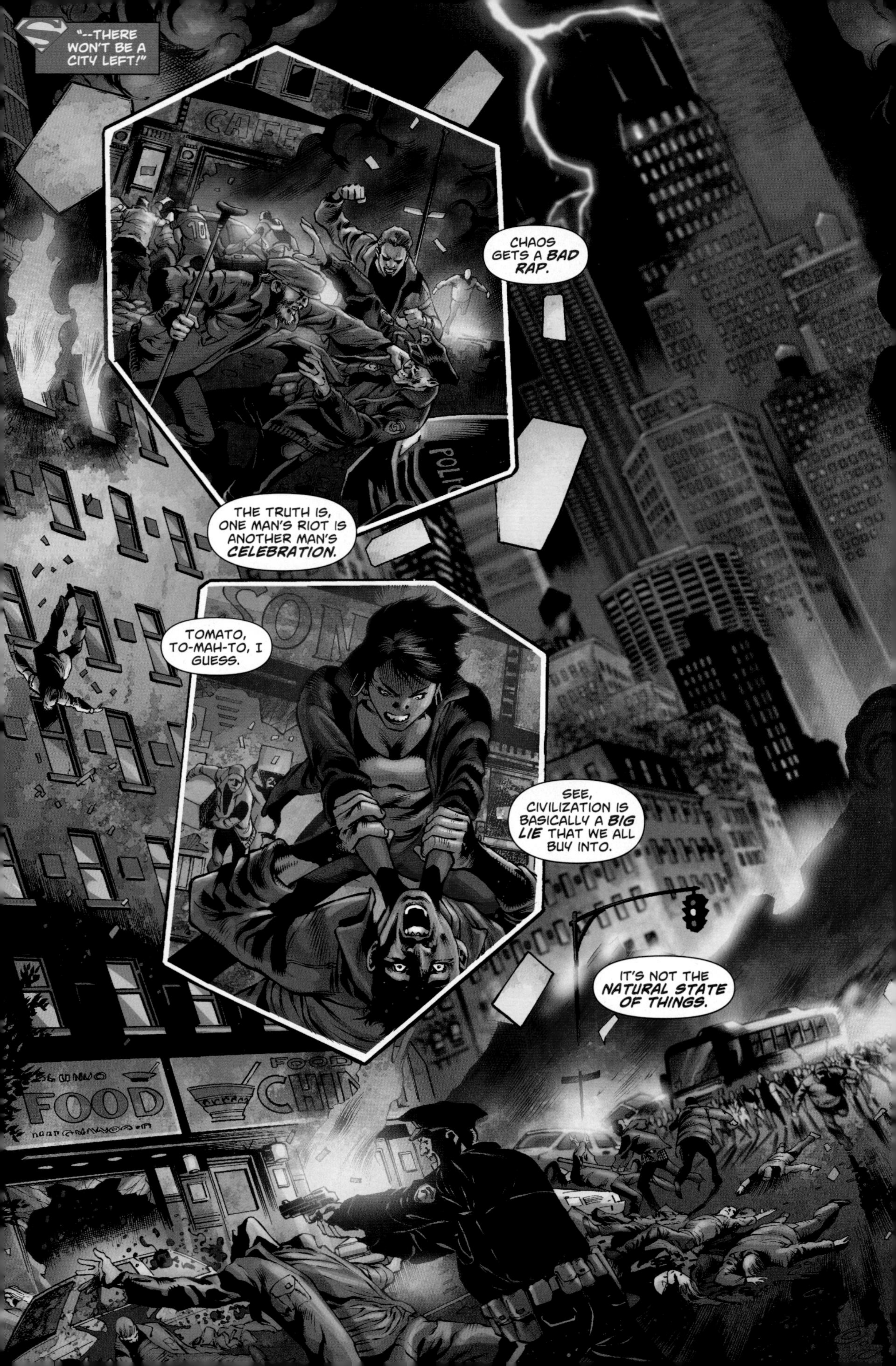
"--THERE WON'T BE A CITY LEFT!"
CAFE
CHAOS GETS A BAD RAP.
THE TRUTH IS, ONE MAN'S RIOT IS ANOTHER MAN'S CELEBRATION.
TOMATO, TO-MAH-TO, I GUESS.
SEE, CIVILIZATION IS BASICALLY A BIG LIE THAT WE ALL BUY INTO.
IT'S NOT THE NATURAL STATE OF THINGS.
FOOD
FOOD

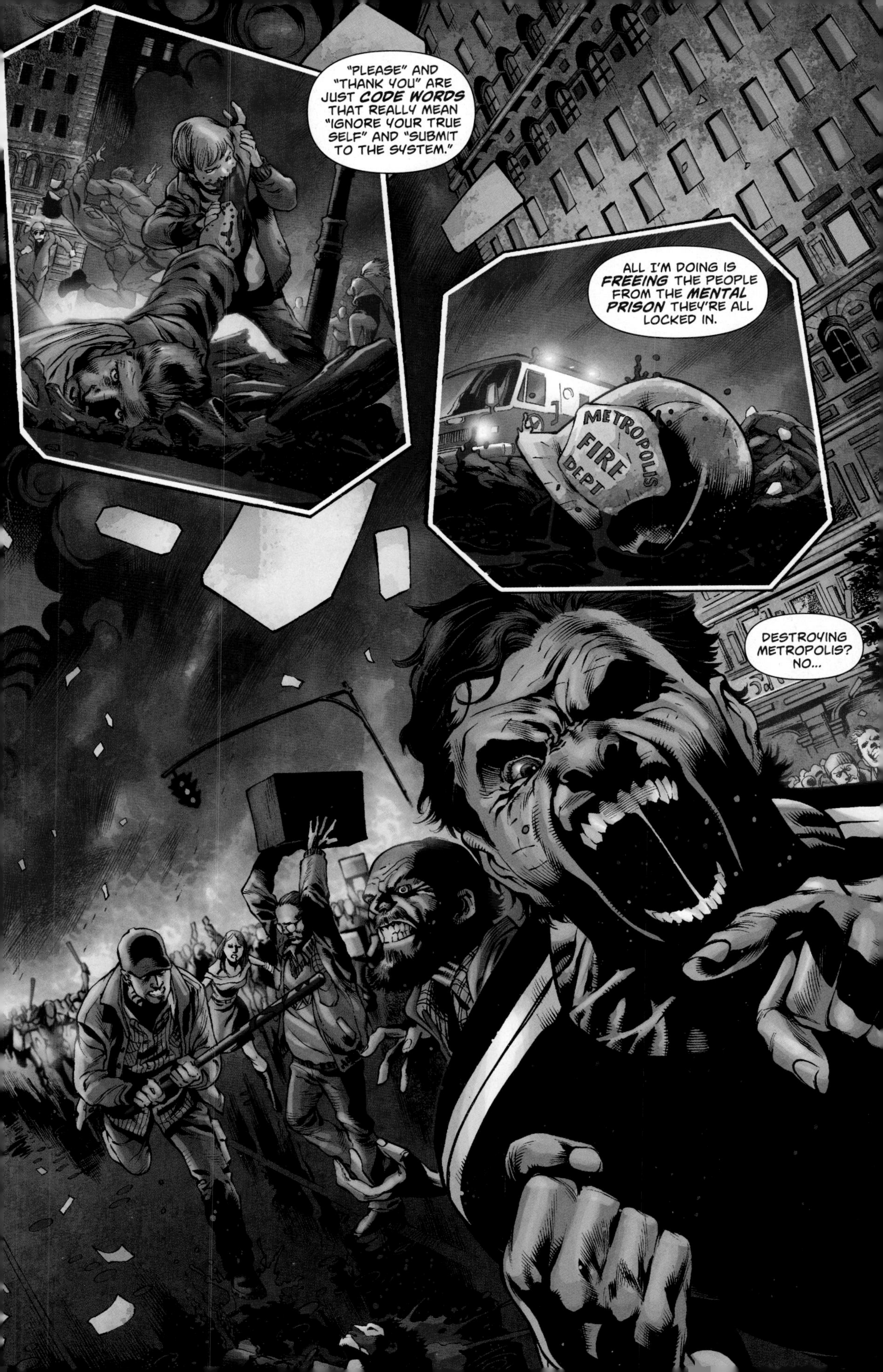
"PLEASE" AND "THANK YOU" ARE JUST CODE WORDS THAT REALLY MEAN "IGNORE YOUR TRUE SELF" AND "SUBMIT TO THE SYSTEM."
ALL I'M DOING IS FREEING THE PEOPLE FROM THE MENTAL PRISON THEY'RE ALL LOCKED IN.
METROPOLIS FIRE DEPT
DESTROYING METROPOLIS? NO...

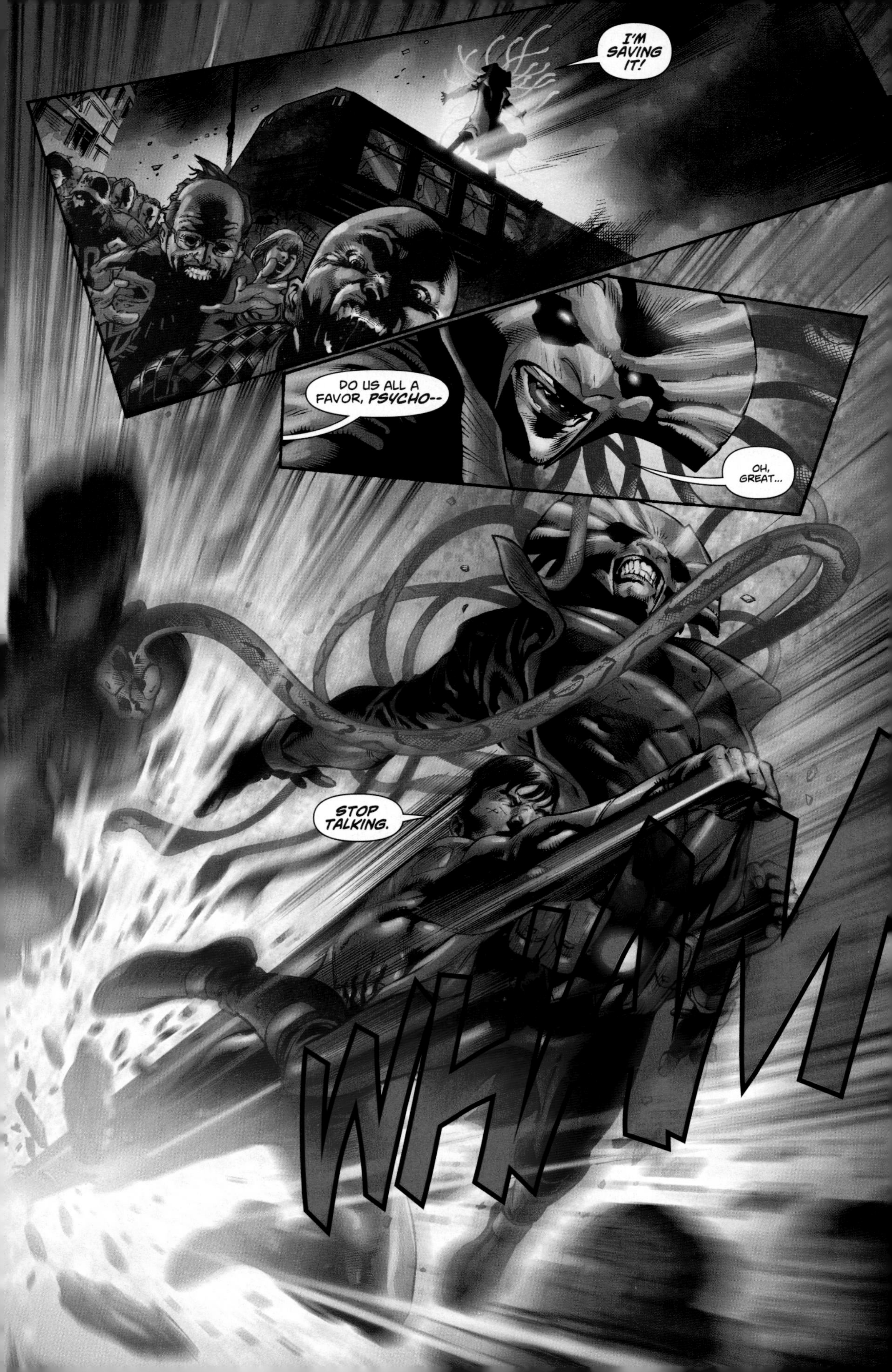
I'M SAVING IT!
DO US ALL A FAVOR, PSYCHO--
OH, GREAT...
STOP TALKING.
WHAM

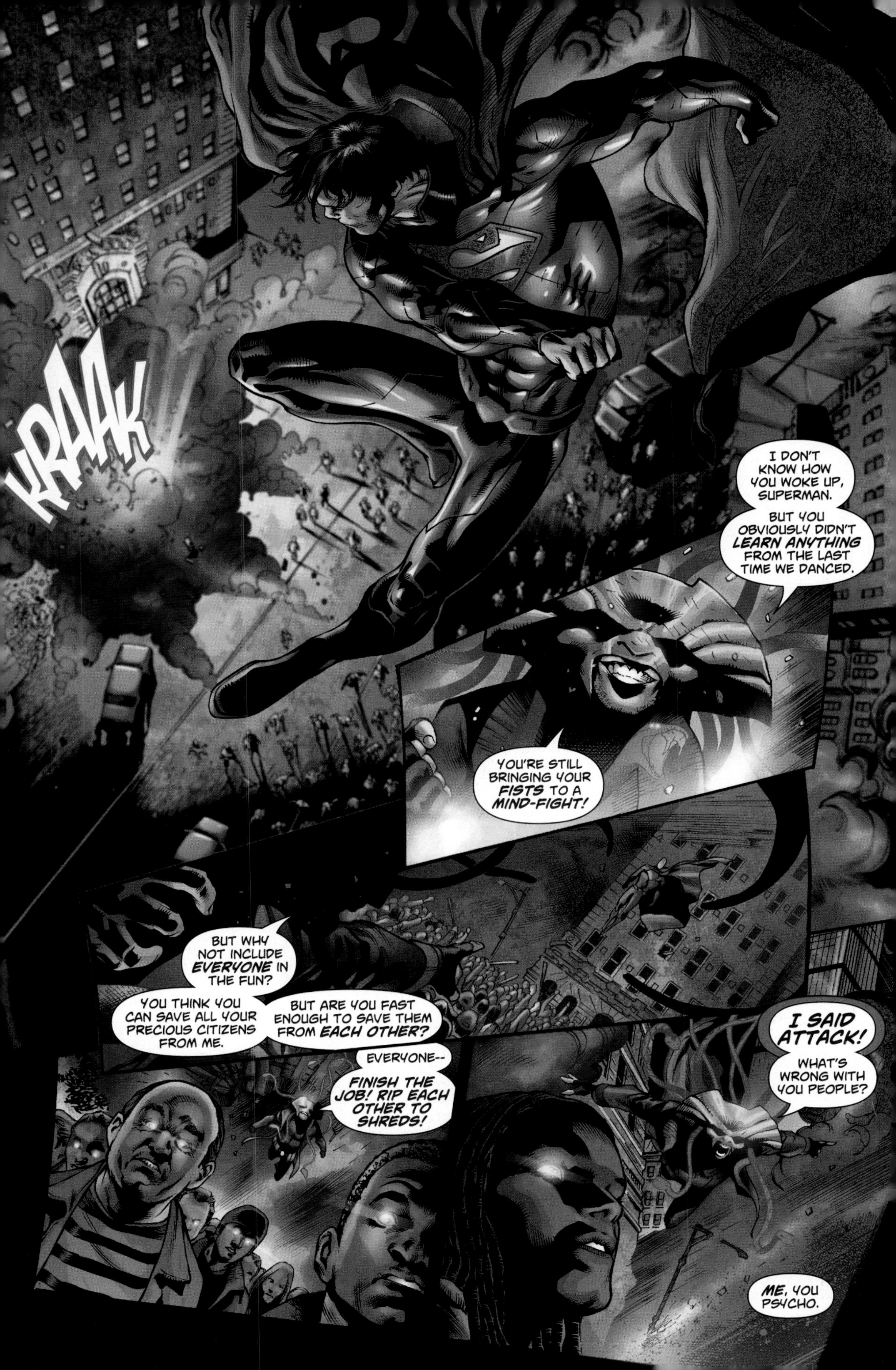
KRAAK
I DON'T KNOW HOW YOU WOKE UP, SUPERMAN.
BUT YOU OBVIOUSLY DIDN'T LEARN ANYTHING FROM THE LAST TIME WE DANCED.
YOU'RE STILL BRINGING YOUR FISTS TO A MIND-FIGHT!
BUT WHY NOT INCLUDE EVERYONE IN THE FUN?
YOU THINK YOU CAN SAVE ALL YOUR PRECIOUS CITIZENS FROM ME.
BUT ARE YOU FAST ENOUGH TO SAVE THEM FROM EACH OTHER?
EVERYONE--
FINISH THE JOB! RIP EACH OTHER TO SHREDS!
I SAID ATTACK!
WHAT'S WRONG WITH YOU PEOPLE?
ME, YOU PSYCHO.

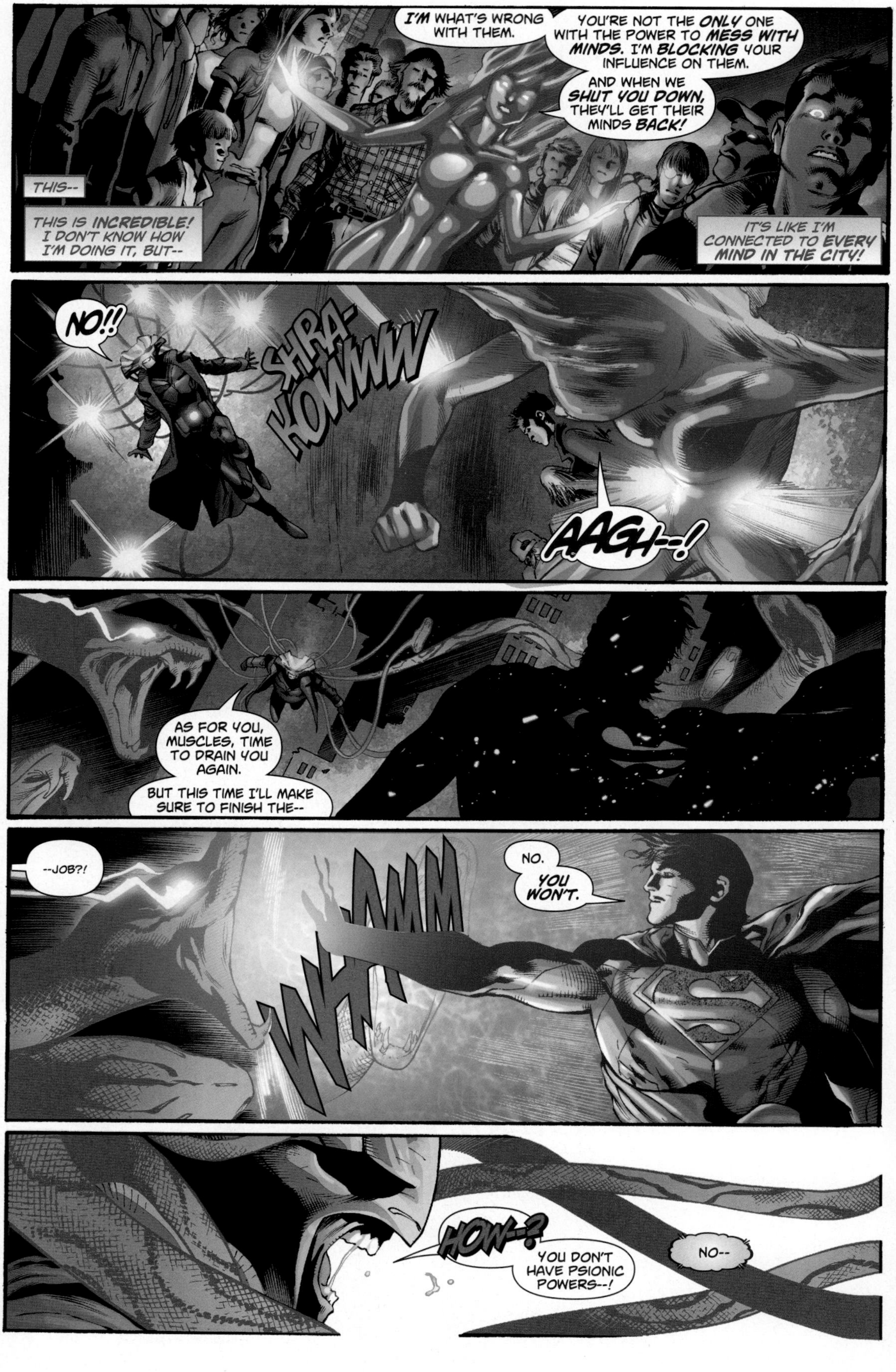
I'M WHAT'S WRONG WITH THEM.
YOU'RE NOT THE ONLY ONE WITH THE POWER TO MESS WITH MINDS. I'M BLOCKING YOUR INFLUENCE ON THEM.
AND WHEN WE SHUT YOU DOWN, THEY'LL GET THEIR MINDS BACK!
THIS--
THIS IS INCREDIBLE! I DON'T KNOW HOW I'M DOING IT, BUT--
IT'S LIKE I'M CONNECTED TO EVERY MIND IN THE CITY!
NO!!
SHRA-KOWWW
AAGH--!
AS FOR YOU, MUSCLES, TIME TO DRAIN YOU AGAIN.
BUT THIS TIME I'LL MAKE SURE TO FINISH THE--
--JOB?!
WHAMM
NO. YOU WON'T.
HOW--?
YOU DON'T HAVE PSIONIC POWERS--!
NO--

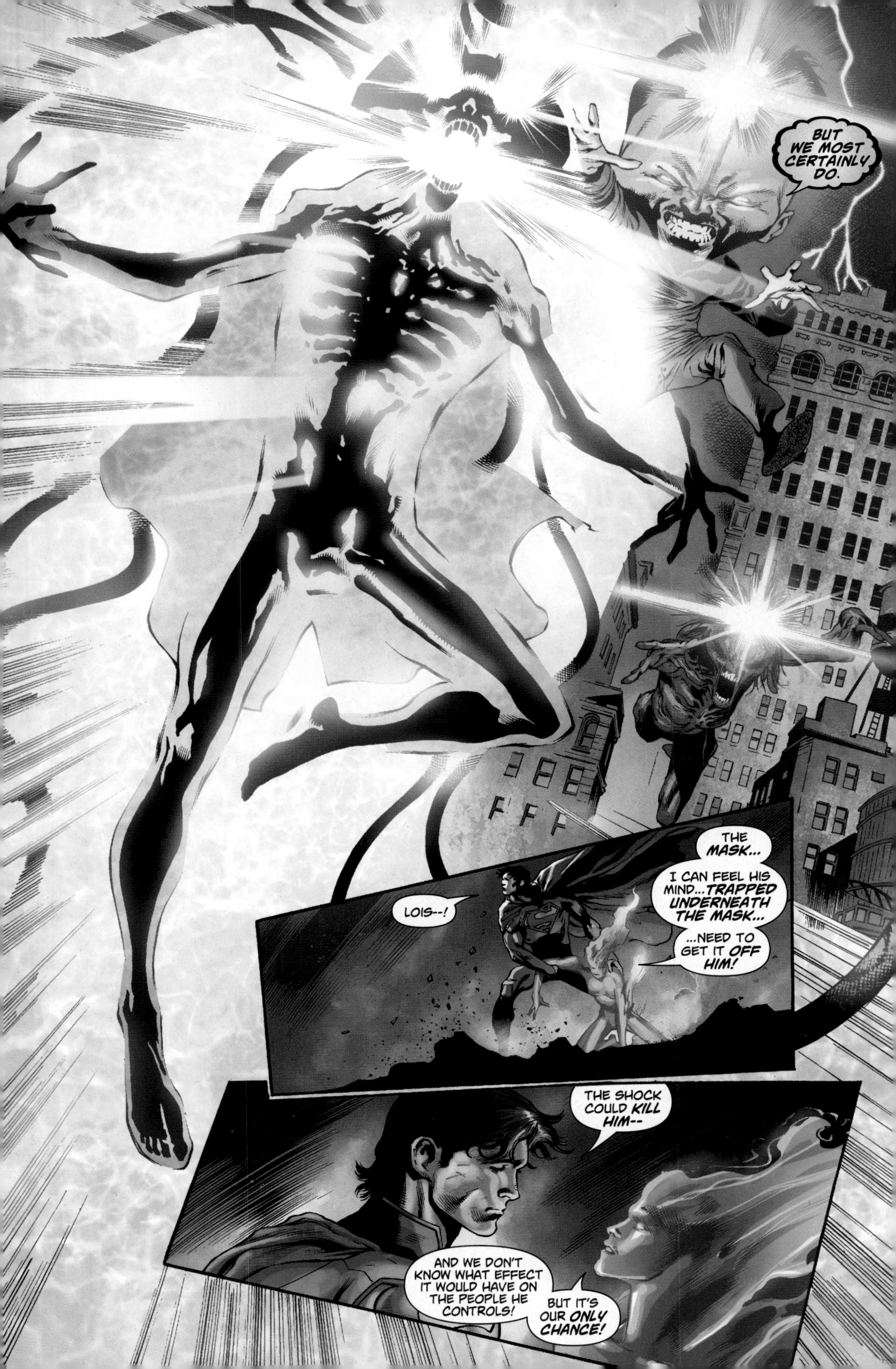

BUT WE MOST CERTAINLY DO.
THE MASK...
I CAN FEEL HIS MIND...TRAPPED UNDERNEATH THE MASK...
LOIS--!
...NEED TO GET IT OFF HIM!
THE SHOCK COULD KILL HIM--
AND WE DON'T KNOW WHAT EFFECT IT WOULD HAVE ON THE PEOPLE HE CONTROLS!
BUT IT'S OUR ONLY CHANCE!

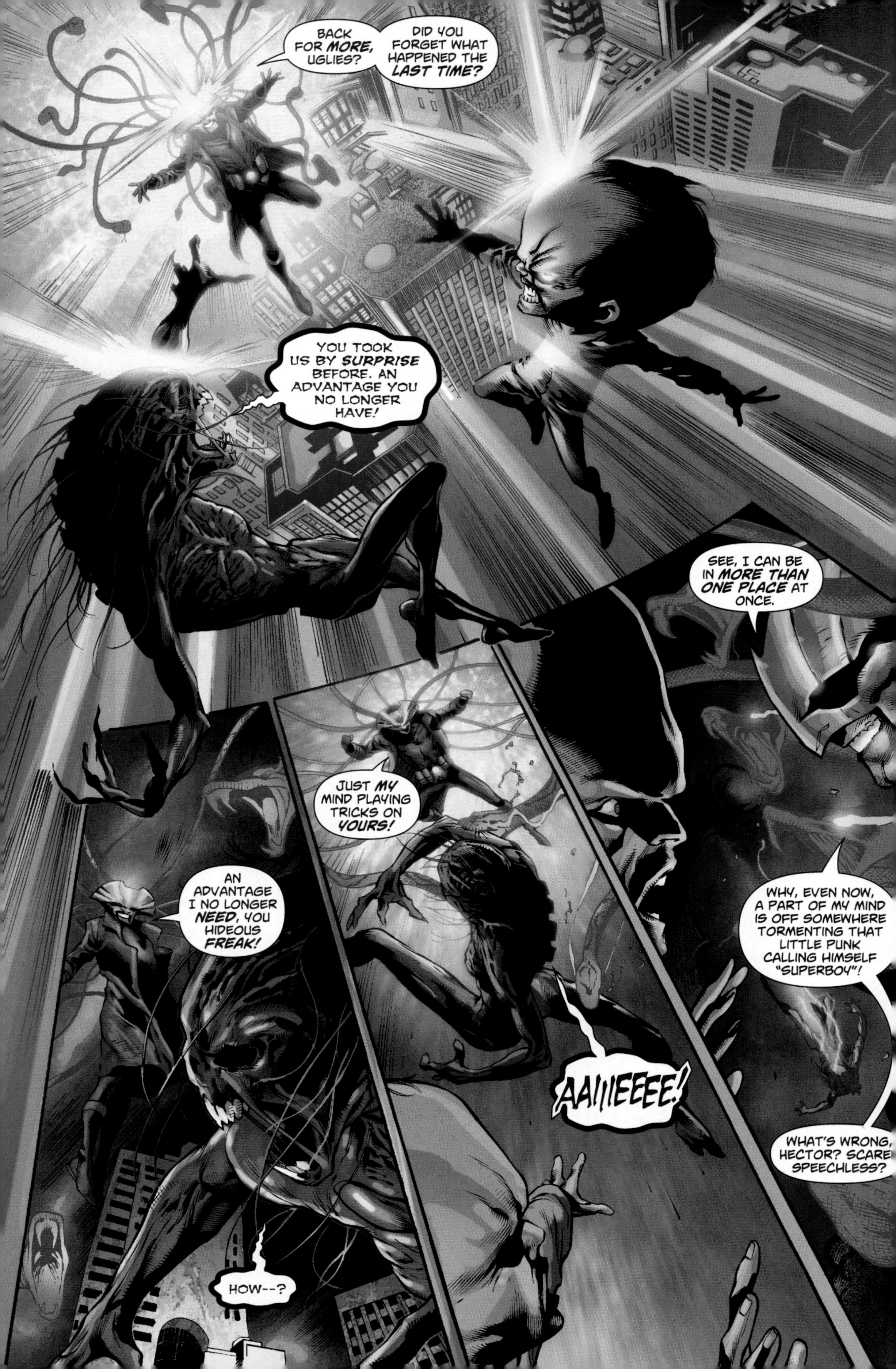
BACK FOR MORE, UGLIES?
DID YOU FORGET WHAT HAPPENED THE LAST TIME?
YOU TOOK US BY SURPRISE BEFORE. AN ADVANTAGE YOU NO LONGER HAVE!
SEE, I CAN BE IN MORE THAN ONE PLACE AT ONCE.
JUST MY MIND PLAYING TRICKS ON YOURS!
AN ADVANTAGE I NO LONGER NEED, YOU HIDEOUS FREAK!
WHY, EVEN NOW, A PART OF MY MIND IS OFF SOMEWHERE TORMENTING THAT LITTLE PUNK CALLING HIMSELF "SUPERBOY"!
AAIIIEEEE!
WHAT'S WRONG, HECTOR? SCARE SPEECHLESS?
HOW--?

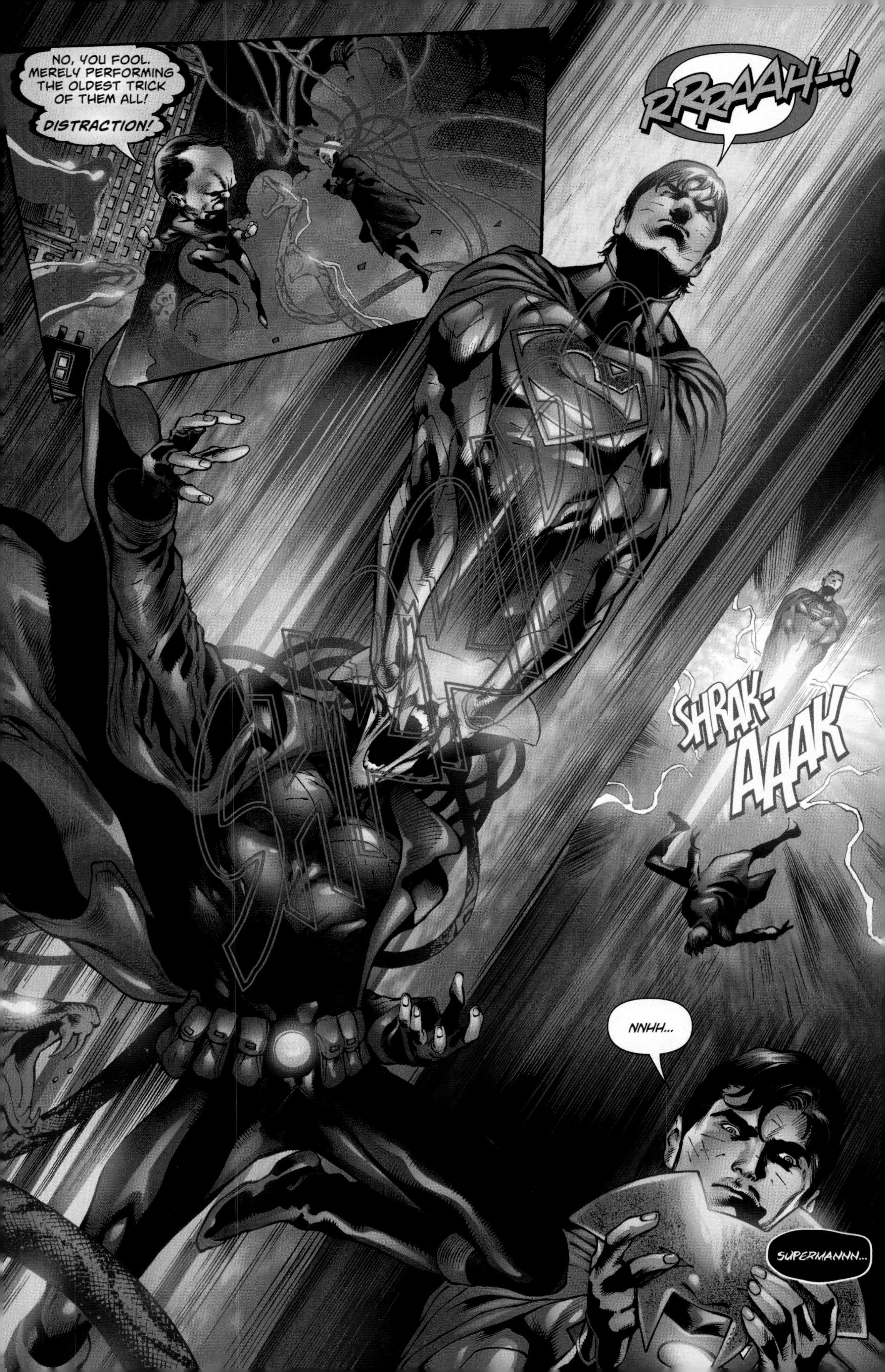
NO, YOU FOOL. MERELY PERFORMING THE OLDEST TRICK OF THEM ALL!
DISTRACTION!
RRRAAH--!
SHRAK-AAAK
NNHH...
SUPERMANNN...

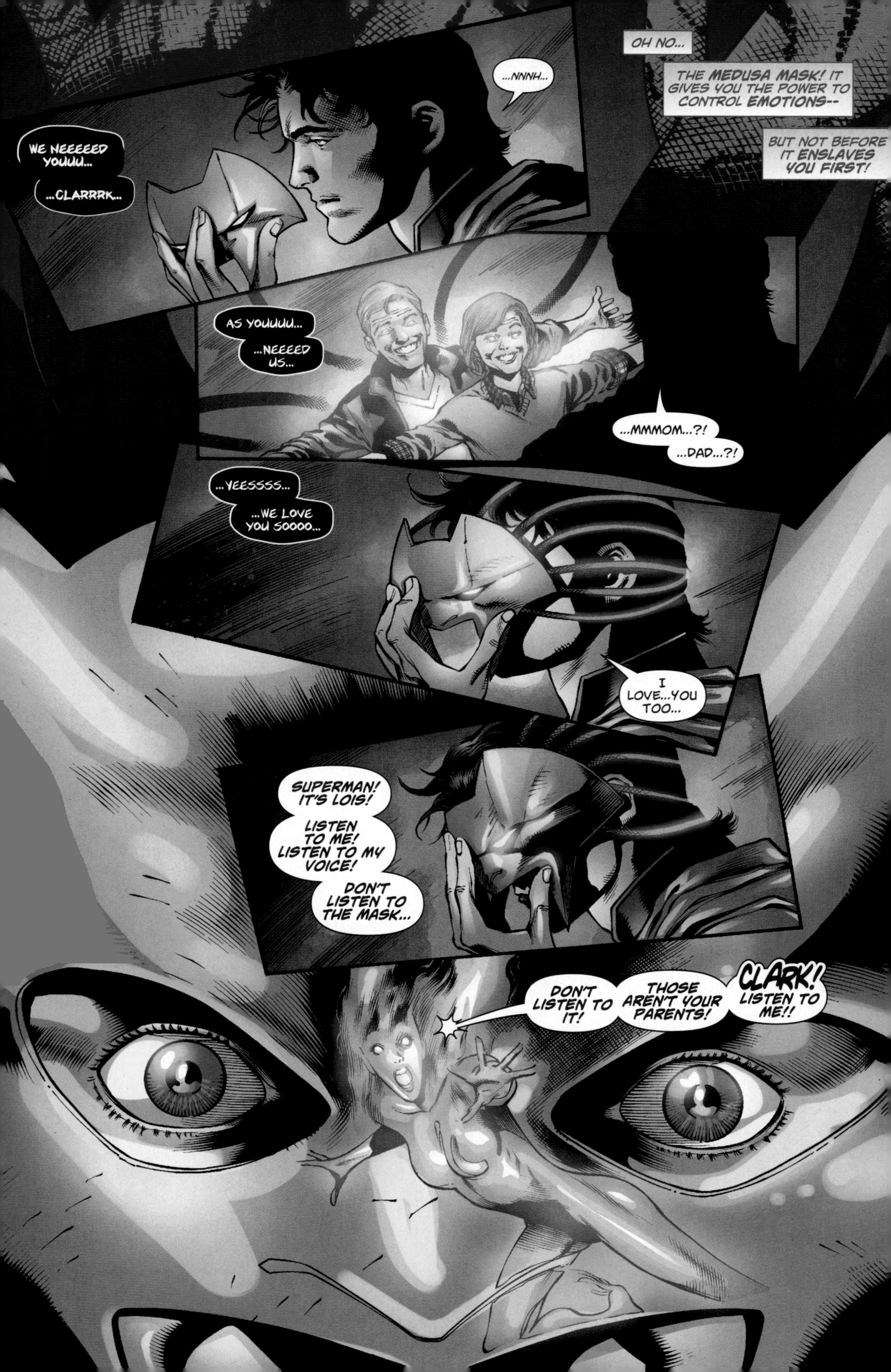
OH NO...
THE MEDUSA MASK! IT GIVES YOU THE POWER TO CONTROL EMOTIONS--
BUT NOT BEFORE IT ENSLAVES YOU FIRST!
...NNNH...
WE NEEEEED YOUUU...
...CLARRRK...
AS YOUUUU...
...NEEEED US...
...MMMOM...?!
...DAD...?!
...YEESSSS...
...WE LOVE YOU SOOOO...
I LOVE...YOU TOO...
SUPERMAN! IT'S LOIS!
LISTEN TO ME! LISTEN TO MY VOICE!
DON'T LISTEN TO THE MASK...
DON'T LISTEN TO IT!
THOSE AREN'T YOUR PARENTS!
CLARK! LISTEN TO ME!!

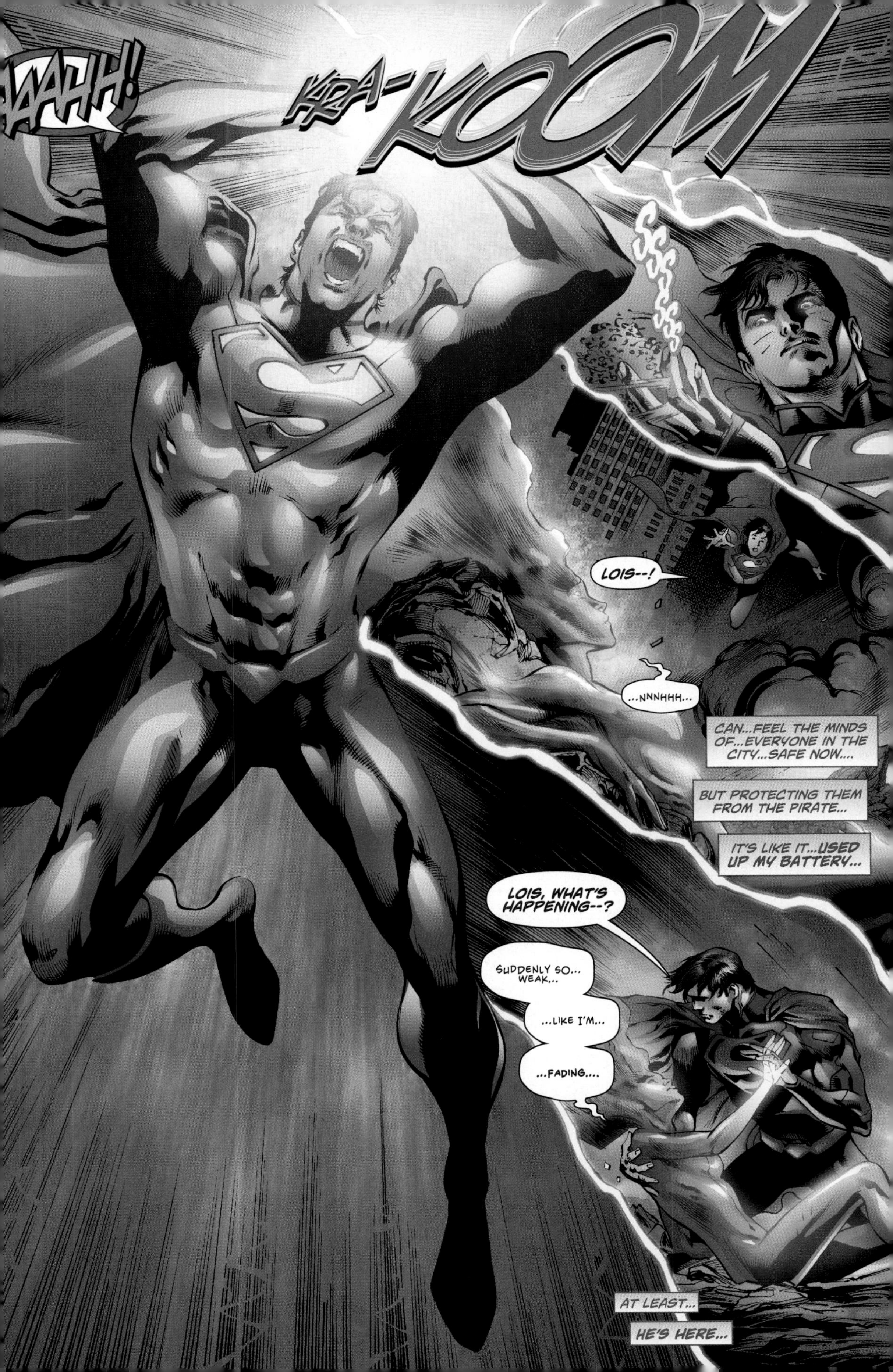
AAAHH!
KRA-KOOM
SSSSSS
LOIS--!
...NNNHHH...
CAN...FEEL THE MINDS OF...EVERYONE IN THE CITY...SAFE NOW....
BUT PROTECTING THEM FROM THE PIRATE...
IT'S LIKE IT...USED UP MY BATTERY...
LOIS, WHAT'S HAPPENING--?
SUDDENLY SO... WEAK...
...LIKE I'M...
...FADING....
AT LEAST...
HE'S HERE...

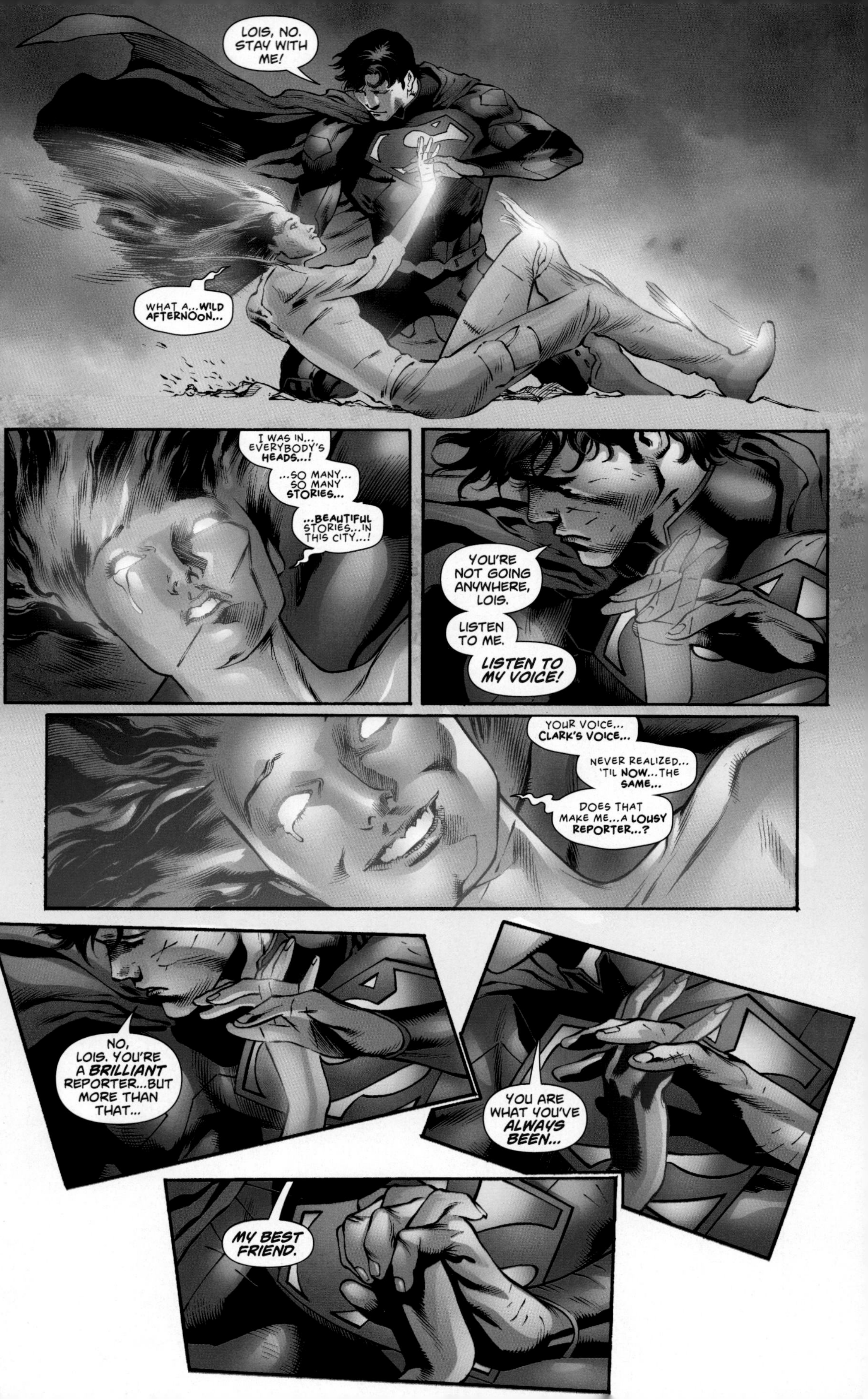
LOIS, NO. STAY WITH ME!
WHAT A...WILD AFTERNOON...
I WAS IN... EVERYBODY'S HEADS...!
...SO MANY... SO MANY STORIES...
...BEAUTIFUL STORIES...IN THIS CITY...!
YOU'RE NOT GOING ANYWHERE, LOIS.
LISTEN TO ME.
LISTEN TO MY VOICE!
YOUR VOICE... CLARK'S VOICE...
NEVER REALIZED... 'TIL NOW...THE SAME...
DOES THAT MAKE ME...A LOUSY REPORTER...?
NO, LOIS. YOU'RE A BRILLIANT REPORTER...BUT MORE THAN THAT...
YOU ARE WHAT YOU'VE ALWAYS BEEN...
MY BEST FRIEND.

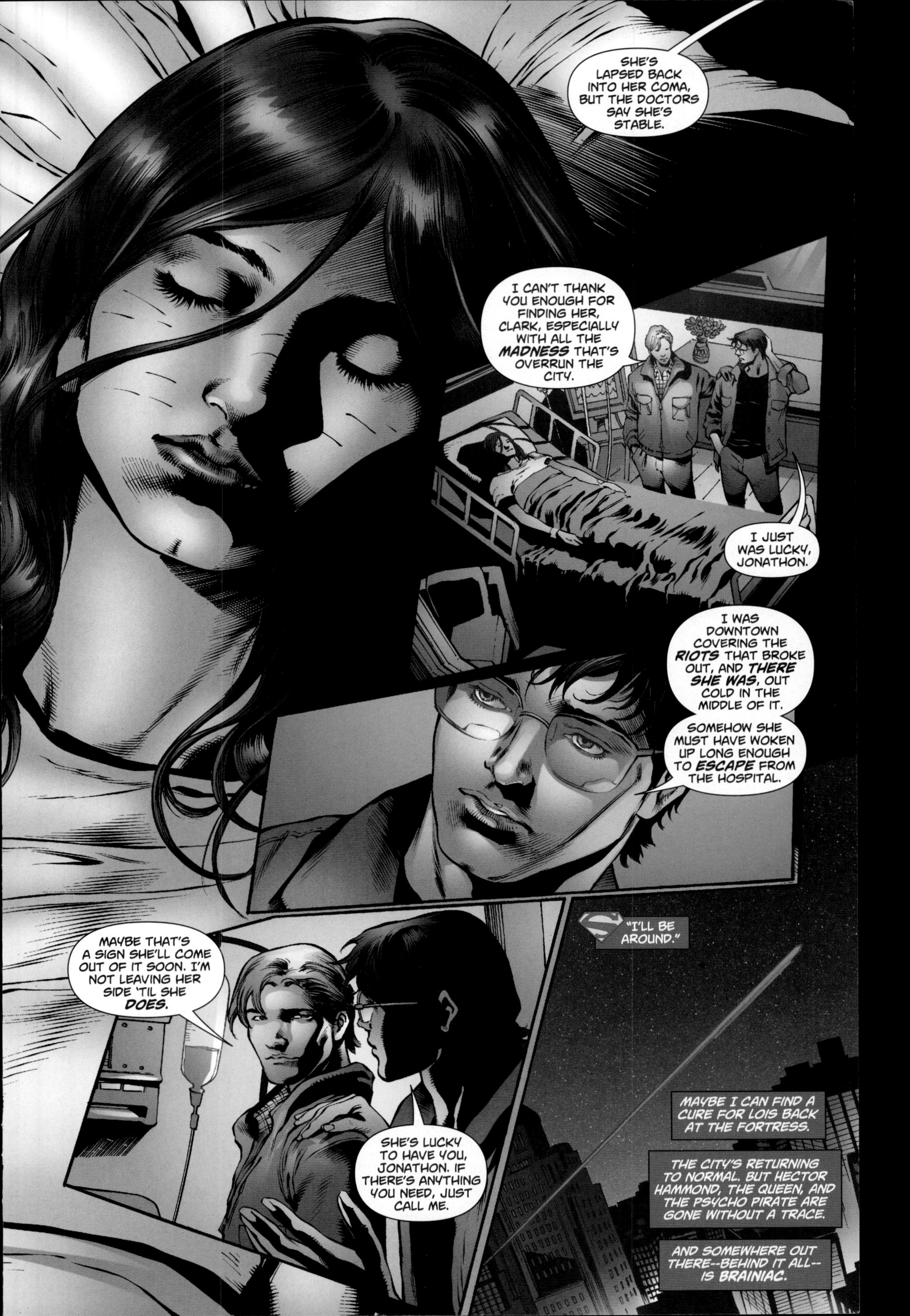

SHE'S LAPSED BACK INTO HER COMA, BUT THE DOCTORS SAY SHE'S STABLE.
I CAN'T THANK YOU ENOUGH FOR FINDING HER, CLARK, ESPECIALLY WITH ALL THE MADNESS THAT'S OVERRUN THE CITY.
I JUST WAS LUCKY, JONATHON.
I WAS DOWNTOWN COVERING THE RIOTS THAT BROKE OUT, AND THERE SHE WAS, OUT COLD IN THE MIDDLE OF IT.
SOMEHOW SHE MUST HAVE WOKEN UP LONG ENOUGH TO ESCAPE FROM THE HOSPITAL.
MAYBE THAT'S A SIGN SHE'LL COME OUT OF IT SOON. I'M NOT LEAVING HER SIDE 'TIL SHE DOES.
SHE'S LUCKY TO HAVE YOU, JONATHON. IF THERE'S ANYTHING YOU NEED, JUST CALL ME.
"I'LL BE AROUND."
MAYBE I CAN FIND A CURE FOR LOIS BACK AT THE FORTRESS.
THE CITY'S RETURNING TO NORMAL. BUT HECTOR HAMMOND, THE QUEEN, AND THE PSYCHO PIRATE ARE GONE WITHOUT A TRACE.
AND SOMEWHERE OUT THERE--BEHIND IT ALL--IS BRAINIAC.

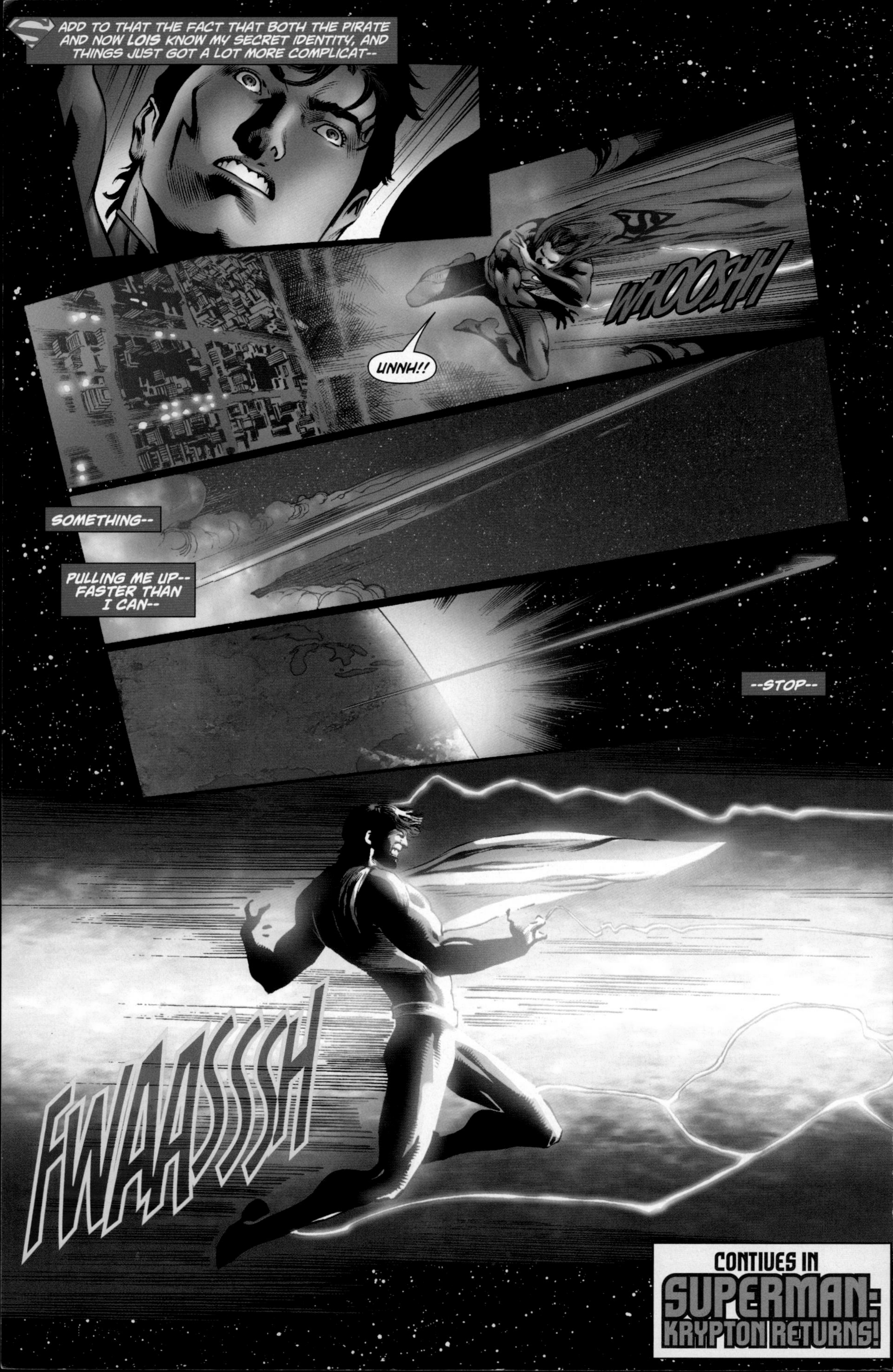
ADD TO THAT THE FACT THAT BOTH THE PIRATE AND NOW LOIS KNOW MY SECRET IDENTITY, AND THINGS JUST GOT A LOT MORE COMPLICAT--
WHOOOSHH
UNNH!!
SOMETHING--
PULLING ME UP-- FASTER THAN I CAN--
--STOP--
FWAAASSSH
CONTIVES IN
SUPERMAN: KRYPTON RETURNS!

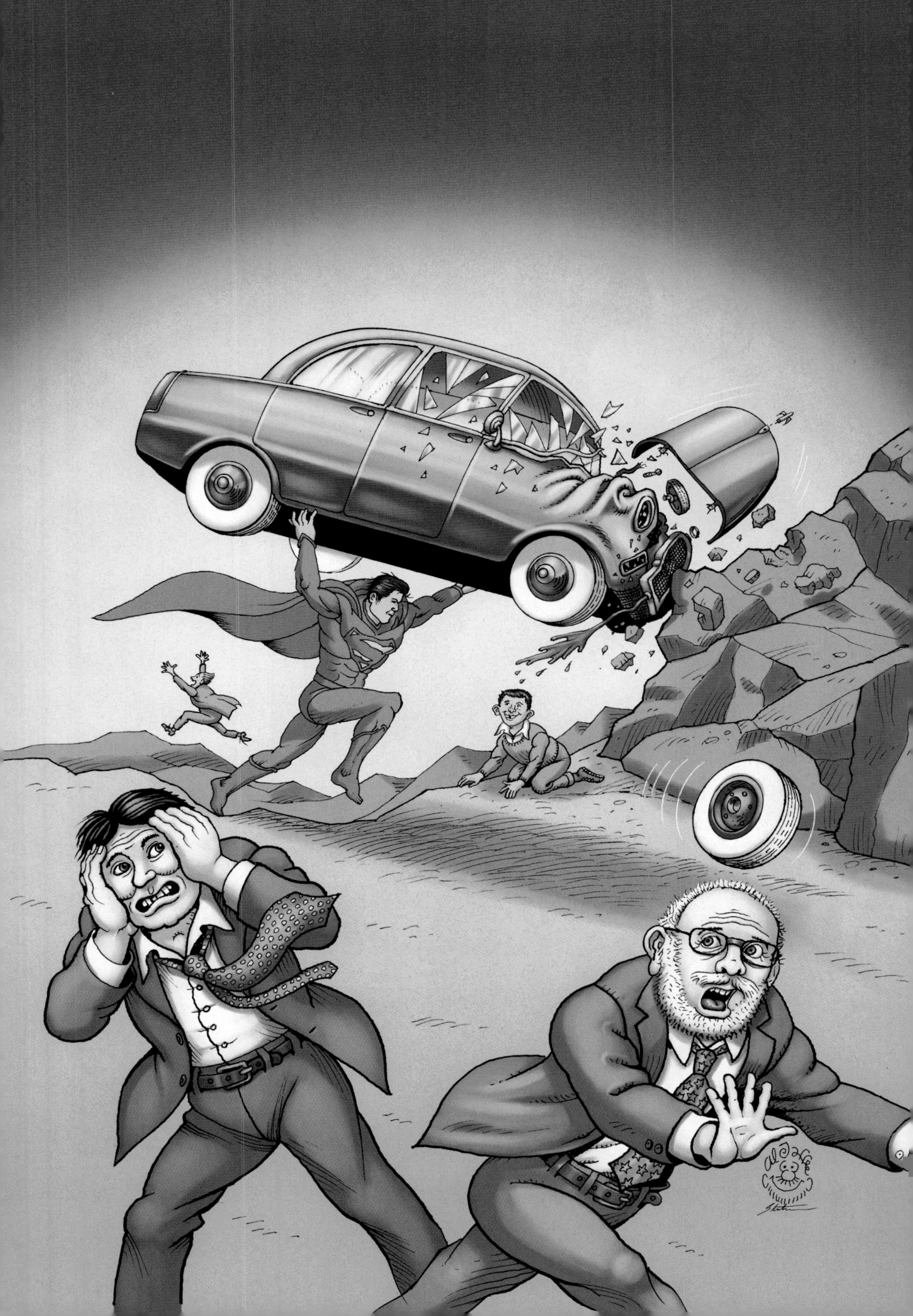

MAD variant cover for SUPERMAN #19
by John Caldwell & Carrie Strachan

Full spread cover for SUPERMAN #19
by Kenneth Rocafort

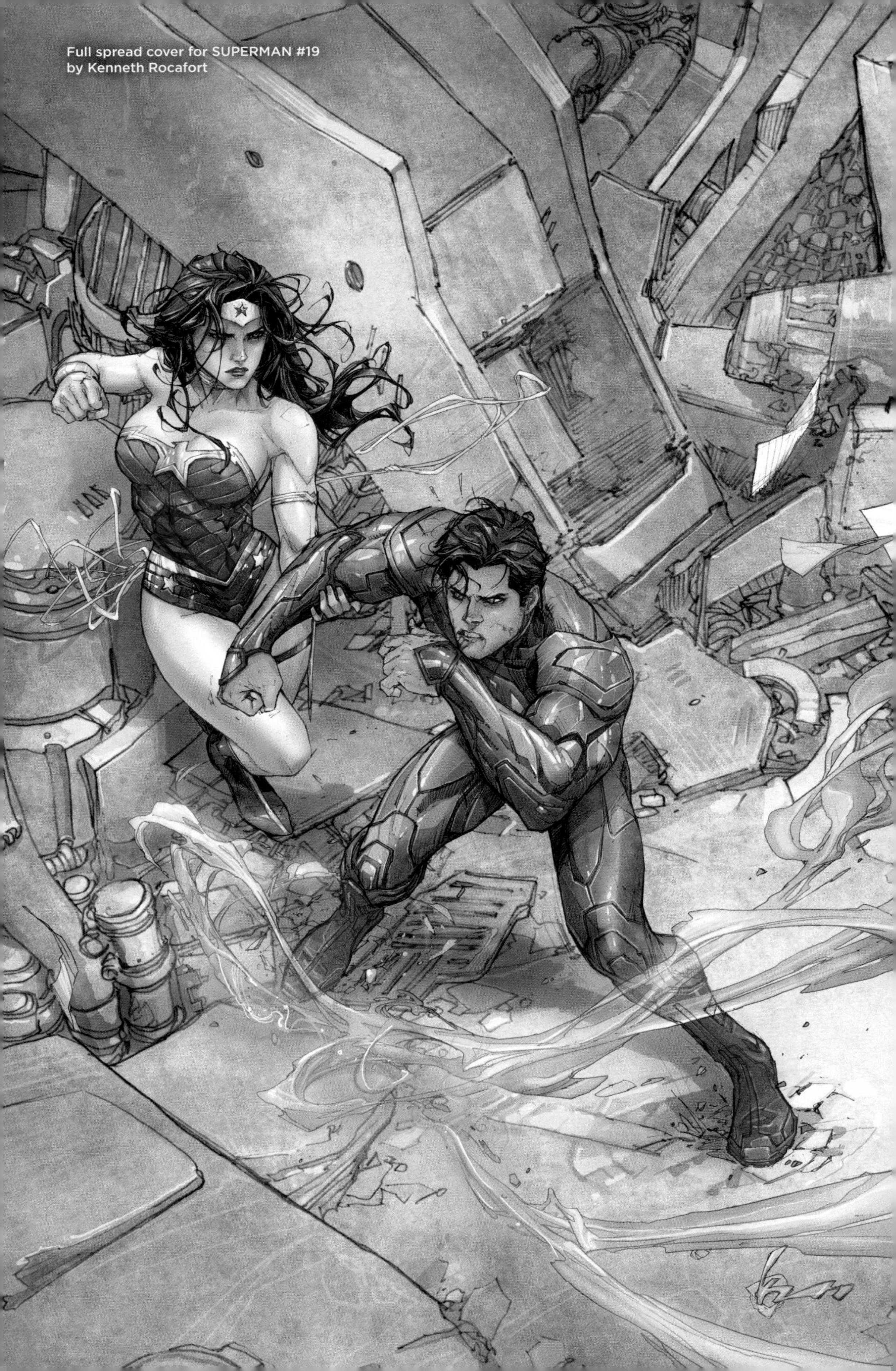

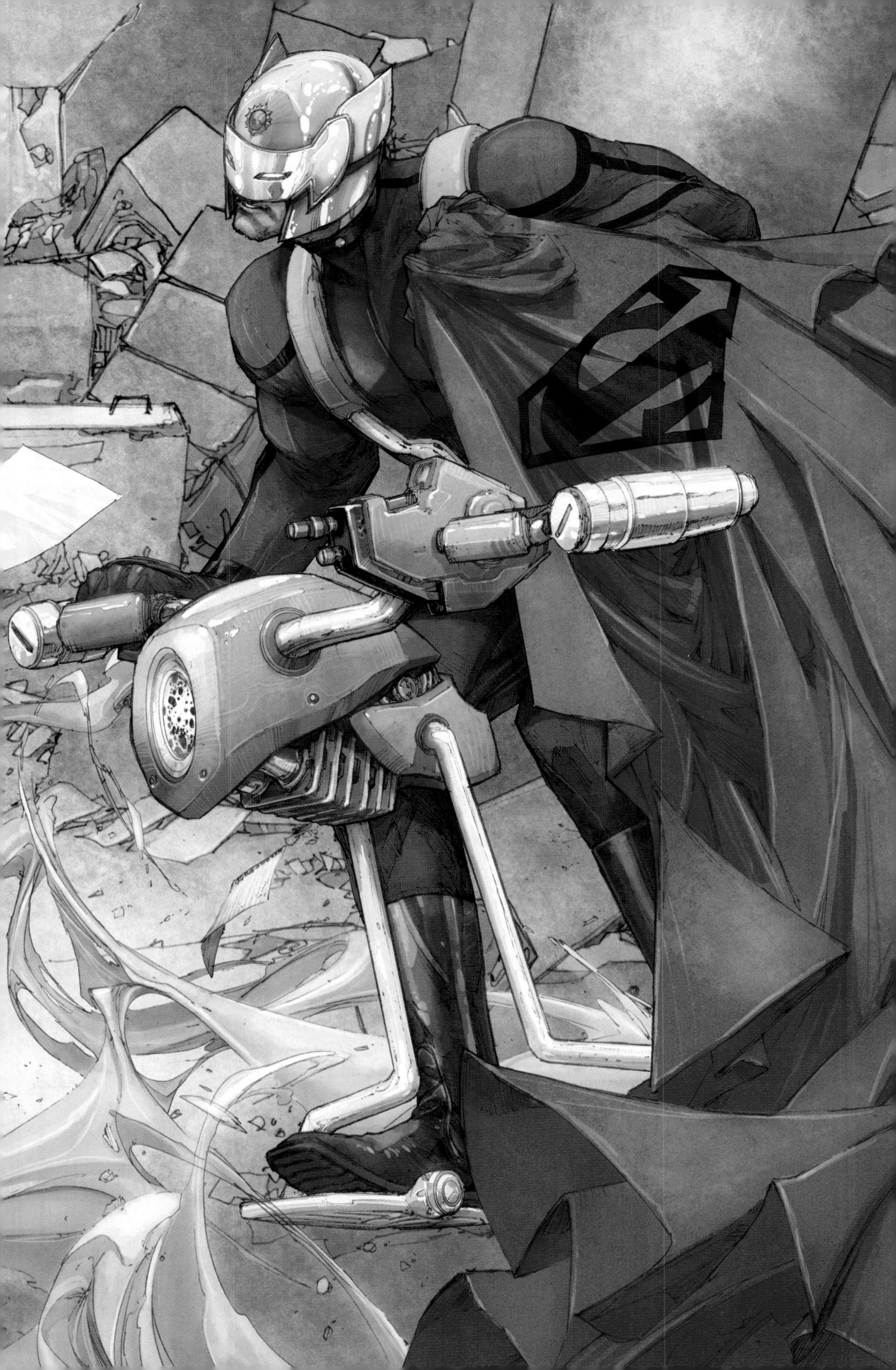

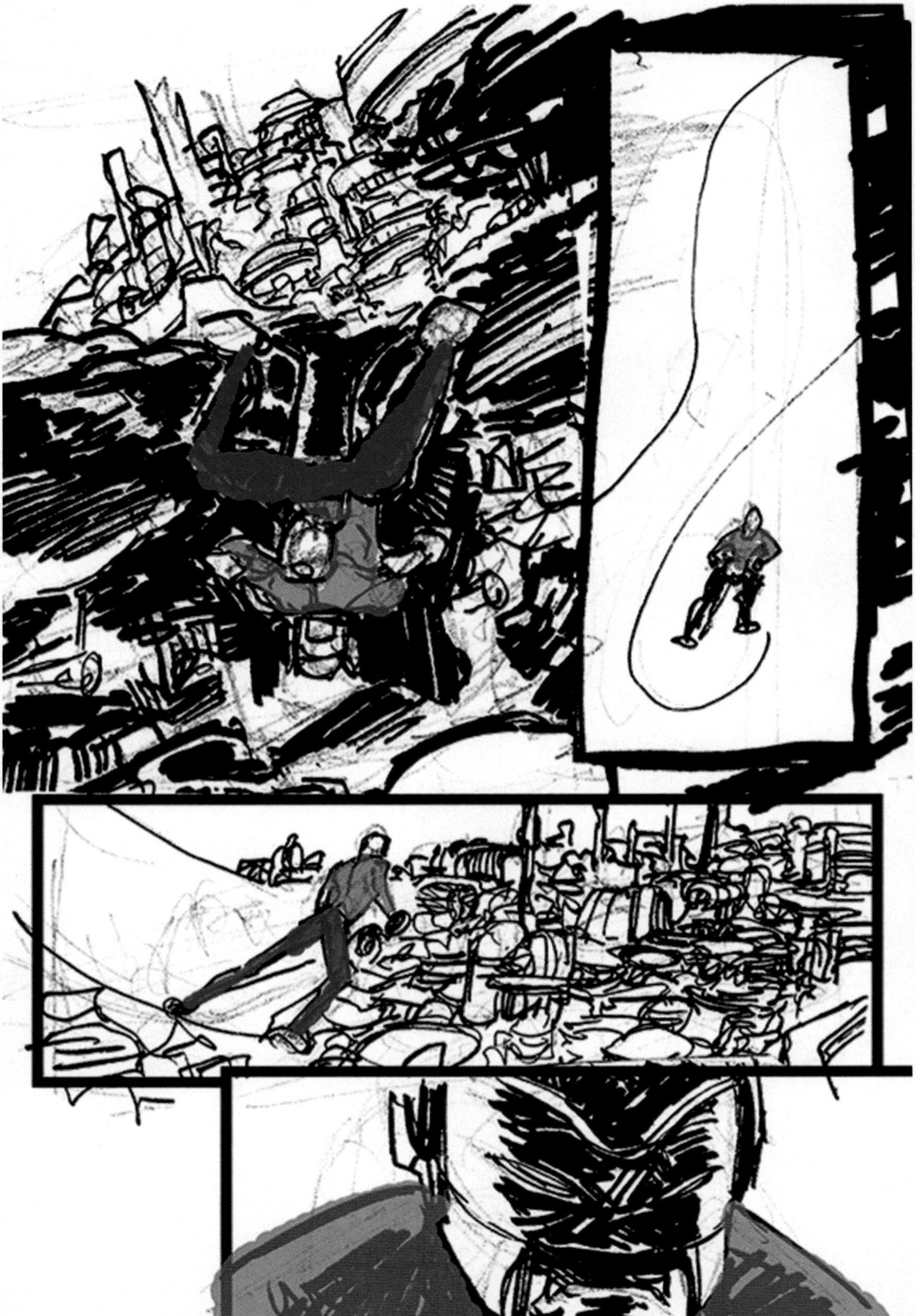

"Superman is still super."
—WALL STREET JOURNAL

"The SUPERMAN world is also
one now where fans new and old, young and
not-so-young, can come to a common ground to
talk about the superhero that started it all."
—CRAVE ONLINE

START AT THE BEGINNING!

SUPERMAN VOLUME 1: WHAT PRICE TOMORROW?

**SUPERMAN VOL. 2:
SECRETS & LIES**

**SUPERMAN VOL. 3:
FURY AT WORLD'S
END**

**SUPERMAN:
H'EL ON EARTH**

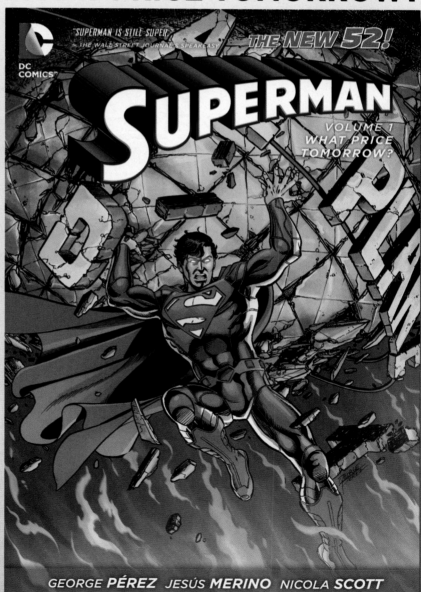

GEORGE PÉREZ **JESÚS MERINO** **NICOLA SCOTT**

"ACTION COMICS has successfully carved its own territory and continued exploring Morrison's familiar themes about heroism and ideas."—IGN

"Casts the character in a new light, opens up fresh storytelling possibilities, and pushes it all forward with dynamic Rags Morales art. I loved it."—THE ONION/AV CLUB

START AT THE BEGINNING!

SUPERMAN: ACTION COMICS VOLUME 1:
SUPERMAN AND THE MEN OF STEEL

SUPERMAN: ACTION COMICS VOL. 2: BULLETPROOF

with GRANT MORRISON and RAGS MORALES

SUPERMAN: ACTION COMICS VOL. 3: AT THE END OF DAYS

with GRANT MORRISON and RAGS MORALES

SUPERBOY VOL. 1: INCUBATION

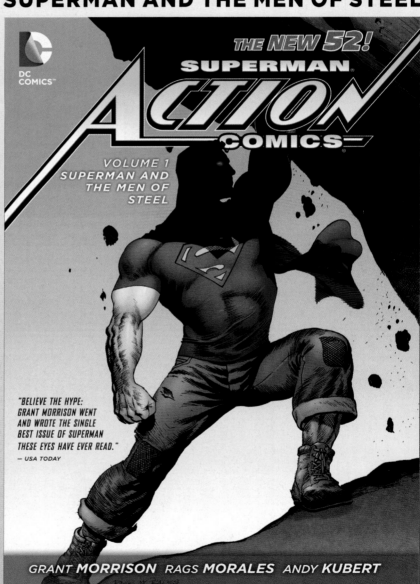

"BELIEVE THE HYPE: GRANT MORRISON WENT AND WROTE THE SINGLE BEST ISSUE OF SUPERMAN THESE EYES HAVE EVER READ." — USA TODAY

GRANT **MORRISON** RAGS **MORALES** ANDY **KUBERT**

"Clear storytelling at its best. It's an intriguing concept and easy to grasp."—THE NEW YORK TIMES

"Azzarello is rebuilding the mythology of Wonder Woman." —CRAVE ONLINE

START AT THE BEGINNING!

WONDER WOMAN VOLUME 1: BLOOD

WONDER WOMAN VOL. 2: GUTS

by BRIAN AZZARELLO and CLIFF CHIANG

WONDER WOMAN VOL. 3: IRON

by BRIAN AZZARELLO and CLIFF CHIANG

SUPERGIRL VOL. 1: LAST DAUGHTER OF KRYPTON

"Welcoming to new fans looking to get into superhero comics for the first time and old fans who gave up on the funny-books long ago."
—SCRIPPS HOWARD NEWS SERVICE

START AT THE BEGINNING!

JUSTICE LEAGUE VOLUME 1: ORIGIN

AQUAMAN
VOLUME 1:
THE TRENCH

THE SAVAGE
HAWKMAN VOLUME 1:
DARKNESS RISING

GREEN ARROW
VOLUME 1:
THE MIDAS TOUCH

"WRITTEN BY GEOFF JOHNS, WITH ART BY THE GODLY JIM LEE, JUSTICE LEAGUE IS A MUST READ."
— COMPLEX MAGAZINE

GEOFF **JOHNS**   JIM **LEE**   Scott **WILLIAMS**